HOME EQUITY AND AGEING OWNERS

The growing use of housing equity to support a range of activities and needs raises complex issues, particularly for older owners. In an environment in which older owners are pushed towards housing equity transactions to meet income and welfare costs, they are required to make choices from a complex and sometimes bewildering range of options. The transactions which facilitate the use of home equity as a resource to spend in later life—from 'trading down' and 'ordinary' secured and unsecured debt to targeted products including reverse/lifetime mortgages, home reversion plans and sale-and-rent back agreements—raise important legal and regulatory issues.

This book provides a contextual analysis of the financial transactions that older people enter into using their housing equity. It traces the protections afforded to older owners through the 'ordinary' law of property and contract, as well as the development of specific regulatory protections focused on targeted products. The book employs the notion of risk to highlight the nature and causes of the 'situational' vulnerabilities to which older people are now subject as 'consumers' of housing equity, showing that older owners' personal situations are crucial in determining whether and why they may seek to release equity, the options and products available to them, and the impact of harms resulting from adverse transactions. The book critically evaluates the extent to which this context is incorporated in the legal frameworks through which these transactions are governed, as a measure of the 'appropriateness' of existing legal provision, as well as considering the arguments surrounding 'special protection' for older owners in housing equity transactions.

Home Equity and Ageing Owners

Between Risk and Regulation

Lorna Fox O'Mahony

·HART·
PUBLISHING

OXFORD AND PORTLAND, OREGON
2012

Published in the United Kingdom by Hart Publishing Ltd
16C Worcester Place, Oxford, OX1 2JW
Telephone: +44 (0)1865 517530
Fax: +44 (0)1865 510710
E-mail: mail@hartpub.co.uk
Website: http://www.hartpub.co.uk

Published in North America (US and Canada) by
Hart Publishing
c/o International Specialized Book Services
920 NE 58th Avenue, Suite 300
Portland, OR 97213–3786
USA
Tel: +1 503 287 3093 or toll-free: (1) 800 944 6190
Fax: +1 503 280 8832
E-mail: orders@isbs.com
Website: http://www.isbs.com

British Library Cataloguing in Publication Data

Data Available

ISBN: 978-1-84946-007-1

Typeset by Columns Design XML Ltd, Reading
Printed and bound in Great Britain by
CPI Group (UK) Ltd, Croydon, CR0 4YY

Preface

The use of home equity by elderly homeowners raises several specific issues, which are linked to income, financial management strategies, indebtedness and attitudes to inheritance, as well as a range of political issues which characterise an asset-based welfare system, including pensions, healthcare in old age, and housing and welfare support for the elderly. What is clear, however, is that 'cashing-in' on home equity by elderly owner-occupiers has become increasingly normalised, and that this trend seems likely to continue. Furthermore, the growing use of home equity by ageing homeowners raises an important set of questions for socio-legal studies and for legal practice, which relate to the vulnerabilities of older owners in property transactions involving their home, as well as a range of systemic issues concerning exposure to risk.

My thinking about the ideas set out in this book was triggered by two conference papers which I gave in 2007 and 2008. The first was a paper Paul McCutcheon of Limerick Law School invited me to give in a panel he was convening on 'Elder Law' at the Annual Conference of the International Association of Law and Mental Health, in Padua in June 2007. While I had been working on issues concerning socio-legal aspects of homeownership, mortgage indebtedness, possession actions and the impact of debt on the meanings of home for some years, this was the first time that I focused specifically on the impact of debts attached to the owner-occupied home for older homeowners, including the particular issues concerning the use of the owned home as a repository of capital in retirement. The second trigger, which gave further shape to the direction the book would take, was a paper which I gave at the Annual Conference of the Society of Legal Scholars in September 2008. This Conference was held at the London School of Economics, and it seemed apposite to focus on the legal issues around equity release and the elderly using the conceptual constructs of 'risk' and 'security',[1] as a sensitising framework for thinking about the impact of a rise in equity release and the issues that this might present for law.

The book explores a range of legal issues relating to the use of home equity by elderly homeowners, in the context of contemporary social, economic, political and demographic factors affecting the elderly. The analysis applies the concepts of risk and responsibility, developed through the theoretical framework of the 'risk society', to locate the law's responses to housing equity transactions in the context of a range of policy and legal factors that have shaped the emergence of home equity use for elders. These contextual factors include the rise of the older homeowner as a self-responsible credit market actor, and the development of 'innovative' (and complex) products to facilitate equity release, which have made the repository of value in the owned home—for many households the main asset and source of wealth—easier to spend than ever before. The intersection of financial, socio-economic, political and policy factors which have brought housing equity

[1] Popularised by Professor Lord Tony Giddens, Director of the LSE from 1997 to 2003; see ch 3 for discussion of Giddens's work as it informs housing equity transactions.

transactions for older owners into the mainstream of financial services raises significant new issues relating to the nature and extent of law's protection for older owners—particularly marginal older owners—as potentially vulnerable parties. This, in turn, casts new light on the older owner as a legal (and financial, and risk) subject, and on the location and degree of responsibilities that flow from such transactions, in various directions: on the State (including through law and regulation), on the market and on the older owner as a self-responsible subject.

Financial transactions that are linked to the owned home raise particular tensions for legal analyses, situated as they are at the juncture between commercial practice and domestic life. The role of law and regulation in intervening with the market to ensure an appropriate balance is struck, and to provide adequate protection for consumers, has been brought to the fore in political and legal discourse following the crisis which housing market collapse triggered in the banking and financial services industry from 2007, and the 'credit crunch' that followed.[2] Debates concerning risk and responsibility in the financial services industry have taken centre-stage in discussions about the future of financial regulation. Meanwhile, the same issues have also shaped contemporary social policy debates relating to the construction and delivery of welfare provision.[3] For older owners, who are increasingly expected to self-provide for financial needs after retirement through transactions that utilise their housing equity, participation in housing equity transactions is central to their status as archetypal neoliberal subjects. As the neoliberal foundations of the UK's 'light-touch', risk-based approach to financial regulation have been brought into question, the self-responsible consumer paradigm has been challenged by a greater emphasis on the vulnerability of consumers, particularly in complex, high-risk financial transactions.[4]

This book focuses primarily on the financial transactions older people enter into with respect to their housing equity, and particularly on the contexts in which older owners make financial decisions concerning housing equity use across the competing paradigms of 'housing as home', 'housing as inheritance' and 'housing as investment-asset-to-spend'. The contexts which shape the market for these transactions, analysed in chapters one to three, provide a foundation for reconsidering how older owners are cast as legal subjects in private law (chapter four) and the difficulties they are likely to face in negotiating their needs through competing housing paradigms (chapter five). In order to challenge the dominant (liberal) legal model of subjectivity, it is necessary to take a real measure of the nature and source of the vulnerabilities that potentially affect older owners in housing equity transactions. At the same time, it is important to be mindful of the potentially countervailing impacts of strategies to protect older owners that are rooted (however benignly) in ideas of paternalism or prejudice. Chapter six examines the vulnerabilities associated with age and financial transactions, and develops an approach which emphasises the contextual or 'situational vulnerabilities' that flow from the policy contexts of housing equity transactions. By locating this understanding of vulnerability within the theoretical framework of the 'vulnerable legal subject', this analysis implicates the State (including law as an institution of the State) and the market to responsive and responsible

[2] See, eg, I MacNeil and J O'Brien, *The Future of Financial Regulation* (Oxford, Hart Publishing, 2010); generally, ch 9.

[3] See, eg, H Kemshall, *Risk, social policy and welfare* (Maidenhead, Open University Press, 2002).

[4] These shifts are discussed in ch 9.

action. Chapters seven to ten evaluate the patchwork of provisions governing different types of housing equity transaction according to the theoretical tropes of vulnerability and responsibility.

The aims of this book are:

a) contextually to examine the housing equity transactions of older owners through the lens of the risk society;
b) to explore the status of (marginal) older owners as vulnerable subjects, and the corresponding responsibilities on law and market actors for the risks associated with home equity; and
c) to consider how law, through a combination of property law, contract law, regulatory provisions and equitable doctrine, has responded to these issues.

These thematic aims are embedded in analyses of the particular significance of the owned home for older occupiers, for example in relation to the preservation of self-identity and independence, and including the potential impact on the mental and physical health of elderly owners of leaving or losing the home. A key theme of the book is the growing tensions which the use of equity for various purposes—including income after retirement, healthcare and home maintenance costs, and the release of equity to fund housing costs for adult offspring—creates between the competing meanings of owned housing for older people. The book seeks to analyse the growing phenomenon of home equity use by older owners within a framework of risk, by combining a focused analysis of the theoretical, contextual and policy issues related to the particular tensions surrounding elders' use of home equity, with a sensitivity to the ways in which they must navigate through different types of risk related to using, not using or selecting particular options from within the different range of mechanisms for using, equity release. The aim is to draw appropriate connections between existing interdisciplinary analyses of housing equity transactions and their contexts, and legal and other perspectives on ageing, and to apply these insights to evaluate the adequacy of the relevant legal frameworks according to the tropes of vulnerability and responsibility. The book attempts to adopt a post-disciplinary, problem-centred perspective on older owners' housing equity transactions by de-centring legal structures and starting from the legal subject, located in her specific context.

While all property in errors and misjudgements remains my own, I owe many debts of thanks for support, encouragement, and useful advice and insights accrued during the gestation of this book. I am, as always, deeply indebted to my colleagues at Durham Law School, which I have found over many years now to be a most collegiate and scholarly environment. I am grateful for generous university research leave which enabled the majority of the research and writing to be completed. Particular thanks go to members of 'GLAD' (Gender and Law at Durham), who provided valuable feedback on aspects of the project drawing on feminist legal theory. During the last few years spent thinking about older owners and their financial transactions, I received valuable feedback on papers presented at various conferences, including the Society of Legal Scholars Annual Conference in 2008, the Association of Law, Property and Society's Annual Conference at Georgetown Law School in March 2011, and Emory Law School's workshop on 'Aging as a Feminist Issue' in January 2011. I owe a particular, longstanding debt to Professor Martha Fineman from Emory Law School, whose 'Feminism and Legal Theory Project' and, more recently, 'Vulnerability and the Human Condition Initiative' have played a major role in shaping how I have approached legal scholarship. Professor Nina Kohn from Syracuse Law

School also offered generous insights which greatly helped me in thinking through the questions of vulnerability and difference for older people. The people at Hart Publishing were once again a pleasure to work with, and I hope to have justified their faith in the project. Lastly, biggest thanks are reserved for David and Conor, the world's best boys and the light of my eyes.

Lorna Fox O'Mahony
Durham
June 2011

Summary Contents

Preface v
Contents xi
Table of Cases xv
Table of Legislation xix

1 **Housing Wealth and the 'Ageing Society'** 1

2 **Political and Policy Contexts** 23

3 **The Consumption of Housing Equity in a Risk Society** 44

4 **The Older Owner as a Legal Subject in Private Law** 72

5 **The Meanings of Home for Older Owners** 118

6 **Vulnerabilities and Older Owners** 157

7 **Older People and 'Ordinary Debt'** 204

8 **Fairness in Contract and Consumer Credit Regulations** 223

9 **Targeted Housing Equity Products and FSA Regulation** 264

10 **Equitable Remedies and Older Owners** 318

Conclusion 379

Index 385

Table of Contents

Preface	v
Summary Contents	ix
Table of Cases	xv
Table of Legislation	xix
1 Housing Wealth and the 'Ageing Society'	**1**
(1) Introduction	1
(2) Ageing Owners: the Demographic Context	5
(a) 'Intergenerational justice'	6
(b) Pensions	8
(c) Home ownership	10
(3) Ageing Owners: the Socio-economic Context	12
(a) Poverty and pensions	12
(b) Savings and housing wealth	15
(4) Conclusions	21
2 Political and Policy Contexts	**23**
(1) Introduction	23
(2) Political Perspectives on Ageing	25
(3) Political Expectations of Home Equity	30
(4) Older People, Rights and (In)Equality	37
(5) Conclusions	40
3 The Consumption of Housing Equity in a Risk Society	**44**
(1) Introduction	44
(2) The Conceptual Framework of Risk and the Rise of the 'Risk Society'	46
(a) Older owners, risk and housing equity transactions	50
(b) Home equity transactions: identifying the risks	54
(c) Welfare benefits, 'moral hazard' and the role of the State	60
(3) Owners as 'Risk Subjects' in Policy and Law	62
(4) Conclusions	71
4 The Older Owner as a Legal Subject in Private Law	**72**
(1) Introduction	72
(2) Legal 'Personality' in Private Law Theories	73
(3) The Liberal Legal Subject	78
(4) Challenges to the Liberal Legal Subject	83
(a) Substantive fairness	87
(b) Relational contract theory	94

(5) Property's Rational Subject 100
(6) Conclusions 115

5 The Meanings of Home for Older Owners 118
(1) Introduction 118
(2) Housing Consumption, Downsizing and Under-occupation 120
(3) Housing as Home: Ageing in Place 125
(4) Housing as Inheritance 138
(5) Housing as Investment: Spending Housing Wealth 146
(6) Conclusions 154

6 Vulnerabilities and Older Owners 157
(1) Introduction 157
(2) Capacity 160
(3) Age, Financial Capability and Economic Decision-making 166
(4) Financial Abuse of Older People 178
(5) Contextual or 'Situational' Vulnerabilities: Charting a Path Between Incapacity and Autonomy 184
(6) Vulnerability and Adverse Impact: The Measure of Harm 188
(7) Re-thinking Responsibility for 'Vulnerable Legal Subjects' 192
(8) Conclusions 202

7 Older People and 'Ordinary Debt' 204
(1) Introduction 204
(2) 'Trading Down' 205
(3) 'Ordinary Debt': Access and Enforcement 206
(a) 'Conventional' mortgage debt 207
(b) Bankruptcy 212
(c) Administration of Justice Act 1970, section 36 218
(4) Conclusions 219

8 Fairness in Contract and Consumer Credit Regulations 223
(1) Introduction 223
(2) 'Unfair Terms': Freedom and Fairness 224
(3) Unfair Contract Terms Act 1977 226
(4) Unfair Terms in Consumer Contracts Regulation 1999 227
(5) The Law Commissions and Unfair Terms 241
(6) Older Owners as 'Non-status Borrowers' 243
(7) The Consumer Credit Act 1974 247
(a) 'Extortionate bargains' 247
(b) Consumer Credit Act 2006 250
(c) Financial Ombudsman Service 252
(d) 'Unfair relationships' 254
(8) Consumer Protection from Unfair Trading Regulations 2008 257
(9) Conclusions 260

9 Targeted Housing Equity Products and FSA Regulation **264**
(1) Introduction 264
(2) The Financial Services Authority's Approach to Regulation 266
(3) The Market for Targeted Housing Equity Transactions 269
(4) The Regulated Products 273
(a) 'Lifetime mortgages' 273
(b) Home reversion plans 284
(c) Sale-and-rent back transactions 290
(d) Regulatory redress and remedies 298
(5) The Limits of the Regulatory Regime 301
(6) Conclusions 309

10 Equitable Remedies and Older Owners **318**
(1) Introduction 318
(2) Undue Influence 323
(a) Presumed undue influence and older owners 326
(b) The relationship of trust and confidence 328
(c) The jurisprudential basis of undue influence 335
(d) Does the transaction call for explanation? 348
(e) The nature and scope of the creditor's responsibilities 352
(3) Unconscionable Bargain Doctrine 369
(4) Conclusions 376

Conclusion **379**

Index 385

Table of Cases

Abbey National Building Society v Cann [1991] AC 56 63
AIB plc v Byrne [1995] 2 FLR 325 (ChD) 354–55
Alec Lobb (Garages) Ltd v Total Oil (Great Britain) Ltd [1983] 1 WLR 87 370–72
Allcard v Skinner (1887) 36 ChD 145 .... 325, 335–36, 340, 348
Archer v Cutler [1980] 1 NZLR 386 163
Ashbourne v Melbourne Money Pty Ltd [1992] ANZ ConvR 95 339
Avon Finance v Bridger [1985] 2 All ER 281 .... 329–31, 353
Backhouse v Backhouse [1978] 1 All ER 1158 370
Bainbrigge v Browne (1881) 18 ChD 188 327
Baker v Monk (1864) 4 De GJ & S 386 371
Banco Exterior Internacional v Mann [1995] 1 FLR 602 (CA) 359, 365
Bank for Credit and Commerce International v Aboody [1990] 1 QB 923 348
Bank of Baroda v Rayarel [1995] 2 FLR 376 359
Bank of Baroda v Shah [1988] 3 All ER 24 359
Bank of Ireland Home Mortgages Ltd v Bell [2001] 2 All ER (Comm) 920 .... 211, 213
Bank of Montreal v Hancock (1982) 137 DLR (3d) 648 (Ontario High Court of Justice) 368
Barclay's Bank plc v Kennedy [1989] 1 FLR 356 353
Barclay's Bank plc v O'Brien [1993] QB 109 (CA); [1994] 1 AC 180 (HL) 327, 331–33, 353–55
Barclays Bank plc v Thomson [1997] 1 FLR 156 359
Barons Finance Ltd v Olubisi Mayor's and City of London Court, 26 April 2010, Claim No: 7BB82089 256
Blomley v Ryan (1956) 99 CLR 362 371
Boustany v Piggott (1995) 69 P & CR 298 371
Bristol &West Building Society v Ellis (1996) 73 P&CR 158 (CA) 219
Broadwick Financial Services Ltd v Spencer and another [2002] EWCA Civ 35 .... 244, 249–50
Buckley v Irwin [1960] *Northern Ireland Law Reports* 98 371
Butler v Miller (1867) IR 1 Eq 195 371
Campbell v Campbell (Ch, 21 February 1996) 349
Castle Phillips & Co Ltd v Wilkinson [1992] *Consumer Credit Law Reports* 83 256
Chaplin & Co Ltd v Brammall [1908] 1 KB 233 353
Cheese v Thomas [1994] 1 All ER 35 .... 327–28, 340
Cheltenham & Gloucester Building Society v Ebbage [1994] *Current Law Yearbook* 3292 226
Cheltenham & Gloucester Building Society v Norgan [1996] 3 FCR 621 218–19
CIBC Mortgages plc v Pitt [1994] 1 AC 200 .... 327, 354, 365
Cityland and Property (Holdings) Ltd v Dabrah [1968] Ch 166 223
Clark v Malpas (1862) 4 De GF & J 401 371
Clarke v Prus [1995] New Property Cases 41 (Ch) 325–26
Claughton v Charalamabous [1999] 1 FLR 740 213
Close Invoice Finance Ltd v Pile [2008] EWHC 1580 (Ch) 213
Commercial Bank of Australia Ltd v Amadio (1983) 151 CLR 447 370–71
Cooke v Lamotte (1851) Beav 234 328
Credit Lyonnais Bank Nederland NV v Burch [1997] 1 All ER 144 .... 119, 370–71
Cresswell v Potter [1978] 1 WLR 255 370–71

Davies v Dobson (ChD, 7 July 2000) 330
Dean v Stout [2005] EWHC 3315 (Ch) 214
Director General of Fair Trading v First National Bank plc [2001] UKHL 52 228–9
Earl of Aylesford v Morris (1873) LR 8 Ch App 484 375
Earl of Chesterfield v Janssen (1751) 2 Ves Sen 125 373
Elgie v Campbell (1865) 12 Gr 132 328
Evans v Llewellin (1787) 1 Cox 333 371
Everitt v Budhram [2009] EWHC 1219 (Ch) 213
First National Bank plc v Achampong [2003] EWCA Civ 487 .... 211, 213
Forsdike v Forsdike (CA (Civ), 21 February 1997) 331
Fry v Lane (1887) 40 Ch D 312 .... 97, 371
Garcia v National Australia Bank Ltd (1998) 194 CLR 395 345
Garvey v McMinn (1846) 9 Ir Eq Rep 526 371
Ghaidan v Godin-Mendoza [2004] UKHL 30 .... 39, 174
Glanville v Glanville [2002] EWHC 1587 (Ch) 349
Goldsworthy v Brickell [1987] 1 Ch 378 338–39
Grealish v Murphy [1946] *Irish Reports* 35 371
Greene King Ltd v Stanley [2001] EWCA Civ 1966 .... 328, 365–67, 377
Grigby v Cox (1750) 1 Ves Sen 517, 27 ER 1178 331–32
Hammond v Osborn [2002] EWCA Civ 885 .... 181, 328
Harry v Kreutziger (1979) 95 DLR (3d) 231 371
Hart v O'Connor [1985] AC 1000 163
Heathcote v Paignon (1787) 2 Bro CC 167 373
Hosking v Michaelides [2004] All ER (D) 147 214
Howes v Bishop [1909] 2 KB 390 332
Howley v Cook (1873) IR 8 Eq 570 371
Humphreys v Humphreys [2004] EWHC 2201 (Ch) 328
Imperial Loan Co v Stone [1892] 1 QB 599 163
Inche Noriah v Shaik Allie Bin Omar [1929] AC 127 327
Investors Compensation Scheme v West Bromwich Building Society [1999] Lloyd's Rep PN 496 .... 304, 329
Jennings v Cairns [2003] EWCA Civ 1935 327
Jones v Morgan [2001] EWCA Civ 995 372
Judd v Brown [1998] 2 FLR 360 213
Ketley v Scott [1981] ICR 241 248
Khodari v Al Tamimi [2008] EWHC 3065 (QB) 256
Kindlance Ltd v Murphy (1997, High Court of Northern Ireland) 228
Kingsnorth Trust Ltd v Bell [1986] 1 All ER 423 (CA) 332, 353
Langton v Langton [1995] 2 FLR 890 .... 325–26, 349
Lavelle v Lavelle [2004] EWCA Civ 223 349
Lloyd's Bank Ltd v Bundy [1975] QB 326 .... 321, 369, 371
Lloyd's Bank plc v Egremont [1990] 2 FLR 351 359
Local Loan Co v Hunt 292 US 234 at 244 (1934) (USA) 191, 215
London Borough of Newham v Khatun [2004] EWCA Civ 44 227
Longmate v Ledger (1860) 2 Giff 157 371
Louth v Diprose (1992) 175 CLR 621 371
Lydon v Coyne [1946] Irish Jurist Report 64 371
Madsen Estate v Saylor [2007] SCC 18 (Sup Ct (Can)) 349
Martin-Sklan v White [2006] EWHC 3313 213
Masterman-Lister v Brutton & Co (No 1) [2002] EWCA Civ 1889, [2003] 1 WLR 1511 162–63
McGinn v Grangewood Securities Ltd [2002] EWCA Civ 522 250

McGuffick v Royal Bank of Scotland plc [2009] EWHC 2386 (Comm) 259
Meredith v Lackschewitz-Martin [2002] EWHC 1462 (Ch) 328–29
Midland Bank Ltd v Greene (1993) 27 *Housing Law Reports* 350 (ChD) 355
Midland Bank plc v Massey [1994] 2 FLR 342 (CA) 354, 359
Midland Bank plc v Serter (1994) 26 *Housing Law Reports* 612 359
Midland Bank plc v Shephard [1988] 3 All ER 17 (CA) 353
Mitchell v 700 Young Street Pty Ltd [2001] VSC 116 (Cummins J, 23 April 2001) 339
Mortgage Agency Services Number Two Ltd v Chater [2003] EWCA Civ 490 328
Mortimer v Capper (1782) 1 Bro CC 156 374
Mrs U v Centre for Reproductive Medicine [2002] EWCA Civ 565 370
Multiservice Bookbinding v Marden [1979] Ch 84 370–71
Mutual Finance v John Wetton & Sons Ltd [1937] 2 KB 389 370
Nash and Staunton v Paragon Finance Plc [2001] EWCA Civ 1466 248
Nash v Paragon Finance Plc [2002] 1 WLR 685; *Paragon Finance plc v Nash* [2001] EWCA Civ 1466 .... 223, 256, 250
National Australia Bank Ltd v Garcia (1998) 194 CLR 395 (High Court of Australia) 368
National Westminster Bank plc v Morgan [1985] AC 686 .... 325, 372
Nicholls v Lan [2006] EWHC 1255 (Ch) 213
Nichols v Jessup [1986] 1 NZLR 226 371
Nine Regions (T/A Logbook Loans) v Sadeer Bromley County Court, 14 January 2009 256
Palk v Mortgage Services Funding plc [1993] Ch 330 211
Paragon Finance v Pender [2005] EWCA 760 256
Patel v Patel [2009] EWHC 3264 (QB) 251
Patel v R (on the application of IFG Financial Services Ltd) v Financial Ombudsman Service Ltd [2005] EWHC 1153 (Admin) 252
Pecore v Pecore [2007] SCC 17 (Sup Ct (Can)) 349
Pesticcio v Huet [2004] EWCA Civ 372 368
Pesticcio v Niersmans [2003] 2 *Planning & Compensation Reports* D22; *Niersmans v Pesticcio* [2004] EWCA Civ 372 .... 319, 326–28
Polonksi v Lloyd's Bank Mortgages Ltd (1997) 31 HLR 721 211
Portman Building Society v Dusangh [1999] EWCA Civ 1331, [2000] 2 All ER (Comm) 221 ... 302, 328–30, 355–57, 371–72
Powell v Powell [1900] 1 Ch 243 327
Printing and Numerical Registering Co v Samson (1875) LR 19 Eq 462 225
R (on behalf of the Incorporated Trustees of the National Council on Ageing) v Secretary of State for Business, Enterprise and Regulatory Reform, Case no C-388/07, 5 March 2009 4
R v Gilbertson [2009] EWCA Crim 1715 183
R v Waveney DC, ex p Bowers [1983] QB 238 158
Radley v Bruno [2006] EWHC 2888 (Ch) 367, 377
Rae v Joyce (1892) LR Ir 500 371
Randall v Randall [2004] EWHC 2258 .... 327, 350
Re A: A v A [2002] EWHC 611 213
Re Bremner [1999] 1 FLR 912 (ChD) 213
Re Brocklehurst's Estate [1978] 1 Ch 14 .... 331, 338, 349
Re Citro (A Bankrupt) [1991] Ch 142 214
Re Craig [1971] 1 Ch 95 338
Re MB (Medical Treatment) [1997] 2 FLR 426 162
Re MM (An Adult) [2007] EWHC 2003 (Fam) 162–63
Re Raval (A Bankrupt) [1998] 2 FLR 718 213
Re Walker [1905] 1 Ch 60 163
Regina (Weaver) v London & Quadrant Housing Trust [2008] EWHC 1377 38

Rooney v Conway [1982] 5 Northern Ireland Judgements Bulletin 371
Ropaigealach v Barclay's Bank plc [2000]1 QB 263 (CA) 218
Royal Bank of Scotland v Etridge (No 2) [2002] 2 AC 773, [2001] 4 All ER 449 ...... 146, 325–8, 335, 342–43, 345, 348, 350, 352–53, 355–56, 358–60, 362–63, 365–368, 377
Sheffield City Council v E [2004] EWHC 2808 (Fam); [2005] Fam 326 163
Simpson v Simpson [1992] 1 FLR 601 338
Slator v Nolan (1876) IR 11 Eq 367 371
State Bank of India v Soni (CA, 17 February 1997) 327
Stovin v Wise [1996] 3 All ER 801 93
Symons v Williams [1875] VLR 199 328
Tessman v Costello [1987] 1 Qd R 283 339
Tew and others v Bank of Scotland (Shared Appreciation Mortgages) No 1 plc and others [2010] EWHC 203 (Ch) 239–40, 274
TSB Bank plc v Marshall [1998] 39 EG 308 211
Tufton v Sperni [1952] 2 *Times Law Reports* 516 368
Turnbull & Co Ltd v Duval [1902] AC 429 (PC) 353
UK Housing Alliance (North West) Ltd v Francis [2010] EWCA Civ 117 .... 84, 235–39, 297
United States v Smith 113 F 3d 737, 741 (10th Cir 1997) (USA) 179
Vale v Armstrong [2004] EWHC 1160 (Ch) 327–28
Vernon v Bethell (1762) 2 Eden 110 373
Watson v Huber [2005] All ER (D) 156 (Mar) 327, 328, 358
Williams and Glyns' Bank Ltd v Boland [1981] AC 487 63
Williams v Bayley (1866) LR 1 LH 200 337
Williams v Williams [2003] EWHC (Ch) 742 327
Wilson v First County Trust Ltd [2003] UKHL 40 257
Wood v Abrey (1818) 3 Madd 417 371
Woods v Hubley (1995) 130 DLR (4d) 119) 371
Woodstead Finance Ltd v Petrou [1986] 1 FLR 158 249
Wright v Cherrytree Finance Ltd [2001] 2 All ER (Comm) 877 357–58
Yerkey v Jones (1939) 63 CLR 649 .... 332, 345
YL v Birmingham City Council [2007] UKHL 27 38

Table of Legislation

Administration of Justice Act 1970, section 36 218–19
Assembly Bill 1046 (2009) (USA) 216
California Code of Civil Procedure §704.730 (USA) 216
Charging Orders Act 1979 210
Colo.Rev.Stat. §38.41.201–212 (USA) 216
Consumer Credit (Advertisements) Regulations 2004 (SI 2004/1484) 252
Consumer Credit (Agreements) (Amendment) Regulations 2004 (SI 2004/1482) 252
Consumer Credit (Agreements) Regulations 1983 (SI 1983/1553) 252
Consumer Credit (Agreements) Regulations 2010 (SI 2010/1014) 252
Consumer Credit (Disclosure of Information) Regulations 2004 (SI 2003/1481) 252
Consumer Credit (Disclosure of Information) Regulations 2010 (SI 2010/1013) 252
Consumer Credit Act 1974 .... 230, 239, 243–44, 246, 247–57, 261, 374
Consumer Credit Act 1974, section 137(2)(b)) 248
Consumer Credit Act 1974, section 138 248–49
Consumer Credit Act 1974, section 140 .... 243, 250
Consumer Credit Act 1974, section 39(A) 256
Consumer Credit Act 2006 .... 239, 243, 245, 250–252, 254–57, 374
Consumer Credit Act 2006, section 140A 251, 255
Consumer Credit Act 2006, section 5 252
Consumer Credit Directive 2008 (2008/48/EEC) 252
Consumer Protection from Unfair Trading Regulations 2008 (SI 2008/1277) 56, 183, 257–60, 293
Consumer Protection from Unfair Trading Regulations 2008 (SI 2008/1277), Reg 7 258
Consumer Protection from Unfair Trading Regulations 2008 (SI 2008/1277), Reg 7(3)(b) 184
Criminal Law Act 1977 218
Employment Equality (Age) Regulations 2006(SI 2006/1031) 4
Enterprise Act 2002 .... 64, 214, 217–18
Enterprise Act 2002, Part 8 252
Enterprise Act 2002, section 313A 214
Equality Act 2010 .... 209–10, 243,
Equality Act 2010, section 5 209
Equality Act 2010, section 13(2) 209
Equality Act 2010, section 29 209
Equality Act 2010, Part 3 209
EU Framework Equal Treatment Directive (2000/78/EC). 4
EU Unfair Commercial Practices Directive 257
European Consumer Credit Directive, Directive 2008/48/EC, Art 5(6), Recital 27 307
European Council Directive on Unfair Terms in Consumer Contracts (Directive 93/13/EEC) [1993] OJ L95/29 227
Financial Services and Markets Act 2000 (Regulated Activities) (Amendment) Order 2009 (SI 2009/1342) 231, 266, 290
Financial Services and Markets Act 2000 (Regulated Activities) Order 2001 (SI 2001/544) 230, 266, 274
Financial Services and Markets Act 2000 .... 244, 266, 312

Financial Services and Markets Act 2000, section 5 302
Financial Services and Markets Act 2000, section 151(2) 312
Financial Services and Markets Act 2000, section 155 266
Financial Services and Markets Act 2000, section 226A 252
Fraud Act 2005, section 4 180
Haw.Rev.Stat. §651–92 (USA) 216
Homeownership and Economic Opportunity Act 2000 (USA) 152
Housing Act 1949 30
Housing Act 1969 30
Housing Act 1988 297
Housing Grants, Construction and Regeneration Act 1996 30
Human Rights Act 1998 .... 38, 39
Human Rights Act 1998, s6 38
Insolvency Act 1986, section 264 212
Insolvency Act 1986, section 276 212
Insolvency Act 1986 267–72
Insolvency Act 1986, section 281 5
Insolvency Act 1986, section 283 .... 214, 215
Insolvency Act 1986, section 330 212
Insolvency Act 1986, section 335A 212
Insolvency Proceedings (Monetary Limits) (Amendment) Order 2004 (SI 2004/547) 214
Interim Permitted Regulated Sale and Rent Back Activities Instrument 2009 .... 266, 290, 294
Land Registration Act 2002 106
Law of Property Act 1925 .... 62, 105
Law of Property Act 1925, section 91(2) 210–11
Law of Property Act 1925, sections 101–103 210
Local Government and Housing Act 1989 30
Me.Rev.Stat. Ann tit 14, §4422 (USA) 216
Mental Capacity Act 2005 .... 161, 162, 180
Mental Capacity Act 2005, section 1(4) 161
Mental Capacity Act 2005, section 2(1) 161
Mental Capacity Act 2005, section 2(3)(a) 161
Mental Capacity Act 2005, section 3(4) 161
Mental Capacity Act 2005, section 16(2) 161
Old Age and Widows and Orphans Contributory Pensions Act 1925 13
Private Tenancies (Northern Ireland) Order 2006 (NISI 2006/1459) 297
Protection from Eviction Act 1977 218
Regulation of Financial Services (Land Transactions) Act 2005 .... 266, 286–87
Regulatory Reform (Housing Assistance) (England and Wales) Order 2002 (SI 2002/1860) 31
Reverse Mortgage Insurance for Older Americans Act of 1989 (USA) 152
Sale of Goods Act 1893 226–27
Senior Citizen Homestead Exemption (35 ILCS 200/15–170) (USA) 216
Senior Citizens Against Marketing Scams Act 1993 (USA) 18 USC §2326 (1994 & Supp III 1998) 179
Senior Citizens Home Equity Protection Act 1997 (USA) 152
South Dakota Codified Laws Ann §43–31–1 (USA) 216
Trusts of Land and Appointment of Trustees Act 1996, section 14 211
Trusts of Land and Appointment of Trustees Act 1996, section 15 211
Unfair Contract Terms Act 1977 .... 89, 224, 226–27, 241–42
Unfair Contract Terms Act 1977, section 2 226
Unfair Contract Terms Act 1977, section 3 226

Unfair Contract Terms Act 1977, section 4 226
Unfair Contract Terms Act 1977, schedule 1, para 1(b) 226
Unfair Terms in Consumer Contract Regulations 1999 (SI 1999/2083) 84, 89, 119, 224, 227–40, 241–2, 248, 255, 260–61, 379
Unfair Terms in Consumer Contract Regulations 1999 (SI 1999/2083), Reg 5 229
Unfair Terms in Consumer Contract Regulations 1999 (SI 1999/2083), Reg 6(2) 228
Unfair Terms in Consumer Contract Regulations 1999 (SI 1999/2083), Schedule 2 ..... 230, 232–33

To Eileen McCullagh
my wonderful grandmother
with love and affection

1

Housing Wealth and the 'Ageing Society'

(1) Introduction

Issues relating to older owners, their homes and the transactions they enter into have attracted considerable attention in recent years.[1] A key aspect of the 'ageing society' in developed countries concerns the ways in which ageing owners use—and are expected to use—their housing equity to support various activities and needs in later life. There has been an exponential growth in recognition of the potential for housing equity to be used

[1] Much of the policy discussion in England and Wales has focused on regulation of the financial services market targeted at the elderly, as discussed in ch 9. In Ireland, the Law Reform Commission (LRC) has published a Consultation Paper on *Law and the Elderly* which included a section on 'Protection against Financial Abuse' in relation to both products aimed at elderly people, and issues relating to undue influence and unconscionable transactions in other contracts involving property; further work in this area was identified in the Commission's 'Third Programme of Work (2007–2014)'. The Commission's 2003 Consultation Paper, *Consultation Paper on Law and the Elderly* (LRC CP 23—2003), formed part of its second programme of law reform (2000–2007) and identified, under 'Vulnerable Groups and the Law', consideration of 'law and the elderly, including the legal protection of older persons transferring assets and "advance care directives"'; see 'Second Programme for Examination of Certain Branches of the Law with a View to their Reform: 2000–2007', available online at <http://www.lawreform.ie/lawunderreview/secondproglawreform.htm>. Although the *Report on Vulnerable Adults and the Law* (LRC 83—2006) was published in 2006, this focused primarily on issues relating to capacity and assisted decision-making amongst vulnerable adults, and did not specifically address issues of financial abuse. The LRC's work in respect of vulnerable adults has continued to focus on mental capacity and the wards of court system (see ch 6 of this book). A recent upsurge in the use of equity release products in Australia also prompted the Australian Securities and Investments Commission to publish a report in 2005 to highlight the risk associated with trading-in the equity in one's owner-occupied home; see Australian Securities and Investment Commission, *Equity release products* (Report 59, November 2005), available online at <http://www.asic.gov.au/fido/fido.nsf/lkuppdf/FIDO+PDFW?opendocument&key=Equity_release_report_pdf>. In the US, considerable academic attention has focused on the use of reverse mortgage products and other forms of equity release amongst the elderly—see, eg, NK Kutty, 'The Scope for Poverty Alleviation among Elderly Home-owners in the United States through Reverse Mortgages' (1998) 35 *Urban Studies* 113–29; IF Megbolugbe, J Sa-Aadu and JD Shilling, 'Oh, Yes, the Elderly Will Reduce Housing Equity under the Right Circumstances' (1999) 9 *Journal of Housing Research* 53; RG Quercia, 'House Value Appreciation among Older Homeowners: Implications for Reverse Mortgage Programs' (1999) 9 *Journal of Housing Research* 201; S Merrill, M Finkel and N Kutty, 'Beneficiaries from reverse mortgage products for elderly home-owners: an analysis of American housing survey data' (1994) 22 *Journal of the American Real Estate and Urban Economics Association* 257; US Department of Housing and Urban Development, *No Place Like Home: A Report to Congress on FHA's Home Equity Conversion Mortgage Program* (Washington, DC, 2000). Although the overriding impetus in US policy since the enactment of the FHA Reverse Mortgage Legislation, the Housing and Community Development Act of 1987 (s 825), has been to facilitate equity release through reverse mortgages to elderly homeowners, following the crash in the sub-prime mortgage lending business in the US which began in 2007, consumer advocates began to call for Congress to investigate the degree of legal protection afforded to elderly consumers by unscrupulous lenders; see US Senate Special Committee on Aging December hearing on 'Foreclosure Aftermath: Preying on Senior Homeowners', available online at < http://aging.senate.gov/hearing_detail.cfm?id=316277&>.

in later life to alleviate poverty rates,[2] subsidise living expenses,[3] cover the costs of housing needs,[4] or fund healthcare or welfare needs after retirement.[5] The growth in opportunities for equity release, and changing expectations regarding the use of housing wealth, have also, crucially, been accompanied by an attitude shift amongst UK homeowners, away from the idea that the owned home provides a repository of wealth to pass on through inheritance, and towards the idea that it will provide a resource of capital and income to spend during the life-course 'either on high days and holidays, or to meet a more sobering array of welfare needs'.[6] This book sets out to consider whether current legal approaches to regulate and, in some cases, remedy these transactions are appropriate in light of the particular risks and vulnerabilities associated with housing equity transactions for (marginal) older owners. This chapter opens the discussion by setting out the demographic and socio-economic policy contexts of housing equity use by a growing population of ageing homeowners, and highlighting the urgent need for socio-legal analysis of the issues which have emerged concerning the use of home equity by older owners.

Official statistics emphasise the need to ensure that governmental and legal policy-makers are sensitive to the issues affecting Britain's ageing population. With birth rates falling and increasing numbers of people living into very old age, the proportion of the population of England aged over 65 years of age is set to grow from 15.6 per cent in 2000 to 19.2 per cent by 2021.[7] Globally, the 'oldest old' (those aged 80 years or over) are the fastest-growing population, currently increasing at 3.9 per cent per year.[8] In Britain, the number of centenarians has been increasing at a more rapid rate than any other population group since the 1950s.[9] As the 'baby-boomer generation' reaches retirement age, policy analysts are increasingly concerned with the implications of this 'Agequake' for economic and social policies,[10] and it is likely that scholarly interest in issues affecting, and affected by, older people will continue to grow in the decades to come. As Kutty has noted

[2] R Hancock, 'Can Housing Wealth Alleviate Poverty among Britain's Older Population?' (2005) 19 *Fiscal Studies* 249; NK Kutty, 'The Scope for Poverty Alleviation among Elderly Home-owners in the United States through Reverse Mortgages' (1998) 35 *Urban Studies* 113.

[3] E Hurst and F Stafford, 'Home Is Where the Equity Is: Mortgage Refinancing and Household Consumption' (2004) 36 *Journal of Money, Credit and Banking* 985.

[4] SF Venti and DA Wise, 'Aging and Housing Equity: Another Look', *NBER Working Paper No W8608*, November 2001, available online at <http://papers.ssrn.com/sol3/papers.cfm?abstract_id=240728>.

[5] S Lowe, 'Capital accumulation in home-ownership and family welfare' in N Manning and C Ungerson (eds), *Social Policy Review 1989–90* (London, Longman, 1990); S Lowe, 'Home-ownership, wealth and welfare: new connections' in A Corden, E Robertson and K Tolley (eds), *Meeting Needs in an Affluent Society* (Aldershot, Avebury, 1992).

[6] SJ Smith, BA Searle and N Cook, 'Rethinking the Risks of Home Ownership' (2009) 38 *Journal of Social Policy* 83, 89; see also K Rowlingson and S McKay, *Attitudes to Inheritance in Britain* (Bristol, Policy Press, 2005); J Smith, 'Exploring attitudes to housing wealth and retirement' (2004) 63 *Housing Finance* 34; SJ Smith, 'Owner-occupation: living with a hybrid of money and materials' (2008) 40 *Environment and Planning A* 520; see further discussion in ch 5.

[7] Statistics available online at http://www.statistics.gov.uk/cci/nugget.asp?id=949.

[8] United Nations Department of Economic and Social Affairs, Population Division, *World Population Aging 2007* (New York, UN, 2007), Executive Summary, xxvii. In 2007, those aged 80 years or over made up about 12.5% of the 60-plus population, but this is set to grow to about 20% by 2050 (*ibid*).

[9] Official statistics available online at <www.statistics.gov.uk/cci/nugget.asp?id=1875>.

[10] See, eg, SA Nyce and SJ Schieber, *The Economic Implications of Aging Societies: The Costs of Living Happily Ever After* (Cambridge, CUP, 2005); A Tinker, 'The Social Implications of an Aging Population' (2002) 123 *Mechanisms of Aging and Development* 729; P Wallace, *Agequake: Riding the Demographic Rollercoaster Shaking Business, Finance and Our World* (London, N Brearley Publishing 1999); J Tavares Alvarez, *Reflections on an Agequake* (New York, UN–NGO Committee on Aging, 1999).

in the US context, 'The economic and social wellbeing of the growing elderly population is ... an important issue for society in general and for policy-makers in particular.'[11]

The demographic and socio-economic contexts set out in this chapter are central to the 'situational' context of older owners in housing equity transactions. In a policy context which is primed for increasing use of housing equity by older owners,[12] it is important to assess the legal protections, regulations and remedies available to older consumers. The analysis in this book starts from the view that in any assessment of the *appropriateness* of legal protections and procedures governing home equity transactions—including when and why law protects, or does not protect, older owners in particular types of home equity transaction—the *context* of financial decision-making by older owners is crucial. The older owner's personal context or situation is central not only to the decision to release equity, but also to the options and products available to any given owner to enable equity release. This is particularly the case for 'marginal owners', owners in lower-value properties, who are also likely to have lower incomes, pensions and savings, and to face multiple demands on their housing wealth, which makes spending housing equity more 'high-risk' for them than for the general population. The growth and diversification of the home-ownership sector has included the substantial growth of marginal ownership.[13] Marginal owners are increasingly likely to face multiple and complex demands on their housing equity,[14] which—with home ownership seen as a proxy for active citizenship, and housing equity a store of wealth to meet a range of welfare needs—they are politically constructed, as 'owners', as 'responsible' for meeting through their own resources.[15]

In assessing the nature and extent of legal protections, regulations and remedies for older owners, the focus of this analysis is on those who are most vulnerable or 'at risk'. In keeping with the importance of affordability in financial transactions, the term 'older owners' is interpreted as referring to those who have passed the 'normal' age for retirement.[16] Although recognising that the point at which a retirement age is set may be viewed as arbitrary, and imposes a particular perspective which treats ageing as the 'problem',[17] the age at which people retire has a significant impact on their income, which in turn drives housing equity transactions. In the UK at present the normal retirement age is usually 65 years of age for men and 60 for women, although some may retire earlier[18]

[11] Kutty, above n 2.

[12] See further ch 2.

[13] See R Burrows, *Home-ownership and poverty in Britain, Findings* (York, Joseph Rowntree Foundation, 2003), indicating that half of the people 'living in poverty' in the UK were homeowners.

[14] Eg, maintenance and repair costs for what are often older properties; R Burrows and S Wilcox, *Half the poor: Home-owners with low incomes* (London, Council of Mortgage Lenders, 2000).

[15] See, eg, Department of Communities and Local Government, *Homes for the Future: More affordable, more sustainable*, Cm 7191 (London, DCLG, 2007); for further discussion of the political and policy contexts of housing equity transactions, see ch 2.

[16] This is the most commonly used definition of 'old age'; see NS Walford and S Kurek 'A comparative analysis of population ageing in urban and rural areas of England and Wales, and Poland over the last three census intervals' (2008) 14 *Population, Space and Place* 365.

[17] Rather than an overall shortage of employment, or a shortage of younger people contributing to the economy, which could be solved by changing immigration policies, or a shortage of suitable and affordable housing; see F Heywood, C Oldman and R Means, *Housing and Home in Later Life* (Milton Keynes, Open University Press, 2002) 43.

[18] Banks and Smith describe 'two distinct groups with very different "retirement" experiences. At the top of the wealth distribution, early retirement has typically been influenced by private, occupational pensions; at the bottom of the wealth distribution, individuals are even more likely to be not working in their 50s, but do not

and some later.[19] Retirement age in the UK has traditionally been influenced by the State Pension Age, which was to be revised upwards from 2010, towards a targeted retirement age of 68 for both men and women by 2046.[20] However, this plan has been displaced by legal challenges to the default retirement age: the Employment Equality (Age) Regulations 2006, which made it lawful for UK employers to impose a mandatory retirement age of 65[21] have been challenged in the European Court of Justice,[22] leading the Coalition Government to publish proposals which will seek to phase out the default retirement age by October 2011.[23] At the time of writing it is not yet clear what the outcome of this initiative will be, or, if the default retirement age is phased out, what the effects will be on real income levels for older people. While the proposals would remove this age-based discriminatory barrier, the conventional retirement age continues to provide a useful rule of thumb for determining when an owner may be designated as 'older' for the purposes of the analysis in this book, based on two linked premises. First, since the proposed changes in legal status would make retirement a matter of choice rather than compulsion, it is not yet clear how dramatic an effect they would have on employment patterns, and particularly on income in old age for marginal as compared to affluent owners, and for the 'older old' as compared to the 'younger old'. Meanwhile, for those who have already retired, for those who will still choose to do so or for those whose transition into older old age makes

typically define themselves as retired and draw on income support or, more usually, disability benefits': J Banks and S Smith, 'Retirement in the UK' (2006) 22 *Oxford Review of Economic Policy* 40.

[19] The Department of Work and Pensions (DWP) has commissioned a number of research projects through its Extending Working Life Social Research Division, which has responsibility for undertaking research in this area; see, eg, A Hedges and W Sykes in association with C Groom, 'Extending working life: changing the culture. Qualitative research into effective messages', *Research Report No 557* (London, DWP, 2009), which was commissioned to help the DWP 'develop messages with the potential to change the way people think about when and how they should retire from paid work, and to encourage them to stay in work up to and beyond State Pension Age (SPA)' (*ibid*, at 1). See also C Phillipson and A Smith, 'Extending working life: A review of the research literature', *Research Report No 299* (London, DWP, 2005).

[20] See The Pension Service (DWP), State Pension forecast, available online at <http://www.thepensionservice.gov.uk/state-pension/forecast/home.asp>.

[21] The Employment Equality (Age) Regulations 2006 (SI 2006/1031) came into force in October 2006 to comply with the EU Framework Equal Treatment Directive (2000/78/EC). These Regulations render age discrimination in employment unlawful in the same way as discrimination on grounds of sex, race, disability, sexual orientation, or religion and belief. The Regulations also set a national default retirement age of 65, which makes compulsory retirement below the age of 65 unlawful unless it is objectively justified.

[22] This aspect of the Regulations has been described as 'an unfortunate and unnecessary step on the road to dealing with the relationship between dismissal and age'—C Kilpatrick, 'The New UK Retirement Regime, Employment Law and Pensions' (2008) 37 *Industrial Law Journal* 1—and was challenged at the European level, with the European Court of Justice finding an interference with the right to non-discrimination and referring the case back to the UK High Court to justify the legitimacy of the aim: see *R (on behalf of the Incorporated Trustees of the National Council on Ageing) v Secretary of State for Business, Enterprise and Regulatory Reform*, Case no C-388/07, 5 March 2009. In September 2009, Mr Justice Blake in the UK High Court deemed the Regulations proportionate, and so lawful, based on the policy environment in place when they were adopted in 2006, so giving the Government some breathing-space to review its policy. For a critique of the Employment Equality (Age) Regulations which describes the UK model as weaker than US, Canadian and Australian counterparts, see R Filinson, 'Age Discrimination Legislation in the UK: A Comparative and Gerontological Analysis' (2008) 23 *Journal of Cross-Cultural Gerontology* 225; for the arguments against mandatory retirement, see PA Lawrence, 'Retiring Retirement' (2008) 453 *Nature* 588.

[23] See, eg, Department for Business Innovation and Skills, *Phasing out the Default Retirement Age: Government Response to Consultation* (London, BIS, January 2011); available online at <http://www.bis.gov.uk/assets/biscore/employment-matters/docs/p/11–536-phasing-out-default-retirement-age-government-response.pdf>.

it impracticable to continue working, the shift from income generation through employment to decreased opportunities for future earnings will continue to feed the need to release housing equity. Furthermore, those who are no longer earning a regular salary are likely to suffer particular harm from disadvantageous financial transactions, when compared, for example, to younger owners who have a greater opportunity to 'recover' from a financial setback[24]—in the terminology of bankruptcy, to have a 'fresh start'.[25]

Chapter two places the housing equity transactions of older owners in their political and policy contexts, while chapters three and four explore the range of risks associated with home equity transactions for older owners, locating these risks within the sensitising framework of risk theories and considering the older owner first as a risk subject and then as a legal subject. Chapter five considers the intersection of a range of competing demands on the older owner's home: as *investment* to yield capital or income for various activities, from lifestyle wants to welfare needs, property maintenance to payment for long-term care; as *housing*, both for the older owner and as housing stock; and as *inheritance* to pass wealth to the next generation. Chapter six builds on these contextual analyses to consider the arguments surrounding the recognition of older (marginal) owners as 'vulnerable' in the context of housing equity transactions, and so in need of 'special protection'. The legal frameworks that regulate housing equity transactions—which range from trading down and 'ordinary' secured and unsecured debt to specialised housing equity products—are analysed in chapters seven to ten. In conclusion, the issues raised in the book are reviewed through a lens of risk and responsibility, to evaluate the appropriateness of the current approaches for marginal older owners and to reconsider law's role in responding to new types of risk related to housing equity use for older owners.

(2) Ageing Owners: the Demographic Context

In 1999, Paul Wallace published the book *Agequake: Riding the Demographic Rollercoaster Shaking Business, Finance and our World*,[26] which highlighted the implications of the unprecedented global population dynamics that have created an 'ageing society'. Falling birth rates, resulting from control over fertility and the tendency to have smaller families, and rising life spans due to advances in health and medical care,[27] have led to population projections showing that

> [t]oday in the developed world, 15 percent of the population is elderly. By 2030, according to the latest UN projections, the share will be closing in on 25 percent; by 2050, it will be closing in on

[24] Notwithstanding the adverse consequences of mortgage default and the threat of repossession, discussed in L Fox, *Conceptualising Home: Theories, Laws and Policies* (Oxford, Hart Publishing, 2006) ch 3.

[25] See Insolvency Act 1986, s 281 on discharge of bankrupts for details of this legislative policy.

[26] Wallace, above n 10.

[27] 'Since World War II, life expectancy at birth has risen from around age 45 to 65—a greater gain over the past 50 years than over the previous 5,000. In the developed countries, it has risen from around age 65 to between 75 and 80. Life expectancy at older ages has also improved dramatically.': R Jackson, *The Global Retirement Crisis: The Threat to World Stability and What to do about it* (Washington DC, Centre for Strategic and International Studies, 2002) 10.

> 30 percent. And that's just the average. In Japan and some European countries, the share will be passing 35 percent.[28]

The UN has described this process of population ageing as 'unprecedented, a process without parallel in the history of humanity'.[29] The global picture shows increases in the proportion of older people (aged 60 and over), with reductions in the proportion of children (aged under 15) as well as a decrease in the population of 'working age' (15–59); and the UN has projected that 'At the world level, the number of older persons is expected to exceed the number of children for the first time in 2047.'[30] With trends set to continue for as long as old age mortality remains in decline and fertility remains low,[31] the older population is expected to continue growing more rapidly than other age groups at least until 2050.[32]

While the global picture demonstrates consistent patterns across developed and developing countries, this 'Agequake' has significant implications for economic and social policies, the effects of which are already apparent in relatively high-wealth developed countries, where the process of population ageing is much more advanced. While the global elderly population was 11 per cent in 2007, UK statistics for the same year recorded 21.8 per cent of the population aged 60 or over,[33] and 2007 was also the first year in which the UK population over State pensionable age was higher than the population aged under 16.[34] Over the last 25 years the number of people aged 65 and over in the UK has increased by 16 per cent, from 8.5 million to 9.8 million.[35] Again, reflecting the global pattern, the rate of growth in the UK population aged 65 and over is only set to increase,[36] with the 'oldest old' (85 and over) currently the fastest growing age group in the UK[37] and projected to more than double again by 2032[38]; while in the same period, the proportion of the population aged between 16 and 64 is expected to fall from 65 per cent to 60 per cent.[39]

(a) 'Intergenerational justice'

One way of looking at the issues raised by these demographic changes is from an 'intergenerational justice' perspective. The exchange of support—practical, financial and

[28] *Ibid*, at 3.

[29] United Nations Department of Economic and Social Affairs, Population Division, *World Population Aging 2007* (New York, UN, 2007), Executive Summary, xxvi. See also S Harper, *Ageing Societies* (New York, Hodder Arnold, 2006).

[30] United Nations, above n 29, xxvi.

[31] *Ibid.*

[32] *Ibid*, at xxvii.

[33] *Ibid*, Table A.III.4.

[34] Office for National Statistics, 'Population Trends', *Report No 136* (Basingstoke, Palgrave Macmillan, 2009) 43; see also Office for National Statistics (2008), *More pensioners than under-16s for first time ever*, available at <www.statistics.gov.uk/cci/nugget.asp?ID=949>, attributed to the combined effect of lower fertility after 1974 and women born in the post-World War II baby boom reaching retirement age.

[35] Office for National Statistics, 'Population Trends', *Report No 134* (Basingstoke, Palgrave Macmillan, 2008) 9.

[36] *Ibid*, at 10.

[37] Office for National Statistics, *Report No 136*, above n 34, at 43, 56; see also E Dini and S Goldring, 'Estimating the changing population of the "oldest old"' (2008) 132 *Population Trends* 8.

[38] Reaching 3.1 million (4% of the total population); H Bray for the Office for National Statistics, '2006-based national population projections for the UK and constituent countries', *Population Trends* (Basingstoke, Palgrave Macmillan, 2008); 2006-based national population projections data available at <www.gad.gov.uk/Demography_Data/Population>.

[39] Office for National Statistics, *Report No 134*, above n 35, at 10.

social—within and across generations is central to our concept of social solidarity, whether at the societal or household level. The impact of the 'Agequake' on the 'generational contract', particularly in relation to housing, care and inheritance,[40] has raised issues of fairness and justice which were explored by the UK's Equality and Human Rights Commission in its *Just Aging?* programme, and which are discussed in chapter two.[41] On the global scale, the UN has described population ageing as 'profound' and as 'having major consequences and implications for all facets of human life'.[42] The issues raised by ageing are also clearly gendered: since women live longer than men, they constitute the majority of older people, nearly twice as many of the over-80 cohort, and four to five times as many centenarians.[43] Furthermore, with evidence to indicate that certain factors, for example living alone, are associated with older people being less financially capable and more vulnerable to financial abuse, and to unfair or exploitative contracts,[44] and longer life-expectancy and lower propensities to remarry meaning that older women are almost 250 per cent more likely to live alone compared to older men,[45] vulnerability and risk in housing equity transactions is also clearly gendered. With global ageing patterns poised to challenge the structural sustainability of the economy, particularly retirement systems, of family arrangements and even threatening to 'rearrange the world order',[46] this book argues that it will also challenge the way in which we need to think about housing equity transactions from socio-legal perspectives.

For governments, this has been captured in terms of policy questions about the balance between caring for the old, including the rising costs of pensions and health care provision, and the 'burden' this places on younger members of society to fund elder care through general taxation, against a backdrop of concerns about fiscal and economic stability and sustainability.[47] Yet the portrayal of the fiscal aspects of the 'ageing society' as involving an inevitable trade-off between care for the old and costs for the young has been challenged by arguments that such accounts rely upon a number of unproven assumptions, for example that increased numbers of older people necessarily means increased

[40] See, eg, M Izuhara, 'Residential property, cultural practices and the generational contract' (2005) 29 *International Journal of Urban and Regional Research* 327; M Izuhara, 'The Generational Contract between Care and Inheritance in Britain and Japan' (2004) 33 *Journal of Social Policy* 649.

[41] See <http://www.equalityhumanrights.com/fairer-britain/just-ageing/> and discussion in ch 2, section (4).

[42] United Nations Department of Economic and Social Affairs, above n 29, Executive Summary, xxvi. The report (*ibid*) claimed that: 'In the economic area, population ageing will have an impact on economic growth, savings, investment, consumption, labour markets, pensions, taxation and intergenerational transfers. In the social sphere, population ageing influences family composition and living arrangements, housing demand, migration trends, epidemiology and the need for health-care services. In the political arena, population ageing may shape voting patterns and political representation.'

[43] *Ibid*, at xxviii.

[44] See ch 6.

[45] 'Globally, an estimated 19 per cent of women aged 60 years or over live alone, whereas just 8 per cent of men in that age group do so': United Nations Department of Economic and Social Affairs, above n 29, Executive Summary, xxviii. The gap created by women's greater longevity is particularly evident amongst the oldest old: from more than 330 women aged 85 and over for every 100 men of the same age, and 155 women aged 65 and over, for every 100 men of the same age in 1982; to projections of just under 140 women aged 85 and over for every 100 men of the same age, and 120 women aged 65 and over for every 100 men of the same age by 2032; Office for National Statistics, *Report No 134*, above n 35, at 11.

[46] R Jackson, *The Global Retirement Crisis: The Threat to World Stability and What to Do About It* (Washington DC, Centre for Strategic and International Studies, 2002) Foreword.

[47] See generally, *ibid*; The World Bank, *Averting the Old Age Crisis: Policies to Protect the Old and Promote Growth* (New York, Oxford University Press, 2004).

health care costs, and that people over the age of 65 will not be economically and financially productive.[48] It is also argued that the current patterns are not 'new' but part of a rising trend which has not yet been proven to produce adverse economic consequences; and that reduced fertility rates may mean that an increased older population turns out to be a short-term problem which is matched by lower costs in other areas, such as providing services such as education for younger people. Herring argued that these limiting factors may mean that only a relatively small amount of economic growth is likely to be needed to compensate for increased costs.[49] This perspective is echoed by research for the Equality and Human Rights Commission which has suggested that claims about intergenerational conflict may be 'overblown'.[50]

With reference to these broader sustainability issues, the role of conserving older owners' financial resources through the avoidance of 'bad transactions' must also carry considerable policy weight. The macro-policy agenda has focused on the promotion of self-provision through the use(s) of housing equity to meet financial costs in old age, as an alternative to State-funded (through taxation) support. However, without a sufficiently robust legal system which provides appropriate levels of protection for older owners entering into such transactions, there is a risk that the self-provision strategy may be exhausted through bad transactions, leaving the older person to fall back on a State-funded safety-net in any event. There is a sympathetic relationship between achieving appropriate levels of legal protection in housing equity transactions and the wider policy context for fiscal sustainability in an ageing society, since strategies involving self-provisioning may potentially be undermined by legal norms which allow the housing assets of vulnerable older owners to be dissipated in ill-advised, unfair or inappropriate transactions. The interconnectedness of the policy agenda for older owners' housing equity use, on the one hand, and the legal framework governing these transactions, on the other, is an implicit theme of the arguments advanced in this book.

(b) Pensions

Concerns about financial provision for the growing population of older people has prompted a global discourse concerning pension provision, with 'the World Bank and the IMF at the forefront of attempts to foster a political climate conducive to the residualization of state welfare and the promotion of private and voluntary initiatives'.[51] The political context of these debates is explicitly and uncompromisingly neoliberal, and has 'largely excluded perspectives which might suggest an enlarged role for the State, and which might question the stability and cost-effectiveness of private schemes'.[52] The discourses of

[48] J Herring, *Older People in Law and Society* (Oxford, Oxford University Press, 2009) 198–99.

[49] *Ibid.*

[50] M Lee, *Just Ageing? Fairness, equality and the life course: Final Report* (London, Equality and Human Rights Commission, 2009) 8.

[51] N Yeates, *Globalisation and Social Policy* (London, Sage Publications, 2001) 122.

[52] CL Estes, S Biggs and C Phillipson, *Social Theory, Social Policy and Ageing: A Critical Introduction* (Maidenhead, Open University Press, 2003) 110; also noting that this discourse has excluded the groups most affected (eg older people, women and those on low incomes). Cesaratto claimed that 'Non-orthodox commentators have always been suspicious of the demographic alarm raised by mainstream scholars and by some international institutions. This suspicion is warranted since the demographic indicators, such as the ratio of old population to the working-age population, are misleading about the economic sustainability of the inactive population which depends, inter alia, on the share of the adult population that is actually employed and on the

self-provision and self-responsibility are also deeply embedded in the UK's political and legal cultures. Successive governments have reduced the cost of the State pension and increased expectations that citizens will provide for their own pension needs through privately-funded schemes (employer pensions or personal pensions),[53] while the cross-party promotion of home ownership and the residualisation of the public rental sector have created a large population of 'owners' (including marginal owners) who are constructed as self-responsible 'consumers' both in the new 'wealth-fare state'[54] and as legal subjects.[55] Indeed, Jackson has suggested that these policies 'have been so successful at controlling costs that some worry the UK may end up trading a budget problem for a poverty problem'.[56] Compared to northern EU comparators,[57] older people under the UK's neoliberal market-led model have a lower average standard of living and higher rates of poverty.[58]

While the promotion of housing equity transactions has been largely premised on a policy of financial self-provision in retirement, it is notable that in 2010, the Demographic Change and Housing Wealth project concluded an EU-wide study which found that wider access to, and use of, equity release products would provide only limited help in addressing Europe's pension shortfall.[59] In response to the European Green Paper on Pensions,[60] which suggested that strengthening the internal market for reverse mortgages could be part of a strategy of extending access to financial provision outside pensions,[61] the project found that equity release could not be relied upon to solve pension problems, since even if most owners spent their housing equity, this would not help the 25 per cent or so of renters, who are also likely to have the lowest income, savings and pension provision. The report also revealed that for those who do enter into housing equity transactions, it is those who have most to gain from releasing equity (that is, owners with high-value homes) who are also most likely to have adequate pension provision. As such, it highlighted reliance on housing equity as a strategy which is likely to increase inequalities, without helping those (including those owners) who are least well-provided

community's choices about the amount of output to be transferred to retirees.': S Cesaratto, 'Pensions in an Aging Society: A Symposium' (2006) 18 *Journal of Political Economy* 295, 296. See also A Walker, 'The economic "burden" of ageing and the prospect of intergenerational conflict' (1990) 10 *Ageing and Society* 377, on the role of the IMF and World Bank in pensions policies.

53 See A Walker and L Foster, 'Caught between virtue and ideological necessity. A century of pension policies in the UK' (2006) 18 *Journal of Political Economy* 427.

54 S Parkinson, BA Searle, SJ Smith, A Stokes and G Wood, 'Mortgage Equity Withdrawal in Australia and Britain: towards a wealth-fare state?' (2009) 9 *European Journal of Housing Policy* 363.

55 See further discussions of the implications of the 'owners as consumers' model throughout this book; and on the older owner as a legal subject, particularly ch 4.

56 Jackson, above n 46, at 55–56.

57 Which operate social democratic or corporatist pensions systems.

58 A Walker, A-M Guillemard and J Alber, *Social and Economic Policies and Older People in Europe* (Brussels, European Commission, 1993); A Walker and T Maltby, *Ageing Europe* (Buckingham, Open University Press, 1997); A Walker and G Naegele, 'Social protection: incomes, poverty and the reform of pension systems' in J Bond (ed), *Ageing in Society* (London, Sage, 2006). Walker and Foster have added that 'The UK ... has consistently had an old age poverty profile that looked more like the Southern EU states than its Northern neighbours': Walker and Foster, above n 53, at 442.

59 <http://www.chasm.bham.ac.uk/documents/press-release-demhow-reverse-mortgage.pdf>; for more details of the project, see generally <www.demhow.bham.ac.uk>.

60 European Commission, *Towards Adequate, Sustainable and Safe Pension Systems in Europe* (Green Paper, SEC (2010) 830) (Brussels, European Commission, 2010); available online at <http://www.eubusiness.com/topics/employment/future-pensions.gp>.

61 *Ibid*, para 3.3.1.

for. In addition, the risks which owners must take when entering into housing equity transactions, and the extent to which these risks are mitigated by appropriate legal protections, have significant implications for the effectiveness of a long-term strategy that treats housing equity use as a means to address the pension shortfall, with direct costs for local authorities where the (perceived) inadequacies of the legal framework require financial incentives to promote low income homeownership and action to guarantee the 'safety' of the products.

(c) Home ownership

The tenure patterns and home equity holdings of older owners also provide important context to the analyses in this book. Older people are more likely than the general population to be owner-occupiers (74 per cent compared to 72 per cent), and much more likely to own their homes outright. In 2006, 68 per cent of retired people owned their homes outright, compared to 32 per cent across all socio-economic groups, with 6 per cent owning subject to a mortgage compared to 40 per cent across all groups.[62] In 2008, 78 per cent of households in which the eldest person was aged 60–74 owned their own homes,[63] with the proportion of older people who own their homes outright projected to rise to 75 per cent by 2026.[64] In 2004, households of people over the age of 60 owned £932 billion of equity in their homes,[65] representing a significant repository of housing equity into which the equity release industry is keen to tap.[66]

For those older owners who are enjoying unprecedented affluence and are able—in an overall context of relative financial security—to use their housing wealth to improve their quality of life, housing equity transactions appear to offer significant opportunities: the 'risk worth taking'. Yet at the same time, government discourse has recognised that while the overarching picture suggests increasing affluence, the reality is much more complex, with statistical evidence pointing to a cohort of older homeowners who are increasingly polarised as affluent or marginal according to housing wealth—forming what the Department for Communities and Local Government has described as 'two nations in old age'.[67] While the current cohort of older owners are much more likely to have concentrated their assets in housing than earlier generations,[68] this wealth is not evenly distributed, and a key feature of the UK's housing profile is the stark contrast between well-off and marginal

[62] Office for National Statistics, *Social Trends 38* (Basingstoke, Palgrave Macmillan, 2008) Table 10.5.

[63] Department of Communities and Local Government, *Lifetime Homes, Lifetime Neighbourhoods: A National Strategy for Housing in an Aging Society* (Wetherby, DCLG, 2008) 29.

[64] *Ibid*; see also Department of Communities and Local Government, *Projected growth in numbers of older households* (Wetherby, DCLG, 2008); available online at <www.communities.gov.uk/housing/housing managementcare/housingolder/>.

[65] Department of Communities and Local Government, above n 63, at 29. See further, S Wilcox, *UK Housing Review 2006/2007* (Chartered Institute of Housing and Council of Mortgage Lenders, 2007), available at <http://www.cih.org/publications/pub361.htm>.

[66] The drive to 'kick-start' the equity release market and the policy agenda to overcome barriers to equity release are discussed in ch 5, section (5).

[67] Department of Communities and Local Government, above n 63, Executive Summary, para 11.

[68] In 2008, housing wealth accounted for 42% of household wealth, up from 22% in 1971: *ibid*, at 33.

older owners.[69] The Department of Communities and Local Government explicitly acknowledged in its *National Strategy for Housing in an Aging Society* that

> [o]n the one hand this is the story of the consolidation of advantage, of a generation of people who have done well for themselves and can afford to fund the next generation of advantage. On the other hand there is also the prospect of the consolidation of poverty. For those who have missed out on life's chances, for whatever reason, those chances become fewer in old age, and the opportunities to replenish meagre resources diminish. And even among those with significant housing assets, income can be low.[70]

A substantial proportion (50.3 per cent) of those older households designated by the Government as 'vulnerable' (defined as those in receipt of principal means-tested and disability benefits) are owner-occupier households[71]; and the risks this presents are compounded by the claim that this figure represents a significant under-estimation of the numbers of vulnerable pensioner households living in 'non-decent owner-occupied homes', in light of the relatively poor take-up of two measures of vulnerability, pension credit and council tax benefit, particularly amongst older owning households.[72]

In a pension system characterised by deregulation, privatisation and individual responsibility to save for retirement (including saving through home ownership as promoted by the Government throughout the latter half of the twentieth century),[73] the issue of wealth and income differentiation across the retired population provides important context to the decision-making in housing equity transactions. Furthermore, to the extent that differentiation in financial well-being has been associated with vulnerabilities—from evidence that the wealth gains from housing are place-specific and socio-economically unequal,[74] to the role of situational factors linked to place, including the effect of social location (for example, lacking contact with others experienced in using complex financial products) in contributing to low financial capability,[75] or linking social isolation (lack of family, friends, neighbours to offer advice) to heightened vulnerability to financial abuse[76]—this context is significant in assessing the appropriateness of legal protections for marginal older owners in housing equity transactions.

[69] Jackson has argued that 'Although the rapid growth in private pension funds is improving the retirement prospects of many workers—the UK now has more pension assets than the rest of the EU put together—others are being left behind. "Two worlds" of pensioners may be emerging: one where employer pensions are common and real incomes are rising, the other where retirees struggle to get by on public benefits that each year fall further behind wages.': Jackson, above n 46, at 55–56.

[70] Department of Communities and Local Government, above n 63, at 33.

[71] *Ibid*, at 32–33.

[72] S Wilcox, *UK Housing Review 2008/2009* (Chartered Institute of Housing and Council of Mortgage Lenders, 2009) 51, available at <http://www.cih.org/publications/pub365.htm>. Wilcox has predicted that 'These issues, and the challenges they present, will inevitably become more significant in the years ahead with the rapid growth in the numbers of older owner-occupied households'; *ibid.*

[73] See, eg, government publications describing home ownership as 'Of all forms of saving … one of the best. Of all forms of ownership this is one of the most satisfying to the individual and the most beneficial to the nation.': *Houses: the Next Step*, Cmnd 8996 (London, HMSO, 1953), Preamble; see also *House Purchase*, Cmnd 571, (London, HMSO, 1958); 'If the householder buys his house on mortgage he builds up by steady saving a capital asset for himself and his dependants': Department of the Environment, *Fair Deal for Housing*, Cmnd 6851 (London, HMSO, 1971) 4.

[74] R Burrows, *Home-ownership and poverty in Britain, Findings* (York, Joseph Rowntree Foundation, 2003); D Dorling, J Rigby, B Wheeler, D Ballas, B Thomas, F Eldin, D Bordon and R Lupton, *Poverty, wealth and place in Britain, 1968–2005* (York, Joseph Rowntree Foundation, 2007).

[75] See ch 6, section (3).

[76] See ch 6, section (4).

(3) Ageing Owners: the Socio-economic Context

The relative financial well-being of older owner-occupiers in the UK is complex and dependent on a combination of factors, including whether owners have been financially productive through employment, the extent to which they have self-provided for their old age through pensions, savings and accumulation of housing wealth (including how they have fared in the housing market), as well as their costs, including living costs, home maintenance costs, health care needs and so on. These variables give rise to a broad spectrum of socio-economic profiles amongst the UK's older population. Nevertheless, there are also a number of common features across the older population, including fewer wage-earners and greater reliance on public or private pensions or other private income streams (for example savings or housing wealth), with more people reliant on non-wage resources which provide relatively fixed incomes and may be subject to political risk (for example, changes in State pension or means-tested benefits) or economic risk (where occupational or private pension funds are linked to investment performance).

(a) Poverty and pensions

The relationship between old age and poverty was one of the central themes of Charles Booth's late nineteenth-century mapping of poverty in London,[77] and played a major role in the campaigns which led to the establishment of the old age pension in Britain in 1909.[78] Before the introduction of the State pension, older people who were no longer 'financially productive' through employment, and who were not independently wealthy, were dependent on either private charity or the public purse in the form of the Poor Laws.[79] Booth's research indicated that

> poverty in old age arose from a general financial inadequacy in earlier life which made long-run saving an economically irrational act for most workers, as there were more pressing and rewarding calls upon the family purse.[80]

When the Royal Commission on the Aged Poor reported in 1898, it estimated that 'of the two million people in Britain aged 65 and over, two-thirds of them were in want'.[81] It was the failure of this Commission to make recommendations to address the issue that fed the political pressure leading to the Old Age Pensions Act 1908.

[77] C Booth, *Pauperism, a Picture, and the Endowment of Old Age, an Argument* (London & New York, Macmillan & Co Ltd, 1892); C Booth, *The Aged Poor in England and Wales* (London, Macmillan & Co Ltd, 1894).

[78] See R Pope, A Pratt and B Hoyle (eds), *Social Welfare in Britain 1885–1985* (London, Croom Helm, 1986) 51 *et seq*.

[79] Charles Booth found old age to be a 'primary marker for poverty' among British households at the end of the nineteenth century, with a third of elderly households in receipt of poor law relief in 1891; PA David and M Thomas (eds), *The Economic Future in Historical Perspective* (Oxford, Oxford University Press, 2003) 490. See also A Walker and L Foster, 'Caught between virtue and ideological necessity. A century of pension policies in the UK' (2006) 18 *Review of Political Economy* 427, 428.

[80] Walker and Foster, above n 79, 428; see also P Johnston, *Saving and Spending—The Working-class Economy in Britain 1870–1939* (Oxford, Clarendon Press, 1985).

[81] Walker and Foster, above n 79, at 429.

Although the introduction of the universal State pension undoubtedly provided assistance for many older people living in poverty, it was not intended to be a 'total rescue'[82] system; rather, it 'provided limited cover for financial and moral reasons'[83] and was to be supplemented by additional funds accumulated through contributory systems, for example through The Old Age and Widows and Orphans Contributory Pensions Act 1925. Walker and Foster described the basic pension as 'a flat-rate income adequate for those lacking other resources but low enough to encourage voluntary additional saving'.[84] This dual system of basic State pension and supplementary private provision underpinned British pension policies from the early twentieth century until the neoliberal policies introduced under Thatcher[85] and followed by subsequent Conservative and Labour governments.[86]

The development of 'old age pension' schemes was regarded as a key element in the twentieth-century 'generational contract' between older, 'less economically productive' members of society on the one hand, and younger workers on the other.[87] In the UK and other welfare State societies, the State, implicitly and indirectly, 'made intergenerational transfers of resource through the mediums of taxation and social expenditure'.[88] This macro-level arrangement was supported by informal, micro-level arrangements in which 'for various reasons including reciprocity and affection, adult children provide care for their aging parents'.[89] The shifting terms of the micro-level 'contract', particularly in respect of housing wealth and inheritance, are discussed in more detail in chapter five. In its analysis of policies to protect older people, the World Bank noted that while the care of older people in traditional societies tends to be characterised by informal, reciprocal arrangements (where the older generation contribute productive labour, for example by

[82] See ch 4, section (3) for discussion of liberal legal arguments against 'total rescue' schemes.

[83] Walker and Foster, above n 79, at 429, also noting that the public pension 'was not, and was not intended to be, sufficient to live on by itself'; see also J Rhodes, *Public Sector Pensions* (London, George Allen & Unwin, 1965).

[84] Walker & Foster, above n 79, at 431.

[85] Walker, above n 52; J Ginn and S Arber, 'Changing patterns of pension inequality: a shift from state to private sources' (1999) 19 *Ageing and Society* 319.

[86] Walker and Foster noted that 'The New Labour governments since 1997 have reformulated welfare as the extension of individual ownership, aimed at promoting an increasing share of private funded schemes, while reducing the share of state spending on pensions. The expressed aim is to move from 60% state and 40% private provision to 40% state and 60% private provision. However, despite this emphasis on individual responsibility and its focus on the importance of paid work and saving in order to achieve financial security in old age, New Labour is also committed to reducing the number of older people in poverty.': Walker and Foster, above n 79, at 437. Measures seeking to alleviate poverty for older people under New Labour included the means-tested Pensions Credit scheme and Savings Credit to incentivise and reward those who save for their old age, and research for Help the Aged in 2008 suggested that these policies had had a positive impact in enabling some older people to benefit from a rise in prosperity: Help the Aged, *Debt and Older People* (London, Help the Aged, 2008), Executive Summary, 4.

[87] Although the generational contract has, historically, focused on various aspects of intergenerational relationships, including in the 1960s between the middle-aged and young people, Walker has noted that 'Now the debate about generations is being focused increasingly on the economic, social and moral obligations of the middle aged and young to the increasing numbers of older people and, in turn, the senior citizens', or future senior citizens' obligations to younger people.': A Walker (ed), *The New Generational Contract* (London, UCL Press, 1997) 2.

[88] *Ibid.* Walker added that 'the welfare state has operated as a system of intergenerational as well as intragenerational transfers and, therefore, has institutionalised and encouraged the expectation of reciprocity … It is the widespread acceptance of this dual responsibility [that the State should offer security in return for service and contribution] and the perceived deservingness of pensioners that gives the social contract its legitimacy in the eyes of tax-payers and voters.': *ibid*, at 2–3.

[89] *Ibid*, at 3.

providing care for grand-children, in exchange for housing and financial support), these types of arrangement have become less common in industrial societies as families become smaller and more dispersed, young people have greater employment opportunities, and, while people live longer, the older person's time and contributions are de-valued, with the result that they 'are likely to withdraw from productive work, to live alone, and to depend on nonfamily sources of income in their old age'.[90]

The demographic changes discussed in this chapter have also been associated with the 'renegotiation' of the macro-level generational contract[91] in discourses supporting neoliberal policies based on privatisation and individual responsibility.[92] The World Bank observed that 'When traditional, informal arrangements for subsistence break down in other spheres, they are replaced by formal market arrangements',[93] but it also cautioned that it is not advisable to rely exclusively on the market in the context of financial support for old age, since while 'Market solutions—such as individuals saving and investing for their old age—help to fill the gaps left by the breakdown of the family system ... they fail to do the job completely'.[94] The limitations of a market approach in the context of provision for old age include the risk effect of short-sightedness amongst the young when it comes to saving enough to provide for old age; the unpredictability of life expectancy; a preference for consuming today rather than saving for tomorrow; and the difficulties associated with anticipating what one's needs will be into old age. Even with the most diligent intentions, and for the most 'skilled' consumers, there are risks and uncertainties to be negotiated, since

> [i]ncome security in old age requires very long-term planning, and many people *lack the information* for this type of planning (including information about future health, cost of living, lifetime earning capacity, and the safety and productivity of alternative forms of investment and insurance).[95]

The World Bank recommended that, for governments, broad diversification across the 'three pillars' of old-age provision—savings,[96] redistribution (for the lifelong poor)[97] and insurance (against risks to which older people are especially vulnerable)[98]—represents the best strategy to insure against adverse outcomes for older people in a very uncertain world.[99] It also argued that where these strategies involve government intervention, this does not necessarily mean tax and transfer of wealth (raising sustainability concerns in an

[90] The World Bank, *Averting the Old Age Crisis: Policies to Protect the Old and Promote Growth* (New York, Oxford University Press, 2004) 5.

[91] Walker (ed), above n 87, at 11.

[92] A Walker, 'The third way for pensioners (by way of Thatcherism and avoiding today's pensioners)' (1999) 19 *Critical Social Policy* 511.

[93] The World Bank, above n 90, at 5.

[94] *Ibid*, at 36.

[95] *Ibid.*

[96] To 'smooth [income] over a person's lifetime: people postpone some consumption when they are young and their earnings are high so that they can consume more in their old age than their reduced earnings would permit': *ibid*, at 10.

[97] Redistribution involves shifting lifetime income from one person to another, on the basis that if low-income workers saved enough to live on in old age, they would plunge below the poverty line when young: *ibid.*

[98] For 'protection against the probability that recession or bad investments will wipe out savings, that inflation will erode their real value, that people will outlive their own savings, or that public programs will fail': *ibid.*

[99] *Ibid*, at 16.

ageing society) but includes strategies such as 'creat[ing] a legal system for reliable financial institutions'.[100] As the Financial Services Authority has recently recognised, reliable financial institutions are dependent on a regulatory framework which, as well as being sustainable for lenders, protects consumers by offering a range of products that meet the needs of different consumer types; where consumers clearly understand the costs and risks of mortgage borrowing; and where consumers understand the implications and risks of treating their housing as an investment asset to spend rather than primarily as a home.[101] In the housing equity context, a legal system for reliable financial institutions requires scrutiny of the legal regulation of the institutions and products that enable the release of housing wealth.

(b) Savings and housing wealth

A central pillar of the UK Pension Commission's approach to future provision has been an emphasis on the need to encourage increases in private savings for retirement,[102] both through savings schemes, such as the Savings Credit element of the Pensions Credit Scheme, and through alternatives to pension income, such as housing wealth which is now most concentrated amongst older population cohorts and which, net of mortgages, exceeds the value of funded pension rights. This emphasis on savings—and, indeed, on the individual's self-responsibility to save for retirement—was highlighted in the Department of Work and Pensions' Five Year Strategy from 2005,[103] and in former Chancellor of the Exchequer Alistair Darling's Budget speech on 22 April 2009,[104] while strategies for the accumulation/decumulation of assets have remained central to the Con/Lib Coalition's asset-based welfare policies.[105]

The emphasis on saving within the UK's strategy for retirement is closely linked with the political and social economy of housing wealth. Considerable research attention has been paid to the 'saving' which takes place through accumulation of housing wealth in the UK, the significance of housing equity as the largest component of the savings and investment portfolio of most households, and the uses to which that equity could, or should, or should not, be put. Smith, Searle and Cook have demonstrated how housing equity has come to dominate people's wealth portfolios, and the individual and systemic

[100] *Ibid*, at 6.

[101] Financial Services Authority, *Mortgage Market Review* (Discussion Paper 09/3) (London, FSA, 2009) para 1.3.

[102] Pensions Commission, *Pensions: Challenges and Choices*, First Report of the Pensions Commission (London, TSO, 2004); Pensions Commission, *A New Settlement for the Twenty-First Century*, Second Report of the Pensions Commission (London, TSO, 2005). In its First Report, the Commission stated that one or more of the following needed to happen: (i) private savings for retirement have to rise; (ii) taxes and/or national insurance contributions devoted to pensions have to rise; (iii) average retirement ages have to rise; or (iv) pensioners have to become poorer relative to the rest of the population. The Second Report proposed a combination of responses (i), (ii) and (iii), while protecting the current standard of living of pensioners in the UK, which is 'still not high in international terms': Second Report, at 6.

[103] Department for Work and Pensions, *Five Year Strategy: Opportunity and Security Throughout Life*, Cm6447 (London, The Stationery Office, 2005).

[104] See *Hansard*, HC Debate, vol 491, part 62 (22 April 2009), col 237 et *seq* (Rt Hon Alistair Darling), available online at <http://www.publications.parliament.uk/pa/cm200809/cmhansrd/cm090422/debtext/90422–0003.htm#09042264000149>.

[105] L Appleyard and K Rowlingson, *Home ownership and the distribution of personal wealth: A review of the evidence* (York, Joseph Rowntree Foundation, 2010), available online at <http://www.jrf.org.uk/sites/files/jrf/home-ownership-personal-wealth-full.pdf>.

risks associated with this strategy of 'over-investment into a single asset, over-dependence on housing wealth, and vulnerability to the under-performance of housing assets'.[106] The owned home is the single most important asset held by the majority of people in the UK,[107] a pattern which—with £2.5 trillion held in unmortgaged housing equity in 2007—Smith *et al* described as 'the British norm of holding their financial "eggs" primarily in an owned housing "basket"'.[108] When people put all of their financial resources into housing, other types of savings dwindle[109]: research has indicated that 'Even ordinary savings rates are low in the UK compared to the rest of Europe, and declining',[110] a phenomenon that has been mapped to the large rises in equity and house prices, and to the fall in inflation which allowed late twentieth-century households to enjoy the same level of wealth and consumption with less saving.[111] While housing wealth in the UK grew at an average of 5.2 per cent per year between 1991 and 2006,[112] around one-quarter of households in the UK had no savings at all in 2006–07,[113] with savings patterns varying considerably with household composition. One in three households with one occupier or both occupiers over the State pension age were most likely to have substantial savings of £20,000 or more, reflecting their greater opportunity to build up savings during their working lives, and perhaps the receipt of a lump sum pension payout on retirement.[114] Nevertheless, this still leaves a substantial majority of older people in the UK without substantial savings, and—perhaps more worryingly—a survey of attitudes to saving for retirement among adults under the State pension age found that while 49 per cent agreed that 'having a pension was the best way to save for retirement' and 60 per cent agreed that 'investing in property is the best way to save for retirement', a significant 39 per cent agreed that they would 'rather have a good standard of living today than save for retirement'.[115]

Although the concentration of housing wealth tends to increase with age,[116] there is a growing concern about the extent to which the stores of housing wealth held in the owned

[106] Smith *et al*, above n 6, at 84.

[107] *Ibid*, at 85; this is also the case in most other countries, especially in the English-speaking world: see also J Muellbauer, 'Housing and personal wealth in a global context', in J Davies and T Shorrocks (eds) *Personal Assets from a Global Perspective* (Oxford, Oxford University Press, 2006); SJ Smith, 'Home-ownership: managing a risky business' in J Doling and M Elsinga (eds), *Home-Ownership: Getting In, Getting Out, Getting From* (Delft, IOS Press, 2006).

[108] Smith *et al*, above n 6, at 85.

[109] SJ Smith, *Banking on Housing: Speculating on the role and relevance of housing wealth in Britain* (Paper prepared for the Joseph Rowntree Foundation Inquiry into Home Ownership 2010 and Beyond, 2005) 9.

[110] *Ibid*, at 19.

[111] M Davey, 'Saving, wealth and consumption', *Bank of England Quarterly Bulletin* (Spring 2001) 92.

[112] Social Trends 38 (London, Office for National Statistics, 2009) 76–77; online at <http://www.statistics.gov.uk/downloads/theme_social/Social_Trends38/Social_Trends_38.pdf>.

[113] *Ibid*, Table 5.21.

[114] *Ibid*, at 77.

[115] *Ibid*, Table 5.22. This is consistent with behavioural economics research on the preference for immediate gratification; see, eg, D Laibson, 'Impatience and Saving', *NBER Reporter: Research Summary* (Cambridge, MA, National Bureau of Economic Research, Fall 2005), available online at <http://www.nber.org/reporter/fall05/laibson.html>.

[116] Most outright owners are in the older age groups, with 94% of outright owners aged 45 or older, and so approaching retirement. In 2005–06, 32% of household reference persons in the 45–64 age bracket owned outright, with 69% of those in the 65–74 bracket, and 66% of the 75 and older cohort being outright owners; see *Housing in England 2005–06* (London, Department for Communities and Local Government, 2007) Table 1.3; further, there has been a significant increase in owner occupation over the last 25 years for households where the household reference person is aged 45 and older: *ibid*, Chart 1.4.

home can be relied upon to fund retirement. In a report for the Institute of Public Policy Research in 2006, Maxwell and Sodha argued that the role of housing wealth for older owners had been overstated; that a house should not be thought of as a pension; and that 'while housing wealth can provide many benefits, and be spent on many things ... it cannot do everything'.[117] The concentration of assets in housing wealth underlines the potential risks associated with housing equity transactions, particularly for marginal older owners, who may have only 'one roll of the dice' when it comes to cashing in their housing wealth.[118]

Meanwhile, successive UK governments continue to promote the expansion of home ownership as a means of enabling more (especially lower-income) people to accumulate asset wealth.[119] The promotion of savings as a strategy for financial support in retirement, and specifically of housing wealth as a beneficial way to save for retirement, raises a number of issues which are contextually significant for the analysis in this book. The accumulation and decumulation of housing wealth by older owners who are 'asset rich, income poor'[120] raises tensions concerning the role of the owned home as a resource for older people. These issues are considered in more detail in chapter five, which explores the emergence of pluralist and competing housing paradigms for older owners, including housing as investment, housing as inheritance and housing as home. As Smith has noted, 'Owned homes are a hybrid of money, materials, and meanings,'[121] and nowhere is this more evident than in respect of older owners in equity release transactions.

The 'hybrid' functions of housing for older people include several positive features associated with saving for retirement through investment in the owned home. For one thing, since the owned home functions as a consumption good (the roof overhead) as well as an investment asset, an owned-outright home should enable older owners to meet a significant portion of their consumption costs in retirement through the 'steady and certain flow of [housing] services at low out-of-pocket cost'[122] that the 'virtual income stream from housing'[123] provides, and which is particularly important in light of the decline in income after retirement. There is also, in theory at least, the opportunity for the older homeowner to 'downsize' or 'trade down' to a less expensive property and release some capital, although there is evidence to suggest that in Britain this is relatively rare for

[117] D Maxwell and S Sodha, *Housing Wealth: First timers to old timers* (London, IPPR, 2006); see also S Sodha, *Housing-rich, Income-poor; the Potential of Housing Wealth in Old Age* (London, IPPR, 2005) 5: 'At the macro level, housing wealth has only a limited role to play in filling the "pensions gap" and we should be cautious about any solution to the inadequacy of pensions savings that relies solely on housing wealth.'

[118] See, further, discussion in ch 3 and ch 4, section (3).

[119] The objectives of the 'Homebuy' scheme, launched in 2005 to help social tenants, key workers and first-time buyers to 'buy a share of a home and get a first step on the housing ladder', included: 'Enabling more people to share in increasing asset wealth: homes are not just places to live. They are also assets—assets which now account for over 40% of wealth, compared to just over 20% in 1971. But this increase in wealth is unevenly spread. Support for home ownership will enable more people on lower incomes to benefit from any further increases in the value of housing assets.' Office of the Deputy Prime Minister, *HomeBuy: Expanding the Opportunity to Own* (London, ODPM, 2005) para 2.1.

[120] See Sodha, above n 117 (using data from the Survey of English Housing), for discussion of the likely growth in the number of pensioners who will be 'income poor' but relatively 'housing rich' in the next 10 to 15 years.

[121] Smith (2008), above n 6, at 521.

[122] J Rouwendal, 'Housing Wealth and Household Portfolios in an Aging Society' (2009) *De Economist* 1, 3; see also Lowe, in Manning and Ungerson (eds), above n 5; Lowe, in Corden *et al* (eds), above n 5.

[123] Smith, above n 109, at 18.

various financial and non-financial reasons,[124] and the Pensions Commission has cautioned against over-estimating how much capital may be released in this way.[125]

The extent to which housing wealth may be relied upon as a source of income for retirement depends on several factors. For one thing, while housing has generally performed well against inflation and as an investment asset in the UK since 1971,[126] the potential for accumulation of wealth through home ownership is unevenly distributed across regional housing markets and according to the socio-economic status of the owner. Homeownership is less profitable and more risky for those on lower incomes,[127] and the mean amount of housing wealth is lower for those who have never had a private pension than for those who have,[128] prompting the claim that rather than 'provide an adequate and dependable income stream for a new generation of retirees ... it seems likely that [housing assets] will simply add to the security of the already well-off'.[129]

The socio-economic heterogeneity of older owners as a group is significant when considering tensions between the construction of older owners as 'autonomous market actors' for the purposes of financial transactions, and arguments about their 'situational vulnerabilities', set out in chapter six. On the one hand, the status of 'owner' provides no reliable indication of socio-economic well-being, with half of those who are categorised as 'living in poverty' in the UK being homeowners[130] and 60 per cent of poor homeowners aged over 60.[131] Housing wealth also tends to be clustered with pension assets and savings, creating a 'polarisation of poverty and affluence in old age'.[132] Also significant for this analysis of financial transactions is evidence that the differentiation of older owners depending on how well their housing investments have fared, as well as how 'income rich' or 'income poor' they are based on other assets (savings, investments and pensions), is likely to correlate with how well they have been able to 'plan reflexively' for retirement. Denton *et al* have suggested that people with high household incomes are more likely to

[124] See R Disney, 'Aging and Saving' (1996) 17 *Fiscal Studies* 83; J Banks, R Blundell, Z Oldfield and JP Smith, 'Housing Price Volatility and Downsizing in Later Life', *NBER Working Paper No 13496* (Cambridge, MA, National Bureau of Economic Research, 2007); for similar findings in the US, see SF Venti and DA Wise, 'Aging, Moving and Housing Wealth', *NBER Working Paper No 2324* (Cambridge, MA, National Bureau of Economic Research, 1989); SF Venti and DA Wise, 'But They Don't Want to Reduce Housing Equity?', *NBER Working Paper No 2859* (Cambridge, MA, National Bureau of Economic Research, 1990); see discussion in ch 5, section (2).

[125] See Pensions Commission, First Report, above n 102, fig 5.18 charting the difference in average price of semi-detached and terraced houses at only £32,000 in 2004.

[126] Smith *et al*, above n 6, at 86.

[127] Maxwell and Sodha, above n 117. Walker and Foster have also noted that higher-income households benefit disproportionately from housing wealth accumulation; see Walker and Foster, above n 79, at 440. See also discussion of income and risk factors in relation to accumulation of housing wealth in L Fox, *Conceptualising Home: Theories, Laws and Policies* (Oxford, Hart Publishing, 2006) 216–20.

[128] J Banks, C Emmerson and Z Oldfield, *Preparing for Retirement: The pension arrangements and retirement expectations of those approaching State Pension Age in England* (London, Institute for Fiscal Studies, 2005).

[129] K Strauss, 'Banking on property for retirement? Attitudes to housing wealth and pensions', draft paper online at <http://www.geog.ox.ac.uk/research/transformations/wpapers/wpg08–04.pdf>, at 3. Strauss adds (at 6): 'In other words, housing wealth does not necessarily substitute for pension wealth—it often compliments it.'; see also J Banks, C Emmerson, Z Oldfield and G Tetlow, *Prepared for Retirement? The Adequacy and Distribution of Retirement Resources in England* (London, Institute for Fiscal Studies, 2005).

[130] R Burrows and S Wilcox, *Half the poor: Home-owners with low incomes* (London, Council of Mortgage Lenders Research Report, 2000).

[131] P Meadows and D Rogger, 'Low-income homeowners in Britain: descriptive analysis', *Department for Work and Pensions Research Report No 251* (London, HMSO, 2005).

[132] Walker and Foster, above n 79, at 445.

recognise risks and engage in reflexive planning for later life,[133] while research drawing on Bourdieu's theories of *habitus*, and the unequal distribution of cultural capital,[134] has emphasised the importance of access to these resources to enable people to function as 'winners' in the risk society,[135] particularly with respect to financial decision-making.[136] These themes, which have important implications for decision-making when entering into home equity transactions, are explored in chapter three (which sets out the conceptual framework of the risk society as it relates to home equity transactions) and chapter six (which explores the question of vulnerability in respect of older owners).

Another dimension of this differentiation is the gender gap in respect of socio-economic risk factors for older owners. Several systemic factors relating to women, incomes, and the accumulation of wealth and assets across the life-course—for example, that women are more likely to be responsible for child-rearing and caring for elderly family members, and so their labour force participation is generally shorter and more irregular than that of men; that women are more likely to engage in part-time work and retire earlier; that women's wages are often lower than men's for the same work; and that they are more likely to work in the informal sector, where wages are lower and access to pensions more difficult—along with longer life-expectancy, combine to make women more likely than men to be poor, and so potentially more vulnerable in financial transactions in old age.[137]

These contexts—age, socio-economic and income profiles—also play key roles in determining the financial products that are available for particular owners to release equity. This underlines the significance of the considerable variations in cost-effectiveness across the sector, with some products carrying high costs and offering low value for money. To some extent this reflects the risks associated with providing these products to older customers,[138] although the UK Government has recognised that there is a need for stricter legislation to prevent inappropriate or arbitrary age discrimination, where this is not relevant to risks or costs.[139] The uneven nature of access to 'conventional' or 'prime' products and concerns regarding the value for money of targeted products[140] are coupled with varying levels of risk to borrowers across different product types, as a result of variations in legal regulation and remedies across procedural matters, the substantive content of terms and enforcement procedures,[141] and depending on the extent to which the consumer is regarded as 'vulnerable'.[142]

[133] MA Denton, CL Kemp, S French, A Gafni, A Joshi, CJ Rosenthal and S Davies, 'Reflexive Planning for Later Life' (2004) 23 *Canadian Journal on Aging Supplement* S71–S82.

[134] See, eg, P Bourdieu and L Wacquant, *An Invitation to Reflexive Sociology* (Cambridge, Polity Press, 1992).

[135] M Cooper, 'The inequality of security: Winners and losers in the risk society' (2008) 61 *Human Relations* 1229.

[136] A Aldridge, '*Habitus* and cultural capital in the field of personal finance' (1998) 46 *The Sociological Review* 1.

[137] See Walker and Foster, above n 79.

[138] This point was emphasised in the Government's Policy Statement on the exclusion of age discrimination in financial services from the Equality Act 2010; see Government Equality Office, *Equality Bill: Making it Work—Ending Age Discrimination in Services and Public Functions, Policy Statement* (London, Government Equality Office, 2010) paras 3.28–3.31, available online at <http://www.equalities.gov.uk/pdf/GEO_EqualityBillAge_acc.pdf>; discussed in ch 2, section (3).

[139] *Ibid.*

[140] See, eg, K Rowlingson, 'Attitudes to housing assets and inheritance', *CML Housing Finance* Issue *10/2005*, 1; and discussion in ch 5, section (4).

[141] See chs 7–10.

[142] See ch 6.

Another factor affecting the relative position of older owners in retirement relates to whether they have already drawn upon housing wealth earlier in the life-cycle, so that they are entering retirement with debts already secured against their home. Smith, Searle and Cook have highlighted the growing trend for owners to withdraw equity from their housing wealth throughout the life-course, whether as a last resort when in dire financial straits or to enhance their lifestyles.[143] By the mid-2000s, the use of housing wealth through mortgage equity withdrawal was described as having

> entered day-to-day decisions around savings, spending and debt, smoothing over dips in income, supporting increased expenditures and helping tackle a suite of unexpected life events … home assets were better positioned than ever before to provide a financial buffer; and borrowers came increasingly to *depend* on owned homes for this function.[144]

The increasing fungibility of housing wealth across the life-course has two important implications for older owners. The first is the likelihood that older owners, particularly those who had lower incomes before retirement and are therefore less likely to have good pension incomes, are increasingly likely to have already leveraged their housing wealth for other (including welfare) purposes before they reach old age.[145] These owners enter retirement with outstanding mortgage debts to be repaid—and potentially subject to enforcement actions for possession and sale against their owned homes if they are unable to meet debt repayments as they fall due—as well as lower stocks of equity to draw upon in the future.

A second consequence of the increased 'spendability' of housing wealth is the change in attitudes amongst the generation of homeowners who will reach retirement in the near future. Smith *et al*'s study of homebuyers and their attitudes to 'spending the home' identified a tendency for participants to 'locate their sense of social and financial security—qualities once rooted in the institutions of the welfare state—in the possession of an increasingly spendable store of housing wealth'.[146] A further consequence of this shift in attitudes was that 'while owner-occupation is popular for all kinds of reasons, it has come to occupy prime position in households' thinking about how to manage financial and other risks'.[147] This will also have implications across the period of retirement: increased longevity has meant that older owners may well be faced with a range of demands on their housing wealth across early to later retirement, requiring decisions to be made between spending on lifestyle and consumption in early retirement and saving for future needs, for example healthcare or nursing care needs, in later old age. When this is layered onto the underlying risks associated with holding retirement wealth in a narrow and undiversified portfolio (one property within one (housing) market),[148] the specific

[143] 'Either way, for one in three of [owners surveyed] … owned housing is experienced as a financial buffer because it is a saleable commodity': Smith *et al*, above n 6, at 87.

[144] *Ibid*, at 88.

[145] This is consistent with economic analyses of the changes in the way that wealth and debt portfolios operate in light of the growing fungibility of housing wealth: J Banks, R Blundell, Z Oldfield and JP Smith, 'House price volatility and housing ownership over the life cycle', *UCL Discussion Papers in Economics 04–09*; S Bridges, R Disney and A Henley, 'Housing wealth and the accumulation of financial debt: evidence from UK households', in G Bertola, R Disney and C Grant (eds), *The Economics of Consumer Credit* (Cambridge, MA, MIT Press, 2006).

[146] Smith *et al*, above n 6, at 88.

[147] *Ibid*, at 90.

[148] Smith, above n 109; Smith (2008), above n 6, at 526.

and definable risks associated with older owners, and the growing expectation that they will use housing wealth to fund retirement, become increasingly evident.

Lastly, it is important to note that older people in the UK are increasingly likely to carry consumer (unsecured) debt, which in turn may drive the need to withdraw equity.[149] A report commissioned by the charity Help the Aged in 2008 indicated that levels of debt amongst older people had risen considerably, and that some older people in debt were struggling to meet their financial commitments in a difficult financial environment, in the same way as their younger counterparts.[150] This study found that people aged between 60 and 65 had increased their debt following retirement, and that for older people in debt in their late 50s or early 60s, the level of unsecured debt in 2005 was four times higher than for the same age group in 1995. Although people are still less likely to get into 'ordinary debt' as they get older, increasing numbers of older people are entering retirement with mortgages and other debt liabilities still to pay off.[151]

(4) Conclusions

The socio-economic context of the UK's ageing ownership society, alongside the growing political expectation that older owners will release equity from their homes to meet a wide range of costs in retirement, provides important context to the legal frameworks of regulation and remedies for various types of housing equity transactions. As a growing cohort of older owners reach retirement, the pressure is on to release housing wealth, although in many cases—particularly for marginal owners—the multiple demands are likely to outstrip the asset long before all needs have been met. This only emphasises the importance of the choices that are made, the need for good quality financial decision-making in housing equity transactions, and the disproportionately adverse impact of bad outcomes for (particularly marginal) older owners. Unpacking the socio-economic context of older owners is also the first step in understanding the situational vulnerabilities which inform some owners' experiences of housing equity transactions.

The idea of older owners as vulnerable consumers (and, specifically, vulnerable due to the context or situation in which they enter into transactions) sits in stark contrast to the neoliberal model of consumers (particularly owners) as autonomous, self-responsible and adept at planning for their own futures. Smith has argued[152] that '*homeownership* has been prescribed, by acts of governance in the UK, as part of the art of responsible citizenship

[149] The legal framework surrounding consumer debt is discussed in chs 7 and 8.

[150] S McKay, E Kempson, A Atkinson and M Crame, *Debt and Older People: how age affects attitudes to borrowing* (London, Help the Aged, 2008).

[151] See also evidence that debt is an increasing problem for high-earning and older Welsh people: in the five years from 2003 to 2008, the number of people in the over-60 age group seeking help with their debts had more than doubled, and those aged 40 to 59 had overtaken the 26 to 40 age group as the largest percentage of clients; see Foundation for Credit Counselling, *Debt in Wales* (2008), available online at <http://www.cccs.co.uk/research/2008/Debt_in_Wales_2008.pdf>.

[152] Smith draws on Flint's theory that 'acts of governance' create 'a discourse of authoritative "grammars of living" [which] seek to shape and prescribe socially accepted acts of consumption, including the consumption of housing'; see J Flint, 'Housing and ethopolitics: constructing identities of active consumption and responsible community' (2003) 32 *Economy and Society* 611, 614.

and ethical living'.[153] The owned home has been constructed not only as 'something you have to pour everything into,' but as 'something you have to wrest all you can from' as 'the grammars of living that write the experience of home ownership have acquired a complexity, even transformativity, around the theme of investment'.[154] This emphasis on investment and consumption has shaped a model of (older) owners as consumers which dovetails neatly with the pre-eminence afforded to the values of autonomy, self-responsibility and choice in neoliberal theory and politics, echoed in the characteristics of the idealised liberal legal subject; and which is challenged by legal initiatives that emphasise vulnerability, unequal bargaining power and the need for legal intervention to ensure fairness for consumers. While the inherently high-risk nature of housing equity transactions has been widely recognised, and the Financial Services Authority has noted that this is compounded because 'these consumers tend to be elderly and vulnerable people who can ill-afford to be unnecessarily exposed to risk',[155] little attention has yet been paid to the nature of these vulnerabilities in legal analyses of housing equity transactions, or to the implications of particular vulnerabilities for the appropriateness of legal protections for older consumers. This book seeks to explore these issues.

[153] Smith (2008), above n 6, at 522.
[154] *Ibid*, at 523.
[155] Financial Services Authority, 'FSA warns advisers that unsuitable equity release advice has got to stop' (24 May 2005), <http://www.fsa.gov.uk/pages/Library/Communication/PR/2005/055.shtml>.

2

Political and Policy Contexts

(1) Introduction

There are various reasons why older owners use housing equity to generate income or capital. One set of reasons is associated with difficulties meeting everyday costs such as food and fuel bills (rising with inflation) after retirement, maintaining a standard of living that cannot be met on pension income alone, or for 'lifestyle expenditure', for example taking holidays, particularly in early old age.[1] Another set of reasons for using home equity relates to expenses such as home maintenance and improvements, or paying for healthcare and nursing care.[2] A third set of reasons for older people to release equity from their owned homes may relate to the desire to gift capital to adult offspring, to help fund their step onto the housing ladder or to give them financial support in a difficult economic climate.[3] Although statistics published in *Social Trends* provide some information on what people spend released housing equity on,[4] these figures relate to *all* owners releasing equity and do not specifically indicate what *older* owners use released funds for. Indeed, there are presently no official statistics to indicate specifically how much of this equity withdrawal is taken by older owners,[5] or how older owners who release equity are spending this money, although a recent study for Age UK indicated that in a significant majority of cases (85 per cent), the equity released was used to supplement rather than substitute for private pension assets; and that plans tended to be used to provide capital rather than a regular income, with the top three uses for released equity identified as house maintenance/repairs (46 per cent), holidays (36 per cent), and to repay mortgages and other forms of debt clearance (35 per cent). Another 33 per cent used the money for

[1] See K Rowlingson, '"Living Poor to Die Rich"? Or "Spending the Kids' Inheritance"? Attitudes to Assets and Inheritance in Later Life' (2006) 35 *Journal of Social Policy* 175.

[2] See below, section (3).

[3] See, eg, M Andrew, 'The Changing Route to Owner Occupation: The Impact of Student Debt' (2010) 25 *Housing Studies* 39; and discussion in ch 5, section (4).

[4] In 2006–07: home improvements/renovations —56%; pay off debts—29%; buy new goods for property—15%; invest or save—13%; buy a car or other vehicle—12%; pay for a holiday—7%; finance towards buying another property for self in UK—6%; finance for business—3%; finance towards buying property for another family member—2%; university costs—2%; school fees—1%; other—10%; data based on Survey of English Housing and published in Office of National Statistics, *Social Trends 38* (Basingstoke, Palgrave Macmillan, 2008), Table 10.20. It is clear, however, that older owners make up a minority of these numbers, since 'The most common methods of equity release borrowing were to increase the size of the current mortgage through a further advance or top-up (used in 33 per cent of cases) or to remortgage the current home (used in 27 per cent of cases)' (*ibid*, at 148)—products which are often not available to older owners.

[5] See S Sodha, *Housing-rich, Income-poor; the Potential of Housing Wealth in Old Age* (London, IPPR, 2005) 7.

home improvements, and 19 per cent used the money to pay for everyday living expenses and regular bills.[6]

This study also underlined the socio-economic heterogeneity of equity release customers, as the purposes for which equity was released mapped across three broad groups:

a) (typically better-off) older owners who were passing on wealth through early bequests and large, one-off purchases;
b) those who used the released funds to enhance their own financial security and enjoy a more comfortable lifestyle through housing and non-housing consumption spending; and
c) those (usually already in debt and experiencing difficulty 'getting by') who turned to equity release as a last resort to relieve financial difficulty.

Across the sample, just over a third of respondents stated that they were just about getting by before taking out the plan, with a further 13 per cent finding it either quite difficult or very difficult,[7] suggesting that a significant proportion of equity release customers are, while perhaps not very poor, towards the 'marginal' side of the ownership spectrum, and certainly likely to be particularly vulnerable to the adverse impact of a bad financial transaction.

This research followed an earlier study for the Joseph Rowntree Foundation which found that the additional income released by older owners made an important contribution to their living standards, and also indicated that, before embarking on equity release, the people who used it had found life financially quite difficult. This study also reported that the equity released was unlikely to be used for major expenditure on housing disrepair or care services,[8] although significant changes in the political context of equity release for older owners since the mid-1990s have set the scene for much more use of housing equity to meet welfare-related expenses, housing maintenance and improvement costs, and health and nursing care costs. The shifting and increasingly complex competing demands on housing equity were underlined in Smith's observation that 'Even governments are hazy on what they expect from housing wealth: currently it is the pot of gold at the end of virtually every ministerial rainbow.'[9]

Another significant set of considerations for owners who are considering transactions to release capital and income from their housing equity are the potential effects on tax liabilities and welfare benefits. The Council of Mortgage Lenders has advised that

> [t]here are likely to be a number of situations where benefit entitlement may be lost or sharply reduced by the receipt of income and/or capital from any form of equity release mechanism. In the worst possible cases, a small weekly rise in income will simply result in an identical amount of

[6] L Overton, *Housing and Finance in Later Life: A Study of UK Equity Release Customers* (London, Age UK, 2010), para 4.1, available online at <http://policy.helptheaged.org.uk/NR/rdonlyres/51C84275–1440–40A1-BE7D-756350AD2A4E/0/ID9116EquityReleaseReport.pdf>.

[7] *Ibid*, para 4.2.

[8] Where expenditure was house-related, this was usually for decorating; see JA Davey, *Equity Release for Older Home Owners: Findings* (Housing Research No 188, York, Joseph Rowntree Foundation, 1996) 3.

[9] SJ Smith, 'Owner-occupation: living with a hybrid of money and materials' (2008) 40 *Environment and Planning A* 520, 530.

lost benefit income, or a rise in capital will result in the loss of benefit but no perceivable gain to the customer.[10]

Cashing in housing equity may reduce the amount of inheritance tax which will be payable, but the income generated will be liable for income tax if the owner's total income goes above the tax-free personal allowance; and where an individual's income, including income from any equity release scheme, goes above £22,900, the individual may lose entitlement to some or all of the 'age allowance',[11] which may increase the overall tax bill.[12] The Financial Services Authority requires those selling regulated equity release products to consider, as part of the advice process, whether potential purchasers will be worse off in terms of tax and benefits if they take out an equity release loan,[13] and a recent study for the Joseph Rowntree Foundation found that the impact on welfare benefit entitlements was amongst the reasons given by older people who were reluctant to cash in their housing equity, along with concerns about reducing inheritance and the fear that spending home equity is risky, not good value for money and complicated.[14]

The political context of home equity transactions, particularly the growing expectation that older people will tap into housing wealth for a variety of purposes, is central to the panoply of risks that arise when older owners enter into these financial transactions. The political agenda has also underpinned the construction of the 'housing paradigms' that frame the meanings and functions of the owned home for older people, influencing the norms that frame decision-making, as well as the extent to which law (for example, through regulation) seeks to facilitate and encourage the market in housing equity transactions. This chapter locates housing equity release by older people in these political and policy contexts by tracing the evolution of political perspectives on ageing from 'cradle-to-grave provision' to asset-based welfare, which in turn has shaped the construction of older people as autonomous and self-responsible consumers, with implications which resonate throughout the book. Lastly, this chapter considers shifting policies on home maintenance and health and nursing care as examples of the specific demands placed on older owners to consume their housing equity.

(2) Political Perspectives on Ageing

The idea that older people should be enabled to tap into their housing wealth for financial support in retirement emerged in the 1980s as a result of a combination of factors, including the expansion of home ownership, the increase in property values and the emergence of new financial products which enabled equity to be withdrawn from owned

[10] Council of Mortgage Lenders, *Equity release and the impact on benefits and tax* (London, CML, 2010) 16, available online at <http://www.cml.org.uk/cml/policy/issues/104>. See also Sodha, above n 5, at 19–22, outlining the interaction of released housing wealth with the benefits system.

[11] In 2010–11, the personal allowance in the UK was £6,475, but for people aged 65–74 this increased to £9,490 and for over-75s to £9,640.

[12] Council of Mortgage Lenders, *Equity release and the impact on benefits and tax* (London, CML, 2010), available online at <http://www.cml.org.uk/cml/policy/issues/104>.

[13] FSA Factsheet, *Equity release—lifetime mortgages and home reversion plans*, available online at <http://www.fsa.gov.uk/smallfirms/resources/factsheets/pdfs/equity_release.pdf>.

[14] R Terry and R Gibson, *Can Equity Release Help Older Home-Owners Improve Their Quality of Life?* (York, Joseph Rowntree Foundation, 2010) 4.

housing.[15] The emergence of this expectation of self-provisioning through the accumulation and decumulation of housing assets can be understood against the backdrop of shifting political perspectives on ageing. In the post-World War II period, older people were promised 'cradle to grave' support, with 'The giants of the welfare state—housing provision, pension provision and social and health care services—... provid[ing] older people with some certainties and some security'.[16] This model came under pressure in the 1970s, when a combination of rising costs of welfare provision, macro-economic decline, and rising unemployment and inflation[17] led to political concern about the sustainability of welfare provision for older people.[18] The crisis in public expenditure brought about significant changes in the portrayals of older people in policy discourses, which, from the 1980s (under Thatcher's Conservative Government in the UK, and under Reagan in the US),[19] increasingly characterised welfare provision for older people as an unsustainable burden on public expenditure.[20]

This perspective was challenged, largely through the discipline of social gerontology, with the argument that the dependency of older people was not inherent but socially created through policies such as compulsory retirement, which are based not on physical or mental decline at a specific age but on structural social and economic factors, such as the need to free up jobs for younger people, described as a form of 'mass redundancy' in an environment of job shortages.[21] Townsend argued that social policies in the twentieth century created the 'structured dependency of the elderly', and portrayed the phenomena of poverty and dependency in old age as the result of individual failures on the part of older people, for example due to a failure effectively to manage their finances by saving and planning for retirement. This 'political economy' perspective argued that by blaming older people for their own hardships—indeed, by constructing 'old age' itself as a social problem—capitalist States concealed the structural causes of dependency in old age.[22]

The political economy perspective also criticised the traditional tendency to treat older people as a distinct and homogeneous social group. More recently, Powell has argued that the traditional 'expert' models of ageing which constructed older people as vulnerable (read as helpless and weak due to physical, social and economic decline), failed to recognise cohort differentiation.[23] In contrast, the political economy perspective emphasised the heterogeneity of older people, arguing that 'different cohorts of adults come to retirement with differentially distributed access to resources and therefore with different

[15] See further discussion in ch 5, section (5).

[16] F Heywood, C Oldman and R Means, *Housing and Home in Later Life* (Buckingham, Open University Press, 2002) 27.

[17] C Phillipson, *Reconstructing Old Age: New Agendas in Social Theory and Practice* (London, Sage, 1998) 2.

[18] P Armstrong, A Glyn and J Harrison, *Capitalism Since World War II* (London, Fontana, 1984); C Phillipson and A Walker (eds), *Ageing and Social Policy: A Critical Assessment* (Aldershot, Gower, 1986); H Glennerster and J Hills (eds), *The State of Welfare: The Economics of Social Spending* (Oxford, Oxford University Press, 1998).

[19] Phillipson, above n 17, at 17.

[20] See Phillipson and Walker (eds), above n 18.

[21] A Walker, 'Towards a Political Economy of Old Age' (1981) 1 *Aging and Society* 73; P Townsend, 'The structured dependency of the elderly: creation of social policy in the twentieth century' (1981) 1 *Aging and Society* 5.

[22] See also Phillipson, above n 17.

[23] J Powell, 'Theorising Gerontology: The Case of Old Age, Professional Power, and Social Policy in the United Kingdom' (2001) 6(3) *Journal of Aging and Identity* 117.

opportunities and post-retirement life chances'.[24] This differentiation was reflected in evidence going back to the mid-1980s, which suggested that older people were now relatively well-off and that their living standards had improved,[25] albeit from a very low base.[26] It is now generally accepted that in rich countries such as the UK and the USA, considerable progress has been made in reducing poverty in old age,[27] with differentiation becoming the key factor in contemporary debates concerning financial security and material deprivation in old age. These inequalities mirror broader societal patterns, since financial security amongst older people reflects the lives (of affluence or insecurity) that they have led.[28] As the discussion in chapter one has indicated, it is crucial to acknowledge that tenure is no indicator of financial security in old age, with significant differentiation within the older home-owning sector.[29] Thus, while older people today are more likely to have pensions and be owner-occupiers than previous generations,[30] it seems that 'the continuing disparities between better-off and worse-off pensioners are likely to continue among future generations of retired people'.[31]

The expectation that older people provide for their own financial security in old age through private means, such as pensions, savings and particularly housing equity, is explained in part by the macro socio-economic context set out in chapter one. The expectation that older people will use their housing wealth as an asset to fund needs in retirement is also rooted in the changing subjectivities of older owners in the post-war period. Social and scientific developments, from the rise of gerontology and increased longevity to the cultural transformation of 'active retirement' lifestyles, have transformed ageing identities. While the period from 1950 to 1970 may be described as 'the high point of the modernisation of aging',[32] the unravelling of the 'twin pillars of old age'—

[24] Walker, above n 21, at 76.

[25] G Figehen, 'Income after retirement' (1986) 16 *Social Trends* 13; A Dawson and G Evans, 'Pensioners' incomes and expenditure 1970–1985' [1987] *Employment Gazette* 243; cited in C Oldman, 'Financial Effects of Moving in Old Age' (1991) 6(4) *Housing Studies* 251.

[26] A Walker, 'Pensioners and the production of poverty in old age' in Phillipson and Walker (eds), above n 18; R Walker and S Hutton, 'Costs of ageing and retirement' in R Walker and G Parker (eds) *Money Matters* (London, Sage, 1988); R Walker, 'The financial resources of the elderly: Paying your own way in old age' in S Baldwin, G Parker and R Walker, *Social Security and Community* Care (Aldershot, Avebury, 1988); J Falkingham and C Victor, *The Myth of the Whoopie?: Incomes, the Elderly and Targeting Welfare* (London, Suntory Toyota International Centre for Economics and Related Disciplines, London School of Economics, 1991); cited in Oldman, above n 25.

[27] See, eg, A Epstein, *Facing Old Age* (New York, Alfred A Knopf, 1922); A Epstein, *The Challenge of the Aged* (New York, Vanguard Press, 1928); M Shearon, *Economic Insecurity in Old Age: Social and Economic Factors Contributing to Old-Age Dependency* (Washington DC, US Social Security Board, 1937); for a criticism of the historical approach to impoverishment theory, including the argument that urbanisation and industrialisation undermined the economic well-being of the elderly, see B Gratton, 'The Poverty of Impoverishment Theory: The Economic Well-Being of the Elderly, 1890–1950' (1996) 56 *Journal of Economic History* 39. Hurd has claimed that 'during most of history, to be old was to be poor': MD Hurd, 'The Economic Status of the Elderly' (1989) 244 *Science* 659, 663; see also TM Smeeding and S Sandstrom, 'Poverty and Income Maintenance in Old Age: A Cross-National View of Low Income Older Women' (Centre for Retirement Research Working Papers, Boston College, 2004).

[28] JA Vincent, *Politics, Power and Old Age* (Buckingham, Open University Press, 1999) 2; Walker, above n 21.

[29] See R Burrows and S Wilcox, *Half the poor: Home-owners with low incomes* (London, Council of Mortgage Lenders Research Report, 2000); see also ch 1.

[30] R Hancock, 'Financial Resources in Later Life' in M Evandrou (ed), *Baby Boomers: Aging in the 21st Century* (London, Age Concern, 1997).

[31] *Ibid*, at 83.

[32] Phillipson, above n 17, at 40.

retirement and the welfare State—in the 1970s can be seen to have prompted a shift in discourses of old age[33] and the 'identity crisis' of the elderly[34] associated with late modernity.

One consequence of this shifting political context is the way in which 'the welfare state [has been] increasingly undermined or "residualised" in respect of providing care and support in periods such as old age'.[35] The construction of the older person as a political subject was fundamentally transformed by the rise of neoliberal governmentality in the closing years of the twentieth century.[36] Rose described the aims of 'advanced liberal governance' as seeking to

> degovernmentalise the State and to de-statize practices of government ... relocating experts within a market governed by the rationalities of competition, accountability and consumer demand. It does not seek to govern through 'society', but through the regulated choices of individual citizens, now construed as subjects of choices and aspirations to self-actualisation and self-fulfilment.[37]

By dismantling some of the central pillars of security in old age, such as pensions and healthcare, neoliberalism has 'cast [older people] loose from the certainties created by full employment and relatively well-funded welfare institutions'.[38] Neoliberal policies seek to discipline older people away from 'structured dependency' on the welfare State, towards self-governance and self-responsibility, as part of a broader socio-political shift towards individuals' self-responsibility as autonomous consumers who negotiate risk through the exercise of prudent choices.[39] Within this perspective, older people are required to act as consumers, making choices in a market-oriented environment characterised by an emphasis on enterprise and in which 'older people are exhorted, indeed expected, to become entrepreneurs in all spheres and to accept responsibility for the management of risk; older people then govern themselves'.[40] Older owners, in particular, have been affected by what Kemeny described as 'the really big trade-off' between homeownership and public welfare, while the 'privatising impact' of rising levels of homeownership on society as a whole,[41] and especially on welfare provision for the elderly,[42] reveals the paradigmatic role of housing equity transactions in the neoliberal strategy for financial support in an ageing society.

[33] *Ibid*, at 1.
[34] *Ibid*, at 2.
[35] *Ibid*, at 3.
[36] See, eg, N Rose, 'Governing "advanced" liberal democracies' in A Barry, T Osborne and N Rose (eds), *Foucault and Political Reason* (London, UCL Press, 1996).
[37] *Ibid*, at 41.
[38] Heywood *et al*, above n 16, at 28; see also Phillipson, above n 17, at 135.
[39] See, eg, P Leonard, *Postmodern Welfare: Reconstructing an Emancipatory Project* (London, Sage, 1997); H Kemshall, *Risk, Social Policy and Welfare* (Maidenhead, Open University Press, 2002).
[40] Powell, above n 23, at 128.
[41] J Kemeny, '"The Really Big Trade-Off" between Home Ownership and Welfare: Castles' Evaluation of the 1980 Thesis and a Reformulation 25 Years On' (2005) 22 *Housing, Theory and Society* 59.
[42] *Ibid*, at 66 *et seq*. Kemeny also explored the causal directions of this relationship: whether homeownership drives down welfare provision, eg, because people paying for 'front-end loading' of household debt themselves are less willing to submit to increased taxation for welfare and social security (*ibid*, at 61–62); or whether welfare cutbacks and privatisation lead people to utilise homeownership as a life-strategy by which they seek to protect themselves from 'grey poverty' (*ibid*, at 66, 71–73). He concluded that further research must be done to delineate more specifically the nature and direction of the symbiotic relationship between homeownership and welfare provision.

These neoliberal strategies require older people to engage with risk,[43] and while the policy narratives accompanying these changes have often emphasised the expansion of *choice* for older people,[44] this has been countered by the claim that 'For many, privatisation of welfare institutions is not a liberalising force but, rather, restricts choice further'.[45] For example, although owner-occupation has long been promoted as the foundation for (self-provided) security for old age, the freedom and autonomy purported to flow from homeownership (and from the accumulation of housing equity) have been undermined as 'significant numbers of older people have no choice but to trade their housing equity for places in the much expanded private nursing and residential home sector'.[46] This political expectation, that older people will trade their home equity for welfare services, is based on a market-led rationality[47]: older people as political subjects are expected to be active, enterprising and responsible citizens, functioning as active 'skilled' consumers within the market. Furthermore, as the discussion in chapter four will indicate, this idealised model of liberal subjectivity is echoed in the underlying orientation of private law, which governs these transactions.

These idealised models of subjectivity are criticised by empirical research that reveals a reality at odds with the expectation: for example, one study of older people's choice and participation in decision-making[48] found that while, on the surface, neoliberalism purports to offer opportunities for self-responsibility and freedom to choose, 'There was little evidence … that elderly people were able to operate as "informed consumers" in their use of care services, either in the community or in the residential sector.'[49] Rather, this study found that the ethos of choice in care provision for older people left many feeling isolated and socially neglected. Gilleard has written more positively about the benefits of consumerism in achieving the expansion of choice and agency for older people,[50] although he has also recognised that 'by no means all older people are engaged in this project',[51] and Heywood, Oldman and Means have argued that 'although there is evidence of rising affluence, it seems there is only a middle-class minority for whom choice is not a hollow concept'.[52] The policy narratives relating to older people as active and responsible consumers also assert a new ideology of citizenship,[53] which has

> enormous implications for how the state has responded to older people who have not been able to 'consume' the right way, to 'be responsible' in the appropriate manner [which] signals a turn towards personal, individual responsibility for one's actions regardless of wider social context.[54]

[43] See ch 3.
[44] See discussion in ch 3 relating to the demands imposed on older people by the expansion of choice.
[45] Heywood *et al*, above n 16, at 28; see also Phillipson, above n 17, at 135.
[46] Heywood *et al*, above n 16, at 27.
[47] Powell, above n 23, at 129.
[48] I Allen, D Hogg and S Peace, *Elderly people: Choice, participation and satisfaction* (London, Policy Studies Institute, 1992).
[49] *Ibid*, at 298.
[50] C Gilleard, 'Consumption and Identity in Later Life: Toward a Cultural Gerontology' (1996) 16 *Aging and Society* 489.
[51] *Ibid*, at 495.
[52] Heywood *et al*, above n 16, at 28.
[53] J Powell and M Edwards, 'Policy Narratives of Aging: The Right Way, the Third Way or the Wrong Way?' (2002) *Electronic Journal of Sociology*, online at <www.sociology.org/content/col006.001/powell-edwards.html>.
[54] *Ibid*, at 3.

The demands which this strategy imposes on older people in relation to home equity transactions, the risks that this creates and the implications of the neoliberal model of older people as active citizens/consumers on legal responses to vulnerability will be a recurring theme throughout this book.

(3) Political Expectations of Home Equity

In an older owner population containing fewer wage-earners, and with more people on fixed incomes (public or private pensions, or other private income streams), products that facilitate the release of housing wealth are potentially attractive to older owners who are 'asset-rich' (or 'house-rich') but 'cash-poor', for a range of reasons. One aspect of the drive towards home equity transactions is a series of UK government policies which (following the more established practice in the USA) increasingly expect older owners to 'use' their homes as a repository of capital to fund expenses, particularly healthcare costs, in their old age. The discussion of housing paradigms in chapter five reveals how the idea of home ownership as a means of accumulating and retaining asset wealth to pass on as inheritance to the next generation[55] has been superseded by a new expectation that 'housing wealth [be used] to meet a range of household expenditures, in particular to meet the costs of care in older age, and to supplement pensions',[56] with the result that wealth tied up in the home is currently regarded as 'more "spendable" now than it will be ever again'.[57] Political expectations of home equity use have played a major part in the emergence of this new paradigm, and this section considers two examples of legal and policy frameworks which have positioned older owners as consumers of their housing equity.

The need to maintain and repair property is one of the responsibilities of ownership that falls on all owner-occupiers, but for older owners who are 'income-poor' this may constitute a considerable financial burden.[58] While the Housing Act 1949 applied a policy of providing capital grants to owners to fund repairs and improvements to their properties, revised and expanded in the Housing Act 1969, recent decades have seen a considerable retrenchment of the system of support for repairs and maintenance to private sector dwellings, with a series of legislative changes that have ensured that owners are increasingly seen as holding primary responsibility for the condition of their properties.[59] The Local Government and Housing Act 1989 residualised grant aid, thus greatly reducing State expenditure in this area, and marking a major shift towards the ethos of personal responsibility. The Housing Grants, Construction and Regeneration Act 1996 went on to

[55] '[T]he asset value of housing … accumulates over the life course, provides a cushion (in the form of low housing costs) for old age, and flows on to the next generation through inheritance.': SJ Smith, *Banking on Housing: Speculating on the role and relevance of housing wealth in Britain* (Paper prepared for the Joseph Rowntree Foundation Inquiry into Home Ownership 2010 and Beyond, 2005) 11.

[56] This has led Smith to conclude that 'the scene is set for more, rather than less, use to be made of the opportunity to use housing equity across the life-course. It may not, for long, remain a resource for old age, much less a component of inheritance. Rather it may be viewed as a store of wealth which can be made available to spend on other things.' (*ibid*, at 12) See further discussion of housing paradigms for older owners in ch 5.

[57] *Ibid*, at 2.

[58] We can contrast the position of older owners in this respect with that of older tenants, who are generally not responsible for the costs of property maintenance in connection with their homes.

[59] See generally, P Leather, 'Grants to Homeowners: A Policy in Search of Objectives' (2000) 15 *Housing Studies* 149.

increase the discretion of local authorities to develop and implement strategic policies for home improvement, and 'heralded a major change in emphasis from [local authority as] provider to enabler'.[60]

The Government has identified a role for housing equity withdrawal to provide the funds for maintenance and repair of owned homes, although there is some evidence to suggest that owners are reluctant to use equity release for this purpose.[61] However, the decision to spend housing equity in this way will become less and less a matter of choice, as local authority grant expenditure continues to decrease and owners are increasingly required to invest their own resources into their homes.[62] The Department for the Environment, Transport and the Regions (DETR) has described its approach in neoliberal terms, as seeking to move towards 'less dependency on grants, and better reinforcement of homeowners' responsibilities towards their properties',[63] with government statements emphasising the ethos of self-responsibility, including the claims that 'it is only right that the responsibility for maintaining privately owned homes, which for many people is their most valuable asset, should rest first and foremost with the owner',[64] and that 'One important part of our policy is to make sure that homeowners are able to recognise and fulfil their responsibilities'.[65] Although it was noted that poor repair can be a particular problem for older people, who are recognised as often being a population at high risk of poor housing,[66] the targeted grant support which local authorities may offer is available only where owners cannot afford to repair the property themselves, including where they do not having the option of withdrawing equity to pay for repairs.[67]

While it has been recognised that many people were reluctant to enter into commercial equity release schemes,[68] in part because of concerns that the withdrawal of equity would have an adverse impact on their benefit entitlements, government policies persist in their promotion of equity release as the solution to housing improvement and maintenance needs.[69] Equity release schemes were identified as part of the 'loan assistance' which local authorities can provide under the Regulatory Reform (Housing Assistance) (England and Wales) Order 2002 (SI 2002/1860), described as potentially providing 'the best method of assisting low-income homeowners if there is substantial equity value in their homes, even though they are in need of repair'.[70] While some grant funding remains available for those

[60] J Stewart, J Clayton and A Ruston, 'Maintenance and repairs: an exploratory study into homeowners' views on alternatives to grants' (2004) 3 *Journal of Environmental Health Research* 62; J Stewart, J Clayton and A Ruston, 'Personal Responsibility for private sector housing renewal: Issues in health improvement' (2006) 65 *Health Education Journal* 73.

[61] Stewart *et al* (2004), above n 60.

[62] *Ibid.*

[63] DETR, *Private sector housing renewal: Reform of the Housing Grant, Construction and Regeneration Act 1996, Local Government and Housing Act 1989 and Housing Act 1985, A consultation paper* (London, DETR, 2001) 5.

[64] *Ibid*, para 3.1.

[65] *Ibid*, para 3.3.

[66] *Ibid*, para 3.4.

[67] *Ibid*, para 3.2.

[68] DETR, above n 63, paras 5.6–5.7.

[69] 'We believe that equity release loans could help bring affordable repairs within reach of a much wider range of homeowners than at present, particularly in areas where property values are high. Equity release could also be a valuable tool for helping older homeowners, many of whom have little or no outstanding mortgages.' (*ibid*, para 5.8).

[70] See Office of the Deputy Prime Minister, *Housing Renewal*, ODPM Circular 05/2003 (London, ODPM, 2003) para 3.13.

who do not have equity to release, the policy requires that owners exhaust their own equity before they will qualify for State-funded grant assistance. While there is a clear logic to this approach when the renewal of private sector housing is viewed in isolation, in reality it forms part of a wider landscape in which home equity is expected to perform multiple functions for the older owner. For example, where housing wealth is also viewed as a substitute or supplement for pension income, the risk of 'running out' of equity in the later stages of retirement could have major implications for the older owner's quality of life.[71]

A second example of a policy area in which the neoliberal mantra of personal responsibility has been explicitly linked to the withdrawal of equity from owned homes, particularly by older owners, is the funding of healthcare and nursing care in old age. The issue of resources to fund healthcare and nursing care for older people has been a vexed political question for several years, with contentious questions concerning the balance between residential care home placements compared to providing care in the older person's own home (and so enabling 'ageing in place'),[72] and the extent to which care for the elderly should be funded from central and local government resources as opposed to from the older person's own resources, specifically their housing equity. The resourcing of long-term care for older people has been high on the political agenda for over a decade, since the Royal Commission on Long Term Care for the Elderly[73] was established to investigate how to provide for needs in old age, including how costs should be apportioned between public funds and individuals.[74]

The current approach to funding for care in England and Wales draws a distinction between health or medical care, which is generally provided free through the National Health Service, and 'non-health' social or personal care, including domiciliary care (in the older person's own home) and residential care, for which local authorities are responsible and for which the relevant local authority assesses need based on locally set criteria and a means-test.[75] Where an individual has capital assets of £23,000 or more—including the value of that person's home, so long as it is not occupied by a spouse, partner or other specified relative—he or she is required to pay the fees for residential care and nursing home fees in full,[76] while people with assets under £23,000 may be expected to make a contribution towards their care costs.

The sharp distinction between healthcare and non-healthcare was challenged in the Report of the Royal Commission, which argued that the relevant distinction should be between the costs of daily living for older people—which the Commission indicated should continue to be the responsibility of the individual—and costs of 'healthcare needs', including intimate personal care, which the majority recommended should be provided free on the basis of assessed need.[77] The Commission argued that this was necessary to ensure, for example, that the personal care available to someone with Alzheimer's Disease

[71] The risks created by these competing demands on housing equity are discussed further in ch 6.
[72] See discussion in ch 5.
[73] Royal Commission on Long Term Care for the Elderly, *With Respect to Old Age: Long Term Care—Rights and Responsibilities*, Cm 4192–1 (London, TSO, 1999).
[74] *Ibid*, Chairman's Introduction, para 1.
[75] *Ibid*, paras 4.9–4.17.
[76] See HM Government, *Shaping the Future of Care Together*, Cm 7673 (London, TSO, 2009) 120.
[77] Royal Commission, above n73, Chairman's Introduction, para 13.

would be equatable with that available for someone with cancer.[78] A minority of the Royal Commission team registered a note of dissent, arguing that free personal care would disproportionately benefit those who were better-off and could afford to pay for it in any event.[79] While the Government accepted many of the recommendations in the Report, the means test was withdrawn only in relation to nursing care. The result was that while health-related care is now free at the point of use, personal care (for example, the mainly 'social' long-term care) remains means-tested.[80]

A system which requires that people use up whatever savings they have before they are eligible for State support has been criticised for 'demand[ing] that people of modest means make themselves poor before it will help'.[81] Those with modest assets can find that they are exhausted very quickly when care is required,[82] leaving little or nothing for other costs in old age. The Royal Commission recognised that for many older people with moderate savings, their assets tend to be tied up in the owned home, leaving them 'asset rich, but income poor'.[83] The Commission was concerned that

> [a] situation where the value of their home effectively dictates whether people are potentially entitled to state help for their care needs does not represent a form of effective pooling of risk of the kind which the Commission thinks is needed.[84]

It also highlighted the difficulties for older people in forecasting the likelihood that they will need personal care in their old age,[85] and the challenges of negotiating these risks as part of their retirement planning:

> Making provision for long-term care is thus different from making provision for a pension. Everyone reaching pensionable age expects to start drawing a pension for their later years. The pension is something which people hope they can rely on for an old age which they would like to be comfortable, and for which many have optimistic expectations. Paying for long-term care on the other hand involves making provision in one way or another against catastrophic and, in principle, unforeseeable costs.[86]

The Royal Commission clearly regarded the ethos of 'self-responsibility' as inappropriate in the context of medical and personal care (which requires the negotiation of risks which even the most careful planning may not address), thus challenging the political culture

[78] *Ibid*, Executive Summary and Report, para 3.7, noting that while Alzheimer's Disease cannot be cured by medical care, so that accompanying personal care would not be designated as 'medical care', people suffering from it need ongoing therapeutic or personal care in order to enable them to live with the condition.

[79] *Ibid*, 'Note of Dissent'; see also discussion in I Heath, 'Redistribution of wealth from rich to poor is not a function of a care service' (1999) 319 (7201) *British Medical Journal* 55, arguing that redistribution of wealth is the function of a taxation system, not a care system.

[80] Except in Scotland, where personal care is also funded by the State; R Hancock, R Wittenberg, A Comas-Herrera and L Pickard, 'Who will pay for long-term care in the UK? Projections linking macro- and micro-simulation models' (2003) 24 *Fiscal Studies* 387; see also R Hancock, L Pickard, R Wittenberg, A Comas-Herrera, A Juarez-Garcia, D King and J Malley, *Paying for Long Term Care for Older People in the UK: Modelling the Costs and Incidence of a Range of Options* (Report to the Nuffield Foundation, PSSRU Discussion Paper 2336, 2007), available online at <www.pssru.ac.uk>.

[81] Royal Commission, above n 73, para 4.16.

[82] *Ibid.*

[83] *Ibid*, para 4.17.

[84] *Ibid.*

[85] 'The point is that people simply do not know whether they will need long-term care until they get old' (*ibid*, para 3.1).

[86] *Ibid*, para 3.2.

that constructs older owners as consumers of care, and calling for greater solidarity in respect of the risks of needing long-term care,

> a risk that is best covered by some kind of risk pooling—to rely on income or savings, as most people effectively have to do now, is not efficient or fair due to the nature of the risk and the size of the sums required.[87]

The Government did not accept this view, older owners remaining responsible through means-testing for personal care, and the push to use housing equity to meet the health and nursing care 'funding gap' as older people live longer continues to be a prominent policy issue.[88] Glendinning *et al* noted that the inclusion of housing assets within the means tests for access to State funding for long-term care tends to be especially controversial,[89] and the ineffectiveness of the requirement to exhaust housing equity is brought home by evidence that in most cases this will not generate sufficient capital to pay for nursing care for any length of time.[90] The requirement that older people fund their own care through savings accounts or housing equity has also been criticised on the basis that while it redistributes resources across the life-cycle, it does not redistribute from those with lesser needs to those with greater needs for long-term care; it is more costly for women, who are likely to have higher needs of care than men and so are more likely to deplete resources earlier[91]; and it involves no pooling of risk.[92] Nevertheless, with the owned home usually the most valuable asset people have, it remains central to the Government's ethos of individual responsibility for long-term care.[93]

The policy of means-testing against private resources in this context has also been criticised on the grounds that the Health Service is 'negating its responsibility for care and making people rely on their own resources', leading to the 'feeling … that a contract with the people has been broken'.[94] This has interesting implications for the idea of 'voluntariness' in housing equity transactions to fund care. The Royal Commission on Long Term Care for the Elderly suggested that it was unfair to require those who have savings or are homeowners to pay for care with large sums of their own resources, in a context where 'Even though they pay the bill this often does not feel like a conscious purchase decision. It is often rushed, and by definition made at a time of personal crisis.'[95] The contexts in which older people execute housing equity transactions (to fund care or for other purposes) are crucial in understanding their vulnerabilities as contracting parties, which in turn enables an assessment of the appropriateness of the legal frameworks that govern

[87] *Ibid*, Executive Summary.

[88] L Sheiner and DN Weil, 'The Housing Wealth of the Aged', *NBER Working Paper No W4115* (2002), available online at <http://papers.ssrn.com/sol3/papers.cfm?abstract_id=226798>; see also in Australia, M Fine and J Chalmers, '"User pays" and other approaches to the funding of long-term care for older people in Australia' (2000) 20 *Ageing and Society* 5.

[89] C Glendinning, B Davies, L Pickard and A Comas-Herrera, *Funding Long-Term Care for Older People: Lessons from Other Countries* (York, Joseph Rowntree Foundation, 2004) 28.

[90] R Hancock, 'Housing wealth, income and financial wealth of older people in Britain' (1998) 18 *Aging and Society* 5.

[91] While men who live to be over 65 have a 1:5 risk of needing residential care, women over 65 have a 1:3 risk; see Royal Commission, above n 73, para 3.1.

[92] Glendinning *et al*, above n 89, at 4.

[93] The Royal Commission noted that 'few people will have capital on the scale needed other than by selling their house': Royal Commission, above n 73, para 3.5.

[94] *Ibid*, para 4.34.

[95] *Ibid*, para 4.37.

these transactions. Having emphasised the risks involved in using equity release products to enable people to buy into private sector schemes for long-term care, the Commission's proposed safeguard was to regulate these products, on the grounds that 'because of the complexity of the nature of the contract which is being entered into, Government should satisfy itself that there are proper regulatory safeguards in place to give potential purchasers peace of mind'.[96] The extent to which regulatory approaches—which seek to control the conduct of the provider, and to prevent harm from occurring[97]—provide an adequate response to the situational vulnerabilities of older owners in housing equity transactions underpins the analysis in this book, and is discussed in chapter nine.

The debate concerning publicly-funded support for long-term care as a universal welfare provision (as opposed to limiting its availability to those older people with low incomes or low levels of assets) was re-opened with the publication of a report for the Joseph Rowntree Foundation in 2004[98] and the Wanless Report in 2006.[99] In 2007, the Government committed to a long-term review of the system, leading to the 2009 Green Paper, *Shaping the Future of Care Together*.[100] Key issues considered in the Green Paper included the impact of charges and means-testing on access to care for those with moderate levels of wealth, often tied up in their housing equity, thus creating a pressure to release equity to fund costs of care. The Paper noted (hinting at the 'moral hazard' in play in this context)[101] that

> [t]here was … little consensus about whether a person's ability to pay for themselves should be taken into consideration when the state is deciding how much support to give … Although people agreed that those who could not afford to pay for themselves had the greatest need for state support, they also felt it was unfair that people who had worked hard and made sensible decisions to save were less eligible for state support.[102]

The Green Paper noted the current practice, whereby

> If someone is in a care home and no one is living in their house, they are expected to use their savings and the value of their house to pay for care and accommodation, until they have used up almost all of them.[103]

The preferred option set out in this Paper was a 'partnership' model, which would recognise the differentiation within the older owner sector, by providing some level of State-funded support for all, with more State-funded care and support for the less well-off, while those with greater assets would be required to fund the balance from their own resources. At the same time, the Paper indicated that 'some people who needed high

[96] *Ibid*, para 5.27.

[97] Contrasted with the *ex post facto* action of remedial legal strategies.

[98] Glendinning *et al*, above n 89.

[99] D Wanless, J Forder, J-L Fernàndez, T Poole, L Beesley, M Henwood and F Moscone, *The Wanless Social Care Review: Securing Good Care for Older People—Taking a Long-term View* (London, King's Fund, 2006), which set out a range of funding options for social care. The conclusions of this Report—that there is a need for partnership between individual and the State and for radical reforms to ensure that good care remains affordable—were reiterated in R Humphries, J Forder and J-L Fernàndez, *Securing Good Care for More People: Options for reform* (London, King's Fund, 2010), available online at <http://www.kingsfund.org.uk/applications/research/index.rm?filter=publications>.

[100] Above n 76.

[101] See ch 3, section (2)(c).

[102] Above n 76, 14.

[103] *Ibid*, Executive Summary, at 16.

levels of care and support ... would need to spend their savings and the value of their homes'.[104] The proposed partnership model would be supported by additional, risk-sharing mechanisms, including the development of a State-led insurance scheme for those who need to 'top-up' the State care to which they are entitled, or a comprehensive scheme which all older people who have resources would be required to pay into in exchange for 'free' care and support. These insurance schemes would have the advantage of spreading some of the risk resulting from the unpredictability of future needs for long-term care, with the stated intention of 'help[ing] people to protect their wealth and the value of their homes'.[105]

Under the Green Paper scheme, older people who moved into residential care would continue to be liable for accommodation costs, food and lodging—'because we would expect people to buy their own food, pay their own bills, and pay their own rent or their own mortgage, if they were living at home'[106]—but rather than requiring this to be paid immediately (for example through housing equity transactions during the owner's lifetime), the Paper proposed a universal deferred payment system, which would allow these costs to be charged upon the individual's estate when he or she died.[107] These proposals have interesting resonances with the housing paradigms for older owners discussed in chapter four. The suggestion that payments would be deferred supports the psychological attachment to housing as home, while also using the paradigm of housing as investment asset to spend (through the claim against the owner's estate). As with equity release, however, shifting these costs towards the care-user's estate would diminish the amount of housing asset available as inheritance.

In fact, the mechanism proposed would presumably operate in a very similar fashion to equity release. The White Paper, published in March 2010,[108] carried forward the proposal for a deferred payment scheme for living expenses. Although it did not explicitly state that the 'deferred payment' (or debt) would be secured by a charge, it seems likely that the only option to ensure that payment would be made is through a fixed 'line of credit' charge,[109] either against the home specifically, or against the fluctuating pool of assets making up the owner's estate.[110] Such a charge would have to be hedged by conditions, for example in relation to other transactions purporting to spend housing equity for the remainder of the owner's life, as the accumulating debt would potentially make a claim against the whole of the equity. If this was the case, the deferred payment scheme would inhibit the use of housing equity for other purposes. It is difficult to see what the difference would be for the owner compared to using equity release, other than that equity release for a fixed sum or to a limit preserves the possibility of retaining some equity for other purposes (for other transactions, or for inheritance), that there may be some perceived psychological advantage in the Government's care scheme labelling the transaction as 'deferred payment' rather than a transaction which has immediate effect (although the difference would be

[104] *Ibid*, at 106.
[105] *Ibid*, Executive Summary, at 18.
[106] *Ibid*, at 87.
[107] *Ibid*, Executive Summary, at 19–20.
[108] HM Government, *Building the National Care Service*, Cm 7854 (London, The Stationery Office, 2010).
[109] The only alternative would be that the debt is unsecured, which seems unlikely as it would leave the local authority vulnerable to (and create a moral hazard towards) the assets being dissipated by the time the care recipient dies.
[110] For discussion of the nature of a fixed charge over fluctuating assets, see *National Westminster Bank plc v Spectrum Plus Ltd* [2004] EWCA Civ 670.

semantic), and that the government-backed nature of the scheme would overcome some of the barriers to trust that have been reported in relation to commercial equity release providers.

Lastly, the Green Paper also acknowledged the counter-argument, raised in the consultation, that the use of housing wealth by older owners for this purpose is preferable to passing on the 'burden' of funding long-term care to younger people through taxation, because the younger generation

> were already paying for many things—such as tuition fees and higher mortgage repayments—that older generations had not had to face. They also argued that the increase in older people's housing wealth was not something that they had earned, so it was not fair that they should have an automatic right to keep it, at the expense of younger generations.[111]

Since it is clear that there is likely to be a significant continuing role for personal responsibility towards the costs of long-term care in old age for those who are designated as having the resources to pay, including, for example, older owners who hold their assets in the form of housing equity, this adds weight to the case for urgent socio-legal scrutiny of the legal framework that governs these crucial transactions for older owners.

(4) Older People, Rights and (In)Equality

A final landmark on the political and policy landscape of housing equity transactions is the issue of older people, their rights and the equality agenda. In 1991, the UN General Assembly adopted the 'United Nations Principles for Older Persons',[112] which recognised the complexity and rapidity of the ageing of the world's population, and provided a common basis and frame of reference for protecting and promoting the rights of the elderly. The UN Principles were rooted in the universal standards set out in the Universal Declaration of Human Rights, the International Covenant on Economic, Social and Cultural Rights, and the International Covenant on Civil and Political Rights, but they recognised the need for specific attention to ensure that these universal standards would be appropriately applied to particular groups.[113] This resolution acknowledged the heterogeneity of older people's experiences, including within countries and between individuals, but called for action in several areas, including 'creating a financial environment that encourages people to save for their old age'[114] and 'Strengthening measures and mechanisms to ensure that retired persons do not fall into poverty, taking into account their contribution to the development of their countries.'[115]

The five key principles articulated by the UN resolution were:

— Independence
— Participation
— Care

[111] *Shaping the Future of Care Together*, above n 76, 91.
[112] UN resolution A/RES/46/91, available online at <http://www.unescap.org/ageing/res/res46–91.htm>.
[113] *Ibid*, Annex.
[114] <http://www.unescap.org/ageing/res/principl.htm>.
[115] *Ibid.*

— Self-fulfilment
— Dignity

and these broad principles were supported by guidelines, for example in respect of care, that 'Older persons should have access to social and legal services to enhance their autonomy, protection and care.'[116] This formulation captured one of the key challenges addressed in this book: how a legal regime governing housing equity transactions for older people can balance the desire to maintain 'autonomy' (in the political and legal sense of allowing, and often requiring, older people to make choices and holding them responsible for the consequences of those choices) with the need for protection and care against the vulnerabilities of ageing. The vulnerabilities of age were also recognised in the 'Dignity' principles, which included reference to the right of older persons to 'live in dignity and security and be free of exploitation and physical or mental abuse'.[117] Again, this reinforces the importance of striking an appropriate balance between autonomy and vulnerability in legal frameworks which seek to ensure fairness and equality for older people.

Rights-based approaches to policy for older people are often welcomed on the grounds that they 'shift the emphasis away from older people as passive and needy consumers of services, to self-reliant and autonomous citizens',[118] but within a more benign context than that offered by the market—in the context of human rights obligations and wider human rights values, such as those articulated in the UN principles, and the FRED principles (fairness, respect, equality, dignity). The age charities have emphasised the role of human rights norms in 'achieving social progress for the many disadvantaged, marginalised and vulnerable people in our society',[119] and have expressed concerns about the 'many older people [who] remain at risk of breaches of their human rights and are unable to achieve redress'.[120] The focus of this literature is mainly on public service provision for older people, since the legal responsibilities which the Human Rights Act (HRA) 1998 imposes in respect of 'Convention Rights' are explicitly aimed at the Government and public authorities, rather than at the private organisations (for example, creditors or equity release providers) with whom older people may transact to release their housing equity.[121] As the neoliberal strategy for meeting the welfare needs of older people has shifted the focus from the public realm to the individual responsibility of the older person, through private market provision, it has marginalised the scope for making 'rights-based' claims within the framework of the HRA 1998, particularly in respect of the 'private law' transactions which have become necessary to fund welfare needs.[122]

[116] UN resolution A/RES/46/91, Annex, principle 12.

[117] *Ibid*, principle 17.

[118] F Butler, *Rights for Real: Older People, Human Rights and the Commission for Equality and Human Rights* (London, Age Concern, 2006) 8.

[119] *Ibid*, at 12.

[120] *Ibid.*

[121] HRA 1998, s 6, although there is an extensive literature exploring the argument that the HRA has indirect horizontal effect through the status of the court as a 'public authority'; see, eg, W Wade, 'Horizons of Horizontality' (2000) 116 *LQR* 217; M Hunt, 'The "horizontal effect" of the Human Rights Act' [1998] *Public Law* 423; G Phillipson, 'The Human Rights Act, "Horizontal Effect" and the Common Law: a Bang or a Whimper?' (1999) 62 *MLR* 824.

[122] HRA 1998, s 6(3)(b); the test of 'public function' was set out in *YL v Birmingham City Council* [2007] UKHL 27, applied in *Regina (Weaver) v London & Quadrant Housing Trust* [2008] EWHC 1377. This test took account of the public nature of the functions performed by the housing trust, that it was permeated by State control and influence, the nature and extent of the public subsidy involved, and its role in the implementation of Government policy. While private and voluntary organisations that exercise a 'public function' are included

At the same time, the HRA 1998 was intended to have an effect beyond strict legal obligations, to create a 'culture of human rights', embedding human rights values in law and policy. This objective offers an alternative rights-based perspective through which to consider the particular needs and vulnerabilities of older people. In Wales, the Older People's Commissioner[123] is legally obliged to have regard to the UN Principles, which it states 'should be considered by all organisations and regarded as a framework for their treatment of older people'.[124] There is no specific governmental agency for older people in England, although age discrimination and age equality fall under the remit of the Equality and Human Rights Commission, whose projects concerning older people have included the 'Just Ageing?' programme, the final report and recommendations of which were published in December 2009. This programme set out to explore inequalities throughout the life-course and their implications for later life by exploring a range of issues, including the implications of longer lives for traditional models of social justice, the concept of intergenerational equity and the impact of trigger events on the later life experiences of different demographic groups.[125]

The 'Just Ageing?' project emphasised the need to ensure fairness and equality across the life-course, particularly seeking to 'build momentum for action on the disadvantage that accumulates across all the different stages of life and results in inequality in old age'.[126] Key insights highlighted by the project included concerns that policy-makers are focused on a short-term agenda rather than planning for the long term, and the need to ensure that the 'systems and structures' designed to address the needs of older people create equality rather than furthering inequality.[127] The research emphasised the importance of responding to the socio-demographic differentiation discussed in chapter one, to address the unequal later life outcomes that result from inequalities across the life-course. A paradigmatic example of this phenomenon is the case of 'marginal owners' in housing equity transactions: low-income owner-occupiers living in lower-value properties who, with perhaps only one roll of the equity release dice to make, can ill-afford a 'bad transaction', with the disproportionately adverse consequences that might have for their financial well-being for the remainder of their lives. The risks that must be negotiated by these marginal older owners are only compounded by the increasing demands placed on their housing wealth. This raises new issues for legal theory and practice, including the question of whether, while fairness and the principle of non-discrimination require that like cases are treated alike,[128] the specific and particular vulnerabilities under which

within the scope of the HRA, the same cannot be said of functions which *were* public but are now redesignated as the private responsibility of the 'consumer'.

123 Established by the Commission for Older People (Wales) Act 2006, and set up in 2008.

124 See Older People's Commissioner for Wales website, <http://www.olderpeoplewales.com/index.php?id=454&L=0>.

125 <http://www.equalityhumanrights.com/fairer-britain/just-ageing/>.

126 M Lee, *Just Ageing? Fairness, equality and the life course: Final Report* (London, Equality and Human Rights Commission, 2009), Executive Summary, ii.

127 *Ibid*, iv.

128 In *Ghaidan v Godin-Mendoza* [2004] UKHL 30, Lord Nicholls, stating the principle of non-discrimination, claimed (at para [9]): 'Of course all law, civil and criminal, has to draw distinctions. One type of conduct, or one factual situation, attracts one legal consequence, another type of conduct or situation attracts a different legal consequence. To be acceptable these distinctions should have a rational and fair basis. Like cases should be treated alike, unlike cases should not be treated alike.'

(marginal) older owners enter into housing equity transactions raise an argument for 'special protection'.

(5) Conclusions

This book examines the legal framework of home equity transactions for older owners to explore the appropriateness of the current law, and to assess the balance struck between the model of the older owner as 'autonomous consumer' and the realities of inequalities and vulnerabilities which leave some older owners exposed to heightened risk compared to the general population. The paradox of the political contexts considered in this chapter, so far as legal regulation and remedies are concerned, is that while on the one hand home ownership is increasingly seen as a proxy for active citizenship, with the push towards homeownership and the accumulation of wealth seen as a cure for many social problems,[129] including financial incompetence and security against unforeseen circumstances,[130] it is frequently recognised that this image of the 'ideal consumer' does not accurately reflect the reality, particularly for marginal owners. Research on financial capability has highlighted the difficulties that much of the UK population has in understanding complex housing finance products,[131] while the very act of getting into debt is *de facto* used as a measure of financial incapability.[132] While the recent global financial crisis has highlighted the vulnerable position of marginal home owners, even in periods of economic prosperity owner-occupiers—particularly older owners in lower-value properties—are exposed to risks where the wealth gains from housing are place-specific and socio-economically unequal.[133] The complex socio-economic circumstances and events to which marginal home owners may be exposed, and the inequalities and vulnerabilities that are created and revealed in these transactions, are compounded by age. This is only exacerbated in a legal context which distinguishes consumers not according to their (financial or legal) capabilities, but as either having capacity—and so 'qualifying' as autonomous consumers—or not.[134]

The demographic, socio-economic and political contexts of home equity use by older owners present a landscape which is poised for increasing housing equity use, for various purposes, particularly following retirement. This book argues that these changing patterns require a new analysis of the legal regime surrounding home equity transactions by older owners which focuses on the risks that flow not only from the transactions *per se*, but from these particular types of transactions in the particular contexts in which older owners find themselves. As such, the book explores a range of legal issues relating to the use of home equity by older owners, applying the concepts of risk and security, vulnerability and

[129] Department of Communities and Local Government, *Homes for the Future: more affordable, more sustainable*, CM 7191 (London, DCLG, 2007).

[130] DETR, *Quality and Choice: A Decent Home for All* (London, DETR, 2000).

[131] For discussion of financial capability, see ch 8, section (3).

[132] M Taylor, S Jenkin and A Sacker, *Financial capability and wellbeing: Evidence from the BHPS, Occasional Papers Series 34* (London, FSA, 2009), available online at <http://www.fsa.gov.uk/pubs/occpapers/op34.pdf>.

[133] D Dorling, J Rigby, B Wheeler, D Ballas, B Thomas, F Eldin, D Bordon and R Lupton, *Poverty, wealth and place in Britain, 1968–2005* (York, Joseph Rowntree Foundation, 2007); R Burrows, *Home-ownership and Poverty in Britain, Findings* (York, Joseph Rowntree Foundation, 2003).

[134] See ch 8, sections (2) and (3).

responsibility, as they have been developed through the theoretical framework of the 'risk society' and in the concept of a 'vulnerable legal subject'. While equity release is a growing industry for various types of owner-occupier, the book focuses on the specific contexts likely to be experienced by older owners to determine whether—bearing in mind the policy and legal factors that have shaped the emergence and development of equity release as an option for older owners, including the emergence of the older owner as a credit market actor, and the development of innovative and complex products to facilitate equity release—law's response to older owners in respect of home equity use is appropriately balanced between autonomy and protection.

In doing so, the approach adopted places considerable emphasis on the economic, social, political and demographic patterns already outlined to explore the importance of context in housing equity transactions along three broad themes. The first theme relates to the importance of contextual factors in economic decision-making (under conditions of uncertainty), as recognised in behavioural economics, for example through analysis of the 'traits' or psychological biases of risk aversion, inconsistency in discount functions, susceptibility to framing effects, anchoring and inefficiency in the use of information.[135] Empirical evidence demonstrating the importance of context to transactional decision-making challenges the strong model of rationality underpinning the 'rational economic man' of classical economic thought, and provides a basis for incorporating the psychology of intuitive beliefs, constraints and choices as they relate to real-world decision-making. Evidence that older owners entering into housing equity transactions are likely to be influenced by their social, economic, political and personal contexts is explored through the lens of contextual or 'situational' vulnerability,[136] as well through challenges to the liberal model of legal subjects as rational market actors.[137]

This feeds into a second theme, concerned with the ways in which the rise of individualism and choice in neoliberal welfare policies has cast older owners as market actors or consumers who are required to manage their finances in retirement through home equity transactions. Strauss has argued that behavioural economics 'has particular salience in societies characterised by the domination of markets, the individualisation of welfare and neoliberal presumptions in favour of self-reliance',[138] so that

> [i]n the UK, for example, strong assumptions are made about the economic rationality and decision-making competence of individuals in areas of government policy such as health, pensions and education ... The 'choice agenda' does not only concern state-provided public services ... Individualised risk, responsibility and choice are at the heart of the [direct contributions pension] model, yet inertia and low levels of personal saving suggest that individuals have difficulty making appropriate decisions.[139]

There are clear parallels between evidence of 'irrational' decision-making concerning pensions and the pressures on older owners to participate in housing equity transactions

[135] See, eg, D Kahneman, 'Maps of Bounded Rationality: Psychology for Behavioural Economics' (2003) 93 *American Economic Review* 1449; S Issacharoff, 'Can There be a Behavioural Law and Economics?' (1998) 51 *Vanderbilt Law Review* 1729; CR Sunstein (ed), *Behavioural Law and Economics* (Cambridge, Cambridge University Press, 2000); see further discussion in ch 3.

[136] See ch 6.

[137] See ch 4.

[138] K Strauss, 'Re-engaging with rationality in economic geography: behavioural approaches and the importance of context in decision-making' (2008) 8 *Journal of Economic Geography* 137, 142.

[139] *Ibid*, at 138.

to fund costs after retirement, which highlight the need to scrutinise the legal response to home equity transactions against the backdrop of the contextual and environmental factors which form the 'real-world' environment of such transactions.

Thirdly, the importance of context also flows back into the content of legal responses which judge transactions as 'normal' or 'abnormal'[140] depending on implicit expectations about the ways in which people are likely to use their housing wealth.

A number of contemporary scholars have argued for the need to build on behavioural economics—which, it is argued, while recognising individual psychological proclivities, presents individuals as autonomous, unconnected agents, and so downplays the role of context and environment[141]—to 'enrich current behavioural approaches by taking seriously the notion of context … by specifying and incorporating contextual factors into studies of "real world" economic decision-making'.[142] Smith *et al* have described the opening of the 'black box' of context in economic decision-making as a 'challenge [to] the economic essentialism invested in … "stylised facts" of economics'.[143] This, in turn, provides a basis to challenge the ways in which private law has been shaped by the perceived demands of market efficiency to serve the interests of creditors,[144] and adds weight to the argument that legal discourse should look beyond efficiency criteria in analyses of financial transactions, and take account of the broader contexts of transactions, both for contracting parties and for the reciprocal relationships between economic, social and legal discourses.

As socio-economic research increasingly emphasises 'the social and power-filled character of markets; their diversity and complexity, their sensitivity to context, their passions as well as their "rationality" and their part in the social construction and performance of the economy',[145] there is a parallel need for areas of private law which have long been aligned with neoclassical economics[146] and dominated by a liberal legal subject[147] to be re-viewed in light both of these new understandings of the role of social context and of the changing character of the context in which the transaction takes place. Where Smith *et al* have sought to 'engage the cutting edge of economic analysis in closer dialogue with the

[140] Eg, in the context of undue influence, see ch 10.

[141] Strauss, above n 138, at 144.

[142] *Ibid*, at 139; see also S Smith, M Munro and H Christie, 'Performing (housing) markets' (2006) 43 *Urban Studies* 81.

[143] Smith *et al*, above n 142.

[144] For a discussion of this phenomenon in the context of mortgages, see L Fox, *Conceptualising Home: Theories, Laws and Policies* (Oxford, Hart Publishing, 2007) 81–108.

[145] Smith *et al*, above n 142.

[146] Eg, Gray and Gray have described English land law as 'display[ing] many of the features of a closed system of logic or an autopoietic order, prompting immediate analogies with mathematics and, more particularly, with the discipline of Euclidean geometry … every strategic move is dictated by an arbitrarily predetermined set of foundational principles … property in land "behaves" in a manner just as predictable and verifiable as any other branch of rational science.': K Gray and S Gray, 'The Rhetoric of Realty' in J Getzler, *Rationalizing Property, Equity and Trusts: Essays in Honour of Edward Burn* (London, LexisNexis, 2001) 204–05. Green described English land law as a discipline in which 'The rules maintain their logic and predictability for rational men; distance and a certain ruthlessness are also persuasive of land law's masculine world view … All the rules are judged rationally, according to their fitness for their purpose: the test is whether they render the market more or less efficient': K Green, 'Being Here—What a Woman Can Say About Land Law' in A Bottomley (ed), *Feminist Perspectives on the Foundational Subjects of Law* (London, Cavendish, 1996) 101; 'Reason is seen to demand that the needs of property owners, self-interested and rational individuals in the market place, override the needs of those who are different: weaker or poorer, or in a different way defined as Other.' (*ibid*, at 93–94).

[147] See ch 4.

rich texture of other social research concerned with economic ideas and practices',[148] there is also an argument for legal analysis to attempt to capture their role in shaping the context of financial decision-making. This endeavour can usefully include a new critical analysis of where, when and why law protects—or does not protect—ageing owners in particular types of home equity transaction.

[148] Smith *et al*, above n 142.

3

The Consumption of Housing Equity in a Risk Society

(1) Introduction

Planning for old age in the early twenty-first century requires the careful negotiation of a range of risks and uncertainties, from personal life events over which one has limited control (including, for example, health/disability risks, longevity risks), to the market risks associated with financial transactions, especially in respect of complex, non-discrete products (for example, investment risk, inflation). The decision to spend housing equity—whether earlier in the life-course or after retirement—clearly involves risk, and with that the possibilities of both positive and negative outcomes. This chapter sets out a conceptual framework for analysing how law determines who is 'responsible' for adverse outcomes in housing equity transactions. There are several possible candidates, including the older owners themselves, or their families; the creditor/housing equity provider who benefits from the opportunity to profit from these transactions; or the State, either through welfare provision or protective schemes (the costs of which are passed on to wider society through general taxation), or through the institutions of law.

The legal framework that governs housing equity transactions in any given case is determined according to a complex web of pathways; the starting point depends on the nature of the transaction (from 'trading down' and 'ordinary' debt to specialised equity release products) and—in the case of the 'targeted' products—on the recognised level of 'product risk'. The attribution of responsibilities for possible harms in each case is shaped by prevailing norms (in the particular context), including the (potential) vulnerability of the older owner and the responsibilities of the other party vis-à-vis that vulnerability. Across these contexts, there is a range of approaches which legal analyses might take regarding the distribution of risk and responsibility: for example, we might ask 'Who is best able to absorb the risks of home equity transactions?', considering factors such as whether older people who are no longer income-generating are less able to absorb risk, adjust to losses and recover from economic setbacks than the young; whether younger borrowers should be protected from the costs of bad outcomes for older owners; how effectively the legal framework that governs decision-making in housing equity transactions ensures personal responsibility on the part of older owners; whether the nature of the uncertainties is such that even older owners who act 'responsibly' cannot avoid the risk of adverse outcomes. These questions inevitably require value judgements about the economic and social policy aims of the legal system, and the nature and extent of its role in the housing equity market. This, in turn, raises tensions between the model of legal subjectivity that requires older owners to be effective autonomous and self-responsible consumers, on the one hand, and challenges to this model and the liberal conception of contract it supports from critical scholarship, for example feminist theories of dependency and vulnerability, on the other.[1]

Expectations that older owners will participate in housing equity transactions, their experiences as consumers in the credit market and the engagement with risk that has resulted from the development of innovative housing equity products, have been transformed in recent decades. This chapter proposes the conceptual framework of the 'risk society' as a useful sensitising framework for analyses of the new legal issues that policies in respect of older owners, debt and housing equity transactions have generated. Key features identified as characteristic of the 'risk society' are helpful in framing the context of these transactions, including the expansion of choice for older owners, their responsibilities to *make choices*—which necessarily involve an element of risk—about how to finance their retirement, the proliferation of information relating to these choices, the unpredictability of their futures[2] and the effects of changing traditions of 'old age', which mean that people no longer 'fade away' after retirement but lead active lives with ongoing financial needs which must be balanced across early and later 'old age', creating a new tension between lifestyle now and potential health and welfare needs into the future.

In particular, this chapter will consider Giddens' three core conceptualisations of the risk society:

a) reflexivity of the self;
b) lifestyles and life planning; and
c) ontological security;

and their significance for housing wealth decision-making by older owners.[3] For generations, home ownership has been promoted as a preferred form of tenure on the promise of ontological security in retirement; but this 'security' is coming under pressure from the increasing range of functions that home equity is expected to perform. The question of who is responsible for the older person's needs in retirement, and particularly the individualisation of older owners[4] as self-responsible credit market actors, has prompted calls for legal intervention, first in the Financial Services Authority's (FSA's) expanding regulatory jurisdiction over equity release products, and again as the regulatory environment responds to broader post-global financial crisis concerns about responsibility in financial transactions.[5] This chapter also begins to unpack the theme of responsibility, from the individual responsibility of the owner as an autonomous subject to the responsibilities of providers to address product risk and consumer risk, and the issue of State responsibility—whether through legal protections at the point of sale or, if not then, through fall-back on the welfare State when the older owner's housing wealth has been

[1] See ch 4 for discussion of these competing models of the legal subject in housing equity transactions.

[2] Both the older owner and the credit provider trade not only on the future value of the property but also on how long the older owner will live.

[3] A Giddens, *Modernity and Self-Identity: Self and Society in the Late Modern Age* (Cambridge, Polity Press, 1991).

[4] U Beck, *Risk Society: Towards a New Modernity* (New Delhi, Sage, 1992).

[5] See, eg, T Williams, 'Open the box: an exploration of the Financial Services Authority's model of fairness in consumer financial transactions' in M Kenny, J Devenney and L Fox O'Mahony (eds), *Unconscionability in European Private Financial Transactions: Protecting the Vulnerable* (Cambridge, Cambridge University Press, 2010).

depleted—for the risks which have been created, in part at least, by political and policy strategies in respect of housing equity.

The socio-economic and political environments of ageing in the early twenty-first century mean that, increasingly, many older owners will have no choice but to engage with some form of risk in relation to the use (or not) of home equity after retirement. The risks associated with spending housing wealth can lead to positive outcomes relating to lifestyle, better quality of life and ameliorating poverty in old age, as well as to potentially negative outcomes, where the older owner enters into a transaction which is extortionate, unfair or simply inappropriate to his or her needs, objectives and circumstances. In either case, the expectation (or requirement) that older owners will accumulate housing wealth during their lives to spend on welfare after retirement, performing as individually responsible 'active subjects', and trading their housing equity in the credit market, raises new questions for legal analysis.

(2) The Conceptual Framework of Risk and the Rise of the 'Risk Society'

Although the conceptual framework of risk and the idea of a 'risk society' are closely associated with late modernity, the idea of risk has been around since pre-modern times. Risk was historically employed as a tool of commerce: in the Middle Ages, it described the dangers a ship might face on a voyage—storms, tempests, 'perils of the sea', what are often referred to as 'acts of God' resulting from the uncontrollable forces of nature—for the purposes of maritime insurance.[6] In this context, the objective of identifying commercial risk was to associate potential dangers with legally-binding consequences, thus enabling the insurance industry to underwrite the risk-taking behaviour of embarking on a voyage, which in turn served the social purpose of developing trade and commerce.[7]

By the late nineteenth century, the concept of 'risk' had evolved from a concern with naturally occurring dangers to a strategy through which to manage the consequences of human agency and to attribute responsibility,[8] on the basis that parties could in some cases be regarded as 'at fault' and so liable for the costs of adverse outcomes.[9] Yet while the development of risk transformed the *way* in which threats and hazards were conceived, Lupton argued that the purpose remained the same: that the idea of risk enables people to deal with uncertainties, both conceptually and behaviourally,[10] including types of changes that resonate strongly with ageing, such as 'the loss of control over our bodies, our relationships with others, our livelihoods and the extent to which we can exert autonomy in our everyday lives'.[11] As the traditional vulnerabilities of ageing are compounded by new financial concerns related to loss of income, inadequate pensions and savings, and the

[6] F Ewald, 'Two infinities of risk' in B Massumi (ed), *The Politics of Everyday Fear* (Minneapolis, Minn, University of Minnesota Press, 1993) 226.

[7] P Bernstein, *Against the Gods: The Remarkable Story of Risk* (New York, John Wiley & Sons, 1996).

[8] Ewald commented that at this stage, risk was 'also in human beings, in their conduct, in their liberty, in the relations between them, in the fact of their association, in society'; Ewald, above n 6, at 226.

[9] J Steele, *Risks and Legal Theory* (Oxford, Hart Publishing, 2004).

[10] See D Lupton, *Risk* (London and New York, Routledge, 1999) 1–3.

[11] *Ibid*, at 3.

expectation that older people—especially older owners—are individually responsible for their own welfare, health and nursing care, the risks of ageing and the anxieties they generate are brought into sharp relief.

The concept of 'risk' as a theoretical framework first appeared in scholarly literature in the 1970s[12] as a means of analysing and improving the 'security' of technological systems in the natural sciences,[13] but it was not until the 1980s and into the 1990s that social science scholarship recognised the significance of the concept of risk in relation to the changes affecting modern, and particularly neoliberal, societies.[14] The idea of a 'risk society' is most strongly associated with the work of sociologists Anthony Giddens[15] and Ulrich Beck,[16] who identified a range of macro-social processes as characteristic of late modern societies (for example, reflexive modernisation, individualisation) and analysed the relationships of these processes to concepts of risk.

A key theme of 'risk society' scholarship reflects on the extent to which the technical concept of risk—making use of the science of probability and statistical calculations—has enabled

> [c]onsequences that at first affect only the individual [to] become 'risks', systematically caused, statistically describable and in that sense 'predictable' types of events, which can therefore also be subjected to supra-individual and political rules of recognition, compensation and avoidance.[17]

Giddens identified a range of factors which have created uncertainty in 'late modernity', and which this notion of risk is employed to manage, including the unravelling of traditional forces such as marriage, the family and other institutions, and the end of lifelong employment. He claimed that these phenomena have fed a continuous state of 'crisis' in which 'There is much to be gained; but there is unexplored territory to be charted, and new dangers to be courted.'[18]

Modern autonomous individuals (or 'risk subjects') are required to negotiate this territory through a process of 'concentrated reflexive monitoring'.[19] Giddens argued that 'Each of us not only "has", but *lives* a biography reflexively organised in terms of flows of social and psychological information about possible ways of life.'[20] This has particular resonance with regard to older people in terms of the opportunities that home equity transactions may present for improved lifestyles in old age, as well as the personal capital and capabilities that are accumulated (or not) across the life-course to support reflexive decision-making in later life. Giddens used the example of ageing to illustrate what he described as the 'end of tradition': that people are no longer expected (or 'fated') to 'fade away' after retirement, with fundamental implications for (financial) well-being in later

[12] Although the modern concept of risk is often linked to the discovery of the theory of probability by lawyer and amateur mathematician Pierre de Fermat and mathematician Blaise Pascal; see Bernstein, above n 7.

[13] A Giddens, *The Consequences of Modernity* (Cambridge, Polity Press, 1990).

[14] *Ibid*, at 7–10; eg, Giddens claimed that 'Trust is usually more of a continuous state … Similar observations apply to risk and danger … Inaction is often risky, and there are some risks which we all have to face whether we like it or not …' (*ibid*, at 32).

[15] See, eg, Giddens, above n 13; Giddens, above n 3.

[16] See, eg, Beck, above n 4.

[17] U Beck, 'From Industrial Society to the Risk Society: Questions of Survival, Social Structure and Ecological Environment' (1992) 9 *Theory, Culture and Society* 97 at 99.

[18] Giddens, above n 3, at 12–13.

[19] *Ibid*, at 16.

[20] *Ibid*, at 14.

life.[21] While improved health, increased longevity or greater financial capacity now present opportunities to enjoy life after retirement which previous generations did not have, these changes also open up a new sphere of risk around the financial transactions which trade on the owned home to fund these activities.

The role of 'reflexive modernity'[22] in the risk society is based around three processes:

a) the redistribution of wealth and risk (goods and 'bads', ie risks);
b) individualisation (the process by which we are required to make choices which necessarily involve risks, so that there is no option but to engage with risk); and
c) the de-standardisation of labour, with the dismantling of traditional work structures (for example, the end of the 'job for life').

Neoliberal policies based on privatisation and individual responsibility heighten expectations that older owners will take responsibility for their own lives (their biographies) by planning for the future, including strategies to ensure financial well-being after retirement and into old age.[23] Yet the socio-economic heterogeneity of older owners (characterised as a 'polarisation of poverty and affluence in old age'[24]) means that the opportunities for people to construct their own lives—including their post-retirement lives—are limited by structural social factors (for example, education, access to information) which are significant in determining who the 'reflexivity winners' and 'reflexivity losers' will be.[25]

One effect of reflexive modernisation that has particular resonance for older people is the perception that the combination of increased risks, on the one hand, and the 'weakening of collective structures', on the other, leaves people without 'traditional life paths to rely on', to produce their own 'self-reflexive' biographies'.[26] While increased longevity, improved lifestyles and more choices in later life are undoubtedly welcome, they also create what Cooper has described as an 'increased … burden to make the right life choices since individuals must make their own personal decisions, rely on their own resources and do their own life planning to determine their destinies'.[27] As Ford, Burrows and Nettleton (discussing the experience of home ownership in a risk society) have noted,

> social and economic life *is* more complex and far less clear cut than once it was. While for the major part of the twentieth century social traditions combined with economic imperatives meant that the trajectory of many people's lives was relatively predictable, now these are far less certain.[28]

[21] A Giddens, 'Risk and Responsibility' (1999) 62 *MLR* 1, 3.

[22] Beck, above n 4.

[23] The 'risk society' thesis claims that 'modernisation helps the self become an agent via processes of individualisation which [Giddens and Beck] see as indicative of neo-liberalism; they advocate that the self becomes less constrained by structures and becomes a project to be reflexively worked on': JL Powell and A Wahidin, 'Aging in a Risk Society' (2005) 25 *International Journal of Sociology and Social Policy* 70, 72.

[24] A Walker and L Foster, 'Caught between virtue and ideological necessity. A century of pension policies in the UK' (2006) 18 *Journal of Political Economy* 427, 445.

[25] See, eg, S Lash, 'Reflexivity and its doubles: structure, aesthetics, community' in U Beck, A Giddens and S Lash, *Reflexive Modernisation: Politics, Tradition and Aesthetics in the Modern Social Order* (London, Sage, 1994), where he uses the example of a 'ghetto mother' to ask 'just how "reflexive" is it possible for a single mother in an urban ghetto to be? … just how much freedom from the "necessity" of "structure" and structural poverty does this ghetto mother have to self-construct her own "life narratives"?' (*ibid*, at 120).

[26] M Cooper, 'The inequality of security: Winners and losers in the risk society' (2008) 61 *Human Relations* 1229, 1232.

[27] *Ibid*, at 1233.

[28] J Ford, R Burrows and S Nettleton, *Home Ownership in a Risk Society: A social analysis of mortgage arrears and possessions* (Bristol, Policy Press, 2001) 4.

Older people—and particularly older owners—are required actively to produce their own lives, with significant emphasis on the use of housing equity to fund later life.

The legal governance of housing equity transactions has a significant normative function in the allocation of risk, attribution of responsibility and allotment of costs in the event of adverse outcomes, between older owners (or a particularly vulnerable sub-group of 'marginal older owners') and those who transact with them. One of the aims of this book is to unpack how the legal and other discourses that shape these norms reflect the tropes of responsibility and vulnerability. Critics of reflexive modernisation have argued that certain social groups—including perhaps the elderly—are particularly vulnerable or 'at risk' as a result of the 'continuing influence of social class, gender, ethnicity, position in the life-course and so on in shaping subjectivity and individuals' life chances'.[29] Yet at the same time, the potentially undesirable consequences of labelling populations as 'vulnerable' for the purposes of legal protection are also recognised:

> The 'at risk' label tends either to position members of these social groups as particularly vulnerable, passive, powerless or weak, or as particularly dangerous to themselves or others. In both cases, special attention is directed at these social groups, positioning them in a network of surveillance, monitoring and intervention.[30]

The implications of 'special protection' for particular 'identity' groups have been extensively rehearsed in critical legal scholarship, where arguments asserting the 'vulnerability' of women have been perceived as creating a dilemma between a reality of dependency or disadvantage, on the one hand, and the undesirability of connotations of incapacity, on the other.[31] The use of the 'vulnerability' label, even when well-intentioned, can be counterproductive where it 'serves to reinforce the marginalised or powerless status of individuals'.[32] The heterogeneity of older owners as an 'identity group' also threatens to render any broad use of an 'at risk' label inherently suspect. The issues surrounding the construction of older owners as 'vulnerable legal subjects' can usefully be analysed through feminist legal theory, and chapter four embarks on the task of reconceiving older owners through this lens. A key task in this endeavour is to identify the specific (sources of) vulnerabilities to which older owners may be subject in this context, as only then is it possible to assess the appropriateness of legal responses and any implications for the subjectivity of older owners.[33] Of course, underpinning the legal subjectivity of older owners and the notion of their 'vulnerability' is their status as subjects of the risk society, to which the next section now turns.

[29] Lupton, above n 10, at 113.

[30] *Ibid*, at 114.

[31] See discussion in L Fox, *Conceptualising Home: Theories, Laws and Policies* (Oxford, Hart Publishing, 2006) 400–07, especially 402–04; also K Green and H Lim, 'Weaving Along the Borders: Public and Private, Women and Banks' in S Scott-Hunt and H Lim (eds), *Feminist Perspectives on Equity and Trusts* (London, Cavendish, 2001); and R Auchmuty, 'Men Behaving Badly: An Analysis of English Undue Influence Cases' (2002) 11 *Social and Legal Studies* 257, 267–68.

[32] Lupton, above n 10, at 113.

[33] The specific vulnerabilities of older owners are examined in ch 6, while the implications of these discursive tropes of vulnerability and responsibility provide the basis for the analyses in chs 7 to 10.

(a) Older owners, risk and housing equity transactions

Although Giddens described the risk society as 'democratising' in the sense that traditional cleavages of inequality related to income and wealth have been overtaken by large-scale manufactured risks to which we are all equally 'at risk' (for example, terrorism, nuclear war or global warming),[34] significant areas of risk remain unequally distributed. Giddens and Beck have been criticised for their portrayal of a 'universal risk subject', a rational and calculating actor who, unhinged from traditional forces, can exercise reasoned judgement through reflexivity and life planning to determine (with the help of expert knowledge systems) his own life course through an uncertain world.[35] While neoliberal governance, neoclassical economics and liberal legal theory conjoin to present their subjects as 'prudent, rational, desiring to be responsible for themselves, and capable of becoming knowledgeable in all realms of risk from finances to health',[36] this view has been criticised as unrealistic, both as a general proposition[37] and in relation to particular contexts.[38] As Lupton explained, the

> self-reflexive individual, as presented by Beck and Giddens, is a socially and economically privileged person who has the cultural and material resources to engage in self-inspection. But many people, however, simply lack the resources and techniques with which to engage in the project of self-reflexivity.[39]

The extent to which people can effectively plan for (and finance) their futures is clearly linked to the social and cultural resources at their disposal, and to (the related matter of) their financial and legal capabilities to understand complex products.[40] Research in the UK has demonstrated a gap between the abilities of 'educated, articulate' households to function as active, informed 'utility-maximising consumers', and the difficulties that those who lack cultural capital—in the form of knowledge and financial proficiency—face in

34 Giddens, above n 13.

35 Cooper, above n 26, at 1234.

36 *Ibid.*

37 M Fineman, *The Autonomy Myth: A Theory of Dependency* (New York, The New Press, 2005).

38 Hacker argued that in the context of employment, no one can manage his own risk: JS Hacker, *The great risk shift: The assault on American jobs, families, health care, and retirement and how you can fight back* (New York, Oxford University Press, 2006).

39 Lupton, above n 10, at 114.

40 Research studies in the US have shown that financial literacy is not evenly distributed, with the least well-off—those on low income, uneducated, and minorities—least well-equipped to make good financial decisions; see Cooper, above n 26, at 1235, citing BD Bernheim, 'Personal saving, information, and economic literacy' in *Tax policy for economic growth in the 1990s* (Washington, DC, American Council for Capital Formation, 1994) 53; D Bernheim, 'Do households appreciate their financial vulnerabilities? An analysis of actions, perceptions, and public policy' in *Tax policy and economic growth* (Washington, DC, American Council for Capital Formation, 1995) 1; D Bernheim, 'Financial illiteracy, education and retirement saving' in OS Mitchell and SJ Schieber (eds), *Living with defined contribution pensions* (Philadelphia, University of Pennsylvania Press, 1998) 38; BD Bernheim and JK Scholz, 'Private saving and public policy' (1993) 7 *Tax Policy and the Economy* 73; MA Hilgert, JM Hogarth, and SG Beverly, 'Household financial management: The connection between knowledge and behavior' (2003) 89(7) *Federal Reserve Bulletin* 309; A Lusardi and OS Mitchell, 'Financial literacy and retirement preparedness: Evidence and implications for financial education' (2007) 42(1) *Business Economics*, 35; YK Ng, 'Do individuals optimize in intertemporal consumption/savings decisions? A liberal method to encourage savings' (1992) 17(1) *Journal of Economic Behavior and Organization* 101; M Zhan, SG Anderson, and J Scott, 'Financial knowledge of the low-income population: Effects of a financial education program' (2006) 33(1) *Journal of Sociology and Social Welfare* 53.

making good, informed decisions.[41] Cooper argued that for those who are not well-informed, well-advised and sceptical consumers, policies based on an idealised risk subject may be regarded as creating 'opportunities for people to participate in their own exploitation',[42] and this seems particularly apt in relation to 'reflexive planning' for retirement.[43] The patterns of inequality set up by unequal distribution of gains from housing wealth[44] are compounded by the claim that planning for later life is not just a matter of having the right personality type (an 'enterprising self') but that calculative and informed risk subjects are more likely to be upper- to middle-class and highly educated.[45] Cooper has noted that 'planning for later life is most common among those who have a future time perspective, feel in control of their lives and are a part of a couple'.[46] This is also linked to socio-economic context, as

> those with the fewest resources, [who] are frequently unemployed, have children, and whose plans have failed them in the past, are the least likely to plan, especially in the long term, and are more concerned with the day-to-day.[47]

This supports the proposition that it is the 'marginal' owners who have most need to release equity (because of inadequate pension or other savings) who are also least well equipped to calculate risks in financial transactions, to make 'good' decisions, and to be informed and active consumers or ideal 'risk subjects'.

Giddens also drew a link between life-planning, self-identities and ontological (in)security in the risk society, which bears consideration in respect of older owners. The emphasis placed by UK (and other neoliberal) governments on financial planning for retirement provides a clear example of the role of lifestyles and life-planning in the contemporary experience of risk. These lifestyle choices are also significant for the constitution of self-identity, as 'individuals are forced to negotiate lifestyle choices among a diversity of options',[48] across 'many areas which used to be governed by taken-for-granted norms'.[49] Although Giddens claimed that 'Risk society, looked at positively, is one in which there is an expansion of choice',[50] he qualified this by adding that 'obviously choice is differentially distributed according to class and income'.[51] While (free) choice is often identified as a

[41] Cooper, above n 26, at 1236. UK studies include A Aldridge, 'Habitus and cultural capital in the field of personal finance' (1998) 46(1) *The Sociological Review* 1; J Baldock and C Ungerson, 'Becoming a consumer of care: Developing a sociological account of the 'new community care' in S Edgell and K Hetherington (eds), *Consumption Matters* (Oxford, Blackwell, 1996) 11.

[42] Cooper, above n 26, at 1236.

[43] M Anderson, F Bechhofer and S Kendrick, 'Individual and Household Strategies' in M Anderson, F Bechhofer and J Gershuny (eds), *The Social and Political Economy of the Household* (Oxford, Oxford University Press, 1994) 19; M Anderson, Y Li, F Bechhofer, D McCrone and R Stewart, 'Sooner rather than later? Younger and middle-aged adults preparing for retirement' (2000) 20 *Aging and Society* 445; MA Denton, CL Kemp, S French, A Gafni, A Joshi, CJ Rosenthal and S Davies, 'Reflexive planning for later life' (2004) 23 *Canadian Journal on Aging Supplement* S71; DA Hershy and JC Mowen, 'Psychological determinants of financial preparedness for retirement' (2000) 40 *The Gerontologist* 687.

[44] See ch 1.

[45] See V Gillies, 'Raising the meritocracy: Parenting and the individualization of social class' (2005) 39 *Sociology* 835.

[46] Cooper, above n 26, at 1237.

[47] *Ibid.*

[48] Giddens, above n 3, at 5.

[49] Giddens, above n 21, at 5.

[50] *Ibid.*

[51] *Ibid.*

necessary stepping-stone to identity, autonomy and agency[52] (thus, the opportunity to choose is a core element of liberal legal subjectivity[53]), this model presumes that the chooser has the option *not to choose* (or, in the case of private law transactions, not to contract).[54] In contrast, choice can be viewed as a burden where people feel pressured to make the 'right' life choices, to 'rely on their own resources and do their own life planning to determine their destinies'.[55] Thus, while modernity has reduced the 'overall riskiness of certain areas and modes of life',[56] the increase in choices and the new requirement to make decisions in certain areas (for example, through the rise in housing equity transactions, as a result of the changing political and policy landscape) have 'introduce[d] new risk parameters largely or completely unknown to previous eras ... risks which previous generations have not had to face'.[57] For example, the choices that must be made about housing equity use range from whether to spend now (perhaps on 'lifestyle' goods such as holidays) or later (saving housing equity for welfare needs in later old age), against the backdrop of an uncertain future (in respect of longevity and future needs). Once a choice has been made to act, the older owner must then negotiate the complex array of available product options.

The negotiation of these new risk environments also has implications for the significance of owned housing within the older owner's self-identity and ontological security. 'Home as self-identity' encapsulates a major cluster of meanings within the idea of 'housing as home'.[58] Embarking on housing equity use, on the other hand, requires a paradigm shift towards the idea of owned housing as an investment-asset-to-spend, with potential implications for the older owner's ontological security.[59] Giddens has argued that while transitions in people's lives 'have always demanded psychic reorganisation',[60] the modern context demands a more active engagement in the process of reflexively mobilising self-identity to create a 'new sense of self'.[61] In doing so, we are increasingly

[52] See, eg, J Raz, *The Morality of Freedom* (Oxford, Oxford University Press, 1988), arguing that autonomy requires that individuals have an array of valuable options to choose from; also TM Scanlon, *What We Owe to Each Other* (Harvard, MA, Harvard University Press, 1998) 251–67, demonstrating the value of choice and its role in responsibility for outcomes, the role of 'voluntariness' of choice, the conditions under which choices are made and the reasonableness of rejecting principles which make the chooser bear the costs of any loss. Legal analyses have also argued that the context of our choices is significant in determining the value of choice for agents; see E Voyiakis, 'Unconscionability and the Value of Choice' in Kenny *et al* (eds), above n 5, at 91: 'our circumstances always "frame" the choices we have and affect the value these choices have for us'. Voyiakis added that 'when it comes to choice, less can be more' (*ibid*, at 92), as sometimes choice can have no value for an agent. See also A Voorhoeve, 'Scanlon on Substantive Responsibility' (2008) 16 *Journal of Political Philosophy* 184. The implications of the 'paradox of choice' with reference to the vulnerabilities of older owners are discussed in ch 6.

[53] See ch 4.

[54] The liberal concepts underpinning classical contract law include the negative freedom *from* contract (as well as the positive freedom *of* contract; see C Willett, *Fairness in Consumer Contracts: The Case of Unfair Terms* (Aldershot, Ashgate, 2007), para 2.3.1.

[55] Cooper, above n 26, at 1233.

[56] The preoccupation with risk in modern social life does not usually relate to life-threatening dangers, since people in developed societies are relatively secure, in their individual life spans, life expectations and freedom from serious disease.

[57] Giddens, above n 3, at 4.

[58] The significance of the owned home for the occupier's self-identity is examined in Fox, above n 31, at 167–73.

[59] See ch 5 for discussion of the competing housing paradigms for older owners.

[60] Giddens, above n 3, at 33.

[61] It is arguable that the need for reflexive mobilisation of identity is just as significant during the shift from adulthood to older life (or working life to retirement), as in the example Giddens gives of adolescence to adulthood.

reliant on 'abstract systems' of expert advice to manage the unfamiliar choices that these transitions generate[62]; in the context of home equity transactions, this can be seen in the extent of older owners' reliance on expert financial and/or legal advice to inform and enable the decisions that must be made about complex financial products, despite concerns about the limited value of such information in improving (especially older owners') decision-making.[63]

The abilities of individuals to be reflexive subjects and to manage (with the help of expert knowledge delivered through abstract systems) the challenges to self-identity that arise at times of transition, feeds into a final concept of 'ontological security', which connotes the emotional security and basic trust that enables us to 'screen off' risks and dangers and get on with our lives.[64] The significance of 'home', and specifically the owned home, for a person's self-identity and ontological security have been analysed extensively in the literature on the meaning of home.[65] The meanings of home as a repository of self-identity underpin Radin's theory of property for personhood,[66] which posits that certain types of property ('personal property') can become so strongly constitutive of a person's self-identity as to become part of their personhood, and so to merit stronger legal protection than other, more 'fungible' property. The home provides a quintessential example of 'personal property', with the owned home a powerful symbol as the storehouse of memories that 'enables its occupiers to project their own self-identities into the future'.[67]

Housing equity transactions engender tensions between the competing meanings of home for older owners, including the effect of commoditising the home as an exchange asset for older owners, the symbolic importance of home for the older occupier's personal identity and independence, and the issues which must be reconciled when negotiating owned housing as home, as inheritance and as an investment asset to spend.[68] The idea of the owned home as a financial resource for old age was a central pillar of the political ideology of home ownership which consistently characterised ownership as a way of controlling one's future into old age (described as 'Of all forms of saving, one of the best'[69]), and a housing strategy which claims to

[62] Giddens, above n 3, at 33. In *The Consequences of Modernity* (above n 13), Giddens related his analysis of *risk* to the concept of *security*, describing modernity as double-edged—it 'created vastly greater opportunities for human beings to enjoy a secure and rewarding existence than any pre-modern system', but also had a 'sombre side', reflected in the globalisation of risk, with risks of greater intensity (eg nuclear war); an expanding number of contingent events which affect everyone, or very large numbers of people (eg global divisions of labour); the nature of modern social organisation, and greater awareness of risk as risk; and institutionalised risk environments, which affect the life chances of millions, eg investment markets. At an individual level, people must deal with the fundamental challenge of finding their daily lives reconstituted through a bewildering array of 'abstract systems'. These knowledge-based patterns of social behaviour, which are coordinated through markets as well as bureaucracies, govern the conditions of individual existence, and potentially pose threats to self-identity.

[63] See ch 6, section (3).

[64] Giddens, above n 3, at 36–40.

[65] For a discussion of home as identity and self-identity, see Fox, above n 31, at 167–73; and on home ownership as ontological security, *ibid*, at 232–37.

[66] MJ Radin, 'Property and Personhood' (1982) 34 *Stanford Law Review* 957; MJ Radin, *Reinterpreting Property* (Chicago, Ill, University of Chicago Press, 1993).

[67] Fox, above n 31, at 170–71. See also GD Rowles and H Chaudhury (eds), *Home and Identity in Late Life: International Perspectives* (New York, Springer, 2005).

[68] See ch 5.

[69] *Houses: The Next Step* (Cmnd 8996) (London, HMSO, 1953) Preamble.

> satisf[y] a deep and natural desire on the part of the householder to have independent control of the home that shelters him and his family … If the householder buys his house on mortgage he builds up by steady saving a capital asset for himself and his dependents.[70]

While home ownership remains a key element in government strategies to encourage people to save for their old age,[71] the demands on housing equity to deliver ever-multiplying functions, during the owner's working life and after retirement, are challenging the idea that this same owned home can continue to be relied on to sustain the owner's self-identity and ontological security.

(b) Home equity transactions: identifying the risks

While risk is inherent to decision-making, and calculations and assessments must be made, the outcome of particular risks are normally incalculable, and even the process of identifying and articulating risks is often contentious,[72] with 'experts' presenting conflicting evidence to dispute questions such as 'how serious the [risks] are; who should be blamed for them; what the most appropriate course of action might be'.[73] Beck has argued that this leaves any enumeration of risks 'open to social definition and construction',[74] while Powell and Wahadin have argued that this 'puts those in a position to define (and/or legitimate) risks—the mass media, scientists, politicians and the legal profession—in key social positions'.[75] Giddens described the 'risk society' as one 'where we increasingly live on a high technological frontier which absolutely no one completely understands and which generates a diversity of possible futures'.[76] The risks to which we are subjected, and 'the patterns of life we follow' in responding to them, are altered 'almost constantly'[77]; yet at the same time, 'It is characteristic of the new types of risk that it is even disputed whether they exist at all.'[78] Nevertheless, Giddens claimed that living in a risk society means that we have no choice but to adopt a 'calculative attitude' to the 'open possibilities of action, positive and negative' with which we are continuously confronted.[79] Certainly, for older owners in need of income, engaging with the risks of financial transactions is unavoidable.[80]

The risks associated with housing equity transactions—particularly as they are perceived by older owners—are crucial to the mental strategies or 'heuristics' that older

[70] Department of the Environment, *Fair Deal for Housing* (Cmnd 6851) (London, HMSO, 1971) 4.

[71] See ch 1.

[72] Although this claim itself is challenged on the basis that risk by definition must be capable of calculation: see M Dean, 'Risk, Calculable and Incalculable' in D Lupton (ed), *Risk and Sociocultural Theory: New Directions and Perspectives* (Cambridge, Cambridge University Press, 1999).

[73] Powell and Wahidin, above n 23, at 73.

[74] Beck, above n 4, at 23.

[75] Powell and Wahidin, above n 23, at 74.

[76] Giddens, above n 21, at 3.

[77] *Ibid*, at 4.

[78] *Ibid*, at 5.

[79] Giddens, above n 3, at 28.

[80] Research for the World Bank has identified two principal risks associated with financial provision in old age: the risk of becoming unproductive through ill-health or disability; and the risk of living long and without sufficient income to meet consumption needs. See the World Bank, *Averting the Old Age Crisis: Policies to Protect the Old and Promote Growth* (New York, Oxford University Press, 2004) 55.

owners use to make particular transactional decisions.[81] Cognitive and behavioural research analysing the process by which the 'objective facts' of risk are filtered through the subjective understandings of the people responding to the risk,[82] has suggested a tendency for people to regard a risk as likely to occur if information about the risk is readily available and easily recalled; and to over-estimate the risk if they can imagine it happening to them.[83] In addition, risks which are serious but rare tend to be over-estimated, with those which are less serious but more common being under-estimated[84]; while risks which are perceived as voluntary are regarded as more acceptable and less likely to occur than those which are imposed.[85]

These findings have interesting implications for housing equity transactions. First, it suggests that the nature and quality of the information older owners have about the risks of different types of transaction are likely to influence their perceptions of risk and so their decision-making process, as is their financial and legal capability to understand and appreciate the content and potential implications of the transaction.[86] Secondly, the attention given to home equity transactions in the popular media, including the specific risks associated with certain types of transaction (product risk), is likely to influence their perceptions of risk. Whether the circumstances in which the older owner enters into the transaction may be regarded as 'voluntary' (for example, spending equity on 'lifestyle' expenses, holidays or luxury items) or needs-driven (to fund essential living costs, home maintenance costs, or health and nursing care costs) may have implications for the value which can be conferred on the 'choice' which the owner has made, and so for the allocation of responsibility for the outcomes of the transaction. Lastly, it seems likely that the socio-cultural and policy environment has gone some way towards 'normalising' the risks associated with housing equity use, with consequences both for the attitudes of the older owners themselves and for the norms (of vulnerability and responsibility) applied by courts and other legal adjudicators when resolving claims following adverse outcomes.

The FSA has classified the equity release sector as 'high risk',[87] and there are arguably at least five types of risk which might be associated with this type of transaction for older owners. The first is the risk that the creditor/product provider acts 'improperly', often described as 'mis-selling'.[88] In theory at least, the appropriate legal response to this 'provider risk' is relatively straightforward, since providers who are 'guilty' of wrongdoing may be deemed responsible for any losses which result from the transaction and have no legitimate expectation that their contracts will be enforced. In practice, whether the

81 On the role of heuristics in making judgements about risk, see Lupton, above n 10, at 19, citing P Slovic, 'Perceptions of Risk' (1987) 236 *Science* 280.

82 Lupton, above n 10, at 19, citing M Douglas, *Risk Acceptability According to the Social Sciences* (New York, Russell Sage Foundation, 1985) 25.

83 Lupton, above n 10, at 20.

84 *Ibid.*

85 *Ibid.*

86 See ch 6 for discussion of financial capability.

87 In 2005, Anna Bradley, the FSA's consumer affairs director, told the *Telegraph*: 'We are very conscious that equity release is an area that is relatively high risk. There is the potential here for people to make some very bad decisions and there is the potential for mis-selling.' See P Farrow, 'FSA launches equity release investigation', *Telegraph*, 23 February 2005, available online at <http://www.telegraph.co.uk/finance/personalfinance/2906443/FSA-launches-equity-release-investigation.html>.

88 In 2005, a mystery shopper exercise for the FSA flushed out widespread poor practice in the sale of equity release products, which in the same year reported that action had been taken against 44 companies for misleading advertising: *ibid.*

provider is in fact held to account depends not only on the legal standards applied to the particular transaction, but also on the strength of the enforcement mechanism against it. The standards of conduct required of providers are to some extent determined by regulations and guidelines issued by the FSA and the Office of Fair Trading (depending on the transaction), relating to advertising, promotional material, information disclosure, unfair or misleading sales practices, and so on[89]; but they are also governed by broader instruments, such as the Consumer Protection from Unfair Trading Regulations 2008 (SI 2008/1277), which regulate commercial practices before, during and after contracts are made.[90] The identification of wrongdoing on the part of the provider is therefore largely dependent on the responsibilities of providers as determined by industry regulators (presently the FSA and the Office of Fair Trading), which in turn can depend on whether the particular consumer base for a product is viewed as 'vulnerable'.[91] The norms that determine the provider's responsibilities in a transaction with a potentially vulnerable consumer also influence the willingness of courts and enforcement agencies to utilise legal tools (from statutory 'fairness' provisions to equitable doctrines) to ensure that providers follow rules of procedural fairness in selling their products.

A second way of capturing the risks of housing equity transactions is by focusing on particular products. The FSA's approach to equity release is explicitly based on 'product risk', with the main categories of housing equity product targeted at older owners positioned on a sliding scale of 'riskiness'—from lifetime mortgages (lowest risk), to home reversions, and lastly (the highest level of risk) sale and rent back transactions—and corresponding regulatory interventions imposing a sliding scale of responsibilities on the providers of such products.[92] The starting point for a product risk approach is with the terms and structure of the products themselves. For example, the regulation of home reversions is shaped by the underlying property transaction, in this case a sale of the owner's interest which is deemed a 'riskier' transaction than a lifetime mortgage. As a result, the FSA has put in place a range of bespoke regulatory protections relating to the owner's/vendor's security of tenure under the lease, the need (in the case of partial reversions) to protect the consumer's residual beneficial interest in the property, and the need (in the case of 'income products', which allow for a series of 'mini-reversions' to provide an income over an agreed and fixed period of time) to protect the consumer's income stream, as well as the overarching protection conferred through the requirement that the provider receive confirmation that the owner has had legal advice before proceeding with the transaction.[93]

The Authority's strategy for regulating risk in housing equity transactions has also demonstrated some sensitivity to 'consumer risk'. This is particularly evident in the regulation of sale and rent back transactions, where the likelihood that consumers will be 'marginal' owners under immediate financial pressure was an important factor in shaping the regulator's approach to this product.[94] Consumer risk can take various forms: some consumers may be particularly vulnerable to decision-making/procedural risks, which are

[89] See ch 9.
[90] See ch 8, section (8).
[91] See, eg, the discourse that preceded the FSA's regulation of sale and rent back transactions, discussed in ch 9.
[92] These regulatory regimes are discussed in detail in ch 9.
[93] Ch 9, section (4)(b).
[94] See ch 9, section (4)(c).

addressed through strategies that focus on procedural fairness. Another aspect of consumer risk is the disproportionate impact of losses on certain types of consumer, for example marginal owners and older owners who lack the capacity and/or the time to recover from bad financial outcomes. Lastly, consumer risk may result from 'situational vulnerabilities',[95] where the context or situation in which the consumer enters into the transaction (for example, when under immediate financial pressure) exposes him or her to the risk of entering into a substantively unfair contract.

As the discussion in chapter nine will show, the FSA's approach to housing equity products recognises these aspects of consumer risk to various degrees in different product contexts, with the nature of the legal response depending on which aspect of consumer risk is being tackled. Procedural protections (for example, relating to information supplied to consumers) aim to address decision-making/procedural vulnerabilities; both situational vulnerabilities and disproportionate impact, on the other hand, require procedural and substantive responses. In addition, where the regulatory response to certain product risks and consumer risks/vulnerabilities has amounted to substantive protections, this has imposed specific responsibilities on the part of the provider, for example to assess the suitability of the particular product to meet the needs, objectives and circumstances of individual buyers.[96] Meanwhile, the broader application of legal interventions to achieve substantive fairness in contracts remains controversial.[97] According to the liberal legal tradition, contracting parties are generally free to obtain the best deal they can, subject to following the procedural rules of the bargaining process, and any departure from this classical philosophy of freedom of contract would have to be justified by showing that the stronger party is not entitled to rely on the contract due to a breach of the agreed bargaining norms for this relationship. This book posits that in housing equity transactions, the discursive tropes of vulnerability and responsibility provide a useful framework in which to review these norms.

One of the objectives of FSA regulation was to support market growth by changing perceptions of equity release products, a key strategic issue for both the equity release industry and the underlying government policy agenda. The very 'normalisation' of these transactions has implications for the application of 'explicability' tests,[98] and for the assumptions that underlie models of legal subjectivity applied to older owners (as autonomous, 'responsibilised' consumers or vulnerable subjects). At the same time, the increase in volume of transactions has heightened older owners' exposure to some risks which are difficult to address within legal frameworks of protection. For example, a fourth set of risks is linked to the inherent complexity of home equity transactions. The FSA's 2007 review of products to finance retirement emphasised both the complexity of financial decision-making to provide for needs in old age (in choosing between the range of options for using home equity, or the impact of not doing so) and the specific complexity of equity release products, so that the detail of how the different products

[95] See ch 6 for a discussion of contextual or situational vulnerabilities.

[96] See ch 9.

[97] However, see SA Smith, 'In Defence of Substantive Unfairness' (1996) 112 *LQR* 138; FH Buckley, 'Three Theories of Substantive Fairness' (1990) 19 *Hofstra Law Review* 33; discussed in ch 4.

[98] Eg, in the case of undue influence, where the second limb of the test for presumed undue influence is whether the transaction calls for explanation; see ch 10, section (2)(d).

work is difficult to understand.[99] The effect of the individual's ability to recall information about risks on their subjective understandings of those risks underlines the relationship between the complexity of equity release and the degree of financial and legal capability required to make good and informed choices.[100]

Lastly, older owners who spend their housing equity face a long-term risk of depleting housing wealth too early in the life-course, leaving them reliant on welfare support to meet their needs in later old age. While the selling point of home equity products is the promise that the owner can raise income from the property while at the same time retaining the housing as home, with important 'safety' features including the 'no negative equity guarantee' in the case of a lifetime mortgage,[101] or security of tenure in home reversions or sale and rent back agreements, there are other situational factors, for example the need to maintain the property, which can threaten the sustainability of the older person's continued occupation of the property, and which are heightened for owners who have already depleted their equity. The prospect of future maintenance costs—and, if equity has already been released, the risk that the occupier will not be able to afford to maintain the house and so will have to move anyway—is a longer-term risk to which owners are exposed by early housing equity use.

It is also important to bear in mind the implications of housing equity withdrawal across the life-course, in light of evidence that younger owners are increasingly tapping into housing wealth rather than saving it as a resource for use in old age.[102] The increasing dependence on housing equity *before* retirement makes it more likely that older owners will already have leveraged their housing wealth before they reach old age, when a new set of needs can emerge. This, in turn, alters the panoply of risk posed by subsequent transactions. For example, use of housing equity for 'lifestyle' costs before retirement will alter not only the impact but potentially the options for releasing equity for need in later life, as some products will not be available depending on the proportion of housing equity the owner holds in the property and the nature of the obligations already incurred to prior creditors. The owner's strategy for releasing equity at different points across the life-course is therefore significant, as this is likely to shape his or her choices at later stages, and to alter the risk environment of subsequent transactions.

[99] See FSA, *Finance in and at retirement—results of our review* (London, FSA, 2007), available online at <http://www.fsa.gov.uk/pubs/other/retirement_review.pdf>; the FSA's findings on product complexity were based on research by Watson Wyatt for the Financial Service Consumer Panel, which highlighted that consumers find it difficult to understand the relative costs of different equity release options: <http://www.fs-cp.org.uk/publications/pdf/report_value_equity.pdf>. The inherent complexity of these products was also recognised by Lord McKenzie, on introducing the second reading of the Regulation of Financial Services (Land Transactions) Bill 2005—which extended the FSA umbrella over home reversion plans—when he acknowledged that 'these are not simple products to understand, hence the need to ensure that potential purchasers receive an appropriate level of advice': *Hansard*, HL Deb, 17 October 2005, col 554 (Lord McKenzie).

[100] The issue of financial capability is discussed in ch 6.

[101] The guarantees which must be provided to consumers, according to the SHIP (Safe Home Income Plans) Code of Conduct, include: 'To allow customers to remain in their property for life provided the property remains their main residence'; and a 'no negative equity guarantee. This means customers will never owe more than the value of their home and no debt will ever be left to the estate.'; see <http://www.ship-ltd.org/shipguarantee.aspx>.

[102] See SJ Smith, BA Searle and N Cook, 'Rethinking the Risks of Home Ownership' (2008) 38 *Journal of Social Policy* 83; see also discussion in ch 1.

There is also arguably a sixth category of risk: the risk of doing nothing and so remaining cash poor—and perhaps living in poverty[103]—in old age.

It is important to emphasise that these risks are qualitatively different from those to which home owners have arguably become accustomed in relation to traditional mortgage lending. In 2007, the FSA claimed that 'Equity release is potentially higher risk than standard mortgages for a variety of reasons including: product complexity; the link with the benefits system; and risk of negative equity.'[104] Both lenders and industry body SHIP tend to refer to lifetime mortgages as 'long-term loans'—'Much like a standard mortgage, the loan is secured against your property and you continue to own your own home'[105]—while the FSA categorises conventional mortgages, equity release products, and sale and rent back collectively as 'regulated home finance activities'.[106] Yet the order of risks associated with equity release is significantly different compared to conventional mortgages, for the lender as well as for the borrower. Most significantly for lenders, there is usually no issue of 'default' as the loan is not scheduled for repayment by instalments: while for conventional mortgages, repossession and sale of the property are a last resort to recover the debt, equity release transactions are planned with the intention that the property will eventually be sold to repay the loan, usually when the owner dies or moves into care.

For lenders, equity release transactions present at least three main types of risks[107]:

a) the 'termination risk', that is, how long the lender will have to wait to recover the capital through sale of the property, and the risk that by the time this happens, the value of the property will be insufficient to discharge the debt, interest and costs (presuming that—according to SHIP guidelines—the lender has given a 'no negative equity guarantee');
b) the interest rate risk, whereby variable rates create uncertainties for the insurers of these loans, since higher rates may increase the likelihood of non-repayment on termination; and
c) the house price depreciation risk.

However, a major difference between equity release and other forms of credit is that equity release providers do *not* face the risk of default. In conventional lending transactions, a key feature of the deal is that: 'Anyone who ever extends credit faces the possibility that repayment will not be forthcoming [so that] [i]nterest is structured, among other things, to pay the creditor for assuming the risk of non-payment.'[108] The risks taken by housing equity providers are of a different order, since they relate not to *whether* repayment will be made, but to *how much* and *when*.

[103] Research has emphasised that being a homeowner in the UK is no indicator of the risk a person faces of living in poverty, with half of all households living in poverty now categorised as 'owner-occupiers'. See generally, R Burrows and S Wilcox, *Half the poor: Home-owners with low incomes* (London, Council of Mortgage Lenders, 2000).

[104] See FSA (2007), above n 99, para 36.

[105] <http://www.ship-ltd.org/howitworks.aspx>.

[106] <http://fsahandbook.info/FSA/html/handbook/PERG/2/Annex2>.

[107] H Chen, SH Cox and SS Wang, 'Is the Home Equity Conversion Mortgage in the United States Sustainable? Evidence from pricing mortgage insurance premiums and non-recourse provisions using the conditional Esscher transform' (2010) 46 *Mathematics and Economics* 371, 374.

[108] E Warren, 'Bankruptcy Policy' (1987) 54 *University of Chicago Law Review* 775, 780.

Lastly, it is worth noting that in its 2006 survey of lifetime mortgage products available in the UK, Watson Wyatt claimed that—taking account of the risks to providers, particularly the potential costs of the 'no negative equity guarantee'—across the market as a whole products were priced on a fair basis.[109] While this suggests a fair market based on the risk posed to the lender, the fair operation of the market depends on consumers being able to understand relative costs and recognise fair value across a complex range of products, to choose those that are both suitable for their needs and good value.

(c) Welfare benefits, 'moral hazard' and the role of the State

Another important dimension of the risk environment surrounding housing equity transactions is link between the role of the State in governing housing equity transactions through the institutions of law, and the State's welfare function as a 'safety-net' for older owners who suffer adverse outcomes as a result of housing equity use. The interrelationships between the State's roles as 'regulator' and 'safety-net' are also apparent at the point of sale: the FSA advises anyone considering equity release to check before going ahead whether they are entitled to any State benefits,[110] since some means-tested benefits may be lost when equity is released from the owned home. At the point of crisis, an older 'owner' who has already used his or her housing equity, whether for lifestyle- or needs-based requirements earlier in the life-course, may become eligible for State-sponsored support in later old age (for example, in the form of nursing and personal care). The rise in housing equity transactions threatens progressively to strip away the store of housing wealth—both through simple depletion of assets and where transactions have adverse outcomes—ultimately placing an increased burden on State welfare responsibilities, as well as re-casting older 'owners' whose equity has been dissipated as 'flawed' consumers,[111] or even as welfare-dependent subjects.

On the one hand, the risks associated with spending housing equity, and potentially falling-back on State resources, may be described as a 'moral hazard' for older owners,[112] with the existence of fall-back provision dis-incentivising the owners themselves from acting responsibly in relation to their housing wealth. On the other hand, the constraints of State-sponsored provision, and the meanings that the owned home represents to the older person (including the implications of the 'badge' of owner for the older person's subjectivity),[113] may militate against excessive risk-taking by the owners themselves. It is also important to recognise that the moral hazard model presumes that older owners' decision-making in housing equity transactions follows an idealised model of rational subjectivity. It is for this reason that Baker has criticised the use of 'moral hazard' in policy discourse to encourage us to assume that these vulnerable people 'are in control of themselves and their situation … [thus] help[ing] to absolve the rest of us of our

[109] Financial Services Consumer Panel, *Report on the value of equity release products to UK consumers*, prepared by Watson Wyatt Ltd (November 2006), available online at <http://www.fs-cp.org.uk/publications/pdf/report_value_equity.pdf>.

[110] FSA, *Equity Release* (London, FSA, 2008), available online at <http://www.fsa.gov.uk/financial_capability/pdfs/equity_release.pdf>.

[111] Bauman has described how those who make the wrong choice are stigmatised as 'flawed' consumers; see Z Bauman, *Work, Consumerism and the New Poor* (Buckingham, Open University Press, 1998) 38.

[112] For a discussion of the concept of moral hazard in law-and-economics, see T Baker, 'On the Genealogy of Moral Hazard' (1996) 75 *Texas Law Review* 237.

[113] See discussion in ch 5.

responsibility for that situation',[114] and so to undermine initiatives that seek to protect vulnerable people.

Housing equity is liable to be dissipated for a range of reasons, from 'high-days and holidays' to pressing welfare needs, at different stages of the life-course, and with different consequences for the 'owner'. Yet in the case of housing equity transactions, it may be argued that 'the real lesson of moral hazard should be that the world is a relational web',[115] characterised by interconnected individual and institutional relationships of cause and effect, that implicates the broader risks these transactions potentially pose to the sustainability of the Government's policy aims concerning housing wealth, as well as casting a new perspective on the attribution of responsibilities between the provider, the consumer/owner and the State. While housing equity transactions are typically characterised in law as 'private' agreements between provider and consumer, the role of the State in this context clearly goes beyond that of a 'residual player' (in the sense of shaping the background rules and institutions on which the parties rely),[116] with adverse outcomes likely to result in direct costs to the public purse. While similar arguments might, in theory, also be made in respect of other types of transaction that are liable to render a (vulnerable) contracting party destitute, the housing equity transaction brings this risk to the State into particularly sharp relief in light of the limited opportunities that older owners are likely to have to recover from financial setbacks.

This adds weight to the arguments for reconsidering how the State through its institutions (including law) can control the distribution of risk and the allocation of loss to prevent or minimise the financial burden that is likely to result when vulnerable parties suffer losses due to adverse housing equity outcomes. There are many possible causes of adverse housing equity outcomes, and while excessive risk-taking in the shadow of the State's safety-net may be one, others include 'wrongdoing', in the sense of failing to satisfy norms of responsibility on the part of the provider, unfair terms or 'unsafe' products, or the unforeseeability of the older owner's needs into an uncertain future. The extent to which these risks are managed through legal regulation of, and responses to, housing equity transactions is the main subject of chapters seven to ten. These legal responses are themselves influenced by the ways in which the construction of (older) owners as 'risk subjects' has filtered into legal discourses, as well as by the theoretical frameworks which offer models for the allocation of risk, the attribution of responsibility and the allotment of resulting losses.

[114] Baker, above n 112, at 243–44. Baker went on to demonstrate that, conversely, the origins of 'moral hazard' were rooted in social responsibility.

[115] *Ibid*, at 240; rather than justifying the withdrawal of fall-back support for older people.

[116] See M Fineman, 'The Vulnerable Subject: Anchoring Equality in the Human Condition' (2010) 20 *Yale Journal of Law and Feminism* 1, 7.

(3) Owners as 'Risk Subjects' in Policy and Law

The concept of 'risk' captures the possibilities of 'good' and 'bad' outcomes, but by the end of the twentieth century, popular use of the term generally anticipated negative outcomes,[117] with the notable exception of 'the esoteric parlance of economic speculation', where

> there remain such things as 'good risks' in relation to making a profit. It is recognised that risks must be taken to make money in speculative enterprises, and that often the greater the risk of losing one's money, the greater the return should things go well.[118]

This type of 'good risk' was typified in the promotion of owner-occupation as an investment strategy: when a buyer purchases property, the hoped-for (and, excepting adverse housing market performance in the short-term, often realised) outcome is that the capital sum paid (including mortgage interest and fees) will be outweighed by the prospect of its future exchange value, while the owner-occupier also enjoys the use aspects of the property itself. This model of risk-taking in respect of the accumulation of housing equity[119] went into overdrive in the most recent housing market boom, when growing numbers of house[120] buyers (encouraged by media and a television industry obsessed by property development and home improvement) acquired owner-occupied properties with the intention of 'flipping' them for profit.[121] The opportunities for financial gain through house purchase had—at least until the crisis in the housing market which began in 2007—created strong positive associations between the idea of risk and wealth creation through owned housing.

The positive 'entrepreneurial' aspects of risk-taking in relation to house purchase have also been a dominant feature in legal discourses, from the 'investment value' model of joint ownership set in place by the Law of Property Act 1925[122] to the idea of a

[117] Lupton, above n 10, at 8.

[118] N Luhmann, *Risk: A Sociological Theory* (New York, Aldine de Gruyter, 1993) 71.

[119] The commodification of the owned home is discussed in Fox, above n 31, ch 5; the competing paradigms of housing as home, housing as inheritance and housing as investment asset to spend are considered in ch 5 of this book.

[120] Although these were primary residences, the label 'house' seems more appropriate than 'home', such was the dominance of the investment motive.

[121] 'Flipping' a house refers to the process of buying a house, fixing it up and selling it on for a profit: see RR Roberts and J Kraynak, *Flipping Houses for Dummies* (Hoboken, NJ, John Wiley & Sons, 2006) in the '... for Dummies' series of manuals; also K Kemp, *Flipping Confidential: The Secrets of Renovating Property for Profit in Any Market* (Hoboken, NJ, John Wiley & Sons, 2007). In the housing market boom of the late 20th and early 21st centuries, it was not even necessary to fix up a house. Buyers purchased properties on which they would never be able to afford repayments in anticipation of re-selling the property for a profit long before the mortgage ever became due. While—so long as the housing market boom lasted—this represented a 'good risk' for the purchaser, legal scholarship in the US has debated a ban on house-flipping due to the wider economic implications: see, eg, G Lefcoe, 'Should We Ban or Welcome "Spec" Home Buyers?' (2010) 36 *Journal of Legislation* 1; CA Pritts, 'Forcing Property Flippers to Show Their Hand: The Prior Purchase Price Disclosure Requirement' (2001) 11 *Journal of Affordable Housing and Community Development Law* 446; see also RP Malloy, 'Mortgage Market Reform and the Fallacy of Self-Correcting Markets' (2009) 30 *Pace Law Review* 79, 107 *et seq* on the problems of over-borrowing and over-lending generated by the practice of house flipping, and for proposals to reduce the incentives to 'flip' your home.

[122] Co-owned land was placed on a statutory trust for sale, and the Law Commission later observed that 'Implicit in this is the notion that this land should be held primarily as an investment asset rather than as a "use" asset.' See Law Com No 181, *Transfer of Land: Trusts of Land* (1989), para 3.1; see further discussion in Fox, above n 31, chs 2 and 6.

jointly-owned (and occupied) family home as an entrepreneurial project. Freeman, discussing the well-known case of *Williams and Glyns' Bank Ltd v Boland*,[123] in which the bank sought to recover possession of a jointly-occupied home when Mr Boland defaulted on a secured (business) loan charged against his home, and Mrs Boland (successfully) defended the possession order on the basis that her joint ownership interest had priority over the bank's charge, reasoned that

> [h]ad Mr Boland's building business prospered, no doubt Mrs Boland would have shared in the increased standard of living made possible by the successful use of capital provided by the Bank. Marriage is, after all, a partnership to which both parties contribute. Is there any justification for departing from the normal principle of partnership, under which profits are shared if things go well, but losses are shared if they go badly?[124]

The portrayal of debt secured against the home as a positive, entrepreneurial risk was not limited to debts to raise business capital, but also informed the policy of prioritising the interests of creditors who provided acquisition finance over the claims of occupiers, on the grounds that

> The acquisition of the legal estate is entirely dependent upon the provision of funds which will have been provided before the conveyance can take effect and which are provided only against an agreement that the estate will be charged to secure them.[125]

Since the property could not have been acquired without the mortgage, the creditor—who enabled the owner-occupiers' entrepreneurial activity by providing the finance which bought the price of admission for the home-buyer into this class of entrepreneurs—typically takes priority in the event of default.

Steele has argued that the idea of a 'good risk', or at least of a 'risk worth taking', remains essential to liberal legal conceptualisations of responsibility[126]: 'Risk in its positive, opportunity-creating sense is compatible with the richer liberal ideal of the autonomous individual who seeks to maximise his wellbeing through pursuit of a good life. It is also linked with profit-making activity.'[127] While it is not difficult to make this argument in relation to conventional mortgage finance, when applying this perspective to housing equity transactions some important distinctions should be noted. First, there is the obvious fact that the 'consumer' in a home equity transaction is not embarking on a potentially profit-making activity, in the way that a house purchaser may do. Products which release equity, such as lifetime mortgages, and more particularly home reversions and sale and rent back agreements,[128] are in this sense the converse to acquisition mortgages: by cashing in their housing equity, homeowners are trading *out* of home ownership as a profit-making enterprise—the real property equivalent of cashing in their chips and leaving the casino. The risks—positive and negative—of future fluctuations in

123 [1981] AC 487.
124 M Freeman, 'Wives, Conveyancers and Justice' (1980) 43 *MLR* 692, 696.
125 *Abbey National Building Society v Cann* [1991] AC 56 at 92.
126 J Steele, *Risks and Legal Theory* (Oxford, Hart Publishing, 2004) 49, fn 50.
127 *Ibid*, at 29.
128 Which involve a total withdrawal from the ownership sector.

the value of the property will be borne by the home equity provider, along with the benefit of any future profit.[129]

Meanwhile, the idea that consumers in domestic property transactions may be viewed as 'responsible risk-takers', enthusiastically engaged in the activity of positive risk-taking in relation to financial transactions,[130] has been challenged as the global financial crisis has demonstrated how the risks inherent in the financial system can filter down to consumers, and calling into question the 'overly optimistic view of self-regulating markets'[131] which has informed much law-and-economics scholarship. Even before the 'credit crunch', the relationships between risk, responsibility and regulation had emerged as important themes in UK policy,[132] with the growing reach of the FSA providing an example of the shift towards regulatory intervention as a response to the risks associated with financial transactions. The way in which risk itself is conceptualised has also been transformed by the global financial meltdown,[133] with a more negative outlook on risk-taking prompting the suggestion that permissive regulatory conditions played a role in creating the conditions for the crisis, and leading to increased calls for fundamental reviews of the ways in which financial transactions are regulated.[134]

The ways in which law responds to risk-taking in the abstract, and to concrete harms, have a central role in defining and legitimating risks, by denoting the acceptability (or 'reasonableness') of certain types of risk. These definitions are not static, rather

> the identification of 'risks' takes place in the specific sociocultural and historical contexts in which we are located. To call something a 'risk' is to recognise its importance to our subjectivity and wellbeing. In some societies at some times, certain phenomena are selected as the focus for anxieties. In other societies and eras, other phenomena become prominent as 'risky'.[135]

The process by which risks are identified is rooted in the perception of threats to our ontological security, and so reflects anxieties which are linked to our individual and group identities. This means, amongst other things, that 'members of social groups that are less powerful tend to be more concerned about risks than members of powerful social groups'.[136] Thus, while there are certain 'objective' risks associated with home equity transactions, for older owners their 'risk selection'—the identification and perception of risk—is likely to be linked to socio-economic profiles,[137] as well as cultural capital and capabilities.[138]

[129] While the owner who takes out a lifetime mortgage retains an ownership interest in the property, the 'no negative equity guarantee' shifts a major aspect of future risk onto the creditor, although the owner remains interested in the property itself to the extent of any remaining equity.

[130] Eg, the Enterprise Act 2002 was intended to encourage entrepreneurship and 'responsible risk taking'; see Government White Paper, *Productivity and Enterprise: Insolvency—A Second Chance* (Cm5234).

[131] Malloy, above n 121.

[132] Better Regulation Commission, *Risk, Responsibility and Regulation: Whose Risk is it Anyway?* (London, Cabinet Office, 2006).

[133] E Heilpern, C Haslam and T Andersson, 'When it comes to the crunch: What are the drivers of the US banking crisis?' (2009) 33(2) *Accounting Forum* 99; V Acharya and M Richardson (eds), *Restoring Financial Stability* (New York, John Wiley & Sons, 2009).

[134] M Wolf, 'Why the credit squeeze is a turning point for the world', *Financial Times*, 11 December 2007. The impact of shifting perspectives on risk and responsibility on the specific regulation of consumer financial transactions in the UK is discussed in ch 9.

[135] Lupton, above n 10, at 13.

[136] *Ibid*, at 23.

[137] See ch 1.

[138] See ch 6.

Analyses of human ageing in the risk society highlight the ways in which neoliberal governance has disrupted the ontological status of older people.[139] The emergence of a neo-liberal approach to social welfare for older people, with market-led provisioning and policies based on privatisation and individual responsibility,[140] requires older owners to engage in financial transactions that carry risks.[141] In the neoliberal paradigm—which emphasises the individualisation of citizens[142] as 'prudent, rational, desiring to be responsible for themselves'[143]—risk has been valorised as enabling the development of an idealised subjectivity—that of the 'autonomous consumer'. Under neoliberal policies 'individuals are encouraged to take risks, since risk is believed to be the source of self-reliance'.[144] Risk-taking has become part of the modern identity of consumers as 'enterprising entrepreneurs', 'mak[ing] "choices" as to which risks he/she will manage, to what degree, and by what provision, and who must live with the consequences of the mistakes they make'.[145]

According to governmentality theorists, concepts of risk construct norms which are applied to encourage individuals to behave in certain ways. From this perspective, the extent to which older (and other) owners are able successfully to negotiate home equity transactions depends on their ability to live up to socially-imposed models of agency, including their responses to—and exercise of judgement in respect of—certain risk phenomena. Where older owners are not 'successful'—where 'bad' outcomes result from the transaction—then whether or not they can obtain a legal remedy is likely to depend on whether they have met the norms of behaviour which inform legal regulation and protections. Applying this perspective to ageing, Powell and Wahidin have argued that the constitution of risk as the centrally defining tenet of neoliberalism 'gives the impression that older people have the capacity to generate their own "human agency" ... irrespective of structural constraints'.[146] Self-provisioning in old age has been presented, through the lens of neoliberal social policies, as an opportunity to achieve autonomy, control and self-governance.[147]

While post-World War II institutional structures—the welfare State, mandatory retirement and inter-generational relationships—provided a framework for calculating and assessing the risks associated with ageing (for example, illness, poverty), from the 1980s onwards this has been disrupted as the concepts of self-responsibility, self-governance and self-care increasingly characterised relationships between older people and the State. Powell and Wahidin argued that this phenomenon demonstrates

[139] Powell and Wahidin, above n 23.

[140] See ch 2.

[141] P Bernstein, *Against The Gods: The Remarkable Story of Risk* (New York, J Wiley & Sons, 1996), which provides a historical account of risk in financial transactions; K Byrne, 'How do consumers evaluate risk in financial products?' (2005) 10 *Journal of Financial Services Marketing* 21; H Van Greuning and S Brajovic Bratanovic, *Analyzing and Managing Banking Risk*, 3rd edn (Washington, DC, The International Bank for Reconstruction and Development/The World Bank, 2009).

[142] N Rose, 'The Death of the Social? Refiguring the Territory of Government' (1996) 25 *Economy and Society* 327; P O'Malley, 'Risk and Responsibility' in A Barry, T Osborne and NS Rose (eds), *Foucault and political reason: Liberalism, neo-liberalism and the rationalities of government* (London, UCL Press, 1996); P Leonard, *Postmodern Welfare* (London, Sage, 1997).

[143] Cooper, above n 26, at 1234.

[144] *Ibid*, at 1233.

[145] *Ibid*.

[146] Powell & Wahidin, above n 23, at 71.

[147] *Ibid*, at 72.

> an ambivalence at the heart of neo-liberalism: on the one hand, older people are to be 'managed' by other administrative powers such as professional experts in modernity; on the other hand, older people are left to govern themselves ... Hence, as consumers older people are distanced further away from the State; rather than a cause for celebration, the dystopian implications are far reaching which provides further risks the self must negotiate with the withdrawal of the State.[148]

Beck described the process by which older owners have become responsible for their own reflexive biographies as 'individualisation',[149] and argued that there are both benefits and challenges to this freedom to create our own biographies:

> Seen from one angle it means freedom to choose, and from another pressure to conform to internalized demands, on the one hand being responsible for yourself and on the other being dependent on conditions which completely elude your grasp.[150]

Creating a self-produced or 'reflexive biography' requires that we participate in the risk society, but in doing so we are expected to behave (and our behaviour is 'judged') according to particular norms. The shift from State provision for welfare needs in old age to individual responsibility through private market-based provision, has also triggered a step-change in the nature of the legal responsibilities in play in such scenarios, and the characteristics, values and expectations of the risk society have influenced legal subjectivity by determining the thresholds for the allocation of risk, the attribution of responsibility, and the allotment of costs when transactions result in bad outcomes for one party.

O'Malley demonstrated the importance of the relationships between risk, the uncertainty of the future and the norms of behaviour which (older) people are expected to perform in his analysis of the role of contract law in constructing legal subjects. He argued that the emergence of 'will theory' in contract allowed the court to 'express ... its acceptance of the idea that legal subjects who are parties to an exchange are calculating actors who act rationally, and as such take full responsibility for the future consequences of their decisions'.[151] Under this legal paradigm, 'It was not the court's concern whether or not the outcomes were fair according to any other criterion.'[152] The court viewed the legal subject who entered into a contract as 'a speculator ... to be protected, or not protected, as such'.[153] Thus, the legal subject of contract was above all an 'entrepreneurial individual', expected to be both prudent (expected to exercise reasonable foresight and everyday prudence in relation to potential harms) and risk-taking (acting as an entrepreneur),[154] when entering into the contracts which would bind his[155] uncertain future.

While this model resonates with the characteristics of the idealised risk subject (rational and self-responsible), O'Malley argued that the key to understanding the liberal legal

[148] *Ibid*, at 78.

[149] 'Individualisation' may be described as 'the requirement in late modernity that individuals must produce their own biographies themselves, in the absence of fixed, obligatory and traditional norms and certainties and the emergence of new ways of life that are continually subject to change': Lupton, above n 10, at 69; referring to U Beck, 'The reinvention of politics: towards a theory of reflexive modernisation' in U Beck, A Giddens and S Lash (eds), *Reflexive Modernisation: Politics, Tradition and Aesthetics in the Modern Social Order* (Cambridge, Polity Press, 1994) 13.

[150] U Beck and E Beck-Gernsheim, *The Normal Chaos of Love* (Cambridge, Polity Press, 1995) 7.

[151] P O'Malley, 'Uncertain subjects: risks, liberalism and contract' (2000) 29 *Economy and Society* 465, 473.

[152] *Ibid.*

[153] *Ibid*, at 474.

[154] O'Malley described this model of legal subjectivity as 'enterprising prudentialism'; see P O'Malley 'Risk and Responsibility' in Barry *et al* (eds), above n 142.

[155] For this subject is a 'he'.

perspective was the concept of 'reasonableness', which provided the vehicle through which the subjects of contract law

> were, and still are, assumed to operate with a form of common-sense rationality and reasonable foresight that common law read into the activities of those engaged in commerce, and by means of which in turn it governed and sought to shape them.[156]

The promotion of commerce required that legal subjects were imagined as exercising common sense, as being pragmatic; that outcomes were treated as foreseeable, if not necessarily calculable; so that contracts governing the future could proceed on the basis of expectations, if not predictions.[157] O'Malley claimed that, while contract law's 'liberal subjects ... [were] expected to govern themselves as rational and responsible agents',[158] this concept of 'reasonableness' softened the calculative edge of rational liberalism by requiring that subjects have only 'reasonable foresight' for the purposes of avoiding liability (responsibility) for adverse outcomes.[159]

The idea of the legal subject as a prudent entrepreneur raises interesting questions in the context of housing equity transactions. The reward of the entrepreneur for taking an unpredictable risk with his capital is the opportunity to make a profit. So, for example, in a conventional mortgage transaction, the prospect that the value of the property will rise provides the profit motive for the buyer (with the possibility of default and repossession representing the risk for the borrower, and with non-payment and negative equity amongst the risks for the lender). Although the paradigm of 'housing-as-investment-asset-to-spend'[160] is a direct consequence of the construction of the home-buyer as an entrepreneur in respect of the commoditised home, housing equity transactions occupy a radically different risk environment compared to conventional mortgages, in which the 'entrepreneurial' activity is not profit-making but (equity) spending. In a traditional mortgage, both parties might expect to make a financial profit (the lender through the payment of interest and the borrower through the rising value of the property); in a housing equity transaction, only the provider is expected to make a profit (through the payment of interest and the rising value of the property). To the extent that profit-making is viewed as a core element of entrepreneurship, owners releasing housing equity are not *entrepreneurs* but *consumers* of their own housing wealth. This potentially calls into question—more so than in the case of conventional mortgages—the assumptions underlying the idealised 'risk subject' of these transactions.

The task of making prudent decisions with reasonable foresight in respect of housing equity is also complicated by the particular uncertainties the older owner must negotiate. Financial products, such as equity release products, may be regarded as 'credence goods', in that their characteristics (and their suitability for the needs, objectives and circumstances of the consumers) often cannot be judged until long into the future. The

156 O'Malley, above n 151, at 471.

157 *Ibid*, at 468. O'Malley went on to claim that 'the standard of the reasonable person is being deployed to require a certain kind of calculation of all contractual subjects ... not that of statistical probability nor that of theoretically based prognostication by expertise. Rather ... [contract law] is employing foreseeability as a technology of everyday life, as deploying the categories of practical experience. In consequence, searching the common law rarely if ever reveals any estimation of likely outcomes expressed in terms of statistical probability ...' (*ibid*, at 477).

158 *Ibid*, at 478–79.

159 *Ibid*.

160 See ch 5.

uncertainties that consumers must plan around—future needs as they grow older, how long they will live, the future value of the property—are likely to remain unknowable for considerable periods, as are the countervailing risks for the lender. The consumer of housing equity is not rewarded for any risk-taking by the possibility of a future profit: while the provider has the opportunity to profit through the future value of the property, the occupier's compensation is the continued use of his or her housing as home. Yet even though the financial costs and benefits of the transaction are largely set at the time of the agreement (at least as far as the consumer is concerned), it is only with hindsight that the older owner will know whether he or she has made the right decision for his or her own future needs.[161] In addition to the more tangible risks of mis-selling and mis-buying, the uncertain future places limits on the reasonable foresight of these (potentially vulnerable) consumers.

Legal strategies to control risk may be either 'forward looking' (seeking to avoid bad outcomes for risks as yet unmaterialised) or 'backward looking' (attributing responsibility and awarding remedies for materialised risks).[162] The presumed rationality of the legal subject as reflected in the UK model for financial regulation is evident in its various 'forward looking' strategies, from information and disclosure requirements to enable consumers to make informed rational choices, to strategies to educate consumers and improve financial capability.[163] The Office of Fair Trading has recognised that 'there are limits to the information which consumers can assimilate, that these limits will vary between individuals and that just providing more information is not necessarily the answer to solving consumers' problems',[164] and has recommended the development of strategies that, rather than seeking to educate consumers about complex products, simplify the products on offer.[165] Yet by keeping the emphasis on the creation of 'knowledgeable consumers' who 'with the right information … can take responsibility for their own financial well-being, shop around and exert the pressures on suppliers which drive a competitive and innovative market',[166] these strategies tend to ignore both foreseeable risks, where the vulnerable consumer has (or perceives that he has) no (real) choice, and those risks which are unforeseeable. There is evidence to indicate that strategies for consumer protection based on information—described as a 'protection for the middle classes'[167]—are of least benefit to those who need them most. Marginal owners are least well-placed to manage their own risks based on information, and they are likely to have little choice due both to pressing financial pressure necessitating the transaction

[161] As Heywood *et al* have noted: 'Older people have to live with the uncertainties of not knowing how long they will live, not knowing what may befall them or how costs may rise and therefore not knowing how long their money will last. These uncertainties make planning difficult and are exacerbated by their feelings of uncertainty of provision if they should need help at a future date.' See F Heywood, C Oldman and R Means, *Housing and Home in Later Life* (Milton Keynes, Open University Press, 2002) 57.

[162] See Steele, above n 126, Preface (John Gardner) ix, and ch 8.

[163] See ch 6, section (3).

[164] Office of Fair Trading, *Vulnerable Consumers and Financial Services: The report of the Director General's Inquiry* (OFT 255) (London, OFT, 1999) para 700.

[165] *Ibid.*

[166] HM Treasury, *Competition in UK Banking: A Report to the Chancellor of the Exchequer* (London, TSO, 2000) Executive Summary, para 50.

[167] G Day, 'Assessing the effects of information disclosure requirements' (1976) 40 *Journal of Marketing* 42, 49; G Howells, 'The potential and limits of consumer empowerment by information' (2005) 32 *Journal of Law and Society* 349, 357.

and to the limited options available to them to raise needed funds.[168] Indeed, Wilhelmsson has described 'measures based on the information paradigm [as liable to] reproduce and even strengthen existing social injustice'.[169]

The reservation of legal liability to 'exceptional' or pathological cases in which the provider is deemed 'culpable' is implicit in the approach of liberal legal theory, which starts from the position that an individual who suffers a harm is responsible for himself (outcomes are attributed back to the actor) unless the creation of a liability is specifically justified. Honoré justified this approach on the basis that without responsibility for outcomes, we lack agency, since it is only as individuals with capacity and the ability to make choices that we acquire identity and status in terms of our 'effects in the world'. Honoré argued that this model of 'outcome responsibility' would ultimately be fair, based on the theory that agents of normal capacity will 'win more than they lose', and so can 'take the rough with the smooth'.[170] Yet this approach might be seen to operate particularly harshly in the case of older owners, who although they may be viewed as having 'normal capacity', do not have the opportunity to roll the dice again, or to recover from bad financial outcomes through future earning potential. Criticisms of outcome responsibility that claim there is no basis for assuming that 'things will somehow even out in the end'[171] are brought into sharp relief in the case of older owners, where there is limited or no opportunity for (financial) risk outcomes to 'even out' due to both limited time to recover and (typically) a steep decline in their income-generating capacity in that period. Furthermore, while Scanlon's 'forfeiture view' asserted that a person cannot complain of a harm suffered as a result of his or her voluntary choice,[172] this is challenged in an emerging literature which asserts that it is sometimes important to protect people against harms that cannot avoid by choosing appropriately, and to protect people against choices through which they might come to harm.[173]

The circumstances in which legal responsibility for the harms that may result from equity release transactions shifts from older owners themselves simply bearing their own losses as they fall, to the provider of home equity services becoming liable for losses, are typically limited to cases in which losses materialise as a result of 'fault' that may be attributed to the provider.[174] These circumstances tend to be limited, for a number of reasons. For one thing, they depend on concrete harms, which are directly attributable to the provider and not remote, and so do not cover cases in which the 'bad' outcomes of the risk do not become apparent until much later in the owner's life-course: for example, when an early release of equity to spend on lifestyle goods or services leaves the owner in

[168] 'Information is only useful if it can be acted upon. The poor may rationally decide not to make use of information, if they feel no alternatives will be available to them.': Howells, above n 167, at 357.

[169] T Wilhelmsson, 'Consumer law and social justice' in I Ramsey (ed), *Consumer law in the global economy* (Aldershot, Dartmouth, 1997) 224.

[170] T Honoré, *Responsibility and Fault* (Oxford, Hart Publishing, 1999) 9; see discussion in Steele, above n 126, at 94.

[171] Steele criticised this aspect of Honoré's approach to outcome responsibility with the example of 'An accomplished surgeon who makes a fatal misjudgement [who] may find all their life-saving work overshadowed by this one event, such is the response to losses as opposed to gains, or to error as opposed to routine excellence.' See Steele, above n 126, at 96.

[172] See Scanlon, above n 52, at, for discussion of the 'forfeiture view'.

[173] A Voorhoeve, 'Scanlon on Substantive Responsibility' (2008) 16 *Journal of Political Philosophy* 184.

[174] Leading to the contract being deemed voidable due to undue influence or misrepresentation for which the provider is deemed to be 'responsible', see ch 10; or because the provider has acted outside the rules of the regulatory framework, see ch 9.

financial difficulties later when there is insufficient housing equity left to meet his or her needs. It is also the case, and deliberately so as a result of the starting-position of 'victim responsibility', and the need for justifications to shift responsibility for harms from the victim to the 'author' of the risk,[175] that 'rescue' avenues based on legal liability are narrowly defined and intended to operate only at the margins of property law, contract and tort.

The framework of risk society draws upon ideas of responsibility which are, perhaps inevitably, broader than those which have been adopted in juridical conceptions of private law or in liberal legal theory.[176] Giddens described 'responsibility' as 'an interestingly ambiguous or multi-layered term', with at least three meanings: being the author of an event; acting in an ethical/accountable manner; and obligation or liability.[177] Private law theories of responsibility tend to focus on 'responsibility as obligation or liability', although the principles and doctrines of private law have been overlaid by regulatory regimes which have altered both the liabilities and the accountability of equity release providers.[178] The last decade has seen significant extensions to the FSA's jurisdiction over housing equity transactions, including the emergence of regulatory techniques which range from requiring advisers to take account of the consumer's circumstances, to requiring that the consumer has legal advice, to fixing the provider with responsibility for ensuring the suitability of the product for the individual consumer. Giddens recognised the particular challenges of maintaining appropriate standards of responsibility in the 'inherently ambiguous' circumstances of manufactured risk where responsibility can be neither easily attributed nor assumed',[179] and particularly in the context of financial markets, where risk is viewed as 'an energising principle'.[180] The neoliberal perspective that tends to dominate in UK law and policy has (largely echoing private law's tendencies) typically emphasised the *self*-responsibility of the individual consumer, rather than regarding the provider of financial services, or the State or the legal system, as bearing responsibility for harms. However, since the global financial crisis, this model of individual consumer responsibility has come under increasing pressure, and the 'decentered regulatory approach', underpinned by a mantra of 'responsible lending and responsible borrowing'—undermined by evidence of failure adequately to protect consumers[181]—seems poised for reform in the shape of a more enforceable set of obligations and liabilities to which providers are legally held to account for abrogating their responsibilities towards consumers.[182]

The development of innovative products which facilitate the use of housing equity to enable 'house-rich, cash-poor' older owners to release income and capital for use during

[175] See, eg, Honoré, above n 170; A Ripstein, *Equality, Responsibility and the Law* (Cambridge, Cambridge University Press, 1999); R Dworkin, *Sovereign Virtue* (Cambridge, MA, Harvard University Press, 2000); J Coleman, *Risks and Wrongs* (Cambridge, Cambridge University Press, 1992). The key ideas set out in these analyses, as they pertain to risk, are discussed in Steele, above n 126, and considered further in ch 4.

[176] These models are discussed further in ch 4.

[177] Giddens, above n 21, at 8.

[178] The nature and content of the financial services provider's responsibilities following the extension of the FSA jurisdiction over certain housing equity products in recent years is discussed in ch 9.

[179] Giddens, above n 21, at 8.

[180] *Ibid.*

[181] See, eg, S Nield, 'Responsible Lending and Borrowing: Whereto low-cost home ownership?' (2010) 30 *Legal Studies* 610.

[182] See ch 9, sections (5) and (6).

their life-course without risking the roof over their heads, has raised new questions about 'Who is to determine how harmful products are, what side effects are produced by them, and what level of risk is acceptable?'[183] The concepts of risk and responsibility[184] render intelligible the proposition that legal subjects can make rational choices despite imperfect information,[185] and support a model of subjectivity that regards rational choice, and responsibility for the consequences of those choices, as the foundations of agency, identity and capacity; that is, the idealised subject of private law. Yet at the same time, the reality that 'consumers'—and perhaps also particular 'identity' categories of consumer—are not idealised rational actors, but are more accurately portrayed as vulnerable subjects, creates tensions which legal theory and practice must attempt to resolve. The tensions between these competing conceptions of the older owner as a legal subject are considered in chapter four.

(4) Conclusions

Housing equity transactions for older owners present a unique set of issues. While the inherent 'riskiness' they present has been widely recognised in the regulatory context, little specific attention has been paid to the broader legal framework of transactions for the use of housing wealth in the UK. For example, property law and contract support and enable these transactions by providing the legal tools by which the provider can obtain deferred exchange rights over the home while the owner continues to live there. At the same time, little attention has been paid to date within property law *per se* to the consequences of increased use of housing wealth,[186] and while the increase in regulation of some housing equity products has been reducing some risks associated with these transactions, further analysis remains necessary to assess the extent to which the range of legal frameworks in play in this context can ameliorate the risks that are now undertaken by older owners, and the effect of the balance struck between risk and regulation for the construction of the older owner as a legal subject.

183 *Ibid.*

184 Which offer 'an understanding of uncertainty … [that] allows us to plan our actions despite not knowing how the future will turn out': Steele, above n 126, at 18.

185 This '"decision-making" heritage of risk also influences those approaches which concentrate their attention on an individual decision-maker or agent. Here, the emphasis is on the way that techniques of protection and rational decision-making can enable individuals to exercise their freedom as active agents even in the face of an uncertain future. No longer governed purely by fate, human beings may reach a decision on rational, or at least, identifiable grounds.' (*ibid*)

186 For a discussion of the relevant property law principles, see ch 7.

4

The Older Owner as a Legal Subject in Private Law

(1) Introduction

Analyses of the impact of the 'risk society' on constructions of the political subject have highlighted the role of the human subject—and particularly questions of 'who gets to be a subject?' and 'what qualities and attributes are subjects expected to have?'[1]—in shaping the emergence of political and legal policies and practices. The extent to which individuals can call upon law, especially in relation to 'private' transactions, depends on the model of legal subjectivity that dominates laws and policies in that particular context. This, in turn, reflects a position on risk which is often expressed in competing private law discourses through the discursive tropes of autonomy, choice, reasonableness, rights, fault, responsibility and liability. The nature and content of legal subjectivity are crucial in defining the parameters within which law is formulated, applied and critiqued. This is particularly evident in the case of older owners in housing equity transactions, where the changing political characterisation of older people, and especially older owners, as individualised, self-responsible consumers and risk subjects, and of the enterprise of releasing equity as a normal step in neoliberal self-provision for older age, has largely coincided with the dominant private law norms of liberal legal theory.

Tensions between neoliberal ideals and expectations relating to older owners (particularly marginal older owners living in lower-value properties, who notwithstanding the realities of inequality in their lives, are characterised as homogeneous, autonomous, self-responsible legal subjects), and their experiences as vulnerable consumers who face a higher order of risk in housing equity transactions (from the riskier terms of the product options available to them, to the impact of inequality and situational vulnerability on economic decision-making, and their heightened exposure to the adverse impacts of 'bad' transactions) are only exacerbated by the complex housing paradigms (housing as home, housing as inheritance, housing as investment-asset-to-spend) they must negotiate as a result of the political and policy contexts in which they are located through their status as 'owners', and so as 'full' financial and risk subjects.

This chapter analyses the significance of competing characterisations of the older owner as a legal subject in creating the frameworks within which the terms, the expectations and the vocabulary of legal discourses concerning housing equity transactions are defined. The chapter begins from the 'barest' model of legal subject, the conception of 'personality'

[1] Boyle described legal subjectivity as the '(purified) fantasy persona that confronts and receives legal knowledge': J Boyle, 'Is Subjectivity Possible? The Post-Modern Subject in Legal Theory' (1991) 62 *University of Colorado Law Review* 489, 517.

advanced in non-instrumentalist private law theories, before considering the portrayal of legal subjects, including older owners, within the normative framework of liberal legal theory. While this model has tended to dominate the law governing private law transactions (primarily contract and property law), it has been challenged from several quarters. The growing sphere of regulatory jurisdiction over housing equity transactions has altered the normative lens through which these transactions, and the 'consumers' who are their subjects, are understood in legal discourse. Meanwhile, critical discourses within contract law and property law have challenged the strict application of liberal legal subjectivity—with its commitment to autonomy and choice—in private law.

(2) Legal 'Personality' in Private Law Theories

The ways in which the idea of 'risk' is understood in private law theories, and the expectations placed on legal subjects to negotiate risk successfully or pay the costs, depend on underlying conceptions about the role and reach of private law, and the mode of legal reasoning adopted by the theorist. At one end of the spectrum are the 'non-instrumentalist', corrective justice theories,[2] in which the theorists seek to detach the 'reason' of the law from political and policy issues in the conviction that private law is not a legitimate vehicle by which to achieve social policy goals.[3] The non-instrumentalist approach, which reasons from private law's 'inner character' rather than its external effects, seeks to achieve an internally coherent justification for the interpersonal rights and obligations which determine the outcomes of claims between the parties to litigation (the plaintiff and the defendant). A central concern of these theories is with correlative corrective justice between the parties, to the exclusion of distributive considerations (for example, underlying inequalities). For example, Weinrib's theoretical framework for private law excluded from consideration all factors that are external to the correlative relationship between the parties,[4] including welfare considerations in respect of either party, evidence of bad conduct ('evil') or socio-economic context ('need'), which were described as 'moral categories that may well figure in other contexts, but they are not pertinent to liability'.[5] This position was justified on the basis that any normative factors

[2] These theories have been largely 'worked out' in the context of tort law theory, although the model of legal personality they offer has been applied by some theorists to contract law, as discussed below.

[3] Eg, Weinrib's anti-instrumentalist theory of private law emphasises private law's 'inner character', seeking to find coherence in the internal characteristics of private law without external referent in the form of policy or 'social interests'; E Weinrib, *The Idea of Private Law* (Cambridge, MA, Harvard University Press, 1995). Weinrib argued that private law 'looks neither to the litigant individually nor to the interests of the community as a whole, but to a bipolar relationship of liability' (*ibid*, at 2). For further examples of anti-instrumentalism in private law, see A Beever, *Rediscovering the Law of Negligence* (Oxford, Hart Publishing, 2007); R Stevens, *Torts and Rights* (Oxford, Oxford University Press, 2007).

[4] This model of corrective justice is 'relational' in the sense that it considers only the relationship between the two parties, plaintiff and defendant, and the concept of 'correlativity' reflects the idea that liability results from 'the defendant and the plaintiff hav[ing] respectively done and suffered the same injustice ... [with] equal normative status as ... doer and sufferer of the same wrong': EJ Weinrib, 'Correlativity, Personality, and the Emerging Consensus on Corrective Justice' (2001) 2 *Theoretical Inquiries in Law* 107, 110. Thus, the unreasonable risk that materialised in the plaintiff's harm must be the same unreasonable risk initiated by the defendant's act; the harm must flow from the risk unreasonably created by defendant.

[5] *Ibid*, at 118.

applied to determine liability, to be fair, must apply equally to both parties.[6] By this model, defendants owe the same duty to everyone, and there is no positive duty to safeguard the welfare of another, regardless of the subjective context or vulnerabilities of that person.[7]

The 'non-instrumentalist' approach to allocations of transactional risk and the costs of transactional harms, seeks to achieve corrective rather than distributive justice[8]; it emphasises the 'private' rather than the 'public' nature of the transactional interactions between individuals, and argues that these categories must remain distinct.[9] From this perspective, law is understood as 'a relatively autonomous universe of normative discourse based on concepts such as "rights", "wrongs", "responsibility" and, of course, "justice"'.[10] While non-instrumentalist accounts, like much private law theory, have little to say about property,[11] where property law features in accounts such as Weinrib's *The Idea of Private Law*, it also 'takes its normative character from the abstractness of right rather than from the promotion of welfare'.[12] The project of private law theorising is conceived not in terms of social justice, but purely as an 'exploration and systematization of the legal rules based on fundamental and immutable moral principles' which avoids external referents, including what are seen as 'messy and controversial discussions about the social consequences of the rules of private law'.[13]

The 'subject' of anti-instrumentalist accounts of private law is not the 'real person' of social analysis, but a 'de-personalised rationality'[14] sometimes described as bearing characteristics of Rawls's essential, stripped-down subject.[15] Weinrib has sought to establish an abstraction of 'personality' within the juridical conception of corrective justice, which he described as 'the idea of purposiveness regardless of one's particular purposes ... the conception of the interacting parties that is presupposed in a regime of rights and their correlative duties'.[16] 'Personality', for Weinrib, was deliberately conceived 'at a high degree of abstraction',[17] to be 'representative' of the parties as bearers of rights and

6 *Ibid*, at 117.

7 *Ibid*, especially at 119–20, and at 123, where he claimed that 'the agency of the parties cannot be conceived in terms of the importance of their welfare to them'. See also A Ripstein, *Equality, Responsibility and the Law* (Cambridge, Cambridge University Press, 1999) 92, arguing that ownership of risk cannot be tied to shifting welfare considerations.

8 Although some writers in this vein allow some scope for mixed corrective/redistributive theories; eg, Jules Coleman applies corrective justice to the 'core' of tort law, but allows for distributive justice in the 'penumbra': J Coleman, *Risks and Wrongs* (Cambridge, Cambridge University Press, 1992) 386. For other mixed theories of tort law, see I Englard, 'The Idea of Complementarity as Philosophical Basis for Pluralism in Tort Law' in DG Owen (ed), *Philosophical Foundations of Tort Law* (Oxford, Oxford University Press, 1997); GT Schwartz, 'Mixed Theories of Tort Law: Affirming Both Deterrence and Corrective Justice' (1997) 75 *Texas Law Review* 1801; GP Fletcher, 'Fairness and Utility in Tort Theory' (1972) 85 *Harvard Law Review* 537.

9 See P Cane, 'The Anatomy of Private Law: A 25th Anniversary Essay' (2005) 25 *OJLS* 203, 212–17.

10 *Ibid*, at 205.

11 N Hopkins, 'Regulating Trusts of the Home: Private Law and Social Policy' (2009) 125 *LQR* 310.

12 Weinrib, above n 3, at 131.

13 H Collins, 'Utility and Rights in Common Law Reasoning: Rebalancing Private Law through Constitutionalization' (2007) 30 *Dalhousie Law Journal* 1, 6. According to this method, 'appeals to coherence, consistency, and fidelity to principle would suffice to resolve the issue' (*ibid*). As an example of this reasoning, see discussion of the Birksian taxonomy of private law in relation to undue influence in ch 9.

14 Eg, in Ripstein's principle of reciprocity, which relies on an image of the 'reasonable person' drawn from Rawls; see Ripstein, above n 7.

15 J Rawls, *A Theory of Justice* (Cambridge, MA, Harvard University Press, 1971). While private law theorists have borrowed the 'stripped-down subject' from Rawls, Rawls himself said 'almost nothing' about private law; Cane, above n 9, at 204, fn 6.

16 Weinrib, above n 4.

17 *Ibid*, at 123.

correlative duties, but 'for whose normative status welfare does not matter except insofar as it forms the content of a right'.[18] Weinrib deliberately distanced this notion of 'personality' from the Rawlsian political subject on which Ripstein based his juridical 'reasonable person', and this barer, even more abstract conception of personality[19] was also the subject of Benson's 'public basis justification' of contract.[20] Weinrib argued that

> [f]or tort law, the formulation of the rational in terms of the agent's conception of the good is misplaced. Tort law is indifferent to judgments about goodness. It therefore does not view the parties' actions as manifesting even personal conceptions of the good, but merely as executing the actor's purpose on a particular occasion.[21]

The Rawlsian conception of the person is, by this measure, too reliant on co-operation, and not sufficiently individualist for a juridical concept, because 'The persons that private law governs are not co-operators concerned with the basic structure of society as a whole. Rather, they are all pursuing their individual purposes subject only to the limits of permissible impingement on each other.'[22] The deliberately limited conception of the person (the legal subject) adopted in this context was reflected in the claim that 'For persons conceived in this way, being better or worse off does not, in itself, constitute an injustice.'[23]

Weinrib's commitment to an inward-facing methodology in his juridical concept of the person required that this model of personality could not even acknowledge the concept of rational agency, as this would require reliance on moral philosophy extrinsic to tort theory.[24] While tort law itself was presented as a 'repository of moral reasoning about responsibility for harm',[25] the precepts of Weinrib's theory required that its ideas must reflect only those ideas that are 'implicit in liability as a normative practice'.[26] As such,

> [p]ersonality in this context is not a psychological but a normative idea: it refers not to the pattern of an individual's behavioural characteristics, but to a presupposition about imputability and entitlement that is implicit in the rights and duties of private law.[27]

[18] *Ibid.*

[19] While the source of Weinrib's 'personality' is internal to law, he acknowledges that this does not mean that political philosophy cannot provide insights into the inner character of law; Weinrib, above n 4, at 112.

[20] P Benson, 'The Idea of a Public Basis of Justification for Contract' (1995) 33 *Osgoode Hall Law Journal* 273, 316: 'In positive terms, individuals are to be viewed as, and *only* as, subjects with a capacity to have, acquire and exercise rightful possession by and for themselves.'; see also P Benson, 'The Unity of Contract Law' in P Benson (ed), *The Theory of Contract Law: New Essays* (Cambridge, Cambridge University Press, 2001).

[21] Weinrib, above n 4, at 145.

[22] *Ibid.*

[23] *Ibid*, at 123. Boyle has argued that the Rawlsian subject is 'only convincing because the values smuggled into his subjects, such a love of material wealth and freedom of action, are too familiar to understand': Boyle, above n 1, at 506–09.

[24] Weinrib claimed that caution about the implications of making tort theory reliant on wider moral philosophies (Kant, Hegel) has led some corrective justice theorists to reject the concept of personality.

[25] Weinrib, above n 4, at 109.

[26] *Ibid*, at 108. The use of 'normative' in this context is as a 'juridical' concept, focusing on 'the justifications internal to tort law, treating them as normative in their own terms rather than as the disguised surrogates for extrinsically justifiable social goals'(*ibid*, at 110).

[27] *Ibid*, at 111. This passage went on to explain that 'This presupposition is that as participants in a regime of liability, the parties are viewed as purposive beings who are not subject to a duty to act for any purpose in particular, no matter how meritorious. This capacity for purposive action underlies the rights and duties that are its juridical manifestations. Personality signifies that all persons possess an equal capacity for rights and duties without being obligated to act towards any particular purpose; it thereby reflects the structure of the law of

Weinrib emphasised that the concept of personality he asserted for corrective justice theory was stripped back to 'the most abstract representation of the parties themselves as interacting beings'.[28]

Although Weinrib's theory was primarily focused on tort rather than private law more generally, it also extrapolated more generally to apply the concepts of correlativity and personality to the right to property in things and the right to contractual performance,[29] and the corrective justice approach has also provided the basis for some contract theories. Like justificatory theories of tort, contract theories may be either instrumental (whereby the justifications for enforcing a contract, or not, may include reference to background social goals, for example economic efficiency) or non-instrumental (whereby the justifications for outcomes are based only on 'internal' principles of corrective justice). The non-instrumentalist, internal approach is reflected in those autonomy theories of contract law[30] which are concerned only with whether contracts are 'voluntary' and 'fair' (in the corrective rather than distributive justice sense), and which argue that it is not necessary or appropriate to look beyond the parties' wills (to external values, such as efficiency or distributive justice) to establish the moral basis for enforcing the contract, or not.[31] While the role of corrective justice in tort theory focuses on whether one party is *responsible* for the other's loss, its application in contract law requires that, so long as agreements are voluntary and fair, the legitimate expectations that flow from such agreements must be satisfied; if not, corrective justice demands that the transaction be reversed and the contract rescinded.[32]

In determining the rights and duties of contracting parties (the non-instrumental notion of obligation), corrective justice theories of contract also rely on a highly abstracted ideal of the legal subject.[33] Benson's account of contract as corrective justice describes 'The conception of the person entailed in personality [as] absolutely minimal'[34]; and he contrasts this with what he describes as Rawls's 'more complex conception of the

obligations as a system of negative duties of non-interference with the rights of others.' This is not to say that such persons have no positive moral duties in other contexts, but describes the extent of their liabilities under private law.

[28] *Ibid.*

[29] *Ibid*, at 122.

[30] See, eg, C Fried, *Contract as Promise: A Theory of Contractual Obligation* (Cambridge, MA, Harvard University Press, 1981); R Barnett, 'A Consent Theory of Contract' (1986) 86 *Colorado Law Review* 269. These non-instrumentalist autonomy theories of contract are criticised on the grounds that they 'do not have the resources to specify "background rules" for contract law … At most, they may require that individuals be free to contract around all or some of the background rules which are adopted on grounds other than autonomy.': Benson (1995), above n 20, at 279. See also R Craswell, 'Contract Law, Default Rules, and the Philosophy of Promising' (1989) 88 *Michigan Law Review* 489, 514.

[31] Benson (1995), above n 20, at 278.

[32] M Ramsay, 'The Buyer/Seller Asymmetry: Corrective Justice and Material Non-Disclosure' (2006) 56 *University of Toronto Law Journal* 115, 133.

[33] See, eg, P Benson, 'Abstract Right and the Possibility of a Nondistributive Conception of Contract: Hegel and Contemporary Contract Theory' (1989) 10 *Cardozo Law Review* 1077, 1192–93, which adopted the abstract, contentless Hegelian model of personality. 'Because personality is knowledge of oneself as undetermined by inclination and thus as indifferent to particularity, it is without particular content and therefore abstractly universal. And since personality is contentless, there is nothing to differentiate one person from another. As purely abstract, persons are necessarily identical. In this sense, and with respect to their personality, individuals are therefore equal.' (*ibid*, at 1160) While it is not suggested that individuals can, in fact, strip themselves of their characteristics, the stripped-down subject is employed to answer the limited question that non-instrumentalist contract theory asks: that is, can individuals conceive of themselves as responsible for their choices, or as 'self-consciously purposive'?

[34] *Ibid*, at 1161.

person'. Rather, Benson draws upon the Hegelian notion of 'will'[35] to argue that contractual obligations result from the common will manifested in a voluntary interaction between free parties. This obligation 'is independent of all considerations relating to the needs and welfare of the parties'.[36] While Benson recognised that 'a decision to enter a contract may be determined by a variety of factors, including a party's particular aims, needs, or abilities',[37] he claimed that the 'common will' of the parties, which constitutes the basis of the obligation, does not incorporate these extrinsic factors as 'elements that constitute the contractual relation. They are as such irrelevant to the analysis of contract'.[38]

The non-instrumentalist approach to private law and its juridical concept of the person does not deny that other values (efficiency, welfare, etc) are persuasive within their own moral and political orders; rather, according to this perspective, these values are simply not relevant to the juridical order governing private transactions between individuals. Similarly, it is not suggested that corrective justice is the only available form of justice, or that juridical norms are the only norms which should determine outcomes; rather, they are the only criteria appropriate to juridical reasoning. Where the outcomes of this closed process of reasoning are unacceptable, non-instrumentalist theories allow that these outcomes may be adjusted by moral and political schema of distributive justice, for example through politics and policy, given effect in the form of legislation.[39] It is only within the confines of private law that such considerations are excluded.

However, in a legal environment that is structured so that the 'subject' has little real option but to contract, the negative conception of liberty invoked in such accounts of private law,[40] and typified in the argument that the party who suffers a loss must bear that loss because he or she 'chose' by his or her own free will to participate as a subject of private law, is undermined. For the claimant, the suggestion that the framework of private law may be bolstered by other, extra-judicial (moral and political) norms, which may provide greater protection, is of little comfort when the political and policy context has (with the exception of those particular products which have been regulated, and subject to the limitations of such regulation) determined that the issue of housing equity use be governed by the application of private law norms. As the discussion in chapter two has shown, political and policy frameworks in the UK have, since the 1980s, progressively privatised the provision of service for older owners. Areas which were previously regarded as the responsibility of the State (for example home maintenance, and health and nursing care) are now the self-responsibility of older owners, who must exhaust their own assets before they can qualify for State support. One of the problems this creates is that it locates the transactions that are necessary to release the equity which the older owners must use within the realm of private law and renders them subject to private law's juridical norms.

[35] GWF Hegel, *Elements of the Philosophy of Right* (ed, AW Wood, transl, HB Nisbet) (Cambridge, Cambridge University Press, 1991).

[36] Benson, above n 33, at 1187.

[37] *Ibid.*

[38] *Ibid.*

[39] Weinrib claimed that 'only a libertarian believes that corrective justice is the only justice there is': Weinrib, above n 4, at 158; on the relationship between 'background principles' and the law governing individual transactions, and between distributive and corrective justice, see, eg, P Benson, 'The Basis of Corrective Justice and its Relation to Distributive Justice' (1992) 77 *Iowa Law Review* 515.

[40] Benson added that 'Because the common will reflects merely the negative imperative of abstract right, it does not oblige individuals to enter contracts.': Benson, above n 33, at 1187. The implications of this negative conception in relation to housing equity transactions are considered further below, section (4)(a).

This, in turn, raises broader questions about the limits of the judicial function in the absence of, or operating subject to, legislative policy, which are deeply contested.[41] Furthermore, while Weinrib attempted to demarcate clear boundaries around the legal subject of private law (which itself was viewed as autonomous and based on an immanent rationality), in reality the implications of this abstract conception of personality potentially reach considerably further than private law doctrine, due to the complex interactions between common law principles and doctrines, and the judicial application of legislative or regulatory provisions which, while giving effect to clear policy goals, often leave considerable scope for judicial discretion.[42] The discussion of 'fairness' regulations in chapter eight illustrates how the abstract 'private law' juridical conception of the legal subject has 'leaked' across to influence judicial applications of statutory provisions which have the explicit goal of protecting vulnerable consumers, to dull their effect.

(3) The Liberal Legal Subject

Non-instrumentalist theories argue that policy and social interests are not relevant to private law, and that the pursuit of goals would threatens its coherence and stability. Critics of this method—which 'tr[ies] to make the authority of the interpretation look as though it were "objective", as though the law came from within the fetishized textual objects rather than from some authoritative Will'[43]—assert that law, in theory and in practice, always has both a subject and a set of goals. The identity of the legal subject is critical to the justificatory goals and values that inform the theory, as 'The subject is loaded up, consciously or unconsciously, with a particular set of qualities or attributes. That subject then reflexively produces a kind of society, a legal decision, or a professional practice.'[44] Choices must be made, explicitly or implicitly, about the rights and duties of legal persons (or subjects), which in turn shape the expectations that inform legal doctrine, policies and practices, as well as the rights and remedies recognised by legal institutions. For example, Cane has argued that there are important differences between Weinrib's de-personalised subject and the liberal legal subject, due to the

> world of difference between a litigation-focused concept of correlativity of remedial rights and obligations, and an account of private law based on a concept of interpersonal responsibility cashed out in terms (for instance) of a reasonable balance between the interests we all share in freedom of action, on the one hand, and security of person and property on the other.[45]

[41] See S Waddams, *Dimensions of Private Law: Categories and Concepts in Anglo-American Legal Reasoning* (Cambridge, Cambridge University Press, 2003) 206 *et seq*; cf Weinrib, above n 3, ch 8, especially section 8.2.2.

[42] The effect of legislative policies on the incremental development of the common law has been recognised: see J Landis, 'Statutes and the Sources of Law' (1965) 2 *Harvard Journal on Legislation* 7; J Beatson, 'Has the Common Law a Future?' [1997] *Cambridge Law Journal* 291; J Beatson, 'The Role of Statute in the Development of Common Law Doctrine' (2001) 117 *LQR* 247. The interconnections between common law and statute are also, as the analysis in ch 8 reveals, a two-way street, along which common law conceptions also influence the interpretation of statutory provisions.

[43] Boyle, above n 1, at 510.

[44] *Ibid*, at 518.

[45] Cane, above n 9, at 212; see also P Cane, *The Anatomy of Tort Law* (Oxford, Hart Publishing, 1997); P Cane, *Responsibility in Law and Morality* (Oxford, Hart Publishing, 2002).

Thus, while non-instrumentalist accounts emphasise law's corrective justice functions (with the central concern on what it means to be responsible), liberal legal theories have a more practical concern with the content of our responsibilities as liberal subjects.[46]

At the same time, and although the 'de-personalised subject' exists only in the most abstract form, the non-instrumentalist accounts share many characteristics with the liberal legal theories which have dominated classical contract law and theory. Classical liberal legal theories also subscribe to the formal transactional equality of corrective justice, underpinned by reference to the individual's capacity to make rational choices which is the hallmark of the autonomous (ie free) subject. The privileged legal subject of liberal private law theories is an individualist, autonomous legal subject who takes responsibility for his own actions and choices, and whose free and equal moral agency must be respected by holding him to those choices, no matter how bad they are. This model of subjectivity—which admits its inspiration in Rawls's political subjects—is subject to the criticism that, while the 'stripped down subject' claims to be 'objective', he

> end[s] up sounding suspiciously like middle class white male American liberals. For example, they decide in their kindly but materially self-interested way that it is acceptable to have inequalities of wealth if those inequalities would put the worst-off people in the society in a better position than they would be in a more egalitarian society. Pareto must be with them behind that veil of ignorance.[47]

This conception of the legal subject is central to the autonomy-centred, deontological structure of the liberal conception of contract, which focuses on the function of contracts in enabling the individual to maximise his or her opportunities, and which treats pre-contractual bargaining as an adversarial 'game' from which each party—so long as they follow the rules of the game—aims to wrest as much as they can to their own self-interest. Bigwood asserted that contract law's commitment to these liberal values ensures that it 'simply complements the free competitive market and processes'.[48] It is a necessary consequence of this ideological orientation that the liberal conception of contract law 'naturally ... allows people to enjoy (disproportional) returns on the basis of inequalities existing between social members'.[49] As a result, for the liberal contract scholar, 'the common law of contract [is seen to] offer little in the way of achieving social (or distributive) justice'.[50] This is consonant with the broader notion that the purpose of private law is to 'deliver on the liberal state's promise to respect the freedom of individuals ... [by] construct[ing] a framework of opportunities for individuals in cooperation with others to become authors of their own lives.'[51]

This justificatory narrative for private law clearly resonates with the socio-political character of the 'risk society', with its emphasis on individuals having the opportunity to take risks, to pursue opportunities and to be held responsible for the outcomes, whether good or bad. As such, it reflects the neoliberal State's support for positive freedom (autonomy) and the responsibilities of, and opportunities for, individuals to exercise that

[46] Cane, above n 9, at 215, fn 72.

[47] Boyle, above n 1, at 506.

[48] R Bigwood, 'Conscience and the Liberal Conception of Contract: Observing Basic Distinctions: Part 1' (2000) 16 *Journal of Contract Law* 1 at 19.

[49] *Ibid.*

[50] *Ibid.*

[51] Collins, above n 13, at 4–5.

freedom to achieve well-being. Collins has argued that the structure of private law as a system of rights and entitlements

> symbolize[s] and make[s] concrete the point that the individual can choose independently or autonomously how to exercise positive freedom. The individual's choices about well-being are protected from interference by the state or by other individuals by recognizing that these choices involve the exercise of rights such as freedom of contract or the enjoyment of private property.[52]

Liberal models of private law are instrumentalist in that they accept the inherent relevance of 'goals', although the range of permissible goals is strictly limited by the liberal individualist requirement of respecting consensual choice.

Bigwood claimed that 'The distinct ideology that underlies the classical conception of contract is *liberal individualism*, the fundamental aim of which is the protection of the individual as an autonomous subject and independent moral agent.'[53] This characterisation of law's subject is rooted in the concept of autonomy, and the goal of equality pertains to opportunity, not outcome; it is concerned to achieve formal, not substantive, equality.[54] This perspective is reflected in Rosenfeld's formulation, which describes

> each individual [as] autonomous and independent, equal to all other individuals, and free from all other individuals ... [E]quality among individuals means ... equality of autonomy and an equal right to freedom from interference by other individuals. Equal freedom, in turn, entails equality of opportunity for each individual to exploit his or her own faculties as he or she best sees fit.[55]

The logic of the liberal perspective posits that subjects—'freely choosing, rationally valuing, specifically efficacious moral personalities'[56]—*deserve* to be held to account for the consequences of their choices,[57] because to do otherwise would be to fail to respect their subjectivity by not 'taking seriously' their equal status as autonomous subjects. It does not recognise that the ability of risk subjects effectively and strategically to manage their lives is unequally distributed, with those who are likely to have most *need* of their housing equity in later life—that is, those who do not have other savings or sufficient pension assets—also likely to have less of the economic, social and cultural capitals needed to navigate the risk society.[58]

The liberal legal model echoes to some extent Dworkin's account of the individual responsibilities on rational agents to make binding choices.[59] Dworkin argued that equality and justice must be understood in terms of the rational choices that people make,

[52] *Ibid*, at 5.

[53] Bigwood, above n 48, at 19.

[54] *Ibid*, at 20.

[55] M Rosenfeld, 'Contract and Justice: The Relation Between Classical Contract Law and Social Contract Theory' (1985) 70 *Iowa Law Review* 769, 778.

[56] Bigwood, above n 48, at 20.

[57] '[W]hether those choices turn out well or badly for them in terms of their ultimate material, psychological, or welfare interests ... For if we are to take autonomy seriously, we must respect the bad bargains that people make as well as the good ones, since to interfere with bad bargains entered into voluntarily is to deny someone the right to self-determination, and hence to deny that person's absolute and equal status as a freely choosing, rationally valuing, specially efficacious moral personality.' (*ibid*, at 21).

[58] Furthermore, to the extent that this norm is decisive in determining the allocation of harms flowing from home equity transactions, it reinforces the patterns of 'winners' and 'losers' in the risk society; see ch 3.

[59] See generally, R Dworkin, *Sovereign Virtue: The Theory and Practice of Equality* (Cambridge, MA Harvard University Press, 2000); discussed in relation to risk in J Steele, *Risks and Legal Theory* (Oxford, Hart Publishing, 2004) ch 5.

based on their own preferences, because (hypothetically, given fair circumstances and a level-playing field) they will rationally make choices (concerning risks, or in Dworkin's terminology 'chances and opportunities') according to what they value most. In the context of older owners making choices concerning their housing equity, the housing paradigms set out in chapter five provide one means by which these preferences may be articulated, while the political and policy contexts discussed in chapter two highlighted the pressures that have constrained those choices, particularly for marginal older owners.[60] The exercise of these (limited) choices is also complicated by the difficulties older owners must face in choosing between their wants and needs, now and later. The inherent tendency towards meeting present wants is revealed in Steele's claim that 'no matter how far we take "improvements" to decision-methods informed by risk, these decisions are still preoccupied above all with "the present"'.[61] In reality, this has implications for the exercise of choice by legal subjects, and may inhibit even a 'rational' older owner's ability to plan safely for his or her financial future.

Steele argued that Dworkin's acceptance of the need for 'limited rescue' through State institutions gives the lie to the claim that legal subjects are free and equal moral agents: 'the individual is neither as free nor as sovereign as may first appear.'[62] This contradiction is also evident in the liberal legal theory of contract law, which acknowledges that the 'platform of neutrality' on which the juridical legal subject is positioned, indifferent to the realities of need and advantage, is an idealised model.[63] The unreality of this liberal legal subject is also implicitly recognised in the role of 'public law' to craft the 'principles of background justice' that determine the 'basic structure of society' according to principles of distributive justice. The result is that, while it is clearly acknowledged that the principles of corrective justice as they are applied to the liberal subject are not sufficient to ensure overall 'justice', thus giving the lie to the myth of the free and equal, autonomous legal subject,[64] these theories effectively abdicate responsibility, on behalf of private law, for persistent inequalities. The ideological constraints of liberal democracy limit the reach of private law and demand that it serve the liberal goal of autonomous rights, and not the competing aim of individual welfare. Thus, common law contract is constructed as 'a prisoner of ineradicable practical and ideological constraints, and is limited to addressing the internal fairness of individual transactions themselves. This is "interpersonal justice" rather than "social" justice—"corrective" justice rather than "distributive" justice.'[65] In the context of housing equity transactions, this means that (setting aside for now the

[60] '"To choose" means giving up some options in favour of others.': Steele, above n 59, at 125.

[61] *Ibid*, at 162.

[62] *Ibid*, at 155.

[63] Benson described the liberal conception of responsibility as a 'limited idea of responsibility, with its essential indifference to need and advantage as such': Benson (1995), above n 20, at 315–16; and Bigwood acknowledged that it is 'indifferen[t] to the parties' needs and welfare, their social and economic positions, and the distribution of society's resources and wealth': Bigwood, above n 48, at 24.

[64] Rawls argued that this emphasis in private law on the pursuit of self-interest means that 'individuals and associations are then left free to advance their ends more effectively within the framework of the basic structure, secure in the knowledge that elsewhere in the social system the necessary corrections to preserve background justice are being made': J Rawls, 'The Basic Structure as Subject' in AI Goldman and J Kim (eds), *Values and Morals* (Dordrecht, D Reidel, 1978) at 47. Bigwood also accepted that the outcomes of the liberal model of corrective justice may be unjust, but argued that 'the corrections necessary to remedy the systematic injustice effected through the non-instrumental use of contract are to take place outside the domain of contract law, via other instruments or within other social institutions': Bigwood, above n 48, at 35.

[65] Bigwood, above n 48, at 19.

regulatory provisions discussed in chapters eight and nine)[66] as neoliberal policies have transplanted responsibility for financial provision for older owners[67] into the domain of private provision funded through private law transactions, corrective justice perspectives on private law bounce this responsibility right back onto the welfare system. For the real people who are required to enter into these transactions, and particularly for the marginal older owners who are arguably most vulnerable and so most far removed from the idealised liberal subject, this creates a responsibility deficit.[68]

Within the liberal framework of private law, individuals are free to pursue their own self-interest, subject only to observing the 'rules of the game', which include respecting the autonomy and equal opportunities of others to do likewise.[69] These rules (the 'criteria' of contract) are set by the institutional framework of contract law, which determines, for example, the standards of responsibility applied to parties when forming a contract. So long as the defendant has kept to the 'rules of the bargaining game', the corrective justice principle of correlativity requires that his or her reasonable expectations in the enforceability of the contract be upheld. While a distributive justice perspective would require that the outcomes of these transactions are substantively fair, with the standards by which the parties are held responsible determined according to principles of mutual benefit, reciprocity and underlying fairness, corrective justice—applying the autonomy model—is concerned only with the voluntariness of the transaction and the process by which it was created.[70]

For creditors or housing equity providers, the principle of correlativity means that they are entitled to rely on the contract unless it is found to be unenforceable due to some 'wrong' that was committed by the defendant to procure the contract (for example, duress or undue influence).[71] This framework looks to the plaintiff for self-responsibility, and to the defendant, who is entitled to rely on his reasonable expectations unless he or she is found to have 'exploited' the plaintiff. According to the liberal model, defendants should not bear the brunt of plaintiffs' losses unless they are *responsible* for those losses:

> From the ideological standpoint of liberal individualism, to refuse to enforce a contract merely because, unknown to D, P failed to bring a genuine consent to the transaction is simply to single out one member of society (D), who happens to have crossed paths with P, and to punish D for states of affairs for which he or she is not responsible.[72]

[66] As the discussions in these chapters will show, while some efforts have been made to address the welfare interests of older consumers through regulation, and good progress has been achieved in some areas, the effects remain limited, leaving a gap between the risks to which older owners are exposed and the reach of regulation.

[67] Eg, in respect of improvements to the owned home, or personal and nursing care.

[68] The possibility for this type of deficit is implicitly recognised in Bigwood's claim that 'The common law could never hope to redress all the inequalities that will inevitably affect contracting parties according to their circumstances.': Bigwood, above n 48, at 36.

[69] *Ibid*, at 20.

[70] The debates concerning procedural and substantive fairness in contract law are discussed further below, in section (4)(a).

[71] Thus, Bigwood argued that 'From a corrective justice perspective, for example, systematic background injustices may be analytically relevant only to the extent that they may transmit into situations opportunities for powerful individuals to commit certain "wrongs" against less powerful individuals in the context of particular social interactions. But the relevant *wrong* must reside in the particular *way* in which the power has been used inter se: it cannot reside merely in the presence of the power itself.': RA Bigwood, 'Conscience and the Liberal Conception of Contract: Observing Basic Distinctions—Part II' (2000) 16 *Journal of Contract Law* 191, 196.

[72] *Ibid*, at 211.

The specific content of D's responsibility in any given circumstance is therefore crucial, within the liberal model, to justify State-assisted rescission for the plaintiff's losses. It is also, as the discussion below explains, crucial in determining what actions (if any) a housing equity provider must take when contracting with (potentially) vulnerable older owners.[73] As Bigwood explained: 'Theories of corrective justice are inevitably parasitic upon more general normative theories: we need a theory of "rights" before we can know what constitutes a "wrong" warranting correction in the name of corrective justice.'[74]

The content of contract law's rights and wrongs, according to the liberal principle of autonomy, is based on the proposition that respecting the (abstract) rights and freedoms of both parties to plan and control their own lives without (wrongful) interference from others promotes their 'individual moral personality and (self-perceived) welfare in an individualistic order'.[75] This individualistic order rejects the idea that contracting parties owe any positive duty to 'benefit others or to meet their needs or desires',[76] underscored by the claim that 'no one is obliged to contract with another'.[77] Yet this claim is contestable in the context of housing equity transactions, where marginal older owners, while not compelled to contract with a specific provider, are increasingly manipulated by neoliberal policies into contractual arrangements to release housing equity, and who are likely to have limited options in terms of the products offered by contracting parties willing to do business with them. The reality of housing equity transactions for marginal older owners may be explored further through the lens of challenges to the unreality of the liberal legal subject (consonant with the political and risk subject) as a self-responsible, autonomous consumer, who chooses to enter contracts as a free and equal moral agent.

(4) Challenges to the Liberal Legal Subject

The idea that contracting parties have no positive duties towards those with whom they contract has been challenged by competing contract theories which reject the strict application of corrective justice, arguing instead that the functions of contract law include matters of distributive justice such as welfare policy and social context considerations. Waddams has described the ways in which private law concepts interact with public policy[78]; while Collins's analysis of judicial decision-making in private law identified what he has characterised as a 'hybrid' form of legal reasoning, in which decisions are justified by reference to both legal principle and social policy.[79] Collins described the style of legal reasoning employed in corrective justice theories as reminiscent of a 'past, and perhaps

[73] This theme is also developed in ch 9, which discusses Bigwood's theory of 'transactional neglect' as a mechanism for determining whether the defendant has met his or her responsibilities in respect of a potentially vulnerable plaintiff.

[74] Bigwood, above n 71, at 217.

[75] *Ibid*, at 203.

[76] *Ibid.*

[77] *Ibid.*

[78] S Waddams, *Dimensions of Private Law: Categories and Concepts in Anglo-American Legal Reasoning* (Cambridge, Cambridge University Press, 2003).

[79] Collins, above n 13. Collins used the example of the 'surety wives' cases (discussed in ch 10) to illustrate the ways in which policy-based reasoning has shaped the development of private law doctrine.

mythical, age of pure private law'.[80] While the 'classical' period of private law from the mid-nineteenth century has been characterised as providing a 'fortress of protections for individual rights',[81] the emergence of a collective 'safety-net' through the welfare State, through regulatory responses to risk and in the development of 'new spheres of private law', including consumer law,[82] also triggered a 'marked shift in private law reasoning as a whole, which became more instrumental or policy oriented'.[83]

Collins argued that through this cross-fertilisation of what were traditionally seen as distinct vehicles to achieve corrective and distributive justice, judicial reasoning in the sphere of private law 'evolved into a hybrid of the old private interest reasoning and modern policy oriented regulatory reasoning'.[84] Indeed, Collins argued that the influence of social policy considerations on English courts is now so significant that

> without the reference to policy, lawyers and judges apparently think today that legal reasoning would not provide a sufficient justification for a particular decision. In this respect private law becomes similar to regulation in that it must be judged by its results measured by welfare criteria, not just its coherent protection of principles and rights. To put the point even more bluntly: a legal decision reached in accordance with strict fidelity to principle that violates important policy considerations which are already reflected in social regulation is now regarded not just as an unfortunate decision but one that is probably a wrong decision in law.[85]

While there are undoubtedly many examples in which the courts have been so influenced by policy considerations in other private law contexts, it is interesting to note that there is little evidence to date that the regulatory policies articulated by the FSA in respect of housing equity transactions have displaced the stranglehold of liberal legal values in cognate private law decisions, even where the courts are applying legislation as opposed to common law doctrine. For example, in *UK Housing Alliance (North West) Ltd v Francis*,[86] Mr Francis invoked the Unfair Terms in Consumer Contract Regulations 1999 (SI 1999/2083) to challenge the fairness of a sale and rent back agreement containing terms which, had it been made after the commencement of the FSA's new regulatory framework for such transactions, would have been specifically prohibited, and to resist a possession action which would have been disallowed under the FSA's regime. Although the Court of Appeal had considerable scope to find the agreement 'unfair' under the broad criteria set out in the Regulations, it opted not to do so, with the Court concluding that it would not disrupt the legitimate expectations of the provider where there was no wrongdoing.[87]

The claim that courts have adopted a 'hybrid' form of legal reasoning in private law coincides with Collins's normative account, in which he argued that 'private law must always struggle with the endeavour of how to cope with the competing concerns of individual and collective interests'.[88] Collins rejected the precepts of correlativity to argue

[80] *Ibid*, at 14.
[81] *Ibid*, at 1.
[82] *Ibid*. The direct impacts of these developments on housing equity transactions is considered further in chs 8 and 9, where it is noted that while they have reduced some of the risks associated with these transactions, there are significant limits to their reach in relation to even potentially vulnerable older owners.
[83] *Ibid*, at 1.
[84] *Ibid*.
[85] *Ibid*, at 13.
[86] [2010] EWCA Civ 117.
[87] The Court held that it could not detect 'any failure to conform with "good standards of commercial morality and practice"' (*ibid*, at [29]).
[88] Collins, above n 13, at 14.

that private law 'can never limit itself to an examination of individual rights and corrective justice between two individuals. It must always have regard to collective interests, to the distributive patterns produced by its rules.'[89] Indeed, from the latter half of the twentieth century, critics of the formalist models have challenged their false claims to objectivity and the unequal effects of their schemas for formal equality. As the non-instrumentalist theorists themselves acknowledge, most contemporary scholarship recognises the relevance of 'goals' (in the form of policy or social interests) to private law, although the question of what those goals are is contested, as is the balance struck between competing goals.

A series of specific debates—the scope for private law to seek to achieve substantive versus procedural fairness, whether it is appropriate to impose liability for nonfeasance as opposed to misfeasance, and the possibility of imposing positive obligations on contracting parties in relation to the vulnerabilities of those with whom they contract—have exemplified the tensions between corrective and distributive models of contract theory, and are discussed further below. These debates are informed by the legal development of the regulatory sphere, as well as by the intellectual challenges mounted against the 'justice theories' in the late twentieth and early twenty-first centuries. For example, Collins argued that the emergence of regulation subverted the traditional paradigm of private law as a 'principles-based' system of rights and entitlements,[90]

> challeng[ing] the implicit values and ideology of the system of private law by curtailing its positive freedoms for what were perceived as more important social goals, such as distributive justice and fairer opportunity ... [This] presented an implicit challenge to the way private lawyers conceived of their subject.[91]

Thus, it was argued, the influence of regulatory reasoning 'leaked' across into common law decision-making,[92] as 'the courts began to consider the protection of consumers as an appropriate role for private law even in the absence of relevant social regulation'.[93] This blurring of boundaries between the autonomous subject of 'private law reasoning' and the vulnerabilities of (certain) consumers reflected (to some extent) in regulatory initiatives, and the *ad hoc* ways in which these patterns of reasoning are liable to overlap and merge, highlights the need for further scrutiny of the constitution of older owners as legal subjects in housing equity transactions.

At the same time, critical legal theories have challenged the assumptions underpinning formal 'equality' theories based on a liberal legal subject, and their claim to legal neutrality. While classical liberal legal thought claimed to have 'stripped its subjects of any of their social and economic power before allowing them through the gates of the law',[94] the unreality of this position was fundamentally undermined by the emergence of the critical school of legal realism. Legal realists emphasised the functions of law as a system created by humans, to govern human conduct, shaped by policies and with real social consequences.[95] From this starting-point, the realists argued that there was 'no coherent

[89] *Ibid.*
[90] *Ibid*, at 9.
[91] *Ibid.*
[92] *Ibid*, at 11.
[93] *Ibid.*
[94] Boyle, above n 1, at 515.
[95] 'The common description of law upon which all are agreed is that it is "a body of rules for the regulation of human conduct," and whether we look to the exercise of the power of legislation, or to the action of judicial

and epistemologically defensible way that [the subject could be "stripped down"] and that the attempt to do it would lead to substantively poor decisions'.[96] The role of the stripped-down subject in justificatory theories of law was also criticised on the basis that it operates as a shield for the implicit smuggling of (liberal) values into legal discourse, with 'profound political consequences that are concealed because they are loaded into the subject at such an early point in the theory'.[97]

The critical legal studies movement explicitly emphasised the distributive consequences of legal doctrine and institutions, and their role in perpetuating and reflecting political choices, social disadvantage, and relations of inequality and oppression.[98] These critiques include analyses of the ways in which law—including private law—affects distributions of risk, wealth and power,[99] and challenge the claim that 'lawyers, and especially common law judges, are to a large extent bound to accept the world as they find it'.[100] Critical legal theorists particularly challenge the 'essentialist subject' of formalist models of justice, on the basis that it 'exclud[es] on supposedly formal criteria large amounts of human experience, social context, class power, and racial, sexual, and gender difference, and thus claim[s] to be a universal and apolitical authority'.[101] Boyle argued that 'The key feature of this [essentialist] subject is that it looks empty but is actually full ... the subject's biases, motivations, and assumptions are the same ones honoured in the dominant culture.'[102] Indeed, debates concerning the essential characteristics of the legal/political subject reveal much about the biases of legal institutions, doctrines and theories. Feminist legal theorists have criticised the presentation of legal doctrine as 'abstract', 'objective' and 'impartial' as privileging what are perceived to be 'masculine' values. So too, feminist scholarship argues that legal methods that justify and privilege the 'contentless' personality of corrective justice, or the liberal legal subject, claim to strip away the context in which transactions occur, and the individual characteristics of the parties—for example, the perspective of the 'reasonable man'—in positing an 'ideal legal subject who, despite claims of neutrality is white, male, middle class, Christian'.[103]

Challenges to the classical doctrinal model of law are variously based on considerations such as economic efficiency (for example, in law-and-economics scholarship), sometimes

tribunals, we find that in every instance the thing, and the only thing, sought to be affected by law is human conduct.': JC Carter, *Law: Its Origin Growth and Function, Being a course of lectures prepared for delivery before the Law School of Harvard University* (New York, GP Putnam's Son, 1907) at 14. Carter went on to argue that 'Of course in connection with human conduct everything which directly bears upon it, including especially the nature and constitution of man, and the environment in which he is placed, becomes part of the field of fact to be studied, for these are causes constantly operating upon conduct and affecting it. Human conduct, therefore, with everything bearing upon and restraining it, constitutes the arena of fact which the student seeking for a knowledge of the true nature of law must explore, and an attentive survey of this field, and a just arrangement of its contents can, I think, scarcely fail to clear up much of the confusion and uncertainty which now obscure our conceptions of the origin, nature and function of the law.' (*ibid*, at 14–15).

[96] Boyle, above n 1, at 515.

[97] *Ibid*, at 518.

[98] Cane, above n 9, at 205.

[99] *Ibid.*

[100] Bigwood, above n 48, at 35.

[101] Boyle, above n 1, at 514.

[102] *Ibid.*

[103] E Bonthuys, 'Accommodating Gender, Race, Culture and Religion: Outside Legal Subjectivity' (2002) 18 *South Africa Journal of Human Rights* 41, 55; see also C Smart, 'Law's Power, the Sexed Body, and Feminist Discourse' (1990) 17 *Journal of Law and Society* 194, 210; MJ Mossman, 'Feminism and Legal Method: The Difference it Makes' (1986) 3 *Australian Journal of Law and Society* 30.

linked to the ideology of market-individualism with its emphasis on competitive exchange, security of transactions, freedom of contract, sanctity of contract and so on[104]; or the welfare of the parties (or 'consumers' as a particular category of party) based on principles of fairness and reasonableness, non-exploitation and so on. Behavioural economics has challenged the classical economic model of efficiency using psychological and empirical evidence that captures the reality of decision-making, and which in turn challenges the ways in which the traditional assumptions of economics have informed law.[105] Critical 'identity-based' analyses that emphasise particular substantive inequalities (and thus discrimination), based on age, gender, race, class, disability and so on, offer alternative frameworks by which to analyse the role of law (as an institution and through legal doctrine and decisions) in perpetuating inequalities. The remainder of this chapter explores alternative perspectives with particular relevance to the issues raised thus far concerning the housing equity transactions of older owners. This analysis provides a basis for thinking about how the range of laws, policies and regulations applied to these 'private' transactions can be most appropriately evaluated, beginning with the challenges that have been made to 'pure' liberal subjectivity within the contract paradigm.

(a) Substantive fairness

The classical model of contract law has always included principles and doctrines which recognise the vulnerabilities of particular subjects (children, parties who enter contracts under duress, undue influence, etc). However, these 'special protections' are consistent with contract law's liberal subject, to the extent that the claimant is treated as lacking capacity or autonomy and the defendant is fixed with agency-responsibility for the plaintiff due to 'advantage-taking' in the transaction.[106] These doctrines do not, therefore, detract from the classical paradigm, which posits that, so long as the parties to a contract have capacity, normative choices about the responsibilities of the 'stronger' party within the liberal model are based on the tenets of the bargaining 'game', the rules of which allow that 'obtaining a material advantage, *per se*, is a valid aim of contractual bargains'.[107] In this model, parties—unless they have, for some exceptional reason, lost their autonomy—are treated as liberal subjects, whose preference to be recognised as 'agents in freedom of action' leads them to want their choices, whether good or bad, to be respected and enforced. This approach places less emphasis on the fairness of outcomes for individual parties and focuses more on overall outcomes, on the basis that

> [p]rovided that [plaintiffs] do in fact gain in the long run, the overall welfare of society is still enhanced as a result, and a wealthy society is better able to provide for its disadvantaged or

[104] See, eg, JN Adams and R Brownsword, 'The Ideologies of Contract' (1987) 7 *Legal Studies* 205.

[105] See, eg, C Sunstein (ed), *Behavioural Law and Economics* (Cambridge, Cambridge University Press, 2000); see also discussions of behavioural analyses relevant to housing equity transactions in the next section, as well as in ch 2, section (5) and ch 6, section (3).

[106] R Bigwood, 'Contracts by Unfair Advantage: From Exploitation to Transactional Neglect' (2005) 25 *OJLS* 65, 74–75.

[107] *Ibid*, at 77–78.

'unlucky' members, through general (minimally intrusive) programmes of redistribution, than an impoverished society.[108]

The corrective justice orientation of both non-instrumentalist and liberal models of private law means that the 'fairness' justification for interfering with the agreements of contracting parties is limited to *procedural* fairness (that is, fairness in the process of contract formation) and does not extend to the *substantive* fairness of the contract that results from this process (ie the terms, and particularly the price, of the contract).[109] Corrective justice approaches to private law justify interventions based on procedural unfairness on the basis that complying with the 'rules of the bargaining game' in the process of contract formation comprises part of the parties' responsibility not to harm others. Yet so long as these rules are observed, corrective justice-based analyses posit that the contract that results is enforceable regardless of any substantive unfairness in its terms, because it represents an agreement which the parties have reached as free and rational moral agents. According to this view, where the choices that a party has made result in a substantively unfair contract, this is not analytically relevant to the doctrinal rules of common law contract. If one accepts the premise that basic liberty includes 'the liberty to make bad, even very bad, bargains'[110] then respecting that liberty requires that parties are held even to substantively unfair contracts, so long as the 'rules of the game' have been respected in the formation of the contract.[111] To do otherwise, the liberal model holds, would be (inappropriately) to protect the parties' welfare interests rather than (the proper concern of private law) to protect their autonomy interests.[112]

As the discussion above has noted, the liberal model is based on an idealised conception of the legal subject, which assumes that transactional decision-making will be based on rational choices making optimum use of the information disclosed at the time of the transaction. The assumptions inherent in this model—which also underpin much of the content of procedural fairness protections, emphasising the clear disclosure of information in the process of contract formation—have been critiqued on several bases. Empirical insights from behavioural economics have shown that consumers do not necessarily make financial decisions according to the classical model of the 'rational economic man', and

[108] *Ibid*, at 88. Bigwood recognised that contemporary perspectives on contract and commercial law do not necessarily view its aims in such stark terms but allow some scope for principles of morality and fair play—so long as they are understood within the liberal framework.

[109] This 'orthodox' model is explained on several grounds, including claims that substantive fairness is meaningless, indistinguishable from procedural fairness, impossible to assess, not valuable, beyond the competence of the courts to assess and so on; S Smith, 'In defence of substantive fairness' (1996) 112 *LQR* 138. See R Epstein, 'Unconscionability: A Critical Reappraisal' (1975) 18 *Journal of Law and Economics* 283, 305–15; AA Leff, 'Unconscionability and the Code—the Emperor's New Clause' (1967) 115 *University of Pennsylvania Law Review* 485, 487; C Fried, *Contract as Promise* (Cambridge, MA, Harvard University Press, 1981) chs 3 and 7; RE Barnett, 'A Consent Theory of Contract' (1986) 86 *University of Colorado LR* 269, 283–86; M Trebilcock, 'An Economic Approach to Unconscionability' in B Reiter and J Swan (eds), *Studies in Contract Law* (Toronto, Butterworths, 1980); A Schwartz, 'Justice and the Law of Contract: a Case for the Traditional Approach' (1986) 9 *Harvard Journal of Law & Public Policy* 107; R Nozick, *Anarchy, State and Utopia* (New York, Basic Books, 1974) at 64–65; L von Mies, *Human Action: A Treatise on Economics*, 2nd edn (New Haven, Conn, Yale University Press, 1963) 94–98, 242, 354, 727–30; J Gordley, 'Equality in Exchange' (1981) 69 *California Law Review* 1587; J Gordley, *The Philosophical Origins of Modern Contract Doctrine* (Oxford, Clarendon Press, 1991).

[110] Bigwood, above n 71, at 199.

[111] Bigwood argued that commitment to the liberal model requires that contract law hold this position, notwithstanding the 'popular sentiment and intuitive appeal' of substantive fairness provisions; 'contract law must sometimes ignore moral intuition of what is fair and unfair' (*ibid*, at 200).

[112] *Ibid*, at 201.

have suggested that, in reality, procedural protections may not be sufficient to enable parties to protect themselves or to avoid harms when making economic and legal decisions. It has also been argued that while substantive fairness considerations are excluded from liberal contract theories, this disjuncture between the assumptions on which the theory is based and behavioural realities has led to substantive fairness considerations in fact being taken into account by courts more often than the dominant theoretical models would permit.[113] The distinction between procedural and substantive fairness (with only procedural fairness recognised as the concern of common law contract doctrine, and substantive justice considerations reserved as the business of political norms as expressed through legislation) is also blurred to the extent that the liberal conceptions of individual freedom and self-reliance have influenced the application of statutory provisions (for example, the Unfair Contract Terms Act 1977 and the Unfair Terms in Consumer Contracts Regulations 1999) which explicitly set out to ensure substantive fairness in consumer contracts.[114]

Some contract scholarship—notably Stephen Smith's seminal article—has sought to establish a theoretical foundation to support the instinctive view that substantive fairness is a 'distinct virtue of good contracts … that should be regulated by the law of contract'.[115] However, Smith's argument in support of legal intervention in substantively unfair contracts is also rooted in liberal legal subjectivity, inasmuch as it bases the justification for intervention on the claim that substantive unfairness harms individual autonomy. Smith argued that unfair prices in contracts 'may disrupt planning and hence our ability to lead self-directed, autonomous lives'.[116] The scope of Smith's model of substantive fairness as a legitimate objective of contract law was limited in several important respects: it was limited to considering the objective 'normality' of the price paid for the contract, and not imprudent (but objectively fair) transactions.[117] Smith argued that a subjective conception of substantive fairness (which 'might focus, for example, on the contracting parties' happiness or welfare'[118]) would be of dubious moral weight, and too difficult to apply in practice. Yet even this objective model departs from procedural fairness to the extent that it accepts that there may be circumstances in which a legal subject—a rational, adequately informed individual trading in a competitive market—might agree to pay more than the normal price for a contract for reasons other than incapacity, lack of autonomy or the 'plausible invalidating procedural defects' reflected in the vitiating factors.[119]

The liberal objection to making substantive fairness a criterion of a valid contract is rooted in the idea that as liberal subjects we are free to make bad bargains, and that it is inconsistent with this position for courts to interfere in 'parties' choices about how to live their lives. Individuals should be free to live their lives as they choose … so long as they do

[113] See, eg, S Waddams, 'Unconscionability in Contracts' (1976) 39 *MLR* 369; M Chen-Wishart, *Unconscionable Bargains* (London, Lexis Law Publishing, 1989).

[114] See generally, C Willett, *Fairness in Consumer Contracts: The Case of Unfair Terms* (Aldershot, Ashgate, 2007); and discussion in ch 8.

[115] Smith, above n 109, at 139.

[116] *Ibid.*

[117] Smith demonstrated that imprudence is wider than unfairness, reasoning that 'People do not normally agree to imprudent contracts. Unfair contracts are imprudent, but so are many fair contracts—for example a contract in which an elderly person invests all her savings in a high risk scheme.' (*ibid*, at 146).

[118] *Ibid*, at141.

[119] *Ibid*, at 142–43.

not coerce, defraud, or manipulate others.'[120] Smith's challenge to this view was rooted in the characterisation of contract law as an enabling or 'power-conferring legal doctrine',[121] which expands rather than contracts the scope of individual freedom by helping people to do certain things which are regarded as good. This starting-point legitimates a sphere of inquiry into the harm that the institution of contract might, directly or indirectly, bring about,[122] offering valuable critical potential for the analysis of housing equity transactions in this book. As the discussion in chapter six will demonstrate, the particular impact of harms resulting from bad housing equity contracts is core to the justification of 'special protection' for vulnerable older owners. This line of scrutiny also anticipates the discussion of Fineman's 'vulnerable legal subject' in chapter six,[123] which emphasises the responsibilities of the State—including its responsibilities through (private) law as an institution of the State—to respond to the real vulnerabilities of actual legal subjects.

Smith argued that while 'the enforcement of contracts is presumably a good thing generally … a substantively unfair contract is not the sort of contract the law should promote.'[124] This justified the State in refusing to enforce substantively unfair contracts, because

> the state should only lend a hand to endeavours that help individuals to achieve well-being and thus to realise fulfilling lives … Contract prices can affect contracting parties' abilities to achieve fulfilling lives [drawing on] … the importance, for well-being, of leading an autonomous, self-directed, life and, more specifically, having a threshold level of material wealth.[125]

This analysis recognised the unreality of the liberal model of legal subjectivity by inherently accepting the subjective inequalities of some contracting parties. It also recognised—with particular implications for the discussion of older owners, vulnerability and housing equity transactions in this book—the differential impact of adverse outcomes for the abilities of the parties who are left to bear the losses of bad transactional outcomes to lead 'autonomous lives'.[126] Yet while Smith recognised that adverse outcomes are clearly instrumental in shaping the instinctive view that some contracts are 'bad', the inequalities that cause particular parties to be especially vulnerable to adverse impacts fall outside the definitional scope of his model of 'substantive unfairness'. Since this concept of 'fairness' is delineated as a 'relational concept', objections to contracts on the basis that they leave someone in poverty carry no weight because they are not necessarily related to the other contracting party.

The role of substantive fairness protections in facilitating and encouraging transactions is also of particular salience in relation to housing equity transactions, in light of evidence that indicates that concerns amongst older owners that equity release products are not

[120] *Ibid*, at 145.

[121] For a discussion of law as power-conferring, see HLA Hart, *The Concept of Law* (Oxford, Clarendon Press, 1961) 27–38.

[122] Smith, above n 109, at 154.

[123] See section 6.

[124] Smith, above n 109, at 145.

[125] *Ibid*, at 150.

[126] 'It is not necessary to be rich to lead an autonomous life, but it is necessary to have one's basic physical needs met. Individuals whose every choice is dictated by the need to survive cannot lead autonomous lives. They are unable to direct their lives in any meaningful sense. A contract at abnormal prices can leave a contracting party in this position.' (*ibid*).

good value for money, or that their complexity makes it difficult for consumers confidently to judge the fairness of their terms, are significant barriers to equity release for many older owners.[127] Smith argued that legal rules requiring substantive fairness in respect of price can help to overcome such barriers, so that

> in situations where one of the contracting parties is unsure of the normal price for a good, a requirement that goods be sold at normal prices can facilitate contracting. The risk of paying more than the normal price for a good can make people hesitate to contract in some situations. The risk can be decreased by studying more carefully the terms of contracts and by researching market prices, but these moves are costly. If contracting parties have an assurance that contracts at above normal price will not be honoured, they will more readily and easily enter into contracts.[128]

The policy drivers supporting such a strategy are strong in light of the State's enthusiasm for self-provision by encashing housing equity use to meet needs in later life. In addition to the reassurance that the possibility of legal intervention when a contract is substantively unfair might offer for individual owners, it could also function to discipline traders against offering products that are not fairly priced, and thereby improve consumer confidence in the equity release market.

This line of reasoning was also evident in Buckley's argument for legal intervention where contracts are substantively unfair. The basis for upsetting such contracts was rooted in an efficiency analysis (rather than welfare considerations), in the belief that legal cover against substantively unfair terms would encourage 'bargainers' to trade, and so to exploit the opportunities for gain that trading presents.[129] The criterion of fairness applied in this analysis was the economic measure of 'whether contractual gains are divided in an equitable manner',[130] and three alternative theories were offered to justify substantive fairness norms. The first line of argument claimed that substantive fairness protections would minimise the socially wasteful 'precaution costs' that arise when parties are excessively anxious about the fairness of contractual terms; a second analysis posited that fairness review by the court would increase the overall level of contracting (by building consumer confidence); and a third model reasoned that the parties' own costs of screening for unfairness are reduced when there is a possibility for judicial review of substantive fairness.

The goals that underpin these justifications for legal intervention against substantive unfairness are not the welfare considerations associated with the adverse impact of substantively unfair outcomes on weaker parties; instead they are the economic efficiency goals of disciplining of traders, facilitating contracting, and the liberal legal argument that substantively unfair contracts make it more difficult for subjects to plan and control their autonomous lives by 'upsetting the material foundations upon which plans and aspirations are built'.[131] A crucial issue for such arguments is whether they differentiate legal subjects based on varying abilities, depending on knowledge, skills and experience, to

[127] See discussion in ch 5, section (5).
[128] Smith, above n 109, at 149.
[129] FH Buckley, 'Three Theories of Substantive Fairness' [1990] 19 *Hofstra Law Review* 33 at 34.
[130] *Ibid*, at 35.
[131] Smith, above n 109, at 151. Smith compared the principle of substantive fairness (in the form of 'normal' pricing) to the rule of law in promoting clarity, stability and prospective planning, arguing that protection against substantive unfairness seeks to ensure that 'avoidable, undesired, uncertainty [is] not promoted by the law': *ibid*.

plan, to avoid harms, to safeguard one's own interests or to prevent harm to others. By locating the argument within contract doctrine, proponents of substantive fairness provisions are committed to focusing on the correlative relationship between contracting parties (the basis on which a party is 'held responsible' for the unfairness must satisfy the criterion of correlativity) rather than broader contextual factors and welfare consequences. Yet at the same time, Smith recognised that the reasons why parties enter into substantively unfair contracts cannot always be referenced to their own capacity or autonomy but may be attributable to contextual factors such as the complexity of contract or the market in which they are transacting: there are circumstances in which self-interested parties may enter into contracts that are substantively unfair.[132]

Smith also recognised that certain 'gaining parties' are in a privileged position to prevent harms in certain transactions, whether because of their relatively superior information or knowledge, or because of their skills or experiences in the market. He argued that it would be 'consistent with ordinary conceptions of fairness' that such parties are held responsible for preventing these harms. This approach also provides a starting-point for the argument that the scope of the responsibilities placed on contracting parties might include preventing harms to transactional partners where the 'stronger' party is specifically equipped to do so.

The proposition that certain parties might bear particular responsibilities towards those with whom they contract raises another complex issue for contract theory: the distinction between misfeasance (duties not to harm others) and nonfeasance (duties to help or prevent harm). For classical contract doctrine, the idea that parties are subject to a duty, within the transaction, to help the other party or protect him from harm is inconsistent with the characterisation of contracting as a game of 'advantage, strategy, and power'.[133] Smith challenged this characterisation of contract, arguing that the function of contract law as a 'power-conferring doctrine' connotes that its purpose is to encourage 'interaction and cooperation' rather than adversarial game-playing; and that the rules of this 'voluntary cooperative venture' require—as a matter of fairness—'that participants do their share in preventing the harm that the venture might bring about'.[134] By this analysis, the individual's freedom from the duty of nonfeasance 'does not apply once individuals enter the world of contract'.[135] This position opens up new possibilities for considering how the potential losses of a joint venture should be allocated, including the possibility that 'responsibility' for losses is more appropriately determined according to a fairness-based strategy of allocating the burden to the party best able to bear it, rather than the classical liberal requirement that there must be 'wrongdoing' before the legitimate expectations of contracting parties can be disappointed.[136]

[132] Smith accepted that even if the harms that result from such unfair contracts are rare, 'the infrequency of a problem is no reason to ignore it': *ibid*, at 156.

[133] Bigwood, above n 71, at 207.

[134] Smith, above n 109, at 155.

[135] *Ibid*, at 154.

[136] Eg, Bigwood argued that, according to the liberal conception of contract, 'only exploitation, which *ex hypothesi* involves wrongful ("unconscientious") conduct on the part of D, *justifies* our taking the transaction from D in order to do it. Only *exploitation* trumps our concern for D's desert or "reasonable expectations."': Bigwood, above n 71, at 210.

Smith's substantive fairness analysis would treat the 'gaining party's' failure to act where he had the opportunity to prevent harm, as a positive act of unfairness.[137] This analysis clearly distinguished the responsibilities of contracting parties from those of the 'mere bystanders' of English tort law. The subject of tort law is not generally liable for 'nonfeasance' or failure to act, as English law does not impose duties to act in protection of others, or to rescue them, except in limited circumstances,[138] for example where a defendant creates the risk (however blamelessly) and then fails to control it[139]; when the defendant has voluntarily assumed responsibility and induced the plaintiff to rely on him; where society as a whole relies on a group of defendants (eg solicitors) to carry out a task once undertaken; and where the defendant is in a position of 'special responsibility' towards the plaintiff.[140] While Bigwood's liberal conception of contract echoed the philosophical commitment to non-liability for nonfeasance,[141] the applicability of this principle within contractual relationships is undermined by the fact that the parties to a contract have clearly established a (voluntarily undertaken) relationship which has generated specific obligations *inter se*. The tortious principle is based on the lack of proximity/relationship between the parties, with the exceptional circumstances all involving cases in which the defendant is no longer a 'bystander' but has an easily identifiable relationship with the plaintiff that has generated a duty to act. Thus, Smith argued:

> The parties [to a contract] are, by their own choice, no longer strangers to each other. If individuals object to being required to consider the well-being of others, they should not enter contracts or at least not ask for the state's help to enforce those contracts.[142]

The idea of contract as a 'power-conferring doctrine', underpinned by values of interaction and cooperation, led Smith to argue that the 'gaining party' in an abnormally-priced contract is subject to a responsibility to prevent harm, where the prevention of the particular harm is more within its power than that of the plaintiff. Indeed, the characterisation of contractual obligation that supported Smith's doctrine of substantive fairness is of as much interest for the purposes of this analysis as the relatively narrow doctrine itself. By re-casting the contractual relationship in terms which direct inquiry towards the responsibilities of 'gaining parties', alongside the conceptualisation of the 'losing party' as 'in a comparatively weak position to avoid paying that [unfair] price',[143] the framework which Smith has built substitutes the discursive tropes of vulnerability (of the losing

[137] '... the gaining party acted unfairly in failing to prevent a harm that he could have prevented more easily than the losing party': Smith, above n 109, at 155.

[138] The distinction between liability for feasance and nonfeasance was confirmed by the House of Lords in *Stovin v Wise* [1996] 3 All ER 801 at 807, when Lord Nicholls stated that for a 'duty to rescue' to arise: 'Something more is required than being a bystander. There must be some additional reason why it is fair and reasonable that one person should be regarded as his brother's keeper and have legal obligations in that regard.' For criticisms of the distinction between feasance and nonfeasance, see AM Honoré, 'Law, Morals and Rescue' in JM Ratcliffe (ed), *The Good Samaritan and the Law* (Garden City, NY, Anchor Books, 1966); AM Honoré, *Making Law Bind, Essays Legal and Philosophical* (Oxford, Clarendon Press, 1987) 256 *et seq*; EJ Weinrib, 'The Case for a Duty to Rescue' (1980) 90 *Yale Law Journal* 247.

[139] Although this is regarded as feasance rather than nonfeasance.

[140] For discussion of the circumstances in which English courts have identified liability for nonfeasance, see J Kortmann, *Altruism in Private Law: Liability for Nonfeasance and Negotiorum Gestio* (Oxford, Oxford University Press, 2005) ch 5.

[141] See Bigwood, above n 48, at 207–13.

[142] Smith, above n 109, at 154–55.

[143] *Ibid*, at 155. Smith defined 'substantively unfair contracts' as abnormal price contracts 'that are harmful and in which the losing party was in a comparatively weak position to protect himself' (*ibid*).

party) and responsibility (of the gaining party, to prevent the harm) for classical contract law's commitment to the autonomy and self-responsibility of the losing party, and freedom to take advantage (up to the point of wrongdoing) on the side of the gaining party. This deployment of the tropes of vulnerability and responsibility opens up new theoretical avenues in which to explore the justificatory norms that govern older owners' housing equity transactions, which are considered further in chapter six, in relation to Fineman's 'vulnerable legal subject'.

(b) Relational contract theory

Relational contract theory offers a powerful critique of orthodox contract law by exposing the assumptions that law makes about the behaviour of contracting parties, and the legal consequences attributed to such behaviour.[144] It posits a conception of contract law which challenges the 'discrete and self-interested' neo-classical paradigm of contracting to argue that the reality of exchange relationships requires a longer-term view of self-interest that looks beyond the gains to be made in an individual transaction and recognises the relational character of contracting, which relies on the parties demonstrating co-operation, trust, flexibility and altruism. This perspective has obvious implications for the norms that give content to contract law[145]; relational contract theory reasons from the reality of the contractual relationship to critique the application of liberal norms which fail to recognise the importance of context to the transactions.

While long-term agreements are often identified as the 'typical' relational contract, the insights offered by relational theory—particularly 'its wider engagement with the role of the social matrix'[146]—have also been applied more broadly to critique the assumptions and values of neoclassical contract law.[147] Relational theory is sceptical about the centrality of 'consent' and agreement in classical contract theory, reasoning that 'almost any contract will have more complicated consequences than anyone can possibly have in mind at once'.[148] It also challenges theories which purport to rely on an objective model of individual autonomy, and specifically consent, as the basis for the contractual obligation, arguing that they are in fact 'using consent-based language to express and justify norms

[144] See, eg, I Macneil, 'Relational Contract Theory: Challenges and Queries' (1999) 94 *Northwestern University Law Review* 877; D Campbell (ed), *The Relational Theory of Contract—Selected Works of Ian Macneil* (London, Sweet & Maxwell, 2001); J Feinman, 'Relational Contract Theory in Context' (1999) 94 *Northwestern University Law Review* 737; J Wightman, 'Commentary on *Baird Textile Holdings v Marks & Spencer plc*' in R Hunter, C McGlynn and E Rackley (eds), *Feminist Judgments: From Theory to Practice* (Oxford, Hart Publishing, 2010) 186.

[145] See, eg, I Macneil, 'Contracts: Adjustments of Long-Term Economic Relations under Classical, Neoclassical and Relational Contract Law' (1978) 192 *Northwestern University Law Review* 854; I Macneil, 'Relational Contract: What We Do and Do Not Know' (1985) 3 *Wisconsin Law Review* 483; D Campbell, H Collins and J Wightman (eds), *Implicit Dimensions of Contract: Discrete, Relational, and Network Contracts* (Oxford, Hart Publishing, 2003).

[146] J Wightman, 'From individual conduct to transactional risk: some relational thoughts about unconscionability regulation' in M Kenny, J Devenney and L Fox O'Mahony, *Unconscionability in European Private Financial Transactions: Protecting the Vulnerable* (Cambridge, Cambridge University Press, 2010) at 100.

[147] Wightman noted that Macneil's work did not regard *only* long-term contracts as having relational elements: *ibid*, at 101–02; while Campbell argued that even discrete (or 'one-off') contracts have 'relational elements', rooted in their dependence on the social institutions and practices that constitute them: D Campbell, 'The Relational Constitution of the Discrete Contract' in D Campbell and P Vincent (eds), *Contract and Economic Organisation* (Dartmouth, Aldershot, 1996).

[148] Wightman, above n 146, at 103.

which are not derivable from explicit consent'.[149] The effect of anchoring contract law in the classical concepts (autonomy, consent, agreement, wrongdoing), relational theorists argue, has been to 'muffle' the real impact of transactional context in the practice of contracting.[150] Thus, Wightman argued, once consent is de-centred, it becomes clear that most contractual norms are socially derived, 'from the nature of the parties' evolving relationship, the practices of a particular market sector, or from society in general'.[151] Since relational theory regards the origin of norms as social rather than individual, it naturally focuses on the social context of transactions to determine the rights and responsibilities of the parties.

The analysis of housing equity transactions in this book is consistent with the fundamental orientation of the relational approach inasmuch as it focuses on the 'transactional context' of the exchange between the older owner and the housing equity provider, to identify 'the whole of the law relating to exchanges in that context … includ[ing] not just private law beyond contract, but all forms of regulation of the subject matter of the exchanges'.[152] The focus on social context allows relational scholars to consider whether the characteristics of the particular type of transaction, in interaction with the conduct of the parties, create unusual risks for one party to the contract. This feature is of particular salience in relation to housing equity transactions for older owners, the particular risk features of which have been implicitly recognised by the FSA through their decision to regulate some equity release products.[153] At the same time, the complex relationships and interplay between common law contract and property doctrines, statutory provisions (and judicial interpretation thereof) and regulatory schema in the governance of housing equity transactions also militate in favour of a 'whole system' approach.

The roots of the relational approach in the social origins of norms (so departing from the liberal emphasis on the individual) allow relational analyses to recognise that particular transactional contexts pose heightened risks for individual claimants.[154] The categories of circumstance in which contracts law recognises that contracting may present particular risks for claimants may be classified as:

a) personal characteristic risk (for example, children as a category of persons with characteristics such as inexperience or lack of foresight, which make contracting a high-risk activity for them);
b) relational risk (for example, the 'relationship of trust and confidence' recognised by presumed undue influence)[155]; and
c) transactional risk (based on the nature of the transaction).[156]

Wightman argued that, where circumstances of heightened risk are recognised in law, this has the effect of shifting the burden of proof of validity to the defendant, who must

[149] *Ibid.*
[150] *Ibid*, at 106.
[151] *Ibid*, at 103.
[152] *Ibid*, at 104.
[153] See ch 9.
[154] Wightman, n 146 at 107, discusses the example of presumed undue influence.
[155] See ch 10.
[156] Wightman, n146.

establish the legitimacy of the transaction by demonstrating that specific requirements have been met (that its responsibilities in respect of the claimant have been discharged).

The particular risks posed by housing equity transactions were considered in chapter three, while the idea that older owners bear particular 'personal characteristic risks' due to inherent vulnerabilities is discussed in chapter six. Yet the contractual risk model employed in relational theory does not—in contrast to the liberal model—limit the scope of the inquiry to the correlative conduct of the contracting parties or their 'internal' individual characteristics (for example, their autonomy/capacity). Rather, it allows other, external contextual factors—viewed by doctrinal lawyers as an 'analytical last resort'[157]—to play a central role in the balance of risk. The relational approach 'is open in attempting to identify the relevant norms in a context, and in assessing how the law may express these'.[158] This ready reference to context is significant in light of the role of situational vulnerabilities and, particularly, the impact of harms in older owners' housing equity transactions; the relational approach explicitly links contractual norms and rules with outcomes.[159] Thus, Wightman has argued that relational contract theory's recognition of contractual risk based on the nature and context of the transaction 'can be seen to have affinities with some regulatory techniques, as well as some pre-classical doctrine'.[160] The shift away from consent-based approaches also opens up scope to consider substantive (rather than purely procedural) unfairness in terms of the responsibilities of a stronger party in a 'high-risk' transactional context.

Wightman offers the example of presumed undue influence, and particularly the shift in the burden of proof to the defendant to establish the legitimacy of the transaction once the 'high-risk' context (the relationship of trust and confidence) has been made out, as

> an example of a distinctive approach … characterised by the way in which the heightened risks to the claimant, posed by features of the contractual context, become the reason for the law to adopt a different approach to assessing the validity of a contract … this approach is more explicit in taking account of contextual factors.[161]

Wightman went on to argue that the contractual risk inherently recognised in undue influence cases is based on 'a perception of increased risk in the claimant's position', which is not dependent on individual conduct in a specific case but which recognises heightened risk across a category of situations.[162] The responsibilities of stronger parties towards those who are vulnerable to heightened risk in these 'contractual risk' situations are reflected in the

> perception that in particular circumstances the degree of risk to the claimant is such that it is justified to require the defendant to demonstrate the legitimacy of the contract. Instead of the claimant having to establish specific evidence which leads to the contract being set aside, the defendant has to establish positive reasons why the contract should stand.[163]

This model of contractual enforceability starts from the view that certain categories of transaction, which involve heightened risk of an adverse outcome for the weaker party,

[157] *Ibid*, at 104.
[158] *Ibid.*
[159] *Ibid.*
[160] *Ibid*, at 100.
[161] *Ibid*, at 107.
[162] *Ibid.*
[163] *Ibid*, at 109.

may be treated differently in law so that the responsibility for protecting the interests of the weaker party shifts to the stronger party.[164]

Applying this analysis to housing equity transactions raises a crucial question about the nature of the vulnerabilities to which, it is suggested, law should respond through contractual norms. As the discussion in chapter six will demonstrate, the practical and theoretical justifiability of any claim for 'special protection' in housing equity transactions must be based on a real assessment of the sources of older owners' vulnerabilities (for example, the internal vulnerabilities linked to capacity and capability; situational vulnerabilities linked to socio-economic and financial contexts; and the differential impact of harm resulting from the older owner's capacity for resilience). Wightman categorised contractual risks according to their source in 'personal characteristics' (for example, minors, or 'poor and ignorant persons'[165]), in particular types of relationship (for example, where undue influence is presumed) and 'where the nature of the transaction itself creates an increased risk that the claimant will suffer disadvantage.'[166] The choice of category is crucial to the implications of any protection offered: for example, where a protection for older owners was based on 'personal characteristic risk', this would necessarily imply vulnerability that is internal to the person, which may be inaccurate and which implies undesirable characteristics of dependency in the older person.

In contrast, the model of transactional risk has significantly greater potential for useful application in the context of older owners. Transactional risk may be based on a combination of factors, including the contextual or situational vulnerabilities of the parties,[167] the complex nature of the transaction and the potentially adverse impact of bad outcomes, which reflect the 'real' vulnerabilities of marginal older owners in housing equity transactions. It shifts the emphasis away from the questions of consent/autonomy on the part of the weaker party and wrongdoing of the stronger party, but responds instead to the '*risk* of disadvantage in a category of transactions, rather than with whether that risk eventuated in a specific case'.[168] Wightman argued that the 'Etridge code' applies a transactional risk approach to non-commercial surety transactions[169] by imposing responsibilities on banks to guard against risks that they have not themselves created. While he recognised that such a move is 'extremely unusual for the judge-made law of contract',[170] he claimed that it is consistent with a shift in the law of undue influence, away from consent/autonomy and wrongdoing considerations, to concerns with substantive unfairness and the responsibilities of the lender. The transactional risk model in common law contract echoes the regulatory approach to financial transactions in that, by articulating the responsibilities of the lender, it seeks to avoid harms across a class of transactions, rather than simply providing for remedies in particular cases (prevention rather than cure).

[164] *Ibid*, at 109–10.

[165] In the context of unconscionable bargain doctrine, see *Fry v Lane* (1887) 40 Ch D 312; see discussion in ch 10.

[166] Wightman, above n 146, at 113.

[167] Wightman uses the example of 'catching bargains', where the expectant heir was poorly-off, in 'necessitous circumstances' and selling a future interest which is subject to hyperbolic discounting (see *ibid*, at 114); this type of transaction has clear parallels with the housing equity transactions of older owners.

[168] *Ibid*, at 115.

[169] *Ibid*, at 117; see discussion in ch 10.

[170] *Ibid*, at 118.

Wightman identified three criteria by which, he argued, it might be possible to identify circumstances in which the transactional risk of a particular type of contract justifies displacing the orthodox 'consent/wrongdoing' paradigm in favour of a vulnerability/responsibility approach. The first is that the transaction has an element of 'futurity' in the claimant's performance of the contract. In the case of housing equity transactions, this is evident in the delayed transfer of possession in home reversions and sale and rent back transactions, or in the future execution of the security attached to a lifetime mortgage (usually, according to the terms of the contract, when the owner dies or ceases to occupy the property). The second criterion identified by Wightman was 'a degree of transactional complexity which makes it more than usually difficult for the claimant to make an informed judgment about what is in their interests'.[171] Again, it has been widely recognised in the regulatory sphere that the products that enable equity release are particularly complex, while the complex risks that older owners must negotiate in planning for their financial futures are redolent with the difficulties of assessing risks and benefits for an uncertain future.[172] Lastly, Wightman suggested that for transactional risk to be present there must be a 'clear disparity between the parties in terms of their experience of entering such transactions',[173] which places the claimant at a specific disadvantage in the process of negotiation.[174]

Wightman argued that the main challenge for law in responding to transactional risk is that the normal orientation of existing theoretical frameworks remains limited, and typically bound to the neoclassical, liberal commitments to choice, consent and autonomy. Even behavioural economics is

> not oriented to address the larger normative question of what obligations are owed when an organisation that is very familiar with the pitfalls (and opportunities for exploitation) of a particular transaction routinely deals with parties who are traversing those pitfalls for the first time; this is ultimately a question about the form of exchange morality which is to be expressed in the law ...[175]

However, relational contract theory foregrounds these norms through its reliance on the 'established understandings, and the practices of a community of regular contractors of which they are part',[176] with limiting implications for vulnerable parties (for example, marginal older owners) who are outside that community of 'regular contractors', and where it is the '*absence* of implicit background understandings which prevents the inexperienced party participating fully in the formation of the contract'.[177]

In the search for alternatives to the theoretical framework offered by (neo)classical liberalism, feminist theories have offered critical challenges to the dominance of the liberal model both generally and specific to contract law. Indeed, many scholars have drawn links between the socially normative nature of contract as expressed in relational contract

[171] *Ibid*, at 123.
[172] *Ibid*, see discussion in ch 3.
[173] *Ibid.*
[174] 'These features mean that "one shot" players will find it especially difficult to make sound judgments in the absence of independent advice. Without such advice, there can be something approaching a trap which requires parties to tread very carefully. This creates the clear opportunity for defendants (or a third party) to take advantage of the fact that claimants may not be in a position to act in their best interests.' (*ibid*).
[175] *Ibid*, at 124.
[176] *Ibid*, at 125.
[177] *Ibid*, at 126.

theory, and the alternative theoretical frameworks offered by feminism.[178] Feminist theories of contract have challenged the privileging of 'masculine' assumptions and values—that people are disconnected, adversarial and strategic game-players, with opposing interests, the absence of obligations not voluntarily assumed—over what are perceived to be the more 'feminine' ethics of care, connection and responsibility, obligation and co-operation.[179] Mulcahy has argued that 'The deficit in the explanatory power of neo-classical ideology and doctrine has created a conceptual lacuna, which feminist writers ... are well placed to inhabit',[180] and that

> [t]he ['feminine'] ethic of care represents a distinctive approach to the understanding of relationships and has its own moral vocabulary, moral epistemology and explanatory force. It offers a direct contrast to the classical model in that it stresses the importance of intimacy, community and relational actors embedded in particular contexts.[181]

Feminist contract scholarship has emphasised norms of responsibility and underlined the importance of context to contract relationships, while also recognising the difficulties posed by claims of dependency and vulnerability against the backdrop of the 'autonomous and independent actor of liberal politics and contract theory'.[182] Feminist theory has also, more fundamentally, challenged the dominance of the liberal legal subject,[183] and offered alternative frameworks within which legal subjectivity could be more realistically, and more appropriately, conceived. Specifically, Fineman's 'vulnerable legal subject' offers an alternative theoretical framework based on the tropes of vulnerability and responsibility. The scope for applying feminist theory to address the transactional risk of housing equity transactions, and the particular contribution of Fineman's 'vulnerable legal subject' in overcoming the problematic connotations of dependency and vulnerability, are considered in chapter six. The following section sets out the characterisation of the

[178] See, eg, J Wightman, 'Intimate relationships, relational contract theory and the reach of contract' (2000) 8 *Feminist Legal Studies* 93; P Vincent-Jones, Contractual governance: institutional and organisational analysis' (2000) 20 *OJLS* 317; A Belcher, 'A feminist perspective on contract theories from law and economics' (2000) 8 *Feminist Legal Studies* 29; and in US scholarship, C Dalton, 'An Essay in the Deconstruction of Contract Doctrine' (1985) 94 *Yale Law Journal* 997; E Mertz, 'An Afterword: Tapping the Promise of Relational Contract Theory—'Real' Legal Language and a New Legal Realism' (2000) 94 *Northwestern University Law Review* 909; DL Threedy, 'Feminists and Contract Doctrine' (1999) 32 *Indiana Law Review* 1247.

[179] Although these values are central to the ongoing relationships of long-term, 'relational' contracts. For discussion of 'masculine' and 'feminine' values in contract, see, eg, L Mulcahy, 'The Limitations of Love and Altruism: Feminist Perspectives on Contract Law' in L Mulcahy and S Wheeler (eds), *Feminist Perspectives on Contract Law* (London, Cavendish, 2005). Similar arguments have been made in respect of the dominant, 'masculinity' of property law: see, eg, K Green, 'Being Here—What a Woman Can Say About Land Law' in A Bottomley (ed), *Feminist Perspectives on the Foundational Subjects of Law* (London, Cavendish, 1996); and in feminist economics, see, eg, SF Feiner and BB Roberts, 'Hidden by the Invisible Hand: Neoclassical Economics Theory and the Textbook Treatment of Race and Gender' in AL Aerni and K McGoldrick (eds), *Valuing Us All: Feminist Pedagogy and Economics* (Michigan, University of Michigan Press, 1999); GJ Hewitson, *Feminist Economics: Interrogating the Masculinity of Rational Economic Man* (Cheltenham, Edward Elgar, 1999); JA Nelson, 'The study of choice or the study of provisioning? Gender and the definition of economics' in MA Ferber and JA Nelson (eds), *Beyond Economic Man: Feminist Theory and Economics* (Chicago, Ill, University of Chicago Press, 1993).

[180] Mulcahy, above n 179, at 3.

[181] *Ibid*, at 5.

[182] *Ibid*, at 11.

[183] See, eg, C Mackenzie and N Stoljar, *Relational Autonomy: Feminist Perspectives on Autonomy, Agency, and the Social Self* (Oxford, Oxford University Press, 2000); J Nedelsky, 'Reconceiving Autonomy: Sources, Thoughts, and Possibilities' (1989) 1 *Yale Journal of Law and Feminism* 7; M Nussbaum, *Frontiers of Justice: Disability, Nationality, Species Membership* (Cambridge, MA, Harvard University Press, 2006).

legal subject of property law, and identifies some challenges to conventional modes of reasoning in relation to property transactions.

(5) Property's Rational Subject

Property law, like other areas of private law, tends to view the relationships between parties to transactions in terms of particular discursive tropes, which have direct, and sometimes explicit, implications for the ways in which legal responsibility for losses or harms is allocated. These discourses, in turn, reflect constructions of the 'legal subject' as a person who is expected to understand legal rules and procedures in a particular way, and behave accordingly to protect his or her own interests.[184] The classical exposition of property law—and particularly of English land law—emphasises its rational, logical, abstract and juridical character, with 'conceptual purity and internal coherence ... unrivalled across the field of contemporary law'.[185] In their essay 'The Rhetoric of Realty' (which while not explicitly concerned with risk and responsibility, or with legal subjectivity, provides a fascinating analysis of the 'character' of English land law), Gray and Gray described land law as characterised by 'many emanations of a strict logic or deep rationality which order the intellectual processes of the land lawyer'.[186] While this model might suggest that land law is determined according to the (non-instrumental) demands of 'pure reason', Gray and Gray identified a series of 'meta-norms'—located within the 'interpretive community' of land lawyers, but reflecting external social, cultural and economic developments[187]—which they perceived as influencing modes of reasoning in land law through their 'persuasive logic'. These 'rhetorical norms' (rationality, reasonableness and reciprocity) variously, they argue, and depending on the nature of the relationship between the parties, shape the development of the rules and doctrines in particular land law contexts. While relationships between neighbours (for example, in relation to restrictive covenants or easements) have been infused by a meta-norm of *reasonableness*, and decisions relating to the wider contexts in which we deal with each other as fellow citizens (for example, in relation to large-scale community issues such as planning or environmental protections) are informed by *reciprocity*, Gray and Gray argued that the 'heightened' norm that influences 'random commercial interactions between strangers'[188]—for example, the sale and purchase of land, mortgage transactions and housing equity transactions—is the ultimate liberal norm of *rationality*.[189]

In the context of land law, 'rationality' can have at least two meanings. On the one hand, it is used in the sense of the 'deep rationality' (the internal 'pure reason' or logic of the juridical concept adopted in non-instrumentalist analyses) that presents the core 'grammar' of land law as 'a closed system of logic or an autopoietic order, prompting immediate

[184] For a discussion of the idea of a 'legal subject', see JM Balkin, 'Understanding Legal Understanding: The Legal Subject and the Problem of Coherence' (1993–94) 103 *Yale Law Journal* 105.

[185] K Gray and SF Gray, 'The Rhetoric of Realty' in J Getzler (ed), *Rationalizing Property, Equity and Trusts: Essays in Honour of Edward Burn* (London, LexisNexis UK, 2003) 204.

[186] *Ibid*, at 205.

[187] *Ibid*, at 206.

[188] *Ibid*, at 242.

[189] *Ibid*.

analogies with mathematics and, more particularly, with the discipline of Euclidean geometry'.[190] On the other hand—and in the particular context of financial transactions—what Gray and Gray describe as the 'meta-norm' of rationality adopts the meaning more usually associated with the classical economic theory of 'rational choice', that is, the assumption that people will behave in a welfare-maximising way.[191]

Gray and Gray's analysis of 'deep rationality' implied that the core respect for logic in land law is specifically and deliberately divorced from any concept of, or reference to, human (or even liberal legal) subjectivity, but rather implies that 'the naked force of reason, is concerned only with the inner order of the scheme of land law and not with the 'fairness' of its outcomes. The propositional logic of realty is both dispassionate and inexorable'[192]; this is an 'arid and impersonal rationality'.[193] In contrast, the 'meta-norm' of (economic) rationality reflects a model of (liberal) legal subjectivity 'in which relationships are strictly commercial, bargaining is hard-nosed, social bondings are minimal and the value attached to land is primarily, perhaps even exclusively, an "exchange value". Altruism is in very short supply; we are talking money.'[194] Gray and Gray's portrayal of these exchange relationships revealed a positivist view of an adversarial transactional environment in which the parties' responsibilities are to their own self-interests, and where there is no responsibility to protect the other from harm beyond following the rules of the game, under which 'the various players owe no overriding obligation to subserve the welfare concerns of any broader community'.[195] This view of property law echoes the rejection of social-welfarist considerations in the liberal legal model of private law, aligning land law (or the types of relationships that pertain to financial transactions between strangers at least) with the liberal, market-individualist model of contract discussed above.

The meta-norm which Gray and Gray identify as informing commercial transactions affecting land (for example, housing equity transactions), and which reflects a construction of the legal subject as a rational agent aggressively pursuing his or her own self-interest, may conceivably be justified on several grounds. These include the need to ensure the security of long-term expectations, the reliability of investment strategies, the rationality of decision-making about future land use, stable forward planning, the need to protect titles taken by purchasers and creditors, and the importance of ensuring that the substantial wealth tied up in land should not be rendered 'economically sterile'.[196] Indeed, the argument for heightened rationality to ensure that land does not become economically sterile has particular resonance in relation to housing equity transactions. Political and policy initiatives in the UK in recent years have placed considerable emphasis on the housing wealth 'locked up' in owned homes, and the development of the housing equity industry—particularly those products aimed at older owners—has been driven by the

[190] *Ibid*, at 204–05.

[191] Although, as noted above, this in turn has been challenged by behavioural economics analyses that emphasise the reality of our 'bounded rationalities': see, eg, J Conlisk, 'Why Bounded Rationality?' (1996) 34 *Journal of Economic Literature* 669.

[192] Gray and Gray, above n 185, at 216–17.

[193] *Ibid*, at 233.

[194] *Ibid*, at 241.

[195] *Ibid*, at 242.

[196] *Ibid*, at 243.

belief that releasing equity is, and will become, an increasingly important strategy to fund retirement for older owners.

Yet the relationship between the precepts of this model, and the advantages it offers to individuals, begins to come apart for older owners as the transaction takes effect. Gray and Gray described the sharpening influence of rationality as reflecting the 'preoccupations of a materialistic and increasingly affluent era',[197] in which 'Security in the enjoyment of accumulated wealth has become essential to the construction of individualist visions of the good life.'[198] This proposition supports a normative argument that rationality should be the dominant mode of legal reasoning in housing equity transactions, so long as we can assume that the *enjoyment* (that is, the use) of accumulated wealth through equity release is the best route to 'the good life' for older owners. At the same time, however, it disconnects the individual transaction from its consequences. Before, and up to the moment of the transaction, the heightened norm of rationality constructs the homeowner as a rational legal subject, with whom the provider can contract, safe in the knowledge that its security will be enforced by law. Gray and Gray argued that this serves the 'owner', because in a 'rationally regulated, contract-based *Gesellschaft*: the crisper the title, the easier the trade … the safer the owner'.[199] From the pre-transaction perspective, this appears to benefit older owners because it creates a safe environment in which the provider will be willing to trade with them. However, the reality is that once the transaction has taken place, it is the provider who enjoys the 'safety' of ownership (through security), and who experiences the '"feel good" factor [enjoyed] in the minds of those who own estates behind the strengthened legal palisade'.[200] This shift in the subject of property law's protections (from older 'owner' to provider) is concealed to some extent by the structure of housing equity transactions, which enable owners to maintain the 'badge' of owner while ceding the legal rights of ownership.

The aim of rhetorical rationality in property law is to make transactions happen as smoothly and effectively as possible, and this has shaped the construction of property law's subject, and the court's outlook on the responsibilities of the parties in respect of harms. Economic rationality has been conflated with 'commercial realities' to create an attitude of 'brutal commonsense reality' in transactional disputes between strangers.[201] This ethos echoes classical and neoclassical contract law's emphasis on consent and voluntariness, to the extent that 'the parties involved in such dealings cannot be heard to disavow the basic implications which flow from their own voluntarily determined strategies'.[202] The assumption that (marginal) older owners enter into housing equity transactions based on planned strategies echoes the (unrealistic) expectations imposed on risk subjects to take responsibility for their own lives through the processes of reflexive monitoring and life planning. Gray and Gray argued that the 'real-world' commercial demand for security in property transactions has necessarily closed out competing arguments for social/welfare considerations in the context of property law.[203] The emphasis on voluntariness as the core justification for enforcing bad outcomes against the

[197] *Ibid*, at 244.
[198] *Ibid.*
[199] *Ibid.*
[200] *Ibid.*
[201] *Ibid*, at 252.
[202] *Ibid.*
[203] They describe such competing arguments as rooted in 'over scrupulous legal scholasticism': *ibid.*

'consumers' of land transactions (for example, mortgages, surety transactions, housing equity transactions) also echoes the liberal legal model of contract, and the view that 'victim responsibility' may be justified so long as the parties (who are rational agents) freely entered into the transaction.

The sharpening influence of the 'meta-norm' of rationality, and its implications for the legal subject of property law transactions, are also challenged by the insights of behavioural science on rational choice theory. Behavioural economics has identified a range of 'anomalies' ('loss aversion',[204] the 'endowment effect',[205] over-optimism or over-confidence in their own decisions,[206] and 'hyperbolic discounting'[207]) which have successfully challenged the claims of conventional rational choice theory by demonstrating that, in reality, even the most educated and well-informed[208] individuals are not always 'rational maximisers'. For example, Kahneman and Tversky's[209] 'prospect theory', which sought to model real-life choices (rather than optional decisions) where outcomes are uncertain, found that there are limits to the classical rationality that may be expected even of seasoned market actors. Research in behavioural economics has also revealed that it is both reasonable and rational for individuals to have varying subjective attitudes towards risk (for example, risk aversion), depending on the values (or marginal utility) they attach to the potential losses and gains in any given transaction.[210]

Housing equity transactions tend to be 'framed'[211] in a way that suggests that they enable owners to 'have it all'—to enjoy their capital now, while also retaining the property

[204] That is, that people are much more willing to take a risk when there is something to gain, so long as the price is low, than if they stand to lose something they already have.

[205] That is, that people place a higher sale price on what they already have than they would pay for the same thing if they did not own it: see C Camerer, 'Individual Decision Making' in JH Kagel and AE Roth, (eds), *The Handbook of Experimental Economics* (Princeton, Princeton University Press, 1995) at 665–70, for an account of empirical studies of the endowment effect, and some possible psychological explanations for such effects; S Issacharoff, 'Can There be a Behavioural Law and Economics?' (1998) 51 *Vanderbilt Law Review* 1729, 1735. On the 'endowment effect' as a status quo bias, see W Samuelson and R Zeckhauser, 'Status Quo Bias in Decision Making', (1988) 1 *Journal of Risk and Uncertainty*; D Kahneman, JL Knetsch and RH Thaler, 'Anomalies: The Endowment Effect, Loss Aversion and Status Quo Bias' (1991)5 *Journal of Economic Perspectives* 193, 197; G Loewenstein and D Kahneman, 'Explaining the Endowment Effect', Working Paper, (Department of Social and Decision Sciences, Carnegie Mellon University, 1991); and discussing its relevance for law, see DA Farber, 'Towards a New Legal Realism' (2001) 68 *University of Chicago Law Review* 279; L Fox, *Conceptualising Home: Theories, Laws and Policies* (Oxford, Hart Publishing, 2006) 281–84.

[206] S Taylor, *Positive Illusions* (New York, Basic Books, 1989).

[207] That is, the tendency to discount future risks compared to present gains; see S Frederick, G Lowenstein and T O'Donoghue, 'Time Discounting and Time Preference: A Critical Review' (2002) 40 *Journal of Economic Literature* 351.

[208] See P Bernstein, *Against the Gods: The Remarkable Story of Risk* (New York, John Wiley & Sons, 1996), ch 16.

[209] See, eg, A Tversky and D Kahneman, 'Judgment under uncertainty: Heuristics and biases' (1974) 185 *Science* 1124; D Kahneman and A Tversky, 'Prospect Theory: An Analysis of Decision under Risk' (1979) XLVII *Econometrica* 263; A Tversky and D Kahneman, 'The framing of decisions and the psychology of choice' (1981) 211 *Science* 453; D Kahneman, P Slovic and A Tversky, *Judgment Under Uncertainty: Heuristics and Biases* (New York, Cambridge University Press, 1982); D Kahneman and A Tversky (eds), *Choices, Values, Frames* (Cambridge, Cambridge University Press, 2000); D Kahneman, 'A perspective on judgment and choice: Mapping bounded rationality' (2003) 58 *American Psychologist* 697.

[210] On the mental strategies or heuristics older owners use in making decisions about entering into particular transactions, see discussion in ch 3, section (2)(b).

[211] That is, the way in which the degree of risk of certain decisions is pitched in comparison to alternative options—so that a high-risk product can be framed as a medium-risk choice if framed by even riskier alternatives: Tversky and Kahneman (1981), above n 209; and applied in the legal context in M Kelman, Y Rottenstreich and A Tversky, 'Context-Dependence in Legal Decision Making' (1996) 25 *Journal of Legal Studies* 287.

for use and occupation as a home for the rest of their lives—with potential implications for the older owner's perception of risk in the transaction.[212] Insights from behavioural economics have revealed that the 'rationality' of decision-making in these transactions depends not only on what the owner stands to lose, but also on how the owner perceives such losses in risk terms (that is, taking account of both the likelihood of losses and the value attached to the loss—'the awfulness of getting the wager wrong'[213]). This emphasises the importance, when confronting present decision-making, of articulating the 'prospects' or risks which the owner is choosing between, their implications for the tensions between the competing paradigms of home, and the potential 'losses'—whether now or later—in the owner's uncertain future. These analyses fundamentally challenge the assumptions underpinning the strong commitment to economic rationality in property law rhetoric, with significant implications for the 'unreality' of property law's putative subject.

The objectives of a rationally oriented system, in which 'individualist visions of the good life' can be pursued through property transactions in which 'the various players owe no overriding obligation to subserve the welfare concerns of any broader community',[214] are consistent with the risk-taking model of homeownership[215] that emerged following the deregulation of the mortgage market, and which privileged risk-taking behaviour as a 'normal' activity for (liberal) citizens. This vision of ownership supported the ideological commitments of the 'ownership society'[216] by 'incentivising individualised opportunity-seeking over group-based rights'.[217] It is also a central tenet of the paradigm of housing as 'an investment asset to spend' with a neoliberal landscape that requires older owners to participate in housing equity transactions to meet their needs after retirement.[218] In the accumulation phase, Dyal-Chand has argued that 'the rhetoric of the ownership society emphasised the importance of building equity, [but] the market incentivised something markedly different: the use of home equity as a means of leverage, a means of risk taking in pursuit of greater wealth.'[219] While the discussion in chapter three has demonstrated the differences between the nature and extent of risk involved in the decumulation phase (compared to strategic moves to accumulate housing wealth, for example 'house flipping'),[220] both types of activity are promoted under the risk-taking model of homeownership, which privileges the (inherently risky) paradigm of 'housing as an investment asset to spend' over (the material security of) 'housing as home'.

The characterisation of homeownership (whether in accumulation or decumulation phases) as an entrepreneurial risk-taking activity also supports the liberalist focus on

[212] This issue is explored further in ch 5, which examines the multiple paradigms of housing for older owners, and the tensions that are created by the increasing range of functions which the owned home is expected to perform.

[213] On 'Pascal's wager', see Steele, above n 59, at 22–23.

[214] Gray & Gray, above n 185, at 242.

[215] See R Dyal-Chand, 'Home as Ownership, Dispossession as Foreclosure: The Impact of the Current Crisis on the American Model of "Home"' in L Fox O'Mahony and JA Sweeney (eds), *The Idea of Home in Law: Displacement and Dispossession* (Aldershot, Ashgate, 2010).

[216] See Fox, above n 205, ch 5.

[217] Dyal-Chand, above n 215, at 46.

[218] See ch 5, section (5).

[219] Dyal-Chand, above n 215, at 47.

[220] Specifically, in the case of equity release, the potential for profit lies with the provider, whereas house flipping may be viewed as 'entrepreneurial' on the part of the owner; see ch 3, section (3).

negative rights (the opportunity to participate in the market) over positive, welfare-oriented conceptions of rights. Dyal-Chand argued that the 'ownership society' model that has developed in the US—focused on individualised opportunity, risk and reward—provided the rhetorical backdrop to the State's policy of delimiting its role in regulating and developing the home finance market.[221] As the 'light-touch' model of State responsibility for financial regulation has come under pressure, in both the US and the UK, following the global financial crisis, the attenuation of the risk-taking model in favour of a heightened concern with (borrower and lender) responsibility which Dyal-Chand identified in the US is echoed in a growing emphasis on creditor responsibility in the UK.[222]

The impact of crises (for example, the current global financial crisis) in producing 'property moments' that can fundamentally alter dominant norms concerning the State's role in regulating the (private) arena of property transactions, or the balance that property law strikes between the interests of the individual and community, was examined by Davidson and Dyal-Chand in a fascinating article in the *Fordham Law Review*.[223] They argued that crises play a significant role in adjusting the tensions underlying property theory, altering the very nature of property, ownership and community, and shifting the balance that property law strikes between norms of individualism and community. Moments of crisis, the argument goes, provide opportunities to disrupt the significant path dependency that tends to act as a conservatising force in property law.[224] Davidson and Dyal-Chand's analysis of US property history suggests that in moments of crisis, 'seemingly settled questions about the balance of individual autonomy and state authority, the role of the state in regulating property, and the role of property in social ordering rise to the cultural and legal surface'.[225] Even if 'the pendulum seems to swing back toward more privatised visions of property' when the crisis subsides, they argue that the experience can leave a lasting impression on property law and theory; that 'the residue of crisis remains'.[226]

Critical property theory in the US often focuses on the protection afforded to property and economic rights under the US Constitution, locating arguments in support of economic liberty and the safeguarding of rights of property owners within the wider political theme of market individualism and the restraint of government power over individuals.[227] Under the UK's 'unwritten constitution', the political nature of property is more implicit, and is achieved and maintained through the institutional commitments of the legislature and the judiciary to core values. Landmark moments where these values have been clearly articulated include the 1925 property legislation,[228] which sought to make land as easily and securely transferable as possible, and as readily exchangeable as

221 Dyal-Chand, above n 215, at 48.

222 See ch 9.

223 NM Davidson and R Dyal-Chand, 'Property in Crisis' (2009) 78 *Fordham Law Review* 1607.

224 *Ibid*, at 1619.

225 *Ibid*, at 1623.

226 *Ibid*.

227 See, eg, JW Ely Jr, *The Guardian of Every Other Right: A Constitutional History of Property Rights*, 3rd edn (Oxford, OUP, 2008); CM Rose, 'What Government Can Do for Property (and Vice Versa)' in N Mercuro and WJ Samuels (eds), *The Economics of Legal Relationships: The Fundamental Interrelationships between Government and Property* (Stamford, CT, JAI Press, 1999).

228 The '1925 legislation' refers collectively to the major overhaul of the property system given effect through the Law of Property Act 1925, the Land Registration Act 1925, the Settled Land Act 1925 and the Trustee Act 1925, the Land Charges Act 1925 and the Administration of Estates Act 1925.

any other asset. In emphasising the *exchange value* of land over its *use value*, the 1925 legislation marked a clear ideological commitment to a market-based political economy which has, in turn, supported specific policies such as the promotion of owner-occupation.[229] In the early 1980s—on the cusp of Thatcherism and the emergence of neoliberalism in UK political and legal discourse—Gray and Symes identified a concern with 'social interests' (including a particular emphasis on security of tenure and rights of residential protection) in the policies and doctrines of land law.[230] The policy pendulum swung back decisively from the 1980s, and property's role was re-cast in terms of fostering market competition and private enterprise in a deregulated environment, with 'owners' constructed as the epitome of self-providing, self-responsible, autonomous neoliberal subjects.[231] The swing towards individualism and alienability in land law more broadly was also evident in the Land Registration Act 2002, with its attempts to 'perfect the register',[232] its protection of the rational, objective and tangible interests recorded on the title over the material, 'irrational' interests subsisting on the ground, and its heightened emphasis on transactional certainty over the protection of informal or occupational interests.[233]

Notwithstanding the dominance of liberal individualist norms in contemporary property law, if we accept that moments of 'crisis' open up new possibilities for re-thinking the orientation of property law, then the roots of the current crisis in the collapse of the residential property market, and particularly the problems generated by over-indebtedness against the security of 'owned' housing, must justify fresh scrutiny of the norms underpinning the dominant paradigm of housing as an investment asset to spend.[234] The factors implicated in the current crisis include the overly-enthusiastic promotion of homeownership for all, specifically including marginal households; the relentless portrayal of the positive risks of entrepreneurial attitudes towards the owned home ('home as investment asset'); and the rhetorical representation of owners and homeownership in terms of autonomy, opportunity, control and freedom to make choices. The impacts of fiscal, economic and property losses resulting from the sub-prime mortgage crisis have blown apart—temporarily at least—the claim that a market-led, non-interventionist strategy, rooted in ideas of possessive individualism and the pursuit of reward through risk, can generate acceptable (in terms of risk) and appropriate (in reflecting prevailing social and economic priorities) property norms.

If the 'perennial dichotomy' within property may be characterised as the tension between 'bottom-up individualistic paradigms' and the 'top-down regulatory nature of property',[235] the current crisis has highlighted the State's role in what had—increasing through the era of financial deregulation and expansion of homeownership that started in the 1980s—been identified as a domain of 'private ordering'.[236] Davidson and Dyal-Chand

[229] See Fox, above n 205, ch 5.

[230] See KJ Gray and PD Symes, *Real Property and Real People* (London, Butterworths, 1981).

[231] See ch 3.

[232] Through streamlined methods of recording information, categories of burdens and incumbrances, and the reduction in the category of overriding interests; see generally, E Cooke, *The New Law of Land Registration* (Oxford, Hart Publishing, 2003).

[233] See, eg, KJ Gray and SF Gray, *Elements of Land Law*, 4th edn (Oxford, Oxford University Press, 2005) [2.48].

[234] See ch 5, section (5).

[235] Davidson and Dyal-Chand, above n 223, at 1614.

[236] *Ibid*, at 1612–13.

have argued that, in contrast, the 'interconnected' vision of property revealed by the global financial crisis is 'as much about collective security and an active state as it is about individual risk and reward'.[237] In terms of its impact, the very nature of the crisis may provide the catalyst for a swing away from rational individualism based on the pursuit of self-interest, so providing a point of entry for more 'communitarian', social conceptions of property, and for richer understandings of the role of State responsibility in respect of property transactions. Specifically, the crisis has already called into question the role of the State in regulating financial transactions secured against property.[238] Davidson and Dyal-Chand claimed that

> as the current crisis has deepened, it has exposed the drawbacks of conceptualising property as the locus for primarily individual opportunity. Given the extent to which the crisis has touched so many people's retirement accounts, savings, and investments—not to mention homes, jobs, and schools—the distributional consequences of crisis are difficult to ignore.[239]

By revealing the reality of property as interconnected, through the large-scale economic, financial and social repercussions of what started as a credit crunch in the residential mortgage market, the crisis has challenged atomised accounts of property based on non-instrumental deep rationality, as well as those that rely heavily on the normative assumptions of economic rationality. In this 'property moment', there is a renewed opportunity for alternative perspectives which challenge the individualist orientation of these conceptions of property to acquire some purchase within property thinking.

Layered on top of the 'general' financial crisis, it is also important to bear in mind the spectre of the demographic 'Agequake' and the social, economic and fiscal pressures that are anticipated on both individual and State resources in the coming years.[240] Concerns about the sustainability of financial provision for older people, and the increasingly central role that privately-held housing equity is expected to play in resourcing needs after retirement, underline the wider community interest in housing equity transactions. Perceptions amongst older owners themselves that these transactions are not adequately protected through law represent a barrier to the facilitation of equity decumulation in the 'wealth-fare State', while the reality of bad outcomes has direct implications for the State in terms of the dissipation of a resource on which it relies for the effectiveness of the self-provision policy. If private law leaves vulnerable parties unprotected, the welfare needs of property owners who suffer adverse transactions (for example, the housing equity owner whose financial resource for old age is dissipated in a 'bad' transaction) will fall on the responsibility of the State (funded through general taxation), to the extent that the State undertakes to provide for the needs of non-property owners in their old age.

In addition to these efficiency concerns, the human costs of insecurity and moral regard for 'capabilities' have informed new schools of property theory that challenge the proposition that the parties to property transactions owe no positive duties or responsibilities towards each other or to the wider community, and which re-assert the role and functions of property law in questions of distributive justice by emphasising human

[237] *Ibid*, at 1611.
[238] See ch 9.
[239] Davidson and Dyal-Chand, above n 223, at 1641.
[240] See ch 1.

welfare and social context considerations.[241] These theories challenge the self-interested perspective that characterises market individualism, and argue for more responsible and responsive approaches to property which recognise claimants as individuals with particular needs, but as members of a community within which property is a valued resource and private ownership of property (including capital interests in property) is a privilege. The idea of property as privilege resonates with Hart's depiction of certain areas of law as 'power-conferring legal doctrine',[242] which expand rather than contract the scope of individual freedom by helping people to do certain things which are regarded as good:

> Such laws do not impose duties or obligations. Instead, they provide individuals with *facilities* for realising their wishes, by conferring legal powers upon them to create, by certain specified procedures and subject to certain conditions, structures of rights and duties within the coercive framework of the law. The power thus conferred on individuals to mould their legal relations with others by contracts, wills, marriages etc, is one of the great contributions of law to social life …[243]

Accepting the idea that property has a social context broadens the meaning of 'responsibility' for property law. If we regard the State's role in respect of property as 'enabling', this raises important questions about the nature of the endeavours that are supported or privileged by property's laws, and the relevance of their consequences or impacts on the community. This wider perspective looks beyond the proposition that law's support for property pursues (only) the goal of economic efficiency, to encompass broader social and welfare considerations.

When the housing equity transactions of older owners are viewed in this wider perspective, the limited conceptions of 'responsibility' inherent in the 'deep rationality' or liberal-individualist models are supplanted by social constructions of property that emphasise the community interest in property transactions. The community interest in property is a dominant trope in the recent work of scholars such as Gregory Alexander and Eduardo Peñalver,[244] who have proposed a substantive (rather than procedural) conception of justice as it applies to property, built around the notion of 'human flourishing'. This school of 'progressive property', which challenges utilitarian and classical liberal theories of property, focuses on the social matrices necessary for the development of 'human flourishing', and offers a rich basis for articulating alternatives to the individualist, negative rights conception of property as opportunity. By emphasising the role of property in promoting or fostering the development of the capabilities that are necessary for human flourishing, and the social obligations this places on the community and the State, progressive property supports the argument for a more protective, interventionist response to individual vulnerability.

[241] Examples of these approaches, including 'progressive property' and the 'freedom-promoting approach to property' are discussed further below.

[242] For a discussion of law as power-conferring, see Hart, above n 121, at 27–38; see discussion above in section (4)(a) in relation to Smith's arguments for substantive fairness in contracts.

[243] HLA Hart, *The Concept of Law*, 2nd edn (Oxford, Clarendon Press, 1994) 27–28.

[244] See, eg, GS Alexander and EM Peñalver, 'Properties of Communities' (2009) 10 *Theoretical Inquiries in Law* 127; GS Alexander and EM Peñalver (eds), *Property and Community* (Oxford, Oxford University Press, 2010); GS Alexander, EM Peñalver, JW Singer and LS Underkuffler, 'A Statement on Progressive Property' (2009) 94 *Cornell Law Review* 743.

Progressive property tempers the individualism of classical property theory with the idea that the individual and the community are mutually dependent[245]; that we are all members of a community, 'an interconnected web', in which an ethic of mutual responsibility around property plays a central role in achieving the common good.[246] Progressive property emphasises the social values of property: values of community, autonomy, personhood, environmental protection and security. According to progressive property, the values that legal subjects ascribe to—on behalf of the community at large,[247] as well as for their own individual well-being[248]—are oriented around 'just social relations', encompassing positive commitments to equality, dignity, respect and justice, as well as the more commonly articulated 'property' values of freedom and autonomy.[249] Indeed, progressive property rejects the negative meanings ascribed to 'freedom' and 'autonomy' by utilitarianism and classical liberal contractarianism, in favour of richer, fuller and more positive understandings of these values.[250] In this sense, the aim of progressive property is to enable 'dependent' individuals to develop into 'autonomous moral agents', able to make meaningful choices, using the medium of property to support their capabilities, and so their human flourishing.

The 'community of rights' invoked in this model of property emphasises a shared commitment to the values of 'life and human flourishing, the protection of physical security, the ability to acquire knowledge and make choices, and the freedom to live one's own life on one's own terms'.[251] The idea of community responsibility invoked in progressive property is based on a form of rationality, but not the self-interested economic rationality discussed in the previous section. Rather, in this context, individuals are held responsible for the wider community interest in property for human flourishing, because we are rationally constrained 'to acknowledge the right of every other human being, as a rational moral agent, to develop the same capabilities [as we value for ourselves]'.[252] This expansive concept of community responsibility draws upon the Aristotelian conception of human beings as social and political animals, in contrast to the neoliberal model of atomised individualism. Crucially, for the purposes of this discussion, it directly relates this community membership—and the responsibilities that brings—to the goal of individual autonomy: Alexander and Peñalver argue that 'although human beings value and strive for autonomy, dependency and interdependency are inherent aspects of the human condition'.[253] When they describe the human condition as including inevitable dependency on communities both for our physical survival and for our ability to function as independent agents, the meaning they ascribe to 'dependency and interdependency' is mutual between members of the community (and so universal, as part of a rational

245 Alexander and Peñalver (2009), above n 244, at 129.

246 GS Alexander, 'The Social-Obligation Norm in American Property Law' (2009) 94 *Cornell Law Review* 745, 818–19.

247 Alexander and Peñalver reason that, to the extent that we (as members of communities that value private property) value property as necessary for us (as humans) to flourish, we have a moral obligation to support social matrices and legal strategies that promote 'human flourishing' for others.

248 Necessarily, they argue, to avoid self-contradiction; Alexander and Peñalver (2009), above n 244, at 141–42.

249 *Ibid*, at 140.

250 Eg, they argue that 'authentic, robust freedom' must include the capacity to make *meaningful* choices: *ibid*, at 135.

251 Alexander *et al*, above n 244.

252 Alexander and Peñalver (2009), above n 244, at 142.

253 *Ibid*, at 134–35.

working-out of their correlative duties towards fellow human beings),[254] and therefore distinctive from the one-sided dependency which has been negatively associated with ageing and heavily criticised within social gerontology and political economy of ageing scholarship.[255]

The account of community dependency offered by Alexander and Peñalver locates the function of property in supporting human flourishing within a broader concern for human autonomy.[256] Yet this model of autonomy leads not to self-interested choices and non-intervention with adverse outcomes in the name of respecting the agency of the autonomous person, but to a solidarity-based web of mutual obligation to support the social matrix that is necessary for every person's development as an autonomous moral agent. Support for the community, they argue, is a necessary step in achieving individual autonomy: 'far from undermining personal autonomy, communities (and the sacrifices that maintain communities) are necessary for it to exist.'[257] Progressive property rejects individualist (self-interested) conceptions of autonomy in favour of a model of property that encompasses the plural and incommensurable values that are implicated in property conflicts and property institutions.[258] The pursuit of 'autonomy' for progressive property requires a contextual approach to property entitlements, which recognises the reality of inequalities between legal subjects, the obligations on property owners to enhance the abilities of those who lack the resources (capabilities) for human flourishing, and the need for State intervention to enforce this social obligation.[259]

The liberal individualist model of property law, its concern with formal not substantive equality/opportunity and the assumptions it makes about the decision-making autonomy of its economically rational legal subjects, are also challenged in Purdy's 'freedom-promoting' approach to property. Purdy's theory is rooted in a re-analysis of Adam Smith's moral philosophy, which challenges the claim that a 'free market economy' denotes that transactions should be valued exclusively according to their economic efficiency and promotion of negative rights (freedom from interference by the State).[260] Purdy's approach to property is substantive and contextual inasmuch as it 'conceives of freedom *functionally*: to inquire how free people are, it asks what they are able *to do*, which forms of human potential they have turned into actual capabilities that they can in fact exercise'.[261] Like progressive property, Purdy draws from Amartya Sen's[262] argument that

[254] Indeed, Alexander and Peñalver's conception of the obligation on fellow members of the community to foster capabilities in others is based on Gewirth's 'universalizability' principle; see A Gewirth, *Reason and Morality* (Chicago, University of Chicago Press, 1978).

[255] See discussion in ch 2, section (2).

[256] Alexander and Peñalver (2009), above n 244, at 137.

[257] *Ibid*, at 145.

[258] Alexander *et al*, above n 244.

[259] Alexander, above n 246.

[260] This theme is also prominent in the work of Robin Paul Malloy, who argued that while economic efficiency is one factor that may be taken into account in the legal frameworks surrounding exchange relationships, it must be tempered by considerations of justice, fairness and morality, and embedded in social and community values; see, eg, RP Malloy, *Law and Market Economy: Reinterpreting the Values of Law and Economics* (Cambridge, Cambridge University Press, 2000); RP Malloy, *Law in a Market Context: An Introduction to Market Concepts in Legal Reasoning* (Cambridge, Cambridge University Press, 2004); RP Malloy, 'Equating Human Rights and Property Rights—The Need for Moral Judgment in an Economic Analysis of Law and Social Policy' (1986) 47 *Ohio State Law Journal* 163.

[261] J Purdy, 'A Freedom-Promoting Approach to Property: A Renewed Tradition for New Debates' (2005) 72 *University of Chicago Law Review* 1237, 1243.

[262] See, eg, A Sen, *Development as Freedom* (Oxford, Oxford University Press, 1999).

both negative protections and positive entitlements should be based on *capabilities*—that is, on what they enable a person to do.[263] Sen's capabilities theory resonates with the idea of *contextual vulnerability* in housing equity transactions, in that it emphasises the limits that life circumstances (for example, social status) place on a person's capability to achieve 'freedom' and so to be able to transact equally within a system that emphasises negative rights to freedom and equality. Where classical and liberal models of contract and property emphasise the 'process' dimension of freedom as non-interference and the protection of autonomous choice, Sen defined freedom as concerned with both process and 'opportunity', based on a real measure of the range of viable choices available to the actual person entering the transaction.

Sen's concern with opportunity resonates strongly with the transactional choices that may be faced by marginal older owners. In assessing the value of negative rights for such subjects, Sen reasoned that

> [f]reedom from interference means little to a person faced with 'a choice over three alternative achievements that are seen as "bad", "terrible", and "disastrous"', even though from the perspective solely of process freedom, this person will enjoy 'exactly as much freedom as [if she had] a choice over ... three alternative achievements which are seen as "good", "terrific", and "wonderful" ... Any person's opportunity freedom encompasses both the *number and variety* of activities and projects actually available to her and the *value* of the alternatives to her in the light of her interests and commitments.[264]

This focus on *opportunity* also echoes Scanlon's 'value of choice' theory in its emphasis on the legal subject's opportunity to make choices, and the implications this has in respect of responsibility for adverse outcomes.[265] Purdy takes up this argument by claiming that (in contrast to classical or neoliberal interpretations of (market) freedom, which focus on actual or hypothetical consent), in evaluating the degree of freedom with which a choice is made, we must consider both the set of viable options which the individual faces in making the choice, and the extent to which the individual conceives of herself as

> the kind of agent whose interests and commitments are self-authorising reasons for her not to act and give others reason to respect her person and projects; or whether, alternatively, she either fails to formulate interests and commitments of her own or is psychologically inhibited from acting on them.[266]

This analysis resonates with older owners' housing equity transactions in several important respects. For example, the challenge to classical or liberal theories based on 'choice' is advanced by emphasising the need for that choice to be 'real', and the importance of context-sensitivity in understanding the *viable* choices within which a person makes a decision.[267] The analysis of housing equity transactions in this book emphasises the contextual (social, economic, political, psychological and risk) constraints within which older owners—particularly marginal older owners—must make 'choices' concerning their use of housing equity to meet needs after retirement. By identifying the goals of property

[263] A Sen, 'Rights and Capabilities' in A Sen, *Resources, Values and Development* (Cambridge, MA, Harvard University Press, 1984).

[264] Purdy, above n 261, at 1260, citing A Sen, 'Markets and Freedoms' in A Sen, *Rationality and Freedom* (Cambridge, MA, Harvard University Press, 2002) at 515.

[265] TM Scanlon, *What We Owe To Each Other* (Cambridge, MA, Harvard University Press, 1998) 251 *et seq.*

[266] Purdy, above n 261, at 1244.

[267] *Ibid*, at 1261, 1286.

as going beyond negative freedom against interference, or economic efficiency, Purdy's freedom-promoting approach recognises the contextual reality of legal subjectivity, and provides a moral basis for recognising and responding to inequalities in property law.

Indeed, Purdy also acknowledges that participation in the market itself, while sometimes increasing capability, also produces vulnerability due to the exogenous risks to which individuals may be exposed, with potentially major negative impacts for their capabilities.[268] The freedom-promoting approach recognises that legal subjects are vulnerable to risk in the market:

> It promotes an image of the individual not as the sole mistress of her talents and her fate, but rather as vulnerable to a variety of social and economic forces that she cannot control. Taken together, an emphasis on the pervasive power of risk to redirect life-paths; a valorization of institutions that can mitigate such risk; and the literal intertwining by contract of the long-term fates of otherwise disconnected persons present a very different picture of personhood and society from that of the stereotyped, atomised individual of the liberal economy and polity. From the standpoint of freedom-enhancing risk reduction, each person is an initiative taker, but is also profoundly vulnerable.[269]

In the context of housing equity transactions, this is manifest through the uncertainty and risk surrounding decision-making in a complex financial transaction, which leaves the older owner vulnerable to exogenous shocks. Where unacceptable levels of risk prevent parties from entering into these transactions—when to do so would improve their lives—this reduces 'freedom' because it 'narrows the domain of viable alternatives from which people choose their life paths'. Purdy argued that 'to be denied viable alternatives is to be restricted along an important dimension of freedom … It may prevent advances that would otherwise have occurred.'[270]

Purdy's aim, and that of progressive property, was to identify ways in which property and property law can *promote autonomy* in contexts of individual and contextual vulnerability.[271] While Purdy does not attempt to give a specific account of the content of this positive liberty, he argues that analyses of property regimes should consider

> whether they promote relationships of domination or subordination, which tend to inhibit self-assertion by the subordinated, or whether, alternatively, they promote reciprocity and cultivate the habit of recognising and pursuing one's own interests and commitments in the course of negotiating cooperation with others.[272]

The goal of this project is to extend property entitlement-based protections: it is concerned with the role of property rights and property law in effecting a transformation from a society of relative vulnerability and incapacity to a society of relative security and capability.[273] It is based on a moral outlook ('human-regarding values'[274]) that tempers the market's efficiency agenda with other considerations, based on the vulnerabilities of

[268] *Ibid*, at 1271; '[F]reedom to enter into market relations produces vulnerability as well as capacity: it means being subject to the sometimes devastating vagaries of markets, whose power to wreck economies and lives seems to grow with their scale.' (*ibid*, at 1263).

[269] *Ibid*, at 1277.

[270] *Ibid*, at 1273.

[271] *Ibid*, at 1272. seeks to 'help people towards the resources, institutional context, and psychologically significant experiences that undergird "positive" self-direction'.

[272] *Ibid*, at 1244–45.

[273] *Ibid*, at 1271.

[274] *Ibid*, eg, at 1296.

legal subjects. Purdy argues that this is necessary because 'property law exists to serve human values … The law of property sets the terms of social and economic cooperation'.[275] Property law is not separate from society but central to the instrumental delivery of freedom and equality; our approach to property reflects the type of society we choose to be.[276]

While Purdy explicitly sets the boundaries of his 'approach' in broad terms,[277] and despite its value in recognising the vulnerabilities of property law's subjects, their inequalities resulting from contextual vulnerabilities and exogenous risk, and the responsibilities of the State to address these inequalities through property law, at present there appear to be—for the purposes of older owners' housing equity transactions—two potentially limiting features. The first is his strategy of meeting the needs of vulnerable subjects through rights and entitlements. While there is obvious strength in this approach (in the 'deep' nature of deontological protections), there are likely to be some practical difficulties in applying this theory to housing equity transactions. It is perhaps natural that a theory with redistribution within its sights focuses on those in most need of resources: as such it emphasises *foundational capabilities* (physical mobility, linguistic capability, literacy, etc) and *metacapabilities* (which enable people to expand, refine or revise their existing capabilities, for example the capacity to participate in self-government) to the exclusion of significant human values which are less 'basic'.[278] Purdy acknowledges that

> the most straightforward way to apply this emphasis in concrete institutional decisions is in distributive terms—specifically in the distribution of the resources that promote foundational capabilities and of political rights and other metacapabilities that promote self-improvement and the revision of contexts.[279]

Older owners, who *have*—or appear to have—a reasonable level of (financial) resources, may not be readily identifiable as a suitable 'target population' for Purdy's freedom-promoting approach. Of course, it must be acknowledged that Purdy himself sets no such boundaries around his theory—indeed, quite the opposite[280]—but the perception of older people who have capacity and are currently holding assets in the form of their owned home as relatively 'capable' already, may operate as a barrier to the political persuasiveness of a 'freedom-promoting' approach in this context.

A potentially more serious limitation of the theory itself is its commitment to 'autonomy' as the destination point for 'capable' subjects. For example, Purdy describes Shiller's proposal[281] for the distribution of risk caused by exogenous shocks in the employment market through complex contractual arrangements as an example of a 'freedom-promoting' approach to property rights.[282] Shiller's solution, which seeks to address the contextual risks that financial subjects are required to undertake, involves

[275] *Ibid*, at 1298.

[276] 'The first contribution to understanding property's appropriate boundaries is the recognition that there is no "outside", or "opposite" of property.' (*ibid*, at 1298)

[277] '[T]he freedom-promoting approach is the very opposite of dogmatic': *ibid*, at 1297.

[278] *Ibid*, at 1292–93.

[279] *Ibid*, at 1293.

[280] Indeed, the example of Shiller's employment sector index lists biology PhDs, genetic specialists, patent attorneys and physical therapists amongst the employees who might be protected; *ibid*, at 1274.

[281] R Shiller, *The New Financial Order: Risk in the 21st Century* (Princeton, Princeton University Press, 2003).

[282] Shiller has also produced house price indices which track the housing market; see, eg, R Shiller, *Irrational Exuberance* (Princeton, Princeton University Press, 2000).

risk-sharing within the vulnerable community—described as autonomy with solidarity—which 'enables people to resist the coercion, not of other individuals, but of enormous and anonymous shifts in the operation of economic life'.[283] The objective is to recognise the reality of 'inevitable interdependence',[284] while helping people move towards greater autonomy. Purdy describes the extension or identification of property rights as desirable when it can make people 'freer' in any of several ways, including 'expanding the set of viable alternatives from which they choose in directing their life courses, [or] by creating the social preconditions for psychological attitudes supporting self-regard and autonomous decision-making'.[285] Yet the very inevitability of interdependence raises important questions about the achievability of 'autonomy',[286] the distinctions between procedural and substantive autonomy, the political content of the concept of the 'autonomous individual', and the nature and extent of the State's enduring responsibilities towards vulnerable subjects.[287]

While the acknowledgement of property law's role in recognising and responding to inequality and interdependence encourages a more realistic and contextual analysis of the subjectivities of older owners, including their vulnerabilities, it also presents challenges both in respect of the extent to which strategies based in property rights and entitlements can protect marginal people, in light of the tendency of the property regime to insulate itself against change[288]; and in its inference that the appropriate response to vulnerability is to build capabilities and so enable people to become autonomous moral agents—converting them from 'flawed consumers' to 'skilled consumers'. In this sense, the commitment to autonomy in both progressive property and the 'freedom-promoting approach' might be viewed as reinforcing the neoliberal agenda of turning vulnerable subjects into responsible citizens who make fewer demands on the State.[289] These challenges are discussed further in chapter six.

[283] Purdy, above n 261, at 1277. The use of property law to achieve this type of risk-sharing was explored in LA Fennell, 'Homeownership 2.0' (2008) 102 *Northwestern University Law Review* 1047.

[284] Purdy, above n 261, at 1278.

[285] *Ibid*, at 1298.

[286] This issue is explored in MA Fineman, 'The Vulnerable Subject: Anchoring Equality in the Human Condition' (2008) 20 *Yale Journal of Law and Feminism* 8; and discussed in ch 6.

[287] These issues are discussed in chs 5 and 6.

[288] See, generally, A van der Walt, *Property in the Margins* (Oxford, Hart Publishing, 2009) viii–ix. The author argues that 'the function of the rights paradigm tends to resist or minimise change … [even] strong reformist legislative efforts to protect weak and marginalised occupiers … are sometimes frustrated by restrictive judicial and doctrinal interpretation and application informed by the underlying assumptions of the rights paradigm.' The effect of this phenomenon in the context of housing equity transactions is particularly evident in respect of the consumer protection provisions discussed in ch 8. See also L Fox O'Mahony and JA Sweeney, 'Re-thinking Responses to Displacement and Dispossession' in L Fox O'Mahony and JA Sweeney (eds), *The Idea of Home in Law: Displacement and Dispossession* (Aldershot, Ashgate, 2010).

[289] See N Rose, 'Community, citizenship, and the third way' (2000) 43 *American Behavioral Scientist* 1395; J Flint, 'Housing and Ethopolitics: constructing identities of active consumption and responsible community' (2003) 32 *Economy and Society* 611; J Flint and R Rowlands, 'Commodification, Normalisation and Intervention: cultural, social and symbolic capital in housing consumption and governance' (2003) 18 *Journal of Housing and the Built Environment* 213.

(6) Conclusions

The socio-economic and political environments of ageing in the early twenty-first century mean that, increasingly, many older owners will have no choice but to engage with some form of risk in relation to the use (or not) of home equity after retirement. While the risks associated with spending housing wealth, and the outcomes of home equity transactions, can be both positive and negative—with positive aspects relating to lifestyle, better quality of life and avoiding poverty in old age—the necessity for many older homeowners to participate in the credit market in one way or another, and to negotiate the risks associated with market participation, present new questions for legal analysis. The expectation that homeowners will accumulate housing wealth during their lives to spend on welfare after retirement, and that they will be individually self-responsible as 'active subjects' under neoliberal governmentality, provide an important context for analysis of the ideas of responsibility and vulnerability as they are applied to older people in the current political and policy landscape.

The dominant themes in political and policy discourse concerning housing equity transactions reflect a particular construction of the older owner as a reflexive risk subject, 'free' to negotiate choices as an autonomous consumer. Yet the extent to which the general population—and, by extension, older owners—are likely to be able to plan effectively for (and finance) their futures is clearly linked to the social and cultural resources at their disposal, as well as to their financial and legal capabilities to understand complex products. Research in the UK on people's abilities to be the type of active, informed consumer they are now expected to be has demonstrated a gap between the abilities of 'educated, articulate' households to function as 'utility-maximising consumers', and the abilities of those who lack the cultural capital—the knowledge and financial proficiency—to make good, informed decisions; and Cooper has argued that this gap 'creates opportunities for people to participate in their own exploitation'[290] if they are not well-informed, well-advised and sceptical consumers. One specific context in which a lower level of cultural capital has been shown to disadvantage some consumers is in relation to life planning for retirement.[291]

This type of inequality is difficult to represent in the legal domain. Liberal legal theory emphasises the values of autonomy and choice, with the positive 'entrepreneurial' aspects of risk-taking in relation to house purchase tending to characterise legal perspectives on these transactions, which are anchored in the typically non-market interventionist approaches of property law and contract as 'private' law domains. Yet this model of consumers in domestic property transactions as 'responsible risk-takers' has been challenged by the recent global financial crisis, which has demonstrated how risks in the financial system can potentially impact on *all* consumers, calling into question the 'overly

[290] M Cooper, 'The Inequality of Security: Winners and Losers in the Risk Society' (2008) 61 *Human Relations* 1229 at 1236.

[291] M Anderson, F Bechhofer and S Kendrick, 'Individual and Household Strategies' in M Anderson, F Bechhofer and J Gershuny (eds), *The Social and Political Economy of the Household* (Oxford, Oxford University Press, 1994) 19; M Anderson, Y Li, F Bechhofer, D McCrone and R Stewart, 'Sooner rather than later? Younger and middle-aged adults preparing for retirement' (2000) 20 *Aging and Society* 445; MA Denton, CL Kemp, S French, A Gafni, A Joshi, CJ Rosenthal and S Davies, 'Reflexive planning for later life' (2004) 23 *Canadian Journal on Aging Supplement* S71–82; DA Hershy and JC Mowen, 'Psychological determinants of financial preparedness for retirement' (2000) 40 *The Gerontologist* 687.

optimistic view of self-regulating markets'.[292] Indeed, even before the 'credit crunch', the relationship between risk, responsibility and regulation had emerged as an important theme in UK policy,[293] with the growing reach of the FSA providing an example of use of (albeit 'light-touch') regulatory approaches as a response to the risks associated with financial transactions. Since the financial crisis, the UK Government has made an explicit commitment to a more responsible regulatory regime.[294] However, the conceptualisation of 'owners as consumers', including in particular 'older owners as consumers', has cast a long shadow over our understandings of older owners as legal subjects, and—as the discussion in later chapters will show—has tended to inhibit the extent to which their vulnerabilities in financial transactions are reflected in the legal frameworks which govern such transactions.

Housing equity transactions—which comprise both a property transaction and a financial services contract—sit on a politically-charged axis between the common law of property (in which the dominant norms are shaped by ideologies of non-State intervention and market individualism) and statutory regulation through the FSA and other consumer protection policies. The interplay between these competing forces—particularly in the moment of 'crisis' engendered by the coincidence of the 'Agequake' and concerns it brings regarding financial provision for older people, on the one hand, and the impact of the global financial crisis on understandings of 'responsibility' within financial services regulation—is a prominent theme throughout this book. Of course, even before the current crisis, the particularly high-risk nature of housing equity transactions prompted a series of regulatory interventions in respect of specific product types. Although the nature and extent of these interventions varied, there is evidence to indicate that the UK's commitment to the portrayal of legal/financial subjects as self-responsible consumers in this specific context has been increasingly challenged by arguments for greater creditor/provider responsibility, given effect through State intervention via the FSA.[295]

The role of the State in respect of housing equity transactions—and, specifically, the *responsibilities* of the State through the institutions of law, including the 'power-conferring' doctrines of contract and property—is a central concern of this analysis, and may be framed in different ways. One area for analysis is the realm of private law, where there is evidence to indicate that in addition to the 'private' ordering achieved through the market, the State plays a key role in shaping the institutions of contract and private property, according to a political agenda.[296] As the wider implications of the global

[292] RP Malloy, 'Mortgage Market Reform and the Fallacy of Self-Correcting Markets' (2009) 30 *Pace Law Review* 79.

[293] Better Regulation Commission, *Risk, Responsibility and Regulation: Whose Risk is it Anyway?* (London, Cabinet Office, 2006).

[294] See 'Statement to the House of Commons by the Financial Secretary to the Treasury, Mark Hoban MP, on Reforming the Institutional Framework for Financial Regulation', 17 June 2010, online at <http://www.hm-treasury.gov.uk/statement_fst_170610.htm>; HM Treasury, *A new approach to financial regulation: judgment, focus and stability*, Cm 7874 (London, TSO, 2010), online at <http://www.hm-treasury.gov.uk/d/consult_financial_regulation_condoc.pdf>.

[295] See ch 9.

[296] KM Wyman, 'From Fur to Fish: Reconsidering the Evolution of Private Property' (2005) 80 *New York University Law Review* 117. This view may be contrasted with 'Demsetzian' accounts of private property, which overlook the political process of property rights formation ('top-down') in favour of the 'private ordering' of underlying economic and social factors as mediated through the market ('bottom-up'); H Demsetz, 'Toward a Theory of Property Rights' (1967) 57 *American Economic Review* 347; H Desmetz, 'Toward a Theory of Property Rights II: The Competition Between Private and Collective Ownership' (2002) 31 *Journal of Legal Studies* S653; I

financial crisis on the nature of financial regulation in the UK remain to be seen, so too does the impact of normative changes in the regulatory environment—including conceptions of the (older) consumer as an autonomous moral agent or a vulnerable legal subject—on common law property and contract discourse. In order to unpack this further, it is necessary to understand the context of housing equity transactions for older people, the real nature of the 'choices' that the older owner makes and the politically-charged 'housing paradigms' within which they are located.

Sened, *The Political Institution of Private Property* (Cambridge, Cambridge University Press, 1997); TW Merrill, 'Introduction: The Desmetz Thesis and the Evolution of Property Rights' (2002) 31 *Journal of Legal Studies* S331. For evidence of the political influence in contract, see, eg, Collins's discussion of the impact of financial services regulation in subverting the traditional paradigm of private law in contract as a 'principles-based' system of rights and entitlements: above, section (4).

5

The Meanings of Home for Older Owners

(1) Introduction

This chapter explores the pluralist and competing paradigms of owned housing for older people, from housing as investment and housing as inheritance, to housing as home for 'ageing in place'. Smith has described owned homes as 'a hybrid of money, materials, and meanings',[1] and nowhere is this more evident than in respect of older owners. This chapter uses the model of pluralist housing paradigms to explore the meanings which have been constructed around the owned home. The 'housing paradigm' approach provides a method of capturing the additional complexities of home meanings for older owners, as they have been layered through a policy context which sits at the intersection of competing demands on the older owner's home: from 'housing as home', the roof overhead for the older owner and home as housing stock; to 'housing as inheritance' to pass on wealth to the next generation; and lastly to 'housing as an investment asset to spend', to be encashed as capital or income to fund various activities, from lifestyle to welfare needs, property maintenance to payment for long-term care.

These competing demands can usefully be characterised as competing 'paradigms',[2] as each constitutes a particular mode of thinking about the owned home, its functions and its meanings for the older owner-occupier. Housing paradigms are the value-laden organising principles that shape housing issues through an on-going social dialogue.[3] Iglesias defines a 'housing paradigm' as

> an organising principle that affects housing law and policy by directing attention to certain kinds of facts and issues as relevant and important for policy and decision-making ... each housing paradigm incorporates a normative dimension; it is poised towards decision and action in a value-laden way, operating as a lens that privileges certain goals by shaping perceptions of the social reality.[4]

Each paradigm focuses on a particular aspect or function of housing, and enables a discourse to debate the issues raised by the problems it explores.[5] Housing paradigms are

[1] SJ Smith, 'Owner-occupation: at home with a hybrid of money and materials' (2008) 40 *Environment and Planning A* 520 at 521.

[2] This use of 'paradigm' in this context is drawn from T Kuhn, *The Structure of Scientific Revolutions* (Chicago, Ill, University of Chicago Press, 1962).

[3] T Iglesias, 'Housing Paradigms' in S Smith *et al*, *The International Encyclopaedia of Housing and Home* (Oxford, Elsevier, 2011); see also T Iglesias, 'Our Pluralist Housing Ethics and the Struggle for Affordability' (2007) 42 *Wake Forest Law Review* 511, where the author re-labelled the paradigms as 'housing ethics'.

[4] Iglesias (2011), above n 3.

[5] Iglesias sets out six paradigms of housing which he observes in US law and policy: 'housing as an economic good', 'housing as home', 'housing as a human right', 'housing as providing social order', 'housing as one land use in a functional system' and 'housing as a focal point for self-governance'; *ibid.*

plural and flexible: there are likely to be several operating paradigms in any given context, and they will tend to vary in content and in emphasis, depending on any given historical moment, from one jurisdiction to another and for different groups—for example, the dominant paradigm applied to child occupiers may differ from that applied to older owners, or disabled occupiers or low-income owners, according to the political and policy contexts.

The value of employing housing paradigms to analyse the meaning of home for older owners is that they provide a series of distinct lenses through which we can analyse the implications of laws and policies against the meanings and values which the property represents to the owners, and so evaluate the extent to which legal and policy perspectives on owned housing coincide with the real-world priorities of older people in respect of their properties. This chapter argues that these paradigms have shaped the context of housing equity transactions, from the panoply of risks they invoke to the way in which the older owner is constructed as a legal subject, and are relevant not only for what they mean for the owner herself, but also in their normative impact on the expectations and demands imposed on older people with reference to owned housing.

The dominance of a particular paradigm, or the tensions between competing paradigms, also determines how home equity transactions, and the risks they bear, are located within legal frameworks of regulation and protection. For example, on a spectrum of transactions from 'normal' to 'abnormal',[6] normal transactions are enforced on the basis that the rational incentive for entering into the transaction can be readily understood as resonating with an accepted paradigm, so that reliance is a matter of 'tacit presupposition'[7]; while 'abnormal' or 'pathological' transactions might be described as 'cry[ing] aloud for explanation',[8] and so qualifying as the type of transaction that requires legal intervention to protect the vulnerable party. The 'normalisation' of transactions may also, in itself, influence legal perceptions of 'voluntariness', and conclusions concerning the adequacy of information for the purposes of informed choice.[9]

A second consequence of 'normalcy' in transactions is linked to the legal and regulatory frameworks which set standards for the conduct of financial services providers (or the rules of the bargaining process), including the requirements that information be clear and comprehensible,[10] and—crucially—the behavioural responses of consumers to such information and advice as is provided. As the discussion in chapter three has noted, the ways in which consumers respond to risk in financial transactions is influenced by the extent to which transactions are perceived as familiar and not particularly risky: behavioural research has shown that risks which are serious but rare tend to be over-estimated, with

[6] See, eg, K Llewellyn, 'What Price Contract? An Essay in Perspective' (1930) 40 *Yale Law Journal* 704, 708–10 on 'Normality and Abnormality of Contract'.

[7] *Ibid*, at 709.

[8] *Credit Lyonnais Bank Nederland NV v Burch* [1997] 1 All ER 144 at 152.

[9] These issues are discussed further in ch 10.

[10] Eg, the Unfair Terms in Consumer Contracts Regulations 1999 (SI 1999/2083) provide that 'core provisions' cannot be challenged provided they are expressed in clear language; and the FSA has stated that providers should ensure that 'Consumers are provided with clear information and are kept appropriately informed before, during and after the point of sale': FSA, *Principles-Based Regulation: Focusing on the Outcomes that Matter* (London, FSA, 2007) 36; see discussion in P Cartwright, 'Conceptualising and understanding fairness: lessons from and for financial services' in M Kenny, J Devenney and L Fox O'Mahony (eds), *Unconscionability in European Financial Transactions: Protecting the Vulnerable* (Cambridge, Cambridge University Press, 2010) 214–18.

those which are less serious but more common being under-estimated. Lastly, the normalcy of a transaction also encourages the assumption that—notwithstanding the complexity of the instrument—the transaction falls within the 'limits of cognition' of the contracting parties, so that the consumer may be deemed capable of weighing potential losses and gains as a rational legal actor.

This chapter shows that the competing paradigms reflect the various needs (and potentially conflicting demands) of older people vis-à-vis their owned homes, depending on their health, financial well-being, whether they have family and friends to support them in a particular location, the suitability of the property for their needs as they age and so on. These issues have attracted considerable policy attention in recent years.[11] The Ministerial Foreword to the report *Delivering Lifetime Homes, Lifetime Neighbourhoods*[12] described the agenda set out in the *National Strategy for Housing in an Aging Society* as adopting a 'whole new approach', whereby ageing issues are considered in the mainstream of housing policy, with the goals of supporting people 'to live independent, active lives for longer' and 'to help people stay in their home for longer'.[13] The factors influencing an individual's choice between the housing options available in any given case are likely to include housing consumption needs, housing as home (for 'ageing in place'), housing as inheritance and housing as investment/housing wealth. This chapter demonstrates that, in light of the heterogeneity of older owners and their needs, there is a need for 'safe' options for home equity transactions which enable older owners to reconcile competing housing paradigms. The competing paradigms highlight the need for choices between different types of products which meet different types of needs, and for appropriate legal protection across the range of housing strategies for older owners.

(2) Housing Consumption, Downsizing and Under-occupation

There are several positive features associated with saving for retirement through investment in housing.[14] For one thing, since the owned home functions as a consumption good (the roof overhead) as well as an investment asset, an owned-outright home should enable the older owner to meet a significant portion of his or her consumption costs in retirement through the 'steady and certain flow of [housing] services at low out-of-pocket cost'.[15] This 'virtual income stream from housing'[16] is particularly important in light of the decline in income after retirement. However, for many owners, and in light of the

[11] See, eg, Department of Communities and Local Government, *Lifetime Homes, Lifetime Neighbourhoods: A National Strategy for Housing in an Aging Society* (Wetherby, DCLG, 2008), available online at <http://www.communities.gov.uk/documents/housing/pdf/lifetimehomes.pdf>, discussed further below.

[12] Department of Communities and Local Government (Wetherby, DCLG, 2008), available online at <http://www.communities.gov.uk/documents/housing/pdf/deliveringlifetimehomes.pdf>.

[13] *Ibid*, at 6.

[14] See discussion in ch 1.

[15] J Rouwendal, 'Housing Wealth and Household Portfolios in an Aging Society' (2009) 157 *De Economist* 3; see also S Lowe, 'Capital accumulation in home ownership and family welfare' in N Manning and C Ungerson (eds), *Social Policy Review 1989–90* (London, Longman, 1990); S Lowe, 'Home-ownership, wealth and welfare: new connections' in A Corden, E Robertson and K Tolley (eds), *Meeting Needs in an Affluent Society* (Aldershot, Avebury, 1992).

emphasis on housing wealth as a form of pension asset, it is not enough that the owned home provides a housing service for the occupier after retirement (housing as home); it has come under increasing demands as a source of capital or income, whether for related housing costs (for example, maintenance and improvements),[17] or for other outgoings and expenses.

The idea that the owned home provides a housing service in old age is complicated by the suggestion that, for some owners at least, homeownership may become more onerous with age. In one study for the Joseph Rowntree Foundation,[18] the researchers found that although one might expect owning to be cheaper than renting in later life, especially after the mortgage has been paid off, repairs and maintenance represent a high cost for older owners. Furthermore, while renters on low incomes can get help with housing costs through Housing Benefit, State support for low-income homeowners has been retrenched in recent decades.[19] As a result, despite large differences in gross costs between owning and renting, the difference in net costs may be small, and some households on low incomes (if they would be entitled to Housing Benefit) could find renting less costly than owning in later life.[20] Home equity transactions may provide one way in which older owners can raise capital or income to meet these costs, but it is not the only option and, as the discussion in chapter two has noted, in light of the reduced support for repairs and maintenance—particularly significant for people living in older properties—moving, whether to a less expensive owned house, or to a private or social rented property, may become an attractive or a necessary option.

Before 'equity release' products became widely available, older owners in need of capital or income would typically 'downsize' or 'trade down' their home in exchange for a less expensive property and some capital release. There is evidence to suggest that this is now a relatively rare practice in the UK, as British homeowners prefer to stay in their original residences if at all possible.[21] On the one hand, the Pensions Commission has cautioned that the price differential between a semi-detached house and a terraced property is not hugely significant, so that the average owner wanting to stay in the owner-occupied sector is not likely to release substantial capital in this way.[22] There are transactions costs associated with moving house within the owner-occupied sector (legal costs, survey, searches, stamp duty, Land Registry fee) which eat into the capital sum released by sale. It has also been suggested that there is a lack of suitable properties for older people to move

[16] SJ Smith, *Banking on Housing: Speculating on the role and relevance of housing wealth in Britain* (Paper prepared for the Joseph Rowntree Foundation Inquiry into Home Ownership 2010 and Beyond, 2005) 18.

[17] See ch 2.

[18] R Hancock, J Askham, H Nelson and A Tinker, *Home ownership in old age: financial benefit or burden* (York, Joseph Rowntree Foundation, 1999).

[19] See ch 2.

[20] Hancock *et al*, above n 18, 'Findings', available online at <http://www.jrf.org.uk/sites/files/jrf/F949.pdf>.

[21] J Banks, R Blundell, Z Oldfield and JP Smith, 'Housing Price Volatility and Downsizing in Later Life', *NBER Working Paper No 13496* (Cambridge, MA, National Bureau of Economic Research, 2007). For earlier, similar findings in the US, see SF Venti and DA Wise, 'Aging, Moving and Housing Wealth', *NBER Working Paper No 2324* (Cambridge, MA, National Bureau of Economic Research, 1989); SF Venti and DA Wise, 'But They Don't Want to Reduce Housing Equity', *NBER Working Paper No 2859* (Cambridge, MA, National Bureau of Economic Research, 1990).

[22] See Pensions Commission, *Challenges and Choices*, First Report of the Pensions Commission (London, TSO, 2004), fig 5.18, charting the difference in average price of semi-detached and terraced houses at only £32,000 in 2004; D Maxwell and S Sodha, *Housing Wealth: First timers to old timers* (London, IPPR, 2006).

into, particularly within the owner-occupied sector,[23] with the result that some owners who sell their homes move into the rental sector instead,[24] including a large proportion of those who move into public-sector sheltered housing.[25]

There is also evidence to suggest that non-economic factors may disincline older owners from trading down. A comparative study modelling the housing transitions of older people in Britain and the US has found that, although greater house price volatility in Britain might be expected to make downsizing amongst older owners more popular than in the US, downsizing[26] is less popular in Britain, where older households are much more likely to stay in their original residences.[27] Housing mobility in later life has typically been relatively rare in Britain, particularly for outright owners, with British owners even more reluctant to move than those in the United States.[28] A 2008 study for the Department of Communities and Local Government,[29] which sought to capture the views, experiences and aspirations of older people concerning their future housing intentions, found that most participants were determined to stay in their current homes for as long as possible, with key influencing factors including attachment to the current home; the complexity of family/caring relationships; neighbours and neighbourhoods (with good neighbours an incentive to stay and *vice versa*); access to services and amenities; and health and well-being, with most people recognising that their health would be the deciding factor if they were to move in the future.[30] Interestingly, this study also found that participants were generally reluctant to think about their future selves and their future needs, with many feeling 'that it was impossible to plan for future uncertainties'.[31] This has significant resonances for the demands placed on older people to plan for the future in their strategies for using housing equity.[32] At the same time, the study also found that some older participants accepted the possibility that they might have to move, but emphasised the importance of choice when the time came; that if necessary, they would want to move when they were still young enough to cope with it, and when they could choose a suitable new home from a range of alternatives.[33] This reinforces the importance for older people of maintaining independence through the active exercise of choice,[34] with

[23] G Mountain and H Buri, *Report of the Evaluation of the Pilot Housing Options Advice Services for Older People* (Sheffield, Sheffield Hallam University, 2005), available online at <http://www.careandrepair-england.org.uk/sisosig/downloads/sheffieldhallamevaluation.pdf>.

[24] K Croucher, *Housing Choices and Aspirations of Older People: Research from the New Horizons Programme* (London, Department of Communities and Local Government, 2008) 52.

[25] See K Croucher, D Sanderson, S Chaplin, D Wright and K Lowson, *Review of Sheltered Housing in Scotland*, (Scottish Government Social Research, 2008), available online at <http://www.york.ac.uk/inst/chp/publications/PDF/shelteredhsgscotland.pdf>.

[26] Whether moving to a smaller owned property, to a rented property, moving in with family and friends, renting out rooms or reducing maintenance and repairs; see T Davidoff, 'Maintenance and the Home Equity of the Elderly', *Fisher Centre for Real Estate and Urban Economics Paper No 03–288* (Berkeley, CA, University of California, Berkeley, 2004).

[27] Banks *et al*, above n 21, at 34–37.

[28] JF Ermisch and SP Jenkins, 'Retirement and housing adjustment in later life: evidence from the British Household Panel Survey' (1999) 6 *Labour Economics* 311.

[29] Croucher, above n 24.

[30] *Ibid*, at 7–8.

[31] *Ibid*, at 8.

[32] See generally ch 3.

[33] Croucher, above n 24, at 8.

[34] *Ibid*, at 48; see also R Clough, M Leamy, L Bright *et al*, *Homing in on Housing: A Study of Housing Decisions of People Aged over 60* (Lancaster, Eskrigge Social Research, 2003).

implications for the construction of, and support of, older owners as financially and legally capable agents, notwithstanding their (contextual) vulnerabilities.[35]

There is a range of programmes in place in the UK to support older people in making decisions about where to live, including the *Should I Stay or Should I Go* (SISOSIG) programme, a national initiative coordinated by Care & Repair England to stimulate the development of housing options services for older people.[36] This programme provides 'information, advice, support and practical help for older people who are living in poor or unsuitable housing and/or considering options for "moving on"',[37] and seeks 'to influence the strategic planning of housing, health, care and support services for older people'.[38] The SISOSIG programme was evaluated in 2005,[39] and the findings indicated that most people using the services were aged 80 and older, that 74 per cent were recorded as experiencing health problems, but that they consistently expressed a 'desire for housing, an environment and community that enabled continuance of an independent life despite the cumulative effects of ageing, disability and illness'.[40] This evaluation underscored the general inadequacy of housing options available for older people: there are limited options available for older people who want to move, and those who do want to move are generally motivated by poor health.[41] Older people's reluctance to leave their homes is considered further below in the context of 'housing as home', to support ageing in place.

Before leaving the subject of downsizing, it is also important to note that the relative unpopularity of downsizing in Britain has implications for debates concerning efficient use of housing stock, with the argument that older owners 'under-occupy' their homes. This issue was explored in a 2007 report by the International Longevity Centre,[42] which found that under-occupancy is a widespread issue, with 24 million people, or 46 per cent of the UK population, judged to be living in under-occupied homes. Under-occupancy rates are higher for the retired population (56 per cent), although the report concluded that since the older population represents a relative minority of all owners, the difference is small, such that

> [t]he explicit linkage of older, under-occupied households with overcrowding and homelessness in wider society is 'ageist' … If society deems it reasonable for all households to occupy as much space as they can afford, it is untenable to label housing shortages as an age-driven problem.[43]

While under-occupancy is to some extent age-driven, it is primarily driven by wealth, and to define it as an issue to be addressed through encouraging older households to downsize is ageist inasmuch as it overlooks—or treats as acceptable—under-occupation by younger households. There is no doubt that downsizing can be a positive decision for a minority of older people who *choose* to move, with benefits including the opportunity to release equity and potential advantages when the move brings the older person closer to supportive

[35] See ch 6.

[36] See <http://www.careandrepair-england.org.uk/sisosig/prog.html> for details of the SISOSIG programme.

[37] *Ibid.*

[38] *Ibid.*

[39] Mountain and Buri, above n 23.

[40] *Ibid*, at 69.

[41] *Ibid*, at 71–72; Croucher, above n 24, at 48.

[42] E Harding, *Older People's Housing and Under-Occupancy: A Policy Brief* (London, International Longevity Centre, 2007).

[43] *Ibid*, at 3.

family and friends, services or facilities. The release of larger properties through older owners downsizing would not be sufficient in itself to solve the problems presented by under-occupancy and over-crowding, although it could make some contribution on this front. The key issue, however, is that if older owners do decide to downsize, they are able to make informed choices.[44]

It is also important to recognise that the definition of under-occupancy depends on how person/space calculations are made, which in turn is linked to assumptions about the need for, and use of, space by older owners.[45] In its *National Strategy for Housing in an Aging Society*, the Department of Communities and Local Government recognised that 'As we grow older, we spend more time in our homes, and they become more important to us and more likely to enhance or undermine our health and wellbeing.'[46] People aged over 65 were found to spend on average over 80 per cent of their time at home, with those over 85 years old spending 90 per cent of their time in their homes.[47] Croucher's report for the Department also recognised the importance of space for older people:

> [O]lder people … need space for visitors, hobbies, possessions, to express identity and individuality, as well as space for living (for example, having family for lunch, or celebrating special occasions). For those who are unwell, space is needed too for storing items like mobility aids, wheelchairs, and importantly to allow carers the space to assist someone if this is required.[48]

In fact, with older people more likely to spend most of their time in the home, the reduction in 'home range' means that the use of the property is maximised.[49] With this in mind, 'ageing in place' has been described as a 'win-win' policy, since it is 'overwhelmingly preferred by older people themselves'[50] as well as reducing the demand for institutional care. Judd *et al*'s study of older Australians also found that they used the 'under-occupied' space in their homes well, and that it had an important role in healthy and active ageing.[51]

The arguments for ageing in place recognise emotional attachments to a long-standing home, but may also reflect the practicalities of housing for older people: it has been argued that explanations for 'non-moving' among older people are as much to do with the lack of suitable properties to move to, and the financial implications of moving, as they are about attachment to the home or a desire to stay put.[52] Oldman's analysis of which older owners would be financially better off and some worse off as a result of moving, and where it would be financially neutral, demonstrated some of the constraints to downsizing, particularly for older people living in low-value properties. Oldman concluded that 'Getting at bricks and mortar wealth through trading down is likely to be considerably less

44 *Ibid.*

45 See B Judd, J Quinn, D Olsberg and O Demirbilek, *Does Size Matter? Under-Occupancy and Older Australian Home Owners*, available online at <http://www.fbe.unsw.edu.au/cf/publications/presentations/attachments/SOAC09Quinn_Judd_Demirbilek_Olsberg.pdf>.

46 DCLG, above n 11, at 24.

47 *Ibid.* See also M Baltes, I Maas, H-U Wilms and M Borchelt, 'Everyday competence in old and very old age: Theoretical considerations and empirical findings' in PB Baltes and KU Mayer (eds), *The Berlin Aging Study* (Cambridge, Cambridge University Press, 1999); MS Moss and MP Lawton, 'Time budgets of older people: A window on four lifestyles' (1982) 37 *Journal of Gerontology* 115.

48 Croucher, above n 24, at 49.

49 C Despres and S Lord, 'Growing Older in Post-War Suburbs: The Meanings and Experiences of Home' in GD Rowles and H Chaudhury (eds), *Home and Identity in Late Life: International Perspectives* (New York, Springer, 2005) 332.

50 Judd *et al*, above n 45, at 3.

51 *Ibid*, 12.

52 C Oldman, 'Financial Effects of Moving in Old Age' (1991) 6(4) *Housing Studies* 251.

complicated legally and financially than taking up one of the equity release schemes currently on the market.'[53] In either case, decision-making about moving in old age is undoubtedly complex as 'There [is] … a series of trade-offs; decisions about timing of moves, where in the market to aim for, and very complex calculations about the interaction between income, capital and access to social security benefits.'[54]

The UK's Department for Communities and Local Government considered the role of downsizing (alongside equity release) in government strategies for older owners in its *National Strategy for Housing in an Aging Society*.[55] It recognised that 'Providing housing options that are attractive to and suitable for older people, particularly those wanting to downsize, will bring benefits to the wider community by increasing the supply of larger housing to meet the needs of new younger families.'[56] The strategy identified a role for local authorities to support older people seeking to downsize, noting that

> [s]ome councils have developed financial and practical packages to help households, particularly older people whose families may have left home, to move to smaller more manageable accommodation, thereby releasing larger family accommodation … As well as providing a cash incentive, Southwark (Council) have offered removal grants, re-decorations to the new home and also 'personal support from a dedicated officer'.[57]

However, this strategy did not emphasise downsizing over other options, rather putting the emphasis on ensuring that guidance and support are also available to help with different housing choices.[58] The key objectives for housing older people as set out in this paper included

> to improve information and advice services so that they know how to make the right choice for them, and are not forced to leave their homes before they are ready, or need to do so … whether staying put or moving home, or considering finance options such as equity release[59]

and 'to make it easier and safer for people to stay in their own homes, near their family and neighbours',[60] which included being able to adapt their homes as physical needs change.

(3) Housing as Home: Ageing in Place

Popular and policy support for 'staying put' reflects the long-established housing paradigm of 'housing as home' for older people. While 'housing as home' is recognised by Iglesias as one of the core housing paradigms influencing US law and policy,[61] and the salience of home meanings for *all* occupiers has been recognised in the context of UK law

[53] *Ibid*, at 253.
[54] S Lowe, 'Home Equity and Elderly People' in C Oldman (ed), *Flexible Tenure: Lessons Learned from an Innovative Housing Project for Elderly People* (York, Joseph Rowntree Memorial Trust/National Federation of Housing Associations) 19; quoted in Oldman, above n 52, at 259.
[55] DCLG, above n 11.
[56] *Ibid*, at 113.
[57] *Ibid*.
[58] *Ibid*, at 114.
[59] *Ibid*, at 13.
[60] *Ibid*.
[61] Above, n 3.

and policy,[62] its particular significance for older people is reflected in the policy agenda linking health and housing with 'ageing in place'. Research suggests that older people overwhelmingly prefer to live in their own homes for as long as they can, and home equity transactions can play a crucial role in supporting 'housing as home' by enabling equity to be released while at the same time preserving the home for use and occupation as housing. Indeed, the development of equity release products provides an explicit example of the influence of 'ageing in place' considerations in the design of legal instruments that seek to respond to the needs and desires of consumers. This section considers these home meanings for older people, and their relevance for decision-making in relation to home equity transactions.

In *Conceptualising Home: Theories, Laws and Policies*,[63] I argued that the legal concept of home should recognise the particular salience of home meanings for certain categories of occupier, and considered in some detail the claims that might be made by specific groups such as child occupiers, families, women and low-income households.[64] In the context of housing equity transactions, it is also useful to consider the *home* claims that might be made in respect of older owners, who may be both particularly vulnerable in light of straitened financial circumstances after retirement, and who are at a stage in their life-course when their relationship with their home can play a critical role in maintaining personal identity and independence.[65] These needs were recognised in the Government's *National Strategy for Housing in an Ageing Society*,[66] which focused on the need for appropriate housing stock for older people, including the design and building of suitable housing, as well as the need to make adaptations to property to enable ageing in place and so 'to provide practical help for today's older people to live independent, active lives for longer'.[67] This report also emphasised the need to improve the advice available to older people about their housing options, with the aim of 'help[ing] people stay in their home for longer'.[68]

The general policy of community care for older people in the UK has long been predicated on the belief that most older people prefer to live in their own homes,[69] and a raft of studies exploring the housing preferences of older people have supported the attachments that they have for their homes, and the preference for 'ageing in place'.[70]

[62] See generally L Fox, *Conceptualising Home: Theories, Laws and Policies* (Oxford, Hart Publishing, 2006).

[63] *Ibid.*

[64] *Ibid*, especially chs 7, 8 and 9.

[65] See, eg, A Dupuis and DC Thorns, 'Meanings of Home for Older Home Owners' (1996) 11 *Housing Studies* 485; A Dupuis and DC Thorns, 'Home, Home Ownership and the Search for Ontological Security' (1998) 46 *The Sociological Review* 24; PC Kontos, 'Resisting Institutionalization: Constructing Old Age and Negotiating Home' (1998) 12 *Journal of Aging Studies* 167; J Mansvelt, 'Working at Leisure—Critical Geographies of Ageing' (1997) 29 *Area* 289; G Mowl, R Pain and C Talbot, 'The ageing body and homespace' (2000) 32 *Area* 189.

[66] DCLG, above n 11.

[67] DCLG, above n 12 at 6.

[68] *Ibid.* The Government's support for 'ageing in place' was also reflected in its statement that 'To meet the challenges—and to make the most of the opportunities—presented by our ageing society, we must plan for homes and communities so that people can live out their lives, as long as possible, independently and safely with their families and friends around them.' (*ibid*, at 19).

[69] C Gurney and R Means, 'The Meaning of Home in Later Life' in S Arber and M Evandrou (eds), *Aging, Independence and the Life Course* (London, Jessica Kingsley Publishers, 1993).

[70] See, eg, C Oldham, 'More than Bricks and Mortar' (1998) 24 *Housing* 13; L Harrison and R Means, *Housing: The Essential Element in Community Care* (Oxford, Anchor Housing Trust, 1990); S Peace, 'The living environments of older women' in M Bernard and K Meade (eds), *Women Come of Age* (London, Edward Arnold, 1993); J Langan, R Means and S Rolfe, *Maintaining Home and Independence in Later Life: Older People Speaking*

These studies have identified a range of practical factors which are important for older owners, including the location of the property, both for access to services and for accessing and maintaining social networks and contacts[71]; the strong social value provided by shared neighbourhood spaces[72]; and the need for access to culturally appropriate shops and services for older people from black and ethnic minority communities.[73] Research has also indicated that older rural residents prefer to remain where they are, even where they do not have access to support, services and facilities.[74] Lastly, home also has symbolic meaning for older owners, with particular attachments to the 'dwelling as home' rooted in its place as a physical representation of the life-course and its achievements and events.[75]

Older owners' attachments to home, and the policy paradigm of 'housing as home' that reflects these needs and their role in health and well-being for older people, provide important context to housing equity transactions, as they will tend to support arrangements which allow owners to continue living in their property for the rest of their lives, or as long as they are able to or wish to. For example, equity release schemes typically promise that the older owner will be able to continue living in his or her home,[76] although not all products targeted at older owners deliver security of tenure.[77] The perceived and popular importance of ageing in place also influences the ways that equity release products are framed by those seeking to promote them[78]—as enabling owners to 'have it all', by enjoying their capital now, while also securing their occupation of the property for the rest of their lives—with the result that it may not be immediately obvious what the owner has to lose from such transactions. On the other side of the transaction, the paradigm of the owned house as home reflects the value which the home represents for the older owner, which in turn is likely to influence the owner's perceptions of risk and reward in home equity transactions: the subjective value of the owned home for the occupier is likely to influence decision-making behaviour, through both the 'endowment effect' and the tendency to 'loss aversion' (the desire to maintain the *status quo*).[79] This, in turn, affects the extent to which the older owner's decisions concerning housing equity transactions are objectively 'rational'. The likelihood that older owners will be influenced by these factors (which represent 'anomalies' within rational choice theory) presents a

(Oxford, Anchor Trust, 1996); R Means, 'Home, independence and community care: time for a wider vision?' (1997) 25 *Policy and Politics* 409; R Means, 'Housing Options in 2020: a suitable home for all?' in M Evandrou (ed), *Baby Boomers: Aging in the 21st* Century (London, Age Concern, 1997); F Heywood, A Pate, R Means and J Galvin, *Housing Options for Older People (HOOP): Report on a Developmental Project to Refine a Housing Option Appraisal Tool for Use by Older People* (London, Elderly Accommodation Counsel, 1999); and more recently, Croucher, above n 24.

[71] Croucher, above n 24, at 48; see also Clough *et al*, above n 34.

[72] K Worpole and K Knox, *The Social Value of Public Space* (York, Joseph Rowntree Foundation, 2007).

[73] Croucher *et al*, above n 25.

[74] M Bevan, K Croucher and D Rhodes, *The Housing and Support Needs of Older People in Rural Areas* (The Countryside Agency/Housing Corporation, 2006), available at <http://www.york.ac.uk/inst/chp/Projects/olderrural.htm>.

[75] F Heywood, C Oldman and R Means, *Housing and Home in Later Life* (Milton Keynes, Open University Press, 2002); F Heywood, 'Adaptation: altering the house to restore the home' (2005) 20(4) *Housing Studies* 531.

[76] The first principle in equity release self-regulator Safe Home Income Plan's (SHIP's) Code of Conduct is 'To allow customers to remain in their property for life provided the property remains their main residence.' See SHIP Guarantee, available online at <http://www.ship-ltd.org/shipguarantee.aspx>; see also ch 9.

[77] See ch 9.

[78] See discussion in ch 4, section (5).

[79] See Chapter Four, section 5; and L Fox, *Conceptualising Home*, above, 281–84.

form of 'contextual vulnerability'[80] which offers valuable insights when evaluating the appropriateness of a legal regime predicated on rational choice.

The risks that must be negotiated in respect of housing equity transactions also require owners to navigate through the competing housing paradigms, and to make decisions which reflect the future utility value which the property will hold as the owner ages. The promise of 'safe' home equity use with a guarantee to protect housing as home is likely to carry considerable weight in this decision-making process. This general point is only heightened for older owners, in light of the importance of housing as home in the context of the life-course, and the significance of 'ageing in place' for the identity and well-being of older adults.[81] The argument for 'ageing in place' is 'based on concepts of preference and self-determination: It is grounded in the preservation of identity and recognition of the perceived value of home.'[82] Rowles described home as the 'fulcrum' of the world for older people[83]; the older person's home has also been described as a 'mnemonic anchor for life experiences',[84] and as 'provid[ing] the tools for both enduring and evolving possibilities for the self',[85] helping the older person to define, preserve and maintain his or her self-identity at a time when the transitions associated with ageing (retirement, the ageing body) present challenges to the continuity of the self. The stability of home in supporting self-identity may therefore represent a base from which the older owner is more able to be self-reflexive, in accordance with the requirements of the risk society.[86]

Rowles argued that the symbolic meanings of home give older people their sense of 'insideness'[87]: the physical insideness that results from familiarity and habitual routines; the social insideness that arises from immersion in a neighbourhood or social setting over a long period of time; and an 'autobiographical insideness' based on the landscape of memories wrapped up in the home, which gives the older occupier a sense of identity.[88] Attachment to places of the past helps to 'keep the past alive' for older people, giving them a sense of continuity at a time of transition, while attachment in the present can help in retaining a 'positive self-image' and in enabling older people to assert their independence.[89] Having their own place provides 'a stable source of security and identity amid the flux and vicissitudes of old age'.[90] Indeed, the positive meanings of home for older people are sufficiently strong that, even against the backdrop of financial demands, Oswald and Wahl claimed that 'An elder's home might be a comforting, familiar place

[80] See Chapter Six.

[81] See, eg, Heywood *et al*, above n 75; Rowles and Chaudhury (eds), above n 49.

[82] E Sherman and J Dacher, 'Cherished Objects and the home: their meaning and roles in later life' in Rowles and Chaudhury (eds), above n 49, at 75.

[83] GD Rowles, 'Aging in rural environments' in I Altman, MP Lawton and J Wohlwill (eds), *Elderly People and the Environment* (New York, Plenum Press, 1984).

[84] Rowles and Chaudhury (eds), above n 49, at 12.

[85] *Ibid*, at 13.

[86] See ch 3.

[87] Rowles, above n 83, at 146–47.

[88] '[T]he sense of belonging to and having one's life expressed within a place that can stem from lifelong residence.': F Oswald and H-W Wahl, 'Dimensions of the Meaning of Home in Later Life' in Rowles and Chaudhury (eds), above n 49, at 23.

[89] RL Rubinstein and PA Parmelee, 'Attachment to place and the representation of life course by the elderly' in I Altman and S Low (eds), *Place Attachment* (New York, Plenum Press, 1992).

[90] C Russell, 'Home, Identity and Belonging in Later Life: The Perspectives of Disadvantaged Inner-City Men', in Rowles and Chaudhury (eds), above n 49, at 238; see also B Donaldson, HL Kendig, F Stephens and V Merrill, *'It's My Place': Older people talk about their homes* (Canberra, AGPS, 1993); SL O'Bryant and D Nocera, 'The psychological significance of "home" to older widows' (1985) 9 *Psychology of Women Quarterly* 403.

despite the fact that it is becoming burdensome to maintain and unsafe (and therefore a source of anxiety).'[91] In addition to the practical and emotional importance of the immediate home environment in light of the amount of time that older people spend at home, Oswald and Wahl argued that the home acquires new meaning in old age, 'because it serves to compensate for the reduced functional capacity of the aging individual, especially in very old age'.[92] They concluded that attachment to home, particularly where an occupier has lived there for a long period of time, becomes representative of the individual's biography. This attachment, combined with competence losses, can give rise to an 'idiosyncratic meaning of home',[93] which is likely to make it more difficult to give up the home, even when that is the 'rational' choice.

These home meanings have implications for the extent to which older owners can function as 'rational' risk subjects in housing equity transactions. Croucher has suggested that the importance of home for self-identity may make it more difficult for older people to plan for the changes that are likely to be necessary in their relationship with housing as they age:

> This attachment to home, and the importance of home in presenting an image of 'self' may explain the reluctance of some older people to consider moving or to prepare their homes for later life (for example, by installing more accessible bathrooms), as this would indicate a recognition of aging, something that people are reluctant to acknowledge.[94]

The expectation, in a 'risk society', that older owners plan for their futures—including the complex role that housing wealth may need to play in supporting them financially after retirement—was considered in chapter three, which noted that the ability of older owners to be self-reflexive and to plan for the future is likely to vary depending on their social and cultural capital, with those who most need to release equity (because of inadequate pension or other savings) also likely to be least well equipped to make 'good' decisions, and to calculate risks as informed and active consumers. The nature of the attachment to housing as home and the importance of ageing in place for continuity and self-identity only complicate the multiple and complex factors that must be negotiated in housing equity transactions.

There is also some debate about whether tenure—being an 'owner-occupier'—remains a priority for older people. For example, one UK study quoted an older owner who reported that

> [o]ne of the great achievements in this country is to own your own property and pay for it. My property was fully paid for and it was time to put my feet up and relax. Everybody has a dream. Mine was to own my own home, fully paid for.[95]

This reflected the 'promise' of homeownership which underpinned much government rhetoric promoting the tenure on the basis that it would provide security for old age. Homeownership was described by the Government in the 1950s (when many of today's retirees were growing up) as 'Of all forms of saving … one of the best. Of all forms of

[91] Oswald and Wahl, above n 88, at 23.
[92] *Ibid*, at 25.
[93] *Ibid*, at 30.
[94] Croucher, above n 24, at 49.
[95] African Caribbean man, quoted in F Heywood and M Naz, *Clearance: The View from the Street* (Birmingham, Community Forum, 1990) at 104; and cited in Heywood *et al*, above n 75, at 57–58.

ownership this is one of the most satisfying to the individual and the most beneficial to the nation.'[96] By the early 1970s, homeownership was described as

> the most rewarding form of housing tenure. It satisfies a deep natural desire on the part of the householder to have independent control of the home that shelters him and his family. It gives him the greatest possible security against the loss of his home: and particularly against the price changes that may threaten his ability to keep it. If the householder buys his house on mortgage he builds up by steady saving a capital asset for himself and his dependents.[97]

By 1995, the aspiration to homeownership was officially explained on the premise that people 'value independence and control over their own home'[98]; and in 2005 the Government reiterated its policy of 'offer[ing] people opportunity and choice—to own their home, to meet their aspirations and to build up assets'.[99]

Some scholars have supported the claim that there is a link between ontological security and retaining home ownership in later life, through the sense of 'constancy' the home can provide, through freedom from surveillance, a sense of control and a secure base around which identities are constructed.[100] Dupuis and Thorns' work with older owners built on Saunders' controversial claim that homeownership enhances 'ontological security' where renting does not,[101] by arguing that (against the backdrop of a political ideology of homeownership in post-Depression era and post-World War II New Zealand) the *owned home* offered a possibility for a generation of people (now 'older people') to re-establish a sense of security.[102] Ownership, they argued, was viewed as part of an 'adult identity',[103] while renting was seen as 'much more of a risky business with vulnerable tenants subject to the whims of the landlord and eviction a constant fear'.[104]

The proposition that remaining an *owner* is important for older people must be reviewed in light of the challenges to Saunders' thesis that home ownership (as opposed to renting) is intrinsically linked with ontological security.[105] In Pia Kontos' study of older tenants living in social housing in Canada, she found that 'Home is an invaluable resource to senior tenants in adjusting to physical decline that comes with old age and in sustaining

[96] *Houses: the Next Step*, Cmnd 8996 (London, HMSO, 1953), Preamble. Similarly, the stated goal of the 1958 White Paper *House Purchase* was 'to enable more people to buy their own homes': Minister for Housing and Local Government, *House Purchase*, Cmnd 571, Sessional Papers (London, HMSO, 1958).

[97] Department of the Environment, *Fair Deal for Housing*, Cmnd 6851 (London, HMSO, 1971) 4.

[98] Department of the Environment, *Our Future Homes*, Cm 2901 (London, HMSO, 1995) 12.

[99] Office of the Deputy Prime Minister, *Extending Home Ownership for All* (London, HMSO, 2005) 1. It was clear, however, that the 'choice' on offer was the choice of buying into the owner-occupied sector, and that the Government's policy position on the implicit advantages of owning your own home remained strong. See also, *Sustainable Communities: Homes for All (A Five Year Plan from the Office of the Deputy Prime Minister)* (Norwich, HMSO, 2005).

[100] A Dupuis and DC Thorns, 'Home, homeownership and the search for ontological security' (1998) 46 *The Sociological Review* 24.

[101] This claim has been widely challenged, most notably in Gurney's research arguing that 'home' meanings are not necessarily dependent on tenure; C Gurney, *The Meaning of Home in the Decade of Owner Occupation: Towards an Experiential Perspective* (Bristol, School of Advanced Urban Studies, University of Bristol, 1990).

[102] Dupuis and Thorns, above n 100, at 26.

[103] *Ibid*, at 37–38.

[104] *Ibid*, at 31.

[105] Eg, Gurney and Means's 1993 paper rejected the idea that home delivers 'ontological security', but suggested rather that the meanings of home include 'emotional security', and called for work that compared the extent to which occupiers derive 'emotional security' from their homes by tenure; C Gurney and R Means, 'The Meaning of Home in Later Life' in S Arber and M Evandrou, *Aging, Independence and the Life Course* (London, Jessica Kingsley Publishers, 1993).

their independence and a sense of personal identity',[106] and that 'Their desire to remain independent and in control of their own lives is linked to home living and to what home signifies to them.'[107] The perception of control in the home environment has been found to be particularly important for older people in maintaining higher levels of health and well-being, and lower rates of hospitalisation and mortality.[108] Yet the evidence suggests that this is linked to the preservation of *home* rather than *ownership*: for example, Kontos found that older tenants' attachments to their rented homes led them to employ diverse coping strategies to avoid relocation to an institutional care facility[109] and to prevent their homes in supportive housing becoming 'institution-like'.

In contrast, the disadvantages of ownership for older people, including the financial costs and ineligibility for welfare support (for example, for care, unless the home is sold), have been linked with increasing disability or ill-health,[110] and the negative psychological effects of ownership for older people include a

> burdensome lack of independence, since people feel constrained by practical imperative and sense of moral duty to maintain their home, by financial duty to keep up mortgage or other payments, and by the housing market which might prevent them moving when or where they wanted.[111]

Of course, the debate about 'ownership' and what it means for older occupiers sits on top of the more fundamental issue about continued occupation in the same place: whether one accepts that owners have enhanced 'ontological security', or that owners and renters both derive 'emotional security' from their homes, the point about remaining in place prevails in either case; the difference is in the facility with which this is made possible within policy and market/legal contexts—through housing policy options, on the one hand, or 'safe' housing equity transactions, on the other.

The proposition that the cultural/symbolic meanings of being an *owner* are specifically important, in addition to the practical and emotional desire to 'stay put', is also potentially challenged by recent research exploring the shifting attitudes of owners towards their homes as inheritance and as investment assets to be used (spent) throughout the life-course. These issues are discussed in more detail in subsequent sections, which note evidence of changing attitudes towards the meanings of owned homes. Even without presuming a relationship between ontological security and homeownership,[112] the attachment to a particular place

[106] PC Kontos, 'Resisting Institutionalization: Constructing Old Age and Negotiating Home' (1998) 12 *Journal of Aging Studies* 167, 168.

[107] *Ibid*, at 173.

[108] R Schultz and J Heckhausen, 'Aging, culture and control: Setting a new research agenda' (1999) 54B *The Journals of Gerontology* 139.

[109] AJ Sixsmith, 'The Meaning and Significance of Home in Later Life' in B Bytheway and J Johnson (eds), *Welfare and the Ageing Experience* (Aldershot, Gower, 1990).

[110] J Askham, H Nelson, A Tinker and R Hancock, *To Have and To Hold: The Bond Between Older People and the Homes They Own* (York, York Publishing Services, 1999) 44.

[111] *Ibid*. This study concluded that the benefits of ownership outweighed its burdens for older people.

[112] While some scholars have argued that ownership enhances ontological security—see eg, RM Rakoff, 'Ideology in Everyday Life: The Meaning of the House' (1977) 7 *Politics and Society* 85; SG Smith, 'The essential qualities of a home' (1994) 14 *Journal Of Environmental Psychology* 31; P Saunders, *A Nation Of Home Owners* (London, Unwin Hyman, 1990); M Bulos and W Chaker, 'Sustaining a sense of home and personal identity' in D Benjamin (ed), *The Home: Words, Interpretations, Meanings And Environments* (Aldershot, Ashgate, 1995)—others have challenged that view, arguing that occupiers can achieve ontological security through their homes regardless of tenure, see Gurney, above n 101; C Gurney, *Meanings of Home and Home Ownership: Myths,*

may influence the older person's decisions concerning the use of his or her housing wealth. Despres and Lord found that older people 'show tenacity and a remarkable capacity to adapt and hold on to their home despite autonomy problems',[113] although they argued that this was not only because of the desire to 'stay put', but also explicitly linked to the sense of security presumed to go with *unencumbered home ownership*. They claimed that 'seniors' perception of security is linked to *home ownership*. Not only their status as homeowner, but also the fact that their mortgage is entirely paid-off, makes people feel secure about their financial future.'[114]

In addition to its functions as a locus of socialisation, a familiar setting, the centre of daily life and for attachment and memories, Despres and Lord argued that the owned home is also important to older people as an indicator of social status, to preserve 'autonomy' and avoid the label of 'dependency'.[115] Yet where housing equity is encashed, the superficial badge of ownership may be underpinned by a deeper and more problematic vulnerability when the *social* 'owner' is no longer a *legal* owner.

The mechanism by which the older person generates equity from his or her home—whether through a reverse mortgage, home reversion scheme, 'sale and rent back', secured (or, *ab initio* unsecured) borrowing or downsizing—will determine the extent to which that person is divested of his or her 'ownership' rights, the '*prima facie*, unlimited privileges of use or abuse over the thing, and, *prima facie*, unlimited powers of control and transmission'.[116] While downsizing completely severs the relationship between the person and the property (perhaps also involving tenure change, thus divesting the older person of both the badge of 'owner' and the occupation of his or her home), a 'sale and rent back' transaction allows the older person to remain in occupation while divesting himself of ownership of the property, which is transferred out-and-out with a new (and potentially vulnerable) new lease granted.[117] Equity release or reverse mortgage products, on the other hand, treat the property as security, although the crucial difference compared to a conventional mortgage is that the debt is not generally intended to be repaid by instalments but with the proceeds of sale of the property itself. Although equity release schemes effectively divest older owners of the exchange rights that are often seen as central to the definition of 'ownership', the agreement that they can continue to live in the property is crucial to enabling them to maintain their physical and social environments, their daily habits and routines, and so preserving their feelings of 'comfort and security'.[118] To some extent, at the equity release/reverse mortgage end of the spectrum, the impact of the transaction on ownership is not very far removed from the conventional mortgage, with the owner/consumer remaining the registered proprietor and, crucially, retaining the 'badge' of owner notwithstanding the substantial property right which has been traded as security. However, as the discussion in chapters seven, eight and nine will show, the extent

Histories, and Experiences (PhD, Bristol, 1996); P Marcuse, 'The Ideologies of Ownership and Property Rights' in R Plunz (ed), *Housing Form and Public Policy in the US* (New York, Praeger, 1980).

[113] C Despres and S Lord, 'Growing Older in Post-War Suburbs: The Meanings and Experiences of Home' in Rowles and Chaudhury (eds), above n 49, at 330.

[114] *Ibid*, at 328.

[115] 'Maintaining homeownership not only reflects enduring values and lifestyles, it contributes to seniors' positive self-image, preserving their social status as autonomous and independent persons. Breaking up with one's house is acquiring the status of a socially dependent person.' (*ibid*, at 329).

[116] J Harris, *Property and Justice* (Oxford, Oxford University Press, 1996) 30.

[117] See ch 9.

[118] Despres and Lord, above n 113, at 330.

to which the 'owner' who has traded on housing equity can bank on ageing in place depends on the terms of the particular transaction and the underlying property rights left to him or her.

Lastly, it is important to recognise that there are, of course, circumstances in which ageing in place becomes too much of a burden, and where the older person may experience adverse home feelings: losses of security, autonomy, independence, social contact; because he or she becomes isolated at home, physically unable to maintain the house or to keep it clean,[119] or because the design or the neighbourhood is no longer suitable for that person's needs.[120] Although 'staying put' has been described as 'ultimately ... less disruptive and more socially just',[121] it may also necessitate the making of adaptations or improvements to property, which require housing improvement finance. While Oldham asserted that 'It cannot be always assumed that older people do not want to move',[122] Heywood *et al* argued that the *reasons* for wanting to move or stay put are primarily about the housing itself, particularly its adequacy and suitability as the occupier ages.[123] Nelson went further in claiming that it was not just the physical suitability of the housing that mattered, but that

> [h]ousing decisions are formed and reformed out of the vast array of experiences and processes taking place in an individual's life. The home, the memories it holds, the neighbourhood, roots in the community, friends, family, money, housing opportunities, the environment, all play a part.[124]

The complexities of *home* and ageing give rise to a relationship that is 'variable and sometimes contradictory',[125] and which reinforces the complexities of decisions for housing after retirement. Even within the paradigm of housing as home, owners must confront challenging issues relating to their needs, identities and attachments; this is only compounded by the tensions between competing paradigms that come into play in housing equity transactions.

Research on ageing in place also suggests that it is important to preserve the older person's sense of autonomy and control over decision-making, which in itself is significant in ensuring that he or she feels 'at home', whatever housing option may be taken. Watkins and Hosier describe three possible scenarios for later-life outcomes in respect of housing and home: first, the older person may successfully 'age in place', maintaining control over his or her home environment and the high level of autonomy and decision-making control that ensure a positive home experience; secondly, the older person may relinquish

[119] Heywood *et al*, above n 75, at 58–59.

[120] *Ibid*, at 87–88.

[121] D Clapham and SJ Smith, 'Housing Policy and "Special Needs"' (1990) 8(3) *Policy and Politics* 183; discussed in C Hamnett and SJ Smith, 'Special Issue on the Housing Implications of an Aging Society' (1991) 6(4) *Housing Studies* 227.

[122] C Oldman, *Developing a Housing and Community Care Strategy for Older People: A Do It Yourself Guide* (Oxford, Anchor Trust, 2000) 18.

[123] Heywood *et al*, above n 75, at 83.

[124] H Nelson, 'To move or not to move: the role of health and well-being' (1997) 2 *Health Care in Later Life* 143, 153.

[125] 'For example, staying in the home may be viewed both as an identifier of old age and therefore something to be avoided, and as a means of resistance to ageing.': G Mowl, R Pain and C Talbot, 'The ageing body and the homespace' (2000) 32 *Area* 189. Mowls *et al* added that 'In both cases, the meaning of the homespace is influenced by ideas about gendered as well as aging bodies ... Attachment to the home was influenced not so much by chronological age ... but factors such as health status (spending time at home was seen to be linked to physical decline, which is viewed as heralding old age), and gender (it was seen as more important for men to spend time outside the home after retirement than women).' (*ibid*, at 193).

much of his or her decision-making authority, in which case 'the experienced home drifts towards the homelessness end of the spectrum as the person becomes increasingly unable to actively pursue the imagined home'[126]; and thirdly, the older person can lose his or her sense of home (becoming 'homeless') not only by having to leave the property, but also when decision-making authority has been stripped away and decisions are made without consultation, leaving that person unable actively to express his or her 'self' in the environment,[127] and with significant negative effects for well-being.[128]

Loss of control over decision-making for older owners may be manifest in a number of ways: at the extreme end it involves incapacity, but along the spectrum it also includes varying levels of 'paternalistic intervention' in decision-making concerning the older person's housing arrangements, through to questioning the enforceability of housing equity transactions, for example based on impaired consent.[129] The threat to 'autonomy' posed by loss of control over decision-making is obviously greater at the more extreme end of the spectrum, in response to (medical) evidence that functional capacities are undermined.[130] When considering the links between the older person's sense of autonomy and control over decision-making for 'feeling at home', and the legal frameworks governing housing equity transactions, it is important to distinguish between the psychological meaning of decisional autonomy and the legal meaning of autonomy.[131]

For one thing, while traditional legal accounts have tended to position autonomy and dependency as opposite ends of one spectrum,[132] psychologists draw a clear distinction between autonomy or self-determination on the one hand, and individualism and independence on the other.[133] According to the psychological theory of self-determination, 'autonomy' occurs when a person's behaviour is 'experienced as willingly enacted and when he or she fully endorses the actions in which he or she is engaged and/or the values expressed by them'.[134] The opposite of autonomy, within these terms, is not dependence but '*heteronomy*, in which one's actions are experienced as controlled by forces that are phenomenally alien to the self or that compel one to behave in specific ways

126 JF Watkins and AF Hosier, 'Conceptualising Home and Homelessness: A Life Course Perspective' in Rowles and Chaudhury (eds), above n 49, at 207.

127 *Ibid.*

128 C Russell, 'Home, Identity and Belonging in Later Life: The Perspectives of Disadvantaged Inner-City Men', in Rowles and Chaudhury (eds), above n 49, at 237.

129 See ch 10.

130 This is reflected in the literature surrounding participation in care decision-making for older people, see eg, S Davies, S Laker and L Ellis, 'Promoting autonomy and independence for older people within nursing practice: a literature review' (1997) 26 *Journal of Advanced Nursing* 408.

131 See, eg, BJ Winick, 'On Autonomy: Legal and Psychological Perspectives' (1992) 37 *Villanova Law Review* 1705.

132 See ch 4, sections (3) and (4), and ch 6 for discussions of the autonomy/dependency dyad in private law.

133 See V Chirkov, Y Kim, RM Ryan and U Kaplan, 'Differentiating Autonomy from Individualism and Independence: A Self-Determination Theory Perspective on Internalization of Cultural Orientations and Well-Being' (2003) 84 *Journal of Personality and Social Psychology* 97; R Koestner and GF Losier, 'Distinguishing Reactive versus Reflective Autonomy' (1996) 64 *Journal of Personality* 465; RM Ryan and J Lynch, 'Emotional autonomy versus detachment: Revisiting the vicissitudes of adolescence and early adulthood' (1989) 60 *Child Development* 340.

134 Chirkov *et al*, above n 133, at 98; 'People are therefore most autonomous when they act in accordance with their authentic interests or integrated values and desires.': *ibid.*

regardless of one's values or interests'.[135] In contrast, 'dependence' connotes reliance on others, and is the opposite of independence (not autonomy).[136]

The psychological meaning of 'autonomy' also emphasises the contextual nature of decision-making capacity as part of 'an ongoing, dynamic process wherein a person's capacity to exercise decisional autonomy depends on a variety of impinging environmental, psychological and social factors'.[137] By recognising the contextual, external nature of decision-making vulnerabilities, the psychological concept of autonomy adopts a broader and more empirically-based perspective on the individual's subjectivity, compared to the 'stripped-down', abstract subject that has informed the liberal legal, political and economic concept of autonomy. This in turn creates space within the psychological concept for consideration of both the 'inherently idiosyncratic' nature of an individual's position on the autonomy spectrum,[138] and the related issue of how to strike an appropriate balance between respect for autonomy and the responsibility to protect potentially vulnerable people,[139] recognising that neither autonomy nor protection can be 'pursued single-mindedly at the expense of the other'.[140]

In contrast, the meaning of autonomy in traditional private law goes beyond actions which support one's values or interests, to conflate choice with decision-making *capacity*, and by extension with the enforcement of those choices (with good or bad outcomes) on the grounds that to do otherwise fails to respect legal subjects as formally equal.[141] The meaning of autonomy in private law has been loaded up with the political ideology of individualism, so that the 'autonomous individual' does not merely pursue his or her own interests, but must do so in a self-responsible, self-reliant, independent way. This concept of autonomy resonates with neoliberal risk subjectivities, by requiring the individual to be self-responsible for determining his or her own life plans within a supposedly neutral context.[142] The politically-charged conflation of autonomy with atomistic individualism, and the 'unreality' of excluding context from traditional legal analyses of autonomy have both been heavily criticised in feminist scholarship on the basis that they conceal both the

[135] *Ibid.*

[136] Thus 'autonomy is seen as largely orthogonal to both independence and individualism': *ibid*; see also RM Ryan, 'Agency and organisation: Intrinsic motivation, autonomy and the self in psychological development' in JE Jacobs and R Dienstbier (eds), *Nebraska Symposium on Motivation Vol 40: Developmental Perspectives on Motivation* (Lincoln, University of Nebraska Press, 1993).

[137] SJ Anderer, 'Integrating Legal and Psychological Perspectives on the Right to Personal Autonomy' (1992) 37 *Villanova Law Review* 1563, 1566; see also WM Altman, PA Parmalee and MA Smyer, 'Autonomy, Competence, and Informed Consent in Long Term Care: Legal and Psychological Perspectives' (1992) 37 *Villanova Law Review* 1671, arguing that 'psychology's process orientation and focus on the complex interplay between personal, environmental and social factors can help expand the otherwise rigid and narrow elements of informed consent': *ibid*, at 1672.

[138] '[T]hey suggest that individuals' "best-interests" are inherently idiosyncratic and can be identified and served only through careful examination of each individual and his or her own circumstances.': Anderer, above n 137, at 1566.

[139] See, eg, D Kennedy, 'Distributive and Paternalist Motives in Contract and Tort Law, With Special Reference to Compulsory Terms and Unequal Bargaining Power' (1982) 41 *Maryland Law Review* 563, 624–47. Indeed, law-and-psychology analysis of decisional autonomy amongst older people has identified 'a complex dialectal relationship between the need for self-determination and the need for security through paternalistic intervention': Anderer, above n 137, at 1566.

[140] JW Ellis, 'Decisions By and For People with Mental Retardation: Balancing Considerations of Autonomy and Protection' (1992) 37 *Villanova Law Review* 1779.

[141] See discussion in ch 4, section (3).

[142] See ch 3.

contextual[143] and the relational nature of 'true' autonomy,[144] and support a 'constructed polarity between autonomy on the one hand and dependence on the state on the other'.[145]

Feminist conceptions of autonomy (and the role of the State in fostering autonomy)[146] also highlight the distinction between substantive and procedural autonomy.[147] While procedural autonomy focuses on whether an individual is *capable* of making autonomous choices, a substantive account is concerned with whether the choices that person makes (including those that are made under constraints) can in fact be regarded as autonomous choices.[148] This echoes Purdy's description of Sen's example of 'a choice over three alternative achievements that are seen as "bad", "terrible", and "disastrous"',[149] as 'process freedom', and emphasises the ways in which contexts can compromise substantive autonomy at a given moment, without necessarily negating the possibility of autonomy as a capacity.[150] Substantive accounts of autonomy are rooted in empirical realities, not abstract values. They recognise the context of the individual and his or her relational connections to others and within dominant social structures, so 'allowing us to discern between contexts that appear to grant "free choice" but maintain relations of domination and exclusion, and those that are genuinely supportive of autonomy'.[151] This vision of 'genuine autonomy' also reflects the choice or decision that is most consistent with 'future autonomy'.[152] In contrast, Ben-Ishai argued that

> [a] procedural account will not provide us with the tools to distinguish between the options that are based on oppressive socialization and those that are not, or between those that are more or *less* autonomy fostering in the long run.[153]

[143] '[T]he substance of autonomy is always constituted within a given political and social context.': E Ben-Ishai, 'The Autonomy-Fostering State: "Coordinated Fragmentation" and Domestic Violence Services' (2009) 17 *Journal of Political Philosophy* 307, 318. The importance of context, and challenges to the individualistic notion of autonomy in favour of 'relational autonomy', have been extensively analysed in feminist critique of the legal concept of autonomy: see, eg, J Anderson and A Honneth, 'Autonomy, Vulnerability, Recognition, and Justice' in JP Christman and J Anderson (eds), *Autonomy and the Challenges of Liberalism: New Essays* (Cambridge, Cambridge University Press, 2005); M Friedman, *Autonomy, Gender, Politics* (Oxford, Oxford University Press, 2003); EF Kittay and EK Feder, *The subject of care: feminist perspectives on dependency* (Lanham, Md, Rowman & Littlefield Publishers, 2002); C Mackenzie and N Stoljar, *Relational autonomy: feminist perspectives on autonomy, agency, and the social self* (New York, Oxford University Press, 2000); J Nedelsky, 'Reconceiving Autonomy: Sources, Thoughts and Possibilities' (1989) 1 *Yale Journal of Law and Feminism* 7; so has the 'stripped-down subject' of private law: see also M Nussbaum, *Frontiers of Justice: Disability, Nationality, Species Membership* (Cambridge, MA, Harvard University Press, 2006); see further, ch 6.

[144] Ben-Ishai, above n 143.

[145] *Ibid*, at 328.

[146] *Ibid.*

[147] For an account of substantive autonomy, see N Stoljar, 'Autonomy and the Feminist Intuition' in C Mackenzie and N Stoljar (eds), *Relational autonomy: feminist perspectives on autonomy, agency, and the social self* (New York, Oxford University Press, 2000).

[148] As the discussion in ch 6 will show, the legal doctrine of capacity, along with the theories of consent and voluntariness that have drawn on the notion of capacity in private law, is focused on the individual's specific capacity to make a particular decision, or in relation to a particular transaction, rather than on that person's overall competency or capabilities.

[149] A Sen, 'Markets and Freedoms' in A Sen, *Rationality and Freedom* (Cambridge, MA, Harvard University Press, 2004), at 515; quoted in J Purdy, 'A Freedom-Promoting Approach to Property: A Renewed Tradition for New Debates' (2005) 72 *University of Chicago Law Review* 1237, 1260; see discussion in ch 4, section (5).

[150] Ben-Ishai, above n 143, at 319.

[151] *Ibid.*

[152] *Ibid*, at 320.

[153] *Ibid*, at 321.

In the context of housing equity transactions, the liberal legal commitment to 'procedural autonomy' would emphasis the importance of respecting the older owner as an 'autonomous individual' by enforcing his or her choices (whether they lead to good or bad outcomes) in the individual transaction. In contrast, substantive autonomy would be concerned with the impact on the individual's autonomous life, including that person's (future) substantive autonomy, and (since neither dependence nor State intervention is anathema to this understanding of autonomy) with the question of appropriate protections where there is a real risk that his or her capabilities may be severely compromised by an adverse (financial) transactions from which he or she will have limited opportunity to recover. This model of autonomy recognises the external effects of context on an individual's ability to exercise autonomy; the need for a balance between autonomy and protection[154]; and the risk that vulnerable populations may be subjected to harms in the name of 'autonomy' where it is posited as an antonym to 'dependence'. Friedman argued that attracting the protection of the State in certain circumstances does not exclude the possibility of living an *autonomous life*[155]; indeed, she argued that in some circumstances or contexts, it is only through State protection that such an autonomous life becomes possible.[156] These analyses are helpful in negating any suggestion that the psychological need for control over housing choices necessarily supports the (neo)liberal legal and political 'autonomy' agenda.

The meanings of 'housing as home' for older people, to support 'ageing in place' or the desire to 'stay put', are complex, multiple and contingent, with housing decisions based on an array of factors, including health and physical ability, social and family context, neighbourhood environment and financial well-being. There is, however, no doubt that 'home' is loaded with meanings for older people, for the memories it holds, for its role in supporting their current lives and for housing their ageing selves. This section has demonstrated the practical, emotional/symbolic and cultural meanings underpinning the desire to remain in place, and which are likely to influence the ways that people perceive the options available to them, so affecting individual action and choice when making decisions about the use of housing wealth (for example, favouring financial solutions which allow them to hang on to their homes). The paradigm of 'housing as home' demonstrates that notwithstanding its increasing 'fungibility'—especially for older owners—the owned home is often still regarded as 'personal' property,[157] so demanding stronger legal protection than fungible property. The hybrid functions which the owned home must perform for older people again underline the complexity of financial decision-making in this context, with implications for the construction of the older owner as a legal subject.

Smith explored these tensions in her research into the changing character of housing assets, the owned home, and perhaps owner-occupiers themselves, as households shift

[154] See, eg, Ellis, above n 140; Kennedy, above n 139.

[155] '[O]ne lived by someone who has the capacities for autonomy and is able to exercise them frequently over a substantial stretch of time.': Friedman, above n 143, at 13.

[156] The nature of the State's responsibility for vulnerable populations, including Fineman's argument that making the goal of intervention 'greater autonomy', ultimately supports the neoliberal agenda of creating self-responsible citizens rather than recognising inherent vulnerabilities is discussed in ch 6.

[157] The idea of a spectrum from fungible property to personal property is based on Radin's theory of 'property for personhood'; see MJ Radin, 'Property and Personhood' (1982) 34 *Stanford Law Review* 957; MJ Radin, *Reinterpreting Property* (Chicago, Ill, University of Chicago Press, 1993).

towards deliberate strategies of 'banking on housing'; as property-holding citizens become 'asset-accumulating investors'; and as the growing fungibility of housing wealth stimulates an 'ethically charged encounter between the governance of housing and the micropolitics of home'.[158] Smith identified a generation gap in relation to the types of values which 'housing investors' embody: while younger people today are more likely to enter the owner-occupier market as 'investors', consciously buying into the 'grammars of living' that define responsible citizens as 'enterprising, home-owning individuals' with 'seemingly autonomous self-directed lives',[159] this model of ownership may be less germane for older people, who are more likely to have bought their homes more by accident than by design at a time when there was little to choose between the main tenure sectors,[160] and who continue to view their housing as home (for use, rather than as an investment asset). This has implications both for the application of the 'investor model' of legal rationality to older owners in home equity transactions, discussed further in section (5) below, and for the idea of owned housing as inheritance.

(4) Housing as Inheritance

A second housing paradigm for older owners emphasises the role of the owned home as an element of inheritance. The role of housing wealth as inheritance has attracted considerable attention since the 1980s, as a result of the growth of the homeownership sector combined with a rapid rise in the value of housing inheritance. In *Safe as Houses: Housing Inheritance in Britain*,[161] Hamnett, Harmer and Williams charted the ways in which the growth of homeownership in the twentieth century set the scene for the accumulation, release and transfer of housing wealth. For the newly-elected Thatcher Government in 1979, the paradigm of housing as inheritance was a key factor in the promotion of homeownership, including the sale of public-sector 'council housing', which Thatcher argued would 'give to more of our people that freedom and mobility and that prospect of handing something on to their children and grandchildren which owner-occupation provides'.[162] While housing as inheritance already existed as a housing paradigm for a small minority of well-off owners, the growth in home ownership (including lower-income homeownership) through the 1980s meant that by the 1990s it was 'rediscovered as an important issue',[163] and became a 'mainstream' housing paradigm. In the 1990s, 'housing as inheritance' was perceived as consonant with 'housing as investment'; Hamnett *et al* observed that

[158] Smith, above n 1.

[159] *Ibid*, at 522.

[160] S Power, *Grey Areas: Housing Experience of Older People*, unpublished PhD thesis, Dept of Geography, University of Edinburgh, 2004; cited in Smith, above n 1, at 523.

[161] C Hamnett, M Harmer and P Williams, *As Safe as Houses: Housing Inheritance in Britain* (London, Paul Chapman, 1991).

[162] *Hansard*, HC Deb, 15 May 1979, vol 967, col 80 (Mrs Thatcher).

[163] Hamnett *et al*, above n 161, at 151.

> [we] have ... gone from a situation where ownership was valued for the assumed benefits it carried regarding thrift, independence and stability, to a position where more emphasis is placed on the investment/inheritance value the dwelling represents.[164]

As this section and section (5) will demonstrate, in the last two decades the paradigm of housing as investment has been separated from inheritance value through the development of products and attitudes that support the spending of housing wealth.

There are various ways of analysing the paradigm of 'housing as inheritance'. On the one hand, the question may be framed in terms of whether the older owner should be required to spend his or her housing wealth on care (and other needs) rather than passing it on to adult offspring as inheritance. Meanwhile, attitudes towards 'housing as inheritance' may be shifting, with a generation of adult offspring who are more likely than their parents to become home-owners themselves though purchase (rather than inheritance) and with their own growing perception of transactions that spend housing wealth as 'normal'—for themselves across the life-course as well as for their parents in retirement.[165] The paradigm of housing as inheritance is also challenged by the argument that while traditionally resources typically flowed down the generations,[166] rising longevity and the retrenchment of welfare provision may leave adult offspring facing (growing) responsibilities to support their parents financially in old age. A report in 2009 for Liverpool Victoria, a UK insurance and investment company, claimed that supporting elderly parents was costing adult offspring the equivalent of £39 billion a year in financial contributions and unpaid care.[167] Research has indicated that while the norms governing these relationships are sensitive to the personal circumstances of adult children, the capacity of adult offspring to provide support is coming under increasing pressure due to declining mortality rates leading to longer periods of care, adult offspring's financial responsibility towards their own children, and the reduced capacity of adult children to provide informal support and care due to the demands of paid work.[168]

As the political question of how to fund old age has gained momentum, the subject of filial responsibility for the care of ageing parents has attracted scholarly attention.[169] There is no legal obligation of support for ageing parents in England and Wales.[170] While there is considerable sympathy (and empathy) for the needs of older people, arguments against a legal obligation include the (neoliberal, risk society) expectation that they will have planned for themselves, and the risk of resentment if younger people are forced (through

[164] *Ibid*, at 3.

[165] See Smith, above n 1; SJ Smith, BA Searle and N Cook, 'Rethinking the Risks of Home Ownership' (2008) 38 *Journal of Social Policy* 83.

[166] BS Low, 'The evolution of human life histories', in C Crawford and DL Krebs (eds), *Handbook of evolutionary psychology: Ideas, issues, and applications* (Mahwah, NJ, Erlbaum, 1998) 131.

[167] See Press Release at <http://www.lv.com/media_centre/press_releases/uk-elderly-parents-unpaid-care>.

[168] See discussion in ch 1; also D Gans and M Silverstein, 'Norms of Filial Responsibility for Aging Parents Across Time and Generations' (2006) 68 *Journal of Marriage and Family* 961.

[169] See chs 1 and 2; also J Herring, *Older People in Law and Society* (Oxford, Oxford University Press, 2009) 228–34; J Herring, 'Together Forever? The Rights and Responsibilities of Adult Children and Their Parents' in J Bridgeman, H Keating and C Lind, *Responsibility, Law and the Family* (Aldershot, Ashgate, 2008), on the extent to which families should be financially responsible for the needs of older people.

[170] M Oldham, 'Financial Obligations Within the Family—Aspects of Intergenerational Maintenance and Succession in England and France' (2001) 60 *Cambridge Law Journal* 128; M Oldham, 'Maintenance of the Elderly and Legal Signalling—Kinship and State' in F Ebtehaj *et al* (eds), *Kinship Matters* (Oxford, Hart Publishing, 2006).

taxation) to pay for them.[171] A legal requirement that younger people pay could also be viewed as an intrusion into family privacy.[172] The idea of intergenerational financial responsibilities sits more easily as a moral, than a legal, obligation, with philosophical arguments for filial responsibility alternatively based on reciprocation,[173] the debt owed by the offspring to parents, gratitude for the good things that parents have done for their children, friendship between the adult children and ageing parents, or the 'special goods' theory, which focuses on the unique relationship between parents and children, enabling them to provide a unique type of 'good' in the form of care and support.[174] It is the idea of *forcing* offspring to fulfil that moral obligation—as a matter of law or public policy—that is problematic,[175] and by the twentieth century, economic, social and political trends in England had displaced the idea of 'kinship' responsibility for support of the elderly with a public welfare model,[176] which has in turn been diluted by the neoliberal expectation of self-provision. As the fiscal burden involved in providing this support from the public purse is widely regarded as a growing crisis to which there is no obvious solution,[177] self-provision by older owners through the release of accumulated housing wealth is seen to play a central role, with obvious implications for the idea of intergenerational support and for the correlative transfer of accumulated wealth as inheritance.

This is not necessarily a bad thing: for those who have (housing) wealth left at the end of their life-course, intergenerational transfers of wealth (whether *inter vivos* or on death) have obvious financial benefits for the recipients, but are also criticised for contributing to social inequality and reproducing class relations.[178] These concerns provide a justification for inheritance tax (which draws a portion of privately-transferred wealth into the public purse), justified in legal discourse in the US on the grounds of equality of opportunity, protecting democracy (against plutocratic wealth concentration) and protecting children from being corrupted by unearned wealth.[179] Taxation consequences may also influence decision-making in housing equity transactions, as older owners may seek to divest themselves of property in advance of their death—either through an *inter vivos* transfer, or by spending their wealth—to avoid inheritance tax. Herring has claimed that

> [t]he expectation of an inheritance means that relatives sometimes feel they are being 'robbed' of their inheritance if older people's assets are used up in their case, and older people feel guilt at not being able to leave their relatives the inheritance they were expecting.[180]

[171] P Wald, 'Looking Forward to the Next Millenium: Social Previews to Legal Change' (1997) 70 *Temple Law Review* 1085, 1091, quoted in Herring (2009), above n 169, at 231.

[172] Herring (2009), above n 169, at 231.

[173] See M Collingridge and S Millar, 'Filial Responsibility and Care of the Aged' (1997) 14 *Journal of Applied Philosophy* 119; H Lindemann Nelson and J Lindemann Nelson, 'Frail Parents, Robust Duties' (1992) 3 *Utah Law Review* 747.

[174] S Kellett, 'Four Theories of Filial Duty' (2006) 56 *The Philosophical Quarterly* 233; although Herring has noted that financial support is not unique in this sense: Herring (2009), above n 169, at 232.

[175] See Herring (2009), above n 169, at 233; Collingridge and Millar, above n 173, at 120.

[176] See Oldham (2006), above n 170.

[177] See chs 1 and 2; Herring (2009), above n 169, at 234.

[178] R Forrest and A Murie, 'Accumulating evidence: housing and family wealth in Britain' in R Forrest and A Murie, *Housing and Family Wealth* (London, Routledge, 1995); M Szydlik, 'Inheritance and Inequality: Theoretical Reasoning and Empirical Evidence' (2004) 20 *European Sociological Review* 31.

[179] J Beckert, *Unearned wealth: Discursive structures and the regulation of wealth transmission in France, Germany and the United States* (Bremen, mimeo, 2003).

[180] Herring (2009), above n 169, at 308–09.

On the other hand, older owners who have wealth—in many cases, housing wealth—may feel a desire or an obligation to provide capital to help their adult offspring onto the housing ladder, or to act as sureties (using the parental housing as security) for the borrowing needs of adult offspring, so creating what Burns described as 'intergenerational debt'.[181]

The 'housing as inheritance' paradigm is central to the context of home equity transactions, and likely to impact significantly on the decision-making process, including the role that adult children play in making decisions involving the home and housing equity. In their study of older owner-occupiers, Askham *et al* reported

> an interesting continuum of reported influence of children over their parents' housing decisions, from at one end decisions taken by the parents alone, even in opposition to the children's wishes, to—at the other—decisions which appeared to be taken by the children on their parents' behalf.[182]

The influence that adult children may have over home equity decision-making is considered further in chapter ten, which explores the role of the equitable doctrine of undue influence in governing the home transactions of older owners. Issues raised by Askham *et al* ranged from cases where the adult offspring reportedly told the parent what to do—which in some cases was welcome, in some cases not—to cases in which the adult children played an important role in discussing the decision with their parents, and advising them, but without taking over the decision-making function.[183] This study noted a 'wide variation in the extent to which adult children are involved with decisions about their parents' home',[184] as well as sometimes strikingly different perspectives between parent and offspring on the degree of influence the adult offspring had on the decision-making process.[185]

Another important aspect of the decision-making context was the meaning of the (parents') housing as a specific type of property. Askham *et al* found that adult children were often closely involved with their parents' home, expecting to use it (in some cases moving back in, but more often through frequent contact) and sometimes to inherit either the property itself or its capital value.[186] Dupuis and Thorns have argued that 'The meanings attached to "home" ... are generation specific rather than universal',[187] with the owned home bearing distinct meanings for older owners compared to the younger generation. The idea of the owned home as a financial investment to pass on to your children was cited as a significant aspect of home meanings for owner-occupiers.[188] For example, Perkins and Thorns claimed that

[181] See, eg, F Burns, 'Protecting elders: Regulating intergenerationally transmitted debt in Australia' (2005) 28 *International Journal of Law and Psychiatry* 300.

[182] J Askham, H Nelson, A Tinker and R Hancock, *To Have and To Hold: The Bond Between Older People and the Homes They Own* (York, York Publishing Services, 1999) 38.

[183] *Ibid*, at 38–39.

[184] *Ibid*, at 39.

[185] *Ibid*, at 38.

[186] *Ibid*, at 34–40.

[187] A Dupuis and DC Thorns, 'Meanings of Home for Older Home Owners' (1996) 11 *Housing Studies* 485, 500.

[188] See, eg, KO Doyle, 'The Symbolic Meaning of House and Home' (1992) 6 *American Behavioural Scientist* 790, 796; Dupuis and Thorns, above n 187.

> housing serves not only to provide shelter but is also a source of potential income and wealth. In societies in which owner-occupation of houses has become well established they are a source of wealth both for the present occupants and also potentially for the next generation through inheritance.[189]

Dupuis and Thorns' study of the meanings of home for older homeowners in New Zealand in the 1990s also suggested that elderly homeowners were particularly concerned about passing their assets on to their children to enhance their children's security. The components of 'housing as inheritance' were themselves complex, and comprised the intergenerational transfer of wealth as well as the more symbolic meanings of the home.[190]

Empirical analysis of this context raises some interesting issues with regard to the meaning of housing as inheritance, and its tensions with the competing paradigms of housing as home and housing as investment asset. Finch and Hayes' study of inheritance analysed both the way in which testators viewed the home in the context of making their wills, and the meaning of the inherited home to beneficiaries,[191] and found that in both contexts the meaning of housing as a financial investment appeared to be dominant. Testators tended to view the housing as simply another financial asset making up their estate, 'as property to be disposed of', rather than 'try[ing] to pass on their own house intact as a home'.[192] Beneficiaries also preferred to view the property as an inherited asset rather than an inherited home, although this was in response to 'pressures which militate against occupying an inherited house as one's own, if the beneficiary is already occupying a home which she or he has personally created'.[193] For example, in one of the cases reported by Finch and Hayes, where the testator 'was proud of having built up a comfortable home and, in essence, saw himself as having established a "family home" which he wished to pass on to succeeding generations',[194] the testator's adult daughter, who had already established her own home elsewhere, did not wish to use the property as housing or feel that it could be her home.[195] For the purposes of inheritance, this study suggested that while 'housing as investment asset' is capable of being inherited, 'housing as home' is not.

This has implications for the weight which should be attached to the 'housing as inheritance' paradigm in home equity transactions. The characteristics of a 'normal' transaction, as filtered through the paradigm of housing as inheritance, are shaped according to perceptions of the bequeathing intentions of the older owner, as well as the

[189] HC Perkins and DC Thorns, 'House and Home and their Interaction with Changes in New Zealand's Urban System, Households and Family Structures' (1999) 16 *Housing, Theory and Society* 124, 126.

[190] Dupuis and Thorns also found that while male respondents focused on the desire to pass on an investment asset to the children, for female respondents 'it is the question of family history rather than investment value which was given prominence when they are discussing their bequeathing intentions': Dupuis and Thorns, above n 187, at 498. This reflects, to some extent, studies which have differentiated home meanings, more generally, along gender lines: see, eg, J Hayward, 'Psychological Concepts of Home' (1977) *HUD Challenge* 10; S Saegert and G Winkel, 'The Home: A Critical Problem for Changing Sex Roles' in GR Wekerle, R Peterson and D Morley, *New Space for Women* (Boulder, Col, Westview Press, 1980); M Csikszentmihalyi and E Rochberg-Halton, 'Housing as Symbolic Environment' in M Csikszentmihalyi and E Rochberg-Halton (eds), *The Meaning of things: Domestic Symbols and the Self* (New York, Cambridge University Press, 1981).

[191] J Finch and L Hayes, 'Inheritance, Death and the Concept of Home' (1994) 28 *Sociology* 417.

[192] *Ibid*, at 420.

[193] *Ibid*, at 424.

[194] *Ibid.*

[195] The daughter, who inherited this property, 'did not view favourably the prospect of occupying her father's home in the way that he had anticipated. As far as [the beneficiary] was concerned the house was her parents' home, and everything about it reminded her that they were no longer there.' (*ibid*, at 425).

inheritance expectations of offspring. While the development of equity release products allows the meaning of 'housing as home' to co-exist, to some extent, with the paradigm of 'housing as investment asset', the rising dominance of 'housing as investment asset' has squeezed out the meaning of 'housing as inheritance'. The impact of demands on housing equity use on the owner's ability to bequeath the home to heirs was described in one study as angering some older owners:

> Older home owners are incensed by the thought that they may not be able to hand their hard-won asset to their children because of what they see as the policy requiring them to sell their home to pay for institutional care.[196]

Although the evidence suggests that beneficiaries are likely to see their inheritance as one of capital rather than of the property *as a home*, the older owner's attitude to bequeathing could cause anxiety and hardship if it inhibited the use of housing wealth as investment-asset-to-spend, where the older person is in need.[197]

More recently, empirical evidence has suggested that the significance of housing as a financial investment to pass on to one's children is limited. In *Attitudes to Inheritance in Britain*, a Joseph Rowntree study published in July 2005 which explored the significance of homeownership on attitudes towards bequeathing and inheriting assets,[198] it was reported that while inheritance plays an important part in many people's lives, it has not generally become entrenched as an expectation or a duty. In a study of 2,000 people, the researchers found that while 46 per cent of adults have inherited something, in most cases it was a relatively small amount, with only 5 per cent inheriting £50k or more. With professional white owner-occupiers most likely to inherit, it seemed that those who did inherit were most likely to be well-off already and so need it least,[199] and more than half the population did not expect to inherit at all. It is also worth noting that, with increased longevity delaying the receipt of any inheritance from aged parents into late-middle age, the 'younger generation' are increasingly likely to be homeowners long before their parents' home becomes available for inheritance, again making it all the more likely it will be seen as an asset (and perhaps used to fund the offspring's own retirement).[200]

Arguably more important than what the adult offspring want or expect in terms of inheritance is how the older owner feels about having (or not having) a home to bequeath, and how that may influence his or her decision-making in housing equity transactions. From the older owner's perspective, the Rowntree study found that the majority of older

[196] Joseph Rowntree Foundation, 'Older owner-occupiers' perceptions of home-ownership' (1999), at 4, available online at <www.jrf.org.uk/sites/files/jrf/F939.pdf>; see also Askham *et al*, above n 182.

[197] Askham *et al*, above n 182, also reported an expectation of inheriting amongst adult children, who expected to have access to their parents' home during their lifetime and to inherit after their death.

[198] K Rowlingson and S McKay, *Attitudes to Inheritance in Britain* (Bristol, The Policy Press, 2005); see also K Rowlingson, 'Living poor to die rich or spending the kids' inheritance? Attitudes to assets and inheritance in later life' (2006) 35 *Journal of Social Policy* 175; K Rowlingson and S McKay, 'Retirement Resources: The Role of Housing Assets and Bequests' (2006) 6(4) *Quality in Ageing* 12.

[199] Rowlingson and McKay (2005), above n 198; E Grundy, 'Heirs will have to forgo their inheritance' (1999) 319 (7201) *British Medical Journal* 55; R Disney, P Johnson and G Stears, 'Coverage, level and changes in financial assets' in R Disney, E Grundy and P Johnson (eds), *The dynamics of retirement: analyses of the retirement surveys* (DSS Research Report No 72) (London, Stationery Office, 1997).

[200] J Hills, 'A new pension settlement for the twenty-first century? The UK Pensions Commission's analysis and proposals' (2000) 22 *Oxford Review of Economic Policy* 113. Although some countries, eg in Southern Europe, have a dominant housing style in which inheritance of an owned home is expected to provide the route to homeownership for the next generation, most adult offspring in the UK expect to enter the owner-occupier sector through purchase.

people favoured using their assets for themselves, to meet their needs in later life, rather than feeling bound to save the financial investment tied up in their homes to provide an inheritance for their children.[201] Two-thirds of those with some potential to leave a bequest said they would not worry too much about doing so. There also appeared to be some evidence of a generation gap in attitudes to using accumulated wealth, with people over 80 least likely to put their own needs first rather than bequeathing; but even in that cohort, the majority indicated that they intended to 'enjoy life' rather than worry about leaving an inheritance.

When it came to spending housing equity, only one-quarter of the current or former owner-occupiers interviewed in the Rowntree study had accessed housing equity, and few had taken up equity release schemes.[202] While older people liked the idea of releasing equity in theory, only one in 20 said that they would consider equity release because they viewed the available products as complex, risky and difficult to understand, and indicated that they had little trust in providers.[203] A significant 55 per cent of people reported that while they liked the idea of equity release in theory, they had concerns about the schemes,[204] with the perception that they are 'very risky' the strongest factor against equity release.[205]

This research suggested that, when it comes to using some of their lifetime assets to meet needs in later life, older people in the UK are able and prepared to make rational decisions about spending housing wealth *per se*, but that the particular risks associated with the mechanisms for releasing equity present an obstacle to the purchase of housing equity products which could offer opportunities to satisfy the desire for ageing in place while also releasing some capital or income to support other needs. Rowlingson and McKay claimed that 'most of those with assets are willing to use up savings and access housing equity if they need to do so to maintain a reasonable standard of living'.[206] The desire to preserve housing as inheritance did not dominate decision-making, leading the researchers to conclude that

> [t]his picture supports neither the stereotype of older people being excessively frugal in order to pass everything on nor the more recent image of older [people] irresponsibly spending family assets on luxuries ... Instead, it highlights people's willingness to draw down assets as part of the normal course of managing resources throughout their lifetime, using accumulated wealth to meet current needs.[207]

[201] This was consistent with an earlier report on the attitudes of older people towards equity release against their homes: JA Davey, *Equity Release: An option for older home-owners* (York, Centre for Housing Policy, University of York, 1996).

[202] Rowlingson and McKay (2005), above n 198, at 42–45.

[203] *Ibid*, 'Findings', available online at <http://www.jrf.org.uk/publications/attitudes-inheritance-britain>.

[204] K Rowlingson, 'Attitudes to housing assets and inheritance' (2005) 10 *Council of Mortgage Lenders Housing Finance* 1.

[205] *Ibid*, Chart 3. This survey pre-dated the expansion of FSA regulation over the equity release sector (see ch 9), which may be expected to have an impact on perceptions of 'safety' of equity release products. The most common reported method for generating income was to borrow against the value of the home (see ch 7), followed closely by trading down; with the main reasons for releasing housing wealth being to carry out property repairs or make improvements, to pay bills or debts, and to buy essential items.

[206] Rowlingson and McKay (2005), above n 198, 'Findings', available online at <http://www.jrf.org.uk/publications/attitudes-inheritance-britain>.

[207] *Ibid.*

The researchers concluded that a suitable acronym for this practice might be 'Older people Withdrawing Loot Sensibly' (OWLS). It is important to emphasise, however, that the principal barrier to this (rational) approach to housing equity transactions was concern that home equity products were not 'safe'.[208] The role of law—from theory to a wide range of practices—in this process is a central theme of this book.

Lastly, it is important to recognise that the idea of the older owner's 'housing as inheritance' has broadened in recent years, and to some extent has been blurred with the idea of using the housing as an asset to release wealth, *inter vivos*, to support adult offspring. In addition to the indirect financial benefit which parents provide when adult children (described as 'Baby Boomerangers') move back in to the family home,[209] there is evidence of a growing tendency for young adults to rely on parental financial assistance to enter the homeownership sector,[210] representing yet another demand on housing wealth for older owners. Chamberlin noted that

> [m]ortgage products have adapted to allow for greater parental involvement in their children's house purchases. For example, not only do parents increasingly pay higher proportions of deposits, they can also secure mortgage repayments against their own equity or income. Rising house prices have had the effect of redistributing wealth from the young to older owner-occupiers, so parental assistance may be thought of as an early inheritance or living bequest.[211]

In addition to the suggestion that 'there is now little evidence of younger generations even attempting to save for deposits and a high expectation that parental assistance will be required',[212] the growing practice of parents leveraging their own housing wealth to help children onto the housing ladder is enabled through a range of new mortgage products, for example the 'Lend a Hand' deal from Lloyds TSB, which allows borrowers to take out a mortgage with only a 5 per cent deposit 'plus the backing of someone who wants to help you onto the property ladder by putting their savings up as additional security for the mortgage'.[213] Similarly, the 'family offset' mortgage allows borrowers to link savings accounts owned by family members to offset mortgage accounts.[214]

These products, along with the more 'traditional' mechanisms of offering a guarantee or acting as surety for the offspring's debt, or entering a joint mortgage, facilitate another source of demand on the housing equity of ageing parents, and highlight another type of home equity transaction which may have its own set of issues, for example in the

[208] The policy recommendations from the report included the need to develop safe equity release products, and to forge partnerships between central and local government, and the voluntary and private sectors, including targeted support for older homeowners with low levels of income and equity.

[209] A recent survey has indicated that 23% of 'twenty-somethings' now live with their parents because they are unable to enter the housing market; see R Wicks and J Asato, *Lifelong Parenting* (London, Social Market Foundation, 2003). Recent Office of National Statistics figures have also revealed a growing tendency for older offspring to move back home when affected by the credit crunch; see L Denyer, 'When the Kids Move Back Home', *The Times*, 24 October 2008, available online at <http://property.timesonline.co.uk/tol/life_and_style/property/article5006577.ece>; and in the US, 'Middle Aged Kids Moving Back in with Parents', online at <http://www.msnbc.msn.com/id/23744629/>.

[210] See M Andrew, 'The Changing Route to Owner Occupation: The Impact of Student Debt' (2010) 25 *Housing Studies* 39.

[211] G Chamberlin, 'Recent Developments in the UK housing market' (2009) 3(8) *Economic and Labour Market Review* 29, 34.

[212] *Ibid.*

[213] See <http://www.lloydstsb.com/mortgages/lend_a_hand.asp>.

[214] The family offset mortgage is offered by some providers, eg, Yorkshire Building Society and Newcastle Building Society.

relationship between parents and their adult children. Even where there is no suggestion of illegitimate pressure, the 'contextual' pressure[215] of wanting to provide for one's children in an environment where they are increasingly reliant on parental contributions—and where adult children's needs compete with a complex range of other demands on housing wealth—may require re-analysis of legal perspectives on these transactions, in relation to both the informational context and the regulation of creditors, and the ways in which the courts apply the tests for equitable remedies such as the unconscionable bargain doctrine or undue influence.[216]

The evolution of the paradigm of housing as inheritance, and the emergence of countervailing models for the intergenerational transfer of housing wealth, emphasise again both the heterogeneity of older owners and the wide range of complex and competing demands linked to the use of housing wealth. While the social, economic and familial contexts described in this section all fall within the boundaries of 'normal' transactions—that is, there are rational grounds on which some older owners might choose to use their housing wealth in these ways, so that the transactions would not appear, *prima facie* to 'call out for explanation'—they still carry significant risks for an older owner. It is therefore reasonable to argue that the nature and extent of the protections which law can extend to (potentially vulnerable) older owners requires careful calibration. The following section completes the analysis of competing housing paradigms by considering the (increasingly dominant) paradigm of 'housing as investment' in light of the growing political, social and financial pressures to spend housing wealth, both before and after retirement.

(5) Housing as Investment: Spending Housing Wealth

The transformation of housing discourse in Britain in recent decades has been so significant that it is easy to forget that, until the 1970s, the paradigm of 'housing as home' was clearly dominant. Hamnett *et al* described how, until a few decades ago,

> home ownership was primarily seen in terms of its role of providing a roof over people's heads … Although homeownership was generally viewed as a sound investment and a hedge against inflation or a 'store' of wealth, it was not generally seen as a source of substantial capital gains or as an important retirement nest-egg.[217]

To the extent that there was a competing paradigm of housing as financial asset, it focused upon the idea that 'the asset value of housing … accumulated over the life course, provides a cushion (in the form of low housing costs) for old age, and flows on to the next generation through inheritance'.[218] The paradigms of housing as home and housing as inheritance have, however, been displaced in recent years, through a combination of increased political expectations that owners will spend housing wealth, the development

[215] See L Fox O'Mahony and J Devenney, 'The Elderly, Their Homes and the Unconscionable Bargain Doctrine' in M Dixon (ed) *Modern Studies in Property Law*, vol 5 (Oxford, Hart Publishing, 2009) 265.

[216] Eg, in applying the test that the transaction 'calls out for explanation'; *Royal Bank of Scotland v Etridge (No 2)* [2002] 2 AC 773 at [14] *per* Lord Nicholls, discussed in ch 10.

[217] Hamnett *et al*, above n 161, at 150.

[218] Smith, above n 16, at 11; available online at <http://dro.dur.ac.uk/71/1/Smith_speculating.pdf?DDD14>.

of new financial products to enable housing wealth to be released, and the gradual normalisation amongst owners of, first, the paradigm of 'housing as investment' and, latterly, 'housing as investment-to-spend'. As a result, Smith has argued that the owned home 'may not, for long, remain a resource for old age, much less a component of inheritance. Rather it may be viewed as a store of wealth which can be made available to spend on other things.'[219] Wealth that is tied up in the 'owned home' is not only a financial investment with a view to capital appreciation, but is also regarded as 'more "spendable" now than it will ever be again'.[220] By the late 1980s, a political expectation that this newly 'spendable' wealth would be used to support welfare needs after retirement was articulated by the UK Government, for example in the Griffiths Report on *Community Care: An Agenda for Action*, which put forward the idea that

> growth in individually held resources could provide a contribution to meeting community care needs … There are already a number of interesting schemes for encouraging owner occupiers to use their equity to provide income which can be used to pay for services in retirement and I believe that similar innovative schemes should be encouraged.[221]

In the decades since then, as the idea of encashing housing equity to fund welfare and other needs (both after retirement and, increasingly, earlier in the life-course) has gained traction, the Government has become increasingly explicit in its designation of owned housing as an investment asset.[222]

The idea of 'housing as investment', especially for older owners, was traditionally reflected in the goal of becoming 'mortgage-free' in old age, so that the property could provide 'housing as home' without the major costs of rent or mortgage repayments after retirement. This was reflected in Despres and Lord's interviews with older people, which found that, alongside the practical and symbolic importance of the housing as home, 'The house is also seen as a financial investment that is finally starting to pay off. It was an early desire for most respondents to have a house free of mortgage for their old age.'[223] This model of housing as investment is distinct from the more recent phenomenon of housing as an investment-asset-to-spend. Recent research has highlighted the changing character of housing assets, owned homes and, it has been suggested, owner-occupiers themselves,[224] and Smith has argued that the new generation of financial services (epitomised in the flexible mortgage), has 'blur[red] the boundary between (fixed) capital and (fluid) money',[225] enabling owners to treat their housing wealth as 'interchangeable with the cash economy'[226] and altering the ways in which people think about their owned homes.

Smith's research also has significant implications for the ways in which owners are constructed as legal subjects in relation to mortgage equity withdrawal transactions. Smith

[219] *Ibid*, at 12.

[220] *Ibid*, at 2.

[221] R Griffiths, *Community Care: An Agenda for Action* (London, HMSO, 1988) para 6.61.

[222] 'Homes not just places to live, they are also assets' and the aims of widening home ownership include 'enabling more people to share in increasing asset wealth': Office of the Deputy Prime Minister, *Homebuy: expanding the opportunity to own*, Consultation Paper (London, Office of the Deputy Prime Minister, 2005); cited in Smith, above n 1.

[223] C Despres and S Lord, 'Growing Older in Post-War Suburbs: The Meanings and Experiences of Home' in Rowles & Chaudhury (eds), above n 49, 331.

[224] Smith, above n 1.

[225] Smith, above n 16.

[226] Smith, above n 1, at 520.

charted the 'emendation of an "investor figure" in the new financial order of housing',[227] which resonates with the model of legal subjects as rational, reasonable and responsible market actors.[228] The importance of this subjectivity for citizenship is reflected in the 'grammars of living' which, Smith argues, 'shape and prescribe' the owner's consumption of housing, and have defined homeownership 'as part of the art of responsible citizenship and ethical living'.[229] The model of homeowners as enterprising investors, leading 'seemingly autonomous self-directed lives',[230] is supportive of liberal theories of responsibility which conceive of legal subjects as 'autonomous individuals', or market-actor consumers, whose capacity to make (binding) choices undergirds their self-identity and agency. Smith's critique reveals the ways in which the political discourses which create these 'grammars of living'—for example 'the way in which a home of one's own—an owned home—has turned into something you have to have, pour everything into, and, crucially, wrest all you can from'[231]—are value-laden, and seek to prioritise or even valorise some types of value (competitive, individualised, market-oriented) over others.

The paradigm of housing as investment-asset-to-spend also plays an important role in constructing the 'housing investor' as a favoured financial subject, 'more justified and just than the stockbroker: more respectable still than the most rational of speculators'.[232] While risk-averse investors tend to avoid volatile assets, this does not appear to apply in the case of owned housing, with the suggestion that the multiple functions that the home performs (housing, inheritance, investment) temper owners' perceptions of risk in respect of housing transactions. Smith argued that the materiality of housing as bricks and mortar, and its function as a home, encourage 'investors' to regard homeownership as 'better' than other investments, even though this is a less 'rational' financial strategy than diversifying one's assets so that not all the eggs are in the housing basket, and so it is possible to cash in the more fungible investments in later life.[233] While this strategy[234] could relieve some of the pressures associated with reconciling the competing paradigms for older owners, the current generation—who are likely to have over-invested in property,[235] or those who cannot fund an owned home plus other investments so that they have no fungible assets to cash in—are left only with the options of downsizing—and so surrendering housing as home—or using financial products to release equity.

Another important issue to emerge from qualitative research into the paradigm of housing as investment-asset-to-spend is the generational difference between attitudes of different cohorts of homeowners towards releasing equity. Research for the Council of Mortgage Lending has suggested that different age groups have different attitudes to the (increasingly dominant) paradigm of housing as investment-asset-to-spend. The research,

[227] *Ibid*, at 521.
[228] See discussion in ch 4.
[229] Smith, above n 1, at 522.
[230] *Ibid*.
[231] *Ibid*, at 523.
[232] *Ibid*, at 527.
[233] *Ibid*, 528.
[234] If 'housing investors' could be persuaded to adopt it, and for those who could afford to pay for adequate owned housing as well as holding other investments.
[235] Smith described UK owner-occupiers as holding a 'uniquely high proportion of their personal wealth—62%—in their homes': Smith, above n 1, at 526.

carried out in 2004, collated responses from owners aged 45–54, 55–64 and 65–80,[236] and found that the likelihood that owner-occupiers expected to access their housing wealth depended on their age cohort. While overall, nearly half (46 per cent) of owners expected to spend housing wealth during their lifetime, those in their 40s and 50s were much more likely to hold this view than older cohorts.[237] Conversely, only 46 per cent of owners aged 45–54 wanted to leave the whole of their housing wealth as inheritance, compared to 69 per cent of those aged over 65.[238] The younger cohorts were most likely to indicate that they would be prepared to move from their current homes (downsizing).[239] Explanations for these differences included the possibility that older people, having entered the sector before the emergence of the paradigm of home-as-investment-to-spend,[240] did not necessarily subscribe to this ethic, while the younger cohorts were more open-minded about the prospect of moving between the competing paradigms, or more accepting of the need to make compromises between financial and other needs in later life (although it is also possible that the attitudes of younger cohorts might become more conservative as they get older).[241]

Attitudes towards the use of equity release products also varied across the age cohorts, with younger mortgage holders more likely to indicate that they would consider using such a scheme in the future (13 per cent in the 45–54 age group, compared to 2 per cent in the 65–80 cohort).[242] Jackie Smith, senior research analyst at the Council of Mortgage Lenders, suggested that 'This may indicate that households already accustomed to releasing equity, for example, through re-mortgaging, are more likely to see the benefits of equity release when they are older.'[243] This, in turn, suggests that 'pre-mature equity withdrawal', earlier in the life-course, could in fact be an indicator of a propensity to withdraw equity after retirement. Lastly, this study found that, in talking about reasons *not* to use equity release schemes, while younger owners were more likely to be wary of schemes (35 per cent) or to resist equity release because they want to leave an inheritance (29 per cent), the reasons given by older owners were more likely to be about not needing the money (37 per cent), as well as wanting to leave an inheritance (24 per cent).[244] Smith concluded that these attitudes pointed towards the need for a positive strategy of 'improving understanding of the products and how they work [to] help overcome owners' wariness'.[245]

Wariness about and distrust of equity release products, perceived as poor value for money and high risk, have often been cited as explanations for the relatively low uptake to date of equity release products in the UK.[246] The introduction of FSA regulation[247] has been heralded as potentially triggering significant growth in this sector, with the very fact

[236] J Smith, 'Exploring attitudes to housing wealth and retirement' (2004) 63 *Housing Finance* 22; available online at <www.cml.org.uk/cml/filegrab/pdf_pub_hf_63-3.pdf.pdf?ref=3384>.
[237] *Ibid.*
[238] *Ibid.*
[239] *Ibid,* at 26–27.
[240] Power, above n 160.
[241] Smith, above n 236, at 27.
[242] *Ibid,* at 30.
[243] *Ibid.*
[244] *Ibid,* at 30–31.
[245] *Ibid,* at 31.
[246] See also Croucher, above n 24, at 51.
[247] See ch 9.

of regulation expected to improve the reputation of equity release products and so contribute to increased market confidence.[248] With a series of projections in the last decade emphasising the potential in this market, the industry view is that the market for equity release is primed for expansion. This is supported by the financial and demographic contexts, which suggest that equity release targeted at older owners is (over) due for major growth, and in 2008 industry self-regulator SHIP (Safe Home Income Plans) claimed that it was 'only a matter of time' before predictions of market growth were actualised.[249] Yet the expected growth has not occurred, and the reasons for this clearly pre-date the recession which began in 2008. In a report for the Council of Mortgage Lenders, which examined the reasons for the market's under-performance[250] 'against what appear to be strong fundamentals that should drive significant annual growth',[251] Williams argued that the UK Government must play a stronger role in building confidence in a sector which has been identified as offering a sensible strategy for some older owners.[252]

Williams stated that there was some evidence that attitudes to equity release were changing, thus lending support to the industry mantra that a period of significant growth is likely to be imminent,[253] but that barriers such as mistrust and perceptions of high risk prevent people from utilising equity release schemes.[254] In contrast, the equity release markets in Australia and New Zealand have thrived relative to the UK market,[255] with one industry study in New Zealand reporting that the sector more than doubled from 2005 to 2006.[256] The US market is also well-developed relative to the UK, with reports of 70 per cent growth in 2006,[257] although research in the US has identified a number of factors which inhibit further growth, including transaction costs, moral hazard issues,[258] the risk that taking out a loan too early could inhibit choices in later life (for example, in healthcare), reluctance to incur debt later in life and the suggestion that advice concerning the risks of home equity transactions tends to put consumers off.[259]

Legal regulation and protection also have a significant role to play in ensuring that housing equity transactions can provide 'safe' options for older owners. This would perform the dual functions of supporting the equity release market, while also ensuring that older people have choices which allow them to sustain 'housing as home' if this is a priority for them. Research in the US has suggested that market growth in the UK (and in the early 2000s in the US) has been inhibited by 'the fact that these loans sit at the intersection of many "different, confusing and incomplete" regulatory systems'.[260] While

[248] See discussion in ch 3, section (2)(b).

[249] <http://www.ship-ltd.org/uploads/27-mar-08.pdf>.

[250] P Williams, *Please Release Me! A Review of the equity release market in the UK, its potential and consumer expectations* (London, Council of Mortgage Lenders, 2008).

[251] *Ibid*, at 4.

[252] *Ibid*, see, eg, at 26–27. Williams noted that while there has been continued steady growth, 'underlying demographics (and pension shortfalls) continue to point strongly towards a steady equity release market sometime in the future': *ibid*, at 4.

[253] *Ibid*, at 14.

[254] Rowlingson, above n 198; Smith, above n 236; Williams, above n 250, at 1617.

[255] Williams, above n 250, at 18–21.

[256] Trowbridge Deloitte, *New Zealand Reverse Mortgage Study* (New Zealand, Trowbridge Deloitte, 2007).

[257] Williams, above n 250, at 21.

[258] See discussion in ch 3, section (2)(c).

[259] See Williams, above n 250, at 21–22.

[260] *Ibid*, at 22, citing A Caplin, 'The Reverse Mortgage Market: Problems and Prospects' in O Mitchell (ed), *Innovations in Housing Finance for the Elderly* (New York, New York University, 2001); see also A Caplin, 'Turning

equity release transactions present a complex and challenging array of risks for older owners,[261] the realities of financial needs after retirement are such that 'The question ... is not whether to have an equity release market or not but how best to structure it.'[262] While the FSA's remit has been extended to cover lifetime mortgages, home reversions, and more recently sale and rent back transactions, the limits of the regulatory regime led Williams to conclude that 'it is evident that this in itself has not transformed perceptions of the marketplace[,] in part ... because there are still problems with the way the product is sold.'[263] The UK independent consumer advice organisation Which? has advised older people with financial needs that they should use equity release only as a last resort,[264] following a 2006 study which described the schemes on offer in the UK as 'high risk products' (expensive, inflexible and risky, potentially leaving people facing later life with little or no equity left in their homes).[265] A 2009 survey for *Which?* magazine reported that two-thirds of advisers failed to reach a set of benchmarks for adequate quality advice and information, which included meeting the standards set by the FSA, as well as conducting a 'thorough fact-find' of the older person's circumstances and determining why that person thought he or she wanted an equity release scheme; talking through the different schemes available and the pros and cons of each; talking through the alternatives to equity release, including downsizing; discussing the risks and making sure the customer was comfortable with those risks; and making a suitable recommendation, explaining why it met the customer's needs.[266] While the benchmarking standards used in the Which? investigation went beyond what is legally required by the FSA regulations, they do capture many of the problems associated with equity release, as well as the limits of the current regulatory approach.[267]

While the UK strategy for equity release has primarily been focused on FSA regulation, the US Government has played a much more instrumental role in building confidence in the equity release sector, in several different ways. One route has been to encourage major lenders to enter the market, for example by offering lenders a guarantee against losses in equity release transactions,[268] funded through an insurance fund collected from all borrowers (so spreading the risk of bad outcomes). The US Government has also addressed one of the 'moral hazard' issues, in respect of the condition and upkeep of the property, through inclusion of a standard term which requires that the loan is repaid if borrowers do not keep the property insured and well-maintained; and the Department of Housing and Urban Development (HUD) has developed a standardised, mandatory

Assets into Cash: problems and prospects in the reverse mortgage market' in O Mitchell, Z Bodie, PB Hammond and S Zeldes (eds), *Innovations in Retirement Financing* (Philadelphia, Pa, University of Pennsylvania, 2002) 244.

261 See discussions in ch 3.

262 Williams, above n 250, at 25.

263 *Ibid.*

264 M Wallace and P Spiers, *Care Options in Retirement* (London, Which?, 2008).

265 <http://www.which.co.uk/news/2006/01/equity-release-schemes-cost-homeowners-dear-57986>.

266 <http://www.which.co.uk/news/2009/07/two-thirds-of-equity-release-advisers-fail-test-180694>.

267 This is discussed in detail in ch 9.

268 The US Department of Housing and Urban Development authorised the 'Home Equity Conversion Mortgage' programme in the Housing and Community Development Act 1987, and since 1990 it has made loans to more than 300,000 elderly Americans; see H Chen, SH Cox and SS Wang, 'Is the Home Equity Conversion Mortgage in the United States Sustainable? Evidence from pricing mortgage insurance premiums and non-recourse provisions using the conditional Esscher transform' (2010) 46 *Mathematics and Economics* 371; also L Wang, EA Valdez and J Piggott, *Securitization of longevity risk in reverse mortgages* (Working paper, 2007, available at SSRN <http://ssrn.com/abstract=1087549>).

programme of consumer education and counselling for all borrowers. Other strategies have targeted protections at borrowers, by building greater flexibility into the products, allowing changes between different types of payment plan during the course of the mortgage and enabling homeowners to conserve part of their home equity for other purposes, as well as regulating lenders, for example by requiring lenders explicitly to inform borrowers that their repayment liability is limited by insurance, and requiring lenders to provide a statement of the projected total cost of the mortgage prior to completion.[269]

Other specific protections surrounding equity release include the 'non-recourse' nature of the US Home Equity Conversion Loan (that is, it carries a 'no negative equity guarantee'), which has no maturity date (so does not require repayment so long as the borrower continues to live in the property as a home). Products which allow for 'equity sharing' or 'shared appreciation' of the future value of the home are no longer offered. There are also a number of regulations relating to advance disclosure of total transaction costs over the projected life of the loan, standard and capped interest rates, limitations on fees, no penalty for pre-payment and a requirement for independent counselling before the transaction can be processed. The Senior Citizens Home Equity Protection Act 1997 prohibited intermediaries from charging commissions to potential clients for introductions, while the American Homeownership and Economic Opportunity Act 2000 permitted refinancing of home equity conversion loans with minimal additional insurance premium, authorised the Federal Housing Administration (part of HUD) to impose a limit on origination fees and required HUD to waive up-front mortgage insurance premiums in cases where the funds generated from the reverse mortgage were used to fund long-term care.[270]

In the UK, a report for the independent think-tank Social Market Foundation has similarly argued for a greater government role in regulating and participating (by co-producing an ethical equity release product with a financial services provider) in the equity release market to lower costs for consumers.[271] Another approach explored in the UK has been the idea of partnerships between the charitable sector and private providers: in 2005, the charity Age Concern linked with the (then private sector) bank Northern Rock to offer a branded roll-up lifetime mortgage with no arrangement fee, no exit fee and no charges for advice or repayment. More recently, the Joseph Rowntree Foundation set up an 'Equity Release Task Force', to overcome the three main types of barrier to equity release: reluctance to reduce inheritance; anxiety that spending home equity is risky, not good value for money and complicated; and concerns that withdrawing equity will affect welfare benefit entitlements.[272] In 2010, this Task Force launched a pilot scheme (which was due to report in Autumn 2011) which partnered local authorities, private-sector equity release providers, voluntary/charitable agencies and government departments (such as the Department of Work and Pensions) to develop equity release products which

[269] Reverse Mortgage Insurance for Older Americans Act of 1989 (HR 3006); discussed in BH Irving and T Roughan, 'The development of the reverse mortgage market' (2005) 15 *The Capco Institute Journal of Financial Transformation* 137, 141.

[270] See Irving and Roughan, above n 269, at 141.

[271] Social Market Foundation, *Home made money: a co-production approach to equity release* (London, SMF, 2006).

[272] R Terry and R Gibson, *Can Equity Release Help Older Home-Owners Improve Their Quality of Life?* (York, Joseph Rowntree Foundation, 2010) at 4.

will help older people access funds without reducing their welfare benefit entitlements, and which seeks to ensure that, in the course of the information and advice offered, other financial solutions to equity release are explored with older owners, including ensuring that they are claiming all benefits to which they are entitled.[273]

To date, there is no empirical research that has specifically investigated whether the wariness and suspicion of older owners regarding equity release are linked to their perceptions of the adequacy or not of legal regulation, or what the extent of consumers' legal awareness is concerning the nature and extent of other protections, for example against mis-selling. Terry and Gibson have suggested that 'It appears that improved consumer protection introduced over the last few years [by the FSA and self-regulation through SHIP] is not widely known about.'[274] The policy arguments in support of equity release alongside reluctance in take-up have, however, clearly been deemed sufficiently strong to justify these (central and local[275]) government efforts to improve market confidence, and research exploring the equity release market's failure to thrive has frequently emphasised the significance of lack of trust (of products/providers) on the part of older owners. Overcoming this and other obstacles would clearly support current government policies which have sought to embed the paradigm of 'home-as-investment-to-spend'.

At the same time, this paradigm is increasingly reinforced by the 'normalisation' of housing equity withdrawal for younger cohorts, for whom 'it has never been easier or cheaper … to dip routinely into their housing wealth, spending it sooner rather than saving it for later'.[276] This, in turn, introduces a new set of risks associated with leaving inadequate housing equity for old age, although the impact of 'premature wealth extraction' in middle life will depend on what the money is spent on (whether it is invested, for example, in improvements to property, a second home, or a business, as opposed to being either 'dissipated' on holidays or plasma screen televisions, or spent on welfare/living costs). The purposes for withdrawing funds are not actively regulated in the UK (by government or the lenders),[277] and while the majority of participants in Smith, Cook and Searle's study of UK mortgage holders were resistant to government intervention in this area, some popular unease is reflected in the sizeable minority (nearly two in five) who were 'sympathetic to a stronger government steer on spend from home equity'.[278] The reasons put forward by those participants who did support government intervention on spend from housing equity withdrawal included their fears about the risk of over-indebtedness; the riskiness of 'equity leakage'; the moral hazard of spending on

[273] *Ibid.*

[274] *Ibid*, at 4.

[275] In promoting this pilot scheme to local authorities, the Joseph Rowntree Foundation report highlighted a range of factors which make good quality equity release products valuable to local authorities, principally to support the paradigm of housing as housing for older people to age in place. Terry and Gibson reported that 'Two possible roles [of equity release in supporting local authority policies] are helping older people stay in their own housing as long as possible by enabling them to draw on the equity in their home to pay for additional help; and improving the well-being of older residents.': *ibid*, at 10. See also R Terry and R Gibson, *Local Authority Support for Equity Release* (York, Joseph Rowntree Foundation, 2007), which sets out in some detail the advantages of good quality housing equity products for local authorities.

[276] S Smith, N Cook and B Searle, *From Canny Consumer to Care-full Citizen: Towards a Nation of Home Stewardship* (ESRC Cultures of Consumption Programme Working Paper No 35, 2007) 3.

[277] *Ibid.*

[278] *Ibid.*

lifestyle now and under-resourcing welfare needs later; the dangers facing people who lack financial capability; and vulnerability to mis-selling of unsuitable products.[279]

It is clear that policy considerations strongly support the paradigm of 'housing-as investment-asset-to-spend', but at the same time, that owners who opt to go down this route must negotiate through the multiplicity of risks outlined in chapter three, as active and engaged 'risk subjects', self-reliant and self-responsible for their own life planning. While, for younger cohorts at least, 'the grammars of living that constitute homeownership are more rooted in money ... than they have ever been',[280] with 'freedom, choice, autonomy, and opportunity ... shaping the whole *character* of owner-occupiers',[281] older owners' engagement with the paradigm of housing as investment-asset-to-spend is much more qualified, with barriers principally rooted in their perceptions of the risks that home equity transactions carry, and their fears about lack of protection and adverse impact should bad outcomes result.

(6) Conclusions

Analysis of the emergence of pluralist housing paradigms for older owners reveals much about the evolving and competing meanings of home for older people, and these meanings provide an important part of the context for decision-making in housing equity transactions. While chapter three delineated the 'risk environment' for home equity transactions, this chapter has demonstrated that the competing demands which have come to be placed on housing equity, and the risks they bear for older owners, have been 'normalised' as succeeding generations become more accustomed to the idea—the expectation and the experience—of withdrawing housing equity, not just after retirement but throughout the life-course. 'Housing as home' is clearly important for the practical, emotional, symbolic and identity needs of the ageing person, and this is reflected in the strategy underpinning UK housing policies for older people. At the same time, 'housing as inheritance' taps into the complexities surrounding intergenerational transfers of (housing) wealth, including the debate between private transfers, which tend to concentrate wealth in the hands of those who are already well-off (that is, those who need it least), and the pressures that the ageing society is placing on the public purse. The rise of the paradigm of housing as inheritance may be linked to the rhetoric of the political ideology of homeownership, although recent research has indicated that, while the bequest motive remains significant for some owners, housing as inheritance has not become entrenched as a duty or an expectation. Rather, it has to some extent been superseded by the increasingly dominant paradigm of 'housing as investment-asset-to-spend'.

The emphasis on 'housing as investment-asset-to-spend' is clearly rooted in the financial needs that flow from the socio-economic and political contexts discussed in chapters one and two. In addition, while it has sometimes been suggested that downsizing is a desirable strategy to meet these needs in later life, the discussion in this chapter has demonstrated that UK policies for housing older people do not promote downsizing as a

279 *Ibid*, at 9–10.
280 Smith, above n 1, at 529.
281 *Ibid*.

particular paradigm approach. While downsizing may meet the needs of some older people, it is contingent on a range of factors, including the availability of suitable property to move to, and a sufficiently significant price differential between the current home and the new property to make the move worthwhile. It is also now recognised that older people living in family-sized homes, sometimes described as 'under-occupying' the property, may in fact be making good use of—indeed have a need for—the additional space, for example for visiting children and grandchildren. Housing policies in the UK now recognise that older people represent only a small portion of households who could be described as under-occupying, so that a policy of targeting older people to give up their homes would be ageist. Rather, while seeking to support downsizing for those people who choose to, the current UK strategy supports 'ageing in place', or the paradigm of 'housing as home', with financial needs to be met through using the home as an investment asset which can be spent while still retaining the use of the property as a home.

It is clear that each of the housing paradigms explored in this chapter—housing as home, housing as inheritance, and housing as investment-asset-to-spend—has (varying degrees of) currency with older owners, and may form part of the context of their decision-making. Dupuis and Thorns described the meaning of home for older people as 'a complex interweaving of the quest for security and identity with the accumulation of assets and other markers of achievement and the transfer of these to subsequent generations'.[282] On the one hand, older owners' attitudes to housing equity transactions have shifted according to changes in their financial needs, the withdrawal of welfare, political expectations of housing equity use and the wider range of financial opportunities available to them. The meanings of housing as home for older people are also deeply rooted in the individual's physical and social needs, and their attachment to home (and perhaps to homeownership) for autonomy,[283] self-identity and continuity during a period of transition (from working adulthood to retirement).[284] It is also evident that there is no single or simple 'model' of needs in respect of owned housing after retirement, as needs, attitudes and opportunities vary depending on the situation or context of the individual owner, including their financial and social/family/support resources, the impact of their physical health and mobility on the suitability of the home, and so on. These factors are also interrelated: when a home becomes physically unsuitable it may be possible to adapt it, but this depends on financial resources, and the success of strategies for ageing in place may also depend on the availability of family or other support for independent living. It is also clear that while the competing paradigms are sometimes in tension (for example, using housing as investment to spend may necessitate giving up housing as inheritance), they may also coincide (for example, when home equity transactions enable owners to maintain housing as home while also using the property as an investment to spend).

The development of financial products which enable older (and other) owners to spend housing wealth effected a significant shift into a new 'risk' era, with increased choice and opportunity, but also greater demands in terms of life-planning, reflexive strategising and threats to security where risks are realised as bad outcomes. Before the mechanisms for

[282] Dupuis and Thorns, above n 187, at 500.

[283] Within the psychological meaning of 'autonomy'.

[284] Giddens claimed that this type of transition requires 'psychic reorganisation', an active process of reflexive mobilising of self-identity to protect ontological (or emotional) security which, in the 'risk society', is increasingly carried out in reliance on 'abstract systems' of expert advice; A Giddens, *Modernity and Self-Identity: Self and Society in the Late Modern Age* (Cambridge, Polity Press, 1991) 33.

equity release were developed from the mid-1970s, many older owners had no choice but to leave their housing as inheritance, even if it meant spending their old age living in poverty.[285] The development of alternative housing paradigms, and the role of new financial products targeted at older people that purport to enable 'housing as investment-asset-to-spend' to coincide with 'housing as home', has presented older owners with more choices. This expansion of choice is, however, also linked to higher risk and greater uncertainty. There can be no doubt that the landscape of home equity transactions has fundamentally shifted, but while the UK Government has made significant progress in 'financialising the British welfare citizen in the move towards an asset-based system of welfare',[286] yet with increasing numbers of older owners prepared to consider releasing equity from their homes, the risks associated with products which purport to enable 'housing as investment-asset-to-spend' while preserving the owned home for occupation continue to present obstacles to the anticipated growth in this sector. It has already been noted that older owners are a differentiated population[287] for whom the appropriateness of housing options will obviously vary. This underlines the need for a *range* of 'safe' options: it is not sufficient for law to regulate in one corner of the market; rather, there is a need for appropriate legal protection across the spectrum of options.

The paradigm of housing as investment-asset-to-spend emerged from the 1980s as a result of the financial deregulation of the UK's mortgage market,[288] including the development of a new generation of flexible mortgage products.[289] This (dominant) paradigm supports a particular, politically-driven type of market in which housing wealth is viewed as fungible, and legal subjects are presumed to fit the 'investor model' of legal rationality. The extent to which this perspective has influenced the general legal framework for home equity transactions is examined in chapters seven to ten which analyse the legal frameworks that govern these transactions in the UK. An important thematic question to bear in mind when assessing the appropriateness of the current frameworks is the extent to which *older* owners as a particular group should be regarded as context-neutral subjects, or whether, in light of their particular subjective or contextual vulnerabilities, they should be viewed as a distinctive category of legal subject. As the UK Government's *National Strategy for Housing in an Ageing Society*[290] seeks to 'mainstream' older people's housing issues, highlighting the need to consider the particular needs and circumstances of older people within the mainstream of housing policy, the arguments for adopting a similar approach to legal protections in home equity transactions are likely to depend on whether a particular need for specific consideration can be established based on the heightened vulnerabilities of older people in relation to this type of transaction. These issues are explored further in chapter six.

285 Hamnett *et al*, above n 161, at 160.

286 M Watson, 'When is a House not just a Home? Asset-Based Welfare and the British Housing Market', paper to the Annual Conference of the Housing Studies Association, Cardiff University, 15–17 April 2009, available online at <https://www.york.ac.uk/inst/chp/hsa/papers/spring09/WatsonPAPER.doc>.

287 See ch 1.

288 SJ Smith, 'Risky Business? The Challenge of Residential Mortgage Markets' (2005) *Housing Finance International* 3, available online at <http//www.jrf.org.uk/knowledge/consultation/homeownershipinquiry/documents/housingwealth.pdf>.

289 SJ Smith, J Ford and M Munro with R Davis, *A review of flexible mortgages* (London, Council of Mortgage Lenders, 2002).

290 DCLG, above n 11, available online at <http://www.communities.gov.uk/documents/housing/pdf/lifetimehomes.pdf>.

6

Vulnerabilities and Older Owners

(1) Introduction

Although there are clear and specific risks associated with home equity transactions for any owner (and particularly marginal owners), regardless of age,[1] the particular tensions between competing housing paradigms for older owners emphasise the ways in which their decision-making concerning use of housing equity is framed by specific contextual factors.[2] While older owners are a widely differentiated population, in terms both of socio-economic circumstances and financial and legal capabilities, this chapter considers whether the economic, demographic, social, housing preference and risk contexts of housing equity use for older owners create specific vulnerabilities which affect their ability to negotiate housing equity transactions or the impact of adverse transactions on their well-being. By exploring the factors which may render older owners particularly vulnerable in relation to financial transactions affecting their homes, this analysis begins to consider how these vulnerabilities map onto the legal concepts that potentially trigger protection for vulnerable populations, and to evaluate the appropriate theoretical and practical bases for any legal protections deemed necessary in this context.

One area of vulnerability considered in this chapter relates to the decision-making process when the older owner enters into a transaction. Within this category, the most obvious cause of vulnerability is impaired capacity, although this is not the only nor necessarily the most prevalent issue, particularly in light of improved health and well-being in (especially early) old age. Another potential type of vulnerability, also falling within this category, relates to the impact of age on the ability to make economic decisions, and includes what the FSA has termed 'financial capability' as well as psychological research exploring the impact of age *per se* on healthy older people's abilities to make decisions under uncertainty, to think strategically and to plan their futures. These issues are brought into sharp relief by the demands on older consumers following the 'emancipation from traditional aging'[3] which has made later life in the period of late modernity a time of increased choice (and so increased risk),[4] and which is brought into sharp relief by the inherent complexity of financial products that release housing equity.[5]

[1] See ch 3.
[2] See ch 4.
[3] C Phillipson, *Reconstructing Old Age* (London, Sage, 1998) at 124; see ch 2.
[4] See ch 3.
[5] See ch 3, section (3)(b), where it was noted that the FSA's 2007 review of products to finance retirement emphasised both the complexity of the decisions that older people need to make regarding the funding of their old age and the specific complexity of equity release products, so that the detail of how the different products work is difficult to understand; see Financial Services Authority, *Finance in and at retirement—results of our review* (London, FSA, 2007), available online at <http://www.fsa.gov.uk/pubs/other/retirement_review.pdf>.

A third source of vulnerability in respect of financial decision-making relates to the risk of financial abuse of older owners, either by inappropriate targeting by financial product providers, or by family members or carers who exert pressure on the older person to enter into particular transactions.

Last in this category, a fourth cause of vulnerability relating to the decision-making process is rooted in the social and economic circumstances or contexts of the transaction. This type of systemic vulnerability stems from the pressures on older people to make choices which enable them to take individual responsibility for their old age, and to engage in effective life-planning. The political and policy contexts have set the scene for increasing use of housing equity after retirement, while the tensions between the competing housing paradigms highlight the complexities of the choices that must be made. This 'contextual vulnerability' is distinct from considerations of capacity or consent inasmuch as it is external to the individual's mental abilities or capacities, but it does reflect the constraints that may shape these choices, particularly for marginal owners. This in turn locates the issue of contextual vulnerability within the realm of inequalities, in both financial resources and the social and cultural capitals which play a crucial role in determining the 'winners' and 'losers' in a risk society.[6]

The second category of vulnerability considered in this chapter shifts the focus away from the 'point of sale' of home equity transactions, towards the 'point of crisis', when bad outcomes result from decisions taken. In this context, the issue of vulnerability relates to the differential impact of adverse consequences on (certain) older consumers. In discussing the risks of equity release schemes, the FSA has recognised that 'What makes matters worse in this area is that these consumers tend to be elderly and vulnerable people who can ill-afford to be unnecessarily exposed to risk.'[7] This meaning of vulnerability has also been recognised in the English courts: for example, in *R v Waveney DC, ex p Bowers*,[8] the Court of Appeal defined vulnerability (for the purposes of 'priority need' for local authority housing) as meaning 'less able to fend for oneself so that injury or detriment will result where a less vulnerable man will be able to cope without harmful effects'. The 'impact' dimension of vulnerability shifts the focus from the older owner's ability to make choices at the point of sale, to consider how detrimental the consequences of choosing badly might be for an older owner, compared, for example, to a younger person who has greater opportunity to absorb risk, adjust to losses and recover from economic setbacks by earning more money.[9] These two dimensions of vulnerability (decision-making and impact) also map onto the two dimensions of risk:

a) the probability that the harm will occur; and
b) the magnitude of associated losses or gains.[10]

[6] See discussion in ch 1, section (3)(b).

[7] Clive Briault, Managing Director of Retail Markets at the FSA, quoted at <http://www.fsa.gov.uk/pages/Library/Communication/PR/2005/054.shtml>.

[8] [1983] QB 238.

[9] See discussion in ch 4, section (3).

[10] D Lupton, *Risk* (London, Routledge, 1999) 8.

While decision-making vulnerability captures the likelihood of loss, the impact dimension denotes the value attached to the loss, or 'the awfulness of getting the wager wrong'.[11]

The intersections between vulnerabilities and ageing also raise politically- and emotionally-loaded connotations of 'dependency'. While feminist (and some progressive property)[12] scholarship has attempted to de-bunk the negative connotations of 'dependency',[13] the labelling of populations as 'dependent' continues to carry a political subtext.[14] While it is recognised that dependency creates vulnerability, and both 'dependent' and 'vulnerable' subjects depart from the classical 'rational subject' of neoliberal economics and liberal legal theory, the characteristics which are presumed to set them apart as subjects differ significantly, with potential implications for claims to legal protection. Leonard described the 'dependent subject' as a preoccupation of the New Right critique of the 'culture of dependency': a person who is reliant on State support, and who in turn does not engage with the reproduction of capitalist social relations, for example through his or her reduced ability to consume.[15] Dependent subjects do not display the neoliberal virtues of commitment to work, family responsibility and competition, and so attract social and moral opprobrium, which has sometimes been reflected in legal discourse.[16]

In other cases, dependency has been equated with vulnerability, and has given rise to protections for the older person: for example, a person who is old and homeless will be classified as 'vulnerable', which will usually mean being swiftly re-housed,[17] without the need to demonstrate incapacity. Clapham, Kemp and Smith have argued that this reflects the construction of older people as 'dependent subjects', who

> have, for the most part, no direct relationship with the labour market [and] can be defined as deserving of assistance, in that the provision of state help would not be expected to inhibit the qualities of initiative and self-reliance which the undeserving homeless (those who could, theoretically compete in the labour market and provide for themselves) are deemed to lack.[18]

The discussion in chapter two highlighted the policy narratives which have increasingly constructed older people as active and responsible consumers in relation to care, through the shift from welfare provision to housing equity use, while the particular emphasis on older *owners* as consumers in the neoliberal environment was noted in chapter three. While age has been recognised as a factor which heightens vulnerability in the case of older homeless people for the purposes of local authority housing, it is through the lens of dependency, which is viewed by older people as an unattractive 'label', and which casts them, as a population group, as 'non-subjects', in diametric opposition to the 'autonomous individualism' that underpins the construction of older owners in neoliberal

[11] See J Steele, *Risks and Legal Theory* (Oxford, Hart Publishing, 2004), discussing 'Pascal's wager', at 22–23.

[12] See ch 4, section (5).

[13] See, eg, MA Fineman, *The Autonomy Myth: A Theory of Dependency* (New York, The New Press, 2004).

[14] See discussion below, section (7).

[15] P Leonard, *Postmodern Welfare: Reconstructing an Emancipatory Project* (London, Sage, 1997) 50.

[16] See, eg, T Ross, 'The Rhetoric of Poverty: Their Immorality, Our Helplessness' (1991) 79 *Georgetown Law Review* 1499.

[17] D Hawes, *Older People and Homelessness* (Bristol, Policy Press, 1997) 9.

[18] D Clapham, P Kemp and S Smith, *Housing and Social Policy* (Basingstoke, Macmillan, 1990) 121; quoted in J Morgan, *Housing Law* (London, Blackstone Press, 1998) 276. Morgan goes on to note (*ibid*, at 277) that 'Customarily, people at or past retirement age were considered vulnerable on account of old age. The Code of Guidance suggests that authorities should look at whether age has made it hard for the applicant to fend for himself or herself, and that all applications [to be housed] from people over 60 should be looked at carefully.'

governance as self-providing consumers.[19] As the discussion in chapter five has indicated, the terms 'autonomy' and 'dependence' are heavily loaded with political meanings which have been deployed to justify the dominant tropes of self-provision and self-responsibility. The challenges of reconciling the realities of vulnerability within the dominant political framework are considered in section (7) below.

The analyses of vulnerabilities in this chapter provide a lens through which to evaluate the nature and extent of legal protections for older owners in housing equity transactions. This in turn provides a platform from which to think about the arguments for treating older owners (or older consumers) as 'vulnerable legal subjects'. On the one hand, it has often been argued that the extension of 'special protections' to particular groups should be viewed with caution as it may have adverse implications of dependency, lack of capacity and lack of autonomy.[20] Fineman's concept of the 'vulnerable legal subject' offers a fresh opportunity to move away from the (political) conflation of 'autonomous individualism' and independence (the autonomy/dependence dyad) to 'develop a more complex subject around which to build social policy and law'.[21] Fineman has argued that this vulnerable subject 'must replace the autonomous and independent subject asserted in the liberal tradition'.[22] This chapter seeks to take a 'real measure' of the vulnerabilities which (marginal) older owners may face in housing equity transactions, and to consider how these vulnerabilities reflect on older owners as legal subjects. In doing so, the chapter draws on Fineman's challenge to the normative framework of legal subjectivity to consider its implications for older owners in housing equity transactions. Specifically, the last section considers the critical potential offered by the discursive tropes of vulnerability and responsibility when analysing the justifications for law's outlook on the housing equity transactions of older owners.

(2) Capacity

While capacity provides the obvious starting point for any discussion of older people and vulnerability in financial transactions, it is important not to overplay the significance of questions of capacity in this context,[23] or to focus (as legal analysis often does) on

[19] The social, economic and political contexts of financing retirement mean that housing equity transactions straddle a fluid boundary between private financial transactions executed by homeowners as consumers, and the realm of social welfare support for the care, pensions and housing needs of older people. However, older *owners* are constructed not as 'dependent subjects' but (despite their 'market dependency') as 'independent' and self-determining; see Leonard, above n 15, at 53–54.

[20] See, eg, Green and Lim discussing women entering financial transactions, and arguing against special protections on the grounds that 'We do not want always to be victims.' K Green and H Lim, 'Weaving Along the Borders: Public and Private, Women and Banks' in S Scott-Hunt and H Lim (eds), *Feminist Perspectives on Equity and Trusts* (London, Cavendish, 2001) 98.

[21] MA Fineman, 'The Vulnerable Subject: Anchoring Equality in the Human Condition' (2008) 20 *Yale Journal of Law and Feminism* 1.

[22] *Ibid*, at 2.

[23] 78% of those aged 85 and older have no cognitive impairment at all; T Poole, *Housing Options for Older People* (King's Fund, 2005), at 2; cited in J Herring, *Older People in Law and Society* (Oxford, Oxford University Press, 2009) 52.

(in)capacity to the exclusion of other forms of vulnerability.[24] Nevertheless, questions of capacity do arise, and so this section considers the impact of the current law in this context. The law on capacity in England and Wales is currently to be found in the Mental Capacity Act 2005, which sets out the default position, that a person is assumed to have capacity unless it is established that he or she does not, and that 'A person is not to be treated as unable to make a decision merely because he makes an unwise decision.'[25] The Act goes on to provide that a person is mentally incapable if he is 'unable to make a decision for himself in relation to the matter because of an impairment of, or a disturbance in the functioning of, the mind or brain'.[26] In these circumstances, the legislation empowers the court to make a declaration of incapacity and then either make an order through which the court makes the decision on the incapable person's behalf, or authorise another person to make decisions on his or her behalf.[27]

Although reference is made to age in this Act, it is only in the negative sense that section 2(3)(a) prohibits establishing lack of capacity merely by reference to a person's age. The criteria by which the inability to make a decision is judged are set out in section 3 and include:

a) the ability to understand information relevant to the decision;
b) the ability to retain that information;
c) the ability to use or weigh that information as part of the process of making the decision; and
d) the ability to communicate the decision.

It is interesting to note that section 3(4) provides:

> The information relevant to a decision includes information about the *reasonably foreseeable* consequences of—
>
> (a) deciding one way or another, or
> (b) failing to make the decision.[28]

In light of their unknown future needs, housing equity transactions may well have unforeseeable adverse consequences for older owners.[29] However, the capacity legislation clearly does not extend to difficulties in making decisions that result from the nature and

[24] See, eg, the Report of the Irish Law Commission on *Vulnerable Adults and the Law* (LRC 83–2006), available online at <http://lawreform.ie/_fileupload/Reports/Report%20Vulnerable%20Adults.pdf>, which focused almost entirely on issues relating to capacity. Although the Consultation Paper preceding this Report dedicated a full chapter to protections against financial abuse of vulnerable elders and abuse in property transactions (Law Reform Commission, *Consultation Paper on Law and the Elderly* (LRC CP 23–2003)), this was addressed in four pages of the final Report, which made only one recommendation, ie that equity release schemes should be regulated under the statutory scheme for the financial services regulator. The Scottish Law Commission's *Report on Vulnerable Adults* (Scot Law Com 158, Edinburgh, The Stationery Office, 1997) defined 'vulnerable adults', in terms resounding of incapacity, as 'people aged 16 or over who are unable to safeguard their welfare or property and are (a) in need of care and attention due to age or infirmity, (b) suffering from illness or mental disorder or (c) substantially handicapped by a disability': *ibid*, at vi.

[25] Section 1(4).

[26] Section 2(1).

[27] Section 16(2).

[28] Emphasis added.

[29] See discussion in ch 3, section (3)(b).

context of the transaction, but only to those cases in which 'The inability to make a decision [is] caused by an impairment of or disturbance in the functioning of the mind or brain'.[30]

The statutory definition of incapacity is relevant in cases where the Court of Protection has made a declaration based on the 'diagnostic test' of inability to make decisions. Examples of the problems which may give rise to such an assessment include 'psychiatric illness, learning disability, dementia, brain damage or even a toxic confusional state, as long as it has the necessary effect on the functioning of the mind or brain, causing the person to be unable to make the decision'.[31] In such cases, the court or another nominated person takes over decision-making relating to a range of issues, including health, welfare and the financial affairs of the incapable person, and manages these decisions in the 'best interests' of the incapacitated person. This may include making orders or decisions relating to the use of housing equity to fund health and nursing care. The person making the decision will have to weigh the needs of the older person (across the competing housing paradigms of home, investment and inheritance) and balance the risks of the alternative options to make a choice in the best interests of the owner.[32] While these mechanisms are undoubtedly important in circumstances of medical incapacity, they are to some extent peripheral to the primary focus of this chapter, as the vulnerable person is not in fact making a decision himself.

Older (and other) owners may also be deemed to lack legal capacity under the common law, and this may potentially invalidate extant transactions. In these cases, no order has been made under the Mental Capacity Act, so that the person is not under the control of the court but purports to make his or her own choices and decisions concerning financial transactions which use housing equity. In *Re MM (An Adult)*,[33] Mumby J indicated that the definition of 'incapacity' in the Mental Capacity Act 2005 merely replicated the common law definition,[34] which was explained by Butler-Sloss LJ (in the context of capacity to consent to medical treatment) in *Re MB (Medical Treatment)*.[35] It arises when

> some impairment or disturbance of mental functioning renders the person unable to make a decision [because he or she is] unable to comprehend and retain the information which is material to the decision, especially as to the likely consequences of having or not having the treatment in question [and] the patient is unable to use the information and weigh it in the balance as part of the process of arriving at the decision.[36]

A similar formulation was set out in *Masterman-Lister v Brutton & Co (No 1)*,[37] in relation to the capacity to litigate, when Kennedy LJ held that

[30] Ministry of Justice, *Mental Capacity Act 2005, Code of Practice* (London, The Stationery Office, 2007), s 22.
[31] *Ibid.*
[32] It has been argued that the 'best interests' test is not unproblematic, but that there are tensions between the abstract concept and its everyday application which could have a negative impact on the implementation of the mechanisms for devolved decision-making; see, eg, MC Dunn, ICH Clare, AJ Holland and MJ Gunn, 'Constructing and Reconstructing "Best Interests": An Interpretative Examination of Substitute Decision-making under the Mental Capacity Act 2005' (2007) 29 *Journal of Social Welfare and Family Law* 117.
[33] [2007] EWHC 2003 (Fam), at [74].
[34] See Herring, above n 23, at 54.
[35] [1997] 2 FLR 426.
[36] *Ibid*, at 437.
[37] [2002] EWCA Civ 1889, [2003] 1 WLR 1511.

> the mental abilities required include the ability to recognise a problem, obtain and receive, understand and retain relevant information, including advice; the ability to weigh the information (including that derived from advice) in the balance in reaching a decision, and the ability to communicate that decision.[38]

Mr Justice Mumby added that these various tests are simply different ways of expressing the same 'general theory', which 'applies, in principle, to all "problems" and to all "decisions"'.[39] The common law doctrine may be relevant where the older owner has already purported to enter a contract but then seeks to avoid the transaction on the grounds of incapacity: thus, while the legislation applies to 'before the decision' orders, the common law is likely to be invoked in 'after the decision' disputes.

If a person was acting under incapacity at the time he or she entered into a contract, this renders the contract voidable at the hand of the incapable party,[40] provided that the incapacity was known to the other party at the time of the transaction.[41] It has been argued, and in the New Zealand decision of *Archer v Cutler* the court accepted, that a contract with a person acting under incapacity might be unenforceable even if the other party was not aware of the incapacity, where the contract itself could be viewed as 'unfair' or 'unconscionable'.[42] This argument was rejected by the Privy Council in *Hart v O'Connor* (on appeal from the New Zealand Court of Appeal).[43] Mr O'Connor, aged 83 and—unknown to the purchaser—of unsound mind, had agreed to sell some land to Mr Hart. The Privy Council held that since Mr Hart was not aware of Mr O'Connor's incapacity at the time of the transaction, and there had been no unconscionable dealing, the agreement could not be set aside. Lord Brightman stated that

> the validity of a contract entered into by a lunatic who is ostensibly sane is to be judged by the same standards as a contract by a person of sound mind, and is not voidable by the lunatic or his representatives by reason of 'unfairness' unless such unfairness amounts to equitable fraud which would have enabled the complaining party to avoid the contract even if he had been sane.[44]

The use of stark language ('lunatic') in delineating the scope of the capacity doctrine emphasises its extreme nature, and underlines the unattractiveness of self-identifying within this group. This principle seeks to strike a balance between the protection of the incapable person and the interests of the other party who had no knowledge of the incapacity, although it has been suggested that 'in most cases the latter interest will prevail'.[45] As such, this condition applies a significant limitation to the circumstances in which contracts may be avoided for incapacity, and demonstrates the 'defendant-sided' nature of this doctrine.[46]

[38] [2002] EWCA Civ 1889 at [26].
[39] *Re MM (An Adult)*, above n 33, at [72]; see also *Sheffield City Council v E* [2004] EWHC 2808 (Fam) at [134]–[135], [2005] Fam 326..
[40] *Re Walker* [1905] 1 Ch 60.
[41] *Imperial Loan Co v Stone* [1892] 1 QB 599.
[42] *Archer v Cutler* [1980] 1 NZLR 386 at 398.
[43] [1985] AC 1000. The burden of proving this knowledge rests on the person claiming incapacity; *Molton v Camroux* (1848) 2 Exch 487.
[44] [1985] AC 1000, at 1027.
[45] TA Downes, *A Textbook on Contract* (London, Blackstone Press, 1993) 159.
[46] See P Birks and M Chin, 'On the Nature of Undue Influence' in J Beatson and D Friedmann (eds), *Good Faith and Fault in Contract Law* (Oxford, Clarendon Press, 1995), for discussion of the differences between 'claimant-sided' (responding to vulnerability) and 'defendant-sided' (responding to wrongdoing) protections; see further ch 10.

The use of incapacity to invalidate the contracts by which financial transactions for home equity use are carried out is both limited and potentially problematic, for several reasons. For one thing, it is likely to come into play in only the more extreme cases of 'medical' vulnerability. In fact, as the following sections will indicate, many of the vulnerabilities which are likely to affect older people in home equity transactions are both less extreme and emanate from different sources, including factors which are 'external' to the person—for example, vulnerability resulting from the social context of the transaction. Heywood, Oldman and Means have criticised the tendency of social policy and practice to focus on 'a medical model of disability focusing on the functional limitations',[47] and contrast this with the social model of disability which 'does not see the "problem" as lying with the impairment of the individual but within society itself'.[48] They argued that the role of society in creating the structured dependency of the elderly[49] is particularly evident in the case of suitable housing for older people. The emphasis on contextual factors in creating vulnerability might suggest that the social model of disability would offer more potential to align vulnerability as it is experienced by older people in the context of home equity transactions with capacity doctrine. A more contextual approach also enables vulnerability to be protected without necessarily treating the vulnerable person as a 'victim'.[50] However, even with such a recalibration within the legal doctrine, it remains the case that 'disability' affects only a minority of older people. Any approach which sought to utilise the idea of 'disability' as a broader solution to the issues raised in this book would be both inappropriate and unattractive to the majority of older people.

In *Conceptualising Home*, I set out the reasons—both in principle and in practice—why arguments rooted in dependency or presumptions of incapacity are unattractive as a route through which to address gendered vulnerabilities in the context of financial transactions affecting the home.[51] In principle, arguments for legal protection which are based on incapacity are flawed where they rely on the assumption that age (or gender) can be equated with incapacity *per se*, and where they rely on a model of dependency which can be both inaccurate and have adverse practical implications. Legal discourse has long recognised a risk that 'special treatment' of a particular group of contractors might adversely affect the willingness of creditors to enter into contract with them,[52] with the suggestion that any incursion into the protection of the creditor would inhibit transactions and make it more difficult for that group of consumers to access much-needed capital. This argument—though frequently made and implicitly accepted by the courts—has rarely been subjected to empirical scrutiny, despite the suggestion that there has been a 'tend[ency] to over estimate heavily the effects of law'.[53] Neither is it universally accepted

[47] F Heywood, C Oldman and R Means, *Housing and Home in Later Life* (Buckingham, Open University Press, 2002) 28.

[48] *Ibid.*

[49] That it is not that the individuals who are 'disabled' but society that 'disables' them.

[50] *Ibid*, at 29. See also M Oliver, *The Politics of Disablement* (London, Macmillan, 1990); and C Barnes, G Mercer and T Shakespeare, *Exploring Disability: A Sociological Introduction* (Cambridge, Polity Press, 1999), contrasting the medical model and social model of disability.

[51] See L Fox, *Conceptualising Home: Theories, Laws and Policies* (Oxford, Hart Publishing, 2006), ch 8, especially at 365–66, 401–07.

[52] *Ibid*, at 366; also discussion at 88–92 of the complex relationship between creditor protections and the availability of credit.

[53] K Llewellyn, 'What Price Contract? An Essay in Perspective' (1930) 40 *Yale Law Journal* 704, 725.

that the availability of credit is the most important measure of economic efficiency in credit markets[54]; and even within the efficiency model, there is a need to balance the ready availability of credit against disincentives for effective gate-keeping by creditors who may be induced to take unjustified risks where they are assured of legal protection of their interests in any event.[55]

This set of issues has important ramifications for the housing equity transactions executed by older owners. The policy arguments in support of greater home equity use by older owners include the strategic benefits of (safe) home equity use for local and central government; but barriers to older owners' willingness to spend their housing wealth include concerns about the complexity, riskiness and value for money of such schemes,[56] with the perception that they are 'very risky' the strongest factor against equity release.[57] The discussion in chapter four noted that the equity release industry has for many years been poised for market growth, but that building confidence in the sector—by addressing issues of mistrust—will be a crucial step in achieving that growth. In this context, the arguments for striking the balance between creditor protections and consumer protections on the side of the creditor (rather than providing special protections for potentially vulnerable consumers) are undermined by the importance—both for the industry and for the achievement of government policy—of building confidence in equity release products by providing adequate protection for vulnerable owners.

The arguments against 'special protections' for certain groups have also been extensively rehearsed in the context of undue influence, where the proposition that one party (often a woman) is particularly vulnerable to undue pressure has been viewed as problematic since, while it responds to a reality that women have sometimes been adversely affected by structural socio-cultural inequalities in relation to rights in the owned home, the connotations of female dependency and incapacity—whereby the woman has to 'fit herself within a stereotype of the down-trodden and uninformed housewife'[58]—are unattractive. Similarly, in the case of older people, it has been noted that 'incapacity is often difficult to prove and represents a degrading method of protection'.[59] Relying on incapacity requires the older person seeking the protection of the law to demonstrate weakness or disempowerment; this form of protection echoes of paternalism, carries stigma, has negative connotations for personal dignity, denies the older person the opportunity to make choices and appears to undermine his or her 'autonomy'.

[54] AJ Padilla and A Requejo, *The Costs and Benefits of the Strict Protection of Creditor Rights: Theory and Evidence* (Washington, DC, Inter-American Development Bank, Research Network Working Paper #R-384, 2000); M Manove and AJ Padilla, 'Banking (Conservatively) with Optimists' (1999) 30 *Rand Journal of Economics* 324; M Manove, AJ Padilla and M Pagano, 'Creditor Rights and Project Screening: A Model of Lazy Banks' (Boston, MA, mimeo, 1999); see generally ch 4 for discussion of challenges to the 'efficiency' model of contract and property transactions.

[55] RA Posner, *The Economic Analysis of Law* (Boston, Little, Brown and Company, 1992) 440–41.

[56] K Rowlingson, 'Attitudes to housing assets and inheritance' (2005) 10 *Council of Mortgage Lenders Housing Finance* 1.

[57] *Ibid*, Chart 3; see ch 4, section (5).

[58] B Fehlburg, 'The Husband, the Bank, the Wife and Her Signature—the Sequel' (1996) 59 *MLR* 675, 694.

[59] WC Rossiter, 'No Protection for the Elderly: The Inadequacy of the Capacity Doctrine in Avoiding Unfair Contracts Involving Seniors' (1999) 78 *Oregan Law Review* 807, 808. See also MD Green, 'Proof of Mental Incapacity and the Unexpressed Major Premise' (1944) 53 *Yale Law Journal* 271; JE Rein, 'Clients with Destructive and Socially Harmful Choices—What's An Attorney to Do? Within and Beyond the Competency Construct' (1994) 62 *Fordham Law Review* 1101.

The discussion of ageing in place in chapter five emphasised the importance of maintaining control over decision-making and preserving the older person's sense of personal autonomy in order to support well-being in later life,[60] including control over the home environment. It noted that the loss of the ability to make choices and of personal autonomy may have particularly adverse effects for older people, and so counter the aims of policies supporting 'ageing in place'.[61] Any presumption that older people lack capacity would also potentially undermine their subjectivity within current legal/financial/risk frameworks by creating a stark choice between 'autonomous individualism' and incapacity. The blunt tool of setting an upper age limit on capacity to contract would present similarly stark alternatives, which would not only make it exceedingly difficult for older people to self-provide through housing equity transactions, but would overlook the heterogeneity of older people and discriminate against those who remain highly competent into advanced old age.

Capacity doctrine offers an 'all or nothing' position between autonomy and no autonomy, characterising people as either able to choose (and so responsible for the outcomes of their choices) or unable to choose (and so 'dependent'). This relegates protection for vulnerable older people to claims based on incapacity or disability, and does not address social or contextual vulnerabilities. The usefulness of capacity doctrine in this context is also limited by the medical model of incapacity, which does not capture the cause of vulnerability in many cases, and by the fact that in the context of financial transactions (where an order has not been made under the Mental Capacity Act 2005), parties who do not have knowledge of the incapacity at the time of the transaction are not affected by the fact that someone was acting under incapacity. There is clearly a wide field between capacity and incapacity, in which additional protections against vulnerability must be considered. The following sections consider three other perspectives on the vulnerabilities of older owners when entering into transactions:

a) the relationship between age and economic decision-making;
b) the issue of targeting and financial abuse of the elderly; and
c) the question of contextual vulnerabilities in housing equity transactions.

(3) Age, Financial Capability and Economic Decision-making

While it is recognised that a minority of older people may be affected by impaired capacity, it is by no means the only source of vulnerability in the context of housing equity transactions. Another cause of vulnerability, which falls short of incapacity but which affects the ability to make economic decisions, is related to financial capability. The subject

[60] JF Watkins and AF Hosier, 'Conceptualising Home and Homelessness: A Life Course Perspective' in GD Rowles and H Chaudhury (eds), *Home and Identity in Late Life: International Perspectives* (New York, Springer, 2005) 207; see ch 4, section (3).

[61] See ch 4, section (3); see also C Russell, 'Home, Identity and Belonging in Later Life: The Perspectives of Disadvantaged Inner-City Men', in Rowles and Chaudhury (eds), above n 60, at 237.

of financial capability has been examined in some detail in recent years by the FSA,[62] whose statutory objectives include promoting public understanding of the financial system. In 2003 it published the *National Strategy for Financial Capability*.[63] This initiative was a response to the increasing demands placed on individuals by the State to take responsibility for their own financial affairs, to plan ahead (particularly for retirement) and to choose financial products.[64] It sought to improve financial capability through education and information, particularly for specific populations identified as 'vulnerable'.

In 2006, the FSA carried out a 'baseline survey' to assess levels of financial capability in the UK population. It found that large numbers of people at all income levels lacked financial capability and were unable to plan ahead or to make adequate provision for the future, for example by saving sufficiently for retirement. It also found that while younger people (under-40s) had less financial capability overall than older people,[65] the over-60s were particularly strong at making ends meet.[66] Although planning for the future was a particular weakness across the survey, older people were more capable of planning for the future than younger people. It is these strengths in two specific aspects of financial capability that likely informed the FSA's decision not to focus on older people as a 'vulnerable group', despite the fact that the over-70s were much weaker than the general population at choosing financial products[67]—the specific capability which is most essential in housing equity transactions. The baseline survey also found that 21 per cent of people who have already retired find their income insufficient to give them the standard of living they hoped to have.[68]

The general findings of the financial capability survey indicated that many people take on financial risks without realising it because they have difficulty choosing products that meet their needs.[69] The FSA described capability in choosing financial products as requiring 'an understanding of risk: both what risks they face, and the trade-off between risk and reward … complemented by a good general awareness of the types of financial products that can help them achieve their goals'.[70] The survey found that people in the UK both under-estimated and over-estimated the risks they faced, sometimes taking risks without realising they were doing so, or over-estimating risks, for example purchasing

[62] See, eg, FSA, *Financial Capability in the UK: Establishing a Baseline* [hereafter '*Establishing a Baseline*'] (London, FSA, 2006), available online at <http://www.fsa.gov.uk//pubs/other/fincap_baseline.pdf >; FSA, *Levels of Financial Capability in the UK: Results of a baseline survey* [hereafter '*Results*'], Consumer Research Report No 47 (London, FSA, 2006), available online at <http://www.fsa.gov.uk/pubs/consumer-research/crpr47.pdf >; FSA, *Financial Capability in the UK: Delivering Change* (London, FSA, 2006) available online at <http://www.fsa.gov.uk//pubs/other/fincap_delivering.pdf>; FSA, *The impact of life events on financial capability: Evidence from the BHPS* [hereafter '*Life events*'], Consumer Research Report No 79 (London, FSA, 2009), available online at <http://www.fsa.gov.uk//pubs/consumer-research/crpr79.pdf>; FSA, *Financial Capability and Wellbeing* [hereafter '*Wellbeing*'], Occasional Paper No 34 (London, FSA, 2009), available online at <http://www.fsa.gov.uk//pubs/occpapers/op34.pdf>.

[63] <http://www.cfebuk.org.uk/pdfs/fin_cap_nat_strat.pdf>.

[64] See ch 3 for analysis of the implications of these demands for older people, and the role of housing equity transactions in the panoply of risk they create.

[65] *Establishing a Baseline*, above n 62, at 18.

[66] *Ibid*, at 10.

[67] *Ibid*, at 8. The survey assessed capability on five components: making ends meet, keeping track of your finances, planning ahead, choosing financial products, and staying informed about financial matters.

[68] *Ibid*, at 16. This in turn raised concerns about the financial problems that lie ahead for future generations of retired people, who are less likely to benefit from defined benefit pension schemes.

[69] *Establishing a Baseline*, above n 62.

[70] *Ibid*, at 17.

insurance that they did not really need.[71] Many people took on inappropriate risks, as a result of poor choices, lack of awareness or failure to shop around for a good deal,[72] with over 4 million people having bought their most complex product without considering any other options.[73] The survey also found that the vast majority of the general population (79 per cent) relied on product information and/or non-independent advice when choosing the most complex product they had bought.[74]

The research also explored the reasons why people chose particular products. It found that only 34 per cent were influenced by the product features, with 21 per cent making their decision because of price, 12 per cent because the product was recommended by someone else, 20 per cent because of the provider or ease of purchase, and 13 per cent because it was the only option they had considered.[75] Only slightly more than half of people (54 per cent) had read the terms and conditions of products they bought in detail, and in 9 per cent of cases the terms and conditions had not been read at all.[76] On the specific issue of product choice, the survey found that the very young had the lowest levels of financial capability, and although the oldest respondents scored below average, the FSA decided that any strategies to raise financial capability with respect to product purchase should be targeted at people aged under 40.[77]

The baseline survey was followed by a series of follow-up reports, including an analysis of the impact of life events on financial capability, drawing on data from the British Household Panel Survey.[78] This research focused particularly on the impact of life stages on financial capability: for example, having a baby, becoming unemployed, divorcing or separating, and retirement. The report found that retirement increased financial problems by 31 per cent, due to reduced income, although it also found that those aged over 55 had higher than average financial capability, and that 'the effect on financial capability of halving an individual's income, while large, is smaller than the effects of age, divorce or separation, being a local authority tenant and being unemployed'.[79] Where financial capability research has considered age as a variable, it has been the broad-brush measure that 'on average financial capability increased with age', and 'that people aged below 45 have ... below average financial capability, while those aged 55 and above have ... above average financial capability'.[80] To the extent that the level of generality adopted by the FSA project distinguished between more and less financially capable older people, it noted indications of a non-linear relationship, with less capability amongst the oldest age groups,[81] and that on the measure of 'choosing financial products', homeowners with

71 *Ibid*, at 4.

72 *Ibid*, at 5.

73 *Ibid*, at 18.

74 *Results*, above n 62, [6.8.4], Table 6.10.

75 *Ibid*, [6.8.5], Table 6.11.

76 *Ibid*, [6.8.6], Table 6.12.

77 *Ibid*, [6.9.2]. Another measure of capability used in the survey was whether people complained and/or pursued remedies when they discovered that they had been mis-sold a product. Only 49% of those who felt they had been sold an unsuitable financial product complained to the provider, and 39% of those felt that the problem had been resolved, leaving 51% who took no action at all, and 81% who had not resolved the issue. These results were not disaggregated by age; *ibid*, [7.2].

78 *Life events*, above n 62.

79 *Life events*, above n 62, [8].

80 *Wellbeing*, above n 62, [6.2].

81 *Ibid*.

mortgages scored considerably higher than local-authority and housing-association tenants, even after regression analysis to allow for differences in income and work status. The researchers suggested that this could be attributable to an 'area effect', with access to friends and family who are experienced in using financial products for advice enhancing the capabilities of older owners.[82] Crucially, these findings did not identify 'older owners' as a vulnerable population in relation to financial/decisional capability.

The FSA's strategy in response to the low overall levels of financial capability across the population has included programmes to educate people and help them develop the skills that are needed to navigate through the demands of financial decision-making.[83] This reflects the neoliberal agenda of improving 'citizenship' by transforming 'flawed' consumers into 'skilled' consumers.[84] While the FSA indicated that the financial capability research would also be used to 'help inform our wider regulatory work to help retail consumers achieve a fair deal', its emphasis in this regard also reinforced the goal of greater self-reliance, 'to develop more capable and confident consumers and to produce clear, simple and understandable information for consumers to use'.[85] To the extent that these aims are targeted at particularly vulnerable groups,[86] the focus has been on schools, higher education institutions, organisations that help young and often excluded adults (for example, new parents and former offenders were identified as vulnerable groups), and the workplace. The emphasis on younger people is justified inasmuch as they scored lowest on many of the measures of financial capability, over-70s being the next weakest group, with adults in middle-age usually scoring the highest levels of capability, and the over-70s were identified as particularly weak at choosing financial products.[87] Older people have not been identified as a vulnerable group for the purposes of the FSA's work on financial capability, although they can of course benefit from the support and advice offered by the FSA and the CFEB to the general population.

The financial capability agenda may be described as a 'pro-market' response,[88] directed towards improving consumers' abilities to make rational, informed choices as 'self-responsible' citizens. Yet at the same time, the FSA itself published a detailed review of behavioural economic literature which suggested that it is psychological rather than

[82] *Results*, above n 62, [6.9.3].

[83] See Financial Capability Targets 2009–10, online at <http://www.cfebuk.org.uk/pdfs/fc_targets.pdf>. The Consumer Financial Education Body (CFEB) was established by the FSA to help consumers understand financial services and manage their finances better, see <www.cfeb.org.uk>, and given statutory footing in the Financial Services Act 2010. The CFEB also hosts a website 'Moneymadeclear', which seeks to provide impartial information and tools to help people make financial decisions, <http://www.moneymadeclear.org.uk/>.

[84] See, eg, Z Bauman, *Work, Consumerism and the New Poor* (Maidenhead, Open University Press, 1998) 38, describing how those who make the wrong choice are stigmatised as 'flawed' consumers; and N Rose, 'Community, citizenship, and the third way' (2000) 43 *American Behavioral Scientist* 1395; J Flint, 'Housing and Ethopolitics: constructing identities of active consumption and responsible community' (2003) 32 *Economy and Society* 611; J Flint and R Rowlands, 'Commodification, Normalisation and Intervention: cultural, social and symbolic capital in housing consumption and governance' (2003) 18 *Journal of Housing and the Built Environment* 213, discussing the neoliberal agenda of enabling vulnerable citizens to become more self-responsible. See further, ch 4, section (5).

[85] *Establishing a Baseline*, above n 62, at 8.

[86] *Ibid*, at 22.

[87] Although the detailed *Results* paper suggested that more work could be done to investigate what were described as 'groups that are relatively unusual', for example less capable older people, this seems to suggest that less capable older people are anomalous amongst older people, despite evidence of lower than average levels of capacity, particularly in choosing financial products, and especially amongst the over-70s; *Results*, above n 62, [8.2].

[88] See P Cartwright, *Banks, Consumers and Regulation* (Portland, Ore, Hart Publishing, 2004) 62.

informational differences that account for the differences in financial capability, so that 'people's financial behaviour may primarily depend on their intrinsic psychological attitudes rather than information and skills or how they choose to deploy them'.[89] This report suggested that in light of their emphasis on information and education, the financial capability initiatives the FSA is employing could be expected to have a 'positive but modest impact'. The report argued that, to overcome the problems of financial incapacity,[90] institutional design and regulation, which take account of deep-seated psychological biases (procrastination, regret and loss aversion, mental accounting, status quo bias and information overload),[91] are likely to be much more effective than education.[92] Both the educational strategy[93] and providing generic financial advice[94] are very expensive, and the suggestion that lack of information is not what really matters in financial capability underlines the limited value of this strategy. It also raises significant policy questions concerning the 'gap' that education and information cannot fill, and the extent to which alternative, protective measures are justified to bridge the chasm between expectations of financial capability in the neoliberal State and the realities of financial decision-making. The role of institutional design and regulation on housing equity transactions for older people is considered in more detail in chapter nine.

The specific impact of age on the psychological biases underpinning behavioural economics has been examined in a wide range of studies assessing the effect of ageing on decision-making.[95] In one study that focused on economic decisions, the researchers compared the results of experiments with healthy elderly individuals (highly-educated relative to their age group, aged 70–95, average age 82) and younger students (also healthy and well-educated, aged 18–26, average age 20), to ascertain their levels of confidence, ability to make decisions under uncertainty, differences between willingness to pay and willingness to accept, and strategic thinking. This study—which focused on economic decision-making behaviour rather than financial knowledge or skills—found that, contrary to the 'widely held notion … that decision making faculties decline with aging',[96] adults' decision-making behaviour was similar to that of young adults. While the older subjects were found to have less over-confidence, the study did not find significant differences in the behaviours of younger and older subjects, so belying the common stereotype that older people are 'conservative, dislike taking risk and are set in their

[89] FSA, *Financial Capability: A Behavioural Economics Perspective* (London, FSA, 2008), Foreword.

[90] *Ibid*, at 4.

[91] See ch 3, section (3)(b) for discussion of loss aversion and status quo (eg endowment effect) biases in the context of older people and housing equity transactions.

[92] This claim also has significant implications for legal strategies which rely on information as a safeguard against adverse outcomes.

[93] In 2008, programmes to support personal finance education in schools included the Government's new £11.5m three-year programme 'My Money' and the FSA's £16m 'Learning Money Matters' programme.

[94] In 2009 the FSA launched a new £12m programme to deliver free advice on money matters including budgeting, money management and planning, which aims to help between 500,000 and 750,000 people across the North West and North East of England as part of the Money Guidance 'pathfinder' recommended by the Thoresen Review of generic financial advice; see also O Thorensen, *Thorensen Review of Generic Financial Advice* (London, HMSO, 2008) (hereafter 'Thorensen Review'), available at <http://webarchive.nationalarchives.gov.uk/+/http://www.hm-treasury.gov.uk/thoresen_review_index.htm>.

[95] S Kovalchik, CF Camerer, DM Grether, CR Plott and JM Allman, 'Aging and Decision Making: A comparison between neurologically healthy elderly and young individuals' (2005) 58 *Journal of Economic Behaviour and Organisation* 79.

[96] *Ibid*, at 90.

ways'.[97] In experiments testing endowment effect and loss aversion, the study found no significant differences between the young and the old, and on strategic thinking they behaved similarly,[98] leading the researchers to argue that decision-making behaviour remains stable with age, and that

> [a]side from a minor propensity to make more confused responses on [one of the strategic thinking games], there is no evidence of impairment in the reasoning and choices of the elderly population we studied on any of the areas of the survey.[99]

This research suggests that healthy, well-educated older people do not experience a *decline* in economic decision-making resulting from aging *per se*. However, this does not mean that older people's decision-making is *the same* as that of younger people, or that they may not be more vulnerable in financial decision-making as a result of other factors linked to the nature of the decision or the context in which it is made. Some recent psychological studies have emphasised the importance of age-related changes in deliberation, affect and emotion on decision-making,[100] reflecting what Posner described as the 'knowledge shift' from 'fluid' intelligence (the ability to analyse, solve problems, think deductively) to 'crystallised' knowledge (reliance on one's own knowledge base, the accumulation of concrete experiences and inference of lessons from them, inductive abilities and 'common sense').[101] For example, the examination by Peters *et al* of the implications of 'dual process theory'[102] (the theory that decision-making has both deliberative and affective dimensions) on older people found that while

> age-related declines in the efficiency of deliberative processes predict poorer-quality decisions as we age … age-related adaptive processes, including motivated selectivity in the use of deliberative capacity, an increased focus on emotional goals, and greater experience, predict better or worse decisions for older adults depending on the situation.[103]

Peters *et al* claimed that in identifying areas where older adults are vulnerable as well as those areas where they retain high levels of competence, it is important to recognise the interplay between the 'rational' bases of decision-making and the affective and emotional processes which are 'fundamental to older-adult decisions'.[104] They cited several factors, for example decline in deliberative processes leading to an enhancement in more 'implicit and automatic forms of knowledge (eg affect) in decisions',[105] to argue that 'reliance on affect will increase as people age, or at least increase relatively over reliance on more

[97] *Ibid*, at 80.

[98] These findings contrasted with the earlier findings of NL Denburg, A Bechara, D Tranel, AR Hindes and AR Damasio, 'Neuropsychological evidence for why the ability to decide advantageously weakens with advancing age' (1999) 25 *Society of Neuroscience Abstracts* 32, which found that older adults had tendencies similar to patients with frontal-lobe damage.

[99] Kovalchik *et al*, above n 95, at 90.

[100] See eg, E Peters, TM Hess, D Västfjäll and C Auman, 'Adult Age Differences in Dual Information Processes: Implications for the Role of Affective and Deliberative Processes in Older Adults' Decision Making' (2007) 2(1) *Perspectives on Psychological Science* 1; Q Kennedy and M Mather, 'Aging, Affect, and Decision Making' in KD Vohs, RF Baumeister and G Loewenstein (eds), *Do emotions help or hurt decision making? A hedgefoxian perspective* (New York, Russell Sage Foundation, 2007).

[101] RA Posner, *Aging and Old Age* (Chicago, Ill, University of Chicago Press, 1995) 68–69.

[102] See, eg, D Kahneman, 'A perspective on judgment and choice: Mapping bounded rationality' (2003) 58 *American Psychologist* 697.

[103] Peters *et al*, above n 100.

[104] *Ibid*, at 2.

[105] *Ibid*.

deliberative abilities that require greater conscious effort or do not help meet social goals'.[106] 'Affect' increases with experience over the lifespan as a particularly effective way of making decisions. Affective decision-making is particularly prominent in certain contexts, say, when the decision is complex or must be made under conditions of pressure.[107] The effect of declining cognitive/deliberative processes and increasing affective processes with ageing mean that—depending on the context of the decision—older people's decisions may appear better than younger people's *in some cases*, and worse in others.[108] For example, older people may be more vulnerable to salespeople who use affective techniques to induce them into scams, or deceptive or misleading transactions.[109]

The ways in which individuals make decisions, and what they choose, is highly contingent on the properties of the decision problem and on the characteristics of the individual decision-maker at the point that the decision is made. While older people may be better equipped than younger people to make decisions in familiar life situations or where they have past experience,[110] research suggests that they may make worse decisions 'when complex or changing rules must be learned'.[111] It should not be assumed, however, that this necessarily decreases their overall decision-making ability. Some studies have found that we all adaptively select decision-making strategies, and that older people prefer simple, less cognitively demanding strategies, that use less information.[112] As a result, they are likely to search for less information when making decisions compared to younger people. The logic of this strategy is also supported by research that has shown that the probability of a person selecting the optimal option declines as the number of options increases, and that this is more pronounced for older subjects.[113] These findings clearly undermine the application to older people's decision-making of the standard economic assumption that good decision-making results from having a wide range of choices supported by information.[114]

It is important to emphasise that these studies do not suggest that healthy older people lack capacity, or are less able to make decisions than younger people. Rather, they demonstrate that the cognitive processes and behavioural biases that guide decision-making are *different* for older people. This means that assumptions adopted in legal reasoning, for example that a 'rational man' would act in a particular way, are doubly challenged in the case of older owners: the standard critical argument that law must recognise realities of human subjectivity as evidenced in behavioural economics is compounded by the claim that the 'information paradigm' underpinning the liberal model of choice is particularly inept in respect of older adults.[115] The claim that increasing information is likely adversely to affect the quality of decision-making for older people,

[106] *Ibid*, at 2.

[107] ML Finucane, A Alhakami, P Slovic and SM Johnson, 'The affect heuristic in judgments of risks and benefits' (2000) 13 *Journal of Behavioral Decision Making* 1.

[108] Peters *et al*, above n 100, at 7.

[109] These findings are valuable when considering the vulnerability of older people to financial abuse; see section (4) below.

[110] Peter *et al*, above n 100, at 16.

[111] *Ibid*, at 17.

[112] R Mata, LJ Schooler and J Rieskamp, 'The aging decision maker: Cognitive aging and the adaptive selection of decision strategies' (2007) 22 *Psychology and Aging* 796.

[113] *Ibid*.

[114] T Besedeš, CA Deck, S Sarangi and M Shor, 'Age Effects and Heuristics in Decision Making' (25 January 2009), available at SSRN <http://ssrn.com/abstract=1332564>, at 1.

[115] *Ibid*.

with more options linked to worse choices, raises the concern that the standard liberal model of autonomy has created laws of general application that affect older people differently. In his book, *The Paradox of Choice: Why More is Less*,[116] Schwartz claimed that as options multiply, overwhelming our ability to sort and evaluate, 'choice' shifts from a liberating phenomenon to become debilitating or even tyrannical.[117] At this point, he argued, 'Having the opportunity to choose is no blessing if we feel we do not have the wherewithal to choose wisely.'[118] The behavioural research suggests that older people are likely to reach that point much quicker than younger people, so suggesting a further layer of constraint on the choices 'freely' made by older owners as liberal subjects: in addition to the reality of constraints on the actual range of available choices (for example, the product options open to a particular older owner to release equity), the capability of processing those choices that are available to make the 'right' decision presents a further challenge which, according to the behavioural findings discussed above, may be particularly problematic for older people.

These issues are brought into sharp relief when people are required to make decisions under conditions of uncertainty. With affect, or emotional processes, found to play a prominent role in risky choice, a range of studies have focused on the specific effect of normal ageing on decision-making under uncertainty or ambiguity, and under conditions of risk.[119] Kennedy and Mather have argued that older people are likely to be affected in decision-making for risk in various ways which adversely impact the effectiveness of their decisions, including 'greater reliance on the affective heuristic, greater effort to maintain positive mood during the decision making process, greater attention to the emotional aspects of the decision making process, and positively biased memory for past decisions'.[120] Zamarian *et al* found that older people were better equipped to make good decisions under 'risk' (when the uncertainties can be predicted by well-defined or estimable probabilities so that the risk may be understood) than under 'ambiguity' (where the uncertainties are completely unknown and incalculable).[121] Older people were 'more likely to make advantageous decisions when full information on the problem situation, the options, probabilities and the associated gains and losses is given', but had greater difficulty making good decisions when 'the problem situation is poorly defined, information about risk is missing or conflicting, and they have to learn about the options' utility by contingencies'.[122]

These findings suggested that for older people to make good decisions, for example, in relation to financial transactions, it is better not to have a large *quantity* of information but to have a smaller amount of more specific, precise information concerning the particular situation, the risks, and the associated gains and losses. A crucial question for this book is where responsibility lies for providing this type of qualitative information, which should ideally be contextually tailored to the needs, objectives and circumstances of

[116] B Schwartz, *The Paradox of Choice: Why More is Less* (New York, Harper Perennial, 2004).
[117] *Ibid*, at 2.
[118] *Ibid*, at 104.
[119] See, eg, Kennedy and Mather, above n 100; L Zamarian, H Sinz, E Bonatti, N Gamboz and M Delazer, 'Normal Aging Affects Decisions Under Ambiguity but Not Decisions Under Risk' (2008) 22 *Neuropsychology* 645.
[120] Kennedy and Mather, above n 100, at 259.
[121] Zamarian *et al*, above n 119.
[122] *Ibid*, at 656.

the individual owner. Empirical studies suggest that where the information strategy applied to older people is the same as that for younger people; and where the amount and type of information is more appropriately tailored to the younger person's needs (more choice, greater quantity of information), this is likely to disadvantage the older decision-maker.

The issue of 'difference' in the effects of formally equal legal treatment has been extensively critiqued in feminist scholarship.[123] A fundamental principle of non-discrimination is that while like cases should be treated alike, unlike cases should be treated differently.[124] Yet determining whether a particular difference is, or should be, legally significant presents dilemmas. When difference is recognised in law or policy, the meanings it imbues have (sometimes unintended) consequences.[125] We must be cautious about 'labelling' a person or group as 'different', particularly where such labels draw boundaries between normal/abnormal, or competent/incompetent people[126]; within law's 'bounded vocabulary', labels provide a blunt tool to differentiate people, and may generate legal disability. Concerns regarding the unintended consequences of singling out 'vulnerable' groups for 'special protection', and so reinforcing the stereotype that they are less capable, led 'equal treatment' advocates within feminism to argue that equality requires equal treatment regardless of differential vulnerability,[127] because emphasising the differences of a particular social group can 'underscore their incapacities and special needs as the defining feature of their social identities and, ultimately, place them in subordinate positions within both public and private spheres of social life'.[128]

An alternative strategy in pursuit of equality is to argue for 'special treatment' or a 'positive action' approach,[129] where differences between people mean that formal equality leaves them substantively unequal because they cannot live up to the accepted norm. 'Difference' sets some people apart from the normative model of liberal legal subjectivity.[130] While the unreality of the idealised liberal subject[131] is such that many consumers are likely

[123] See, eg, M Minow, *Making All the Difference: Inclusion and Exclusion in American Law* (Ithaca, NY, Cornell University Press, 1990).

[124] In *Ghaidan v Godin-Mendoza* [2004] UKHL 30 at [9], Lord Nicholls, stating the principle of non-discrimination, claimed that 'Of course all law, civil and criminal, has to draw distinctions. One type of conduct, or one factual situation, attracts one legal consequence, another type of conduct or situation attracts a different legal consequence. To be acceptable these distinctions should have a rational and fair basis. Like cases should be treated alike, unlike cases should not be treated alike.'

[125] 'When we identify one thing as unlike the others, we are dividing the world; we use our language to exclude, to distinguish—to discriminate.': Minow, above n 123, at 3.

[126] *Ibid*, at 8.

[127] See, eg, WW Williams, 'The Equality Crisis: Some Reflections on Culture, Courts, and Feminism' (1982) 7 *Women's Rights Law Report* 175, collected in KT Bartlett and R Kennedy (eds), *Feminist Legal Theory: Readings in Law and Gender* (Boulder, CO, Westview Press, 1991); C Smart and J Brophy, 'Locating Law: A Discussion of the Place of Law in Feminist Politics' in C Smart and J Brophy (eds), *Women in Law: Explorations in Law, Family and Sexuality* (London, Routledge & Kegan Paul, 1985); for discussion of the 'sameness/difference' debate, see JC Williams, 'Dissolving the Sameness/Difference Debate: A Post-Modern Path Beyond Essentialism in Feminist and Critical Race Theory' (1991) 40 *Duke Law Journal* 296.

[128] V Jenness, 'Engendering Hate Crime Policy: Gender, the "Dilemma of Difference" and the Creation of the Legal Subject' (2003) 2 *Journal of Hate Studies* 73, 89.

[129] LJ Kreiger and PN Cooney, 'The Miller-Wohl Controversy: Equal Treatment, Positive Action, and the Meaning of Women's Equality' (1983) 13 *Golden Gate University Law Review* 513; MA Fineman, 'Challenging Law, Establishing Differences: The Future of Feminist Legal Scholarship' [1990] 42 *Florida Law Review* 25.

[130] Minow noted that 'Especially troubling is the meaning of equality for individuals identified as different from the norm.': Minow, above n 123, at 9.

[131] Discussed in ch 4.

to have difficulty living up to its norms (as illustrated by the FSA's findings on financial capability), marshalling this lack of capability to argue for additional protections along group difference lines runs a risk of reinforcing negative stereotypes, for example concerning the capacity and capability of older people. Minow recognised this paradox in her observation that

> [l]aw has treated as marginal, inferior, and different any person who does not fit the normal model of the autonomous, competent individual. Law has tended to deny the mutual dependence of all people while accepting and accentuating the dependency of people who are 'different'.[132]

Minow described the philosophical, legal and strategic questions of how and when society and law should recognise difference as generating 'dilemmas of difference': while recognising that difference may reinforce negative connotations, and so threaten neutrality, equality and freedom,[133] ignoring differences 'may make them continue to matter in a world constructed with some groups, but not others, in mind'.[134]

Minow outlined three distinctive approaches to the issue of difference in law. The first she described as the 'abnormal person' approach, where categories are used to label people with different statuses (for example, capacity/incapacity). In this category, the difference is often seen as 'inherent' to the person, who is classified as 'abnormal'. Minow argued that 'The price of these legal categories has been borne disproportionately by the most marginal and vulnerable members of the society.'[135] The 'labelling' approach is problematic inasmuch as it tends to treat the difference as the private, internal problem of the different person, and by extension it 'only hide[s] human responsibility for their treatment, [and does] not solve the problems of organising perceptions and responsibilities'.[136] Minow argued that if we are to achieve equality and justice for people who are identified as different from the norm, it is necessary to go beyond the 'abnormal person' approach and—by examining assumptions about the sources of difference and debating the dilemmas that difference presents—explore alternative options for addressing them.[137] Merely perpetuating assumptions about two classes of people fails to offer a way out of the dilemma of difference[138] and, for older people, could potentially reinforce negative stereotypes about capacity and capability to make decisions, with implications beyond the immediate context to other areas of decision-making for older people. In this way, what is intended as 'benevolent prejudice' can result in harmful consequences or even hostile prejudice.[139] Lastly, the 'abnormal person' approach offers an 'either/or choice'—as noted

[132] Minow, above n 123, at 10.

[133] *Ibid*, at 74.

[134] M Minow, 'Justice Engendered' (1987) 101 *Harvard Law Review* 10, 12.

[135] Minow, above n 123, at 10.

[136] *Ibid*.

[137] See *ibid*, ch 2.

[138] Minow also rejects Kennedy's modified capacity test, which would focus not on the person's general capacity, but on his or her 'capacity-to-make-this-decision' (see D Kennedy, 'Distributive and Paternalist Moves in Contract and Tort Law, with Special Reference to Compulsory Term and Unequal Bargaining Power' (1982) 41 *Maryland Law Review* 563), on the basis that this still treats the matter as a 'problem in a person—in a given situation—to be judged by another person': Minow, above n 123, at 169. Minow criticises Kennedy for being caught on the dilemma of individual autonomy, in that he cannot shift his focus away from the individuals to the relationships. While Kennedy recognises that many of the 'traits of dependence' result from social or contextual circumstances rather than intrinsic personal qualities, by preserving the separate individual as the focus of the difference, Minow claims that his approach offers no way out of the dilemma; *ibid*, at 170–71.

[139] 'Labeling and stereotyping others as different carries consequences in private and even intimate settings as well as public ones. You have the power to label others "different" and to treat them differently on that basis.

above, capacity or no capacity/autonomy or no autonomy—which may perpetuate inequality by including or excluding the person from the 'norm', without challenging the assumptions of the norm.

A second approach to difference employs a traditional rights paradigm to argue that equal rights for people with 'real differences' justifies different treatment. Minow argued that the rights approach, which challenges the exclusion of the 'different' person from the community inhabited by 'normal' people, is also problematic in that while it permits different treatment for those who are 'really different', it preserves the 'either/or' construction of the problem.[140] Minow argued that

> [w]hen reformers seek to apply the language of rights, taking the rhetoric of equality and freedom literally, they encounter the dilemma that rights crafted for the norms reiterate the differences of those at the margin, and special rights crafted for those at the margin risk perpetuating the negative effects of difference.[141]

Another weakness of the rights approach, according to Minow, is its reliance on empirical 'realities' that are themselves situated within normative structures as sources of knowledge about differences between people.[142] In the case of older owners, a rights analysis could bolster the protections afforded to vulnerable parties in housing equity transactions, but the risk is that it would do so (or would be perceived as doing so) on the basis that they are 'inherently' weaker than the dominant group, rather than challenging the unreality of the idealised norm. As such, a rights-based remedy for discrimination risks creating new forms of discrimination and becoming a new source of stigma.

Minow argues that the route out of the 'double-bind' dilemma of difference is to focus not on the 'different' individual but on the unstated norms and assumptions that characterise some people as conforming to the norm while others do not. 'Difference' depends on a relationship, on 'a comparison drawn between people with reference to a norm'.[143] Since all differences are relational—if one person appears 'different', it is only because the other (in relation to whom he is different) meets the criteria of the dominant norm—Minow argues that responses to difference must adopt a 'social relations' approach. This approach sees difference as 'a function of social relationships and invites a challenge to the patterns of relationships and knowledge that assign the burden of differences between people to only some people'.[144] From this perspective, 'special treatment' simply recognises that the 'different' person does not fit the assumptions of the

Even if you mean only to help others, not hurt them, because of their difference, you may realise the dilemma. By taking another person's difference into account—in a world that has made difference matter—you may recreate and re-establish both the difference and its negative implications. Any remedy for discrimination that departs from neutrality seems a new discrimination and risks a new source of stigma. Yet you cannot avoid trouble through ignoring difference; you cannot find a solution in neutrality. Ours is a world that has made difference matter. Being neutral about the past and ignoring someone's difference assigns remaining burdens of difference to that person.' See Minow, above n 123, at 374–75.

[140] *Ibid*, at 215.

[141] *Ibid*, at 224.

[142] 'Rights analysis … assumes the existence of reliable empirical sources of knowledge about differences between people, and it presumes that such real differences can be discerned—or dissolved—upon scrutiny, without concern about the way in which the observer constructs what is "real".' M Minow, 'When Difference has its Home: Group Homes for the Mentally Retarded, Equal Protection and Legal Treatment of Difference' (1987) 22 *Harvard Civil Rights-Civil Liberties Law Review* 111, 183.

[143] Minow, above n 123, at 377.

[144] *Ibid*, at 13.

norm against which she is judged, and 'special rights' create false dichotomies which are slanted against the person who is different. Minow argues that it is the norms themselves which must be evaluated, not simply accepted as neutral, if we are to achieve equality and justice in cases of difference, so that difference does not mean disadvantage.

The 'social relations' approach rejects the construction of problems of difference in either/or terms. Rather, it is concerned with the relationships in which difference is manifest, the power that is expressed in the process of categorising people or problems, and the institutional practices that determine a norm against which some people seem different.[145] By being so, it forces the statement of norms that have remained implicit.[146] Once stated, Minow argues, these norms 'become a subject for contest; alternative norms can be articulated and defended'.[147] By articulating these differences, 'the social and institutional patterns that ignore this perspective themselves become questionable. The status quo no longer seems natural and inevitable but is revealed instead as a reflection of choices made and choices that can be remade.'[148]

Iris Marion Young illustrated this approach in relation to older people in her work on the 'politics of difference'.[149] Young described one of the differences of ageing as a form of 'bodily difference', and used the example of older people in the workplace to illustrate a case for 'special rights'. She emphasised the relational basis of her approach to difference:

> [T]he circumstance that calls for different treatment should not be understood as lodged in the differently treated workers, *per se*, but in their interaction with the structure and norms of the workplace ... in the relationship of bodies to rules and practices ... the political claim for special rights emerges not from a need to compensate for an inferiority, as some would interpret it, but a positive assertion of specificity in different forms of life.[150]

This disjuncture between specific needs and the normative framework is crucial in determining the goals of legal strategies to address difference. Young asserted that 'The goal is not to give special compensation to the deviant until they achieve normalcy, but rather to de-normalize the way institutions formulate their rules by revealing the plural circumstances and needs that exist, or ought to exist, within them.'[151] This reflects Minow's argument that 'difference' can only exist with reference to a relationship between two persons, and 'that their relationship in turn depends on other relationships embedded in the social, economic, and political structure of society'.[152]

In the context of financial transactions, this strategy could amount to a rejection of the 'norm' of the consumer as an 'autonomous individual', for a more realistic model of legal subjectivity that takes account of real, contextual vulnerabilities. Rather than branding older owners as 'abnormal' and so lacking capacity to contract, or seeking to 'train' the older person in capability so that he or she might better fit the model of 'skilled consumer', a social relations approach to difference might challenge the norms of the neoliberal model of autonomous, self-responsible consumer on the basis that these norms

[145] *Ibid*, at 215.
[146] *Ibid*, at 218.
[147] *Ibid.*
[148] *Ibid.*
[149] IM Young, *Justice and the Politics of Difference* (Princeton, Princeton University Press, 1990).
[150] IM Young, 'Difference and Policy: Some Reflections in the Context of New Social Movements' (1987) 56 *University of Cincinnati Law Review* 535, 547.
[151] *Ibid*, at 550.
[152] Minow, above n 123, at 169.

generate inequalities. Indeed, Minow made a similar argument concerning the need for a 'difference' approach to counter liberal individualism in the law of contract:

> The conception of individual rights exemplified by classical contract law neglected patterns of unequal power—called private but reinforced by public authority—which defeated any ideal of free and equal relationships ... Scholars have started to urge acknowledgement of people's mutual reliance and dependence, and recognition of obligations growing from these relationships.[153]

These challenges to the liberal norm were discussed in chapter four and are considered further in section (7) below. The advantages of the social relations approach as a strategy to respond to difference underline critiques of the dominant paradigms in private law, and help to establish the case for a debate about the law governing financial transactions which challenges its unstated norms and assumptions, and seeks to generate more creative, more appropriate, and more equality and justice-oriented solutions. While Minow acknowledged that the limits to the relational approach become clear when relational strategies do not seek to challenge the dominant ideology of individualism, or are unsuccessful in displacing the dominant norm, she argued that opening up debate around these normative questions is crucial if we are to 'think seriously about difference'.[154]

In the contexts of financial capability and economic decision-making, the source of the older owner's 'difference' is clearly located within the normative liberal model rather than being 'inherent' to the older person. Indeed, in the case of financial capability, the difficulties that older people face in living up to the idealised expectations of financial/risk subjects are not so very different from those experienced by the general population, but reflect a 'capability gap' that cuts across age. Behavioural research has clearly established, and it is widely recognised in critical legal discourses, that the norm on which the institutional expectation of financial capability rests is unrealistic for the population as a whole. Research into economic decision-making and age only reinforces the *extent* to which the dominant normative perspective generates inequalities for older people. Behavioural economics has challenged law's reliance on the 'information paradigm' in relation to consumers in general; evidence indicating that the information paradigm is *particularly* unhelpful for older people may be viewed less as 'difference' than as an exemplar of the unsuitability of this approach in law more generally.

(4) Financial Abuse of Older People

The particular vulnerabilities of older people to financial abuse has attracted considerable attention in recent years, from the scandals of UK telesales companies aggressively targeting older people for charitable donations they could not afford,[155] to the US case in which a charity specifically targeted older people because they were 'perceived as lonely, trusting and more polite, hence less likely to hang up before the telemarketer could make

[153] *Ibid*, at 388.

[154] *Ibid*, at 374. These issues are discussed further below in relation to Fineman's 'vulnerable legal subject'; see section (7).

[155] 'Charity Call Centre Scandal: Shock hard sell tactics—Elderly? Sick? Hassle them for cash till they hang up', reported in *News of the World*, 14 February 2010, available online at <http://www.newsoftheworld.co.uk/news/727531/SHOCKING-CHARITY-CALL-CENTRE-HARD-SELL-TACTICS.html>.

his pitch'.[156] The vulnerabilities of older people to sales pressure were recognised and given specific legal protection in the US through the Senior Citizens Against Marketing Scams Act 1993,[157] enacted in response to evidence that the elderly are targeted for fraud more than any other group.[158] The source of this vulnerability is largely 'situational' rather than 'inherent': older people are more likely to live alone, with the result that they are more available to parties seeking to take advantage, and tend to be isolated in their decision-making. Peters *et al* suggested that 'geographically dispersed families mean that older individuals may have limited access to knowledgeable and supportive family members',[159] while recent statistics from the UK's FSA also suggest that older people are more likely to be targeted for, and are especially susceptible to, fraud, financial scams and other financial abuse, because they are the 'most vulnerable'.[160]

There is no legal definition of 'financial abuse' in the UK, although various charitable and governmental bodies have sought to develop definitions in recent years in an attempt to capture the exposure of older people to various forms of abuse and mistreatment. The broad definitions that are typically used encompass acts which are crimes or civil wrongs, and in some cases not necessarily punishable in law. In 1993 the UK charity Action on Elder Abuse drafted a definition of 'abuse'[161] as:

> A single or repeated act or lack of appropriate action, occurring within any relationship where there is an expectation of trust, which causes harm or distress to an older person.[162]

This definition 'has at its heart the "expectation of trust" that an older person may rightly establish with another person, but which is subsequently violated'.[163] There is also a sub-definition of 'Financial Abuse', 'stealing or defrauding someone of goods and/or property'. Common examples include cases in which adult children attempt to justify their actions on the basis that they are simply obtaining their inheritance in advance, or where

[156] *United States v Smith* 113 F 3d 737, 741 (10th Cir 1997). For discussions of financial scams, consumer frauds and distraction burglaries targeted at vulnerable older people, see B Alt and S Wells, *Fleecing Grandma and Grandpa: protecting against scams, cons, and frauds* (Westport, CT, Praeger, 2004); K Anders, *Elder Fraud: financial crimes against the elderly* (Denver, CO, National Conference of State Legislatures, 1999); CA Cohen, 'Consumer fraud and the elderly: a review of Canadian challenges and initiatives' (2006) 46 *Journal of Gerontological Social Work* 137; W Reiboldt and RE Vogel, 'A critical analysis of telemarketing fraud in a gated senior community' (2001) 13 *Journal of Elder Abuse & Neglect* 21; D Rosato and M Gallardo, 'Keeping the bad guys away from mom and dad' (2005) 35 *Money* 80.

[157] 18 USC § 2326 (1994 & Supp III 1998).

[158] RA Starnes, 'Consumer Fraud and the Elderly: The Need for a Uniform System of Enforcement and Increased Civil and Criminal Penalties' (1996) 4 *Elder Law Journal* 201, 202, 204, cited in WC Rossiter, 'No Protection for the Elderly: The Inadequacy of the Capacity Doctrine in Avoiding Unfair Contracts Involving Seniors' (1999) 78 *Oregon Law Review* 807, 810; see also RJ Bonnie and RB Wallace, *Elder Mistreatment: Abuse, Neglect and Exploitation in an Aging America* (Washington, DC, National Academies Press, 2003), discussing the conceptual, methodological and logistical issues needed to create a solid research base, as well as the ethical concerns that must be considered when working with older subjects.

[159] E Peters, TM Hess, D Västfjäll and C Auman, 'Adult Age Differences in Dual Information Processes: Implications for the Role of Affective and Deliberative Processes in Older Adults' Decision Making' (2007) 2(1) *Perspectives on Psychological Science* 1.

[160] See FSA Press Release, 'Over 65s most likely to be targeted by share fraudsters, warns FSA', 27 April 2009, available online at <http://www.fsa.gov.uk/pages/Library/Communication/PR/2009/055.shtml>.

[161] This definition was subsequently adopted by the World Health Organisation, is promoted by the International Network for the Prevention of Elder Abuse, and has been variously adopted in other countries throughout the world.

[162] See the website of Action on Elder Abuse, <http://www.elderabuse.org.uk/About%20Abuse/What_is_abuse%20define.htm>.

[163] *Ibid.*

people misuse powers of attorney. Age UK[164] add that financial abuse may also involve undue pressure to hand over money or sign over property.[165] While some (but not all) cases of financial abuse incur criminal sanctions, Action on Elder Abuse claim that these criminal acts are not always prosecuted either 'because very often the perpetrator can be someone's son or daughter', or because 'age prejudice means that other people assume it is not happening or that the older person is to blame'.[166]

In *No Secrets*,[167] a UK Government publication providing guidance on the development and implementation of policies to protect vulnerable adults from abuse, a 'vulnerable adult' was defined as someone

> who is or may be in need of community care services by reason of mental or other disability, age or illness; who is or may be unable to take care of him or herself, or unable to protect him or herself from significant harm or exploitation.[168]

This document describes financial abuse as a situation in which 'a vulnerable person is persuaded to enter into a financial or sexual transaction to which he or she has not consented, or cannot consent',[169] and later as 'financial or material abuse, including theft, fraud, exploitation, pressure in connection with wills, property or inheritance or financial transactions, or the misuse or misappropriation of property, possessions or benefits'.[170] The breadth of the category was also reflected in a report for the UK charity Help the Aged, which identified financial abuse as including the more subtle acts of 'exerting undue influence to give away assets or gifts' and 'putting undue pressure on the older person in order to accept lower-cost/lower-quality services in order to preserve more financial resources to be passed on to beneficiaries on death'.[171]

[164] This UK charity was formed by the merger of Help the Aged and Age Concern.

[165] The issues surrounding 'undue influence' for older people are discussed in ch 10. To be 'financial abuse', it is clear that there must be some degree of *mala fides* or bad faith on the part of the abuser. Age UK indicated that 'crimes' associated with financial abuse of older people include theft, undue influence (undue influence is not, of course, a crime according to English law but a private law 'vitiating factor' which may render a contract voidable at the suit of the unduly influenced party), or forgery. Section 4 of the Fraud Act 2005 prohibits a person from abusing a position in which he or she is expected to safeguard the financial interests of another person. See Age UK, *Safeguarding older people from abuse* (Factsheet 78, April 2010), available online at <http://www.ageuk.org.uk/Documents/EN-GB/FS78%20%20%20Safeguarding%20older%20people%20from%20abuse%20April%202010.pdf?dtrk=true>. The Mental Capacity Act 2005 does not specifically mention financial abuse, although protecting older people who lack capacity is implicit in the whole of the Act; the Explanatory Notes mention it only once, in relation to the prohibition against bankrupts holding lasting power of attorney where the power covers property and affairs, in ss 10(2) and 13(8) and (9); see Explanatory Notes to Mental Capacity Act 2005, para 13; available online at <http://www.opsi.gov.uk/acts/acts2005/en/ukpgaen_20050009_en_1>.

[166] <http://www.elderabuse.org.uk/About%20Abuse/What_is_abuse_signs%20financial.htm>. This underlines the potentially adverse consequences of 'special treatment' which identifies older people as lacking capacity or cognitive awareness.

[167] Department of Health and Home Office, *No Secrets: Guidance on developing and implementing multi-agency policies and procedures to protect vulnerable adults from abuse* (London, HMSO, 2000), online at <http://www.dh.gov.uk/dr_consum_dh/groups/dh_digitalassets/@dh/@en/documents/digitalasset/dh_4074540.pdf>.

[168] *Ibid*, para 2.3.

[169] *Ibid*, para 2.6.

[170] *Ibid*.

[171] G Crosby, A Clark, R Hayes, K Jones and N Lievesley, *Financial Abuse of Older People: A review of the literature carried out by the Centre for Policy on Aging on Behalf of Help the Aged* (London, Help the Aged, 2008) 11.

The risks associated with an older person's family or carers exerting undue influence or pressure were highlighted in *Hammond v Osborn*,[172] in which a substantial gift from a vulnerable older man to his carer was set aside on a finding of undue influence. Although the court did not consider that the carer's behaviour was sinister or amounted to 'abuse' (wrongdoing), it emphasised that the protections which the doctrine of presumed undue influence seeks to provide extend to intervention, on public policy grounds, where the relationship between the parties 'requires it to be affirmatively established that the donor's trust and confidence in the donee has not been betrayed or abused'.[173] This focus on 'a relationship of trust and confidence' for presumed undue influence emphasises a distinction between acts which may be viewed as exploitative when carried out by a person in whom the older owner has reposed trust and confidence, but potentially not so when carried out by a stranger.[174] Yet in other cases, definitions of financial abuse have looked beyond existing relationships to include 'stranger abuse',[175] which could include 'being persuaded to buy equity release products that offer very poor value for money'.[176]

The *UK Study of Abuse and Neglect of Older People* found that financial abuse was the second most common type of mistreatment of older people in the UK (after neglect), with 57,000 people over 66 reporting that they had experienced financial abuse in the previous year.[177] The risk factors for financial abuse included people who lived alone, people who were in receipt of services, people in bad or very bad health, older men (both men aged over 65 and then, with significantly greater prevalence, men aged over 85), women who were divorced or separated, and women who had experienced loneliness.[178] Older people with lower quality of life or who suffered from depression also reported a higher prevalence of financial abuse.[179] While over 50 per cent of financial abuse was perpetrated by a son or daughter, and nearly 70 per cent by a family member,[180] it was noted that this may be skewed by the high volume of help given by family members, rather than indicating that they are necessarily less trustworthy than non-family. Another study indicated that older people are more likely to experience financial abuse than other groups of 'vulnerable' adults.[181]

[172] [2002] EWCA Civ 885.

[173] *Ibid*, at [32].

[174] This issue is considered in ch 10, alongside the broader debates surrounding undue influence and older people.

[175] Brown's proposed definition of financial abuse included 'the intentional or opportunistic appropriation of the income, capital or property of a vulnerable person through theft, fraud, deception, undue influence or exploitation; including the hoarding of a vulnerable person's resources for future gain': H Brown, 'What is financial abuse?' (2003) 5 *Journal of Adult Protection* 3.

[176] Crosby *et al*, above n 171, at 20.

[177] The *UK Study of Abuse and Neglect of Older People*, carried out by the National Centre for Social Research (NatCen) and King's College London (KCL) (hereafter '*UK Study*'), was commissioned by Comic Relief and the Department of Health. See M O'Keeffe, A Hills, M Doyle, C McCreadie, S Scholes, R Constantine, A Tinker, J Manthorpe, S Biggs and B Erens, *UK Study of Abuse and Neglect of Older People: Prevalence Survey Report* (London, Department of Health, 2007); available online at <http://assets.comicrelief.com/cr09/docs/elderabuseprev.pdf>.

[178] *Ibid*, at 6.

[179] *Ibid*, at 52.

[180] Crosby *et al*, above n 171, at 9.

[181] P Cambridge, J Beadle-Brown, A Milne, J Mansell and R Whelton, *Exploring the Incidence, Risk Factors, Nature and Monitoring of Adult Protection Alerts* (Canterbury, Tizard Centre, 2006); cited in Crosby *et al*, *ibid*, at 15.

The argument for 'special protection' of older people in financial transactions was asserted in 2007 when the UK charity Help the Aged published proposals to address concerns that older people are not getting the financial services or advice they need.[182] The review noted that 'At present older people are often denied access to financial products, regardless of their individual risk profile, and products targeted towards older people can be more costly than for people in other age groups.'[183] These proposals included recommendations for a 'new legal framework' to combat the abuse of vulnerable adults, enforceable against the financial services industry, and argued that the FSA 'should actively engage in issues relating to financial abuse and publish its own plans for prevention',[184] although they did not specify how this would be achieved beyond indicating that where previous legal interventions have been 'patchy' (across criminal and civil law), in future 'law' should be more proactive in relation to financial abuse.[185] The strategy for achieving this goal—however, benignly—appeared to follow the 'abnormal person' approach to difference, asserting that legal protections for older people 'should be based on capacity rather than age'.[186] This is perhaps explicable, to some degree, by the emphasis on 'physical and/or cognitive impairments'[187] (with connotations of 'disability') in the review's analysis of the sources of vulnerability.

This is to some extent borne out in a 2005 study of susceptibility of older people to 'undue influence', which identified a wide range of factors—both 'inherent' and contextual—which render people vulnerable to financial exploitation. These included advanced age (75+), being female, being unmarried, having suffered organic brain damage, cognitive impairment, physical, mental or emotional dysfunction (especially depression), recent loss of spouse or divorce, living alone, social isolation, being estranged from children, being financially independent with no designated financial carers, being in the middle or upper income brackets, taking multiple medications and frailty.[188] Other studies have placed greater emphasis on the contextual nature of vulnerability to financial abuse. Choi and Mayer found that financial exploitation was most common among older people and those who owned their own homes.[189] Starnes identified several factors which render older people more vulnerable to consumer fraud, including living alone (with no one to consult about questionable transactions); relying only on the information given by the salesperson; having a greater desire for social contact than younger members of the population; limited access to transport and lack of nearby family adding to social isolation; and (particularly for elderly widows who had allowed their husbands to take responsibility for family finances) lacking experience in financial matters.[190] The significance of *contextual* vulnerability has

[182] Crosby *et al*, above n 171.

[183] *Ibid*, at 7.

[184] *Ibid*, at 5.

[185] *Ibid*, at 10.

[186] '[T]here is … a premise that older people require statutory protection because of the association of age with physical and/or cognitive impairments that increase vulnerability to abuse': *ibid*.

[187] *Ibid*.

[188] RCW Hall, RCW Hall and MJ Chapman, 'Exploitation of the elderly: undue influence as a form of elder abuse' (2005) 13 *Clinical Geriatrics* 28; cited in Crosby *et al*, above n 171, at 16–17.

[189] NG Choi and J Mayer, 'Elder abuse, neglect, and exploitation—risk factors and prevention strategies' (2000) 33 *Journal of Gerontological Social Work* 5.

[190] RA Starnes, 'Consumer Fraud and the Elderly: The Need for a Uniform System of Enforcement and Increased Civil and Criminal Penalties' (1996) 4 *Elder Law Journal* 201, 204. Health problems, physical incapacity and the suggestion that the older generation 'are generally more trusting and willing to talk to strangers than younger individuals' (*ibid*, at 205) were also identified as compounding the 'victimisation' of older people by

also been explicitly recognised in research on financial abuse of older people. For example, it has been suggested that

> [t]he fact that more women than men are identified as suffering abuse is likely to reflect the fact that women live longer than men and are consequently more likely to be living alone. It is their circumstances that make women vulnerable to abuse, not their gender.[191]

Meanwhile, in the UK, social policies focused on older people explicitly moved away from traditional ideas of vulnerability on the grounds that the label of vulnerability 'can be misunderstood, because it seems to locate the cause of abuse with the victim, rather than in placing responsibility with the actions or omissions of others'.[192] This appeared to move away from the 'abnormal person' approach; however, the language of the prevailing policy approach is on supporting 'well-being'[193] and 'safeguarding' older people[194] to maintain their status as autonomous individuals, 'to retain independence, wellbeing and choice'.[195] The emphases on independence and choice reinforce the model of older people as autonomous 'responsibilised' consumers of care, and this is underlined by the proposed strategies, which typically have focused on information, advice and advocacy.[196] While this is positive in the sense that (in light of the adverse impact of harms for older people[197]) 'prevention is better than cure',[198] it tends towards an expectation of self-provision/self-protection, which in turn is premised on the information paradigm.[199]

Many of the trading practices that would be likely to be viewed as 'financial abuse' are prohibited by regulations on commercial practices, for example in the Consumer Protection from Unfair Trading Regulations 2008 (SI 2008/1277),[200] which impose a general duty on traders not to trade unfairly and to seek to ensure that they act honestly and fairly towards customers. While these Regulations include potentially powerful enforcement mechanisms—for example, fraud offences[201]—they are primarily 'provider-facing' in the

fraudsters. Rossiter argued that the same characteristics which leave older people vulnerable to fraud also make them 'equally vulnerable to unfair contracts in which seniors are either pressured into unfair transactions, or volitionally enter into transactions harmful to their interests': Rossiter, above n 158, at 810, adding that 'Seniors are particularly vulnerable to unfair contracts because of their physical impairments, loneliness, and limited resources.' (*ibid*, at 821)

[191] Crosby *et al*, above n 171, at 19; see G Fitzgerald, *Hidden Voices: older people's experience of abuse—an analysis of calls to the Action on Elder Abuse helpline* (London, Action on Elder Abuse in association with Help the Aged, 2004). McCreadie also found that older people living alone are at greater risk of financial abuse than those who live with others; see C McCreadie, 'Review of Research Outcomes in elder abuse' (2002) 4 *Journal of Adult Protection* 3.

[192] Commission for Social Care Inspection, *The state of social care in England 2005–06* (London, Commission for Social Care Inspection, 2006); quoted in *UK Study*, above n 177, at 11.

[193] Eg, through the *No Secrets* guidance, above n 167.

[194] See *UK Study*, above n 177, at 8–9.

[195] Commission for Social Care Inspection, above n 193; quoted in *UK Study*, above n 177, at 11.

[196] Eg, Cripps has argued that 'rights-based strategies', which seek to advise older people of their rights and support them in upholding them through an advocacy model, are more effective than other strategies in addressing elder abuse; D Cripps, *Rights Focussed Advocacy and Elder Abuse* (Adelaide, Aged Rights Advocacy Service, 2000), available online at <http://www.sa.agedrights.asn.au/pdf/Rights%20Focussed%20Advocacy%20and%20Elder%20Abuse.pdf>.

[197] See section (6) below.

[198] Crosby *et al*, above n 171, at 23.

[199] As the discussion in section (3) above has indicated, there are risks in viewing more information as necessarily reducing the risks of adverse outcomes or facilitating good decision-making for older owners.

[200] See ch 8, section (8).

[201] For an illustration of their application in a case involving two women aged 85 and 65, see *R v Gilbertson* [2009] EWCA Crim 1715.

sense that they do not provide direct redress for consumers, or affect the enforceability of the contract. These Regulations also clearly demonstrate a commitment to the information paradigm: for example, 'undue influence' is defined as

> exploiting a position of power in relation to the consumer so as to apply pressure, even without using or threatening to use physical force, in a way which significantly limits the consumer's ability to make an informed decision.[202]

The gaps which this leaves in the protections for potentially vulnerable consumers are discussed further in chapters eight and nine. Before that, the following sections consider some alternative perspectives on the sources of vulnerabilities which, it will be argued, provide a stronger platform on which to rest critical analyses of the current legal frameworks.

(5) Contextual or 'Situational' Vulnerabilities: Charting a Path Between Incapacity and Autonomy

One of the persistent difficulties with the use of 'vulnerability' as a basis for enhancing the legal protection afforded to older people is the way in which it has traditionally been presented as a 'victim' status, involving loss of capacity and/or autonomy. From this perspective, 'real differences' between people are portrayed as generating an 'all-or-nothing' choice: to be constructed as a 'vulnerable person', and so attract protection, you must present as unable to make choices; alternatively you are cast as an autonomous consumer who can make choices, but who must be self-reliant and self-responsible for the outcomes of those choices. This choice is not neutral but is heavily couched in socio-political subjectivities, and given effect within a framework of norms: it is a fundamental tenet of the liberal legal system that a person (an autonomous individual) has the right to make his or her own choices so long as he or she has 'capacity'. This starting point skews the normative structures that govern housing equity transactions towards autonomous individualism, notwithstanding the evidence that these are high-risk transactions, in which the complex decisions that many people (including, but not exclusively, older people) are required to make require a level of financial capability that—the evidence suggests—is not manifest in the general population.

In cultural understandings of 'risk', epitomised in the work of Mary Douglas,[203] the idea of being vulnerable or 'at risk' is increasingly associated with 'victimhood' and an awareness of the exposure that results from being part of a world system. Douglas argued that, particularly in the environmental context, the moral and political pressures that are brought to bear in relation to risk have largely been directed at large organisations rather than the individuals who experience the adverse effects when risk is realised. This

[202] Reg 7(3)(b).

[203] See, eg, M Douglas, *Purity and Danger: An Analysis of Concepts of Pollution and Taboo* (London, Routledge & Kegan Paul, 1966); M Douglas, *Risk Acceptability According to the Social Sciences* (New York, Russell Sage Foundation, 1985); M Douglas, *Risk and Blame: Essays in Cultural Theory* (London, Routledge, 1992).

socio-cultural approach emphasises the responsibilities (or attribution of blame) that flow from the creation of risk.[204] In this frame,

> [b]eing 'at risk' … entails being placed in the role of victim, threatened by risks imposed upon oneself by other agents, rather than being seen as bringing risk upon oneself through one's own actions … The political pressure that is brought to bear in relation to risk disputes is largely against exposing others to risk.[205]

While the discussion in this book has noted that the orientation of much of the political and policy framework for housing equity transactions has been strongly tilted towards individual self-responsibility, this is countered, to some extent, by the growing reach and rigour of regulatory responses to a range of specific housing equity products.[206]

The tensions that exist between the individual responsibility of consumers and the responsibilities of the large organisations which profit from financial transactions have been brought into sharp relief by the global financial crisis which began in 2007, which has triggered a widespread review of regulatory practices and provided fertile ground for arguments that lenders must bear more of the responsibility for risk, particularly in the context of mortgage lending, for example through more effective affordability checks, clearer product explanation and more stringent product regulation.[207] In this 'moment' of reflection, this book identifies a number of important questions to be resolved in respect of housing equity transactions. There are a number of strategies which might be adopted to address these questions. One set of strategies would work within the dominant framework to re-evaluate:

a) how to strike an acceptable balance between protecting (potentially) vulnerable older people and respecting their 'autonomy'; and
b) how to balance the responsibilities of older people as 'autonomous consumers' against the responsibilities of the financial providers who are actively seeking to encourage the growth of the equity release market.

A second set of strategies, which in the first instance might also lend support to these rebalancing efforts, would raise broader challenges to the normative framework, for example by critiquing the false dichotomy of autonomy/dependency,[208] or by challenging the institutional structures that create situational vulnerability for older people,[209] from compulsory retirement to the attenuation of the welfare State, the expectations of self-provision and the emergence of the dominant paradigm of housing as investment asset to spend, all of which have contributed to creating the risk environment.[210]

[204] Lupton, above n 10, at 45.
[205] *Ibid*, at 47–48.
[206] Discussed in ch 9.
[207] See, eg, S Nield, 'Responsible lending and borrowing: whereto low-cost home ownership?' (2010) 30 *Legal Studies* 610.
[208] See discussion in ch 5, section (3).
[209] See below, section (7).
[210] Minow, above n 123 at 229, discussed the importance of addressing the impact of difference without losing sight of the larger patterns of power (see, eg, the political construction of ageing discussed in ch 2): '[E]ven when pursued fully, relational ideas carry risks for vulnerable people if the underlying patterns of power remain unchanged. Defining procedures and policies that acknowledge people's mutual needs for one another may exacerbate the dependence of those who have historically been more dependent without remaking the underlying social arrangements that produced the pattern … Developing a method of attending to relationships without losing sight of larger patterns of power will be critical to those who want to redress the legal treatment of difference.'

The association between age and vulnerability, with concomitant risks of ageism, is problematised by the tendency for law to focus almost exclusively on (lack of) capacity as the cause of later life vulnerability. Yet neither incapacity nor lack of autonomy is the primary source of older owner vulnerability in financial decision-making. Rather, the research on financial capability, economic decision-making and financial abuse suggests that contextual factors, from living alone to financial inexperience, from poor health to loneliness and social isolation are much more significant. There is clearly not a perfect relationship between advancing age and vulnerability, with many older people highly capable, competent and often well-off. At the same time, there are also many marginal owner-occupiers, across the life-course, who experience social isolation, financial inexperience, poor health, loneliness and who have lower quality of life, all characteristics associated with vulnerability to financial abuse and a higher risk of entering into unfair contracts. The distinctive factors for older people are the changes to income patterns after retirement which create new types of financial pressure, and the policy context which pushes them towards equity release to fund a range of needs increases the likelihood that they may be required to make complex financial decisions under conditions of financial pressure, leaving (marginal) older owners with lower-value properties at particular vulnerability to disadvantageous equity release transactions.[211]

In seeking to establish an acceptable mode of protection for vulnerable older people, 'situational vulnerability' is strategically valuable inasmuch as it does not rely upon stereotyping older people in need of legal protection as weak or incapable but recognises that the circumstances of ageing in the UK in the early twenty-first century may expose people to specific risks in respect of financial provision. Situational vulnerability not only leaves the individuals at heightened risk of harms (the adverse impacts of which are discussed in section (6) below), but also contributes to market failure. When a sufficient sector of consumers is not focused on value for money, does not 'shop around', or enters transactions while experiencing difficult financial or emotional situations that impair the individuals' ability to assess the transaction against alternatives,[212] this undermines the competitiveness of the market, with adverse consequences across the sector. The prelude to FSA regulation of 'sale and rent back' transactions, discussed in chapter nine, exemplified this risk, and triggered the highest-level of FSA intervention in financial transactions to date. It is also important to recognise that situational vulnerability itself is not randomly distributed but is related to income patterns, differential opportunities to accumulate housing wealth, levels of cultural capital and financial capability, and the success with which people have planned for retirement across their life-course. These contexts are crucial in shaping the 'rational choices' that individuals make as autonomous consumers', so that

> [i]n a world of individualised risk, responsibility and choice, some individuals are likely to be worse off in old age not because they make less rational decisions than others in similar

[211] In addition to the question of whether a low-value loan justifies the transaction costs, there is a higher risk of mis-selling to less well-off people in lower-value properties; see R Terry and R Gibson, *Obstacles to Equity Release* (York, Joseph Rowntree Foundation, 2006).

[212] See Office of Fair Trading, *Sale and rent back—An OFT Market Study* (OFT 1018) (London, OFT, 2008), paras 5.18, 5.21, 5.26; available online at <http://www.oft.gov.uk/shared_oft/reports/consumer_protection/oft1018.pdf>.

situations, although this might sometimes be true, but because the context of their retirement planning is very different.[213]

Those who are worse off are also most vulnerable to the adverse impacts of 'bad' transactions. The arguments for rooting any legal response to 'difference' in the differential impact of adverse outcomes for older people are considered in section (6) below.

Another strategy that might follow from an acknowledgement of the situational vulnerability of (marginal) older owners concerns the balance of responsibility between older consumers and the providers with whom they contract. While contract law tends to be shaped by the 'underlying assumption that individuals are by and large best placed to look after their own affairs',[214] with legal intervention justified only in those 'marginal cases where the assumption does not work',[215] its assumption of 'individual self-responsibility' exists in tension with the outlook of consumer regulation, particularly when (as has recently been the case) renewed arguments are advanced for 'responsible lending', a concept that may be viewed as inherently 'person related and need oriented'. Howells argued that

> [i]t seeks to place into the contract paradigm a concern to respect the needs of the poor consumer and the position she finds herself in. It also requires of creditors an ethical standard … and requires them to acknowledge their responsibilities towards clients whom they dominate economically, socially and psychologically.[216]

These motivations may be found, to varying degrees, in the regulatory regimes that govern housing equity products and transactions.[217] Williams summarised the situational risks inherent to equity release transactions when she claimed that

> [t]oday's equity release industry has been built around a strong recognition that it is a product area where there has been past abuse and where, without appropriate safeguards, there are serious risks to both borrowers and lenders. These concerns flow out of a number of issues:
>
> — Potentially vulnerable customers
> — Potentially complex family dynamics around inheritance
> — Complex products not least in illustration and understanding terms and where house price dynamics can produce unexpected outcomes
> — Limited number of specialist brokers with full understanding of the market, risks and alternatives and relatively high commission payments
> — A regulatory regime that has taken some while to get fully into place
> — Taken together, a market place where risks for all parties are seen by some to be too high.
>
> Counterbalancing this, the simple reality is that households have a major asset, their home, which many need to access.[218]

[213] K Strauss, 'Re-engaging with rationality in economic geography: behavioural approaches and the importance of context in decision-making' (2008) 8 *Journal of Economic Geography* 137, 151.

[214] M Richardson, 'Contract law and distributive justice revisited' (1990) 10 *Legal Studies* 258. Richardson explained that 'the law cannot afford to protect people from themselves. It is simply too costly in terms of the effects on others …': *ibid*, at 262.

[215] *Ibid.*

[216] G Howells, 'Poor consumers in credit markets' in P Cartwright (ed), *Consumer Protection in Financial Services* (The Hague, Kluwer, 1999) 257.

[217] See ch 9.

[218] P Williams, *Please Release Me! A Review of the equity release market in the UK, its potential and consumer expectations* (London, Council of Mortgage Lenders, 2008) 25.

While this account clearly demonstrates the case for regulatory intervention, the context reflected also raises broader normative questions about vulnerability in financial transactions, with implications that go beyond the defined remit of a regulatory regime. These questions are considered in section (7) below.

(6) Vulnerability and Adverse Impact: The Measure of Harm

A further, distinctive aspect of situational vulnerability concerns the impact, or measure of harm, that a person would suffer if a transaction leads to adverse outcomes. The particular vulnerability of older people to the adverse impact of bad financial outcomes was captured in a 2007 study on financial abuse for Help the Aged, which claimed:

> Financial exploitation has a devastating effect on older people. Not only can a comfortable lifestyle disappear, but also older people do not have the time or opportunity to recover financially. In addition, such a profoundly disturbing experience can be a life-threatening event 'characterised by fear, lack of trust and the onset, often, of acute and chronic anxiety.'[219]

It has often been recognised that older adults, who are no longer income-generating, are more vulnerable both to the practical effects of financial set-backs, and to the physical, emotional and psychological consequences of having made a bad decision which has led to financial loss. The UK Government explicitly acknowledged this in its *National Strategy for Housing in an Ageing Society*, noting that, while homeownership has delivered substantial financial rewards for well-off older people, for marginal owners 'there is also the prospect of the consolidation of poverty. For those who have missed out on life's chances, for whatever reason, those chances become fewer in old age, and the opportunities to replenish meagre resources diminish.'[220]

In addition to the limited opportunities that older people are likely to have to earn more money after retirement to make up for losses (or, to use the terminology of insolvency, to make a 'fresh start'), psychologists have noted that while 'poor decisions early in life may be remedied by learning from mistakes and making better decisions in the future … as one ages, diminished physical capacity and less time can translate into reduced opportunities to recover from the "normal" ups and downs of everyday decision outcomes'.[221] This fundamentally undermines the liberal argument that agents of normal capacity will 'win more than they lose', and so can 'take the rough with the smooth'.[222] Rather, it indicates an additional source of vulnerability linked to limited opportunities to recoup financial losses. This is especially pertinent where it is housing equity, which may represent the

[219] Crosby *et al*, above n 171, at 5.

[220] Department of Communities and Local Government, *Lifetime Homes, Lifetime Neighbourhoods: A National Strategy for Housing in an Aging Society* (Wetherby, DCLG, 2008) 33.

[221] E Peters, M Finucaine, DG MacGregor and P Slovic, 'The Bearable Lightness of Aging: Judgment and Decision Processes in Older Adults' in PC Stern and LL Carstensen (eds), *The Aging Mind: Opportunities in Cognitive Research* (Washington, DC, National Academy Press, 2000) 144.

[222] T Honoré, *Responsibility and Fault* (Oxford, Hart Publishing, 1999) 9; see also discussion in J Steele, *Risks and Legal Theory* (Oxford, Hart Publishing, 2004) 94.

older person's main form of saving, accumulated over a lifetime of work,[223] that has been lost. The multiple functions of the family home—as housing, investment and inheritance—also mean that losses associated with this particular asset are likely to be particularly keenly felt. Lastly, the experience of financial victimisation also has specific impacts on older people, including psychological impacts (emotional distress, loss of self-confidence, depression, thoughts of suicide and self-harm),[224] social isolation, deteriorating physical health, loss of independence, financial loss, and adverse impacts on relationships with family and friends.[225] Whether the incident is resolved also has a bearing on the abused person's resilience,[226] as do their personal circumstances and characteristics, including their beliefs and norms, whether they were living alone, health and previous life experiences.[227]

As the discussion of 'dilemmas of difference' in section (3) has shown, a crucial question in analyses of differential vulnerabilities, and the strategies with which we seek to address them, is which differences matter, and in what contexts. This section considers whether, both for individual equality and justice, and for the collective interest, the particular impact of adverse housing equity transactions on older owners is a difference that matters. The idea that particular types of harms, or harms which particularly affect certain groups, justify specific legal intervention was explored in Robin West's work on 'gendered harms'.[228] West identified a phenomenon of differentiated harms experienced by women which have little or no counterpart in men's lives.[229] She argued that

> [w]omen suffer harms in this culture that are different from those suffered by men. And partly because they are different, they often do not 'trigger' legal relief in the way that harms felt by men alone or by men and women equally do. As a result women are doubly injured: first by the harm-causing event itself, and second by the peculiarity or non-existence of the law's response to those harms.[230]

While West's analysis of harm, and her argument for a relational jurisprudential concept of harm, is based on women's experiences and relies heavily on women's bodily and biological differences, her general approach—which critiques the focus of economic instrumentalism on the preference satisfaction of rational men and the avoidance of transaction costs, and its failure to recognise social harm—can be usefully extended to capture the 'invisibility' of the harms that older owners suffer in adverse housing equity transactions, and to posit the argument that greater legal intervention is required to avoid

[223] S Moskowitz, 'Saving Granny from the Wolf: Elder Abuse and Neglect—the Legal Framework' (1998) 31 *Connecticut Law Review* 77.

[224] A Canadian study also reported that 29% of those who had been financially abused reported 'wishing their life would end', compared with only 8% in the rest of the sample: E Podnieks, 'National survey on abuse of the elderly in Canada' (1992) 4 *Journal of Elder Abuse and Neglect* 5; cited in Crosby *et al*, above n 171, at 14.

[225] A Mowlam, R Tennant, J Dixon and C McCreadie, *UK Study of Abuse and Neglect of Older People: Qualitative Findings* (2007); available online at <http://www.dh.gov.uk/en/Publicationsandstatistics/Publications/PublicationsPolicyAndGuidance/DH_078333>.

[226] Or in Kirby's terminology, their 'assets', ie 'advantages, coping mechanisms, or resources that cushion us when we are facing misfortune, disaster and violence'; M Fineman, 'The Vulnerable Subject: Anchoring Equality in the Human Condition' (2008) 20 *Yale Journal of Law and Feminism* 1 at 13, citing P Kirby, *Vulnerability and Violence* (London, Pluto Press, 2006).

[227] *UK Study*, above n 177, ss 7.1, 7.2.

[228] For an introduction to West's concept of 'gendered harms', see R West, *Caring For Justice* (New York, NYU Press, 1999), ch 2.

[229] *Ibid*, at 100.

[230] *Ibid*, at 96, 99.

or rectify these harms. West argued that where difference renders women vulnerable to special types of harm, equality and justice demand that the legal culture recognises and responds to these differences.

From one perspective, while ageing obviously presents different issues and different examples of differential harms compared to gender, the disproportionately adverse impact of bad financial transactions on older people is derived, in part at least, from the impact of the 'ageing body' on opportunities to work and generate financial resources.[231] Another approach might highlight the fact that, in light of their longer life-spans, ageing issues *are* women's issues[232]; similarly, in light of constraints on income and capacity to accumulate wealth and assets throughout the life-course, which combine to make women more likely than men to be poor, issues relating to vulnerability in financial transactions in old age are also women's issues.[233] Longer life-spans mean that women are more likely than men to have ongoing health and personal care needs,[234] to face the medical, social, cultural, economic and legal issues associated with ageing, often without a partner, while their greater propensity to live alone places older women at higher risk of victimisation in financial transactions.[235] The harm of adverse housing equity transactions impacts disproportionately on older people because they are likely to have significantly less opportunity (in terms of remaining lifetime and ability to generate new financial assets after retirement) to recover from financial loss compared to their younger counterparts; and this harm is likely to be disproportionately (although not exclusively) experienced by women.

Indeed, West used the example of 'grossly unjust contractual bargains' to illustrate her discussion of the ways in which legal culture legitimates harms, so causing the harmed individual to lose consciousness of himself or herself as 'harmed'.[236] Noting that in a market-led political and economic framework, 'contract law enforces wise and unwise contracts against "losers" and winners equally',[237] she argued that

> [t]he larger culture justifies this outcome with a sort of harsh, Emersonian, ethic of self-reliance: we have to learn to take our lumps, it's the price of freedom. *Legal* culture, however, goes one step further: the harm is not simply justified, it is *legitimated*, which means in effect that the harm disappears.[238]

The role of legal culture in legitimating, and so obscuring, the harms that result from adverse housing equity transactions also has particular resonance in light of the documented reluctance of older people to pursue legal remedies when they suffer losses in

[231] See above, section (3).

[232] Women constitute the majority of older people, nearly twice as many of the over-80 cohort, and four to five times as many centenarians; see ch 1, section (2)(a).

[233] See ch 1, section (3)(b).

[234] While women live longer than men, older women tend to have poorer health, greater levels of disability and are at greater risk of institutional care; S Arber and J Ginn, 'Gender Dimensions of the Age Shift' in ML Johnson (ed), *The Cambridge Handbook of Age and Ageing* (Cambridge, Cambridge University Press, 2005); E Schroeder-Butterfill and R Marianti, 'A framework for understanding old age vulnerabilities' (2006) 26 *Ageing and Society* 9.

[235] Older women are almost 250 per cent more likely to live alone, compared to older men; see ch 1, section (2)(a).

[236] West, above n 229, at 151 *et seq.*

[237] *Ibid*, at 151.

[238] *Ibid*, at 151–52.

financial transactions.[239] West demonstrates how this view is perpetuated by a legal culture shaped according to the rational precepts of law-and-economics, which have imported the political ideology of 'market individualism' into contract and property law,[240] and which demand:

> If the contract was 'free' then all parties *must*, by definition, have gained. There is, in effect, no loser in a market economy, where one invariably consents to only what one wants and one only wants what will benefit one. No one's actually been harmed.[241]

Indeed, to the extent that the vulnerable parties themselves subscribe to the dominant norms, West argues that they will 'eventually view themselves as not only not entitled to legal relief, but as not harmed. Their acquiescence in the larger system is thereby secured.'[242] From this perspective, the risk of fostering ageism where older people are identified as 'different', in the negative sense of being unable to live up to the 'norms' attendant on being a 'market actor' (and which the older person has internalised as required from a 'market actor', so that failure to live up to the ideal is experienced as a failure in personal identity), is clear. Yet when the experience of specific harms 'fades from view'—because they result from differences that are not 'discriminatory' within a model of formal equality law, so that law and legal culture do not recognise the harm—West cautioned that 'Those harms become, in effect, not harms at all, but rather, the result of well-functioning private and cultural markets, free of pernicious and inefficient state intervention. They become something to celebrate rather than worry over.'[243]

The particularly harmful impact of adverse financial transactions for older people has been recognised in the laws of some US states, which have provided particular protections for older people in the event of bankruptcy. Bankruptcy laws provide a classic example of the liberal legal idea that people can take the rough with the smooth, weather financial failures and then start again with a clean sheet—a 'fresh start'—the aim of which is to allow debtors to discharge their debt through bankruptcy and continue their lives free of debt.[244] The inaptness of the philosophy of bankruptcy, which aims to give 'the honest but unfortunate debtor ... a new opportunity in life and a clear field for future effort, unhampered by the pressure and discouragement of pre-existing debt',[245] is discussed in chapter seven. The specific harms which result when older people experience adverse financial transactions are ignored by a model which relies on 'future earnings as the key to

[239] Research into financial abuse of older people has reported that it can be difficult to detect because victims are reluctant to report it; because they are embarrassed to admit that they have made a poor decision; because of stigma and loss of personal dignity; because they do not know where to turn for help, or do not have the mobility to access help; because they consider the situation to be their own fault or part of the normal risk of transacting; or because they do not realise that an actionable wrong has taken place. See, eg, JI Kosberh and D Nahmiash, 'Characteristics of Victims and Perpetrators and Milieus of Abuse and Neglect' in LA Baumhover and SC Beal (eds), *Abuse, Neglect and Exploitation of Older Persons: Strategies for Assessment and Intervention* (London, Jessica Kingsley, 1996); CL Dessin, 'Financial Abuse of the Elderly' (1999) 36 *Idaho Law Review* 203, 211–13.

[240] See ch 4 for discussion of the dominance of these values in the construction of private law's subjects.

[241] West, above n 229, at 152.

[242] *Ibid.*

[243] *Ibid*, at 153.

[244] See, eg, Insolvency Service, *Bankruptcy: A Fresh Start* (Consultation Document), March 2000, available online at <http://www.insolvency.gov.uk/insolvencyprofessionandlegislation/con_doc_register/con_doc_archive/consultation/freshstart/foreword.htm>; I Livshits, J MacGee and M Tertilt, 'Consumer Bankruptcy: A Fresh Start' (2007) 97 *The American Economic Review* 402.

[245] *Local Loan Co v Hunt* 292 US 234 at 244 (1934).

rehabilitation'[246]: bankruptcy is clearly a law of general application that affects older people differently from younger adults. This difference is recognised when specific provision is made for older owners in bankruptcy proceedings, by allowing them to retain additional 'exempt' property (for example, 'homesteads') with which to make their 'fresh start', compared to younger bankrupts.[247]

A claim to difference that is rooted in the differential impact of adverse financial transactions after retirement avoids ageist stereotypes based on individual physiological traits or 'inherent' characteristics: it is a form of situational vulnerability, inasmuch as the difference does not reside in the person but in the circumstances in which he or she is placed; it is based not on an 'essentialised' image of the older person but on the broader political, social and demographic contexts which shape participation in housing equity transactions. Indeed, an emphasis on the impact of adverse transactions has the potential to be as universal as ageing itself,[248] while also exhibiting 'across-category sameness' with other (younger) marginal owners who are likely to face particular difficulties in recovering from financial setbacks. Similarly, while the 'non-financial' impacts for older owners, resulting from the experience of adverse transactions, have been identified in targeted studies, the Financial Services Consumer Panel's definition of 'consumer detriment' recognised that as a general group, consumers may experience non-financial detriment from adverse financial transactions, including 'social exclusion, confusion, stress and anxiety and associated health consequences, irrespective of whether a financial loss has occurred'.[249] Focusing on impact or harm raises new critical possibilities for an understanding of vulnerability that challenges dominant norms of legal subjectivity, and through which ageing may (in light of the specific social, political, demographic and policy drivers towards housing equity transactions) be viewed as a paradigmatic illustration of more universal sources of vulnerability affecting (particularly marginal) owners across the life-course; of the inappropriateness of the idealised model of the autonomous legal subject in the context of complex financial transactions; and of the universal vulnerability of the human condition.[250]

(7) Re-thinking Responsibility for 'Vulnerable Legal Subjects'

The socio-economic and political environments of ageing in the early twenty-first century mean that, increasingly, many older owners will have no choice but to engage with some form of risk in relation to the use (or not) of home equity after retirement. While the risks

[246] JAE Pottow, 'The Rise of Elder Bankruptcy Filings and Failure of US Bankruptcy Law', *University of Michigan Law School Empirical Legal Studies Center Working Paper 17* (2010), at 22; available online at <http://papers.ssrn.com/sol3/papers.cfm?abstract_id=1669298>.

[247] Examples include California, Colorado, Hawaii, Maine and New York; see ch 7, section (3)(b).

[248] Minow recognised that ageing is universal in the sense that it will happen to us all, making it easier to see, than in many cases of 'difference', that 'we could be like them'; Minow, above n 123, at 385.

[249] See J Wells and M Gostelow, *Financial Services and Later Life: A Scoping Project for the Financial Services Consumer Panel*, para 1.3; available online at <http://www.fs-cp.org.uk/publications/pdf/fscp_laterlife0609.pdf>.

[250] See below, section (7).

associated with spending housing wealth, and the outcomes of housing equity transactions, can be both positive and negative—with positive aspects relating to lifestyle, better quality of life and avoiding poverty in old age—this book argues that the necessity for many older homeowners to participate in the credit market in one way or another, and to negotiate the risks associated with market participation, presents new questions for legal analysis. The expectations that homeowners will accumulate housing wealth during their lives to spend on welfare after retirement, and that they will demonstrate individual responsibility as 'active subjects' under neoliberal governmentality, provide important context for analysis of the ideas of responsibility and vulnerability as they are applied to older people in the current political and policy landscape.

While the dominant themes in political and policy discourse concerning housing equity transactions reflect a particular construction of the older owner as a reflexive risk subject, 'free' to negotiate choices as an autonomous consumer, the extent to which the general population—and, by extension, older owners—are likely to be able effectively to plan for (and finance) their futures is related to the social and cultural resources at their disposal, and their financial and legal capabilities when it comes to understanding complex products.[251] The gap between the idealised neoliberal consumer and the reality of high-risk transactions which leave marginal older owners (and other marginal owners) vulnerable to adverse outcomes, highlights the potential for injustices and inequalities within the dominant (neo)liberal normative domain of housing equity transactions. The relationship between socio-economic inequality (marginality) across the life-course and heightened exposure to risk in housing equity transactions has also been clearly established. Furthermore, as West's concept of harm reveals, the dominance of a particular normative framework can inhibit law's ability to recognise and remedy these adverse outcomes; indeed, where 'victims' themselves internalise the norms, they may not recognise, or pursue legal recompense for, harms they have suffered.

Representing this type of inequality within the dominant liberal norms that have shaped English 'private' law is not straightforward. Liberal legal theory emphasises the values of autonomy and choice, with the positive 'entrepreneurial' aspects of risk-taking in relation to house purchase tending to characterise legal perspectives on these transactions, which are anchored in the typically non-market interventionist approaches of property law and contract as 'private' law domains. Yet this model of consumers in domestic property transactions as 'responsible risk-takers' has been challenged by the recent global financial crisis, which has demonstrated how risks in the financial system can potentially impact on *all* consumers, calling into question the 'overly optimistic view of self-regulating markets'.[252] Indeed, even before the 'credit crunch', the relationship between risk, responsibility and regulation had emerged as an important theme in UK policy,[253] with the growing reach of the FSA demonstrating the use of (albeit 'light-touch') regulatory approaches as a response to the risks associated with financial transactions. Since the financial crisis, the UK Government has made an explicit commitment to a more

[251] See ch 1, section (3)(b); ch 3, section (2)(a).

[252] RP Malloy, 'Mortgage Market Reform and the Fallacy of Self-Correcting Markets' (2009) 30 *Pace Law Review* 79.

[253] Better Regulation Commission, *Risk, Responsibility and Regulation: Whose Risk is it Anyway?* (London, Cabinet Office, 2006).

responsible regulatory regime.[254] This section argues that this process, and other responses to vulnerability in housing equity transactions, is usefully informed by reconceiving the norm of (older) owners as (self-responsible) consumers towards a more realistic concept of older (and potentially other marginal) owners as 'vulnerable legal subjects'.

The (co-)existence of competing characterisations of the consumer as a legal subject, with implications for the nature and extent of legal interventions in 'private', market transactions, has been recognised in a range of legal contexts. For example, Dyal-Chand contrasted US mortgage law's paradigm of the 'ignorant borrower' with credit card law's 'enlightened borrower'.[255] While mortgage law recognised 'situational vulnerability',[256] leading to specific and meaningful substantive legal protections, the 'enlightened borrower' (read 'autonomous consumer') of credit card law attracted only the procedural protections of the 'information paradigm',[257] despite being drawn from the same constituency of borrowers. In a similar vein, Hunter and Nixon's analysis of judicial attitudes towards owners ('autonomous consumers') and tenants ('vulnerable subjects') facing actions for financial default in English courts revealed the significance of these characterisations for judicial interpretations of statutory provisions,[258] resulting in a higher risk of eviction for the owner relative to tenants.[259]

Yet while the paradigm of autonomous consumer clearly leaves the owner exposed to heightened risks, the basis of any claim to legal protection poses a dilemma: how can a claim to legal protection, recognising the realities of situational vulnerability, avoid falling into the trap of perpetuating ageist stereotypes? This section proposes that the resolution to this dilemma may be found in feminist critiques of the core content of the 'autonomous consumer' model (with its roots in the contested concepts of 'rational choice', 'consent' and 'autonomy'); in the realisation that the 'differential' vulnerability experienced by marginal older owners in fact reflects a 'sameness' with other marginal or 'vulnerable' populations; and in the universal and inevitable nature of ageing. While the dominant normative framework presents autonomy/capacity (within the liberal legal meaning of the term)[260] and dependency/vulnerability as opposite poles, challenges to the

[254] See 'Statement to the House of Commons by the Financial Secretary to the Treasury, Mark Hoban MP, on Reforming the Institutional Framework for Financial Regulation', 17 June 2010, online at <http://www.hm-treasury.gov.uk/statement_fst_170610.htm>; HM Treasury, *A new approach to financial regulation: judgment, focus and stability*, Cm 7874 (London, TSO, 2010), online at <http://www.hm-treasury.gov.uk/d/consult_financial_regulation_condoc.pdf>.

[255] R Dyal-Chand, 'From Status to Contract: Evolving Paradigms for Regulating Consumer Credit' (2005) 73 *Tennessee Law Review* 303.

[256] Dyal-Chand explained that the use of 'ignorant' in US mortgage law discourse was not intended to be pejorative but to reflect the relative lack of sophistication of mortgage borrowers compared to lenders, their relative inexperience in this type of transaction, their 'choicelessness' in many circumstances and the likelihood that they may be overreached.

[257] R Dyal-Chand, above n 255, at 315: 'The regulatory focus was on the adequacy of the disclosure made to the borrower about the terms of the lending contract, rather than on directly protecting the borrower from loss of collateral.'

[258] C Hunter and J Nixon, 'The Discourse of Housing Debt: The Social Construction of Landlords, Lenders, Borrowers and Tenants' (1999) 16 *Housing, Theory and Society* 165. For discussion of the implications of social constructions of older owners as autonomous consumers, see ch 2, section (3).

[259] For a detailed analysis of the significance of the identity of both borrower/tenant and lender/landlord in eviction cases, see S Bright, 'Dispossession for Arrears: The Weight of Home in English law' in L Fox O'Mahony and JA Sweeney (eds), *The Idea of Home in Law: Displacement and Dispossession* (Farnham, Ashgate, 2011).

[260] See ch 5, section (3).

assumptions that underpin the conventional 'autonomous consumer' model provide a way out of this dilemma.

Feminist scholarship has long recognised the conflict between autonomy and welfare/protection in the context of contracts and the market,[261] and the problematic nature of the economic conception of 'rational choice'. Hadfield captured the 'dilemma' of choice in her claim that while feminists seek to overcome the historical subjugation that has deprived women of autonomy and choice, they remain anxious 'that autonomy and choice through contract and the market are traps that will only further ensnare women in disadvantage and degradation'.[262] The legal, economic and political subject of 'rational economic man',[263] the norms of liberal market individualism[264] and the conception of the 'autonomous individual' that has been adopted by liberal institutions,[265] have all been widely criticised in feminist analyses on the basis that they are based on unrealistic portrayals of human subjectivity that reinforce privilege and perpetuate inequality. 'Rational choice', while widely regarded as the legitimate basis for liberal approaches in classical and neoclassical contract law,[266] is heavily contested as an epistemological concept[267] and as an explanation for human motivation.[268] Claims that individuals are rational (that they take purposive action, have consistent preferences and are utility maximising), self-interested and individualist are challenged by behavioural evidence of 'imperfect rationality'.[269] Feminist and critical contract scholarship has often demonstrated that choices are not necessarily shaped by the drive to maximise well-being or autonomy.[270] The argument

[261] See, eg, GK Hadfield, 'The Dilemma of Choice: A Feminist Perspective on *The Limits of Freedom of Contract*' (1995) 33 *Osgoode Hall Law Journal* 337.

[262] *Ibid*, at 338.

[263] See, eg, GJ Hewitson, *Feminist Economics: Interrogating the Masculinity of Rational Economic Man* (Cheltenham, Edward Elgar, 1999); MA Ferber and JA Nelson (eds), *Beyond Economic Man: Feminist Theory and Economics* (Chicago, Ill, University of Chicago Press, 1993); MA Fineman and T Dougherty (eds), *Feminism Confronts Homo Economicus* (Ithaca, NY, Cornell University Press, 2005).

[264] Hadfield, above n 262, at 340, described a 'deeply felt concern that market relations, contract relations, reflect an impoverished and destructive view of human relationships. The market and contracts, it is thought, squeeze out from human interaction qualities of love, care, responsibility, duty, fellowship, and community.'

[265] For a discussion of the competing meanings of 'autonomy' in liberal (private law) legal theory, in psychology and in feminist 'relational' theory, see discussion in ch 5, section (3).

[266] See, eg, R Dworkin, *Taking Rights Seriously* (Cambridge, MA, Harvard University Press, 1977); R Posner, *The Economics of Justice* (Cambridge, MA, Harvard University Press, 1981), chs 3 and 4; R Bigwood, 'Conscience and the Liberal Conception of Contract: Observing Basic Distinctions: Part 1' (2000) 16 *Journal of Contract Law* 1; and discussions in ch 4 sections (3), (4)(a) and (5). For a critique of this approach, see, eg, GK Hadfield, 'An Expressive Theory of Contract: From Feminist Dilemmas to a Reconceptualisation of Rational Choice in Contract Law' (1998) 146 *University of Pennsylvania Law Review* 1235.

[267] See, eg, PK MacDonald, 'Useful Fiction or Miracle Maker: The Competing Epistemological Foundations of Rational Choice Theory' (2003) 97 *American Political Science Review* 551; J Friedman (ed), *The Rational Choice Controversy: Economic Models of Politics Reconsidered* (New Haven, CT, Yale University Press, 1996).

[268] BA Pescosolido, 'Beyond Rational Choice: The Social Dynamics of How People Seek Help' (1992) 97 *American Journal of Sociology* 1096; AK Sen, 'Rational Fools: A Critique of the Behavioural Foundations of Economic Theory' in H Harris (ed), *Scientific Models and Man* (Oxford, Oxford University Press, 1979); MR Somers, '"We're No Angels": Realism, Rational Choice and Relationality in Social Science' (1998) 104 *American Journal of Sociology* 722; R West, 'Authority, Autonomy, and Choice: The Role of Consent in the Moral and Political Visions of Franz Kafka and Richard Posner' (1985) 99 *Harvard Law Review* 384.

[269] Behavioural economics has established that 'Individuals make mistakes. They suffer from imperfect information and imperfect rationality, and consequently might fail to make choices that maximise their preferences. Few people question the truth of this proposition': O Bar-Gill, 'The Behavioural Economics of Consumer Contracts', in RA Epstein and O Bar-Gill, *Consumer Contracts: Behavioural Economics vs Neoclassical Economics* (NYU School of Law, NYU Law and Economics Working Papers, Paper 91, 2007) at 1; available online at <http://lsr.nellco.org/nyu/lewp/papers/91>.

[270] West, above n 269.

that 'choice' can be regarded as synonymous with 'autonomy' is challenged by evidence that even 'free' choices can sometimes be harmful to welfare, and so *reduce* the legal subject's autonomy.[271]

One of the risks for older owners entering housing equity transactions is that the exercise of autonomy might reduce their (future) welfare, for example where the product is inappropriate or poor value for money, or where the option taken is not suitable to the needs, objectives and circumstances of the older person. As such, the relationship between autonomy and welfare in this context is not fixed but fluid. This perspective has significant implications for arguments concerning legal intervention, since it posits that 'endorsing autonomy does not imply choosing the market over regulation or ignoring actual welfare in favour of deference to private ordering'.[272] Once autonomy is de-coupled from choice and welfare, the relevant question is not how law can promote autonomy (in the belief that welfare will automatically follow), but how 'various institutions might be coordinated so as to promote both autonomy and welfare',[273] taking account of the risks to the various parties to the contract and the relative impact of harms (including non-financial harms) on each party.[274] Through this process, law may be seen to have a role in 'structur[ing] the relations that establish the preconditions for truly autonomous choice'[275]; that is, for choices that genuinely enhance well-being *and* promote autonomy.

The development of a legal strategy that pursues both well-being and (the broader meaning of) autonomy is usefully supported by feminist critiques of the conventional conception of rational choice, which emphasise the tensions between the narrow, abstract, economic and legal concept of autonomy and the situational realities of inequality.[276] To the extent that the enforcement of contracts is justified by principles of voluntariness and informed choice, arguments for non-enforcement must 'demonstrate a defect in the circumstances of choice: a failure of voluntariness or an absence of adequate information'.[277] If enforceability turns on establishing voluntary and informed choice, the inquiry undertaken by a court when petitioned to intervene is shaped around fact of choice, not the wisdom or consequences of the choice that was in fact made, or the question of whether the choice in fact enhanced or reduced the claimant's autonomy or welfare.[278] Hadfield argued that a better juristic understanding of 'rational autonomous choice' would require reasons beyond the fact of contemporaneous choice when the contract was made to justify the enforcement of obligations,[279] to recognise the complexities of what it means to chose and the evolving nature of the parties' rational choice(s).

271 Hadfield, above n 262, at 341, considering M Trebilcock, *The Limits of Freedom of Contract* (Cambridge, MA, Harvard University Press, 1993). For discussion of the differences between 'choice' and 'autonomy', see ch 5, section (3).

272 Hadfield, above n 262, at 348. Hadfield argued (*ibid*) that 'In many cases, when close attention is paid to the actual relationship between a particular goal such as autonomy or welfare and a particular instrument, such as contract law, it is possible to use a multi-pronged approach so as to vindicate multiple values.'

273 *Ibid.*

274 *Ibid*, at 349.

275 *Ibid.*

276 Hadfield, above n 267.

277 *Ibid*, at 1247, 1248.

278 *Ibid*, at 1248.

279 For example, reliance or a policy interest in the protection of the convention of contractual choice: *ibid*, at 1251. The 'expressive' approach advocated by Hadfield would distinguish between different types of contract depending on whether the contract was framed as a deliberate trade in future risk allocation (in which case contract choice could be collapsed with contemporaneous choice); in other cases, choice would (only) be the starting point for the enforcement of contractual obligations.

The conventional commitment to contractual enforcement based on consent, resting on the belief that respecting the rational choices of 'autonomous consumers' is morally justified because it fosters autonomy and increases individual and societal well-being, has also been criticised on the basis that it 'rests on a severely inadequate picture of human nature and human motivation'.[280] In her critique of the moral value which Posner attached to consent, West argued that the rational, autonomous consumer paradigm 'defines the problem of victimisation out of existence'[281] by allowing the experiences of 'wealth-maximising winners' to shape the normative context in which we judge the enforceability of transactions:

> Posner teaches us that when the risk of a loss is voluntarily assumed, the ultimate suffering of that loss is consensual and we consequently need concern ourselves no more with losers in the market than with those in a lottery.[282]

West argued that legal theories based on rational choice minimise, trivialise and ignore the differences between 'winners' and 'losers', describing the theoretical step of 'dismiss[ing] losers on the basis of a facile judgment that they consented to play the game'[283] as 'morally indefensible'. Rather than viewing the 'failure' of these losers as a matter of individual responsibility, West argued that, in circumstances where the assumption of risk is not rational, justified, morally appealing and so worthy of respect, the community has a moral responsibility to intervene.

This community responsibility is underlined, in the case of housing equity transactions, by the extent to which the decision to spend housing equity is embedded in social contexts and political and policy agendas.[284] While the idea of rational, self-interested, utility maximising, autonomous individuals is compelling,[285] the reality of decision-making is that it does not involve isolated choices but is embedded in social contexts; decision-making subjects are not 'isolated and ever-consciously rational' but social and pragmatic. [286] This portrait of the legal subject as part of an ongoing relational dynamic, who operates within a social network rather than as an atomised individual,[287] echoes a fundamental tenet of relational feminism[288] and enables us to recognise the reality of social context without diminishing the actor's agency.

[280] West, above n 269, at 391, critiquing Posner's theory of rational choice, see RA Posner, *The Economics of Justice* (Cambridge, MA, Harvard University Press, 1983); see also RA Posner, 'Utilitarianism, Economics and Legal Theory' (1979) 8 *Journal of Legal Studies* 103; RA Posner, 'The Value of Wealth: A Comment on Dworkin and Kronman' (1980) 9 *Journal of Legal Studies* 243; RA Posner, 'The Ethical and Political Basis of the Efficiency Norm in Common Law Adjudication' (1980) 8 *Hofstra Law Review* 487.

[281] West, above n 269, at391.

[282] *Ibid*, at 409.

[283] *Ibid*, at 410.

[284] See chs 1, 2 and 3.

[285] '[I]t matches the world view of most people living in advanced capitalist democracies, which includes the ultimate importance of agency (whatever structural constraints may exist); the conjoint nature of modern society, autonomy, and rational thinking; and the everyday notions of the inescapable need to balance pros and cons': Pescosolido, above n 269, at 1100. The impacts of social structure and context in decision-making theory are recognised in the 'social organisation strategy', which identifies social interaction as the primary building block for decision-making.

[286] *Ibid*, at 1103.

[287] *Ibid*.

[288] See discussion of 'autonomy' in ch 5, section (3).

The proposition that 'thinking' and decision-making are not isolated but contextual and situated underpins arguments for contextual approaches to law and legal theory.[289] Minow and Spelman argued that, in addition to their case-by-case relevance, contextual analyses also signal patterns of difference from the dominant norm, and thus 'expose how apparently neutral and universal rules in effect burden or exclude anyone who does not share the characteristics of privileged, white, Christian, able-bodied, heterosexual, adult men for whom those rules were actually written'.[290] They argued that since all rules must be shaped against some context,[291] the 'default' choice of context 'implies a preference for one set of analytic categories rather than another'[292]; for example, for 'autonomous individualism' over group-based claims for legal protection or social justice.

Considering legal subjects in context is also crucial when reasoning about the morality of legal intervention (or non-intervention) in respect of risks or harms. Gilligan argued that

> [o]nly when substance is given to the skeletal lives of hypothetical people is it possible to consider the social injustice that their moral problems may reflect and to imagine the individual suffering their occurrence may signify or their resolution engender.[293]

In the context of housing equity transactions, a contextual approach would seek to capture the specific vulnerabilities of the older owner (including situational vulnerabilities such as the impact of adverse transactions) within the legal frameworks that regulate the creation, content and enforcement of obligations, so that law can seek to 'capture the complexities of [the] moral and political situations and thereby address [the] moral and political dilemmas more responsively and responsibly'.[294] A crucial question, of course, is which contexts should matter. Minow and Spelman argued that

> in many contemporary political and legal discussions, the demand to look at the context often means a demand to look at the structures of power, gender, race, or class relationships, or the effects of age and physical vulnerability on people's abilities to protect themselves ... against the backdrop—the context by default—created by Western liberal legal and political traditions that emphasise as ideals individual freedom, equality, universal reason, and abstract principles.[295]

One aim of this analytical move is to challenge false claims of universality, and so expose the role of power in controlling definitions of difference to work in favour of the dominant group, thereby providing a basis for critical scrutiny of difference based on gender, race, class or age.[296]

In attempting to re-think the question of who bears responsibility for losses resulting from adverse transactions, and when the 'mistakes' that individuals make merit legal intervention,[297] one approach is to focus on those cases which are likely to result in a

[289] 'Thinking is something particular people do as they try to resolve specific problems in specific situations.': M Minow and EV Spelman, 'In Context' (1989) 63 *Southern California Law Rev* 1597, 1600.

[290] *Ibid*, at 1601.

[291] *Ibid*, at 1605.

[292] *Ibid.*

[293] C Gilligan, *In a Different Voice* (Cambridge, MA, Harvard University Press, 1982) 100.

[294] Minow and Spelman, above n 290, at 1615.

[295] *Ibid*, at 1651.

[296] *Ibid.*

[297] Bar-Gill, above n 270.

substantial welfare loss. For example, where the neoclassical approach to law and economics relies on the assumptions that consumers who 'lose' in an individual transaction will learn from their mistakes and from those made by others, a contextual analysis recognises that this is not universally true. An older owner who experiences an adverse housing equity transaction is likely to have little time and no opportunity to recover their losses and re-engage in the market to repeat the exercise, thus limiting his or her 'intrapersonal learning',[298] while 'interpersonal learning' amongst marginal and older consumers is inhibited by a range of factors including social isolation, being less likely to complain and lack of access to a wider community with financial capability/experience in the area of specialised housing equity products.[299] Bar-Gill argued that consumer learning is further inhibited by the different uses to which individuals may put the same product,[300] also underlining the need for contextual understandings of the needs, objectives and circumstances of the individual consumer in the particular transaction.[301]

Contextual analyses do not rely on demonstrating that the individual who has suffered a loss lacked capacity to consent, was 'weak' or incapable, but locate the grounds for enforcing the contract, or not, in a real measure of the transaction, including situational vulnerabilities (marginality or inequality) affecting consent, and the welfare consequences of enforcement (the impact) for that person. The inadequacy of 'consent' as a basis for individual responsibility, and the moral argument for a shift away from individual (self-) responsibility towards a more community-oriented framework when dealing with serious social needs, have also been central themes of Fineman's work on autonomy,[302] dependency[303] and, most recently, vulnerability. Fineman is critical of the rhetorical use of privatisation ('self-responsibility') as a solution to complicated social problems which reflect persistent inequality and poverty.[304] As the discussion in previous chapters has shown, the political and policy moves that have transferred responsibility for financial provision in old age onto private individuals, through self-provision and specifically through housing equity release, provide a paradigmatic example of the ways in which the State has asserted 'that the private market can better address historically public issues than can the public government'.[305] Fineman criticised the weight attached to 'consent' as the

[298] Bar-Gill argued that how quickly consumers learn depends on the individual's 'intrapersonal' context, including how frequently the product is used and how frequently the risk materialises; and on the 'interpersonal' context: *ibid*, at 5–6.

[299] For discussions of the limitations of 'interpersonal' learning, see sections (3), (4) and (5) above.

[300] Bar-Gill, above n 270, at 2. Bar-Gill reinforced his claims concerning the significance of consumer mistakes by highlighting sellers' strategic responses to these mistakes, evidenced in the continual emergence of new types of product. In the case of housing equity transactions, one of the limitations of the regulatory approach flows from the emergence of new types of product, targeted at older owners and structured to fall outside the current parameters of the FSA's regulatory umbrella; see ch 9, section (4)(a).

[301] See ch 9 for discussion of circumstances in which tailoring advice to the needs, objectives and circumstances of the owner has formed part of the provider's responsibility in certain housing equity transactions. Bar-Gill also argued for disclosure mandates that address not only objective product attributes, but also the consumer's individual use of the product: *ibid*, at 4–5.

[302] Fineman, like many other feminist scholars, has critiqued the idealisation of the values of independence, autonomy and self-sufficiency for the liberal subject as 'empirically unrealistic and unrealizable': Fineman, above n 227 at 11.

[303] See, eg, MA Fineman, 'Contract and Care' (2000) 76 *Chicago-Kent Law Review* 1403; MA Fineman, *The Autonomy Myth: A Theory of Dependency* (New York, The New Press, 2004).

[304] Fineman (2000), above n 304, at 1405.

[305] *Ibid*, at 1405.

justification for self-responsibility within this 'private' market, and as 'the basis for withholding public (or other) aid from someone in a needy position'[306]:

> The argument may be phrased as getting what one 'asked for' or as the justice of having to 'lie in the bed' that one has 'made'. The idea is the individual circumstances are the result of individual choices, freely made, and, therefore, that consequences, even if negative, are justified.[307]

Within this rhetoric, the State and the market avoid responsibility for inequalities by holding individuals to be 'self-responsible' not only for their specific contractual choices, but also for the 'life circumstances' in which they find themselves, thus ignoring the significant role of contextual or situational vulnerabilities, as well as the policies that constrain individual choices by 'funnel[ling] decisions into prescribed channels and … operat[ing] in a practical and symbolic manner to limit, or practically eliminate, options'. [308]

Fineman argued that the idealised paradigm of the autonomous self-responsible consumer is given effect as a dominant norm by the 'public' support of private contracting through the legal system.[309] Yet to the extent that housing equity transactions have come to serve an essential public function in society—enabling self-provision for financial well-being after retirement in an economic and policy landscape where this is increasingly necessary—the ways in which they are supported by legal institutions is a crucial pillar in the administration of justice, particularly for those older owners who are already vulnerable due to existing inequalities. If the institutions of the State (including law) are to play a role in supporting the policy drive towards equity release after retirement, they must be responsive to the consequences of these transactions,[310] including thinking seriously about the responsibilities of the market and the State for the risks inherent in such transactions.

Fineman's most recent work on 'vulnerable legal subjects'[311] provides a valuable critical framework for conceptualising this shift from older owner as autonomous consumer to consumers as vulnerable legal subjects. Traditional legal analyses (utilising the reasoning paths offered by property law and contract) have long been trapped in the autonomy/capacity dilemma, where the only alternative to being an autonomous consumer taking responsibility for one's own choices, was incapacity.[312] Fineman's 'vulnerable legal subject' offers the possibility of shifting from the restrictive domain of autonomy/capacity, to a new paradigm of vulnerability/responsibility. It challenges the rhetoric of non-intervention, the 'idealisation' of contract and the 'reification of individual choice'; and accepts the potential for the broader socio-economic and political contexts in which parties (eg older owners) make decisions (to enter housing equity transactions) to perpetuate inequality. Fineman's strategy is rooted in the human experiences of 'real-life subjects'[313] and seeks to move beyond the 'sameness of treatment' response to inequality to emphasise the particular vulnerabilities of older owners as a category of consumer, and so to devise appropriate responses to 'past circumstances and future obligations'—that is,

[306] *Ibid*, at 1419.
[307] *Ibid*.
[308] *Ibid*, at 1419.
[309] *Ibid*, at 1424.
[310] This responsibility is recognised in the context of FSA regulation of some housing equity transactions; see ch 9.
[311] As articulated in Fineman, above n 303.
[312] This dilemma is particularly clear in the context of 'undue influence' doctrine; see ch 10.
[313] Fineman, above n 303, at 10.

to the circumstances, needs and objectives which drive these transactions and which can render older owners vulnerable in this context, as well as to the impact of the transaction on their future well-being.

Lastly, by negotiating the 'theoretical and empirical pitfalls' that arise from the heterogeneity of identity groups—including the relative privilege enjoyed by some members of the group—Fineman's theory seeks to offer a 'universal' strategy to address vulnerabilities. Applying the idea of universality to the context of housing equity, it is possible to recognise that while sources of vulnerability are to some extent specific to older owners, they are not experienced by *all* older owners but tend to be concentrated amongst marginal owners; and that younger, marginal owners are also exposed to similar vulnerabilities due to their inequalities. Since the vulnerability approach emphasises the *possibility* of harm, its approach is universal in the sense that 'Constant and variable throughout life, individual vulnerability encompasses not only damage that has been done in the past and speculative harms of the distant future, but also the possibility of immediate harm.'[314] This susceptibility to harm is conceptualised as fundamental to the human condition. Fineman argued that

> [w]e are beings who live with the ever-present possibility that our needs and circumstances will change. On an individual level, the concept of vulnerability (unlike that of liberal autonomy) captures this present potential for each of us to become dependent based upon our persistent susceptibility to misfortune and catastrophe.[315]

Reconceiving older owners as vulnerable subjects offers an alternative way out of the dichotomy of autonomy and dependence. Fineman claimed that her new understanding of vulnerability, which is not bound to ideas of 'victimhood, deprivation, dependency, or pathology'[316] but describes 'a universal, inevitable, enduring aspect of the human condition that must be at the heart of our concept of social and state responsibility',[317] is 'freed from its limited and negative associations [to become] a powerful conceptual tool'.[318] This 'vulnerable legal subject' also resonates with the concept of risk, with its universal character 'understood as a state of constant possibility of harm'.[319] In this respect, vulnerability is both universal and particular, 'experienced uniquely by each of us and this experience is greatly influenced by the quality and quantity of resources we possess or can command', and clearly present in the differential exposure to risk for older owners, especially where transactional vulnerabilities are 'situational' or 'impact-based'.

This chapter's analyses of older owners in financial transactions has revealed the distinctive vulnerabilities that housing equity transactions, and the risks they carry, engender for older owners; and also the importance of grounding any claim to 'difference' in situational vulnerabilities such as the differential impact of adverse financial transactions on (marginal) older people (as opposed to specific claims that older people lack autonomy or are incapable of contracting). This reflects the 'life-course' approach of the vulnerability thesis: while the lived realities of human subjects involve a range of 'possible

[314] *Ibid*, at 12.
[315] *Ibid.*
[316] *Ibid*, at 8.
[317] *Ibid.*
[318] *Ibid*, at 8–9.
[319] *Ibid.*

stages' within the 'normal' lifespan, the adult liberal subject reflects only one such stage,[320] whereas 'human reality encompasses a wide range of differing and interdependent abilities over the span of a lifetime'.[321] Fineman's approach places particular emphasis on the responsibilities of the State[322] to 'ensure that institutions and structures within its control do not inappropriately benefit or disadvantage certain members of society'.[323] The remaining chapters of this book take forward the call for more responsive and responsible responses to vulnerability by applying the discursive tropes of vulnerability and responsibility to consider the extent to which English law has responded to the vulnerabilities of older owners in housing equity transactions. The remaining chapters consider how the axes of legal analyses could be recalibrated to reflect the realities of older owners' vulnerabilities, and the responsibilities of credit providers (as agents of financial market institutions) and legal institutions (as organs of the State) in respect of the risks of adverse transactions. Where the liberal approach emphasises the individual responsibility of the consumer, this analysis argues that the State, through legal institutions, bears responsibilities in respect of vulnerable older owners to ensure that they are treated equitably.[324]

(8) Conclusions

With many older owners facing no choice but to engage with some form of risk in relation to the use (or not) of home equity after retirement, the expectations that homeowners will demonstrate individual responsibility as 'active subjects' under neoliberal governmentality by spending their housing wealth on needs in later life provide an important context for analysis of the ideas of responsibility and vulnerability as they are applied to older people. Yet, the 'autonomous consumer' paradigm has been challenged by the recent global financial crisis, which has demonstrated the injustices that can result from assumptions of self-responsibility in relation to risky financial transactions. Furthermore, one of the prominent features of the latest housing market and general economic recessions is the impact of harms that begin with individual default and consumer losses for society as a whole, and the welfare budget in particular. It is with an eye to these wider social costs that—while recognising the costs and risks of regulation/legal intervention—we need to scrutinise carefully the circumstances in which the scale and scope of potentially adverse impacts justify these costs and risks, and support a moral argument that such costs and risks as must be borne are distributed equitably across the State, the market and the individual, rather than falling to the 'self-responsibility' of the consumer. This book argues

320 *Ibid*, at 11–12. 'The vulnerable subject approach does what the one-dimensional liberal subject approach cannot: it embodies the fact that human reality encompasses a wide range of differing and interdependent abilities over the span of a lifetime. The vulnerability approach recognises that individuals are anchored at each end of their lives by dependency and the absence of capacity … Constant and variable throughout life, individual vulnerability encompasses not only damage that has been done in the past and speculative harms of the distant future, but also the possibility of immediate harm.' (*ibid*, at12).

321 *Ibid*, at 12.

322 In the broad sense, which includes the 'organised and official set of linked institutions that hold coercive power, including the ability to make and implement mandatory legal rules': *ibid*, at 6, fn 14.

323 *Ibid*, at 20.

324 *Ibid*, at 7.

that the differential impact of adverse outcomes on older owners is one such circumstance, not least because the 'externalities' (for example, the requirement of financial support from family, friends or the State) are particularly evident.

The remaining chapters of this book focus in more detail on the nature and extent of legal interventions in the creation, content and consequences of housing equity transactions. While it is necessary that any case for legal intervention in commercial activities must be 'market-specific'[325]—justified by reference to typical patterns of knowledge, skills, risks and costs between parties to a specific type of transaction—this chapter has identified some of the overarching and intersecting themes which cut across the different types of transaction by which older owners may seek to leverage their housing wealth. There is also a wide spectrum of possible legal interventions, which apply at different stages of the transaction (creation, duration, enforcement), and with varying degrees along a spectrum running from minimal interference[326] to bars against enforcement, and encompassing procedural and substantive, common law and regulatory initiatives. Lastly, the method utilised to access funds in retirement—from conventional secured and unsecured borrowing to bespoke equity release products—anchors the transaction in a particular legal context that shapes the underlying norms that will govern the relationship. As the following chapters will demonstrate, these 'default' norms are also significant in determining the likely success of arguments based in the concepts of vulnerability and responsibility.

[325] Bar-Gill, above n 270, at 40.

[326] Bar-Gill described disclosure mandates as 'the mildest form of legal intervention, legal intervention that facilitates rather than obstructs the efficient operation of markets': *ibid*.

7

Older People and 'Ordinary Debt'

(1) Introduction

For older owners wishing to, or needing to, raise capital or income to supplement pensions or other savings, there are (in theory at least) several options which they may take. This chapter and those which follow explore these options and the legal frameworks which govern various types of housing equity transaction, from the formation of contracts to the regulation of terms, from procedures for enforcement to the remedies which may be available to older owners seeking redress. The legal frameworks applicable in any given case depend on the option which the older person takes to raise funds, which in turn is shaped (and often constrained) by the older person's context, needs, objectives and circumstances. There are three main avenues to releasing housing wealth:

a) 'trading down', whereby the older owner simply sells the property and moves either into a lower-value owner-occupied property or out of the owner-occupier sector;
b) 'ordinary debt', using conventional mortgages, secured loans and charges, and/or consumer (unsecured) debt. This type of debt comes with an expectation of repayment by instalments, and where the older owner is not able to make repayments, this can lead to a forced sale of the home through bankruptcy; and
c) housing equity products specifically targeted at older people, including equity release products, lifetime mortgages, home reversion plans, and sale and lease back transactions.

In theory the older owner can choose between these alternatives; however, in practice the options available to any particular owner are likely to be curtailed by various factors, including the value of the owned home and the socio-economic circumstances of the borrower, and influenced by a combination of preferences and politically-influenced expectations, shaped within what chapter five identified as the competing paradigms of 'housing as home', 'housing as investment' and 'housing as inheritance'. The tensions between the competing paradigms are illustrated by attitudes to 'trading down': while in many respects 'trading down' may appear to offer the most straightforward option for older owners seeking to access equity, there is evidence to suggest that this is now a relatively rare practice in the UK, for several reasons including the tendency of British homeowners to prefer to stay in their original residences, data suggesting that the average owner wanting to stay in the owner-occupied sector is not likely to release substantial capital in this way, high transaction costs associated with moving house within the owner-occupied sector[1] which eat into the capital sum released by sale, a lack of suitable

[1] Eg, legal costs, surveys, searches, Land Transfer Stamp Duty, Land Registry fee.

properties for older people to move into, particularly within the owner-occupied sector, and evidence to suggest that non-economic factors may also disincline older owners to trade down.[2]

It is also important to emphasise that for many owners, particularly 'marginal owners', the 'options' discussed in this chapter are differentially available. Providers of both conventional mortgages and products targeted at older owners generally set out requirements including in some cases lower and upper age limits, as well as criteria relating to the property and other financial matters (eg income). This has significant implications when exploring the risks associated with different options, as well as the varying nature and extent of legal regulation and protections offered to older owners according to the transactions for which they opt. As the discussion below will illustrate, age is also a factor in determining the options that are available to realise housing equity, particularly in relation to 'conventional' mortgages. This chapter introduces these legal frameworks and begins to explore the relevance of being an older owner, including being a marginal older owner, for legal regulation and remedies.

(2) 'Trading Down'

Where 'trading down' is a viable and desirable option for the owner, it presents the most straightforward option so far as legal regulation is concerned. The owner simply sells his or her home, and either purchases another (a sale-and-purchase transaction which may echo earlier transactions in the owner's housing career) or moves into the rental sector. While the decision to trade down and the question of where to live (for example, moving into social housing or sheltered housing) may require support and advice,[3] the legal issues are straightforward. The 'risks' involved in the transaction are relatively low, primarily relating to whether the decision to move will turn out to be the right one for the personal needs of the owner, and the question of when to sell. A sale, or a sale-and-purchase transaction, routinely requires legal advice, and it is desirable for that advice to be given by a solicitor with particular competence in advising older clients.[4] There is a growing awareness within the profession in England and Wales of the need for specialised legal services for older people, and 'Solicitors for the Elderly' (SFE), an independent, national organisation of lawyers (solicitors, barristers and legal executives) was launched in 1999 with the aim of supporting bespoke legal advice services for older and vulnerable people,[5] and now boasts in excess of 1,000 members who specialise in issues affecting older clients and follow the SFE Code of Practice.

[2] The role of market constraints, property value and financial circumstances, as well as the personal contextual factors that influence the older owner's decision to trade down or to stay put, are discussed in more detail in ch 5.

[3] See, eg, F Heywood, A Pate, R Means and J Galvin, *Housing Options for Older People (HOOP): Report on a developmental project to refine a housing option appraisal tool for use by older people* (London, Elderly Accommodation Counsel, 1999).

[4] For a discussion of specialised qualifications in advising older clients, see ch 9, section (6).

[5] See <http://www.solicitorsfortheelderly.com/industry/what-is-sfe12>.

While it is important for practitioners advising elderly clients to understand the complex trade-offs that sit behind a decision to trade down,[6] the legal procedures are straightforward, not least because this option does not involve the use of any new financial product or additional debt. One issue of which the legal practitioner should be mindful is the possibility that the decision to trade down could be induced by undue influence, for example by family members seeking to cash in early on a future inheritance.[7] In the absence of abuse or exploitation by family members, it is likely that once the decision is made, the transaction itself will present no particular risks; rather, for the (former) owner, the uncertainties attending to his or her future life concern dwindling assets and future financial provision. Indeed, trading out of homeownership altogether marks a transformation in the legal subjectivity of the owner, who shifts from owner to (public or private sector) renter, and so becomes a (potential) subject of welfare and social policy—contexts in which he or she is more likely to be viewed as a 'dependent' or 'vulnerable' subject—rather than the 'autonomous consumer' imagined by private law.

(3) 'Ordinary' Debt: Access and Enforcement

For the reasons discussed in chapter five, for many people seeking to realise equity or raise cash, trading down may not be an option, or not an attractive option, leading them to look instead to the credit market, either in the form of 'ordinary' debt or using the specialised products discussed in chapter nine. Of course, some older people will already be carrying 'ordinary' debt as they reach retirement, and this is likely only to increase with the rise in mortgage equity withdrawal throughout the life-course using products such as flexible mortgages.[8] There is also evidence to indicate that older people increasingly accrue unsecured (consumer) debt before and after retirement. Research for the UK charity 'Help the Aged' in 2008 found that about 25 per cent of people approaching retirement age had consumer debts, with some increases in the propensity for credit use after the age of 60 and again after 65[9]; and that the mean amounts owed by credit users in their late 50s and early 60s were higher than for any other age group,[10] and four times as high in 2005 as they were in 1998.[11] This represents a significant burden of unsecured credit for older people, with particular socio-demographic predictors for debt including being separated or divorced, having dependent children and having a mortgage. The research suggested

[6] See ch 5, section (2).

[7] This is discussed further in ch 10.

[8] For details of the increase in mortgage equity withdrawal across the life-course, see SJ Smith, BA Searle and N Cook, *Banking on housing; spending the home*, End of Award Report (ESRC) (2007), <www.esrcsocietytoday.ac.uk>; S Parkinson, BA Searle, SJ Smith, A Stokes and G Wood, 'Mortgage Equity Withdrawal in Australia and Britain: towards a wealth-fare state?' (2009) 9 *European Journal of Housing Policy* 363; BA Searle, SJ Smith and SE Curtis, *Pathways of Housing Wealth and Well-being*, End of Award Report (ESRC) (2010), <www.esrcsocietytoday.ac.uk>. Flexible mortgages are subject to the usual enforcement procedures (action for possession and sale), outlined below, if the mortgage holder reaches retirement carrying an outstanding mortgage debt which, where there is a drop in income, the older owner cannot continue to service.

[9] Help the Aged, *Debt and Older People* (London, Help the Aged, 2008), Executive Summary, available online at <http://policy.helptheaged.org.uk/NR/rdonlyres/B89CE52C-CAB0–44CC-84FF-C3A0CC24F38E/0/debtandolderpeople250308.pdf>.

[10] *Ibid.*

[11] *Ibid*, at 4.

that 'some older people experience financial strain that results in both unsecured and mortgage borrowing; conversely it might indicate that having a mortgage puts a strain on the household budget that necessitates unsecured borrowing'.[12] The socio-economic spread of unsecured debt is also significant: although the use of unsecured credit was highest amongst higher earners, this study found that '25 per cent of the over-50s living in the poorest 40 per cent of households in Britain had outstanding credit commitments'.[13] This underlines the particular problem of consumer debt amongst marginal owners. It also reveals the increasing gap between affluence and marginality: while some older people have benefitted from a rise in prosperity, those who are carrying debt tend to owe significantly larger amounts than they did 10 years previously, and tend to be owners with outstanding mortgages.[14]

(a) 'Conventional' mortgage debt

The development of innovative mortgage products has played a significant role in disrupting the traditional picture of owner-occupiers reaching retirement after having discharged their acquisition mortgage, and with an owned-outright home that provides a 'steady and certain flow of [housing] services at low out-of-pocket cost'.[15] While acquisition mortgages were traditionally granted for a term calculated to end by the time the mortgagor reached retirement age—to coincide with expectations regarding the ability to pay—there is now a diverse range of products designed for, or available to, older owners, and which utilise the security of the owner-occupied home, either *ab initio* or *ex post facto*.[16] Mortgage deregulation has led to a wide range of products that use the traditional mortgage structure but with non-standard features—such as longer terms (of up to 50 years or longer)[17] or interest-only payments[18]—offering greater flexibility for all borrowers, including older people, but with greater choice accompanied by an increase in risk.[19] An increase in borrowing by older owners is likely to lead to an exponential increase in default; as one economic analysis noted, traditionally low rates of default amongst older people were due to the fact that they borrowed very little, whereas 'if old people *were*

[12] *Ibid*, at 3.
[13] *Ibid*, at 4.
[14] *Ibid*.
[15] J Rouwendal, 'Housing Wealth and Household Portfolios in an Aging Society' (2009) *De Economist* 3.
[16] In the form of unsecured (consumer) debt which may be charged against the property under the Charging Orders Act 1979.
[17] K Scanlon, J Lunde and C Whitehead, 'Mortgage Product Innovation in Advanced Economies: More Choice, More Risk' (2008) 8 *European Journal of Housing Policy* 109.
[18] On the basis that the mortgagor is willing to sell up and downsize at the end of the term to meet the capital repayment. The FSA has highlighted the risks associated with interest-only mortgages for those who do not have a strategy in place to repay the capital at the end of the term: see FSA, *Interest-only mortgages: Consumer Risks* (Consumer Research 56) (London, FSA, 2006). Product sales data reported to the FSA in 2006 indicated that 19% of interest-only mortgages were sold to people aged 55 and older: *ibid*, section 9.3. Research in the UK has also shown that most borrowers do not understand the nature of the contract and the risks involved in interest-only mortgages in general terms; see Scanlon *et al*, above n 17, at 128.
[19] '[T]his expanded range of choices makes much greater demands on consumers' financial acumen, and has generally increased market and credit risk (for the individual borrowers, lenders and society as a whole)': Scanlon *et al*, above n 17, at 111.

borrowing as much as people in the middle age groups, then their default rates would be much higher'.[20]

The lender's responsibilities in respect of the borrower's ability to repay such mortgages are set out in the *Mortgages and Home Finance: Conduct of Business* sourcebook, and have been emphasised in the FSA's 2010 Mortgage Market Review.[21] In 2007, the FSA published a paper discussing good and poor practice in relation to mortgages running into retirement,[22] in which it reminded firms of the rules regarding the borrower's ability to repay, as part of the firm's duty to 'pay due regard to the interests of its customers and treat them fairly'.[23] The credit crunch which started in 2007 has focused the attention of the FSA on the particular issues relating to lenders' fair treatment of customers in arrears.[24] For example, the FSA has provided examples of good practice and poor practice to guide lenders as to what is considered 'fair' in this context. While these guidelines are generic in the sense that they apply to lenders dealing with borrowers in arrears of any age, work on arrears handling, for example, has emphasised the importance of considering the individual circumstances of the borrower in arrears[25] and directed lenders to tailor their approach accordingly,[26] to be practical and realistic, and to take court action only as a last resort.

While the fair treatment of borrowers in arrears is expressed as guidelines rather than rules, customers who believe they have been unfairly treated, and who are not satisfied with the firm's response, may make a complaint to the Financial Ombudsman Service (FOS).[27] The FOS determines complaints according to what is 'fair and reasonable in all the circumstances of the case',[28] taking account of rules, guidelines and good industry practices. As the discussion in chapter nine will show, the FOS has attached considerable weight to the contextual vulnerabilities associated with age, lack of financial expertise, the

[20] I Livshits, J MacGee and M Tertilt, 'Consumer Bankruptcy: A Fresh Start' (2007) 97 *The American Economic Review* 402 at 412.

[21] The *Mortgages and Home Finance: Conduct of Business Sourcebook* (MCOB) (see <http://fsahandbook.info/FSA/html/handbook/MCOB>), includes requirements that: '(1) A *firm* must be able to show that before deciding to enter into, or making a further advance on, a *regulated mortgage contract*, or *home purchase plan*, account was taken of the *customer's* ability to repay. (2) A *mortgage lender* must make an adequate record to demonstrate that it has taken account of the *customer's* ability to repay for each *regulated mortgage contract* that it enters into and each further advance that it provides on a *regulated mortgage contract*. The record must be retained for a year from the date at which the regulated mortgage contract is entered into or the further advance is provided.' (MCOB 11.3.1) The FSA's responsible lending rules are currently under review as part of its 2010 Mortgage Market Review; see FSA, *Mortgage Market Review—Responsible Lending* (Consultation Paper 10/16) (London, FSA, 2010), available online at <http://www.fsa.gov.uk/pubs/cp/cp10_16.pdf>.

[22] FSA, *Mortgages Running into Retirement: Examples of good and poor practice for mortgage lenders* (London, FSA, 2007), available online at <http://www.fsa.gov.uk/pubs/other/mortgage_lender.pdf>.

[23] FSA Principle 6—'Treating Customers Fairly' (TCF); for a discussion of TCF, see P Cartwright, 'Conceptualising and understanding fairness: lessons from and for financial services' in M Kenny, J Devenney and L Fox O'Mahony (eds), *Unconscionability in European Private Financial Transactions: Protecting the Vulnerable* (Cambridge, Cambridge University Press, 2010) at 205–26; and T Williams, 'Open the box: an exploration of the Financial Services Authority's model of fairness in consumer financial transactions' in Kenny *et al*, *ibid*, at 227–45.

[24] <http://www.fsa.gov.uk/pages/Library/Other_publications/Miscellaneous/2009/mortgage_arrears_1/arrears.shtml>.

[25] In this context, the 'individual circumstances' of the borrower are specified as including the reason for arrears; the borrower's income and expenditure; and the borrower's short- and medium-term financial outlook.

[26] <http://www.fsa.gov.uk/pages/Library/Other_publications/Miscellaneous/2009/mortgage_arrears_1/handling.shtml>.

[27] See further, ch 9, section (4)(d).

[28] FSA Handbook, DISP 3.6.1, online at <http://fsahandbook.info/FSA/html/handbook/DISP/3/6>.

limitations of information and the particularly adverse impact of financial losses on older people. In 2009–10, the FOS reported that mortgages and unsecured loans were the fourth and fifth most complained-about products.[29] The approach of the FOS in respect of the particular issues and concerns of older consumers is discussed in more detail in chapter eight,[30] but it is worth noting that despite indications that older people may be less likely to complain or to bring legal action,[31] a significant proportion of complaints to the FOS are from older consumers,[32] and their published reports reveal a particular sensitivity to the needs and circumstances of older consumers.[33]

Another issue pertaining to the fair treatment of older borrowers relates to 'age discrimination' in the availability of conventional products on fair and reasonable terms. Some UK lenders explicitly set maximum age criteria on their conventional mortgage products[34]; for others there is no 'official' upper age limit, but where the repayment period extends past the normal retirement date lenders will require evidence that the owner will have the means to make repayments during retirement, and many mainstream lenders are reported to have adopted 'unofficial' policies imposing upper age limits.[35] The question of access to conventional mortgage products raises issues of equality and age discrimination in financial services. 'Age' has been identified as a 'protected characteristic' under section 5 of the Equality Act 2010, and Part 3 of the Act makes it unlawful for providers of services and products to discriminate on grounds of age,[36] except where the treatment can be shown to be a 'proportionate means of achieving a legitimate aim'.[37] The Government has proposed a 'tailored specific exemption allowing age to be used where this is fair and reasonable. For example, in the pricing of financial services, price must be a proportionate response to risks or costs associated with age.'[38] This approach would seek to avoid 'inappropriate age discrimination', but would allow for prices to vary where this is in line with risk or costs and not arbitrary; where 'it can be justified by data showing that it fairly reflects the varying risk profiles of different age groups'.[39] The majority of the provisions of the Equality Act became effective in October 2010, although provision specifically pertaining to the use of age by the financial services sector has not been included in the

[29] <http://www.financial-ombudsman.org.uk/publications/ar10/about.html#3>.

[30] See ch 8, section (7)(c).

[31] See ch 10, section (1) for discussion of the reasons why older, marginal and vulnerable consumers may not take steps to enforce their rights, ie whether because they are not aware of their rights, because they do not have access to advice or resources to help them assess whether any remedy is available, or because they lack the financial, social, emotional or psychological resources to bring a case to court.

[32] In 2007–08, 14% of the consumers who brought complaints to the FOS were between 55 and 64, and 23% were over 65; see <http://www.financial-ombudsman.org.uk/publications/ombudsman-news/74/74-older-customers.html>. See also <http://www.financial-ombudsman.org.uk/news/updates/older_consumers.html>.

[33] See ch 8, section (7)(c).

[34] Eg, Halifax Intermediaries has a criterion that 'The maximum age at the end of the mortgage term is 75 years for **all** lending, with the exception of the Retirement Home Plan.'; see 'Mortgage Lending Criteria', online at <http://www.halifax-intermediaries.co.uk/criteria/default.aspx>.

[35] On 20 February 2010, the *Independent* newspaper reported that 'Lenders appear to operate unofficial upper age limits on mortgages and personal loans and often won't lend to people aged 65–75 plus'; see <http://www.independent.co.uk/money/spend-save/calm-down-if-we-say-youre-too-old-you-wont-get-cover-1905089.html>.

[36] Equality Act 2010, s 29.

[37] Equality Act 2010, s 13(2).

[38] Government Equality Office, *Equality Bill: Making it Work—Ending Age Discrimination in services and public functions, Policy Statement* (London, Government Equality Office, 2010), para 3.28; available online at <http://www.equalities.gov.uk/pdf/GEO_EqualityBillAge_acc.pdf>.

[39] *Ibid*, para 3.29.

2010 Act. Furthermore, in its 2011 Consultation Paper, the Government Equalities Office indicated that while it recognised concerns about age discrimination in financial services, age remained a sufficiently 'relevant risk factor' to default to justify exempting financial services providers from the Equality Act when assessing risk, deciding prices, and using age bands and age limits on specific products and services,[40] so long as the approach is based on relevant information from a reasonably reliable source.[41]

Even with limited access to conventional (prime) mortgages, there are other routes by which consumer debt accrued by older owners may result in a charge against the property. While 'safe' equity release and reverse mortgage products generally have terms which guarantee that the owner will not face repossession and forced sale during his or her lifetime, older people who carry conventional mortgage debt, or those who have unsecured credit (which may be securitised on the property *ex post facto* through a charging order),[42] may be at risk of losing their home in an action for possession and sale if they are unable to make repayments as they fall due. When it comes to enforcing a mortgage, the standard provisions which govern these actions apply regardless of the identity (for example, age cohort or financial status) of the borrower.[43] A mortgagee seeking to force the sale of the debtor's property may, depending on the circumstances, conduct an out-of-court sale or seek a judicial order for sale of the property. The mortgagee has an automatic power to conduct an out-of court sale where the mortgage was made by deed and the criteria set out in sections 101 to 103 of the Law of Property Act 1925—including default in the payment of instalments or interest due—are satisfied.[44] Where these criteria are not satisfied, the creditor may still seek an order for sale from the court under section 91(2) of the Law of Property Act 1925,[45] which confers discretion on the court to

[40] Government Equalities Office, *Equality Act 2010: Banning Age Discrimination in Services, Public Functions and Associations* (London, TSO, 2011), paras 1.17, 6.6–6.10; available online at <http://www.equalities.gov.uk/pdf/110301%20Consultation%20doc.pdf>.

[41] *Ibid*, para 1.18.

[42] Under the Charging Orders Act 1979; this confers discretion on the court to grant a charging order, in turn giving the creditor all the rights and remedies available to secured creditors, including the right to apply to the court for an order for sale.

[43] For a discussion of the relevance, or not, of identities in possession actions, see S Bright, 'Dispossession for Arrears: the Weight of Home' in L Fox O'Mahony and JA Sweeney, *The Idea of Home in Law: Displacement and Dispossession* (Farnham, Ashgate, 2011).

[44] Section 101 of the Law of Property Act (LPA) 1925 provides that the power of sale arises once 'the mortgage money has become due', ie after the legal date of redemption, as specified in the mortgage deed. The power of sale becomes exercisable whenever one of three conditions is satisfied: '(i) notice requiring payment of the mortgage money has been served on the mortgagor or one of two or more mortgagors, and default has been made in payment of the mortgage money, or of part thereof, for three months after such service; or (ii) some interest under the mortgage is in arrear and unpaid for two months after becoming due; or (iii) there has been a breach of some provision contained in the mortgage deed or in this Act, or in an enactment replaced by this Act, and on the part of the mortgagor, or of some person concurring in making the mortgage, to be observed or performed, other than and besides a covenant for payment of the mortgage money or interest thereon' (LPA 1925, s103).

[45] 'In any action, whether for foreclosure, or for redemption, or for sale, or for the raising and payment in any manner of mortgage money, the court, on the request of the mortgagee, or of any person interested either in the mortgage money or in the right of redemption, and, notwithstanding that— (a) any other person dissents; or (b) the mortgagee or any person so interested does not appear in the action; and without allowing any time for redemption or for payment of any mortgaged money, may direct a sale of the mortgaged property, on such terms as it thinks fit, including the deposit in court of a reasonable sum fixed by the court to meet the expenses of sale and to secure performance of the terms …': LPA 1925, s 91(2).

'authorise sale "in any action" on "such terms as the court thinks fit"'.[46] While the court's power to order sale is unfettered, and there is some support for the proposition that the court will look beyond merely financial matters to take account of 'social considerations',[47] there has been no reported case to date in which home arguments have been successfully advanced to prevent the sale of property under section 91(2), or in which age was raised as a relevant factor against sale.

When property is co-owned, the creditor's application for sale is made under section 14 of the Trusts of Land and Appointment of Trustees Act 1996, which again grants the court a discretion to order sale, to be exercised with reference to a list of factors set out in section 15, including the intentions of the person who created the trust, the purpose for which the trust was formed (for example, occupation as a home) and the welfare of any minor occupant, as well as the interests of any secured creditor.[48] Section 15(3) also directs the court to consider the interests of persons of full age entitled to interests in possession—that is, adult co-owners—with a consideration of the value of their interests. Judicial policy has tended to favour sale under section 14,[49] particularly where the application for sale is made by a creditor and the borrower is in arrears, unless the circumstances are exceptional.[50] The Court's view was encapsulated in Gibson LJ's comments in *Bank of Ireland v Bell*, that

> a powerful consideration is and ought to be whether the creditor is receiving proper recompense for being kept out of his money, repayment of which is overdue. In the present case it is plain that by refusing sale the judge has condemned the bank to go on waiting for its money with no prospect of recovery from Mr and Mrs Bell and with the debt increasing all the time, that debt already exceeding what could be realised on a sale. That seems to me to be very unfair on the bank.[51]

While there is no case law dealing specifically with age, marginality and dire financial straits on the part of the occupier are common features of the case law concerning forced sale. The impacts of losing the roof overhead are (except in the most exceptional cases) routinely outweighed by the priority afforded to creditors seeking to recover the debt.

It is interesting to reflect on the specific implications of this philosophy for older owners as opposed to younger borrowers. The development of targeted equity release products is premised on the idea that the likely period of time for which the borrower will continue to live in the property (the period until the creditor can realise its capital value) is limited and decreases as the borrower ages. Equity release products are designed to compensate the lender for the fact that the borrower is not making repayments and is continuing to live in the property through the pricing of interest rates, which are typically considerably higher than short-term rates governing savings and the variable rate on

[46] M Dixon, 'Combating the mortgagee's right to possession: new hope for the mortgagor in chains?' (1998) 18 *Legal Studies* 279, 292.

[47] *Polonksi v Lloyd's Bank Mortgages Ltd* (1997) 31 HLR 721; *Palk v Mortgage Services Funding plc* [1993] Ch 330.

[48] Trusts of Land and Appointment of Trustees Act 1996, s 15(1).

[49] See L Fox, *Conceptualising Home: Theories, Laws and Policies* (Oxford, Hart Publishing, 2006) ch 2.

[50] See, eg, *TSB Bank plc v Marshall* [1998] 39 EG 308; *Bank of Ireland Home Mortgages Ltd v Bell* [2001] 2 All ER (Comm) 920; *First National Bank plc v Achampong* [2003] EWCA Civ 487. The meaning given to 'exceptional' was developed in the context of the bankruptcy cases, and is discussed below.

[51] *Bank of Ireland v Bell*, above n 50, at [31].

mortgage loans.[52] Yet, on the other hand, conventional mortgages, with their expectation of periodic repayment, in default of which the lender may seek to force the sale of the property, are ill-suited to borrowers who have limited income sources after retirement. As mortgage equity withdrawal and the use of flexible mortgages throughout the life-course seem poised to leave an increasing number of owners carrying their existing mortgage into retirement, the nature of the arrangement between creditor and borrower, expectations concerning periodic repayment and the specific issues that flow from mortgage enforcement actions against older mortgagees are likely to assume increasing importance.

(b) Bankruptcy

It has been suggested that the court's tendency to favour sale where a creditor makes an application reflects the 'practical reality that unless the mortgage payments can be met, sale is inevitable'.[53] Indeed, even if the creditor was not able to recover the debt through these methods, it may still force the sale of the property by suing on the debtor's personal covenant to repay and so forcing the owner into bankruptcy. This standard principle applies equally to older owners carrying 'ordinary debt': a creditor may instigate proceedings for bankruptcy to ensure satisfaction of the debt,[54] the owners themselves may present a petition for bankruptcy or the bankruptcy may follow a failed 'individual voluntary arrangement' (IVA),[55] and the court may order a declaration of bankruptcy if the debtor is unable to pay money due.[56] The emphasis on recovering the debt for creditors is particularly emphasised in the bankruptcy case law, even where this includes the forced sale of the bankrupt's home.

Section 335A of the Insolvency Act 1986[57] gives the court a discretion to make such order as it thinks just and reasonable having regard to various factors, including the interests of creditors, the conduct, needs and financial resources of any (current or former) spouse or civil partner, and the needs of any children[58]; the court is explicitly directed *not* to take account of the needs of the bankrupt himself.[59] In addition, section 335A(4) provides:

> Where such an application is made after the end of the period of one year beginning with the first vesting … of the bankrupt's estate in a trustee, the court shall assume, unless the circumstances of the case are exceptional, that the interests of the bankrupt's creditors outweigh all other considerations.

[52] See R Terry and R Gibson, *Can Equity Release Help Older Home-Owners Improve Their Quality of Life?* (York, Joseph Rowntree Foundation, 2010) 4. In addition to the structural differences, the authors add that 'Currently, the gap is particularly large as short-term rates are at an all-time low and the interest rate on an equity release loan is for the life of the deal, which could be for more than 25 years.' (*ibid*)

[53] N Hopkins, 'Regulating trusts of the home: private law and social policy' (2009) 125 *LQR* 310 at 324.

[54] Insolvency Act 1986, s 264(1).

[55] Insolvency Act 1986, s 276.

[56] Insolvency Act 1986, s 264(2); ss 267–272. The procedure in cases of bankruptcy includes appointing a trustee in bankruptcy in whom the bankrupt's estate vests (Insolvency Act 1986, s 306), and who is under a statutory duty to realise and distribute the bankrupt's assets amongst secured and unsecured creditors (Insolvency Act 1986, s 330).

[57] Inserted by the Trusts of Land and Appointment of Trustees Act 1996, sch 3, para 23.

[58] Insolvency Act 1986, s 335A(2).

[59] Section 335A(2)(c) orders the court to take account of 'all the circumstances of the case other than the needs of the bankrupt'.

Judicial policy in determining whether circumstances are 'exceptional' has established a strict approach, with only the most extreme cases accepted as 'exceptional circumstances' to justify refusing the order for sale,[60] for example where an occupier of the property (say, the bankrupt's spouse) is suffering from a serious illness.[61]

While the court is explicitly directed not to take account of the needs of the bankrupt himself, in *Re Bremner*,[62] which involved a 79-year-old bankrupt who was terminally ill with cancer, the court reasoned that although the bankrupt's own needs were not relevant, sale should be refused based on his 74-year-old wife's separate and distinct need to continue providing care in the home during the final months of her husband's life. The court held that the ages of both the bankrupt and his wife, and the fact that the bankrupt was terminally ill, fell outside the 'ordinary range of problems associated with a bankruptcy'[63] and so were exceptional circumstances. The medical evidence suggested that eviction 'would probably lead to a fatal stroke or heart attack',[64] and the court reasoned that forced sale would exacerbate the distress caused to Mrs Bremner, which would result not only from her husband's death, but from 'her own inability to ease his final months'.[65] There are other examples of cases in which serious or terminal illnesses and other contextual factors have justified a delay in sale of the bankrupt's home,[66] although in none of these cases has the age of the bankrupt (and other occupiers) alone been determinative.

[60] *Bank of Ireland Home Mortgages Ltd v Bell* [2001] 2 All ER (Comm) 920; *Re A: A v A* [2002] EWHC 611; *First National Bank plc v Achampong* [2003] EWCA Civ 487.

[61] *Judd v Brown* [1998] 2 FLR 360; *Claughton v Charalamabous* [1999] 1 FLR 740; *Re Raval (A Bankrupt)* [1998] 2 FLR 718; *Nicholls v Lan* [2006] EWHC 1255 (Ch).

[62] [1999] 1 FLR 912 (ChD).

[63] *Ibid*, at 915.

[64] *Ibid*, at 913.

[65] *Ibid.*

[66] In *Martin-Sklan v White* [2006] EWHC 3313, the bankrupt's partner's alcoholism, the fact that the property was the home of their two children, and the 'very particular properties [of the house] so far as the family was concerned, having regard to its position in a community which was supporting the children against their family difficulties' (at [22]) were taken into account. The court also referred to the identity of the creditors, noting that 'The Inland Revenue is hardly short of money, neither is a bank.' (at [30]), before concluding that 'It seems to me that when one contrasts the difficulties occasioned to the bankrupt and his family by this house being sold, and the difficulties in particular occasioned to his partner by having no house to return to with which she is familiar and the loss to his children of their web of support which is around them, when one compares the difficulties which that family would be presented with by being removed from their house with any possibility of difficulty to the creditors, there is only one possible result. It seems to me that, if anything, the creditors will do quite well out of leaving their money in the estate of the bankrupt' (at [31]) In *Re Raval*, above n 61, the bankrupt's wife suffered from paranoid schizophrenia, and a report from her psychiatrist suggested that her condition might be exacerbated by forced rehousing away from her support network; the court in this case noted that 'exceptional circumstances' might include a short and sudden illness, or a long-term illness of indeterminate duration. 'Exceptional circumstances' were also found in *Judd v Brown*, above n 61, where the court held that 'a sudden and serious attack of cancer was an exceptional event … and was clearly distinguishable from problems such as organising substitute housing or rearranging children's schooling'. In *Claughton v Charalamabous* [1999]1 FLR 740, the bankrupt's wife suffered from renal failure and chronic osteoarthritis, which imposed severe restrictions on her mobility, and this justified a delay in the order for sale. In *Nicholls v Lan*, above n 61, the court allowed a delay of 18 months in light of Mrs N's long-term chronic schizophrenia, to give time for her to raise the capital to buy out the secured interest in the home through sale of a second property. In *Close Invoice Finance Ltd v Pile* [2008] EWHC 1580 (Ch), the court postponed the order for sale for a year because of the wife's cancer and disruption to other family members (which included the bankrupt's elderly mother), particularly the 17-year-old daughter whose education might be affected. In *Everitt v Budhram* [2009] EWHC 1219 (Ch), the court held that while the bankrupt wife's medical condition was not relevant, her husband's severe mental impairment was an appropriate factor to take into account and justified delaying the sale of their home for one year.

The courts' approach to 'exceptional circumstances' to justify delaying sale of the home in bankruptcy demonstrates the weight attached to context in these cases. In *Dean v Stout*,[67] Lawrence Collins J indicated that 'typically the exceptional circumstances in the modern cases relate to the personal circumstances of one of the joint owners, such as a medical or mental condition'.[68] While the court emphasised that the categories of exceptional circumstances are 'not to be categorised or defined and the court makes a value judgment after looking at all the circumstances',[69] it is clear that the circumstances must be 'exceptional' in the sense that they are 'out of the ordinary course, or unusual, or special, or uncommon',[70] 'compelling reasons not found in the ordinary run of cases'.[71] This is significant in light of the discussion in chapter one, which highlighted the substantial number of older marginal owners who might seek to call in aid the contextual impact of eviction in circumstances of bankruptcy. With the number of bankrupts aged over 65 increasing eight-fold from 2002 to 2007,[72] the likelihood of persuading a court that the circumstances of being old and bankrupt are 'exceptional' seems likely to have declined. While the provision that the bankrupt's home may cease to form part of the estate if, after three years from the bankruptcy order, the trustee in bankruptcy has not taken steps to realise the value of the property,[73] and the total exemption of certain 'low value homes'[74] from applications for sale or possession, may protect a small proportion of the most marginal owners, the general approach which prioritised the interests of the bankrupt's creditors over all other considerations applies equally to older bankrupts as to any others.

This is despite the inappropriateness of the 'fresh start'[75] aspect of bankruptcy to the context of older people. 'Fresh start' systems allow debtors to discharge their debt through bankruptcy and continue their lives free of debt.[76] The philosophy of 'fresh start', which provides the policy orientation of the UK's Enterprise Act 2002[77] and is deeply embedded in the US bankruptcy literature, seeks to give 'the honest but unfortunate debtor … a new opportunity in life and a clear field for future effort, unhampered by the pressure and

[67] [2005] EWHC 3315 (Ch).

[68] *Ibid*, at [7].

[69] *Ibid*, at [8].

[70] *Hosking v Michaelides* [2004] All ER (D) 147.

[71] *Ibid*, at [9]; citing Bingham LJ in *Re Citro (A Bankrupt)* [1991] Ch 142 at 157–61.

[72] See 'Number of pensioners going bankrupt rises by 700% in five years', *Independent*, 5 October 2007, available online at <http://www.independent.co.uk/news/uk/this-britain/number-of-pensioners-going-bankrupt-rises-by-700-in-five-years-396042.html>.

[73] Insolvency Act 1986, s 283A; inserted by the Enterprise Act 2002. This 'use it or lose it' provision was intended to benefit bankrupts in the sense that 'they and their families will at least know where they stand within a reasonable period of time in relation to what may often be the main asset in the bankruptcy': A Walters, 'Personal Insolvency Law after the Enterprise Act' (2005) 5 *Journal of Corporate Law Studies* 65, 79.

[74] Enterprise Act 2002, s 313A. A 'low value home' is defined in the Insolvency Proceedings (Monetary Limits) (Amendment) Order 2004 (SI 2004/547) as a property with equity worth less than £1,000 after deductions for mortgages or other charges, third-party interests and the reasonable costs of sale.

[75] 'Bankruptcy … offered traders (and *only* traders) the opportunity of a fresh start free of old debt': D Milman, *Personal Insolvency Law, Regulation and Policy* (Aldershot, Ashgate, 2005) 3. See also Insolvency Service, *Bankruptcy: A Fresh Start* (Consultation Document) (hereafter '*Fresh Start*'), March 2000, available online at <http://www.insolvency.gov.uk/insolvencyprofessionandlegislation/con_doc_register/con_doc_archive/consultation/freshstart/foreword.htm>.

[76] See Livshits *et al*, above n 20.

[77] See *Fresh Start*, above n 75; and Department of Trade and Industry, *Productivity and Enterprise —Insolvency: A Second Chance* (Cm 5234) (London, HMSO, 2001), available online at <http://www.insolvency.gov.uk/cwp/cm5234.pdf>.

discouragement of pre-existing debt'.[78] From the debtor's perspective, bankruptcy offers the dual opportunities of discharge from debts and rehabilitation, the latter reflected in the 'exempt' assets, which include clothing, bedding, furniture, household equipment and provisions necessary to satisfy the basic domestic needs of the bankrupt and his or her family, as well as tools, books, vehicles and other equipment necessary for the personal use of the bankrupt to continue his or her employment, business or vocation.[79] The definition of 'exempt property', in combination with the one-year period before the presumption that the trustee in bankruptcy can force the sale of the bankrupt's home unless circumstances are exceptional, and the exclusion of future assets and income from the bankruptcy estate, underline the emphasis on 'fresh start' to give the debtor 'scope to resume participation in the credit economy and liberat[ing] him to make a productive contribution to society free from the burden of his debts'.[80] This model, which is based on 'future earnings as the key to rehabilitation',[81] is irrational for older bankrupts on two grounds:

a) because (depending on age, health, etc) they have less remaining life-course in which to generate future income; and
b) because they have less income-earning capacity or opportunity after retirement.[82]

Bankruptcy policies which offer discharge from debt and a 'fresh start' may be viewed as a form of 'insurance' against '"bad luck" such as divorce, job loss or medical problems',[83] and the more persistent these 'expense shocks', the more attractive the fresh start system is.[84] This has important implications for the negotiation of financial risk,[85] as bankruptcy plays an important role in providing a safety-net against bad financial outcomes[86] and offering a second chance after financial failure. Furthermore, the conclusion that fresh-start bankruptcy systems are 'welfare improving'[87] was based on a model in which retired people were presumed to experience no uncertainty, no income shocks and no expense shocks[88]—an assumption that cannot be viewed as realistic in the UK policy environment, where the political expectation of financial self-responsibility in relation to unpredictable life events, such as the need for personal and nursing care as well as maintenance of owned housing stock,[89] leaves older people exposed to considerable uncertainty in their financial futures.[90] While this is not to say that 'no-fresh start' systems, where the debt remains extant but is restructured and garnished from future income, are necessarily preferable for older people, it is important to note that the extent to which bankruptcy can function to

[78] *Local Loan Co v Hunt* 292 US 234 at 244 (1934).
[79] Insolvency Act 1986, s 283(2).
[80] A Walters, 'Personal Insolvency Law after the Enterprise Act' (2005) 5 *Journal of Corporate Law Studies* 65, 70.
[81] JAE Pottow, 'The Rise of Elder Bankruptcy Filings and Failure of US Bankruptcy Law', *University of Michigan Law School Empirical Legal Studies Center Working Paper 17* (2010) at 22; available online at <http://papers.ssrn.com/sol3/papers.cfm?abstract_id=1669298>.
[82] As Pottow recognised, 'The quintessential asset exemption of 'tools of the trade' seems of limited financial help to a retiree'; *ibid*, at 22.
[83] Livshits *et al*, above n 20, at 402.
[84] *Ibid*, at 403.
[85] See further, discussion in ch 5.
[86] TA Sullivan, E Warren and JL Westbrook, *The Fragile Middle Class: Americans in Debt* (New Haven, CT, Yale University Press, 2000).
[87] Livshits *et al*, above n 20, at 416.
[88] *Ibid*, at 409–10.
[89] See ch 2.
[90] See discussion in ch 3.

smooth bad outcomes across the life-course when it occurs after retirement, with little or no future earning capacity and short remaining life-spans, is limited.

As such, bankruptcy may be identified as a law of general application that affects older people differently. Some US states have responded to this by making specific provision for older owners in bankruptcy proceedings, allowing them to retain additional 'exempt' property (for example, 'homesteads') with which to make their 'fresh start', compared to younger bankrupts. 'Homestead' laws provide an explicit and systematic scheme of legal protection for the home by exempting it—to a greater or lesser extent—from the pool of assets which creditors may access to recoup their losses on default. In a small number of states, the family home has a total homestead exemption, and in those cases the age of the borrower is not relevant.[91] However, in many other states, there are specific homestead exemptions for senior citizens, and these are often also targeted at lower-income (marginal) older owners, 'who, unlike younger persons, have less time and capacity to enjoy the "fresh start" afforded by a bankruptcy discharge'.[92] This clearly responds to vulnerability to 'impact', or reduced resilience, discussed in chapter six. For example, in California, the amount of homeowner's equity protected from creditors is $75,000 for individuals, $100,000 for married couples, and $175,000 for seniors (over 65), the disabled or people over 55 with limited income.[93] In Hawaii, a judgment debtor who is a head of household or aged 65 or older can claim homestead exemption of up to $30,000, compared to the single person exemption of $20,000.[94] The Colorado homestead exemption increases from $60,000 to $90,000 when the debtor is aged 60 or over,[95] while in Maine the standard homestead exemption on bankruptcy of $47,500 increases to $95,000 if the debtor is aged over 60.[96] New York offers a Senior Citizen Homestead Exemption which exempts a proportion of the value of the home, on a sliding scale that is inversely proportionate to the older owner's income to a maximum of 50% exemption for incomes between $0 and $28,999.[97]

Although there has been much criticism of the 'crazy quilt' pattern of bankruptcy exemptions across the US, as well as the complexities of the numerous exemptions and application rules within them,[98] the existence of these provisions explicitly recognises the particular issues that bankruptcy presents for older people, resulting from their 'inherent limitations in income enhancement and 'fresh start' capacity'.[99] The development of a

[91] Florida, Kansas, Oklahoma, South Dakota, Texas. Age is not referred to in any of these states, with the exception of South Dakota which, as well as a total exemption for all homesteads, provides an additional exemption for owners aged 70 and older against sale for taxes; see South Dakota Codified Laws Ann §43–31–1.

[92] DL Skoler, 'The Elderly and Bankruptcy Relief: Problems, Protections, and Realities' (1989) 6 *Bankruptcy Developments Journal* 121, 136.

[93] The amendment was contained in Assembly Bill 1046 (2009), which amended California Code of Civil Procedure §704.730.

[94] Haw.Rev.Stat. §651–92.

[95] Colo.Rev.Stat. §38.41.201–212.

[96] Me.Rev.Stat. Ann tit 14, § 4422; this matches the raised exemption for households where the debtor is physically or mentally disabled, or has minor dependants in residence.

[97] See <http://www.nyc.gov/html/dof/html/property/property_tax_reduc_individual.shtml#sche>. In Illinois, the Senior Citizen Homestead Exemption, offered in addition to the general homestead exemption (35 ILCS 200/15–170), provides a reduction on the assessed value of the property for the purposes of property taxes, and the Senior Citizen Tax Freeze Homestead Exemption also allows a qualified senior citizen (that is, one below the income threshold) to freeze the assessed value of homestead property.

[98] DL Skoler, 'The Elderly and Bankruptcy Relief: Problems, Protections, and Realities' (1989) 6 *Bankruptcy Developments Journal* 121, 127–28.

[99] *Ibid*, at 126.

specific strategy to address the differential impact of bankruptcy across the life-course is particularly salient in light of increasing evidence that bankruptcy is a real issue for older people, and the irrationality of applying principles developed to facilitate the financial rehabilitation of younger, wage-earning households to (particularly lower-income) older owners in light of their specific vulnerabilities. The difficulties that older debtors face in overcoming financial difficulties[100] are reflected in the state-level 'homestead' provisions, although the federal framework of the US Bankruptcy Code with its emphasis on 'fresh start' continues to be a 'theoretical and doctrinal mismatch' for older people.[101] Further weight has been added to the case for special protection for older bankrupts by recent analysis demonstrating that the marked rise in the proportion of older Americans applying for bankruptcy (largely because of a dramatic rise in credit card debt) is now a 'pronounced and persistent trend'.[102] Furthermore, the US data indicate that the financial collapse of older debtors is largely triggered by simply running out of money,[103] and that the effects this has are severe. Evidence that a substantial proportion of older bankrupts go without food underlines the differential impact of financial setbacks for older people: '[A]lthough all bankrupts are in tough financial straits, the elder files are in really tough straits.'[104]

Bankruptcy law in the UK echoes the US Federal Bankruptcy Code in its general approach, to the extent that it is a fresh-start system and it does not distinguish between debtors based on age.[105] The idea that the bankrupt's *context* should be taken into account in the framework of personal insolvency policy was recognised to some extent—albeit not in relation specifically to age—in the UK Government's 2000 Consultative Document *Bankruptcy: A Fresh Start*.[106] This paper proposed a legal distinction between honest but unlucky bankrupts, on the one hand, and those viewed as 'culpable' because they were reckless or dishonest.[107] The philosophy of a two-track system is supported by reasoning that

> [i]n modern society where economic growth depends to a significant degree on consumer spending which, in turn, is structurally dependent on high levels of consumer credit and personal indebtedness, the provision of legal mechanisms for the relief of consumer debtors is a moral imperative.[108]

The contextual or situational framework in which 'innocent' consumers incur debt has particular resonance when that consumer is a marginal older owner in light of the complex and competing demands upon such a person's financial resources, as well as the expectation that he or she will negotiate these demands through the choices he or she

[100] See, eg, RL Meadows, 'Bankruptcy Reform and the Elderly: The Effect of Means-Testing on Older Debtors' (1999) 36 *Idaho Law Review* 227, 240–41; S Moskowitz, 'Saving Granny from the Wolf: Elder Abuse and Neglect—The Legal Framework' (1998) 31 *Connecticut Law Review* 77, 101.

[101] Pottow, above n 81, at 22–23.

[102] *Ibid*, at 2.

[103] *Ibid*, at 17.

[104] *Ibid*, at 18.

[105] The protections for low-value homes, eg, in the Enterprise Act 2002 are likely to help only the most marginal owners.

[106] Above n 75.

[107] The proposals met with considerable criticism, and it was a much pared-down version which was published as the White Paper, *Enterprise and Productivity—Insolvency: A Second Chance*, above n 77, and substantially given effect in the Enterprise Act 2002.

[108] Walters, above n 80, at 72.

makes as a self-responsible, autonomous consumer. While the Enterprise Act 2002 aimed to 'provide honest and unfortunate debtors with a fresh start free from the burden of indebtedness and from stigma, while at the same time penalising the dishonest and irresponsible minority',[109] its emphasis was on entrepreneurial business debtors rather than consumer bankrupts. More recently, the arguments for a separate system for innocent consumer bankrupts has focused on NINAs (debtors with 'no income and no assets'),[110] which obviously excludes the older *owner* consumer debtor. As such, it remains the case that older owners who face bankruptcy continue to fall under the general bankruptcy jurisdiction, despite the various factors which render its underlying philosophy inappropriate to their circumstances.

(c) Administration of Justice Act 1970, section 36

When a defaulting debtor is subject to forced sale at the hands of creditors, a final option of last resort may be to attempt to delay possession proceedings under section 36 of the Administration of Justice Act 1970. Unless the owner-occupier voluntarily gives up the property, it will usually be necessary for the creditor to make an application for possession through the court,[111] and in these cases the court has a limited discretion to intervene on behalf of the occupier who wishes to stay in his or her home. In addition to the court's inherent equitable jurisdiction to adjourn possession proceedings for a short time—probably no longer than 28 days—to allow the mortgagor to find the money to pay arrears, section 36 gives the court a discretion to delay repossession for a limited period of time, so long as the disputed property is a dwelling-house and 'it appears to the court that in the event of its exercising the power the mortgagor is likely to be able within a reasonable period to pay any sums due under the mortgage'.[112]

The value of the section 36 discretion in cases involving older owners, particularly marginal older owners, is likely to be extremely limited. The conditions for the exercise of the discretion are strict and wholly focused on the debtor's financial ability to make good on arrears within a 'reasonable time' whilst continuing to meet instalments as they fall due. While the Court of Appeal in *Cheltenham & Gloucester Building Society v Norgan*[113] held that in quantifying the 'reasonable period', the 'logic and spirit of the legislation' required that the court take as its starting point the whole remaining term of the mortgage,[114] this is wholly dependent on the debtor demonstrating the ability to repay arrears and future instalments as they fall due, and the court is likely

[109] *Ibid*, at 85–86.

[110] Department of Constitutional Affairs, *Choice of Paths—Better Options to Manage Over-indebtedness and Multiple Debt* (Consultation Paper 23/04) (London, DCA, 2004); Insolvency Service, *Relief for the Indebted: An Alternative to Bankruptcy* (NINA Consultation) (London, Insolvency Service, 2005).

[111] Both the Criminal Law Act 1977 and the Protection from Eviction Act 1977 impose criminal sanctions against the forcible eviction of residential occupiers, although in *Ropaigealach v Barclay's Bank plc* [2000]1 QB 263 (CA) the court held that if the mortgagee manages to re-take possession without a court order, the court has no basis on which to intervene on behalf of the occupier.

[112] Administration of Justice Act 1970, s 36(1).

[113] [1996] 3 FCR 621.

[114] *Ibid*, at 631, *per* Waite LJ.

> to demand a more detailed analysis of present figures and future projections than it may have been customary for the courts to undertake until now. There is likely to be a greater need to require of mortgagors that they should furnish the court with a detailed 'budget'.[115]

The emphasis in *Norgan* on the debtor's future financial credibility makes it unlikely that a marginal older owner, with limited future income or earning capacity, will be in a position to persuade the court to adjourn the possession proceedings. This was further underlined in *Bristol & West Building Society v Ellis*,[116] when the Court of Appeal added that a section 36 delay would 'not [be] available to a mortgagor who cannot discharge the arrears by periodic payments and whose only prospect of repaying the entire mortgage loan and accrued and accruing interest is from the sale of the property'.[117]

(4) Conclusions

With evidence to indicate that older owners are increasingly likely to carry ordinary debt—whether in the form of unsecured consumer credit or outstanding mortgage debt—into retirement, it is significant to note that the property law framework of enforcement in the event of default in England and Wales eschews the idea of special protection for older debtors. Furthermore, this is clearly an example of a case in which the 'general' law operates differently—and adversely—for a particular group of consumers. Older people who cannot show that their finances will improve are unlikely to satisfy the financial criteria for the exercise of the court's discretion under section 36 of the Administration of Justice Act 1970, while the assumption that the *quid pro quo* of losing one's assets in bankruptcy (including the owned home) is the discharge from debt (with tools of the trade) to allow the debtor to make a fresh start is cold comfort for an older owner who lacks the future earning capacity, and perhaps the time and energy, to re-build financial security. This is compounded by the likelihood that the main alternatives to bankruptcy (for example, the IVA or other debt management arrangements) will be unavailable to older debtors who

> are much less likely to have predictable future income and expenses than the population as a whole ... the elderly debtor is more likely to have reductions in future income and increases in future expenditures, both of which will affect the success of any repayment plan.[118]

Lastly, when it comes to losing the home in a forced sale, it is clear that judicial policy continues routinely to favour creditors once the debtor is in default, and there are no cases to suggest that the age of the defaulting owner—without other extreme circumstances, such as serious mental or medical illness—is taken into account when the court is exercising its discretion to order sale.

This may be contrasted with some of the US jurisdictions discussed in section (3)(b) above, which have extended additional protections to older owners who experience debt problems by exempting a larger portion of their equity from creditor enforcement actions

[115] *Ibid*, at 631, *per* Waite LJ.
[116] (1996) 73 P&CR 158 (CA).
[117] *Ibid*, at 161.
[118] Meadows, above n 100, at 237.

though homestead and similar provisions. As the chapters that follow will show, in the UK, any 'special provision' for older owners is achieved through the regulation of a small number of specifically targeted 'equity release' products rather than through the regulation of 'ordinary' debt. This is significant in light of the factors that may influence the different routes by which older people ultimately 'spend' their housing wealth. Targeted products are more likely to be taken out by those who have—to some extent at least—made a planned decision to spend their housing wealth. This may be contrasted with those who 'drift' into debt in old age, whether through equity withdrawal on a flexible mortgage (which, for the purposes of regulation, is treated as a species of 'conventional' mortgage and so attracts a relatively low level of regulatory scrutiny),[119] or by accruing unsecured debts which may be *ex post facto* securitised against the owned home or lead to bankruptcy.

In cases where debt is accumulated *ad hoc* rather than according to a planned strategy for decumulation of housing wealth, the older owner must rely on the application of the 'ordinary' rules. This will also apply to those who do not 'qualify' for the regulated equity release products, for example because they are already carrying debt against their homes or through consumer credit transactions by the time they pass the age threshold for the targeted products. There has been no specific research to date to map the socio-economic profiles of older people who carry 'ordinary debt' into retirement. A 2002 study of flexible mortgages found that these products are typically designed to meet the needs of better-off borrowers, and that 'Households who cannot afford to build up overpayments or sustain higher borrowings against accumulating housing equity are less likely to benefit from these products.'[120] While a decade ago, flexible mortgages were more likely to be used by slightly higher-income borrowers,[121] the 'normalisation' of mortgage equity withdrawal may indicate a trend towards the use of flexible mortgages by lower-income households, notwithstanding the suggestion that they are less beneficial for marginal households. The use of mortgage equity withdrawal to meet financial pressures by households whose financial circumstances are seriously deteriorating,[122] alongside indications that older people are increasingly carrying 'ordinary' debt into retirement, raises new questions concerning the adequacy of the protections offered under the current system.

These issues have come under review in the context of the FSA's remit for enforcement practices.[123] The nature and extent of the borrower's 'self-responsibility' for default has been questioned in the wake of the global financial crisis. The discussion of the FSA's approach in chapter nine includes analysis of its evolving approach towards 'conventional' mortgage debt,[124] where it has been suggested that greater emphasis may be placed on the

[119] See ch 9.

[120] SJ Smith, A Ford and M Munro, with R Davis, *A Review of Flexible Mortgages* (London, Council of Mortgage Lenders, 2002); see also Office of the Deputy Prime Minister, *A Review of Flexible Mortgages* (Housing Research Summary, No 166, 2002), available online at <http://www.communities.gov.uk/documents/housing/pdf/140759.pdf>.

[121] Smith *et al*, above n 120.

[122] S Parkinson, BA Searle, SJ Smith, A Stoakes and G Wood, 'Mortgage Equity Withdrawal in Australia and Britain: Towards a wealth-fare state?' (2009) 9 *International Journal of Housing Policy* 365.

[123] See ch 9, sections (5) and (6).

[124] See ch 9, section (4)(a), and S Nield, 'Responsible Lending and Borrowing: Whereto low-cost home ownership?' (2010) 30 *Legal Studies* 610, for analysis of the concepts of responsible lending and borrowing in home finance, and the impact of the Turner Review on the concept of lender responsibility.

suitability of particular products for particular individuals, on greater lender responsibility for affordability and suitability, and a re-balancing of decision-making responsibilities between borrower and lender,[125] as well as continued efforts to improve the quality of rational decision-making through strategies for consumer education and financial capability. The FSA has also emphasised the importance of good practice in arrears management amongst regulated lenders. The *Mortgages and Home Finance: Conduct of Business* sourcebook[126] sets out the standards expected of a firm when dealing with arrears relating to (conventional) regulated mortgage contracts, which in turn are regarded as part of the firm's compliance with the high-level principle that it must 'pay due regard to the interests of its customers and treat them fairly'.[127] The FSA's rules governing arrears (revised in June 2010) specify that the firm must:

(1) make reasonable efforts to reach an agreement with a customer over the method of repaying any payment shortfall or sale shortfall, in the case of the former having regard to the desirability of agreeing with the customer an alternative to taking possession of the property;
(2) liaise, if the customer makes arrangements for this, with a third party source of advice regarding the payment shortfall or sale shortfall;
(3) allow a reasonable time over which the payment shortfall or sale shortfall should be repaid, having particular regard to the need to establish, where feasible, a payment plan which is practical in terms of the circumstances of the customer;
(4) grant, unless it has good reason not to do so, a customer's request for a change to:
    (a) the date on which the payment is due (providing it is within the same payment period); or
    (b) the method by which payment is made;
    and give the customer a written explanation of its reasons if it refuses the request;
(5) where no reasonable payment arrangement can be made, allow the customer to remain in possession for a reasonable period to effect a sale; and
(6) not repossess the property unless all other reasonable attempts to resolve the position have failed.[128]

The rules also require firms to consider whether, given the individual circumstances of the customer, it is appropriate to extend the mortgage term, change its type, defer payment of interest due, treat the payment shortfall as part of the original sum, or make use of government forbearance initiatives.[129] Firms are also required to provide customers in arrears with specific information, including prior to any action for repossession and/or sale.[130]

These rules respond, to some extent, to the concerns that emerged through the 2009 Mortgage Market Review[131] and follow-up work focusing on responsible lending and responsible practices in arrears management. The use of 'rules' rather than 'guidance'

[125] See Nield, above n 124, at 622 *et seq*.
[126] MCOB, above n 21, available online at <http://fsahandbook.info/FSA/html/handbook/MCOB/>.
[127] Principle 6; see <http://fsahandbook.info/FSA/html/handbook/PRIN/2/1#D3>.
[128] MCOB 13.3.2A; online at <http://fsahandbook.info/FSA/html/handbook/MCOB/13/3>.
[129] MCOB 13.3.4A; online at <http://fsahandbook.info/FSA/html/handbook/MCOB/13/3>.
[130] MCOB 13.4 and 13.5; online at <http://fsahandbook.info/FSA/html/handbook/MCOB/13/4>, <http://fsahandbook.info/FSA/html/handbook/MCOB/13/5>.
[131] FSA, *Mortgage Market Review* (London, FSA, 2009), online at <http://www.fsa.gov.uk/pubs/discussion/dp09_03.pdf>; FSA, *Mortgage Market Review: Responsible Lending* (London, FSA 2010), para 2.80; online at <http://www.fsa.gov.uk/pubs/cp/cp10_16.pdf>.

underlines what the FSA described as its 'commitment to intensive and intrusive supervision to ensure firms treat their customers fairly'.[132] This mandatory approach may be contrasted with the 'good practice' guidance provided by the Civil Justice Council through the Mortgage Arrears Pre-Action Protocol,[133] although the FSA's more stringent approach was a direct response to the intervening decline in market conditions[134] and evidence of poor practices.[135] Nevertheless, as the discussion in chapter nine will show, there are some disadvantages to the administrative enforcement mechanisms under a regulatory scheme, compared to judicial enforcement, not least the reliance of individual consumers on the compliance of firms, as well as on the administrative agency's ability to monitor compliance and promote good practice.[136] Lastly, since the steps which the firm is required to take are premised on reaching a reasonable payment arrangement with the customer, those mortgagors who cannot demonstrate their future financial credibility will continue to be vulnerable to repossession.

This chapter has demonstrated that when it comes to enforcement, the property and bankruptcy rules are likely to yield particularly harsh outcomes for a marginal older owner who has little future earning capacity. In these cases, a borrower who cannot pay is in most cases cast as self-responsible, with little regard (except in the most exceptional circumstances) to that person's context or to the impact that losing his or her home will have. This suggests that, so far as ordinary debt is concerned, by the time the borrower defaults, there is little relief available under the law unless there is evidence that the borrower's financial circumstances are likely to improve. With this in mind, chapter eight now shifts the focus to an earlier stage in the transaction, to consider the terms of consumer credit contracts, and specifically to analyse the extent to which older owners may avail themselves of the 'fairness' protections set out in the general law of contract and consumer credit.

[132] FSA, 'FSA demands tough standards from firms dealing with arrears and sale and rent back customers' (FSA/PN/106/2010), 25 June 2010, online at <http://www.fsa.gov.uk/pages/Library/Communication/PR/2010/106.shtml>. See also FSA, *Mortgage Market Review: Arrears and Approved Persons* (CP 10/3), January 2010, online at <http://www.fsa.gov.uk/pubs/cp/cp10_02.pdf>; FSA, *Mortgage Market Review: Arrears and Approved persons—Including feedback to CP10/2* (Policy Statement 10/9), June 2010, online at <http://www.fsa.gov.uk/pubs/policy/ps10_09.pdf>.

[133] Available at <http://www.justice.gov.uk/civil/procrules.fin/contents/protocols/prot_mha.htm>; for discussion of the non-mandatory nature of the Pre-Action Protocol, see L Whitehouse, 'The Mortgage Arrears Pre-Action Protocol: An Opportunity Lost' (2009) 72 *MLR* 793. Although the Protocol sought to encourage greater communication between borrowers and lenders, to ensure that lenders act 'fairly and reasonably' in the event of arrears and avoid repossession except as a last-resort, Whitehouse argued that its reliance on good practice rather than enforcement was likely substantially to reduce its impact on lenders, so that its potential for helping borrowers would be minimal, particularly since reliance on rules of good practice had already proven ineffective in this context, 'leaving borrowers vulnerable to inconsistent and potentially adverse treatment at the hands of lenders'; *ibid*, at 812.

[134] FSA, 'FSA demands tough standards from firms dealing with arrears and sale and rent back customers' (FSA/PN/106/2010), 25 June 2010, online at <http://www.fsa.gov.uk/pages/Library/Communication/PR/2010/106.shtml>.

[135] FSA, 'FSA refers firms to enforcement in clampdown on poor mortgage arrears handling' (FSA/PN/080/2009), 22 June 2009, online at <http://www.fsa.gov.uk/pages/Library/Communication/PR/2009/080.shtml>.

[136] See ch 9, section (4)(a).

8

Fairness in Contract and Consumer Credit Regulations

(1) Introduction

While the Financial Services Authority (FSA) is responsible for regulating specific categories of housing equity product,[1] for products which fall outside its scope, as well as for those within, the 'general law' has also developed a range of protections which seek to safeguard consumers against unfair credit agreements. Where a credit agreement is deemed to be unfair under these provisions, the agreement (or an unfair term within the agreement) may be rendered unenforceable. This potentially provides a valuable protection for vulnerable consumers, particularly in light of the limited scope for avoiding hardship at the enforcement stage. The fairness provisions are also significant to the extent that they purport to respond to substantive as well as procedural unfairness,[2] and so depart from the liberal model of legal subjectivity. Furthermore, the legal frameworks for determining whether a consumer credit contract is enforceable have explicitly emphasised the importance of contextual or social factors (for example, age, experience, business capacity, state of health or financial pressure). To this end, they appear to offer an opportunity for the situational vulnerabilities of consumers[3] to be taken into account in determining whether a specific obligation should be enforced. This chapter analyses the nature and extent of the protection that such provisions offer to potentially vulnerable older owners who transact on their housing equity.

There is an important distinction to note between regulatory and remedial approaches to unfairness. For example, contract law's 'vitiating factors'[4] may render a contract voidable at the behest of the borrower. These doctrines are remedial: they operate after the event, and are dependent on the vulnerable party making a complaint and seeking to

[1] See ch 9.

[2] See discussion in ch 4, section (4)(a).

[3] Discussed in ch 6.

[4] Mistake, misrepresentation, undue influence, duress and unconscionability; see ch 10. 'Unconscionability' includes the equitable jurisdiction to strike down oppressive or unconscionable bargains on the grounds that the interest rates charged are 'excessive': in *Cityland and Property (Holdings) Ltd v Dabrah* [1968] Ch 166 the court held that a capitalised interest rate of 57% was excessive and unconscionable; or 'unreasonable'. In *Paragon Finance plc v Nash* [2001] EWCA Civ 1466, the Court of Appeal held that a term setting a variable rate of interest in a mortgage contract did not give the mortgage lender an unfettered discretion as to the setting of the interest, as lenders are subject to an implied term that they should 'not set rates of interest unreasonably'; nor should lenders exercise their discretion 'in the way that no reasonable lender, acting reasonably, would do' [at 41], or act 'dishonestly, for an improper purpose, capriciously or arbitrarily'; *ibid.* Note, however, that although 'unreasonable' behaviour involves taking account of arbitrary (irrational) factors, pursuing the (rational) commercial goal of maximising profit is not viewed as unreasonable *per se*, and the lender is not prevented from setting 'unreasonable rates' ([at 41]).

avoid the contract. In contrast, regulatory protections[5] seek to make the environment in which (older) owners enter into credit agreements safer, so avoiding the occurrence of harm in the first place.[6] The contract and consumer credit provisions considered in this chapter contain elements of both models. While the remedial aspects of the 'fairness' doctrines potentially may play a role in resolving individual complaints, as well as setting standards of conduct for lenders, relief is only triggered by litigation, when the vulnerable party has already suffered harm. The regulatory aspects of the fairness protections, on the other hand, seek to prevent the harms arising, by setting explicit minimum standard rules and good practice guidance for the conduct of business by lenders. The extent to which both aspects of the regime are effective in protecting consumers depends, amongst other factors, on the type of 'consumer' they seek to protect and on the extent to which contextual information concerning the consumer is taken into account by the court when applying standards of fairness.[7] This chapter considers the fairness provisions provided through the 'general' law regulating credit bargains, and assesses their appropriateness for marginal older owners.

(2) 'Unfair Terms': Freedom and Fairness

While the 'property law' remedies discussed in chapter seven do not take particular notice of the context in which the debtor enters into the loan arrangement, or defaults on repayments (other than to determine the likelihood of repayment, or unless the circumstances are particularly extreme), the context of the transaction appears to play an important role in consumer law's 'fairness' tests. The 'person-oriented' perspective,[8] which emphasises the context of the transaction, is a key feature of the 'fairness-oriented' regulation of credit bargains under the Unfair Contract Terms Act 1977 and the Unfair Terms in Consumer Contract Regulations 1999 (SI 1999/2083). This approach recognises the parties'

> *characteristics* as consumers and traders … [and] the way in which the physical, property, social and economic interests of such parties are affected by the substantive terms. It is also concerned with the factors that may affect the abilities of such parties to protect their interests in the process leading to the contract … the agenda is to fairly balance the interests of the parties. Normally this means protecting the interests of the perceived 'weaker' party, ie the consumer.[9]

The fairness perspective that has developed in the specific context of consumer credit transactions exists in tension with a competing philosophy of contract law as 'freedom-oriented', and with an understanding of 'freedom of contract' as a vehicle for the 'self-interested, self-reliant'[10] activities of rational economic man.

[5] Such as those which have developed in respect of specific housing equity products, discussed in ch 9.

[6] It is, of course, recognised that to the extent that both the regulatory regime and the equitable remedies respond to vulnerability and unfairness, the same set of circumstances may give rise to claims under both.

[7] The discussion of older owners as vulnerable subjects in ch 6 unpacked some of the contextual factors which may affect how marginal and older owners are likely to invoke these different types of protection.

[8] T Wilhelmsson, *Social Contract Law and European Integration* (Dartmouth, Ashgate, 1995) 29–31.

[9] C Willett, *Fairness in Consumer Contracts: The Case of Unfair Terms* (Aldershot, Ashgate, 2007) 33.

[10] *Ibid*, at 17.

The 'freedom approach' applies minimal procedural standards and emphasises the parties' freedom to agree terms. Its ethos is 'non-contextual, abstract and concerned with self-reliance'.[11] In contrast, the fairness perspective views consumers as potentially vulnerable in light of their relative inability to absorb the impact of losses (both financial and non-financial) compared to the trader, and the reality that consumers may be relatively disempowered compared to the trader when it comes to 'doing battle' against the system to complain.[12] While the 'freedom approach', broadly speaking, reflects the neoliberal model of legal subjectivity that requires consumers to be self-responsible,[13] the 'fairness' agenda allows scope for consideration of contextual vulnerabilities.[14] In practice, most provisions display elements of both approaches, and Willett has argued that 'the best way of describing most rules is that they are *more* oriented towards freedom than fairness or vice versa. However, rules that are more oriented in one direction will still tend to have elements of the other approach.'[15]

Consumer contract regulations may be targeted at the *process* of contract formation, emphasising, for example, transparency of terms or the options available to the consumer, or taking account of the particular parties' abilities to protect their own self-interests at the contract formation stage; or they may be focused on the *substance* of the contract, for example the substantive terms to which the parties agree. 'Freedom' and 'fairness' cut across procedural and substantive considerations: while the freedom approach eschews concerns about the subjective abilities of the parties to protect their self-interest in the decision-making or contract-formation processes, as well as the effect that their contextual vulnerabilities may have on the substantive terms to which they agree, the fairness approach explicitly recognises the role of context in creating an inequality of bargaining power, and, in principle, purports to adjust the outcome—either by regulating the process, or by altering the substance of the contract—to achieve a fair result.

The political and economic expectations imposed on older owners, and the growing pressure to spend housing equity,[16] cast an interesting perspective on their experiences of 'freedom' in housing equity transactions. For marginal owners, the pressure to use housing equity to meet their welfare needs means that in addition to their restricted choices in relation to the *terms* on which to contract,[17] there is also pressure *to contract*. This presents a particular challenge to the freedom perspective, which is premised on the idea of 'utmost liberty of contracting'[18]: that the parties have freedom to decide whether or not to enter into contracts and on what terms (freedom of contract); or, where the freedom to negotiate favourable terms is limited, that the contracting party is still free to decide to walk away from the deal (freedom from contract). While the marginal older owner may in theory have freedom *from* contract and freedom *of* contract, that there is pressure to release equity to meet needs means that in practice both freedoms are

[11] *Ibid*, at 34.
[12] *Ibid*, at 39.
[13] See chs 3 and 4.
[14] See ch 6.
[15] Willett, above n 9, at 17.
[16] See chs 1 and 2.
[17] In this respect, marginal owners may be contrasted with 'prime' borrowers, who are generally offered more favourable credit terms.
[18] *Printing and Numerical Registering Co v Samson* (1875) LR 19 Eq 462, *per* Sir George Jessel MR.

constrained; economic context as well as age can therefore leave marginal older owners with limited choices between providers and products.

The free exercise of those choices which do exist depends on the consumer achieving an adequate understanding of what are often complex products, and that the available offerings meet minimum standards of objective fairness. According to the freedom approach, competition between providers in a functioning market drives down the price and so benefits the consumer. However, in some cases the market participation of certain types of consumer is limited, and their options constrained, by the risks to the provider of transacting with them. The freedom perspective emphasises the legitimacy of traders responding to these risks through the prices they set and the terms they offer; legal interference in either the contracting process or the content of the contract restrict the freedom of the trader, and so must be justified, both in the law-making process and in the minds of the judges who apply these provisions to individual cases. In contrast, the provisions discussed in this chapter, which may broadly be identified as 'fairness' provisions, provide some evidence of law's sensitivity to context and willingness to interfere—in principle at least—on the grounds that *consumers* are a relatively vulnerable group. While this necessarily restricts the freedom of the trader to some extent, the scope and application of such provisions are limited in ways that are significant for older owners entering housing equity transactions, and which indicate that the freedom perspective (and the underlying model of liberal legal subjectivity) remains prominent in the reasoning of courts when applying these provisions.

(3) Unfair Contract Terms Act 1977

The legal regulation of the terms of consumer contracts through the Unfair Contract Terms Act (UCTA) 1977 was rooted in concerns about the risks that flow from lack of transparency in consumer contracts, as well as the inequality of bargaining power between the consumer and the trader when it comes to negotiating or bargaining over individual terms.[19] The 1977 Act regulated the substantive liabilities of the trader to the consumer, but was strictly limited in scope to exclusion and limitation of liability clauses, and indemnity clauses in consumer contracts.[20] Furthermore, the Act does not apply to any contracts that relate to land,[21] including mortgages[22] and home equity products.

The exclusion of land contracts from the UCTA 1977 regime appears to be rooted in the historical emergence of the Act from a Law Commission initiative to amend the Sale of

[19] Law Commission and Scottish Law Commission, *Exemption Clauses: Second Report* (Law Com No 69; Scot Law Com No 39) (London, HMSO, 1975) para 11.

[20] Section 2 provided that the trader cannot exclude or unreasonably restrict negligence liability; s 3 provided that in cases where the parties deal on the trader's standard terms of business, they cannot unreasonably exclude or unreasonably restrict liability arising under the contract; and s 4 provided that the trader cannot unreasonably require the consumer to indemnify another party for negligence or breach of contract.

[21] UCTA 1977, sch 1, para 1(b).

[22] *Cheltenham & Gloucester Building Society v Ebbage* [1994] *Current Law Yearbook* 3292.

Goods Act 1893 rather than a principled decision,[23] although one might speculate that landowners were expected to be less vulnerable than other 'consumers'; that it was presumed that land contracts would be regulated under the land law regime; or, as the Law Commission suggested in relation to small business-to-business contracts concerning land, that they 'involve specialised categories of activity in which either certainty is usually highly-prized in the market or where it is customary for parties to seek legal advice so that harsh terms are not usually agreed to unwittingly (or both)'.[24] Each of these possibilities has interesting implications for the analysis in this book. The idea that landowners are more capable consumers is seriously challenged by the growth of marginal or low-income ownership,[25] and by the high proportion of owners who are elderly and so potentially susceptible to specific inherent and situational vulnerabilities associated with ageing and financial transactions.[26] As this chapter, along with chapters seven, nine and ten, will demonstrate, the specific protections afforded to land contracts and to financial transactions affecting land are a patchwork of varying approaches and standards. Lastly, the limitations of legal advice and the 'information paradigm' in addressing contextual vulnerabilities—particularly for parties who are already subject to social and economic inequalities—are a recurring theme throughout the book.

(4) Unfair Terms in Consumer Contracts Regulation 1999

In contrast to the 1977 Act, the Unfair Terms in Consumer Contracts Regulations 1999, which apply to all 'standard-form' consumer contracts,[27] include within their scope contracts relating to land,[28] in accordance with the EU Directive which prompted their enactment.[29] This reflects the significant growth of consumer credit contracts which are effectively a hybrid of a land transaction and a contract for the delivery of financial services: for example, mortgages and other housing equity products, where the use of the land as security plays a 'supporting' role to the financial arrangement.[30] The view that the context of the transaction is a crucial factor in the court's assessment of the fairness of terms in these contracts was reflected in the EU Directive itself, Article 4(1) of which

[23] Law Commission and Scottish Law Commission, *Exemption Clauses in Contracts: First Report, Amendments to the Sale of Goods Act 1893* (Law Com No 24; Scot Law Com No 12) (London, HMSO, 1969); Law Commission and Scottish Law Commission, *Exemption Clauses: Second Report*, above n 19.

[24] Law Commission and Scottish Law Commission, *Unfair Terms in Contracts* (Law Com No 292, Scot Law Com No 199), Cm 6464 (London, TSO, 2005) para 5.76.

[25] See ch 1.

[26] See ch 6.

[27] That is, contracts which are not individually negotiated.

[28] *London Borough of Newham v Khatun* [2004] EWCA Civ 44; see also C Bright and S Bright, 'Unfair terms in land contracts: copy out or cop out?' (1995) 111 *LQR* 655, discussing whether the precursor 1994 Regulations (SI 1994/3159) applied to land contracts. While Bright and Bright expressed some doubts as to whether land transactions were caught by the 1994 Regulations, this led to concerns about whether the Directive had been implemented correctly, and the position has now been clarified under the 1999 Regulations expressly to include land contracts.

[29] European Council Directive on Unfair Terms in Consumer Contracts (Directive 93/13/EEC) [1993] OJ L95/29. While the English term 'goods' excludes land, the French term 'biens', Italian 'beni', Spanish 'bienes', and Portugese 'bens' may include both goods and land.

[30] Bright and Bright, above n 28, at 663.

indicated that the nature of the goods or services covered by the contract, the circumstances surrounding the drafting of the contract, and other terms of the contract would be taken into account in assessing the unfairness of a term.

These Regulations withdraw binding effect from any term deemed to be 'unfair', and apply to all terms with the exception of 'core' terms (those that relate to the main subject matter of the contract) or terms setting the price, for which the only requirement is that they are expressed 'in plain intelligible language'.[31] Although Bright and Bright argued that the provision relating to core terms 'Potentially … has a large exclusionary effect—could it not be said that all of the terms in a contract define the goods and services sold or supplied and therefore relate to the adequacy of the price?',[32] there is some evidence to suggest that the courts should not apply a wide definition to 'core terms'. For example, in *Director General of Fair Trading v First National Bank plc*,[33] the House of Lords held that a term which specified the interest rates payable in the event of default was not the main subject matter of the contract but an 'ancillary term'. Lord Bingham indicated that the court would *not* apply a broad definition to the Regulations, since

> [t]he object of the regulations and the directive is to protect consumers against the inclusion of unfair and prejudicial terms in standard-form contracts into which they enter, and that object would plainly be frustrated if regulation 3(2)(b) were so broadly interpreted as to cover any terms other than those falling squarely within it.[34]

The adequacy of the financial bargain and the nature of the proprietary rights which form the provider's security are likely to be viewed as 'core terms', which would mean they are subject to the plain language requirement.[35] The exclusion of core terms from the substantive fairness review reflects the proposition that 'the regulations do not look to assess whether or not the bargain was advisable, but whether the terms imposed were unfair',[36] and reveals the presence of the 'freedom approach' within the Regulations. The Regulations

> protect the ability of the parties to contract freely with regard to the underlying substance of the agreement without allowing other elements of the contract to bring an unfair advantage to one party.[37]

On the other hand, 'non-core' terms—which have included terms relating to price variation in the event of default, and terms in housing equity transactions relating to the rights and responsibilities of the parties regarding management of the property during the course of the product life, or the sale of the property and administration of proceeds of

[31] Reg 6(2).

[32] Bright and Bright, above n 28, at 670.

[33] [2001] UKHL 52.

[34] *Ibid*, at [12], *per* Lord Bingham. Bright explained the distinction between 'core' and 'non-core' terms as follows: 'A term is seen as "core" only if the consumer would have treated it as such and it relates to the price or defining the subject matter. This means that even a provision that does relate to the price or subject matter will not be excluded from review if it was not brought to the consumer's attention, and therefore could not have been something which the consumer focused on.' See S Bright, 'Winning the Battle against Unfair Contract Terms' (2000) 20 *Legal Studies* 331, 346–47.

[35] See *Kindlance Ltd v Murphy* (1997, High Court of Northern Ireland); *Director General of Fair Trading v First National Bank* [2000] 2 WLR 1353.

[36] S Brown, 'The unfair relationship test, consumer credit transactions and the long arm of the law' [2009] *Lloyd's Maritime and Commercial Law Quarterly* 90, 99.

[37] *Ibid*, at 99–100.

sale when the product terminates—are subject to the fairness test,[38] with the consequence that, if deemed by a court to be 'unfair', they would not be binding on the consumer.

The test of fairness for 'non-core terms' is set out in regulation 5(1), which states that

> a contractual term which has not been individually negotiated shall be regarded as unfair if, contrary to the requirement of good faith, it causes a significant imbalance in the parties' rights and obligations arising under the contract, to the detriment of the consumer.[39]

The test for unfairness is clearly contextual, with considerable emphasis placed on the nature of the transaction and on 'all circumstances attending the conclusion of the contract'.[40] The meaning of 'good faith' was explored by the House of Lords in *Director General of Fair Trading v First National Bank plc*,[41] when Lord Bingham described it as 'not an artificial or technical concept'. The House of Lords described the good faith requirement as demanding 'fair and open dealing':

> Openness requires that the terms should be expressed fully, clearly and legibly, containing no concealed pitfalls or traps. Appropriate prominence should be given to terms which might operate disadvantageously to the customer. *Fair dealing requires that a supplier should not, whether deliberately or unconsciously, take advantage of the consumer's necessity, indigence, lack of experience, unfamiliarity with the subject matter of the contract, weak bargaining position or any other factor listed in or analogous to those listed in Schedule 2 of the regulations.* Good faith … looks to good standards of commercial morality and practice.[42]

The 'good faith' requirement emphasises the conduct of the firm (the lender or financial service provider), rather than the way the transaction is experienced by the consumer, and in this sense adopts an objective and 'defendant-sided' approach to the risks of unfair terms: the firm should not 'take advantage' of the customer. At the same time, Lord Bingham's statement emphasised the personal circumstances of the consumer, and this is echoed in the FSA's increasing emphasis on the personal contextual circumstances of the consumer as part of its judgement as to whether the firm has treated the customer fairly.[43]

The second limb of the 'fairness' test is concerned with whether the term creates a significant imbalance in the parties' rights and obligations, to the detriment of the consumer. In *First National Bank*, Lord Bingham indicated that this test is met

> if a term is so weighted in favour of the supplier as to tilt the parties' rights and obligations under the contract significantly in his favour. This may be by the granting to the supplier of a beneficial option or discretion or power, or by the imposing on the consumer of a disadvantageous burden or risk or duty … This involves looking at the contract as a whole.[44]

Again, this test is oriented towards a contextual approach to the substantive impact of a specific term on the consumer, although the 'context' here is that of the 'contract as a whole' rather than the individual's (socio-economic) context.

[38] *Director General of Fair Trading v First National Bank* [2001] UKHL 52.
[39] Reg 5(1).
[40] Reg 5(2).
[41] Above n 38.
[42] *Ibid*, at [17], *per* Lord Bingham (emphasis added).
[43] The FSA's broad jurisdiction to ensure that firms treat customers fairly is discussed in ch 9, sections (3) and (4), and in this section, below.
[44] *DGFT v First National Bank*, above n 38, at [17], *per* Lord Bingham.

Schedule 2 to the 1999 Regulations provides guidance on the *types* of term that might be viewed as 'unfair', but the Regulations themselves, and the FSA as administrative enforcer of the Regulations in respect of relevant regulated financial services contracts, also place considerable emphasis on the context of the term, both in relation to the contract as a whole and in relation to its potential impact on the consumer, when exercising judgement as to substantive fairness in any given case. For example, the FSA has stated that

> an unfair term in a mortgage contract might cause greater detriment to the consumer if he is unable to avoid the term by withdrawing from the contract because of various applicable fees and, possibly, an early redemption charge. By contrast, a similar term in, for example, a contract for an instant access savings account might cause little or no detriment as the consumer can walk away from it more easily.[45]

Katherine Webster, speaking as manager of the FSA's Unfair Contract Terms Team, added that

> when considering whether a term gives rise to a 'significant imbalance in the parties' rights and obligations', [the FSA] take a step back and consider whether each party to the contract would have thought the term fair from the other's perspective at the time the contract was formed between them. We find that this helps us to take a balanced approach to the issue of fairness ...[46]

While these comments suggest that the FSA is adopting and promoting a 'context-sensitive' approach, the FSA is not the only arbiter of fairness according to the Regulations: while the FSA may state its *view* that a term would be deemed to be unfair, only a court can *declare* a term to be unfair and so render the term unenforceable.

The distribution of enforcement responsibilities for the 1999 Regulations has implications for the extent to which the context of the borrower is, in fact, taken into account in applying the Regulations. While the Office of Fair Trading (OFT) is the lead enforcer of the provisions, following a concordat between the OFT and the FSA in 2001 it was agreed that the FSA would be responsible for enforcing the Regulations where specific contracts fell within its jurisdiction, ie financial services contracts from authorised and regulated firms; while the OFT would have jurisdiction over the fairness of other financial services contracts which involved activities governed by the Consumer Credit Act 1974, including second-charge mortgage loans, buy-to-let mortgages and non-mortgage personal loans (including credit card debts).[47] The 'regulated activities' under the FSA umbrella are discussed in more detail in chapter nine, and include first-charge mortgages as well as arranging, administering, advising on or entering into the principal specialised financial services products targeted at older owners (home reversion plans,[48] home purchase plans,[49] and sale-and-rent back (SRB) agreements[50]). The FSA has a dedicated team

[45] 'FSA's interpretation of the Unfair Terms in Consumer Contracts Regulations 1999', Speech by Katherine Webster, Manager of the Unfair Contract Terms Team, FSA, CML's 7th annual legal issues for mortgage lenders conference (13 January 2009), available online at <http://www.fsa.gov.uk/pages/Library/Communication/Speeches/2009/0113_kw.shtml>.

[46] *Ibid.*

[47] See <http://fsahandbook.info/FSA/html/handbook/UNFCOG/1/1>.

[48] Financial Services and Markets Act 2000 (Regulated Activities) Order 2001 (SI 2001/544) (as amended by the Financial Services and Markets Act 2000 (Regulated Activities) (Amendment) (No 2) Order 2006 (SI 2006/2383), Arts 25B(1), 25B(2), 53B, 63B(1) and 63B(2).

[49] *Ibid*, Arts 25C(1) and 25C(2), 53C, 63F(1) and 63F(2).

addressing issues with unfair terms, which it describes as 'a key and very visible factor in treating ... customers fairly'.[51]

The FSA's approach to dealing with complaints concerning unfair terms is set out in its *Unfair Contract Terms Regulatory Guide* (UNFCOG 1),[52] while 'Statements of Good Practice' on the fairness of terms in consumer contracts are contained in UNFCOG 2. Under the Regulations, the FSA has a statutory duty to consider all complaints made to it about unfair contract terms, two-thirds of which come directly from consumers, with others referred from the OFT, Citizens Advice Bureaux and trading standards services, and internal intelligence from supervisory departments.[53] The FSA may respond to complaints by investigating (if the issue affects a considerable number of consumers with a particular contract, in line with the FSA's risk-based proportionate approach to regulation)[54] and, if appropriate, by negotiating with the firm to delete or amend the unfair term, but the FSA does not have the power under the Regulations to resolve individual disputes for consumers who have suffered loss because of an unfair term, or to provide compensation. Consumers seeking redress must complain directly to the firm and, if the firm does not resolve the matter, may choose to refer the complaint to the Financial Ombudsman Service (FOS) or to a court. While the FSA carries out a regulatory role in relation to the Regulations, which includes encouraging firms to be aware of the provisions and to have systems in place to review their own terms for fairness, an individual who suffers harm as a result of an unfair term must pursue his or her own case against the contracting firm, and potentially through the FOS and/or the courts.

If the use of an unfair term *also* amounts to a breach of the FSA's rules, and that breach causes loss to consumers, the FSA can apply to the court for restitution or require restitution from the firm.[55] For this reason, it is important to consider the 1999 Regulations within the broader regulatory framework in which the FSA reviews complaints concerning unfair terms: while the Regulations themselves have a defined remit, applying a specific statutory criterion of fairness to non-core terms and requiring plain, intelligible language of all terms, the FSA may consider all aspects of the firm's practice that may be unfair. For example, the FSA's Principles of Business, which focus on how terms are applied in practice, stipulate that a firm must not use an unfair (or fair) term (including a core term) in a way that is unfair in practice.[56] The FSA may also take action against a firm where the use of an unfair term involves a breach of an FSA Principle,[57] or

[50] Above n 48 (as amended by the Financial Services and Markets Act 2000 (Regulated Activities) (Amendment) Order 2009 (SI 2009/1342)), Arts 25E(1) and 25E(2), 53D, 63J(1) and 63J(2).

[51] Speech by Katherine Webster, above n 45.

[52] *Financial Services Authority Handbook*, UNFCOG 1.4 The Unfair Terms Regulations: the FSA's role and policy; online at <http://fsahandbook.info/FSA/html/handbook/UNFCOG/1/4>.

[53] FSA, *Fairness of terms in consumer contracts: a visible factor in firms treating their customers fairly* (London, FSA, 2008); online at <http://www.fsa.gov.uk/pubs/other/consumer_contracts_report.pdf>, para 2.3.

[54] *Ibid*, para 2.4.

[55] See *FSA* Handbook, UNFCOG 1.6.1, online at <http://fsahandbook.info/FSA/html/handbook/UNFCOG/1/6>.

[56] FSA Principles of Business, principle 7; online at <http://fsahandbook.info/FSA/html/handbook/PRIN/2/1>.

[57] The FSA has 11 Principles of Business: (1) Integrity—A firm must conduct its business with integrity; (2) Skill, care and diligence—A firm must conduct its business with due skill, care and diligence; (3) Management and control —A firm must take reasonable care to organise and control its affairs responsibly and effectively, with adequate risk management systems; (4) Financial prudence—A firm must maintain adequate financial resources; (5) Market conduct—A firm must observe proper standards of market conduct; (6) Customers'

a rule in one of its Codes of Practice (for example, the *Conduct of Business Sourcebook* (COBS) or the *Mortgages and Home Finance: Conduct of Business Sourcebook* (MCOB)).[58] Part of the 'regulatory tool-kit' of the FSA is the setting of good practice norms,[59] for example:

> We expect firms not to rely on narrow and technical interpretations of the Regulations to seek to justify a contract term that may be, in the wider context, unfair and in which context it may be open to challenge.[60]

Since December 2008, all firms are also expected to be able to demonstrate that they are consistent in 'Treating Customers Fairly'[61]; the FSA has indicated that 'Unfair terms pose a threat to this, and firms should consider the implications of having unfair terms in their consumer contracts more widely than as simply breaches of the Regulations.'[62] The FSA also seeks to discipline regulated firms by reminding them that contracts containing unfair terms present a risk to their business, since the terms themselves are unenforceable and may give rise to 'prudential risks' where the firm is exposed to unexpected costs as a result of unenforceable terms, to 'operational risk' where management time must be spent re-drafting terms to meet fairness requirements and to 'reputational risk' where they damage the relationship of trust with their consumer base.[63]

While the 1999 Regulations overlap significantly with the regulation of specific products that fall under the FSA's remit, they are distinguished here for the purposes of analysis, with this chapter focusing on the general Regulations and their use in relation to housing equity transactions. Schedule 2, paragraph 1 to the Regulations sets out an 'indicative and non-exhaustive' list of the terms which may be regarded as unfair, including:

> (e) requiring any consumer who fails to fulfil his obligation to pay a disproportionately high sum in compensation;
>
> ...
>
> (i) irrevocably binding the consumer to terms with which he had no real opportunity of becoming acquainted before the conclusion of the contract; and
>
> (j) enabling the seller or supplier to alter the terms of the contract unilaterally without a valid reason which is specified in the contract.

interests—A firm must pay due regard to the interests of its customers and treat them fairly; (7) Communications with clients—A firm must pay due regard to the information needs of its clients and communicate information to them in a way which is clear, fair and not misleading; (8) Conflicts of interest—A firm must manage conflicts of interest fairly, both between itself and its customers and between a customer and another client; (9) Customers: relationships of trust – A firm must take reasonable care to ensure the suitability of its advice and discretionary decisions for any customer who is entitled to rely upon its judgement; (10) Clients' assets—A firm must arrange adequate protection for clients' assets when it is responsible for them; (11) Relations with regulators—A firm must deal with its regulators in an open and co-operative way and must disclose to the FSA anything relating to the firm of which the FSA would reasonably expect notice. See *FSA Handbook*, PRIN, online at <http://fsahandbook.info/FSA/html/handbook/PRIN>.

[58] <http://fsahandbook.info/FSA/html/handbook/MCOB>.

[59] J Black, 'Mapping the Contours of Contemporary Financial Services Regulation' (2002) 2 *Journal of Corporate Law Studies* 253, 255–61.

[60] FSA, *Fairness of Terms in Consumer Contracts: Statement of Good Practice* (London, FSA, 2005), para 1.10.

[61] For details of the Treating Customers Fairly (TCF) initiative, see <http://www.fsa.gov.uk/Pages/Doing/Regulated/tcf/index.shtml>.

[62] FSA, *Fairness of Terms in Consumer Contracts: A Visible Factor in Firms Treating Their Customers Fairly* (London, FSA, 2008) para 2.14; online at <http://www.fsa.gov.uk/pubs/other/consumer_contracts_report.pdf>.

[63] *Ibid*, at para 2.12.

Willett argued that the types of terms set out in schedule 2 established the 'reasonable expectations' of both trader and consumer as a benchmark of fairness under the Regulations,[64] with particular concern for terms that vary the trader's rights or the consumer's obligations and so potentially cause a 'significant imbalance' between the parties. The weight that may be attached to reasonable expectations is modified, however, in relation to financial services contracts: paragraph 2 of Schedule 2 qualifies paragraph 1(j) (above) to add that firms that supply financial services can alter terms where there is a 'valid reason', so long as the other party is informed at the earliest opportunity and the consumer is free to dissolve the contract. The validity of reasons would be determined on the facts of individual cases, but the exception for financial services suggest that it might include, for example, a change of interest rate, so long as this was a proportionate response to a changing financial environment.

There have been relatively few examples of challenges to unfair terms under the 1999 Regulations in respect of housing equity products (equity release/lifetime mortgage schemes, home reversions and SRB schemes). The FSA has taken actions in respect of a number of unfair terms within lifetime mortgage products, and there has been one significant reported case concerning a SRB agreement. In 2006, the FSA published undertakings which followed a challenge to the terms of a lifetime mortgage contract offered by Scottish Widows plc.[65] The term under review related to buildings insurance claim monies (payable in the event of fire, etc), and provided that in the event of such monies being paid, the lender could determine whether to apply the payment to reinstate the property, or to pay off or reduce the debt owed under the mortgage. The FSA noted that a consequence of this term might be that the occupier holding a lifetime mortgage could, in the event of damage to the property rendering it uninhabitable, be left with nowhere to live if the lender opted to pay off or reduce the mortgage rather than reinstating the property. Losing the roof over his or her head (the use of housing as home) could potentially undermine the whole basis of the arrangement from the consumer's perspective, and the FSA indicated its view that this term might have been unfair under regulation 5(1) on the grounds that, contrary to the requirement of good faith, it caused a significant imbalance in the parties' rights and obligations to the detriment of the consumer. Following a challenge by the FSA, the firm agreed an undertaking to amend the term so that the discretion to apply insurance monies to reinstatement of the property or repayment of monies due under the mortgage was at the consumer's option, and to read the amended term into all its lifetime mortgage customers' agreements.

In another case, the FSA challenged two terms in an equity release contract offered by the firm, In Retirement Services (Reversions) Ltd. The first term stated that in the period between the consumer's death and the date that the property was sold, the consumer's estate would be responsible for the costs flowing from a series of obligations such as insurance, repairs and taxes, but with no documented obligation on the provider to sell the property within a reasonable time.[66] While the firm stated that its practice was to sell properties within a reasonable timeframe, the FSA was concerned that the term had the potential to go further than was necessary to protect the legitimate interests of the firm. Following the FSA challenge, the firm undertook to introduce a new term which explicitly

[64] Willett, above n 9, at 240–53, especially 240–42.

[65] <http://www.fsa.gov.uk/pubs/other/undertaking_sw.pdf>.

[66] See <http://www.fsa.gov.uk/pubs/other/undertaking_irs.pdf>.

stated that it would take reasonable steps to sell the property within a reasonable time, with examples of the types of circumstances which might lead to a legitimate delay.[67]

The second term addressed in this challenge gave the firm an absolute discretion in dealing with any management, repair and maintenance of the property which it considered necessary pending sale, with no requirement that the discretion be exercised reasonably, and without reference to the MCOB guidance which states that firms may not be treating their customers fairly if they require consumers to maintain the property to a standard which exceeds the standard it was in when the contract began.[68] While the firm stated, again, that it did not use the term unfairly in practice, it also undertook to clarify the meaning of the term to reflect the MCOB guidance, as well as adding new wording to explain that any costs beyond those for which the consumer was directly liable would be shared between the parties in proportion to their beneficial interests in the property, and that the share due from the consumer would be paid by deduction from the proceeds of sale when the property was sold.

In both cases, these terms were potentially unfair and caused a significant imbalance between the parties to the detriment of the consumer by virtue of the risk that unanticipated costs would accrue against the consumer or his estate. By requiring that the property be sold within a 'reasonable' time, and by invoking the MCOB rule which 'grey-lists' requirements on consumers to maintain the property to a standard which exceeds the standard it was in when the contract began, the FSA was clearly trying to strike a balance between the legitimate interests of the provider in the good repair, and in due course the realisation of the capital value, of the property, and the consumer's interest in protection against terms that go beyond what is reasonably needed to protect the firm's legitimate interests.

It is worth noting that while an individual undertaking binds only the firm which makes it, the FSA publishes these undertakings with the advice that

> firms that have not given an undertaking or been subject to a court decision should remain alert to undertakings or court decisions concerning other firms. These will be of potential value in showing the likely attitude of the courts, the FSA, the OFT or other qualifying bodies to similar terms or terms with similar effects.[69]

This is based on the FSA's risk management approach to regulation, although its impact in preventing other instances of the term identified as unfair is limited. In a 2008 review of awareness of, and compliance with, the Unfair Terms in Consumer Contracts Regulations 1999, and the use of the Regulations to secure an appropriate level of consumer protection, the FSA claimed that while it 'expects' firms to be proactive in reviewing all their contract terms and other firms' undertakings, firms need to do more to ensure that their terms are drafted fairly.[70] Many of the firms whose contracts had previously been

[67] The new term complies with the rules set out in MCOB rule 2.6A.15R, which requires firms to take reasonable steps to sell the property within a reasonable time and for the best price that might reasonably be obtained, but which recognises that 'a balance has to be struck between the need to sell the property as soon as possible, and other factors, such as market conditions, which may prompt the delay of the sale. Legitimate reasons for deferring action might include the expiry of a period when a grant is repayable on re-sale, or the discovery of a title defect that needs to be remedied if the optimal selling price is to be achieved.' See online at <http://fsahandbook.info/FSA/html/handbook/MCOB/2/6A>.

[68] MCOB 2.6A.11G(1), online at <http://fsahandbook.info/FSA/html/handbook/MCOB/2/6A>.

[69] See, eg, preamble to sample undertakings referenced above.

[70] FSA, above n 62, para 3.5.

reviewed still had unfair terms in their contracts (in a few cases, the same unfair terms in other regulated contracts with consumers),[71] including one firm which 'had amended its general contract terms to specifically state that the unfair term applied to all products other than the product the undertaking was provided for'.[72] The issue of 'variation terms' was a particular problem, with over half of the sample of contracts reviewed containing at least one variation term (giving the firm power to impose a change in the contract that the consumer has not explicitly agreed to in advance and that does not require the consumer's agreement when the change is made) that the FSA would deem to be unfair. These findings were described as 'disappointing', leading the FSA to conclude that 'firms need to do more and we encourage them to use the information we provide to help them ensure their contract terms are drafted fairly'.[73] While the FSA claimed that the issues would not be difficult to remedy,[74] progress continues to depend on firms' proactive engagement with the guidance and good practice provided by the FSA.

Of course, where a consumer believes that a term does not comply with the Regulations, there is the option of bringing a court action. In *UK Housing Alliance (North West) Ltd v Francis*,[75] Mr Francis, a consumer who had sold his home to the appellant housing company on a SRB agreement, argued that the terms of that agreement—specifically, a term providing that if the Assured Shorthold Tenancy Agreement under which he had rented back his former home was terminated within six years of the original transaction he would not receive the 'Final Payment' (30 per cent of the agreed purchase price)—were unfair under the Regulations and so unenforceable. The Court of Appeal applied the Regulations, having rejected the appellant's argument that the terms were 'individually negotiated' by virtue of Mr Francis having received legal advice and so having had the opportunity to influence the terms.[76] Longmore LJ held that while there is an absolute prohibition on a finding of individual negotiation where the consumer has not had the opportunity to influence the substance of the term, it does not follow that just because the consumer did have the ability to influence the substance of the term that it was 'individually negotiated'; that remains a matter for the supplier to prove. The Court of Appeal applied the 'twin requirements' of good faith and significant imbalance in the parties' rights and obligations to the term under review. Longmore LJ held that 'Looking at the contract as a whole, I am unable to conclude that the retention of the Final Payment, on the grant of a court order for possession, creates a significant imbalance.'[77]

This decision has several interesting implications for analysis of the role of the 1999 Regulations in protecting potentially vulnerable, older consumers in housing equity transactions. For one thing, it provides a reminder of the powerful effect of the particular device used to release equity. While an owner is likely to perceive equity release, reverse mortgages and SRB agreements in common functional terms—as products which release equity while allowing the (former) owner to continue living in the property[78]—the

[71] *Ibid.*
[72] *Ibid*, para 3.18.
[73] *Ibid*, para 3.46.
[74] *Ibid*, para 3.48.
[75] [2010] EWCA Civ 117.
[76] *Ibid*, at [18]–[19].
[77] *Ibid*, at [27].
[78] Thus enabling the use of the housing as an investment asset to spend while preserving housing as home; see further ch 5.

underlying land law transaction makes a crucial difference in the way the fairness of the terms is reviewed. Although the FSA categorises a SRB agreement as a 'regulated home finance activity' alongside mortgage contracts and home purchase plans,[79] equity release products are clearly structured as securitised loans[80] whereas a SRB agreement requires the owner to divest himself of his legal and beneficial interest in the property in a sale and, in a separate transaction (in Mr Francis's case, on the same day), to form a new relationship with the purchaser company as a tenant.

In *Francis*, the parties' underlying land law rights were a prominent factor in informing the court's approach to the fairness of terms in the contract. Longmore LJ centred his analysis around a 'construction of the tenancy agreement'[81]; he emphasised the limited rights that Mr Francis held as an assured shorthold tenant under the Housing Act 1988 and the nature of the court's role in overseeing this type of tenancy. When counsel for Mr Francis argued that he should be permitted to make a claim for relief against forfeiture, the court refused this avenue on the basis that Mr Francis had no proprietary or possessory right in the property:

> Mr Francis … has merely lost a contingent right to payment of a debt. That is not a proprietary right in the sense that he has any proprietary right to the amount of the Final Payment in the hands of the landlord … That is not a right the loss of which can give rise to relief against forfeiture.[82]

Mr Francis's status as a tenant who had defaulted on payments of rent also informed the court's analysis of the good faith and significant imbalance tests, although the emphasis of the Court's reasoning was on the landlord's perspective. Longmore LJ held:

> I am unable to conclude that the retention of the Final Payment, on the grant of a court order for possession, creates a significant imbalance. It is possible to conceive of circumstances where it might, especially if the original contract price was below the market price and the rental market (or perhaps the sale market) was buoyant at the time of the possession. But the matter has to be judged at the time when the contract is made and it would be equally possible to envisage a stagnant market in which the landlord would find it difficult to re-let the property or even to re-sell it. In those circumstances the retention of what is less than a third of the price does not cause any imbalance let alone a significant one.[83]

While this 'contextual' approach took account of the impact of the court's decision on the landlord, it did not extend to Mr Francis's expectations: the Court limited its consideration of his side of the bargain to the transparency (and not the substance) of the agreement and the fact that he had legal advice going into the transaction (although, as noted above, it was not inferred that this meant he had any influence over the substance of the term). This approach adopted a lower threshold than that reflected in the FSA's 'key

[79] <http://fsahandbook.info/FSA/html/handbook/PERG/2/Annex2>.

[80] While mortgage contracts historically involved a conveyance of the legal estate in land, the charge by deed is now the only method of creating a legal mortgage: s 87 of the Law of Property Act (LPA) 1925, and s 23(1)(a) of the Land Registration Act 2002 which prohibited the creation of a mortgage by demise (originally saved by ss 85 and 86 of the LPA 1925).

[81] *Francis*, above n 75, at [24].

[82] *Ibid*, at [14].

[83] *Ibid*, at [27].

messages' on fair terms, which seek to encourage firms to consider the fairness of their terms from the consumer's perspective, taking account of 'consumers' legitimate interests'.[84]

The Court of Appeal in *Francis* was satisfied to find that 'It cannot be suggested that the term is not fully, clearly and legibly expressed or was not given appropriate prominence.'[85] With the assessment of the term under the Regulations turning on this observation, it is difficult to see what the substantive 'fairness' test added in this case to the more limited plain language obligation which applies to core terms, and which is targeted at ensuring that consumers understand the contract and can make an informed choice. Discussion of the circumstances in which Mr Francis entered into the transaction was limited to the observation that 'No doubt Mr Francis was short of money when he made the contract for sale and lease back of the property but it cannot be said that he has been "taken advantage of" unfairly.'[86] This conclusion was drawn without reference to Mr Francis's personal characteristics (the report does not mention, for example, his age or business experience, or attach much weight to the context in which he entered into the transaction), and the 'context' taken into account by the court was limited to the legal context of the landlord's grounds for possession and the commercial/market context that would inform the landlord's ability to raise capital or income from what was now its property, by re-selling or re-letting it. The value of the property as Mr Francis's home, or his (former) interest in it as an owner, was clearly irrelevant. While some reference was made to the financial context which likely led Mr Francis to enter the SRB agreement, the court implied that the pressure of his financial circumstances was countered by the fact that he had received legal advice. While the evidence that his solicitor had drawn to his attention the effect of the disputed term—that if the landlord were to be granted an order for possession because he breached the terms of the tenancy, he would lose the Final Payment—was described as 'probably inadmissible', the Court of Appeal concluded that

> the fact is that Mr Francis necessarily had the protection of a solicitor at the time and he would have had the protection of the court if and when a possession order was sought by the landlord. I cannot see here any failure to conform with 'good standards of commercial morality and practice'.[87]

The suggestion that independent legal advice provides an adequate safeguard against substantive unfairness runs counter to the intended effect of the Regulations. In their discussion of the 1994 Regulations, which were expressed in identical terms so far as relevant to this issue, Bright and Bright stated that

> [e]ven if the consumer is told to take independent legal advice on the agreement, it will still be subject to the regulations as the emphasis is upon the non-negotiable nature of the agreement, not on the consumer's lack of awareness of the agreement's meaning.[88]

This analysis may have been based on the guidance in schedule 2 to the 1994 Regulations (but omitted from the 1999 version) which indicated that 'In making an assessment of

[84] FSA, *Fair Terms—key messages*, FSA webpage, online at <www.fsa.gov.uk/pages/Doing/Regulated/uct/terms/fair/index.shtml>.

[85] *Francis*, above n 75, at [29].

[86] *Ibid.*

[87] *Ibid.*

[88] Bright and Bright, above n 28, at 661.

good faith, regard shall be had in particular to the strength of the bargaining positions of the parties', and which echoed the recital to the Directive on which the Regulations were based. The Court of Appeal's approach in *Francis* also effectively negated the idea that the context of the contract (on the consumer's side) is taken into account in determining the fairness of the term: if the receipt of legal advice is sufficient to ensure that a consumer, who was acknowledged to be in straitened financial circumstances, has received the 'protection' of the law, such that the court does not look beyond legal advice, then the court inevitably attaches no weight to contextual factors. In *Francis*, the 'protection of the court' meant the fact that termination of the tenancy was only possible by court order. The Court noted that the breach was non-payment of rent, a mandatory ground for possession under the Housing Act 1988,[89] and that 'It is agreed that rent which is due has not been paid. It does not look as if it will be; there are therefore good reasons why possession should be ordered.'[90] The court process was therefore treated as a formality to ensure due process rather than a substantive opportunity to review the fairness of the contract.

The Court of Appeal's approach in *Francis* is particularly striking in light of the fact that, while the SRB agreement in this case preceded the regulatory framework for these transactions announced by the FSA in 2009, under the new regime—which had been published although not yet given effect by the date of the Court of Appeal's judgment—it would now be dealt with in Mr Francis's favour. The FSA rules, which are discussed in chapter nine, prohibit the setting up of an agreement which contains this type of retention provision, and would also have prevented the firm from taking possession of Mr Francis's home in the way that it did. Although this judgment post-dated the announcement of the interim regulatory rules, the Court of Appeal did not refer to the FSA regulation or its effects; neither did the way in which the contract would be viewed under the new regime appear to influence its judgment as to whether the terms under scrutiny were substantively fair.

The FSA regime is oriented around risk, and the decision to regulate was based on findings from a 2008 OFT market study, launched in response to widespread concerns raised by Citizens' Advice, Shelter and the Council of Mortgage Lenders (among others), that there is a substantial level of risk specifically associated with SRB transactions, 'particularly for consumers already in stressful and difficult financial and emotional situations'.[91] This study noted, in particular, that in SRB transactions, often vulnerable consumers 'currently bear almost all of the risk in the transaction'.[92] The study also indicated that the general consumer protection legislation was inadequate to protect consumers in relation to these transactions. The 1999 Regulations were described as 'likely to provide less protection to sale and rent back consumers' on the basis that they 'will not apply to sale and rent back agreements which are individually negotiated. Nor do they provide protection for the main subject matter of the contract, or its price.'[93] Yet the decision in *Francis* suggests that the Regulations may be of even more marginal value because of the significant gap between what the court regards as 'fair' for non-core terms

[89] The mandatory ground for possession based on non-payment of rent is set out in Ground 8 of the second schedule to the Housing Act 1988.

[90] *Francis*, above n 75, at [3].

[91] OFT, *Sale and Rent Back: An OFT Market Study* (OFT 1018) (London, OFT, 2008) para 1.9.

[92] *Ibid*, para 1.11.

[93] *Ibid*, para 3.66.

under the Regulations and the standard of consumer protection which the FSA has deemed appropriate under its new regime.

While the regulatory activities of the FSA have resulted in some unfair terms being removed from lifetime mortgage products, on the whole the 1999 Regulations appear to have a limited role in protecting consumers in housing equity transactions. The reasons for this were recognised, in part, by the FSA itself in its report on the effectiveness of the Regulations, which described their limited impact as disappointing and called for a more proactive approach by the firms on whose successful engagement the effectiveness of the Regulations are dependent. While it would be wrong to read too much into one case, the gap between the decision in *Francis* and the standards required in the new regulatory regime for sale-and rent-back transactions suggests that the protection offered by the 1999 Regulations is likely to be of general but limited value for older marginal owners when it comes to ensuring that the terms of housing equity transactions are substantively 'fair'.

While the Unfair Terms in Consumer Contracts Regulations 1999 purport to provide a contextual assessment of fairness, this was not much in evidence in *Francis*. In contrast, the courts placed a much heavier emphasis on context in *Tew and others v Bank of Scotland (Shared Appreciation Mortgages) No 1 plc and others*.[94] This case concerned an appeal against a group litigation order (GLO) which had been made in respect of litigation seeking to challenge the fairness of terms in a shared appreciation mortgage product under the earlier 1994 Regulations, and the fairness of the relationship under the Consumer Credit Act 1974, as amended by the Consumer Credit Act 2006.[95] The shared appreciation mortgage is another example of a product which is targeted at older owners: the mortgage loan is not repayable at any fixed time but only in the event of sale or on the death of the mortgagor. When the loan is repaid, the amount owed is calculated according to the principal debt outstanding and a specified percentage[96] increase in value of the property over the purchase costs. In considering whether the case was appropriate for a GLO, the court noted the 'fact-sensitive nature of the inquiry' and the 'wide-ranging inquiry ... required' under the Regulations.[97]

The claimants argued that the court could determine the fairness (or not) of the terms by looking at the terms themselves to ascertain 'their potential effect, and their actual effect in monetary terms, but excluding any consideration of the personal circumstances and qualifications of the borrowers or the actual circumstances of any of the loans'.[98] The reasons advanced in support of this approach included the claimants' argument that the terms themselves were so unfair that

> there was a real chance that the court, without being referred to any actual individual circumstances, could conclude that the returns to the bank were so great, and so much greater than a proper retail banking risk-reward ratio would normally justify, that the transactions would inevitably be characterised as unfair under the two sets of the legislation and the individual circumstances were irrelevant.[99]

[94] [2010] EWHC 203 (Ch), (22 January 2010, transcript available on Lexis).

[95] See below, section (4)(b).

[96] The specified percentage is a multiple of the loan to value ratio, depending on the category into which the mortgage falls: in one category, there is no interest payable but the multiple is usually three times the loan to value ratio; in another category, there is a fixed interest charge and the multiple is one.

[97] *Tew*, above n 94, at [9], [11].

[98] *Ibid*, at [12].

[99] *Ibid*, at [19].

In this case, the claimants were concerned that there would be evidential difficulties in examining the individual circumstances because 'many of the borrowers were elderly and they would not [be] able to remember precisely what they did and did not know, or understand, in a transaction which took place over ten years ago, so there would not be much evidence available anyway'.[100]

Mann J rejected the claimants' proposals concerning the framing of the GLO issues on the basis that it would be

> quite wrong to allow the GLO issues to be phrased in such a way as to involve a shutting out of individual circumstances from the scope of the litigation. It is not an accurate way of describing the litigation and amounts to a form of pre-judgment of the issues.[101]

The court held that the legislation required it to look at all the circumstances of the transaction, including the qualities and circumstances of each debtor. It was recognised that this focus on context could work both ways: for example, the bank might argue that the terms were fair because the context demonstrated that the claimant had sufficient understanding and that 'the transaction made personal sense for that individual'.[102] Mann J added:

> The inquiry as to fairness is a one stage inquiry looking at both sides of the transaction ... The whole notion of fairness or unfairness involves the impact of matters on a person ... I do not think that any finding of fairness can arise without asking 'fairness to whom?'[103]

He added that while the role of an administrative regulator such as the FSA could include giving guidance in the abstract, the court's function was to decide individual cases.[104] The suggestion that this type of litigation could be tried without reference to the individual circumstances was rejected as

> neither sensible nor practical. It does not reflect the likely real issues, nor does it encapsulate a sensible method of trying them. On the face of the legislation, the facts of individual cases are capable of affecting the assessment of fairness, and they cannot be disregarded as such ... one cannot ignore them as a matter of law.[105]

While the court was prepared to allow the GLO, the issues could not be framed to close off the individual circumstances of the claimants but was only permitted to proceed with the issues defined in such a way as to describe the individual claims being made, including specific contextualised allegations of unfairness.[106] It remains to be seen whether the claimants' substantive claims of unfairness will be successful in the litigation proper, but this case when heard seems likely to provide further insight to the judicial application of the Unfair Terms in Consumer Contract Regulations in relation to older owners' housing equity transactions.

[100] *Ibid.*
[101] *Ibid*, at [22].
[102] *Ibid*, at [21].
[103] *Ibid*, at [27].
[104] *Ibid*, at [26].
[105] *Ibid*, at [25].
[106] *Ibid*, at [37].

(5) The Law Commissions and Unfair Terms

Before leaving the 1999 Regulations, it is worth noting that in 2005 the English and Scottish Law Commissions published a joint report on unfair terms which proposed to replace UCTA 1977 and the Unfair Terms in Consumer Regulations 1999 with a single unified piece of legislation which would preserve the existing level of consumer protection.[107] These proposals, which have not yet been implemented, include within their scope housing equity transactions. The Commissions proposed that land contracts executed by individual consumers would fall within this regime 'as they are subject to [the 1999 Regulations]',[108] and that land contracts would be included within the provisions proposed to replace the UCTA 1977 regime within the new combined regime.[109] Significantly, the legislation would apply to all terms, whether individually negotiated or not, in recognition of the largely illusory power of negotiation in consumer contracts.[110] Beale argued:

> Negotiation may ensure that the consumer knows the clause exists, but unless she has a reasonably full understanding of what the term means and the impact the term is likely to have on her, the negotiation will be pretty meaningless even if she is offered any choice. The number of cases in which consumers are able to negotiate in any meaningful way a term that is not a 'core' term will, we think, be very small.[111]

Although land contracts between businesses and small businesses would not be covered by the new regime,[112] this is not likely to be relevant to marginal older owners in housing equity transactions who generally contract as consumers rather than business-to-business.

[107] Law Commission and Scottish Law Commission, *Unfair Terms in Contracts* (Law Com No 292; Scot Law Com No 199; Cm 6464) (London, TSO, 2005); see also Law Commission and Scottish Law Commission, *Unfair Terms in Contracts: A Joint Consultation Paper* (Law Com CP No 166; Scot Law Com DP No 119) (London, TSO, 2002).

[108] *Unfair Terms in Contracts: A Joint Consultation Paper*, above n 107, para 4.79; see also *Unfair Terms in Contracts*, above n 107, para 4.81–4.84. The Commissions' stated policy was that: 'Our aim is to produce a single, unified regime to cover the whole of the UK that preserves the existing level of consumer protection. Where the Act and Regulations differ, we have rounded up rather than rounded down.' See *Unfair Terms in Contracts*, above n 107, Summary, para 9; online at <http://www.lawcom.gov.uk/docs/lc292sum.pdf>.

[109] *Unfair Terms in Contracts: A Joint Consultation Paper*, above n 107, para 4.37; *Unfair Terms in Contracts*, above n 107, para 3.46–3.47. The Commissions noted that 'None of the other exemptions in Schedule 1 appear to affect consumer contracts, either because there is an express saving in favour of persons dealing as consumer or because the nature of the contract (eg for the formation of a company: para 1(d)) makes it implausible that either party could be dealing as a consumer': *Unfair Terms in Contracts: A Joint Consultation Paper*, *ibid*, para 3.43, fn 101.

[110] *Unfair Terms in Contracts: A Joint Consultation Paper*, above n 107, paras 4.42–4.54; *Unfair Terms in Contracts*, above n 107, para 1.9.

[111] H Beale, 'Unfair Terms in Contracts: Proposals for Reform in the UK' (2004) 27 *Journal of Consumer Policy* 289, 293.

[112] These 'involve specialised categories of activity in which either certainty is usually highly-prized in the market or where it is customary for parties to seek legal advice so that harsh terms are not usually agreed to unwittingly (or both). Insurance contracts are also exempted; many would in any event be covered by the larger exemption we have recommended for financial services contracts': *Unfair Terms in Contracts*, above n 107, para 5.76. The Commissions also noted that 'protections are largely unnecessary in areas where businesses dealing with small businesses are already regulated. In extending protections to small businesses in these situations we run the danger of over-regulating the market. The most obvious situation in which this might occur is that of contracts for the provision of financial services. Most contracts of this kind are already subject to regulation by the Financial Services Authority (FSA)': *ibid*, para 2.39.

One of the Law Commissions' key proposals was that the current tests, of 'reasonableness' under UCTA 1977 and 'fairness' under the Regulations, be combined into a single test of whether a term is 'fair and reasonable'. This new test would replace the 'good faith' and 'significant imbalance' requirements under the current test in the 1999 Regulations. The Law Commissions indicated that they did not view this as a 'change' in the substance of the test, because if the tests are properly understood there is no difference between them.[113] Nevertheless, the use of 'fair and reasonable' would confirm that the requirement of 'good faith' is not purely procedural but both substantive and procedural, so that some terms may be deemed unfair whatever procedure has been followed to secure the consumer's agreement.[114] In applying the 'new test', factors to be considered would include:

a) the transparency of the term, encompassing factors such as the clarity and accessibility of the term;
b) the substance and effect of the term; and
c) the circumstances existing when the contract was made, including the parties' knowledge of those circumstances.

The guidelines which the Commission proposed to include in their draft legislation would cover 'the risks to the party adversely affected by the term'[115]; the knowledge and understanding of the party adversely affected by the term[116]; the strength of the bargaining position of the parties[117]; and the nature of the goods or services for which the contract was concluded.[118]

The Commissions also listed 11 further factors as relevant to the knowledge and understanding of the party adversely affected by the term. This approach would support a structured contextual assessment of the consumer's perspective, including the subjective knowledge and understanding of the particular consumer, the objective test of what 'other persons in a similar position would normally expect in a similar transaction',[119] the complexity of the transaction,[120] and the way in which relevant information, explanations and advice were provided.[121] In assessing the relative strength of bargaining power of the parties, the Commissions' proposed guidelines included: whether the transaction was an unusual one for either of the parties[122]; whether the party adversely affected was offered a choice over the term or had an opportunity to seek a more favourable term[123]; whether that party had an opportunity to enter into a similar contract with other persons without that term; and whether there were alternative means by which that party's requirements could have been met.[124] This last factor is of particular interest in relation to the

[113] *Unfair Terms in Contracts: A Joint Consultation Paper*, above n 107, paras 3.70–3.71.
[114] See Beale, above n 111, at 307.
[115] *Unfair Terms in Contracts: A Joint Consultation Paper*, Draft Bill, sch 1, para 1(b).
[116] *Ibid*, para 2(a).
[117] *Ibid*, para 2(b).
[118] *Ibid*, para 2(c).
[119] *Ibid*, para 3(1)(d).
[120] *Ibid*, para 3(1)(e), 3(2).
[121] *Ibid*, para 3(1)(f)–(j). See ch 6, sections (5), (6) and (7), for discussion of the importance of contextual analyses to capture realities of vulnerability amongst legal subjects.
[122] *Ibid*, para 4(a).
[123] *Ibid*, para 4(b)–(c).
[124] *Ibid*, para 4(d)–(e).

designation of both marginal and older owners as 'high-risk' borrowers. The current exemption of financial services from the age discrimination provisions in the Equality Act 2010[125] reflects an acceptance of the reality that pricing of financial services will respond to risks or costs associated with age.[126] While the Government proposed that age remain a sufficiently 'relevant risk factor' to justify exempting financial services providers from the Equality Act 2010 when assessing risk, deciding prices, and using age bands and age limits on specific products and services,[127] the factors enumerated above would offer some possibility that (for non-core terms at least) the situational vulnerability of marginal or older owners—including the (lack of) options available to them—would be taken into account in determining the fairness of the terms agreed. Even in relation to core terms, the proposals would clarify the importance of considering the term from the consumer's perspective: the Draft Bill proposed that to be exempt from the general test of fairness, a term would have to be transparent, set out the main subject matter of the contract and be 'not substantially different from what the consumer reasonably expected'.[128]

In July 2006, the Government informed the Law Commissions that it accepted these recommendations, subject to a regulatory impact assessment. In 2011, the Government confirmed that implementation of the recommendations is on hold pending negotiation of the Draft EU Consumer Rights Directive, which is expected to conclude late in 2011.[129] There is therefore good reason to believe that, notwithstanding the delay in taking action on the Commissions' 2005 Report, these recommendations may yet be implemented, with potentially valuable consequences for marginal older owners. If the Law Commissions' proposals for unfair terms are implemented, the 'clarifications' in approach evidenced in the Draft Bill, particularly the more detailed emphasis on context, could help in making the general consumer protection regime of greater relevance for marginal older owners. Of course, the application of the 'fair and reasonable' test would remain a matter of judgement on the facts of the individual case, but the more detailed guidance in draft schedule 1 seems likely to direct the courts towards taking account of the types of 'situational' factors that may influence the 'choices' that marginal older owners make in housing equity transactions when making their assessment of the 'fairness' of terms.

(6) Older Owners as 'Non-status Borrowers'

The Consumer Credit Act (CCA) 1974 (as amended by Consumer Credit Act 2006) also empowers the court to intervene where there is an 'unfair relationship' between a creditor and debtor,[130] although the exemptions to this provision are likely to exclude most

125 See ch 7, section 3(a).

126 Government Equality Office, *Equality Bill: Making it Work—Ending Age Discrimination in Services and Public functions, Policy Statement* (London, Government Equality Office, 2010), para 3.28, available online at <http://www.equalities.gov.uk/pdf/GEO_EqualityBillAge_acc.pdf>; see ch 7, section (3)(a).

127 Government Equalities Office, *Equality Act 2010: Banning Age Discrimination in Services, Public Functions and Associations* (London, TSO, 2011), paras 1.17, 6.6–6.10, available online at <http://www.equalities.gov.uk/pdf/110301%20Consultation%20doc.pdf>. This principle would apply so long as the approach is based on relevant information from a reasonably reliable source: *ibid*, para 1.18.

128 *Unfair Terms in Contracts: A Joint Consultation Paper*, above n 107, Draft Bill, cl 6(3).

129 <http://www.justice.gov.uk/lawcommission/unfair-terms-in-contracts.htm>.

130 CCA 1974, ss 140A–140B.

housing equity transactions. First, the Act applies only to credit transactions, so the 'sale-and-rent back' agreement—structured as an outright conveyance followed by the creation of a tenancy—clearly falls outside its ambit, as would a home reversion plan, which is structured as a sale of a share in the property rather than as a credit transaction. Other forms of mortgage product used to release housing equity—for example, lifetime mortgages, shared appreciation mortgages and so on—are also often excluded because the protections offered under the CCA 1974 do not apply to consumer credit agreements secured on land where those agreements are regulated by the Financial Services and Markets Act 2000.[131] However, second mortgages and unregulated housing equity transactions qualify for protection under the Act in respect of unfair relationships, and both are potential risk areas for marginal older owners if they do not opt for, or are not eligible for, the more 'mainstream' housing equity products.

Although the number of mainstream lenders offering targeted products to older owners has, on the whole, increased in the last few decades, recourse to the secondary and 'non-status' lending markets may result where the borrower's age, perhaps combined with a relatively low-value property, leaves him or her unable to obtain finance from primary lenders. The OFT has described 'non-status borrowers' as 'those with a poor credit rating who often find it difficult to obtain finance from traditional sources on normal terms and conditions'.[132] This lack of choice places these borrowers at a heightened risk of financial transactions which involve loans they cannot repay, high up-front fees or commissions which are not properly disclosed or explained,[133] and variable interest rates triggered by default.[134] The Court of Appeal has recognised that 'Non-status borrowers are a particularly vulnerable group of borrowers.'[135] Since much of the non-status market is for secured loans, these borrowers are most likely to be marginal owners,[136] with either low credit ratings (based on lack of verifiable income) or impaired credit ratings (where they have had financial difficulties in the past). Research has shown that

> the most vulnerable of them borrow because they face financial difficulties … usually to pay off existing commitments that have become unmanageable … People in this position usually have no other option for borrowing money and often take out agreements they have not read properly.[137]

The OFT has recognised that non-status borrowers 'may be less knowledgeable or experienced in financial matters than a generality of customers, and on the whole they are more vulnerable'.[138] The socio-economic vulnerabilities that expose these marginal older owners to non-status lending, in combination with the heightened risk of financial exclusion among elderly homeowners,[139] suggest that the protections against unfair relationships in the amended CCA 1974 may be of particular relevance.

[131] CCA 1974, s 16(6C).

[132] Report by the Comptroller and Auditor-General, *The Office of Fair Trading: Protecting the Consumer from Unfair Trading Practices* (HC 57, Session 1999–2000), para 2.17.

[133] *Ibid.*

[134] *Ibid.*

[135] *Broadwick Financial Services Ltd v Spencer and another* [2002] EWCA Civ 35 at [19].

[136] DTI, *Extortionate Credit in the UK: A Report to the DTI*, by E Kempson and C Whyley (London, DTI, 1999) at 26; available online at <http://webarchive.nationalarchives.gov.uk/+/http://www.dti.gov.uk/ccp/topics1/extortionate.htm>.

[137] *Ibid.*

[138] OFT, *Non-status Lending Guidelines for Lenders and Brokers* (London, OFT, November 1997), para 2.

[139] FSA, *In or Out? Financial Exclusion: A Literature and Research Review* (Consumer Research 3) (London, FSA, 2000) paras 3.1, 3.27, 3.30, 3.40, 4.4.

The OFT has taken various steps to discourage unfair practices in the non-status lending market,[140] including threatening to revoke licences where lenders do not comply with guidelines. In July 2009 it published guidelines for businesses engaged in second charge lending which have superseded its specific guidelines for non-status lenders,[141] and which sit alongside the OFT's *General Fitness Guidance*[142] and its guidance on *Irresponsible Lending*.[143] There is not space in this context to do justice to the considerable volume and complexity of regulatory activity in this area, although it is noted that this type of regulation is very much targeted at the conduct of the lender, seeking to discipline lenders into following acceptable procedures, and encouraging good practice in the ways in which they advertise, provide information to prospective consumers, draft terms in their agreements and enforce their claims. Prior to the enactment of the Consumer Credit Act 2006, the OFT emphasised the need for additional protections for 'vulnerable consumers',[144] although the provisions of the Act itself followed their general approach of encouraging lenders to follow fair commercial practices with all consumers rather than targeting protections at particular categories of borrower.

There are various reasons why vulnerable borrowers use non-status lenders. Research for the Policy Studies Institute has found that when older people use moneylenders, it is to manage the ups and downs of their household budget, or to pay specific household bills.[145] Research into the factors that make non-status borrowers vulnerable is also useful when considering more generally the 'borrower-sided' vulnerabilities associated with housing equity transactions. For example, research for the Department of Trade and Industry has found that the value of providing borrowers with information is greater where people borrow for 'discretionary or "*life enhancing*" reasons',[146] because they have the choice to shop around, or to choose not to borrow at all. Conversely,

> [t]hose borrowing to meet pressing needs, without other resources to draw on, frequently lack this choice and have little, if any, opportunity to shop around. Consequently, information imbalances are intensified by inequalities in bargaining power. It is the interaction between these two forces that provides the context for an extortionate credit market.[147]

This study also found that the total cost of credit is of limited relevance to low-income households when deciding to enter financial transactions, with greater weight given to factors such as accessibility of credit and manageability of repayments.[148] Crucially for any assessment of the value of legal protections under the 'information paradigm', despite the 'health warning' required on secured loans to advise borrowers that their home is at risk if

[140] OFT, above n 138 .

[141] OFT, *Second charge lending—OFT guidance for lenders and brokers* (OFT1105) (London, OFT, July 2009); online at <http://www.oft.gov.uk/about-the-oft/legal-powers/legal/cca/second-charge-lending>.

[142] OFT, *Consumer credit licensing: General guidance for licensees and applicants on fitness and requirements* (OFT 969) (London, OFT, 2008); available online at <http://www.oft.gov.uk/shared_oft/business_leaflets/credit_licences/oft969.pdf>.

[143] OFT, *Irresponsible Lending—OFT Guidance for Creditors* (OFT1107) (London, OFT, 2010); available online at <http://www.oft.gov.uk/shared_oft/business_leaflets/general/oft1107.pdf>.

[144] OFT, *Protecting vulnerable consumers—A note by the Office of Fair Trading in response to the DTI's consultation document on extortionate credit* (London, OFT, 2003); online at <http://www.oft.gov.uk/shared_oft/press_release_attachments/extcredit.pdf>.

[145] K Rowlingson, *Moneylenders and their customers* (London, Policy Studies Institute, 1994); cited in DTI, above n 136, at 16.

[146] DTI, above n 136, at 21.

[147] *Ibid.*

[148] *Ibid*, at 22.

they do not keep up repayments, the OFT has suggested that many consumers do not take any notice of these warnings, with 'Consumers who are most desperate to get a loan seldom read[ing] the agreements they are signing'.[149]

With evidence that consumer debt is increasing amongst older people,[150] older owners could also fall under the jurisdiction of the CCA 1974 when a debt[151] is incurred as an unsecured consumer debt but later charged against the owned home through a charging order, sometimes after taking out a debt consolidation loan. This area of vulnerability to extortionate credit can lead to some marginal older owners not so much *using* their housing equity as *losing* it. Research in this sector of the market has also emphasised that the nature of older people's vulnerability is rooted not in a lack of capacity, autonomy or inherent decision-making ability, but in the impact of transactions that do not meet their particular needs, objectives and circumstances.[152] Burden argued that older people should be recognised as a vulnerable consumer group because 'they may be exposed to a greater loss of welfare than other consumers as a result of buying inappropriate goods or services, or of failing to buy something when it would be in their interests to do so'.[153] Vulnerable older owners may also overlap with other vulnerable consumer groups, so compounding their vulnerability: for example, the discussion in chapter one has highlighted the overlap between low income and ageing; no formal educational qualifications also correlates strongly with low income and age[154]—older people are much less likely to have no formal educational qualifications than any other group[155]; and older people are more likely than the average population to suffer from limiting, longstanding illnesses,[156] as well as being most likely to suffer from deteriorating eyesight, hearing and mobility.[157]

The response of the Director General of the OFT to this evidence of vulnerability amongst consumers acknowledged that

> [m]uch consumer policy and regulation appears to assume that all consumers are the same. They are not. Some ... may experience greater difficulty in obtaining the information they need on particular goods and services. Others ... may suffer disproportionate losses when markets fail ... In initiating an inquiry into vulnerable consumers and financial services, I was therefore keen that we should not only develop a clearer idea of what is meant by consumer vulnerability but we should also apply this understanding in a practical way to a sector where I have concerns that the problems of vulnerability and exclusion are severe: the financial services sector.[158]

The report went on to suggest that, taking account of 'who benefits from financial services regulation and who pays for it ... the conclusion that financial regulation, in its widest sense, has failed to address the interests of vulnerable consumers is almost inescapable'.[159]

[149] *Ibid*, at 23.

[150] See ch 7, section (3).

[151] Until 2006 up to a maximum of £25,000, but since the Consumer Credit Act 2006 with no financial limit.

[152] For a discussion of various sources of vulnerability amongst older people, see ch 6.

[153] R Burden, *Vulnerable consumer groups: quantification and analysis* (Report prepared to the Office of Fair Trading, OFT Research Paper 15, OFT 219) (London, OFT, 1998) para 1.1.1.

[154] *Ibid*, para 2.1.4.

[155] *Ibid*, para 3.1.3, suggesting that this is probably a reflection of past educational and cultural trends.

[156] The 1995 *General Household Survey* indicated that two-fifths of elderly people suffered from a limiting, longstanding illness (Burden, above n 153, para 1.4.1), classified as including arthritis, asthma, recovering from heart attacks and mental illnesses: *ibid*, para 1.3.5.

[157] *Ibid*, paras 3.1.8–3.1.10.

[158] OFT, *Vulnerable Consumers and Financial Services: The Report of the Director General's Inquiry* (OFT 255) (London, OFT, 1999) Foreword at 3.

[159] *Ibid*.

This statement coincided with the creation of the FSA's regulatory regime, which in turn has gradually expanded its regulatory remit over housing equity products in the last decade.[160] A key message at the outset of the FSA's existence was the importance of adopting a contextual approach to regulation, specifically, that 'in assessing the benefits that flow from any regulatory or policy initiative intended to benefit consumers, government, regulators and those responsible for self-regulation should take far more account of consumers' relative incomes'.[161] Indeed, the OFT argued that the disproportionate impact of a financial loss to someone with a lower income 'makes a strong case for weighting consumer losses inversely to income in order to attach a greater importance to the problems of the vulnerable'.[162]

The OFT's 1999 report into vulnerable consumers and financial services focused on basic financial services, banking, home contents insurance, short-term consumer credit and long-term banking, rather than on the more complex products used by older owners to release housing wealth (and now regulated by the FSA). Nevertheless, its approach to contextual vulnerability (in this case, based on low income) supports the framework of analysis applied to the range of housing equity transactions considered in this book. In looking ahead, the OFT argued that the embryonic FSA 'should take more account of low-income consumers'[163] by weighting 'consumer detriment' according to income for the purposes of applying cost–benefit analysis to policy and regulatory initiatives aimed at consumer protection.[164] The OFT argued that 'From society's point of view, the costs of regulation should not outweigh the benefits. If this approach is not followed then regulation, however well-intended, will reduce consumption or exclude some products and consumers from the market altogether.'[165] The importance of contextual approaches to legal strategies relating to older owners and housing equity transactions have been emphasised throughout this book. However, as the analysis in chapter nine will show, the FSA's approach has been primarily oriented around product risk rather than consumer risk,[166] and has not specifically differentiated consumers based on their income levels or any other measure of vulnerability.

(7) The Consumer Credit Act 1974[167]

(a) 'Extortionate bargains'

Although many of the 'mainstream' housing equity transactions entered into by older owners are likely to fall outside the provisions of the CCA 1974, the provisions themselves remain of interest both because of their relevance for the most vulnerable borrowers, and as an example of a legislative framework which purports to emphasise the situation and

[160] See ch 9.
[161] OFT, above n 158.
[162] *Ibid*, Summary at 5.
[163] *Ibid*, at 6.
[164] *Ibid*, para 106.
[165] *Ibid*, para 400.
[166] Although, as the discussion in ch 9 will show, in some contexts, particularly sale and rent back, the consumer base has been taken into account when assessing the level of product risk.
[167] As amended by the Consumer Credit Act 2006.

context of the debtor as a central element of the assessment of fairness. The protection of the consumer credit legislation against unfair relationships was initially focused (in the 1974 Act) on 'extortionate credit bargains', thus to some extent filling the gap in the Unfair Terms in Consumer Contracts Regulations, which exclude consideration of the fairness of terms relating to price. Where the court found a credit bargain[168] to be extortionate, it was entitled to re-open the credit agreement so as to 'do justice' between the parties, which could include altering the terms, ordering the return of any security, setting aside the outstanding debt or ordering the creditor to repay money to the debtor.[169] A credit bargain could be deemed to be 'extortionate' if it required 'the debtor or a relative of his[170] to make payments (whether unconditionally, or on certain contingencies) which are grossly exorbitant',[171] or if the agreement 'otherwise grossly contravenes ordinary principles of fair trading'.[172]

In determining whether a credit bargain was 'extortionate', the court was directed to have regard to a wide range of factors, including prevailing interest rates at the time of the transaction,[173] a range of factors relating to the debtor and the creditor,[174] and 'any other relevant considerations'.[175] The factors relating to the debtor included:

a) his age, experience, business capacity and state of health; and
b) the degree to which, at the time of making the credit bargain, he was under financial pressure, and the nature of that pressure[176];

while factors relating to the creditor included:

a) the degree of risk accepted by him, having regard to the value of any security provided; and
b) his relationship to the debtor.[177]

The enumeration of these factors explicitly required the court to analyse the types of contextual factor which are likely to be particular relevant for marginal older owners, as well as the balance of risk and security for the creditor.

In applying the factors relating to the debtor, the court has taken account of the reason the borrower needed the money. For example, in *Ketley v Scott*,[178] the court noted that the 'financial pressure' on the consumer was caused by his desire to complete the purchase of his house, having already paid a deposit, but concluded that

[168] The 'credit bargain' was defined as the 'total charge for credit', which may be spread across one or more related transactions (CCA 1974, s 137(2)(b)) but which does not include variations in interest rates: *Nash and Staunton v Paragon Finance Plc* [2001] EWCA Civ 1466.
[169] CCA 1974, s 139.
[170] In recognition of the circumstances in which the debt is repaid after death from the debtor's estate.
[171] CCA 1974, s 138(1)(a).
[172] CCA 1974, s 138(1)(b).
[173] CCA 1974, s 138(2)(a).
[174] CCA 1974, s 138(2)(b).
[175] CCA 1974, s 138(2)(c).
[176] CCA 1974, s 138(3).
[177] CCA 1974, s 138(4).
[178] *Ketley v Scott* [1981] ICR 241.

> he could have forfeited the deposit and remained there under his protected tenancy. There was no question of his finding that he had no roof over his head. The fact that he wished to keep the reduced purchase price does not, in my judgment, amount to any real financial pressure.[179]

This potentially reflects a valuable distinction between cases in which the borrower makes a 'real' choice to enter the financial transactions—for example, where an older owner chooses to release equity to fund lifestyle-spending in retirement—and 'constrained' choices—where, for example, the money is needed for day-to-day living costs, for essential improvements to the property, or for health or personal care costs, and where the borrower could be viewed as under 'real financial pressure'.

While the 'extortionate credit bargain' provisions appeared, in theory, to be sensitive to the context of the transaction, including the age and experience of, and financial pressure on, the borrower, the provisions were not often invoked, and rarely successfully.[180] Even amongst those transactions which qualified for protection under the Act, the protection against 'extortionate credit bargains' was limited to the most extreme cases: the test of 'extortionate' was high, requiring 'gross contravention' of the principles of fair dealing.[181] This has been interpreted as meaning that, despite the legislative direction to the court to take account of factors relating to the debtor, the vulnerability of a debtor would not in itself be sufficient to re-open even an unreasonable bargain without there being 'morally reprehensible conduct on the part of the creditor in taking grossly unfair advantage of the debtor's circumstances [and an] element of moral culpability, in the form of abuse of power or bargaining position'.[182] While the burden was on the lender to demonstrate that the bargain was *not* extortionate, courts have been cautious in the application of the provisions, with even relatively high interest rates held to be defensible based on poor credit risk and the financial difficulties of the borrower.[183] In *Broadwick Financial Services Ltd v Spencer*, the Court of Appeal held that interest rates should be assessed against industry standards *for that type of loan*, for example, where it is a non-status loan, against the rates prevailing for other non-status loans at the time of the agreement, and taking account of the degree of risk accepted by the lender.[184] Notably, failing to follow the guidance issued by the OFT on good lending practice was not regarded as 'grossly contraven[ing] ordinary principles of fair dealing' for the purposes of section 138 of the 1974 Act.[185] Even where the court is prepared to find that relevant information has not been provided to borrowers, this has not amounted to 'a serious contravention of ordinary principles of fair dealing, still less a gross contravention' where there is no evidence that the borrowers would not have gone ahead with the transaction had they

[179] *Ibid*, at 247, *per* Foster J.

[180] Brown, above n 36, at 91.

[181] See, eg, *Broadwick Financial Services Ltd v Spencer* [2002] EWCA Civ 35.

[182] R Goode, *Consumer Credit Law and Practice* (para 27.26); cited in *Broadwick Financial Services Ltd v Spencer*, above n 181, at [79]. Professor Goode also stated that 'the concepts of extortion and unconscionability are very similar. "Extortionate", like "harsh and unconscionable", signifies not merely that the terms of the bargain are stiff, or even unreasonable, but that they are so unfair as to be oppressive' (*ibid*).

[183] See *Woodstead Finance Ltd v Petrou* [1986] 1 FLR 158, in which the court accepted evidence that a relatively high interest rate is normal for a short-term loan.

[184] *Broadwick Financial Services Ltd v Spencer*, above n 181, at [30]. Although it is also worth noting that while the fact that a term is usual is described as 'powerful evidence that the agreement is not extortionate'(at [77]), the court stopped short of allowing this to be conclusive (at [75]).

[185] *Ibid*, at [44].

received the information, and the policy is not regarded as 'inherently oppressive or unconscionable'.[186]

While agreeing with the leading judgment of Dyson LJ in *Broadwick v Spencer*, Walker LJ added that this was with some regret, as he was

> concern[ed] ... as to whether in a significant number of cases the provisions in sections 137ff of the Consumer Credit Act 1974 fail to achieve their purpose of protecting consumers, and especially 'non-status' borrowers who are unable to obtain credit on more favourable terms from primary lenders.[187]

Indeed, judges repeatedly commented on the complexity of the 'extortionate credit' provisions, and the limited protection they conferred.[188] It is particularly interesting to note that, in relation to the fact that the consumers in this case had not read the documents nor taken advice as recommended in the contract. Walker LJ suggested that failure adequately to comprehend the terms of an agreement may be a normal consequence of the pressure under which borrowers enter into non-status contracts:

> [T]o my mind there is no inconsistency between the notion that Mr Spencer's unemployment may have induced a sense of panic in him and his wife (they were first-time buyers with very limited means) and the sad fact that they did not adequately read or understand, or take advice about, the terms of the credit agreement.[189]

Walker LJ went on to add that the use of 'legislative safeguards', such as plain language, prominent warnings and 'cooling-off periods', 'may not in practice provide adequate protection for borrowers who do not have ready access to professional advice, and who feel that they have no alterative but to grasp what they can get as non-status borrowers'.[190] While there is no doubt that borrowers are best advised to seek advice as soon as they encounter financial difficulties, the court clearly recognised that in reality, the context or situation from which vulnerable borrowers enter into financial transactions can render this type of protection illusory.

(b) Consumer Credit Act 2006

The Consumer Credit Act (CCA) 2006 replaced the 'extortionate credit bargain' provisions of the CCA 1974 with sections 140A–140C. These provisions set out a new 'unfair relationship' test which gives the court far-reaching powers to intervene in credit transactions 'if it determines that the relationship between the creditor and the debtor arising out of the agreement ... is unfair to the debtor'[191] due to the terms, the way the terms are exercised, or resulting from 'any other thing done (or not done) by, or on behalf of, the creditor (either before or after the making of the agreement or any related agreement)'.[192] In determining whether the relationship is 'unfair', the court is directed to have regard to 'all matters it thinks relevant', including matters relating to the creditor and to the

[186] *Ibid*, at [57].

[187] *Ibid*, at [85].

[188] See also *McGinn v Grangewood Securities Ltd* [2002] EWCA Civ 522 at [1], [89], *per* Clark LJ; *Nash v Paragon Finance Plc* [2002] 1 WLR 685, 708–09, *per* Dyson LJ.

[189] *Broadwick Finanical Services Ltd v Spencer*, above n 181, at [88].

[190] *Ibid*, at [89].

[191] CCA 2006, s 140A(1).

[192] CCA 2006, s 140A(1)(c).

debtor.[193] Regulated mortgage contracts and regulated home purchase plans remain exempt from the Act,[194] which continues to apply to secondary mortgages, non-status credit agreements and unsecured credit. The court's powers under the Act include powers to amend the terms of the agreement, set aside a transaction, require the court to repay any money paid by the borrower, direct the return of property and discharge the debt.[195] Yet while Brown described the 'underlying basis of the desire for change [as] protection for the consumer, more particularly the vulnerable consumer and his/her exposure to unfair creditor behaviour',[196] and the new provisions have been heralded as offering 'wider and more flexible powers',[197] the Act provides little guidance on how those powers should be exercised in practice.

The 2006 Act followed a long period of pressure for reforms to make it easier for consumers to challenge extortionate credit agreements. From its 1991 report on *Unjust Credit Transactions*,[198] the OFT took the view that the courts' narrow interpretation of the CCA 1974 meant it had failed to protect vulnerable consumers, and that changes were needed to make it easier for consumers to challenge extortionate terms. The OFT recommended that the term 'extortionate credit' be replaced with 'unjust credit transaction', a test triggered by 'grossly excessive payments' or 'unfair or oppressive business activities'. In 1999, the Department of Trade and Industry published a report on extortionate credit by Kempson and Whyley[199] which argued that these proposals did not go far enough. Although this report emphasised that the problem of 'extortionate credit' was linked to practices followed by only a small number of lenders,[200] it highlighted a particular concern relating to non-status secured borrowing, or 'equity lending', 'where creditors are more interested in the security a borrower can offer than they are in the borrower's ability to meet the loan repayments'.[201] The Department of Trade and Industry's 2003 White Paper *Fair, Clear and Competitive—The Consumer Credit Market in the 21st Century*,[202] went further in arguing that the existing provisions had 'not been effective in dealing with the margins of the market, in particular, regarding credit to consumers on low incomes'.[203] This report went on to argue that 'The existing definition should be replaced with a test that would make agreements easier to challenge.'[204]

The amended Consumer Credit Act seeks to protect consumers who enter into 'regulated agreements' (within its scope) through a range of provisions which cover:

a) regulation of the form and content of agreements;
b) controlling credit advertising;
c) requiring detailed information to be given by creditors to consumers; and
d) providing relief from unfair relationships.

[193] CCA 2006, s 140A(2).
[194] CCA 2006, s 140A(5); CCA 2006, s 16(6C).
[195] CCA 2006, s 140B.
[196] Brown, above n 36, at 90.
[197] *Patel v Patel* [2009] EWHC 3264 (QB) at [55].
[198] OFT, *Unjust Credit Transactions – a report by the Director General of Fair Trading on the provisions of sections 137–140 of the Consumer Credit Act* (London, OFT, 1991).
[199] DTI, above n 136.
[200] *Ibid*, at 29.
[201] *Ibid*, at 34.
[202] Cm 6040, December 2003; available online at <http://www.berr.gov.uk/files/file23663.pdf>.
[203] *Ibid*, para 3.30.
[204] *Ibid*.

The first three areas are primarily 'provider-facing', inasmuch as they set minimum standards for, and impose obligations on, providers in the conduct of their business. Providers are required to give pre-contractual information,[205] and to present key information relating to the agreement clearly and prominently, with failure to comply potentially rendering an agreement unenforceable or subject to a court order.[206] The Consumer Credit (Advertisements) Regulations 2004 (SI 2004/1484) control the form and content of advertisements relating to consumer credit, including specifying the prominent display of a typical APR rate, and the 'health warning' on secured loans concerning the risk to the borrower's home. The 2006 Act has also put in place new post-contract transparency provisions and reformed the licensing system, with enhanced powers for the OFT. The OFT also has enforcement powers under Part 8 of the Enterprise Act 2002, which cover situations in which businesses infringe their legal obligations under EU regulations or breach domestic UK law, and as a result harm the collective interests of consumers.[207] However, contracts involving land have been excluded from these provisions, since they fall under the jurisdiction of the FSA regime, with the result that this additional level of enforcement is not available to consumers even within the limited category of Consumer Credit Act transactions affecting housing equity.

(c) Financial Ombudsman Service

An important aspect of the 2006 Act is the extension of the Financial Ombudsman Service's (FOS's) jurisdiction to allow consumers to refer complaints about licensed creditors, which the FOS can resolve based on what is fair and reasonable in all the circumstances.[208] The FOS has power to make a money award to compensate for financial loss, or other loss or damage suffered by the consumer, up to a limit of £100,000. While the court in *R (on the application of IFG Financial Services Ltd) v Financial Ombudsman Service Ltd*[209] held that the Ombudsman does not 'apply the law' but determines what is fair and reasonable in the circumstances, the County Court Judgments Rules in the *Financial Services Authority Handbook* indicate that the FOS will take account of the relevant law, regulations, guidance and codes of practice, as well as what he considers to have been good industry practice at the relevant time.[210] Brown has argued that it is likely, in practice, that the FOS will always be the consumer's favoured option, since the service is

[205] Consumer Credit (Disclosure of Information) Regulations 2004 (SI 2003/1481); while the implementation of the Consumer Credit Directive 2008 (2008/48/EEC) has triggered revised regulations on the information provided to consumers before they enter a credit agreement, the revised regulations do not apply to agreements secured on land: Consumer Credit (Disclosure of Information) Regulations 2010 (SI 2010/1013).

[206] Consumer Credit (Agreements) Regulations 1983 (SI 1983/1553), as amended by the Consumer Credit (Agreements) (Amendment) Regulations 2004 (SI 2004/1482). Again, the amendments in the Consumer Credit (Agreements) Regulations 2010, (SI 2010/1014) do not apply to land, although they will apply to agreements which are not secured on land *ab initio* but later charged against land under a charging order.

[207] See, eg, OFT, *Consumer Reforms: A Consultation Paper* (OFT No 502) (London, OFT, 2002), available online at <http://www.oft.gov.uk/shared_oft/business_leaflets/enterprise_act/oft502.pdf>.

[208] CCA 2006, s 5; Financial Services and Markets Act 2000, s 226A.

[209] [2005] EWHC 1153 (Admin).

[210] See *FSA Handbook*, DISP section 3.6.4; online at <http://fsahandbook.info/FSA/html/handbook/DISP/3/6>.

free and less onerous than going to court, with the consumer (but not the creditor) still having the option to appeal to court if he or she is unhappy with the outcome.[211]

The FOS has recognised its role in addressing the particular issues and concerns of older consumers.[212] Outreach initiatives to improve awareness and use of the service by older people, and to remind them of their right to use this free service, utilise hospital radio, magazines and websites aimed at older people, drop-in complaints clinics and presence at major events focused on older people, as well as partnerships with advice workers and community groups that work with older consumers. Recent cases involving older consumers have included alleged age discrimination in access to financial services and the need for the bank to provide an explanation when a loan was refused[213]; and a case upheld on the grounds that the salesperson had misrepresented the benefits of a product to persuade the consumer to buy it.[214]

In one case where an 80-year-old woman complained that she had been wrongly advised concerning an investment in a with-profits fund, the complaint was upheld notwithstanding the firm's argument that the consumer's previous employment meant that she understood investment risk. The FOS noted that she had already been retired for many years at the time she received the advice, and held that she was entitled to receive *appropriate* advice, regardless of what the firm assumed she might already know about investments.[215] It is particularly interesting to note that the product literature had explained the product sufficiently clearly, but that the FOS placed greater weight on the context of the transaction than the information provided, finding against the firm on the grounds that

> there was no evidence that the firm had considered the potential impact of these MVRs [market value reductions for cashing in the investment early] on the value of Mrs C's investment, given her age and the fact that she was unlikely to want her capital tied up for a lengthy period.[216]

The firm was penalised for failing to consider the appropriateness of its product for the specific, contextual needs, objectives and circumstances of this older borrower. Lastly, the FOS noted that

> [m]any firms consider it good practice, in cases where the investor is elderly or otherwise vulnerable, to suggest that a family member, friend or solicitor might wish to attend the discussion with the adviser. It is, of course, entirely up to the consumer to decide whether they want to be accompanied when dealing with their financial affairs. But in this case, Mrs C was not told this was an option.[217]

The importance of good quality *advice*, rather than merely *information*, was also emphasised in another case which was upheld by the FOS, and in which the FOS told the firm

211 Brown, above n 36, at 109.

212 In 2007–08, 14% of the consumers who brought complaints to the FOS were aged between 55 and 64, and 23% were over 65; see <http://www.financial-ombudsman.org.uk/publications/ombudsman-news/74/74-older-customers.html>. See also <http://www.financial-ombudsman.org.uk/news/updates/older_consumers.html>.

213 FOS case 74/02, details online at <http://www.financial-ombudsman.org.uk/publications/ombudsman-news/74/74-older-customers.html>.

214 FOS case 74/03, details online at <http://www.financial-ombudsman.org.uk/publications/ombudsman-news/74/74-older-customers.html>.

215 FOS case 74/04, details online at <http://www.financial-ombudsman.org.uk/publications/ombudsman-news/74/74-older-customers.html>.

216 *Ibid.*

217 *Ibid.*

that 'it could not fulfil its responsibility for providing a client with suitable advice by simply handing her a brochure'.[218] Advisers are clearly expected to take account of the risks that the consumer faces in making financial decisions for retirement.[219] The particular vulnerability of older consumers to risky financial transactions was also recognised in the controversial FOS decision against Norwich & Peterborough Building Society, in which the core of the Ombudsman's reasoning was that the bond was 'inherently too risky' for older consumers, and that it was not accepted that a retired couple would have been prepared to purchase this product at this stage of their lives if they were fully aware of the risks.[220] It is also interesting to note that, in addition to the 'damages' ordered for financial losses by consumers in cases it has upheld, the FOS has often also required the payment of an additional sum, to compensate the consumer for the 'distress and inconvenience' caused.[221]

While the case reports from the FOS suggest that it is sympathetic to the idea that older consumers experience a specific, heightened risk environment which lenders and advisers who offer financial services must take into account, this approach is not typical of the judicial application of fairness provisions in contract and consumer credit regulations, in which, as the discussion below illustrates further, 'freedom' rather than 'fairness' perspectives have continued to dominate the courts' reasoning. Wadsley has suggested that the statutory status of the FOS[222] 'allows him to take a more independent, less respectful view of the banks' claim to freedom from restraint in commercial decisions'.[223] This appears to be borne out in cases involving older consumers, where the FOS has attached considerably greater weight to the contextual vulnerabilities associated with age, lack of financial expertise, the limitations of information and the particularly adverse impact of financial losses on older people than has typically been evident in judicial decisions under the fairness provisions.

(d) 'Unfair relationships'

The CCA 2006 also introduced a new 'unfair relationships' test that confers wider powers on the court to provide remedies where the relationship between the creditor and the borrower is deemed to be unfair. The language of the 'unfair relationships' test is not only wider than the limited practical protection offered by the 'extortionate bargain' test,[224] it

[218] FOS case 74/05, details online at http://www.financial-ombudsman.org.uk/publications/ombudsman-news/74/74-older-customers.html.

[219] FOS case 74/06, details online at http://www.financial-ombudsman.org.uk/publications/ombudsman-news/74/74-older-customers.html.

[220] See news reports at http://www.bbc.co.uk/news/business-11011507; http://www.thisismoney.co.uk/news/article.html?in_article_id=512585&in_page_id=2.

[221] FOS cases, 74/02, 74/03, 74/06, details online at http://www.financial-ombudsman.org.uk/publications/ombudsman-news/74/74-older-customers.html.

[222] The FOS emerged out of several private Ombudsmen from the early 1980s before receiving statutory footing in the Financial Services and Markets Act 2000, extended in the CCA 2006.

[223] J Wadsley, 'Bank lending and the family home: prudence and protection' [2003] *Lloyd's Maritime and Commercial Law Quarterly* 341, 358.

[224] Office of Fair Trading, *Review of High Cost Credit, Interim Research Report*, Annexe D (OFT 1150d), (London, OFT, 2009), para 4, available online at <http://www.oft.gov.uk/shared_oft/reports/consumer_credit/oft1150d.pdf>. The 'extortionate bargain' test was been described as 'not in practice a significant tool to protect consumers', since the courts were prepared to intervene only in 'outrageous circumstances': *ibid*, para 8.1, whereas the new 'unfair relationships' test, on paper at least, gives the court power to intervene in relation to

also appears to cast the spotlight more firmly onto the particular circumstances between the individual borrower and lender, rather than the more objective question of the terms of the agreement *per se*. While contextual factors could be taken into account under the old test, this was only to determine whether the agreement was extortionate. The new test allows the court to consider all matters, at any stage of the relationship, to determine whether the relationship was unfair, and (in contrast to the Unfair Terms in Consumer Contracts Regulations) to consider both 'core' and 'non-core' terms, potentially empowering the court to set aside 'a valid but inexpedient bargain'.[225] The DTI White Paper indicated that the factors to be taken into account by the court could include unfair practices,[226] unfair credit costs,[227] irresponsible lending[228] and other relevant circumstances, such as the borrower's circumstances, including his or her age, experience, business capacity and state of health.[229] Brown suggested that the emphasis on responsible lending in the Discussion Paper which prompted the 2006 Act, particularly in relation to careless lending to debtors in financial difficulty which may exacerbate the problems of vulnerable consumers already struggling with over-commitment, may inform the application of the unfair relationship test.[230] These factors have not, however, been carried across into any statutory guidance concerning the meaning of unfairness in a credit relationship, and it remains to be seen whether judicial interpretation of sections 140A–140C will result in a more contextual approach, or lead the court to attach weight to the subjective characteristics of the borrower.

One continuing concern under the new provisions is that the emphasis on the nature and type of the loan, while explicitly intended to protect the lender by recognising the higher risk associated with certain types of loans, may also have the effect of nullifying the protection for the most vulnerable consumers. While

> onerous terms, hidden in the small print of the agreement and imposed on the debtor will also readily fall within the category of unfair [as will] ... excessive costs, for example interest disproportionately high within the market-place or other charges or costs of which the borrower may be unaware[,][231]

the reference to 'context' has been used by the courts to justify these terms, so that 'What may seem unfair, expensive or onerous may be justified where, for example, the debtor is

credit agreements not only as regards the cost of credit or the financial terms of the agreement, but also where it considers that the credit relationship is unfair, so enabling consumers to challenge credit bargains in more ways than before.

[225] Brown, above n 36, at 100.

[226] Eg, misleading, harassing, coercing or otherwise unduly influencing the borrower in connection with the transaction; mis-selling of products, unacceptable high-pressure selling techniques or aggressive debt-collection practices.

[227] Eg, considering whether credit payments substantially exceed market levels, although this must be considered in light of the nature and type of the agreement and the circumstances in which it was made, or how the lender has subsequently acted.

[228] Including failing to take reasonable steps to ensure the consumer's creditworthiness and ability to meet the full terms of the agreement at the time it was concluded, but also bearing in mind that different approaches to responsible lending are required for different sectors of the market.

[229] DTI White Paper, *Fair, Clear and Competitive: The Consumer Credit Market in the 21st Century* (Cm 6040) (London, TSO, 2003) para 3.37.

[230] Brown, above n 36, at 102–03.

[231] *Ibid*, at 99.

very high risk.'[232] For example, in *Khodari v Al Tamimi*,[233] the court held that the high costs of the loan were balanced against the credit risk to the lender. In this case, the defendant could afford the repayments, and had clearly wanted the loan,[234] although these factors may not have been decisive. In *Nine Regions (T/A Logbook Loans) v Sadeer*,[235] the court held that since a 'last resort' loan[236] was of higher risk for the lender, it naturally attracted a higher interest rate (in this case, 384.4 per cent APR), and so did not give rise to an unfair relationship. In *Barons Finance Ltd v Olubisi*,[237] the court found that there was an unfair relationship within section 140A. Although the facts were quite extreme—the agreement had not been properly executed, the interest rate on the loan was 3.5 per cent per month calculated on a day-to-day basis of the balance outstanding each month, and there had been flagrant breaches of the Consumer Credit Act and the 1983 Consumer Credit (Agreements) Regulations, as well as the fact that the loan was made in circumstances in which the borrower desperately needed to obtain the loan in order to stave off possession proceedings (the loan took place two days before the date fixed for the possession hearing)—it does indicate that the court will take account of the borrower's vulnerability and the lender's exploitation of that vulnerability to charge 'usuriously high' interest rates.

Together these cases strike a cautionary note concerning the 'contextual' approach, which in this context led to greater emphasis being placed on the risks taken by a lender who provided credit to a consumer in financial difficulties, perhaps for a lower-value security,[238] than on the financial pressure on the debtor. Thus, while the ability of the consumer to challenge any term in the agreement offers a potentially useful protection for some consumers,[239] the courts have continued to protect the freedom of commercial lenders to conduct their business according to their own best interests,[240] and it is not evident that the adverse circumstances of the borrower will necessarily make a court more sympathetic to the consumer rather than the lender who was willing to take on the higher risk of transacting with an improvident borrower.

Raising minimum standards in relation to the licensing system, enhanced powers of the OFT to act against traders who breach its requirements,[241] as well as the development of stricter rules regarding advertising, information and the form, content and execution of

[232] *Ibid.*

[233] [2008] EWHC 3065 (QB).

[234] Brown, above n 36, at 99.

[235] Bromley County Court, 14 January 2009; discussed in OFT, *Review of High Cost Credit, Interim Research Report*, Annexe D (OFT 1150d) (London, OFT, 2009) para 8.46 *et seq*; available online at <http://www.oft.gov.uk/shared_oft/reports/consumer_credit/oft1150d.pdf>.

[236] Usually made to a debtor with poor credit records and, in this case, with limited security.

[237] Mayor's and City of London Court, 26 April 2010, Claim No: 7BB82089; see <http://www.oft.gov.uk/shared_oft/business_leaflets/consumer_credit/unfair-relationships/barons-finance-olubisi.pdf>.

[238] See also *Castle Phillips & Co Ltd v Wilkinson* [1992] *Consumer Credit Law Reports* 83 on the importance of the value of the security in determining whether a credit bargain is extortionate.

[239] Eg, an unfair relationship was established in *MBNA Europe Bank Ltd v Thorius* (South Shields county court, 21 September 2009), where the failure of the lender to disclose that it received a commission from the sale of a payment protection insurance policy with a credit card was held to give rise to an unfair relationship; discussed in OFT 1150d, above n 236, para 8.52 *et seq.*

[240] *Paragon Finance v Pender* [2005] EWCA 760; see also *Paragon Finance v Nash* [2001] EWCA Civ 1466 at [47], where Dyson LJ stated that 'The claimant is not a charitable institution. Its aim is to make a profit by lending money.'

[241] CCA 1974, s 39(A).

credit agreements,[242] will benefit all consumers, including the most vulnerable. However, on the limited case law available there is little evidence that the 'unfair relationships' test will be dramatically more effective than the extortionate bargain test in enabling the contextual vulnerabilities of consumers to be met with enhanced protection. It is clear that the most vulnerable consumers are likely to be those who fall into more than one of the groups identified in the OFT's research,[243] for example, elderly and low-income (marginal), with low-income identified as the most common unifying factor across the range of categories of vulnerability.[244] While it is important to weigh the context on both sides of the transaction, higher exposure to risk goes hand in hand with lending to low-income borrowers,[245] and the evidence that higher risk for the lender weighs more heavily in the balance than the financial pressure on the borrower suggests that the redress available to marginal older borrowers under the 'unfair relationship' provisions of the consumer credit legislation will be limited. In addition, the onus remains on the debtor to raise the issue, and while the scope of the new test may be wider, the lack of guidelines is unhelpful in overcoming judicial reluctance to interfere with voluntary agreements.

(8) Consumer Protection from Unfair Trading Regulations 2008

The last category of general protection considered in this chapter is the Consumer Protection from Unfair Trading Regulations 2008 (SI 2008/1277) ('the 2008 Regulations'), which regulate commercial practices before, during and after the contract. These Regulations implement the EU Unfair Commercial Practices Directive[246] by imposing a general duty on traders not to trade unfairly and to seek to ensure that they act honestly and fairly towards customers. They apply to any act, omission and other conduct by businesses before, during or after a contract is made, which is directly connected to the promotion, sale or supply of a product to or from consumers. The definition of 'products' to which the 2008 Regulations apply has been drafted widely to include 'any goods or service and includes immovable property, rights and obligations', thus explicitly including land contracts.[247]

The definition of 'unfair commercial practices' includes those practices which are misleading (by action or omission, for example, concerning the risks of the product)[248] or aggressive and which cause the consumer to take a transactional decision he or she would not otherwise have taken.[249] Traders must not omit, hide or fail to provide in a clear, intelligible, unambiguous and timely way, the 'material information' relating to the product, defined as 'the information which the average consumer needs, according to the

[242] See *Wilson v First County Trust Ltd* [2003] UKHL 40 for an example of the court's willingness to render agreements unenforceable where a lender fails to comply with the documentary formalities.

[243] Burden, above n 153.

[244] OFT, above n 158.

[245] See, eg, G McCarthy, S Van Zandt and WM Rohe, *The Economic Costs and Benefits of Home Ownership: A Critical Assessment of the Research* (Washington, DC, Research Institute for Housing America, 2001) 31–32.

[246] Directive 2005/29/EC.

[247] Reg 2(1).

[248] Regs 5(4)(b) and 5(5)(c).

[249] Reg 3.

context, to take an informed transactional decision'.[250] This formulation is interesting for the purposes of the different types of vulnerabilities examined in this book. Measuring material information according to what the 'average consumer' needs implies an objective approach to vulnerability—that is, to the capabilities of the person to process the information cognitively—but at the same time the reference to context allows scope for considering the effects of situational vulnerability, for example the degree of financial pressure on the consumer when making the decision.

The 2008 Regulations also apply where firms provide false or deceptive information, or engage in pressure selling or prohibited practices (for example, falsely claiming to be a signatory to a code of conduct). Regulation 7, dealing with aggressive commercial practices, identifies harassment, coercion and undue influence as prohibited practices, and again emphasises the importance of context or situational vulnerability in determining whether an offence has been committed. It specifies that

> In determining whether a commercial practice uses harassment, coercion or undue influence account shall be taken of—
>
> (a) its timing, location, nature or persistence;
> (b) the use of threatening or abusive language or behaviour;
> (c) the exploitation by the trader of any specific misfortune or circumstance of such gravity as to impair the consumer's judgment, of which the trader is aware, to influence the consumer's decision with regard to the product…

While the 2008 Regulations are clearly 'provider-facing', the duty on traders is measured with reference to the (discoverable) impact on the individual consumer's decision-making abilities. Regulation 7 also provides an interesting formulation of 'undue influence', which is described as

> exploiting a position of power in relation to the consumer so as to apply pressure, even without using or threatening to use physical force, in a way which significantly limits the consumer's ability to make an informed decision.[251]

The emphasis on the effect of the pressure on the consumer's ability to make an informed decision raises issues which are considered further in the discussion of undue influence as an equitable remedy in chapter ten.

Schedule 1 to the 2008 Regulations sets out a list of 31 specific commercial practices which are unfair in all circumstances and prohibited, and which include:

> 25. Conducting personal visits to the consumer's home ignoring the consumer's request to leave or not to return, except in circumstances and to the extent justified to enforce a contractual obligation;
>
> 26. Making persistent and unwanted solicitations by telephone, fax, e-mail or other remote media except in circumstances and to the extent justified to enforce a contractual obligation.

These types of practice have been associated with financial abuse of older people, discussed further in chapter six, and their explicit inclusion in the 2008 Regulations is welcome. The OFT has also suggested that the Regulations may be of particular value for SRB consumers, as misleading statements about the security of tenure they acquire under

[250] Reg 6(3)(a).
[251] Reg 7(3)(b).

the rent-back transaction, or misleading advertisements, would be covered by the prohibitions.[252]

It is also notable that the 'consumer benchmark'—the 'average consumer' by which it is determined whether practices would be viewed as misleading, or allegedly aggressive practices would be likely significantly to impair freedom of choice—can shift according to the characteristics of particular groups of consumers who are 'particularly vulnerable to the practice or the underlying product because of their mental or physical infirmity, age or credulity in a way which the trader could reasonably be expected to foresee',[253] or where practices are directed at a particular group.[254] Willett has argued that this 'articulated consumer benchmark' should allow scope for considering the procedural capabilities of the average member of the relevant consumer group (ie, his or her ability to protect his or her own interests in the decision-making process), while the foreseeability test on the trader's side requires that—for the particular consumer group—the trader bear some responsibility for meeting a higher standard of fairness for more vulnerable consumers.[255] It is also worth noting that in relation to practices targeted at particular consumer groups, there is no requirement to demonstrate vulnerability in order for the standard to be adjusted. Willett—correlating the mischief of the protection and the characteristics of the benchmark group—argued that in relation to these particular consumer groups, the differentiated impact of substantive risks and consequences could also be taken into account when assessing whether a practice is 'unfair' within the meaning of the Regulations, but that this would be relevant only where particular consumer groups are identified by financial resources, for example where a financially vulnerable group are targeted with a particular product.[256] The 2008 Regulations thus provide an example of a fairness regime where the standard required from the trader is directly linked to the characteristics—the procedural and substantive vulnerabilities—of particular categories of consumer.

A distinctive, and significantly limiting, characteristic of the enforcement provisions of the 2008 Regulations is that they do not provide any route to direct redress for consumers who have been harmed by breaches of the prohibitions, neither do they affect the enforceability of the contract; at present there is no private law remedy for breach of the unfairness standard set out in the Regulations.[257] Regulations 8 to 13 identify various criminal offences which are constituted by the unfair practices identified in regulations 3 to 7, and regulation 19 imposes a duty on enforcement authorities to enforce the Regulations; the UK Government deliberately excluded any civil law remedies from the Regulations.[258] As a result, the consumer has no private right of action in relation to

[252] OFT, OFT 1018, above n 91, para 3.65.

[253] Unfair Commercial Practices Directive, above n 247, Art 5(3)(i).

[254] *Ibid*, Art 5(3)(ii).

[255] C Willett, 'Unfairness under the Consumer Protection from Unfair Trading Regulations 2008' in M Kenny, J Devenney and L Fox O'Mahony (eds), *Unconscionability in European Private Financial Transactions: Protecting the Vulnerable* (Cambridge, Cambridge University Press, 2010) 368–69.

[256] *Ibid*, at 371.

[257] Although the Government has raised the issue of private redress and asked the Law Commission for advice on introducing such a remedy: see Law Commission, *A Private Right of Redress for Unfair Commercial Practices* (London, Law Commission, 2008); online at <http://www.lawcom.gov.uk/docs/rights_of_redress_advice.pdf>.

[258] *McGuffick v Royal Bank of Scotland plc* [2009] EWHC 2386 (Comm) at [91].

breaches of the provisions and regulation 29 provides that agreements shall not be rendered void or unenforceable by reason only of a breach of the Regulations.[259]

This may be contrasted with the hybrid administrative/judicial approach of the Unfair Terms in Consumer Contracts Regulations 1999, which combines private judicial redress with systemic administrative sanctions, in recognition of the limits of reliance on private action alone in addressing the widespread use of unfair terms.[260] On the one hand, private action is limited by the fact that the most vulnerable debtors are rarely likely to seek relief from the courts, due to receiving no, or inadequate, legal advice or being unaware of their rights.[261] Vulnerable debtors may also lack the financial resources to bring a case to court, or experience practical, psychological or cultural barriers to litigation.[262] These factors are compounded by the relatively short time a district judge will have to assess terms and contextual issues.[263] For the most vulnerable consumers, the disciplinary model of the 2008 Regulations may prove effective in addressing unfair commercial practices, including cases where these practices are deemed unfair by reference to particular groups. To date there has been little case law through which to explore this issue. While the content of the Regulations appears to offer some protection for older owners who are vulnerable to unfair commercial practices because of situational factors, the approach taken is 'provider-facing', inasmuch as it seeks to discipline traders into good practices rather than to address harms to individual consumers. While this is a legitimate medium-term goal for any regulatory provision, and may prevent harms occurring in some cases, it does not provide any mechanism to ameliorate the harms suffered by consumers where the trader does not respond appropriately to the disciplinary regime. This gap between the risk of harms, and the mechanisms by which disciplinary or regulatory measures seek to protect consumers, is discussed further in chapter nine. Its significance in relation to marginal older owners is emphasised in light of the argument that older people are disproportionately disadvantaged through the impact of financial harms because they are not well-placed to recover from bad outcomes.[264]

(9) Conclusions

The provisions discussed in this chapter are illustrative of the approach taken in the general law towards fairness in contracts and consumer credit agreements. Since the regulation of specialised housing equity products has been taken over by the FSA, many of these general provisions apply primarily at the margins of the market. In one sense, this emphasises their particular importance, since it is the non-status borrowers, or those whose debt expands, quantitatively and qualitatively, from consumer credit to securitised

259 See also *ibid* at [86]–[97].

260 See Bright, above n 36, p352.

261 OFT, *Protecting Vulnerable Consumers—A note by the Office of Fair Trading in response to the DTI's consultation document on extortionate credit* (London, OFT, 2003) para 24; online at <http://www.oft.gov.uk/shared_oft/press_release_attachments/extcredit.pdf>.

262 DTI, *Extortionate Credit in the UK: A Report to the DTI*, by E Kempson and C Whyley (London, DTI, 1999) 31–32; available online at <http://webarchive.nationalarchives.gov.uk/+/http://www.dti.gov.uk/ccp/topics1/extortionate.htm>.

263 *Ibid*, at 32.

264 Discussed in ch 6.

borrowing, perhaps via debt consolidation, who are least able to be strategic about how they spend their housing equity and are most vulnerable to unfair transactions. The OFT has claimed that 'Our job is to make sure that consumers can exercise choice across all the different sectors of the economy while companies compete for their business. When consumers have choice they have genuine and enduring power.'[265] Yet the idea of consumer 'choice' in a competitive market is constrained when the products available to those who are viewed as 'high-risk' borrowers—also likely to be the most marginal or vulnerable consumers—contain terms which are unfair and likely to be non-negotiable.

The provisions discussed in this chapter demonstrate how law has intervened to achieve a greater measure of 'fairness' for all consumers, including—and sometimes with an emphasis on—vulnerable consumers. While there has been considerable activity in recent years to set standards of commercial practice in areas such as control over credit advertising and unfair marketing or sales practices, and the form and content of information given to consumers before, in and after transactions, the immediate impact of these types of measure is largely reliant on the willingness of good lenders to engage with the regulatory frameworks and follow good practices. Where lenders do not engage productively with the OFT and FSA, the authorised agency, or in some cases individual consumers, may bring an action for enforcement or seeking redress (for example, under the Unfair Terms in Consumer Contracts Regulations, or under the 'unfair relationships' provision in the Consumer Credit Act).

Yet when it comes to judicial adjudication, the case law has indicated that, notwithstanding the broad powers given to the courts under these provisions—including explicit direction to focus on the context of the transaction, for example the borrower's age, state of health or degree of financial pressure—context has not, in fact, played a significant role in assisting vulnerable borrowers to achieve redress. Indeed, where it has been influential, this has tended to benefit the lender, with the court recognising the risks associated with lending to marginal or non-status borrowers as a justification for higher interest rates or more stringent terms. Kempson and Whyley, in a report to the Department for Trade and Industry, have suggested that judicial uncertainty concerning the application of the fairness provisions has meant that

> judges have seemed reluctant to be 'too interventionist' particularly in relation to agreements which individuals have entered into of their own free will. Consequently, they have only been prepared to intervene in very clear-cut cases [and] some of the factors which the courts were intended to take into account, such as the borrower's personal characteristics; the financial pressure s/he was under at the time they made the agreement; and the relationship between the lender and borrower, have carried very little weight.[266]

They went on to state:

> In contrast to the limited use of borrower-related factors, those relating to creditors have been applied rather more often in reaching judgments. The level of risk that lenders have accepted in lending to some individuals has been afforded 'considerable importance'.[267]

[265] OFT, *Criminal Enforcement of the Consumer Protection from Unfair Trading Regulations 2008, OFT Policy* (September 2010) (OFT 1273), para 1.2; online at <http://www.oft.gov.uk/shared_oft/policy/OFT1273.pdf>.

[266] DTI, above n 262, at 33.

[267] *Ibid.*

The provisions discussed in this chapter are useful in highlighting the tensions that characterise attempts to use law to protect consumers in financial transactions. At the most fundamental level, there is a philosophical conflict between freedom of contract and market-led competition on the one hand, and intervention to ensure fairness and adequate consumer protection on the other. Debates about freedom of contract and market failure as a moral justification for legal intervention are complex and 'plastic',[268] with the overarching values of 'welfare', 'autonomy' and 'avoidance of harm' variously invoked both to support the freedom principle and to justify limits on the freedom approach in pursuit of fairness. Collins concluded that these arguments

> can do little to contribute to resolving the paradoxes of the debates about freedom of contract ... for, without some criterion for determining the types and degrees of market failure which justify restriction of freedom of contract, these considerations leave the desired scope for freedom of contract indeterminate.[269]

This, in turn, makes it difficult for courts to apply fairness provisions, since the balancing of competing interests, and the philosophical and economic theories underpinning them, are too complex and contested to be properly scrutinised and evaluated in the summary timeframe of typical debt proceedings. Nevertheless, the outcome may well be influenced by the court's implicit value judgements concerning freedom of contract and fairness: for example, even where contextual factors are emphasised in fairness provisions designed to protect consumers, their effect depends on the weight the court gives to the risks taken by the lender as well as the vulnerabilities of the borrower. The paradox of this exercise is that the risks taken by the lender weigh most heavily in cases where the consumer is most vulnerable: there is evidence to indicate that the courts have placed greater weight on the potential losses to the lender who has been willing to lend to a high-risk consumer, than on the consumer who has (in theory, and notwithstanding financial pressure) 'freely' entered into the contract.

The effect of fairness provisions is also dependent on the enforcement mechanisms available to any given individual in the particular context, and these can range from criminal or civil actions by administrative agencies such as the OFT or FSA, to individual judicial actions brought by the consumer. For example, while the right to bring judicial actions may appear to ensure that specific harms are remedied for the individual consumer, the evidence suggests systemic barriers leave the most vulnerable consumers least likely to bring such actions. This is exacerbated in relation to marginal *older* consumers, for whom the impact of the harm may be such that they are further disabled from bringing an action to seek relief.[270] On the other hand, the reach of administrative mechanisms—whether through FSA undertakings or court actions brought by the administrative agency—is inherently limited. The main objective of the good practice guidelines set out by the OFT and FSA, or of criminal sanctions such as those contained in the 2008 Regulations, is to improve trader behaviour over a period of time, so creating a safer environment for future transactions, rather than to control unfairness or achieve remedies specific to individual consumers.[271]

[268] H Collins, 'Review of *Michael J Trebilcock*, The Limits of Freedom of Contract' (1995) 58 *MLR* 446, 448.

[269] *Ibid.*

[270] See further discussion in ch 9 relating to the factors that discourage older people from bringing court actions following adverse financial transactions.

[271] Brown, above n 36, at 92.

The FSA, OFT, FOS and other such bodies have limited resources to pursue actions, and so cannot investigate all complaints but must strategically select the most appropriate cases to pursue from amongst complaints made. At the same time there is evidence of a 'dynamic approach' being taken towards consumer credit in recent years[272]: in addition to a more comprehensive approach towards the regulation of marketing, advertisement and information provided with consumer credit products, the FSA has been active (and seemingly more oriented towards 'fairness' than the courts) in obtaining undertakings from firms in cases involving unfair terms in housing equity products, and the case reports from the FOS suggest that it is sympathetic to the idea that older consumers experience a specific, heightened risk environment which lenders and advisers engaged in financial transactions with them must take into account. The development of regulatory frameworks oriented around the specific needs of older consumers is also implicit to the extension of the FSA's jurisdiction over 'specialised' housing equity products targeted at older owners. These specific regulatory strategies are examined in chapter nine.

[272] *Ibid*, at 109.

9

Targeted Housing Equity Products and FSA Regulation

(1) Introduction

In the last decade, the Financial Services Authority (FSA) has been progressively charged with regulatory responsibilities for specified housing equity products, and this chapter analyses the nature and extent of FSA regulation in this context, including the extent to which it is fit for the purpose of protecting the vulnerable older and marginal consumers at whom these products are often targeted. The Government has recognised that housing equity transactions constitute 'a huge financial decision involving the most important and sometimes only significant asset of elderly people. It can have significant implications for tax, benefits, inheritance and long-term financial planning, which need to be considered very carefully.'[1] The complexity of both the products themselves and the risk contexts in which older owners must plan for their financial futures, has prompted a raft of regulatory rules and guidance to govern three specific types of product targeted either exclusively at older people (lifetime mortgages, home reversion plans) or at marginal owners, including older owners (sale-and-rent back transactions).

One of the main strategies of statutory regulation in this context has been to ensure that firms provide sufficient (and sufficiently clear) information and, in some cases, advice concerning the products on offer, which neoliberal, self-responsible consumers can then apply to make rational, self-interested financial decisions best suited to their needs. The regulatory regimes have been tailored to each product type, in light of the structure of the transaction, the typical risks posed to consumers and the nature of the consumer base. For example, evidence that sale-and-rent back consumers are particularly vulnerable as marginal owners under imminent financial pressure informed a regulatory scheme that fixes the provider with greater responsibility to ensure that the product is suitable for the individual consumer's needs, objectives and circumstances. The sale-and-rent back regime recognises the differential abilities of consumers to manage their decision-making based on factors including their experience in financial transactions and the situation or context in which they are entering the transaction (for example, the financial pressure they are under). It also suggests a new willingness to attribute responsibility to the provider for the risks to which the consumer is exposed, with important implications for the evolving legal subjectivity of marginal (older) consumers.[2]

[1] *Hansard*, HL Deb, 17 October 2005, col 554 (Lord McKenzie).
[2] See especially ch 4.

One consequence of the shift to FSA regulation has been the increasing use of the language of 'safety' in relation to equity release, both by product providers and by charitable organisations such as Age Concern (now merged with Help the Aged to become 'Age UK'),[3] which seek to steer elders towards equity release products which are regulated and so perceived to be 'safe'. The FSA's statutory objectives include ensuring an 'appropriate' level of consumer protection, and it governs creditor activities through a combination of statutory rules and guidance for good practice. The *Mortgages and Home Finance Conduct of Business Sourcebook* (MCOB), which sets out provisions relating to conventional mortgages, lifetime mortgages, home reversion plans and sale-and-rent back (SRB) agreements,[4] emphasises the processes by which the products are advertised, explained and sold to consumers (with specific rules for pre-application disclosure,[5] disclosure at the offer stage[6] and post-sale disclosure[7]).

The analysis in this book has emphasised the extent to which contextual or situational factors may leave even an informed (and advised) consumer vulnerable and unable to make a 'rational' decision.[8] At the same time, the FSA's regulatory regime is intended to build consumer confidence in 'safe' housing equity products targeted at older people.[9] The gap between the limits of the regulatory regime and the risks posed to consumers is brought into sharp relief by the FSA's statutory objective of maintaining confidence in the financial system: if consumer confidence is based on the existence of regulation, so that more older owners enter into regulated transactions (or choose a regulated product rather than an unregulated product), this in turn generates a degree of responsibility on the FSA for ensuring that these products are, in fact, reasonably 'safe'. This chapter outlines the nature and extent of the consumer protection offered by the FSA, and in doing so emphasises the gap between the risks which older people take in financial transactions involving their owned home, and the (in some cases intentionally) limited reach of the regulatory regime. Underpinning this gap are debates about the limits of the information paradigm in addressing the vulnerabilities of (certain groups of) consumers, and the question of whether consumer protections should be limited to 'defendant-sided' issues such as misconduct on the part of providers, or include 'claimant-sided' considerations relating to the vulnerabilities (including the needs, objectives and circumstances) of the particular consumer.

[3] Age Concern, a UK-based charity which seeks 'to promote the well-being of all older people and to help make later life a fulfilling and enjoyable experience' has recognised the advantages of good quality equity release schemes so long as the benefits and pitfalls of different products are properly understood and the product is appropriate for the older owner; see T Hanifan, *Equity Release Made Easy* (London, Age Concern Books, 2008).

[4] As well as home purchase plans, which, since not targeted at older consumers, are not specifically considered in this chapter.

[5] *Financial Services Authority Handbook*, Mortgages and Home Finance Conduct of Business Sourcebook (MCOB) 5, available online at <http://fsahandbook.info/FSA/html/handbook/MCOB/5>.

[6] *Ibid*, MCOB 6, available online at <http://fsahandbook.info/FSA/html/handbook/MCOB/6>.

[7] *Ibid*, MCOB 7, available online at <http://fsahandbook.info/FSA/html/handbook/MCOB/7>.

[8] See also D De Meza, B Irlenbusch and D Reniers, *Financial Capability: A Behavioural Economics Perspective* (FSA Consumer Research 69) (London, FSA, 2008), online at <http://www.fsa.gov.uk/pubs/consumer-research/crpr69.pdf>, as discussed in ch 6; FSA, *Mortgage Market Review* (London, FSA, 2009), ch 6, especially paras 6.7–6.11, online at <http://www.fsa.gov.uk/pubs/discussion/dp09_03.pdf>.

[9] 'Equity release—time to grow?' *Mortgage Finance Gazette* (May 2007), available online at <http://www.mfgonline.co.uk/ccstory/20235/130/Equity_release_%E2%80%93_time_t>.

(2) The Financial Services Authority's Approach to Regulation

The regulation of targeted housing equity products has taken effect principally through four key statutes:

a) the Financial Services and Markets Act (FSMA) 2000 set out the core jurisdiction of the FSA;
b) the Financial Services and Markets Act 2000 (Regulated Activities Order) 2001 (SI 2001/544) gave it jurisdiction over mortgage products, including lifetime/reverse/shared appreciation mortgages;
c) the Regulation of Financial Services (Land Transactions) Act 2005 extended this jurisdiction to include home reversions; and
d) the FSA's Interim Permitted Regulated Sale and Rent Back Activities Instrument 2009, and the Financial Services and Markets Act 2000 (Regulated Activities) (Amendment) Order 2009 (SI 2009/1342)[10] gave the FSA jurisdiction to bring SRB transactions under its regulatory umbrella.

This chapter examines the nature and extent of these regulatory regimes, and their role in protecting older consumers. It focuses in particular on the significance of the context of the transaction in the nature and extent of consumer protections, in light of the specific targeting of these products at older owners and the FSA's responsibility to provide a 'degree of protection that is appropriate in particular circumstances, having regard to the differences in risk and the expertise of different consumers'.[11]

The FSA acts under five statutory objectives set out in the FSMA 2000:

a) maintaining market confidence in the financial system;
b) promoting public understanding of the financial system;
c) contributing to the protection and enhancement of the UK financial system;
d) securing the appropriate degree of protection for consumers; and
e) reducing the extent to which it is possible for a business to be used for a purpose connected with financial crime.

When it comes to assessing the 'appropriate' degree of protection for consumers, this clearly requires an understanding of who the consumers are and where their vulnerabilities lie in relation to these transactions.[12] The FSA's obligations under the 2000 Act also require it to publish a formal cost–benefit analysis in respect of all new financial regulation,[13] to ensure that the restrictions it imposes on the financial services industry are proportionate to the benefits for consumer protection that are expected to result.

[10] Art 33(1).

[11] OFT, *Vulnerable Consumers and Financial Services: The Report of the Director General's Inquiry* (OFT 255) (London, OFT, 1999) para 412.

[12] Although when the FSA has discussed the 'appropriate' level of protection for consumers, it has been to justify its 'non-zero failure' approach to regulation; see discussion below, section (5).

[13] FSMA 2000, s 155.

The FSA's approach to the cost–benefit analysis focuses on the quantifiable economic impacts of proposed initiatives,[14] although some reference is also made to 'countervailing non-economic impacts'[15] and the importance of 'consider[ing] not just impacts on consumers but impacts on different classes of consumers'.[16] The FSA's policy statement has also suggested that

> [t]hough cost benefit analysis itself is neutral with respect to distribution of costs and benefits, the distribution of costs and benefits may be of interest for broader policy reasons. It is therefore worthwhile to state who gains and who loses (and why) as a result of a given policy option.[17]

The cost–benefit analysis has been described as 'a practical and rigorous means of identifying, targeting and checking the impacts of regulatory measures on the underlying causes of the ills with which regulators need to deal, those causes being the market failures that in turn may justify regulatory intervention'.[18] The identification of particular risks as 'market failures' is framed by the assumption that 'it is reasonable to analyse policy options in the context of a reasonably well working, albeit not perfect, free market economy'.[19] This is also underpinned by the presumptions that providers will act to maximise profits and consumers will act to maximise their own welfare, and assumes a degree of reflexive adaptability on the part of consumers as well as traders.[20] Proposed regulatory initiatives are assessed for market impact by projecting changes to direct costs, compliance costs, quantity of products purchased (ie business volume), quality of products (by raising standards across the sector, or by improving suitability match between product and consumer[21]), variety in the market and the efficiency of competition within the market.

The efficiency of competition within the market is likely to be a significant issue in relation to housing equity products. One of the key difficulties older consumers face in this context is assessing good value for money, due in part to the complexity of the financial products used to release housing equity. Consumers who enter into transactions under financial pressure are also less able to assess value for money, as they are less likely to shop around and are not focused on value for money but on the need to release equity

[14] FSA, *Practical Cost–Benefit Analysis for Financial Regulators Version 1.1* (London, Financial Services Authority Central Policy, 2000) at 6, online at <http://www.fsa.gov.uk/pubs/foi/cba.pdf>; 'Obviously, such comparisons are facilitated if one can measure all costs and benefits quantitatively, but that is not always possible. Where one cannot reasonably obtain quantitative estimates for one or more of the options under consideration, one should aim to develop qualitative estimates of costs and benefits that enable one to: A) form a judgement as to whether or not a given policy option yields net benefits; and B) rank the policy options under consideration. Note, however, that under the FSMA the FSA will typically need (where possible) to publish a *quantitative* estimate of the costs, and an analysis of the benefits, of the preferred option encapsulated in the draft rules on which consultation takes place.' (*ibid*, at 13)

[15] *Ibid*, at 8.

[16] *Ibid*, at 11.

[17] *Ibid*, at 14.

[18] I Alfon and P Andrews, *Cost–Benefit Analysis in Financial Regulation: How to do it and how it adds value*, (FSA, Occasional Paper Series, No 3), (London, FSA, 1999) at 5; available online at <http://www.fsa.gov.uk/pubs/policy/p24.pdf>.

[19] FSA, above n 14, at 18.

[20] It also takes account of the knock-on effects of regulation on the market, specifically that 'cost increases will tend to lead to price increases. Price increases tend to lead to lower volumes of transactions and a consequent loss of benefit to all concerned. (On the other hand, greater information, transparency and market confidence can lead to price falls.)' (*ibid*)

[21] Recognising that product quality often depends on the identity of the consumer and their individual needs and wants.

to meet pressing needs.[22] The effectiveness of legal regulation is also a factor in the ability of housing equity to perform the functions that the UK political and policy environments increasingly demand of it: the failure of the UK equity release market to expand on the scale anticipated in recent years has been attributed to consumer distrust of equity release products, which are perceived as poor value for money and high-risk. However, where consumers are not in a position to judge value for money, this creates a market imperfection, since

> [f]irms can then sell poor value products and make a profit. In such a market, firms will have a strong incentive to compete by convincing people to buy poor value products (to compete *for* the market) rather than by offering good value products (to compete *in* the market). The competition to sell poor value products will be fierce, given the profits to be made.[23]

Regulation that discourages the competition to sell poor-value products (for example, by enabling consumers better to understand the product, assess the price paid and shop around for good-value products) justifies the costs of regulating since it reduces the wastage of resources involved in competing to advertise and sell poor-value products, as well as preventing consumer detriment.

The FSA's 'risk-based approach' to regulation and supervision of financial services combines the probability that an event will occur with its likely impact.[24] The FSA defines an 'adverse outcome' as the risk of failing to achieve its statutory objectives.[25] Black has argued that

> [i]t is not an assessment of, for example, the overall level of systematic risk within the markets, or of risks to consumers. Only indirectly does the FSA's risk approach incorporate such risk. Thus, for example, as one of the FSA's statutory objectives is maintenance of market confidence, the issue of systematic risk is relevant as it is one element that will affect market confidence, and thus might threaten the ability of the FSA to achieve this particular statutory objective.[26]

In the wake of the global financial crisis, the links between consumer detriment, market confidence and the stability of the financial system have prompted a shift in regulatory ideology from 'light-touch' regulation to increased lender responsibility and higher levels of consumer protection. This chapter will consider the extent to which the FSA's jurisdiction over housing equity transactions has addressed not only the risks which these specialised products pose for the FSA's statutory objectives, but also the risks which older owners face when making decisions concerning these transactions. This analysis provides a useful platform from which to consider the case for special legal protections for vulnerable consumer groups, for example older consumers, based on the emerging idea of lender responsibility, as well as the responsibilities on the State which encourages these transactions through political and policy strategies.

[22] See OFT, *Sale and Rent Back—An OFT Market Study* (OFT 1018), (London, OFT, 2008), paras 5.18, 5.21; available online at <http://www.oft.gov.uk/shared_oft/reports/consumer_protection/oft1018.pdf>.

[23] FSA, above n 14, at 38.

[24] Known as the ARROW (Advanced Risk-responsive Operating Framework) model of supervision; see FSA, *The FSA's Risk-Assessment Framework* (London, FSA, 2006); J Black, 'The Development of Risk Based Regulation in Financial Services: Just "Modelling Through"', in J Black, M Lodge and M Thatcher (eds), *Regulatory Innovation: A Comparative Analysis* (Cheltenham, Edward Elgar, 2005).

[25] See FSA, *A New Regulator for a New Millenium* (London, FSA, 2000); available online at <http://www.fsa.gov.uk/pubs/policy/p29.pdf>.

[26] J Black, 'Mapping the Contours of Contemporary Financial Services Regulation' (2002) 2 *Journal of Corporate Law Studies* 253, 279.

(3) The Market for Targeted Housing Equity Transactions

The market for targeted housing equity products for older owners is widely regarded as under-developed. The reasons for this include consumers' concerns about risks, value for money and the safety of these options.[27] While statistics from 2005–06 indicated that almost 5 per cent (656,000) of all owner-occupiers in England had withdrawn equity from their home within previous three years,[28] the most common methods for doing so included increasing the size of their mortgage (33 per cent) or remortgaging their current home (27 per cent). Since access to these 'mainstream' methods of releasing equity—which start from the expectation that the debt will be repaid[29]—is based on the ability to repay, opportunities for conventional mortgage equity withdrawal will often be limited for older owners.[30] In addition, the legal framework for the enforcement of 'ordinary debt', based as it is on the ability to pay, is likely to be particularly punitive for older owners where they have reduced or limited incomes.[31]

Older owners in need of additional income or capital are therefore—so the theory goes—more likely to turn to specialised housing equity release products. Housing equity schemes are marketed as facilitative products which enable older owners to tap into the value of their homes—their 'equity'—without having to sell up altogether and move out, and without having to make repayments by instalment. Although the terms of individual products vary, the general idea is that the homeowner receives a payment of capital which is secured against, or in payment for, the borrower's equity. In some cases (lifetime mortgage, shared appreciation mortgage) the repayment of the loan is deferred until the consumer moves into care, decides to sell or dies; while other products involve a transfer of ownership with an agreement that the vendor will continue to occupy the property on terms. In either case, a common feature is that the consumer generates an income from his or her equity while retaining the right to live in the property (for the time being at least). These products may be attractive to older owners because they provide a mechanism for retaining the *use* of the home while unlocking its value to release *capital* in lump sum or income.

The first equity release plans targeted at older consumers were launched in the UK by Hodge Lifetime (then 'Home Reversions Ltd) in 1965; and 'mortgage and annuity' schemes, or 'Home Income Plans'[32] became available from 1972.[33] Several providers were active in the market throughout the 1960s, 1970s and 1980s, although it was the coincidence of the socio-economic and political factors explored in chapters one and two, and the development of increasingly innovative and flexible products following financial

[27] See ch 3, section (3).

[28] To an average amount of £33,300; see *Social Trends 38* (London, Office for National Statistics, 2008) at 148, online at <http://www.statistics.gov.uk/downloads/theme_social/Social_Trends38/Social_Trends_38.pdf>.

[29] The 'ordinary' debt options—structured as they are around repayment by instalments from future income—may be particularly risky for older owners who face reductions in future income or increases in expenditure.

[30] Although it is likely that the increasing use of flexible mortgages across the life-course will, in due course, lead to growing numbers of older owners reaching retirement carrying this type of 'ordinary' debt; see ch 7.

[31] See ch 7.

[32] The 'HIP' is a form of lifetime mortgage in which the lump sum released is used to purchase an annuity, the monthly income from which is divided between servicing the interest on the debt and paying an income to the borrower; the capital debt is repaid when the property is ultimately sold.

[33] See the Safe Home Income Plans (SHIP) website, <http://www.ship-ltd.org/equityreleasemarket.aspx>.

deregulation from the 1980s, that really brought equity release into the popular consciousness. Providers continue to emphasise the flexibility of their products—for example, Hodge Lifetime claims that 'we recognise the individual needs of the customer and have tailored our equity release products accordingly'[34]—although the underlying legal transactions tend to fall into three main categories:

a) lifetime mortgages;
b) home reversion plans; and
c) SRB agreements.

Lifetime mortgages and home reversion plans generally operate a minimum age threshold which varies from product to product and provider to provider, but the consumer must usually be at least 55 years old to qualify for a lifetime mortgage and at least 60 years old for a home reversion plan.[35] This reflects the main risk associated with equity release products for providers, ie the provider will generally have to wait until the owner moves out of the property or dies before money owed (in the form of the capital asset of the house) is recovered.

Although mortgages, equity release products and SRB agreements are collectively grouped by the FSA as 'regulated home finance activities',[36] there is a fundamental distinction between 'traditional' mortgages and other housing equity transactions. While the traditional mortgage is primarily intended as a financial services contract, in which the normal course of events will involve the repayment of the loan and where the securitisation of the home provides an enforcement strategy which will be utilised only as a 'last resort',[37] housing equity products are generally not scheduled for repayment by instalments; rather it is intended that the security of the property will be used to repay the debt. In this sense, housing equity transactions may be described as 'lending against security' or 'equity lending'. This style of lending was anathema to traditional banking practice, which posited that 'To lend money against security knowing full well that one is likely to have to realise that security is bad banking practice.'[38] These products emerged as part of the new financial landscape that followed the deregulation of banking and financial services and the liberalisation of financial markets from the 1980s, and which prompted the emergence of new types of lender as well as a diversification of activities amongst established lenders, from traditional prudential approaches to lending into highly competitive, entrepreneurial and in some cases over-enthusiastic lending.[39]

Until relatively recently, British consumers approached the prospect of equity release with some trepidation, particularly in light of the negative publicity that followed the

[34] See <http://www.ship-ltd.org/shipmembers.aspx>.

[35] See SHIP, *Making Equity Release Safe for You*, online brochure available at <http://www.ship-ltd.org/uploads/FINALBROCHURE2.pdf>; also <http://www.ship-ltd.org/faqs.aspx>.

[36] <http://fsahandbook.info/FSA/html/handbook/PERG/2/Annex2>.

[37] See L Whitehouse, 'The Mortgage Arrears Pre-Action Protocol: An Opportunity Lost' (2009) 72 *MLR* 793, criticising the Civil Justice Council's Pre-Action Protocol for merely encouraging, rather than compelling, lenders to view repossession as a last resort. The idea that repossession should be a last resort is also promoted by the FSA in its statement of 'policy and practice' concerning possession actions under regulated mortgages, as part of its policy of treating customers fairly: the *Mortgages and Home Finance: Conduct of Business Sourcebook* (MCOB), 13.3.2E(1)(f), (available online at <http://fsahandbook.info/FSA/html/handbook/MCOB>).

[38] J Wadsley, 'Bank lending and the family home: prudence and protection' [2003] *Lloyd's Maritime and Commercial Law Quarterly* 341, 342.

[39] *Ibid*, at 343–45.

upsurge in reverse mortgages (a form of lifetime mortgage) during the 'boom and bust' in the British housing market in the late 1980s and early 1990s, when many households lost their homes through repossession.[40] However, recent years have seen a significant growth in the UK's equity release market, and much emphasis has been placed on the potential for further growth.[41] The development of the FSA's regulatory framework is expected to play a major role in facilitating future market growth, by improving the reputation of equity release products and so contributing to increased market confidence.

As is often the case for financial services, collective industry self-regulation pre-dated legal regulation of equity release products through the FSA, and continues to run alongside the statutory schemes. The majority of equity release products sold in Britain (90 per cent by volume) are provided by members of SHIP, which was launched in 1991 and which covers lifetime mortgages and home reversions. All participating companies pledge to observe the SHIP Code of Practice, which binds the companies to provide a fair, easy-to-understand and full presentation of their plans. SHIP describes itself as 'dedicated entirely to the protection of planholders and promotion of safe home income and equity release plans'.[42] While this claim suggests a narrower perspective than the FSA's, focusing wholly on consumer protection rather than balancing the needs of consumers, traders and the market, its impact is limited by the voluntary nature of self-regulation. The Code of Conduct reads as follows:

> The SHIP Code of Conduct provides firms with strict criteria that need to be met in order to become a member. The following guarantees have to be provided to customers:
>
> 1. To allow customers to remain in their property for life provided the property remains their main residence.
> 2. To provide customers with fair, simple and complete presentations of their plans. This means that the benefits and limitations of the product together with any obligations on the part of the customer are clearly set out in their literature. It should include all costs that the customer has to bear in setting up the plan as well as the tax implications, their position on moving house and the effects of changes in house values on their loan.
> 3. The right to move their plan to another suitable property without any financial penalty.
> 4. The right for the customer to choose an independent solicitor of their own choice to conduct their legal work. The firm must provide the solicitor with full details of the benefits their client will receive prior to the completion of the plan. The solicitor only signs a certificate once he or she is satisfied that their client fully understands the risks and benefits of the plan.
> 5. The SHIP certificate signed by the solicitor is there to ensure clients are aware of the terms and implications of the plan including the impact of equity release on their estate.
> 6. All SHIP plans carry a no negative equity guarantee. This means customers will never owe more than the value of their home and no debt will ever be left to the estate.

[40] C Huan and J Mahoney, 'Equity Release Mortgages' (2002) 16 *Housing Finance International* 29, 33: 'During the 1980s [in the UK], equity release came under scrutiny and suffered a bad reputation due to poorly designed and marketed products that led to several court cases.' This analysis uses the examples of home income plans and interest roll-up loans to identify weaknesses in equity release products in the UK, which led to escalating debt, left consumers vulnerable to rising interest rates and falling house prices, and led to forced sale of their homes.

[41] See ch 5, section (5).

[42] See <http://www.ship-ltd.org/about/index.shtml>.

While the first two guarantees are now replicated in FSA regulation, the right to move house, the 'no negative equity' guarantee and the provision for solicitor certification go beyond the FSA's rules for lifetime mortgages.

Founded with four member companies, by 2007 SHIP had 21 member companies, with a market share of £1.279 billion[43] and anticipated growth to £2.19 billion by 2010.[44] Following the credit crunch that started in 2007 and the recession that followed from 2008, initial evidence suggested that the equity release sector was bucking credit market trends, with 14 per cent growth in equity release transactions in 2008 (Q1 to Q2),[45] and a further 10 per cent growth in Quarter 3.[46] Industry research linked this growth to increased costs for general day-to-day living, with 10 per cent more applicants stating they wanted to improve the quality of their everyday life. There were also suggestions that equity was released by older owners to help relatives in trouble as a result of the credit crunch, either to make improvements to their property to accommodate family members moving back into the family home,[47] or to make the capital available to family members, with one survey reporting that 20 per cent of those taking out plans were using some of the money to help out family or friends in difficult times.[48] However, a review of SHIP statistics from 2001 to 2010 shows peaks of over £317 million in Quarter 4 2006, £325.3 million in Quarter 3 2007, and £303.3 million in Quarter 3 2008, followed by a steady but not significant decline in advances.[49]

Since 2008, some 'prime' lenders have withdrawn from the equity release market: in October 2009, Northern Rock withdrew its 'Lifetime' products; and by 2010, Prudential, Newcastle Building Society and Coventry Building Society had closed their doors to new equity release/lifetime mortgage business. The contraction of the pool of providers, and particularly the loss to the market of some high-profile 'mainstream' lenders, will leave borrowers with fewer choices. By late 2010, there were 13 SHIP members in the equity release market (offering lifetime mortgages and/or home reversion plans),[50] including both large sector-wide financial services providers (for example, Aviva Equity Release UK Ltd) and specialised providers (including Bridgewater, which specialises in home reversion plans, and Hodge Lifetime, which has offered equity release plans since 1965, making them the longest-established equity release provider in the UK). SHIP suggested that it was the withdrawal of certain providers that led to a fall in the number of lump-sum mortgages in 2009,[51] while home reversions became more popular in light of the advantages to the customer of selling a fixed portion of equity in a time of uncertainty in

[43] This was an 11% increase on full-year figures for 2006; see SHIP Press Release, 8 December 2007, available online at <http://www.ship-ltd.org/bm~doc/08-dec-2007a.pdf>.

[44] *Ibid.*

[45] SHIP Press Release, 16 July 2008, 'SHIP equity release providers buck the Credit crunch with a 14% increase in Business'; available online at <http://www.ship-ltd.org/bm~doc/16-jul-08.pdf >.

[46] SHIP Press Release, 21 October 2008, 'SHIP reports a 10% increase in equity Release business'; available online at <http://www.ship-ltd.org/bm~doc/21-october-2008.pdf>.

[47] <http://www.prlog.org/10139844-statistics-show-equity-release-is-here-to-stay.html>.

[48] Key Retirement Solutions, UK Equity Release Market Monitor Q2 2008; available online at <http://www.keyrs.co.uk/files/market_monitor_report_q2_2008.pdf>.

[49] <http://www.ship-ltd.org/uploads/SHIP%20business%20Figures%20since%202001.pdf>.

[50] <http://www.ship-ltd.org/shipmembers.aspx>.

[51] <http://www.ship-ltd.org/uploads/Equity%20Release%20Market%20Stabilises%20in%20Q4%202009.pdf>.

house prices.[52] By the end of 2009 and into 2010, drawdown mortgages—which offer a more flexible way to release equity—were the most popular product, accounting for 55 per cent of the equity release market.[53] The next section analyses the nature and extent of the risks and the regulatory regimes that govern these alternative housing equity products.

(4) The Regulated Products

(a) 'Lifetime mortgages'

The 'lifetime mortgage' category includes a range of alternative mortgage products, including roll-up mortgages, drawdown mortgages and shared appreciation mortgages. With a roll-up mortgage (in contrast to a 'traditional' mortgage) the 'borrower' does not make periodic repayments of interest during his or her lifetime; rather, the 'repayments' due are 'rolled up' or added to the mortgage capital, with the whole debt being paid off when the borrower dies, goes into long-term care or for any other reason vacates the property. With this type of mortgage, interest accumulates every month, with the result that providers are generally willing to lend only a small proportion of the value of the property, to ensure that the total amount of the accumulated debt, including interest, will be covered by the realisable value of the property when the mortgage terminates. In theory, the accumulation of interest means that roll-up mortgages may result in negative equity where property prices do not rise in line with the agreed interest rate, although if the lender is a SHIP member, the 'no negative equity' guarantee protects the borrower against this risk.[54]

The drawdown mortgage operates in a similar way, except that a maximum borrowing amount is agreed between the borrower and the lender, based on the value of the property being used as security (normally no more than approximately 80 per cent of the value of the property, at the time of valuation). The drawdown mortgage offers greater flexibility with regard to how much of the maximum is borrowed at any one time, and one of the key advantages of this type of mortgage is that the borrower only pays interest on the amount that has been drawn down, while having the security of knowing that additional funds are available if required. Drawdown mortgages tend to have higher interest rates and larger penalties for early withdrawal. At the less flexible end of the spectrum, in a fixed repayment lifetime mortgage, the amount borrowed and due to be repaid is set from the outset of the plan, with the fixed rate calculated according to criteria such as the borrower's age, his or her state of health and the value of the property.

The shared appreciation mortgage is another example of a lifetime mortgage product targeted at older owners, whereby the mortgage loan is not repayable at any fixed time but

[52] <http://www.ship-ltd.org/uploads/Equity%20Release%20Market%20Stabilises%20in%20Q4%202009.pdf>.

[53] See SHIP statistics, <http://www.ship-ltd.org/uploads/Equity%20Release%20Market%20Stabilises%20in%20Q4%202009.pdf>; <http://www.ship-ltd.org/uploads/EQUITY%20RELEASE%20MARKET%20REMAINS%20ROBUST.pdf>.

[54] Although the 'no negative equity' guarantee is preferable to the risk of negative equity, it is important to be aware that this still puts the whole of the owned home in the hands of the creditor. The guarantee is also of less value where the owned home is the only significant asset the older consumer has (particularly likely if he or she is a marginal consumer) in any event.

in the event of sale or on the death of the mortgagor. The shared appreciation mortgage, which emerged onto the UK market in the mid-1990s, is an arrangement whereby the money repaid includes both the principal debt outstanding and a specified percentage[55] increase in value of the property over the purchase costs. This type of arrangement became controversial in the late 1990s, a period of rapid house price inflation, when it was seen as conferring a windfall on providers. The substantial proportion of equity held by the provider in some cases was criticised as making it difficult for older owners to move house or downsize.[56]

The particular risks associated with each lifetime mortgage product depend on the product type and the individual terms. Risks associated with the roll-up mortgage include the impact of high interest rates over the lifetime of the product. The Government has noted that the amount owed on a rolled-up interest product can double in seven to 10 years, depending on the agreed rate of interest.[57] The availability of different products depends on the value of the property, any outstanding mortgage and the amount of capital the owner needs to release. Typical rates and conditions vary according to the age of the owner: so, for example, lenders on lump-sum lifetime mortgages typically offer 15 to 20 per cent of the value of a property to someone aged 65; 30 per cent to someone aged 75; and a maximum of 50 per cent for someone aged 90. Life expectancy is also central to calculating the terms of the agreement: for example, an income scheme lifetime mortgage is likely to offer 0.13 per cent of property value per month for someone aged 65; up to 1.2 per cent of the property value per month for those aged 90. In a shared appreciation mortgage, the cost of credit is linked to property prices, while for other lifetime mortgage products it may be based on the competitiveness of the interest rate agreed at the time the mortgage is granted (fixed repayment lifetime mortgage, drawdown mortgage) or the penalties for early withdrawal from the scheme (drawdown mortgages).

The FSA's regulatory jurisdiction over lifetime mortgages took effect from October 2004.[58] Since 1 April 2005, product providers have been required to provide the FSA with transaction level data on all sales of regulated mortgages, and statistics covering the period April 2008 to March 2009 showed that approximately 19,700 lifetime mortgages were sold, accounting for just over 1.5 per cent of the mortgage market.[59] There was a 10 per cent drop in volume of sales from Q1 2008 to Q1 2009, with 25 provider firms offering lifetime mortgages and the top five provider firms (ranked by volume of sales) accounting for a 75 per cent market share. A substantial 97 per cent of all lifetime mortgages were sold on an advised basis, emphasising the importance of regulating advisers in this sector. The average age of a person taking out a lifetime mortgage was 70 years old.[60]

[55] The specified percentage is a multiple of the loan to value ratio, depending on the category into which the mortgage falls: in one category, there is no interest payable but the multiple is usually three times the loan to value ratio; in another category, there is a fixed interest charge and the multiple is one.

[56] In *Tew and others v Bank of Scotland (Shared Appreciation Mortgages) No 1 plc and others* [2010] EWHC 203 (Ch) (22 January 2010, transcript available on Lexis), several consumers joined in a group litigation challenge to the Bank of Scotland's shared appreciation mortgage product, based on the CCA 1974's 'unfair relationship' provisions; see further ch 8.

[57] Office of the Deputy Prime Minister, *Housing Renewal* (ODPM Circular 05/2003) (London, ODPM, 2003), para 3.14.

[58] Under the Financial Services and Markets Act 2000 (Regulated Activities Order) 2001.

[59] FSA, *Mortgages: Product Sales Data (PSD) Trend Report* (London, FSA, August 2009) at 17, online at <http://www.fsa.gov.uk/pubs/other/mortgage_report_09%20final.pdf>.

[60] *Ibid.*

The shift from self-regulation of lifetime mortgage products through SHIP to legal regulation under the FSA occurred in the context of the general extension of the FSA's jurisdiction over 'conventional' mortgage sales, but from the outset the FSA proposed to vary the application of its standard tools in the case of lifetime mortgages,[61] recognising that 'lifetime mortgages (which is what we call equity release mortgages targeted at older consumers) were more complex than standard mortgages and posed a higher level of risk, justifying a higher level of regulation'.[62] Although it was noted that home reversion schemes presented a similar order of risk for older consumers, they were not covered in the same tranche of legislation as they did not fit within the definition of 'mortgages'.[63] This emphasis on the form of the underlying legal transaction rather than the substance of the deal from the consumer's perspective is a characteristic feature of the regulatory approach, illustrated more recently when Equity IQ launched its 'Property Income Plan', a new product which performs the functions of equity release, is targeted at older consumers and may appear to the consumer to be an equity release plan. The legal transaction underlying the product falls outside the definitions that demarcate the FSA's jurisdiction (the definitions of 'mortgage', 'home reversion plan', or 'sale-and-rent back') and so is outside the FSA's regulatory scope,[64] leading the Society of Equity Release Advisers to counsel caution on the grounds that the deals do not adhere to industry regulations and the companies involved are not regulated by the FSA.[65]

The main issues which the FSA identified in relation to lifetime mortgages included the importance of ensuring that consumers are advised about other 'substitutable' options that are available to them (including unregulated products) during the sales process,[66] and that firms selling lifetime mortgages take account of other options both in initial disclosure and when making suitability assessments for the individual consumer.[67] In determining the form which regulation would take, the FSA identified a number of specific risks associated with lifetime mortgages, including the risks of rapidly increasing debt and negative equity where the interest is 'rolled-up'; the risk of losing entitlement to means-tested benefits or increasing tax liability; the reduction in any inheritance that consumers may wish to leave; and restrictions on who can live in the property, which

[61] FSA, *The FSA's approach to regulating mortgage sales* (Consultation Paper 146) (London, FSA, 2002), online at <http://www.fsa.gov.uk/pubs/cp/cp146.pdf>; FSA, *Mortgage regulation: Draft conduct of business rules and feedback on CP146—Volume 1* (Consultation Paper 186) (London, FSA, 2003), online at <http://www.fsa.gov.uk/pubs/cp/cp186_vol1.pdf>; FSA, *Mortgage regulation: Draft conduct of business rules and feedback on CP146—Volume 2* (Consultation Paper 186) (London, FSA, 2003), online at <http://www.fsa.gov.uk/pubs/cp/cp186_vol2.pdf>; FSA, *Regulating mortgage sales: final conduct of business rules; Feedback on CP186 and made text Volume 1 & Volume 2* (Policy Statement) (London, FSA, 2002), online at <http://www.fsa.gov.uk/pubs/policy/ps186_vol1.pdf>; National Economic Research Associates, *The Economic Costs of the Proposed Regulation of Mortgage Sales: A Final Report for the Financial Services Authority* (London, NERA, 2003), online at <http://www.fsa.gov.uk/pubs/cp/186/cp186_report.pdf>.

[62] Consultation Paper 146, above n 61, para 2.18.

[63] *Ibid*, para 18.2.

[64] The Property Income Plan does not involve a 'loan' or the sale of (a share in) the property but the creation of a charge against the home (to a maximum of half the equity in the property) which is licensed to an insurance company for a three-year term to enhance its solvency level, with interest payable at a rate of 5% per annum; see website of 'M6 financial', offering this product at <http://www.m6financial.co.uk/>.

[65] See, eg, <http://citywire.co.uk/new-model-adviser/chalk-issues-warning-over-equity-iq-equity-release-plan/a431127>; <http://www.moneymarketing.co.uk/mortgages/advisers-urged-to-be-on-alert-over-property-plan/1018573.article>; <http://www.yourmortgage.co.uk/news/3626986>.

[66] Consultation Paper 146, above n 61, para 18.3.

[67] *Ibid*.

could affect options for care in later years.[68] Alongside these 'product risks', the FSA also recognised that a lifetime mortgage might not be the right choice for the consumer, and that a home reversion, trading down or accessing other sources of funds (for example, obtaining a home improvement grant) could represent a better option.[69]

The key strategy adopted to address these risks was informational, to 'ensure that consumers are fully informed of the risks as well as the benefits of a lifetime mortgage'.[70] Some of the regulatory tools applied to 'ordinary' mortgages were carried across to apply to lifetime mortgages.[71] These included the financial promotion rules,[72] which regulate the form and content of promotional literature, for example by requiring firms to take reasonable steps to ensure that promotions are fair, clear and not misleading,[73] and guidance advising firms to give equal prominence to the disadvantages and advantages of product features.[74] In addition to the standard rules on initial disclosure in mortgage transactions,[75] the FSA identified specific objectives, including making consumers aware of the alternatives for generating capital and income from their homes, to mitigate the risk of firms directing consumers towards unregulated products to avoid regulation, and encouraging consumers to seek advice if they are at all unsure.[76]

The emphasis on professional advice is central to the 'risk statement' for lifetime mortgages. All mortgage product literature must include risk statements (or 'health warnings') identifying the particular risks of the product type: for example, where the product refers to paying off unsecured debts by taking out qualifying credit, the required risk statement is 'Think carefully before securing other debts against your home. Your home may be repossessed if you do not keep up repayments on your mortgage.'; and for standard mortgages, the required wording is 'Your home may be repossessed if you do not keep up repayments on your mortgage.'[77] In contrast, the required statement for lifetime mortgages does not identify the main risks of the product but directs consumers towards obtaining individual advice, with the health warning that 'This is a lifetime mortgage. To understand the features and risks, ask for a personalised illustration.'[78] This reflects the FSA's general approach towards the higher level of risk associated with complex lifetime mortgage products, which is to emphasise the need for consumers to receive individualised professional advice before entering into the transaction.[79] The focus on advice was reinforced through the specific advice requirements set out in MCOB 8.5, which require

[68] *Ibid*, para 18.6.

[69] *Ibid*, para 18.7.

[70] *Ibid*, para 18.8.

[71] While the MCOB 8 sets out specific advising and selling standards for equity release transactions, and MCOB 9 details the product disclosure requirements and good practice guidelines, including standardised content, order and form for illustrations, start of contract and after-sales information, these are largely adapted from MCOB 5 for standard mortgages, to reflect the different features of the products; see *FSA Handbook*, online at <http://fsahandbook.info/FSA/html/handbook/MCOB/5>; <http://fsahandbook.info/FSA/html/handbook/MCOB/8>; <http://fsahandbook.info/FSA/html/handbook/MCOB/9>.

[72] Regulating advertising and product literature: see *FSA Handbook*, MCOB 3, online at <http://fsahandbook.info/FSA/html/handbook/MCOB/3>.

[73] MCOB 3.6.3.1; online at <http://fsahandbook.info/FSA/html/handbook/MCOB/3/6>.

[74] MCOB 3.6.4.1(b); online at <http://fsahandbook.info/FSA/html/handbook/MCOB/3/6>.

[75] Eg, the requirement to provide an illustration that is clear, fair and not misleading, accurate and explained to the consumer; MCOB 5.4, online at <http://fsahandbook.info/FSA/html/handbook/MCOB/5/4>.

[76] Consultation Paper 146, above n 61, para 18.11.

[77] MCOB 3.6.13; online at <http://fsahandbook.info/FSA/html/handbook/MCOB/3/6>.

[78] *Ibid.*

[79] Consultation Paper 146, above n 61, para 18.2.

the provider in an advised sale 'to take reasonable care to ensure the suitability of its advice'.[80] The specific requirements in relation to suitability recognised that while affordability, in the sense of the ability to make payments as they fall due, is the main criterion of suitability in standard mortgages, 'the scope of the suitability requirement for equity release products is necessarily wider'[81] and depends on the consumer's objectives: 'For example … it may be difficult to argue that an equity release product would be suitable if there were an alternative option that met their needs and objectives without incurring an ongoing financial commitment.'[82]

There are three stages to the suitability requirements laid down by the FSA in relation to lifetime mortgages. The first is whether an equity release product is suitable for the consumer.[83] The FSA considered whether this included requiring advisers to discuss trading down, but concluded that the discussion of this issue should be covered by 'training and competence' rather than the suitability rules.[84] It also considered whether advisers should be required to make consumers aware of the possibility of seeking means-tested grants for home improvements[85] (although it was noted that this 'appears to be more the province of the not-for-profit organisations'[86]), and of the impact of equity release on means-tested benefits and tax liabilities. It concluded that since grants, benefits and tax implications are potentially directly relevant to a decision to take out an equity release product, requiring firms to take account of these issues in determining whether a product is suitable would be consistent with the approach taken in the investment conduct of business rules, whereby advisers are required to consider alternative packaged products.[87]

The second stage of the suitability test is to consider suitable type(s) of equity release product, matching the consumer's needs and circumstances to different product features, and not limited to the range of products that is available through the adviser.[88] The factors which advisers should take into account when addressing this question included general issues relating to eligibility, such as the applicant's age, property type and property value, as well as the applicant's bequest motivations, health and life expectancy, future plans and needs ('eg, whether the consumer is likely to need to borrow more, and whether he is likely to want to move house'[89]).

The third stage of the test is to assess which lifetime mortgage(s) or home reversion scheme(s) and which provider(s) best meet the consumer's needs and circumstances.[90] Specifically, this requires that

> the adviser must not recommend a particular lifetime mortgage if he ought to be reasonably aware of another from the range he is advising on that better meets the consumer's needs or

80 MCOB 8.5.1; online at <http://fsahandbook.info/FSA/html/handbook/MCOB/8/5>.
81 Consultation Paper 146, above n 61, para 18.14.
82 *Ibid.*
83 See Consultation Paper 186, above n 61, Table 5.1.
84 *Ibid*, para 18.15. Trading down, grant availability, tax and means-tested benefits are covered in the examination requirements for lifetime mortgages and home reversion schemes; Consultation Paper 146, above n 61, para 18.30.
85 See discussion in ch 2.
86 Consultation Paper 146, above n 61, para 18.16.
87 *Ibid*, para 18.20.
88 Consultation Paper 186, above n 61, Table 5.1.
89 Consultation Paper 146, above n 61, para 18.22.
90 Consultation Paper 186, above n 61, Table 5.1.

> circumstances. This might be satisfied by an adviser recommending the better value lifetime mortgage based on the pricing elements (eg fixed rate) that are most important to the consumer.[91]

While the FSA resisted the suggestion that all sales of lifetime mortgages must be advised on the basis that it would be 'inappropriate to force all consumers in this market to take advice',[92] its strategy of encouraging consumers to take advice if they are at all unsure, both by a warning on the initial disclosure document and in consumer education material,[93] has been quite successful, with the great majority (97 per cent) of lifetime mortgage sales now advised. For those remaining sales which are non-advised, the FSA protection takes effect through a series of 'filtering questions' which cover issues similar to those addressed through the suitability tests, and training and competence requirements for those who design and supervise the administration of such sales.[94] The 'filtering questions' are intended to narrow down the range of mortgages on which the firm offers information. Filtering questions may be described as questions

> that go beyond those needed to assess the consumer's eligibility against the lender's criteria. For example, filtering questions could include questions about the consumer's preferences for particular types of interest rates, whether the consumer has a preference for mortgages without early repayment charges, whether the consumer is interested in mortgages with payment holidays and so on.[95]

Since these are 'non-advised' sales, firms must not make any recommendations to the consumer about the merits of particular products; they may only provide information, and the filtering questions narrow down that information.[96] The areas to be covered by the questions echo those identified in the suitability analysis for advised sales, as well as questions covering the alternative options and the possible effects of alternative choices on

[91] *Ibid. FSA Handbook*, MCOB 8.5.4, available online at <http://fsahandbook.info/FSA/html/handbook/MCOB/8/5>, provides that:

'(1) An equity release transaction will be suitable if, having regard to the facts disclosed by the customer and other relevant facts about the customer of which the firm is or should reasonably be aware, the firm has reasonable grounds to conclude that:

(a) the benefits to the customer outweigh any adverse effect on:
   (i) the customer's entitlement (if any) to means-tested benefits; and
   (ii) the customer's tax position (for example the loss of an Age Allowance);

(b) alternative methods of raising the required funds such as, in particular:
   (i) an equity release transaction from the other market sector; or
   (ii) (where relevant) a local authority (or other) grant;
   are less suitable;

(c) where the equity release transaction requires that payments are made to the equity release provider (for example an interest-only mortgage), the customer can afford to enter into the transaction;

(d) the equity release transaction is appropriate to the needs, objectives and circumstances of the customer; and

(e) the equity release transaction is the most suitable of those that the firm has available to it within the scope of the service provided to the customer.

(2) No recommendation must be made if there is no equity release transaction from within the scope of the service provided to the customer which is appropriate to his needs and circumstances ... '

[92] Consultation Paper 186, above n 61, para 5.9.

[93] *Ibid.*

[94] *Ibid*, para 5.15.

[95] Consultation Paper 146, above n 61, para 13.2.

[96] The importance of limiting the amount of information provided to the most suitable products, particularly for older consumers, is discussed in ch 6, section (3).

the consumer's tax and benefit position.[97] This approach seeks to ensure that the non-advised sales process is geared towards identifying the most suitable product for the individual consumer, although it stops short of fixing the provider with a statutory duty to ensure that the product is suitable for the consumer's needs, objectives and circumstances.

Since lifetime mortgages are classified as 'regulated mortgages', they were broadly clustered with other regulated mortgage contracts so far as the rules covering general conduct of business and fair treatment of consumers were concerned. Many of the general rules address issues identified in the OFT's *Guidelines for Non-Status Lenders and Brokers*,[98] which aimed to protect consumers at the margins of the credit market from unfair practices such as misleading advertising and marketing, cold calling, lack of disclosure or unclear product information, misleading sales practices, unfair treatment of customers in arrears, unsuitable advice and so on.[99] So, for example, the detailed rules set out in MCOB 5.6 regulate the way in which information concerning charges, total cost of product and so on must be set out in the illustration documentation, including itemised information on fees payable. A tailored pre-application illustration (PAI) was designed for lifetime mortgages, and 'road-tested' with older consumers. The FSA claimed that the consumer feedback was positive and enabled it to address issues such as the length of the document (which the research found 'was not an issue for this group of consumers, and that in fact it was helpful to repeat certain information where it was relevant to more than one section of the PAI'[100]). Amongst the information to be included in this document is a section on benefits and risks, with statements or warnings on:

a) the specific circumstances in which the lender is able to repossess the property;
b) how the lender will treat any negative equity arising during the life of the mortgage and at the time the amount borrowed is due to be repaid in full;
c) the effect of the customer wanting or needing to move home (either into another property, or into sheltered accommodation or long-term care or residential care), including the circumstances in which the mortgage is portable and whether early repayment charges are payable (the illustration is not required under this heading to state the exact amount of any early repayment charges);
d) the effect on the lifetime mortgage of another party moving into the property (for example on marriage or where a family member acts as a carer);

[97] Consultation Paper 146, above n 61, para 18.29; see *FSA Handbook*, MCOB 8.6.3, online at <http://fsahandbook.info/FSA/html/handbook/MCOB/8/6>. MCOB 8.6.1 provides:

'The questions used to help a customer select an equity release transaction must cover the following:

(1) the matters regarding eligibility criteria, customer's preferences for his estate, customer's health and life expectancy, customer's future plans and needs, customer's preference or need for stability in the amount of payments, and whether the customer has a preference or need for any other features, set out in MCOB 8.5.8 R;

(2) whether the customer has considered alternative methods of raising the required funds, and in particular:

(a) an equity release transaction from the other market sector; and

(b) where relevant, grant assistance from his local authority (or other provider); and

(3) whether the customer has established whether either his entitlement to means-tested benefits or his tax position or both will be adversely affected.'

MCOB 8.6.2 states: 'A firm should encourage a customer to seek advice on an equity release transaction if the customer is unsure about making their own choice. In relation to grant assistance, means-tested benefits and the customer's tax position, a firm should, where relevant, encourage the customer to seek further information from an appropriate source such as their local authority or Citizens Advice Bureau (or other similar agency).'

[98] See ch 8, section (6).

[99] See Consultation Paper 146, above n 61, Table 16.1.

[100] *Ibid*, para 18.33.

e) the lender's requirements for repair and maintenance of the property, including the lender's right (if any) to enter the property to effect essential repairs, and the circumstances in which this may occur;
f) a warning that taking out this lifetime mortgage may affect the customer's tax and benefits position, and that he or she should consider seeking further information from the Inland Revenue, Benefits Agency or other source of advice such as a Citizens' Advice Bureau;
g) whether the customer can secure borrowing from any other source on the property in the future;

as well as the following specified text:

> Check that this mortgage will meet your needs if you want your family to inherit your home. If you are in doubt, seek independent legal advice.[101]

The MCOB requirement to provide detailed information about the risks of the lifetime mortgage product should, so far as firms are compliant with the FSA's rules, ensure that consumers are *informed* about the nature of the risks they undertake when transacting for a lifetime mortgage. The conduct of the firm is also regulated through the FSA's 'Principles for Businesses', a set of 'high-level standards' which include:

Principle 1—A firm must conduct its business with integrity;
Principle 6—A firm must pay due regard to the interests of its customers and treat them fairly; and
Principle 7—A firm must pay due regard to the information needs of its clients, and communicate to them in a way that is clear, fair and not misleading.[102] For example, provisions regulating initial disclosure also require firms to disclose whether they are going to charge a fee, the amount of the fee and their policy on refunds.[103]

High-pressure selling was addressed through the financial promotion rules for unsolicited communications and the Principles for Business. Guidance is given in MCOB 2.4 regarding high-pressure sales, which unpacks adherence to Principle 6[104] as meaning, in this context, that firms should avoid selling practices that commit customers (or lead customers to believe that they are committed) to any transaction before they have been able to consider the illustration and offer document (for example, by presenting a new customer with an illustration, offer document and mortgage deed at one time, and requiring the mortgage deed to be signed on the same occasion).[105] Principle 7[106] is similarly explained as requiring, for example, that a firm should avoid giving any customer a false impression about the availability of a product, such as describing it as a 'special offer' not available after a certain date unless this is really the case.[107]

[101] *FSA Handbook*, MCOB 9.4.33, online at <http://fsahandbook.info/FSA/html/handbook/MCOB/9/4>; MCOB 9, Annex 1R, online at <http://fsahandbook.info/FSA/docs/mcob/mcob9_annex1R_20100706.pdf>.
[102] *FSA Handbook*, online at <http://fsahandbook.info/FSA/html/handbook/PRIN>.
[103] *FSA Handbook*, MCOB, 5.6.66–5.6.72, online at <http://fsahandbook.info/FSA/html/handbook/MCOB/5/6>.
[104] See above.
[105] MCOB 2.4.2, online at <http://fsahandbook.info/FSA/html/handbook/MCOB/2/4>.
[106] See above.
[107] MCOB 2.4.3, online at <http://fsahandbook.info/FSA/html/handbook/MCOB/2/4>.

Although the provision of a 'cooling-off period' was considered, the FSA was persuaded by industry arguments that this would impose disproportionate costs on lenders, that those most vulnerable to high-pressure selling would be least likely to cancel and that it was unnecessary in light of the protections provided in other elements of the mortgage rules.[108] Interestingly, against the backdrop of the specific development of regulatory regimes for lifetime mortgages, home reversions and SRB agreements, the idea of adopting cooling-off provisions for specific categories of loan where consumer detriment was thought more likely was rejected on the basis that 'the definitional difficulties make this disproportionate—it would be costly for lenders to adopt a different sales process (including a purpose test) just to identify certain types of mortgages'.[109]

The 'light-touch' approach taken to high-pressure sales is evidenced by the use of guidance rather than rules in MCOB 2.4; by the decision not to provide for a cooling-off period; and by the preference for generic consumer protection across the categories of home finance[110] rather than a tailored approach that recognised the heightened vulnerability of certain consumer groups, for example older consumers. The FSA's reluctance to impose a higher burden on lenders with regard to high-pressure sales is striking in contrast to the bespoke approach taken towards different product groups (regulated mortgages, lifetime mortgages, home reversions, SRB agreements) in other parts of the *FSA Handbook*, and in light of evidence that older consumers—at whom lifetime mortgages and home reversions (and to some extent SRB agreements) are targeted—are particularly vulnerable to this type of pressure.[111]

The content of the MCOB *Handbook* is useful and represents significant progress against the unregulated market. It seeks to ensure that firms treat their lifetime mortgage customers fairly, particularly by providing them with clear information about the products on offer and the risks of this type of transaction. A major weakness of the regulatory approach, however, lies in the risk of uneven uptake of guidance and good practice, and in some cases compliance with rules, across the industry. The effectiveness of the FSA's 'principles-based', 'light-touch', 'risk-based' approach to financial regulation has come under intense scrutiny following the global financial crisis from 2007,[112] with some critics describing the FSA's 'light-touch' approach as a lack of (or minimal) regulation.[113] While much of this criticism has been targeted at macro-prudential institutional regulation, the same philosophy of light-touch, principles-based regulation (in contrast to 'an overly legalistic approach'[114]) informed the consumer protection side of the FSA's regime. The FSA has recognised the existence of 'problem areas' when it comes to the effectiveness of its regulation of mortgage lending, particularly in ensuring that all firms are treating

[108] Consultation Paper 146, above n 61, paras 16.14–16.18.

[109] *Ibid*, para 16.17.

[110] Regulated mortgages (including lifetime mortgages), home reversions and sale-and-rent back agreements.

[111] See discussions highlighting the impact of high-pressure sales in relation to age and economic decision-making, and financial abuse and older people, in ch 6, sections (3) and (4).

[112] For discussion of this approach, see eg, R Tomasic, 'Beyond 'Light Touch' Regulation of British Banks after the Financial Crisis' in I MacNeil and J O'Brien (eds) *The Future of Financial Regulation* (Oxford, Hart Publishing, 2010); and J Gray, 'What Next for Risk-based Financial Regulation?' in Mac Neil and O'Brien (eds), *ibid*.

[113] Tomasic, above n 112, at 112.

[114] *Ibid*, at 113.

customers fairly,[115] and especially for consumers with impaired credit histories.[116] Consumers—particularly vulnerable or marginal consumers—may find it difficult to determine at the time of the transaction whether they are dealing with a 'good' lender, who follows regulatory guidance and adopts good practice,[117] or a 'bad' lender, who chooses to pursue greater (short-term) profitability and is prepared to take the risk of FSA sanction.

Industry compliance with the lifetime mortgage advice and sales processes has been evaluated through a series of FSA market reviews (including mystery shops and visits to firms) since 2004. The first project found that more than 70 per cent of advisers were not gathering enough information about their customers before offering them advice on equity release; that more than 60 per cent did not explain the downsides of equity release; and that consumers were being advised to borrow more than they needed and invest some of the additional equity released in products that were not suitable for their needs and could expose them to unnecessary risk.[118] At the time, Clive Briault, Managing Director of Retail Markets at the FSA, recognised that 'What makes matters worse in this area is that these consumers tend to be elderly and vulnerable people who can ill-afford to be unnecessarily exposed to risk.'[119] A second survey in 2006 found some improvements on the previous year, but still identified significant variation in performance across the sector, and variation in the standards of advice offered by intermediaries, from 'unacceptable' to 'effective', and with some exceeding regulatory requirements.[120]

The effectiveness of the FSA's strategy for lifetime mortgages was reviewed again in 2008, when the second stage of the Mortgage Effectiveness Review focused on the 'higher risk areas' of sub-prime and lifetime mortgages.[121] The decision to focus on these areas was prompted by an awareness of greater risk of consumer detriment,[122] and the objective was to evaluate the effectiveness of the MCOB rules against five intended outcomes.[123]

[115] FSA, 'FSA reiterates call for firms to treat customers fairly in current market conditions', online at <http://www.fsa.gov.uk/pages/Library/Communication/PR/2008/087.shtml>.

[116] A 2008 review of 'mainstream' mortgage lenders found that while they were 'largely complying with FSA requirements and have policies and practices that should ensure that customers are generally treated fairly … there were particular concerns with specialist lenders, including that they: operated a 'one size fits all' approach … without reference to the borrower's circumstances; were too ready to take court action; and had lower standards of systems and controls in place to control mortgage arrears handling, including training and competency arrangements': *ibid.* While this review focused on practices in handling arrears and seeking repossession, it reflects the inherent risk of uneven compliance with principles-based regulatory systems. The review also identified a range of issues in respect of lenders more generally, which included that they 'could have done more to consider customers' individual circumstances'.

[117] See S Bright, 'Dispossession for Arrears: The Weight of Home' in L Fox O'Mahony and JA Sweeney (eds), *The Idea of Home in Law: Displacement and Dispossession* (Farnham, Ashgate, 2011) 36.

[118] FSA, 'FSA work discovers consumers are not being properly advised on equity release' (FSA/PN/054/2005) (London, FSA, 2005); <http://www.fsa.gov.uk/pages/Library/Communication/PR/2005/054.shtml>.

[119] *Ibid.*

[120] FSA, 'Lifetime Mortgage Sales and Advice: Improvements made but further to go' (FSA/PN/071/2006) (19 July 2006); online at <http://www.fsa.gov.uk/pages/Library/Communication/PR/2006/071.shtml>.

[121] See FSA, *Mortgage Effectiveness Review, Stage 2 Report* (London, FSA, 2008); available online at <http://www.fsa.gov.uk/pubs/other/MER2_report.pdf>.

[122] FSA, 'Mortgage Effectiveness Review: focusing on higher risk areas' (FSA/PN/047/2007); available online at <http://fsa.gov.uk/pages/Library/Communication/PR/2007/047.shtml>.

[123] The intended outcomes were: (1) Consumers shop around for mortgages; (2) Consumers understand whether they are being given advice or information by firms; (3) Consumers better understand the risks and features of the mortgages they take out, including affordability risks; (4) Consumers take out suitable and good-value mortgages; and (5) Consumers are treated fairly over the life of the mortgage, including when they go into arrears. On this last outcome, the report noted that 'Unfortunately the evidence from the qualitative

This survey judged that the lifetime mortgage market 'works well for most customers most of the time'.[124] Against the intended outcomes, it found that lifetime mortgage consumers generally shop around (doing this for themselves rather than relying on brokers); but that they did not recognise the difference between advised and non-advised sales, neither did they consider the distinction between information and advice to be important, as they assumed that all brokers would recommend appropriate options and at least not suggest inappropriate ones.[125]

While consumers generally (believed they) had a good understanding of the risks and features of the mortgages they had taken out, this was based on their own research into the products, and the Key Facts Illustration (KFI) had not prompted a consideration of the risks and features before purchase.[126] The FSA's findings indicated that, generally, lifetime consumers conducted extensive personal research over a long period of time, weighed up the benefits and disadvantages of products against the alternatives, and discussed the decision with family members.[127] Yet notwithstanding the general conclusion that 'Lifetime consumers take time over their decision',[128] the qualitative research also indicated that the amount of time taken to make the decision depended on the urgency with which the funds were needed. This underlines the heightened vulnerability of more marginal consumers, who make decisions under financial pressure. Although consumers found the KFI 'reassuring', in as much as it set out the risk details in writing, in some cases alerted them to social security/tax implications, and usefully illustrated the mortgage cost over time and how the value of the home could change,[129] this kicked in after the transaction rather than assisting with the decision-making process as it was intended. In fact, the review could not identify any appreciable impact of the MCOB rules and guidance on the suitability and value for money of lifetime mortgages. Rather, consumers tended to be hyperbolic discounters, placing greater emphasis on the short-term costs than on the long-term suitability and value of the product, and tending to rely to a considerable extent on their broker, whom they assumed would sell them a suitable and good-value product.[130]

The evidence from this review does not indicate widespread dissatisfaction—indeed, the qualitative research claimed that 'All lifetime mortgage consumers were happy, confident and comfortable with their final product choice whether they had received advice or not.'[131] Neither does it reflect well on the FSA's strategy to regulate the lifetime

research indicated that some lenders across both the prime and sub-prime markets might have been failing to abide by the MCOB requirements on arrears. So we have been unable to assess and test the effectiveness of our arrears rules': *MER, Stage 2 Report*, above n 121, at 8.

[124] *Ibid*, Foreword, at2.

[125] *Ibid*, at 5.

[126] *Ibid*, at 6.

[127] *Ibid*, at 12.

[128] *Ibid*.

[129] *Ibid*, at 24.

[130] *Ibid*, at 34.

[131] *Ibid*, at 29. The research also showed that 'many lifetime consumers were satisfied with the contact received both at the information/advice stage and subsequently, and felt sufficiently confident to make an independent final decision. Many valued the caution they were encouraged to exercise from their first contact point ... 96% of the respondents who had spoken to a professional adviser did not reject their adviser's recommendation and most purchased the recommended product. 79% of respondents said they were confident that their product was suitable for their needs.'

mortgage market.[132] While the review posited that the market works well for most people most of the time, it is significant that this appears to be based more on consumers' own strategies to acquire and evaluate information about products rather than any appreciable impact of the MCOB rules. This tends to support the behavioural claim that consumers' prior psychological commitment to purchase dilutes the effect of disclosure and other informational strategies.[133] This finding also has significant implications for marginal older owners, who are likely to be particularly vulnerable in complex financial transactions, whether as a result of their relative inexperience or because of the disproportionate impact of adverse outcomes. The discussion of older people as 'risk subjects' in chapter three emphasised the unequal distribution of risk in financial transactions, and the role of cultural capital in determining who will be the 'winners' and 'losers' in the risk society. The heightened vulnerability of marginal older owners when it comes to financial and legal capabilities and situational vulnerabilities[134] underlines the nature of the gap between a market that works well for most of the people most of the time, and adequate legal protections: the evidence all points to those who are most vulnerable being least able to protect themselves.

(b) Home reversion plans

Home reversion plans were brought under the FSA's authority in 2007, to ensure a 'level playing field' within the housing equity market.[135] While a lifetime mortgage involves borrowing against the property, home reversion plans involve sale of the property, or a share in the property in exchange for a lump sum payment, an income for life, or, in some cases, a combination of lump sum and income, alongside an agreement allowing the vendor to remain in occupation, perhaps for a peppercorn rent. In land law terms, a partial home reversion utilises a form of co-ownership whereby the 'vendor' continues to own a portion of the property as tenant in common with the 'purchaser' company. Both co-owners will benefit from any increase in value, proportionate to their shares, and the older owner's share continues to be an inheritable asset for the purposes of his or her estate.[136] A full reversion involves the sale of the whole of the owner's interest in the property to the reversion company in return for a lump sum/income and the agreement that the occupier remain in the property on a lifelong lease. As such, home reversion is a form of 'sale and lease' transaction, although home reversion plans are differentiated from 'sale-and-rent back' transactions by the nature of the contractual arrangement for future occupation.

[132] The FSA acknowledged that 'our market intervention, in relation to disclosure, in particular, may not be working as intended … it seems clear that we need to do something more to ensure consumers understand the implications for them of choosing between an advised and non-advised service': *ibid*, at 34.

[133] C Willett, *Fairness in Consumer Contracts: The Case of Unfair Terms* (Aldershot, Ashgate, 2007), para 2.4.2.2; see also I Ramsey, *Advertising, Culture and the Law* (London, Sweet & Maxwell, 1996).

[134] See ch 6.

[135] See, eg, HM Treasury, *Secondary Legislation for the Regulation of Home Reversion and Home Purchase Plans: A Consultation* (London, HMSO, 2006), para 3.1; available online at <http://webarchive.nationalarchives.gov.uk/+/http://www.hm-treasury.gov.uk/media/4FD/E2/consult_homereversion_300306.pdf>.

[136] In some cases the property may be sold in order to release the remaining equity to fund further expenses, eg the costs of nursing care.

The FSA's definition of home reversion describes a product under which the consumer's right to occupation continues until the occurrence of one of the specified determining events,[137] described as 'qualifying termination events', ie:

a) the occupier becomes a resident of a care home;
b) the occupier dies; or
c) the end of a specified period of at least 20 years.

This definition was based on the products available on the market at the time of the consultation[138] and the Government's specific intention, at that time, *not* to include other SRB products within the regulatory scope of the FSA. More recently, 'sale-and-rent back' has also been brought under the FSA's regulatory umbrella, and it is now negatively defined as an agreement to sell all or part of the owner's interest in the property, where the consumer is entitled to remain in occupation but where the arrangement does not fall within the definition of home reversion,[139] ie where the consumer's occupation is not open-ended subject to these three qualifying termination events. Market experience suggests that a SRB transaction may amount to a less secure arrangement since the consumer's ongoing occupation is usually based on a tenancy for which rent must be paid.[140]

The home reversion company typically pays considerably less than the market value for its share of the property, to reflect the ongoing occupation of the owner. The proportion of the market value paid also depends on the age of the owner, and reflects the lender's risks in taking on the compounded uncertainties of the longevity of the owner and the future value of the property. Home reversion may be considered a more appropriate

[137] MCOB defines a home reversion as an arrangement:
'(a) ... under which a person (the reversion provider) buys all or part of a qualifying interest in land from an individual or trustees (the reversion occupier);
(b) the reversion occupier (if he is an individual) or an individual who is a beneficiary of the trust (if the reversion occupier is a trustee), or a related person, is entitled under the arrangement to occupy at least 40% of the land in question as or in connection with a dwelling and intends to do so; and
(c) the arrangement specifies that the entitlement to occupy will end on the occurrence of one or more of:
(i) a person in (b) becoming a resident of a care home;
(ii) a person in (b) dying; or
(iii) the end of a specified period of at least twenty years from the date the reversion occupier entered into the arrangement;
in this definition 'related person' means:
(A) that person's spouse or civil partner;
(B) a person (whether or not of the opposite sex) whose relationship with that person has the characteristics of the relationship between husband and wife; or
(C) that person's parent, brother, sister, child, grandparent or grandchild.'
See *FSA Handbook*, MCOB Glossary Definition 18, online at <http://fsahandbook.info/FSA/glossary-html/handbook/Glossary/H?definition=G1890>.

[138] HM Treasury, *Secondary legislation for regulation of Home Reversion and Home Purchase Plans: A consultation* (London, HSMO, 2006), para 3.9; online at <http://webarchive.nationalarchives.gov.uk/+/http://www.hm-treasury.gov.uk/media/4FD/E2/consult_homereversion_300306.pdf>.

[139] MCOB defines a 'sale-and-rent back' agreement as an arrangement: '(a) ... under which a person (an agreement provider), buys all or part of the qualifying interest in land in the United Kingdom from an individual or trustees (the "agreement seller"); and (b) the agreement seller (if he is an individual) or an individual who is the beneficiary of the trust (if the agreement seller is a trustee), or a related person, is entitled under the arrangement to occupy at least 40% of the land in question as or in connection with a dwelling, and intends to do so; but excluding any arrangement that is a regulated home reversion plan.' See *FSA Handbook*, MCOB Glossary Definition 32, online at <http://fsahandbook.info/FSA/glossary-html/handbook/Glossary/R?definition=G2646>.

[140] See further below, section (c).

method of equity release than a lifetime mortgage where the owner is not optimistic about the likelihood of house price inflation, since by giving up some or all of his or her ownership there is less (or no) opportunity to benefit from future price increase, or where a larger cash sum is needed than may be obtained on a lifetime mortgage. Home reversion plans also leave the older consumer with less (or no) housing equity to leave as inheritance. A partial reversion may allow the owner to save some equity for later—either for future needs, or for a bequest intention. The discount against market value is typically between 35 per cent and 65 per cent (depending on the consumer's age, life expectancy, the value of the property and the particular product), to reflect the fact that the 'purchaser' will be kept out of use and occupation until a determining event occurs.[141] In some cases it may be possible to 'buy back' equity transferred, or the product may be transferable to another property if the consumer wants to move house, but this depends on the terms of particular agreements.[142]

The market for home reversions is considerably smaller than the lifetime mortgage market: combined figures from the Council of Mortgage Lenders and SHIP for the period 2003–05 suggested that the number of home reversions sold was between 3 per cent and 8 per cent the number of lifetime mortgages.[143] The suggestion that while lifetime mortgages are more popular in times of price inflation, home reversions may be more attractive when house prices stagnate or drop, might have been thought to have prompted an increase in home reversions following the housing market crisis since 2007, although limited data on the volume of sales of home reversion plans have been collected since 1 October 2007. In the six-month period to 31 March 2008, provider firms transacted 620 plans, of which 77 per cent were advised transactions. In the 12-month period to 31 March 2009, the pace of activity was relatively slower, with firms transacting only 750 plans, of which 94 per cent were advised transactions.[144] This in fact reflects a lower volume of sales than the 2003–05 data, suggesting that the housing market recession has not increased the popularity of home reversions,[145] and neither has the extension of regulatory authority to these products.

From the outset of the consultation process for regulation of lifetime mortgages, it was clear that the FSA considered home reversion plans to carry a similar order of risks and was in favour of extending the regulatory umbrella to include these products.[146] This was achieved through the Regulation of Financial Services (Land Transactions) Act 2005,[147]

141 FSA, *Regulation of Home Reversion and Home Purchase Plans, Volume 1—Consultation Proposals* (CP 06/8) (London, FSA, 2006), para 2.4; online at http://www.fsa.gov.uk/pubs/cp/cp06_08.pdf.

142 *Ibid.*

143 *Ibid*, Chart to para 2.7.

144 FSA, *Mortgages: Product Sales Data (PSD) Trend Report* (London, FSA, August 2009) at 17; online at <http://www.fsa.gov.uk/pubs/other/mortgage_report_09%20final.pdf>.

145 While the attractiveness of the alternative options might be expected to vary, it is also noted that since equity release products are based on longer-term risk assessment than mainstream mortgages, immediate changes in the housing market or wider economy have less impact on their pricing; SHIP, 'SHIP Member Survey 2007: Credit Crunch has not affected consumer confidence in equity release but demand for better access to advice remains' (8 December 2007); online at <http://www.ship-ltd.org/uploads/08-dec-2007.pdf>.

146 See, eg, Consultation Paper 146, above n 61, para 2.40.

147 Which extended FSA jurisdiction over financial arrangements involving land in which:

...the person providing the finance either—

(a) acquires a major interest in land from the person to whom the finance is provided, or

(b) disposes of a major interest in land to that person... (s1 inserting paragraph 23A to Schedule 2 of the 2000 Act).

which amended the FSMA 2000 to bring activities relating to financial arrangements involving the acquisition or disposal of land (including Home Reversion Plans, Ijara home financing arrangements and other flexible tenure schemes) within the scope of FSA regulation. In enacting the enabling legislation, the Government reiterated the function of regulation in this context as providing *information* and *advice*. Introducing the second reading of the Bill, Lord McKenzie stated:

> Regulation is not designed to discourage people from purchasing these products, but to help them make informed choices, offer valuable consumer protection and ensure there is a level playing field in the equity release market, most of which already falls within the scope of the FSA mortgage regulation … these are not simple products to understand, hence the need to ensure that potential purchasers receive an appropriate level of advice.[148]

Equity release products are generally both complex and expensive, and the provision of clearer information and advice for consumers—especially elderly consumers—to ensure that they are able to make informed decisions, is undoubtedly welcome. Nevertheless, it is now widely recognised that information and advice are not sufficient in themselves to achieve adequate consumer protection in this context. With the Government anticipating that FSA regulation would

> open the door to important consumer protections to be extended to vulnerable and minority consumers, level the playing field in mortgage regulation, ensure that no artificial distortions go forward, bolster consumer confidence in those products and thus help to ensure that the markets continue to develop.[149]

the adequacy of the protections in preventing consumer harm (in this developing market) merit further analysis.

The detail of the regulatory scheme was worked out in a series of Consultation Papers published by HM Treasury[150] and the FSA.[151] The intention was that the regulation of home reversions would be 'appropriate and proportionate to the nature of and risks inherent to these products, as well as the size of the markets'.[152] Thus it was anticipated that there would be some differences between the approach to home reversions and that taken to regulated mortgage contracts (which is a substantially larger market). At the same time, the FSA emphasised that 'We see HRs [home reversions] (like lifetime mortgages) as higher risk products than standard mortgages.'[153] There were pragmatic and policy arguments for moving towards a single equity release regime,[154] and in many respects the regulation of home reversions followed the approach taken to lifetime mortgages (and sits

[148] *Hansard*, HL Deb, 17 October 2005, col 554 (Lord McKenzie).

[149] *Ibid*, col 558 (Lord McKenzie).

[150] HM Treasury, *Regulating Home Reversion Plans: Consultation Document* (London, HMSO, 2003); HM Treasury, *Defining Home Reversions: Consultation Document* (London, HMSO, July 2004); HM Treasury, *Secondary legislation for regulation of Home Reversion and Home Purchase Plans: A consultation* (London, HSMO, 2006); online at <http://webarchive.nationalarchives.gov.uk/+/http://www.hm-treasury.gov.uk/media/4FD/E2/consult_homereversion_300306.pdf>.

[151] See CP 06/8, above n 141.

[152] HM Treasury (2006), above n 150, para 3.4.

[153] CP 06/8, above n 141, para 1.12.

[154] See, eg, FSA, *Regulation of Home Reversion and Home Purchase Plans—Feedback on CP06/8 and final rules, Volume 1, Policy Statement* (Policy Statement 06/12) (London, FSA, 2006) para 2.5; online at <http://www.fsa.gov.uk/pubs/policy/ps06_12.pdf>.

within MCOB more generally).[155] Indeed, it was the desirability of broad consistency between lifetime mortgages and home reversions that inhibited the application of a 'high-level principles-based approach' to home reversions, the scheme for home reversions falling for consideration at a moment when the FSA was keen to move towards such an approach across its work. The FSA explained that its preference for a high-level approach to home reversions had been 'significantly constrained' by the need to keep the home reversion regulations reasonably consistent with the existing lifetime mortgage regime—to the extent that the risks posed by the products are similar—to avoid creating competitive distortions and potential confusion. Since the FSA took the view that it would not be fair, so soon after the implementation of the lifetime mortgage regime, to require firms to shift their practice once again in compliance with a new single, higher-level set of rules, the lifetime mortgage provisions were allowed to stand; although where bespoke provisions were introduced to address the specific risks associated with home reversions, these were pitched at a higher level.

The generic 'equity release' risks identified in the FSA's paper included:

a) that the target consumer group is older and potentially vulnerable;
b) the risk of mis-buying by consumers;
c) the risk of mis-selling by providers;
d) that consumers will not appreciate the need for legal advice;
e) the risk of not securing appropriate access to redress;
f) insufficient access to information regarding products and risks to make an informed choice; and
g) lack of awareness amongst consumers that they can shop around for a good deal.[156]

In addition, the FSA identified a further set of risks that are specific to home reversions:

a) their impact on tax, benefits and beneficiaries;
b) the discounted sum paid for the property and loss of any future appreciation;
c) unfair valuations;
d) the consumer's rights as a tenant/fair exercise of the provider's rights as a 'landlord';
e) losing security of tenure, or losing a residual financial interest in the property;
f) the fact that the consumer ceases to own his or her home and usually cannot buy it back;
g) that the ability to move house is likely to be restricted;
h) that there may be obligations attached to occupancy, for example an obligation to maintain the property[157]; and
i) with income products, whether the income is guaranteed or whether it ceases to be payable on death.[158]

[155] See, eg, the rules regarding financial promotions, which broadly echo those for lifetime mortgages and require: that promotional material is fair, clear, not misleading and balanced, in giving no less prominence to disadvantages than benefits; and that consumers are advised to request a personalised illustration to understand the product's features and risks. See *FSA Handbook*, MCOB 3.8A, online at <http://fsahandbook.info/FSA/html/handbook/MCOB/3/8A>.

[156] CP 06/8, above n 141, para 3.7.

[157] *Ibid*, para 6.24.

[158] *Ibid*, para 6.62.

These risks are set out in the KFI required text (the 'health warning') for home reversions.[159] Other bespoke requirements for home reversions reflected specific issues relating to the need to preserve the consumer's security of tenure under the lease; the need (in the case of partial reversions) to protect the consumer's residual beneficial interest in the property; and the need (in the case of 'income products', which allow for a series of 'mini-reversions' to provide an income over an agreed and fixed period of time) to protect the consumer's income stream.[160] These issues were viewed as particularly significant in circumstances where the provider made an onward sale of the property to a third party, for example in the secondary market, or where the provider became insolvent. The MCOB rules were therefore extended to any third party who might acquire the title to the property, and this was shored up by proprietary protections ensuring that any new landlord would be subject to the terms of the lease and a requirement that the provider register a restriction on its title at Land Registry.[161] To address the issues arising from the distinctive nature of home reversions as a sale of the property (rather than a mortgage), the FSA rules also require not only that the provider recommend legal advice, but that it receive confirmation from the legal adviser that appropriate advice has been given before proceeding with the sale of a home reversion,[162] unless it is satisfied 'on reasonable grounds, based on the customer's knowledge, expertise and experience that it is unnecessary'.[163] This not only reinforces the standard of information and advice which consumers receive, but was also intended to give the consumer a potential right of action against the solicitor where he or she fails to ensure that the required safeguards are in place.[164]

Bespoke home reversion protections were also provided in respect of valuations, with a requirement that the valuer should be independent and suitably qualified (as part of the obligation to protect customers' interests)[165]; and on an eventual sale of property on partial reversion, through a high-level rule requiring firms to act reasonably alongside a specific rule requiring that they obtain the best price within a reasonable period of time.[166] Where consumers opt for 'income products', there are additional criteria relating to suitability in respect of the investment of the capital to provide income,[167] which are intended to reflect the likelihood that older consumers' risk appetites are lower and that 'They will be using what will probably be their most valuable asset and cannot be expected to rely on long-term factors to enable them to recover from any short-term loss of income.'[168] Lastly, the obligation on firms to treat customers fairly was explicitly worked through in respect of the administration of property sold on a reversion during the post-sale period of occupation. Issues identified here included:

[159] See *FSA Handbook*, MCOB 9, Annex 2R, online at: <http://fsahandbook.info/FSA/docs/mcob/mcob9_annex2R_20100706.pdf>; also MCOB 9.4.145R–9.4.147R.

[160] CP 06/8, above n 141, para 6.41.

[161] See MCOB 2.6A, articulating the provider's duty to protect its customers' interests, and the guidance which follows to explain what this entails: <http://fsahandbook.info/FSA/html/handbook/MCOB/2/6A>.

[162] *FSA Handbook*, MCOB 2.6A.5; online at <http://fsahandbook.info/FSA/html/handbook/MCOB/2/6A>.

[163] *Ibid.*

[164] CP 06/8, above n 141, para 6.53. The issue of shifting responsibility for procedural probity onto solicitors is considered in ch 10 in the context of the equitable remedy of undue influence.

[165] *FSA Handbook*, MCOB 2.6A.12; online at <http://fsahandbook.info/FSA/html/handbook/MCOB/2/6A>.

[166] *Ibid*, MCOB 2.6A.15–2.6A.16.

[167] *Ibid*, MCOB 2.2.5G.

[168] CP 06/8, above n 141, para 6.60.

a) the consumer's obligation to maintain the property;
b) the provider's right to inspect the condition of the property;
c) the amendment and enforcement of the lease;
d) restrictions on the use of the property or who may occupy; and
e) determining whether the property has been 'abandoned' for the purposes of terminating the occupation contract.[169]

These issues were identified as illustrative examples of situations in which a firm would not be regarded as treating customers fairly in matters relating to the reversion.[170] Similar issues have also arisen in relation to SRB transactions, as discussed in the next section.

The bespoke approach to home reversions was strongly focused on the nature of the transaction and the potential risks associated with this type of product. Although some reference was made to the disproportionate impact of adverse outcomes on older consumers, the FSA regime relied on compulsory legal advice as the vehicle through which the individual needs, objectives and circumstances of the consumer would be addressed. This is consistent with the attempt to move away from detailed rules delineating provider responsibilities and towards high-level principles, although, as the discussion below acknowledges, in the wake of the global financial crisis that strategy has now been overtaken by events.

(c) Sale-and-rent back transactions

The SRB agreement was the third type of housing equity product targeted at older people to come under the FSA's regulatory umbrella, first through an interim regime from July 2009, with the final regime put in place in June 2010.[171] An SRB agreement is defined by the FSA as:

> (a) [an] arrangement ... under which a person (an agreement provider), buys all or part of the qualifying interest in land in the United Kingdom from an individual or trustees (the 'agreement seller'); and
> (b) the agreement seller (if he is an individual) or an individual who is the beneficiary of the trust (if the agreement seller is a trustee), or a related person, is entitled under the arrangement to occupy at least 40% of the land in question as or in connection with a dwelling, and intends to do so;
>
> but excluding any arrangement that is a regulated home reversion plan.[172]

In many respects an SRB agreement is very similar to a home reversion: it involves a sale of the property, usually at a significant discount, in return for a leasehold arrangement which allows the (former) owner to continue living in the home. Comparing SRB to the home reversion market, it is noteworthy that while SRB products are relatively new to the market compared to home reversions (which date back to the 1960s), the home reversions market

[169] See CP 06/8, above n 141, para 6.72.

[170] *FSA Handbook*, MCOB 2.6A.11; online at <http://fsahandbook.info/FSA/html/handbook/MCOB/2/6A>.

[171] The decision to regulate followed an OFT market study launched in 2008 to consider SRB arrangements; OFT, *Sale and rent back—An OFT Market Study* (OFT 1018) (London, OFT, 2008), available online at <http://www.oft.gov.uk/shared_oft/reports/consumer_protection/oft1018.pdf>.

[172] FSA Handbook, Glossary Definition 32; online at <http://fsahandbook.info/FSA/glossary-html/handbook/Glossary/R?definition=G2646>.

has remained relatively concentrated.[173] In contrast, the SRB sector is highly fragmented across a few large firms and a large number of small firms, family businesses and individuals.[174]

The terms offered vary from landlord to landlord, and are tailored to individual consumers based on the value of the property, the consumer's existing secured and unsecured debts, and whether financial difficulties are short- or long-term.[175] Rather than offering standard terms, both the amount of discount and the rent payable for continued occupation are therefore 'negotiable' in each individual transaction. On average, the proportion of market value paid is higher than for home reversions, with average estimates ranging from 70 per cent to 90 per cent,[176] although this is countered by the ongoing obligation to pay rent which does not arise in home reversions. The calculations needed to compute varying levels of discount against the market value of the property and different levels of rent add to the complexity of these products and the difficulties for consumers in assessing whether they are being offered good value for money.[177] This was exacerbated by the practices of some SRB providers who did not use independent valuers to assess the market value of the property, did not share written valuations with customers, or in some cases gazundered the consumer[178] who, under the pressure of imminent repossession, was unable to negotiate.[179] The OFT study also reported examples of cases in which the agreed rent increased significantly on completion, or was not agreed until after completion.[180]

The SRB sector has been much more problematic than home reversions: the extension of FSA regulation over home reversions was intended to level the playing field of equity release, but was prophylactic in that there had not been any evidence of actual consumer detriment in the home reversions market.[181] Sale and rent back, on the other hand, has acquired a reputation for misleading consumers, and the OFT study was prompted by issues raised by Citizens' Advice, Shelter and the Council of Mortgage Lenders. For example, one key concern noted by the OFT was that 'Sale and rent back firms often tell consumers that they will be able to stay in their home for years, but in reality the tenancy is rarely guaranteed for more than six or twelve months.'[182] A typical rental agreement used the 'assured shorthold tenancy', common in the private rental sector, under which for a fixed period of 6–12 months the landlord can recover possession only if the tenant breaches a condition, but after the fixed period the landlord enjoys greater latitude to

[173] In 2006, the FSA reported that it was aware of only six provider firms offering home reversion plans, 11 specialist intermediaries, and 50 intermediaries; CP 06/8, above n 141, para 2.10.

[174] OFT, above n 171, para 3.3. The OFT study found that the SRB market 'appears to be highly fragmented, and mainly served by small firms, including non-professional landlords. It is likely that there are upwards of 1,000 firms, together with an unknown number of nonprofessional landlords, who have conducted about 50,000 transactions to date': *ibid*, para 1.2.

[175] *Ibid*, para 3.20.

[176] *Ibid*, paras 3.22–3.23, although by 2008 this figure was thought to be falling in light of the housing market recession; *ibid*, para 3.24.

[177] *Ibid*, para 3.30. The OFT reported that, reinforcing the general issue of widespread lack of financial capability across the general population in the UK, discussed in ch 6: 'Our consumer research suggests that some sale and rent back consumers do not attempt to compute even the basic aspects of the transaction—quite a few had decided to go ahead with sale and rent back without looking at the sums involved.': *ibid*, para 5.14.

[178] By reducing the price offered against the property.

[179] OFT, above n 171, para 3.26.

[180] *Ibid*, para 3.30.

[181] CP 06/8, above n 141, para 3.10.

[182] OFT, above n 171, para 1.1.

recover possession. While the OFT reported that a small number of providers offered the more secure 'assured tenancy' (more typically used in social housing), institutional factors disincentivised this practice since it could breach the terms of the buy-to-let mortgage financing used by the SRB provider to acquire the property.[183] Although it was open to SRB providers to develop the underlying legal transaction to offer greater security (for example, through a collateral agreement not to evict without cause, or to refund a portion of the discount if the occupier was evicted within a specified time period),[184] the enforceability of these agreements remained untested and the availability of this type of assurance obviously depended on the lender.

Of course, SRB is not limited to, nor necessarily targeted at, older consumers: as a product it is sold to marginal consumers across the life-course, often when they are in financial difficulties and facing imminent repossession. For this reason, the SRB sector began to attract more attention as repossession rates rose following the housing market recession from 2007, and to generate more concern as it was feared that the worsening economic climate would exacerbate and multiply the potential for consumer detriment. With repossession a major driver for SRB transactions,[185] it is also a potential avenue for older consumers who find that their 'ordinary debt' (secured or unsecured borrowing)[186] becomes unmanageable. The OFT's research found that a common feature amongst SRB customers was that[187] 'the individual felt the situation was out of control and that he or she could not pay off their debts from income. Some were in imminent danger of repossession.'[188] While not all are retired, SRB consumers are likely to be middle-aged at least, and established rather than recent buyers, since they must have built up a sufficient portion of equity in the property with which to trade. While some SRB firms specifically targeted older consumers approaching retirement,[189] only a small number of consumers actively considered SRB as part of their retirement planning.[190] This underlined the tendency for older consumers to enter into SRB transactions in a context of (perhaps urgent) financial pressure, rendering them particularly (situationally) vulnerable.[191]

The two key concerns identified by the OFT were:

a) that some consumers were opting for SRB when this was not the most appropriate option for them to address their financial difficulties, for example where on-going difficulties meant that they would be unable to pay the rent required for continued occupation, so that staying in the property was not a sustainable solution for them; and
b) that there were significant risks associated with lack of security of tenure after the transaction in many cases.[192]

[183] *Ibid*, para 3.41.
[184] *Ibid*, para 3.43.
[185] *Ibid*, para 2.10.
[186] See discussion in ch 7.
[187] They are typically either out of work and receiving benefits, or in low-paid jobs; and the property is usually a small, low-value (under £200,000) house or flat; OFT, above n 171, para 3.54 and Annexe C.
[188] *Ibid*, para 3.57.
[189] *Ibid*, paras 3.59–3.60.
[190] *Ibid*, para 3.60.
[191] See ch 6 for discussion of contextual or situational vulnerability.
[192] OFT, above n 171, paras 1.6–1.7.

Without the stability of a life-long lease subject to the determining events which signify a home reversion, SRB tenants had been evicted following significant rent increases which they were unable to pay. Another raft of problems emerged where the SRB transaction was funded on a buy-to-let mortgage and the landlord/provider had defaulted, leading to repossession by the landlord's creditor.

The difficulties which have been associated with SRB transactions provide an extreme example of the inadequacies of the current legal framework, outwith FSA regulation, to protect potentially vulnerable consumers.[193] For example, considering the protection against misleading information offered by the Consumer Protection from Unfair Trading Regulations 2008,[194] the OFT noted that while 'The [2008 Regulations] offer some protection from misleading sales ... they do not address the issues around the suitability of the product for individuals, or the risks inherent in the product as it stands.'[195] The Regulations are targeted at misconduct on the part of providers, when there is a clear need for claimant-sided protections in this context, reflected in the OFT's admission that 'We have concerns about sale and rent back, even where it is honestly sold.'[196]

The factors that render SRB consumers particularly vulnerable include the complexity of both SRB products and the alternatives (for example, lifetime mortgages or home reversion plans). This is compounded for consumers who are 'already in stressful and difficult financial and emotional situations'.[197] The OFT recognised that the nature of the risks involved, and the circumstances of SRB, meant that in most cases consumers could not be expected to negotiate the risks as rational legal subjects.[198] It also noted that consumers in financial difficulties may be disinclined to discuss their situation with others, so that the range of advice received could be limited, perhaps to the firm offering the product.[199] The evidence indicated that consumers were not making balanced and informed choices, and that they were particularly vulnerable to 'persuasion' by sales people where SRB was the wrong choice for them.[200] The OFT concluded that the general legal framework left these vulnerable consumers bearing almost all of the risk in the transaction, without being fully aware of the risks they had taken, and unprepared for the adverse outcome where a 'downside risk' materialises.[201] In addition to concerns that SRB consumers were not able to assess the risks they were taking,[202] the market mechanisms that might be thought to contribute to good outcomes for consumers in other retail contexts—for example, price competition and reputational effects—were ineffective because SRB consumers tended not to shop around.[203]

[193] See generally, discussion in OFT, above n 171, ch 8.

[194] For a general discussion of the 2008 Regulations, see ch 8, section (8).

[195] OFT, above n 171, para 8.6.

[196] *Ibid.*

[197] *Ibid*, para 1.9.

[198] '[M]ost consumers are not in a position to make a balanced assessment at the point of sale taking into account the real market value of their home, the price offered, and the cost of renting—in addition to the risks of the firm defaulting on the mortgage, increasing the rent in the future or starting eviction proceedings at the end of the agreed term of the tenancy. We do not believe that many consumers will be aware of, or able to assess, the full costs and risks they face in sale and rent back transactions.' (*ibid*, para 1.9)

[199] *Ibid*, para 1.10.

[200] *Ibid*, para 5.5.

[201] *Ibid*, para 1.11.

[202] *Ibid*, para 5.5.

[203] *Ibid.*

The distinction drawn between being made aware of risks and being in a position to take account of risks is an important one, and echoes the discussion of situational or contextual vulnerability in chapter six, as well as the discussions in section (5) below, and throughout this book, concerning the limits of the information paradigm when it comes to ensuring consumer protection. The OFT's market analysis recognised that it is the context of consumers, or the situation in which they are required to make a decision concerning their housing equity, which makes them vulnerable. Indeed, it was the degree of situational vulnerability which the OFT relied on to distinguish the SRB sector from other regulated housing equity products, and to justify a considerably stronger approach to consumer protection. It reported:

> One of the main differences … is the circumstance in which consumers make their decision. Where consumers are taking a planning decision (as with regulated equity release) reputational effects can be powerful and self-regulation may achieve a high rate of coverage and impose a strong discipline on the sector. Where consumers are taking decisions in a crisis situation, however (as with many sale and rent back transactions) we believe reputational effects to be much less strong.[204]

It also recognised that since most people will enter into only one SRB transaction, there is little scope for 'learning effects'[205] to improve their decision-making. Since consumers did not tend to shop around, there was little scope for price competition or other competitive market effects. The fragmented nature of the market meant that reliance on 'good practice' rather than enforceable rules was recognised as inadequate[206]; and crucially, these vulnerabilities took effect against a backdrop in which the stakes are high and the impact of a bad outcome severe.

The FSA began regulating SRB from 1 July 2009 though an interim regime that sought to address the most immediate problems for consumers (including authorisation to provide SRB, Threshold Conditions that firms must be fit and proper, and the high-level Principles for Business), with the full regime coming into effect by 30 June 2010.[207] The SRB provisions built on the home reversion rules in MCOB, applying many of the generic provisions to SRB, including provisions relating to inducements,[208] high-pressure sales[209] and protecting customers' interests.[210] In light of the risk analyses conducted by the OFT and the FSA, a range of bespoke SRB provisions were also added to address specific risks. The perceived SRB risks and regulatory responses may be clustered across three broad categories:

[204] *Ibid*, para 9.9.

[205] *Ibid*.

[206] *Ibid*, para 9.10.

[207] See FSA, *Regulating sale and rent back—the full regime* (CP 09/22) (London, FSA, 2009), online at <http://www.fsa.gov.uk/pubs/cp/cp09_22.pdf>; FSA, *Sale and rent back (full regime), Feedback on CP09/22, made rules and consultation on reporting* (FSA 10/4), (London, FSA, 2010), online at <http://www.fsa.gov.uk/pubs/cp/cp10_04.pdf>; FSA, *Regulatory reporting for sale and rent back firms, Feedback on CP10/4 and final rules* (PS10/8) (London, FSA, 2010), online at <http://www.fsa.gov.uk/pubs/policy/ps10_08.pdf>.

[208] *FSA Handbook*, MCOB 2.3.

[209] MCOB 2.4.

[210] MCOB 2.6A.

a) transparency and suitability[211];
b) advice; and
c) risk to consumers (especially regarding security of tenure).

The prudential requirements extended to SRB firms included capital resource requirements, personal indemnity insurance for intermediaries and regulatory reporting requirements, while the conduct of business rules addressed a range of issues from financial promotions to post-sale contact, redress and compensation. The financial promotions rules for SRB were particularly sensitive to the vulnerability of consumers who are already in debt and potentially facing repossession. In addition to the standard requirements that the form and content of promotional materials must be clear, fair and not misleading, and the inclusion of specified risk warnings, exploitative advertising practices were addressed through a ban on cold-calling[212] and leaflet-dropping,[213] and a prohibition on 'the use of certain emotive terms and phrases in promotional material'.[214] Further, MCOB 3.8B.8 requires that firms must not exploit their customers or the

> vulnerable nature or circumstances of any customer who may be in financial difficulties and at risk of losing his or her home and must accordingly avoid using in the promotion phrases or terms such as 'fast sales', 'rescue' or 'cash quickly' or any other similar expression.[215]

The FSA undertook to take enforcement action as necessary to ensure that advertising standards for SRB improved.[216] This sensitivity to the particular vulnerabilities of SRB customers reflects an implicit acceptance of the significance of situational vulnerability in exposing consumers to the risk of adverse outcomes in financial transactions. While the SRB provisions were designed to meet the needs of consumers in financial difficulties, including but not necessarily older consumers, the ban on emotive language echoes the discussion of ageing and the shift from cognitive or 'rational' to affective processes in economic decision-making in chapter six.

The provisions relating to the sales process included a series of measures designed to 'remove some of the pressure on consumers and to enable them to properly consider whether SRB is the right option for them',[217] including an FSA consumer factsheet on SRB which firms will be required to provide to, and discuss with, consumers as part of the sales process[218]; protections for the consumer where the provider commissions a valuation, including a duty of care on the valuer to the customer as well as the SRB provider[219]; and a basic affordability and appropriateness test for all sales.[220] In contrast to its approach to lifetime mortgages, the FSA applied a common standard across all sales of SRB (rather

[211] Transparency and suitability are addressed through regulations setting out standards of disclosure, at the pre-offer stage (MCOB 5.9), the offer stage (MCOB 6.9 and Annexes 2 and 3) and post-sale (MCOB 7.9).

[212] MCOB 3.7.3.

[213] MCOB 3.8B.3.

[214] CP 09/22, above n 207, para 9.4; *FSA Handbook*, MCOB 3.8B.8.

[215] Online at <http://fsahandbook.info/FSA/html/handbook/MCOB/3/8B>.

[216] CP 09/22, above n 207, para 9.13.

[217] *Ibid*, para 9.17.

[218] MCOB 4.11.2; online at <http://fsahandbook.info/FSA/html/handbook/MCOB/4/11>.

[219] MCOB 2.6A.12 requires that the valuer is competent and independent, and 2.6A.12A provides that the firm must ensure that the valuation is carried out by someone who has a duty of care towards the customer; see <http://fsahandbook.info/FSA/html/handbook/MCOB/2/6A>.

[220] MCOB 4.11.3; online at <http://fsahandbook.info/FSA/html/handbook/MCOB/4/11>.

than distinguishing between advised and non-advised sales),[221] requiring that, as well as providing certain information disclosures, every SRB must be assessed for affordability and appropriateness before the consumer enters into the agreement. The affordability and appropriateness test requires the firm to scrutinise the consumer's circumstances, and not to enter into a contract with the consumer unless it has reasonable grounds to be satisfied that the customer can afford the payments required under the agreement, and that the agreement is appropriate to the needs, objectives and circumstances of the customer.[222]

The firm must look to evidence to support this assessment: for example, when it comes to affordability of rental payments, the firm must 'stress test' these to take account of future rent increases. There is also a particular emphasis on evidence-based budgeting (taking account of likely future changes) to ensure that the customer will be able to afford the rent payments for the duration of the fixed-term tenancy.[223] In assessing the appropriateness of the product for the consumer, the firm is also required to have due regard to:

a) whether the benefits to the customer in entering into the proposed regulated sale and rent back agreement outweigh any adverse effects it may have for him or her, including on his or her entitlement to means-tested benefits and housing benefits; and
b) the feasibility of the customer raising funds by alternative methods other than a sale of his or her property.[224]

Where the consumer is considering SRB to stave off impending repossession because of mortgage arrears, the provider is guided to consider whether the consumer has attempted to discuss forbearance options with the lender, and other possible options such as local authority or government rescue schemes.

These requirements demonstrate some sensitivity towards the broader context in which consumers enter into SRB transactions, and respond by fixing the lender with responsibility for ensuring that its actions in entering into a contract with the consumer, whether those actions are labelled as 'advice' or not, were appropriate and suitable for the individual consumer in light of his or her situation and circumstances. As such, the SRB requirements go considerably further than FSA regimes for other regulated housing equity products. For example, the final regulations introduced a 14-day cooling-off period, during which time the provider must not contact the customer or, in response to queries, exert any pressure to enter into the transaction.[225] This again reflects a recognition of the situational vulnerabilities of the SRB customer base, due to their marginality and the pressure they are likely to be under when entering into the contract, as well as the particularly adverse impact of bad outcomes, which are central to the justifications for imposing additional burdens (and costs) on firms.

[221] Since many SRB transactions are non-advised, the FSA was concerned that retaining the distinction in this context would enable many providers to avoid the regulatory protections set out in the MCOB, and that this was particularly worrying in light of the specific issue of inappropriate sales of this type of product, and the level of detriment that can result; CP09/22, above n 207, paras 9.18–9.21.

[222] MCOB 4.11.3.

[223] MCOB 4.11.3.1. These assessments must be made net of any capital or income generated by the SRB transaction itself, whether at the time of the transaction or into the future.

[224] MCOB 4.11.5.

[225] MCOB 6.9.4–6.9.8; online at <http://fsahandbook.info/FSA/html/handbook/MCOB/6/9>.

It is also significant that the SRB provisions require firms to take direct responsibility for the appropriateness of the transaction, rather than requiring that they channel customers through legal advice. While firms providing home reversions are required to ensure that customers have received legal advice,[226] SRB firms are only required to ensure that the consumer is made aware of the availability and importance of independent legal or professional advice.[227] It is not clear on the face of the FSA's published policies why firms are required to ensure that the customer has received independent legal advice in the sale of a home reversion but not for a SRB: the underlying legal transaction is remarkably similar, with only the terms of the tenancy distinguishing them, and with SRB widely acknowledged as the higher-risk transaction. The decision to place the burden of ensuring the suitability of the transaction for the individual consumer more directly on the firm may reflect both a recognition of the limits of legal advice in preventing harm to vulnerable consumers, and the importance of fixing the providers themselves with responsibility not only for the product they offer but for the suitability of the transaction for the individual consumer. As such, the FSA's approach to SRB provides an interesting example of its preparedness to hold providers directly responsible for the risk of adverse transactions, notwithstanding the costs this may incur, on the basis that it is a proportionate response to consumer risk.

Lastly, the regulations set out some minimum product requirements, particularly in relation to the tenancy. Lack of security of tenure was identified as one of the key risks for SRB customers, and MCOB section 2.6A.5B provides that the firm's responsibility to protect its customers' interests include ensuring that the tenancy is an assured tenancy (including an assured shorthold tenancy),[228] for a fixed term of no less than five years, the terms of which allow the tenant to terminate on no more than three months' notice, and that each of the terms of the tenancy is fair.[229] The firm must also ensure that the terms of the tenancy do not enable the landlord to bring it to an end without a court order based on one of the grounds for possession applicable to an assured tenancy under the Housing Act 1988,[230] but not including ground 2 (mandatory ground based on landlord's mortgagee exercising power of sale), ground 6 (mandatory ground based on demolition of property), ground 8 (mandatory ground based on non-payment of rent) or ground 9 (discretionary ground based on availability of suitable alternative accommodation). This significantly enhances the tenant's security of tenure, to place the SRB consumer in a stronger position than even an assured tenant for the minimum five-year term, and is shaped to address particular SRB risks, such as the landlord's default on a buy-to-let mortgage, and to allow the court some discretion to refuse a possession order where the breach is non-payment of rent. In addition, during this fixed term, the landlord may rely on any ground for possession only to the extent that this is fair.[231]

[226] MCOB 2.6A.5; discussed in test associated with n 162 above.

[227] MCOB 2.6A.5A.

[228] In Scotland, an assured tenancy including a short assured tenancy; or in Northern Ireland, a private tenancy under the Private Tenancies (Northern Ireland) Order 2006 (NISI 2006/1459).

[229] Online at <http://fsahandbook.info/FSA/html/handbook/MCOB/2/6A>.

[230] See Housing Act 1988, sch 2.

[231] The tenor of the FSA's approach is underlined in MCOB 2.6A.6, which reminds SRB providers that 'Firms remain responsible for ensuring that their customers' interests are protected to a reasonable standard', online at <http://fsahandbook.info/FSA/html/handbook/MCOB/2/6A>.

Concerns about the conduct of landlords in evicting SRB tenants was one of the key factors informing the decision to regulate. As the discussion in chapter eight noted, the English courts were not willing to use the fairness provisions in the general law (for example, the Unfair Terms in Consumer Contract Regulations 1999) to address these types of unfairness: in *UK Housing Alliance (North West) Ltd v Francis*,[232] the Court of Appeal was strongly influenced by the limited rights that Mr Francis had as an assured shorthold tenant under the Housing Act 1988. The loss to Mr Francis when he was evicted from his home for non-payment of rent was compounded by the effect of a term in his SRB agreement that provided that if the Assured Shorthold Tenancy Agreement under which he rented his formerly-owned home was terminated within six years of the original transaction, he would not receive the 'Final Payment', which was 30 per cent of the agreed purchase price. The OFT's *Market Study* noted that 'In some cases, a portion of the consumer's proceeds from the sale is held back by the firm for a period of time … Firms told us that this helped cover arrears or damage to the property.'[233] This practice has been explicitly addressed in the new regulations, with MCOB 2.6A.10 providing:

> A firm is … unlikely to be treating its customer fairly if, upon termination of an agreement under a home purchase plan, home reversion plan or regulated sale and rent back agreement, the customer does not receive (net of any reasonable sums payable by the customer) … [where] the customer retains a beneficial interest in the property, the value of that beneficial interest.[234]

The fact that the outcome for Mr Francis would have been so different under the FSA's regime provides just one example of the enhanced protection offered in relation to SRB.

There is no doubt that FSA regulation has been the principal—if not the only—arena for targeted consumer protection in relation to housing equity products, and that the level of protection deemed appropriate by the FSA is considerably higher than that which the courts have applied under the general fairness provisions. Nevertheless, as the discussion above has recognised in relation to lifetime mortgage regulation, a key challenge with the regulatory approach rests with the compliance of firms and the extent to which the FSA is willing and able (in light of resource constraints) to monitor firms and take enforcement action when appropriate. The next section considers the nature of the remedies available for consumers in respect of the regulatory regime, and assesses their suitability for older consumers.

(d) Regulatory redress and remedies

There are two main regulatory remedies for consumers in respect of the FSA's regime: the Financial Services Compensation Scheme (FSCS), and the Financial Ombudsman Service (FOS). Complaints and compensation in relation to the regulated housing equity products are addressed under the relevant sections of the *FSA Handbook*,[235] which covers matters ranging from requirements for firms to make customers aware of their complaints procedures,[236] to complaint handling[237] and resolution rules,[238] time limit rules,[239] and

232 [2010] EWCA Civ 117; this decision was discussed at length in ch 8.
233 OFT, above n 171, para 3.25.
234 <http://fsahandbook.info/FSA/html/handbook/MCOB/2/6A>.
235 See *FSA Handbook*, Redress, online at <http://fsahandbook.info/FSA/html/handbook/D29>.
236 *FSA Handbook*, DISP 1.2, online at <http://fsahandbook.info/FSA/html/handbook/DISP/1/2>.
237 DISP 1.3.

recording[240] and reporting rules.[241] If a consumer is not satisfied with the firm's response, or if the firm cannot provide a final response within eight weeks, the firm is required to inform the consumer of his or her right to refer the complaint to the FOS.[242] Lifetime mortgages, home reversion plans and SRB agreements (except for disputes which relate purely to the landlord and tenant relationship) fall within the compulsory jurisdiction of the FOS as 'regulated activities'.[243] The FOS's annual review for the financial year 2009–10 reported that from 1 July 2009, when SRB came within its compulsory jurisdiction, it had had few enquiries on the topic, and only one complaint.[244] This may reflect a high level of satisfaction amongst SRB and equity release consumers; alternatively, it may be indicative of consumers' reluctance or reduced capacity to pursue a complaint against a provider, and to persist in bringing it to the FOS where the provider does not resolve it satisfactorily.

Where complaints are referred to the Ombudsman, they are determined according to 'what is, in his opinion, fair and reasonable in all the circumstances of the case'.[245] In considering what is 'fair and reasonable', the Ombudsman may take into account relevant law and regulations, regulators' rules, guidance and standards, codes of practice and (where appropriate) what he considers to have been good industry practice at the relevant time.[246] The FOS's jurisdiction over SRB and regulated equity release products is a valuable tool for the older consumer who makes a complaint, particularly since, in adjudicating complaints involving other financial products, the FOS has attached considerably greater weight to the contextual vulnerabilities associated with age, lack of financial expertise, the limitations of information and the particularly adverse impact of financial losses on older people than has typically been evident in other contexts, for example in judicial decisions under the fairness provisions.[247] If the FOS finds in favour of a consumer, it may make a money award, an interest award and/or a costs award. The FOS's jurisdiction to make a money award against a firm is wide, and empowers it to provide fair compensation for one or more of:

a) financial loss (including consequential or prospective loss);
b) pain and suffering;
c) damage to reputation; or
d) distress or inconvenience; whether or not a court would award compensation.[248]

Where the FSA becomes aware of cases in which the actions of firms expose consumers to risks that are deemed unacceptable, it can take an administrative enforcement action against the firm, with remedies ranging from undertakings from the firm to desist from the inappropriate activity to FSA-imposed fines. For example, in 2007 the Minel Group, a

[238] DISP 1.4.
[239] DISP 1.6.
[240] DISP 1.9.
[241] DISP 1.10.
[242] DISP 1.6.2.
[243] DISP 2.3.1.1; online at <http://fsahandbook.info/FSA/html/handbook/DISP/2/3>.
[244] Financial Ombudsman Service, *Annual Review of Consumer Complaints about insurance, credit, banking, savings, investments, 2009–10* (London, FOS, 2010) at 41; online at <http://www.financial-ombudsman.org.uk/publications/ar10/ar10.pdf>. The *Annual Review* does not mention lifetime mortgages or home reversions, although it not clear whether lifetime mortgages are included within the general figures for mortgages.
[245] DISP 3.6.1.
[246] DISP 3.6.4.
[247] See ch 8, section (7)(c).
[248] *FSA Handbook*, DISP 3.7.2; online at <http://fsahandbook.info/FSA/html/handbook/DISP/3/7>.

buy-to-let mortgage provider, was fined £10,500[249] by the FSA for exposing consumers to the risk of being sold unsuitable lifetime mortgages.[250] The firm was found to have 'persistent record-keeping failures', specifically, failing to record sufficient information about customers' personal and financial circumstances to establish their needs and objectives, and to demonstrate the suitability of its recommendations. The firm also failed to meet the standards of training and competence or effective monitoring of competence required for 'higher-risk' products such as lifetime mortgages. In addition to the fine, the firm was required to review its sales of lifetime mortgages and to compensate customers for any loss caused by unsuitable advice; the firm also agreed to stop selling lifetime loans. This was the first time the FSA had taken enforcement action against a lifetime mortgage adviser, and it demonstrated its willingness to take enforcement action where it identifies market activity that poses unacceptable risks to consumers. This particular investigation was prompted by a thematic review of the lifetime mortgage market, and the FSA indicated its intention to continue monitoring this market in light of its high-risk nature.

While the administrative action is valuable in that it does not depend on individual, vulnerable consumers pursuing their own remedies in circumstances where they have already suffered potentially debilitating harm, the FSA operates within resource constraints which require it to focus on the most significant risks for consumers (either in terms of how widespread the risk is, or in terms of the extent of the detriment). The Government's White Paper on *Reforming Financial Markets* has indicated its intention to enhance the current arrangements for redress by enabling consumers to take group or representative action to obtain collective redress in the case of widespread complaints,[251] and this would potentially strengthen the raft of remedies available for consumer redress, although its impact will depend on the availability of adequate support for consumers to take collective action.

Where a provider breaches FSA standards but cannot meet its financial obligations to compensate the consumer, the consumer may apply for compensation under FSCS. Section 150(1) of the FSMA 2000 provides that a consumer who suffers a resulting loss may bring a court action for breach of statutory duty to recover damages against a firm in breach of FSA rules, although it is important to note that the remedy is limited to damages. Section 151(2) provides that 'No such contravention makes any transaction void or unenforceable',[252] so that for the older consumer who has lost the title to his or her property as a result of the transaction, this avenue of redress will not restore his or her 'housing as home'. Further, the FSCS cannot compensate for losses such as loss of security of tenure under a SRB agreement.[253]

[249] The firm agreed to settle at an early stage of the FSA's investigation, to qualify for a 30% discount on the fine.

[250] FSA, 'FSA fines mortgage firm for lifetime mortgage selling failures' (FSA/PN/109/2007) (London, FSA, 2007); online at <http://www.fsa.gov.uk/pages/Library/Communication/PR/2007/109.shtml>.

[251] HM Treasury, *Reforming Financial Markets* (Cm 7667) (London, TSO, 2009), ch 8, especially paras 8.58–8.69; online at <http://news.bbc.co.uk/1/shared/bsp/hi/pdfs/08_07_09_markets.pdf>.

[252] This may be contrasted with the Consumer Credit Act regime discussed in ch 8, which covers unsecured lending and secured credit which falls outside the FSA's regulatory scope, and under which the court could challenge the enforceability of the transaction if the lender failed to comply with rules concerning pre-contractual information or the form and execution of the agreement (CCA 1974, s 17), although s 127(3) and (4) were repealed in the CCA 2006 so that these provisions now apply only to agreements executed before 6 April 2007.

[253] CP 06/8, above n 141, para 8.10; CP 09/22, above n 207, para 10.17.

Lastly, while the MCOB has set out minimum standards for the terms of the tenancy, the FSA does not have jurisdiction over the landlord and tenant relationship beyond compliance with these minimum terms.

Intervention by the FSA in the equity release and SRB markets was an explicit response to the heightened vulnerability amongst consumers transacting in this sector, the high-risk nature of the products and recognition that there are not likely to be orderly market solutions to protect these vulnerable consumers from detriment.[254] While the FSA has made significant progress in the last decade towards addressing the most serious risks to housing equity consumers, and the regulatory model remains particularly attractive for older consumers (compared, for example, to a remedial model) in light of its focus on disciplining firms to avoid harms rather than relying on the injured party seeking redress, there are also several factors which limit the reach of the FSA in this field. The last section of this chapter reflects on the limits of the regulatory regime in protecting older consumers, from lack of compliance and the ineffectiveness of some regulatory tools (for example, disclosure) to the limited scope of redress (which is restricted to damages). It considers some broader issues in relation to the nature of regulation and the extent to which it may be relied on as a mechanism for protecting individuals from harm.

(5) The Limits of the Regulatory Regime

Following the global financial crisis, the UK's model for financial regulation has come under increasing scrutiny, both through the FSA's own *Turner Review* and *Mortgage Market Review*,[255] and from commentators.[256] While the *Mortgage Effectiveness Review* was planned as part of a move towards greater reliance on principles and high-level rules,[257] this 'light-touch' strategy has come into question. Long before the crisis, the FSA had 'already attempted to dampen down unrealistic and unachievable expectations of financial regulation in its discussion of the persistence of failure in regulated markets'.[258] In its 2003 report on the reasonable expectations of a regulatory regime, the FSA emphasised

[254] This is particularly an issue in relation to SRB. The FSA noted: 'The market failure analysis indicates that the sale and rent back (SRB) market is a fragmented market with little competitive pressure on SRB providers. Evidence from the Office of Fair Trading (OFT) report suggested that there is neither competition on price or quality of SRB products. It is a market characterised mainly by sole traders that act locally and target consumers with high levels of arrears, many of whom are facing repossession. We have identified the existence of informational asymmetries, mainly arising from the valuation of the property and the price discount in combination with the terms of the tenancy agreement, which may not be understood by consumers. It is likely that this lack of knowledge has been exploited by some SRB providers and consumers enter into an SRB agreement when it is not the best option for them. In this context the terms and features of a SRB agreement are of particular importance. The OFT also reported that SRB transactions are carried out very quickly and high-pressure sales tactics are prevalent in the market, inducing consumers to enter into an SRB agreement when it may not be the best option for them.' (CP 09/22, above n 207, Annex A, paras 1–3).

[255] Lord Turner, *The Turner Review: A Regulatory Response to the Global Banking Crisis* (London, FSA, 2009), online at <http://www.fsa.gov.uk/pubs/other/turner_review.pdf>; FSA, *Mortgage Market Review* (London, FSA, 2009), online at <http://www.fsa.gov.uk/pubs/discussion/dp09_03.pdf>.

[256] See, eg, Tomasic, above n 112, at 103, claiming that 'the use of these risk-based and self-regulatory models has been seen by many to be seriously flawed'.

[257] *Mortgage Effectiveness Review, Stage 2 Report*, above n 121, Foreword, at 3.

[258] Gray, above n 112, at 126; FSA, *Reasonable Expectations: Regulation in a Non-zero Failure World* (London, FSA, 2003), online at <http://www.fsa.gov.uk/pubs/other/regulation_non-zero.pdf>.

that it did not aim to prevent all lapses of conduct by firms,[259] and that this approach was implicit in the FSMA 2000 (from which the regime was derived). Section 5 of the Act, dealing with the protection of consumers, provided:

> In considering what degree of protection may be appropriate, the Authority must have regard to—
>
> (a) the differing degrees of risk involved in different kinds of investment or other transaction;
> (b) the differing degrees of experience and expertise that different consumers may have in relation to different kinds of regulated activity;
> (c) the needs that consumers may have for advice and accurate information; and
> (d) the general principle that consumers should take responsibility for their decisions.

The FSA emphasised that these objectives 'Do not require us to protect consumers from all risks'[260]; that a regime that guaranteed no lapses of conduct would be excessively costly[261]; and that it would create a moral hazard for consumers by discouraging prudent behaviour in financial decision-making.[262] The FSA's general approach was to treat customers as self-responsible in their financial decision-making, particularly in excluding from its intended reach the problem of 'mis-buying'. In delineating the reasonable expectations of a regulatory system, the FSA claimed that 'Regulation can limit cases of mis-selling but consumers need to take responsibility for cases of mis-buying (eg where a buyer makes an error of judgement when buying a product but is not misled).'[263]

The question of which categories of risk vulnerable consumers should be protected against echoes the debate that has emerged in relation to the equitable remedies for vulnerable parties,[264] as to whether the protections offered by vitiating factors such as undue influence are 'claimant-sided' or 'defendant-sided': while claimant-sided protections are motivated by the vulnerability of the claimant/consumer, defendant-sided protections are concerned with the defendant/lender's 'exploitation' or mis-conduct in the transaction.[265] Contrary to its general position, in its regulation of both home reversions and SRB the FSA included the claimant-sided problem of 'mis-buying' amongst the risks from which it sought to protect consumers.[266] This reflects the extent to which home reversion and SRB consumers are viewed as vulnerable, as well as the 'high-risk' nature of the products. The FSA's attempts to protect against mis-buying in the home reversion and SRB markets demonstrated its view that consumer protections in this context must go beyond 'defendant-sided' regulation to become more sensitive to the vulnerabilities (sometimes expressed in terms of the individual personal and financial circumstances,

[259] *Reasonable Expectations*, above, para 1.2.
[260] *Ibid*, para 1.7.
[261] The report claimed (*ibid*, para 4.25) that 'it would be excessively resource intensive for us to try to prevent all conduct of business failures. This would, in theory, require us to monitor every sale made to a consumer, and would run counter to the principles of proportionality and management responsibility.'
[262] *Ibid*, para 2.3.
[263] *Ibid*, para 2.8.
[264] See further, ch 10.
[265] These modes of protection were developed in P Birks and Y Chin, 'On the nature of undue influence' in J Beatson and D Friedmann (eds), *Good Faith and Fault in Contract Law* (Oxford, Clarendon Press, 1995); criticised in R Bigwood, 'Undue Influence: "Impaired Consent" or "Wicked Exploitation"' (1996) 16 *OJLS* 503; and discussed in *Portman Building Society v Dusangh* [2000] 2 All ER (Comm) 221, 233, *per* Ward LJ. See further, ch 10.
[266] CP 06/8, above n 141, para 3.7; CP 09/22, above n 207, para 3.4.

needs and objectives) of the consumer when entering into the transaction. This recognition of situational vulnerabilities supports the framework set out in chapter six for conceptualising the transactional vulnerabilities of older consumers. It also raises issues for further consideration in relation to the nature and extent of the protections extended to individuals through the equitable remedies, discussed in chapter ten.

The FSA's efforts to enhance consumer protection apply a sliding scale of rigour from conventional mortgages to lifetime mortgages, rising significantly (for example through the requirement for legal advice) where the transaction is a home reversion and for SRB (where the provider is fixed with a much clearer direct responsibility in respect of the suitability of the product for the individual consumer). Nevertheless, it is the nature of the regulatory approach that it does not seek to prevent all lapses in conduct which might result in consumer losses. For one thing, regulation tends to be specific to defined product types, and, as noted above, this can cause a time-lag between the emergence of innovative products bearing new types of risk on the market, the decision to regulate and the implementation of that regulation. The discussion of the 'Property Income Plan' in section (4)(a), above, illustrated the gaps that can result from a legal regime which is oriented around specifically defined regulated products. The FSA's jurisdiction is triggered by the form of the underlying property transaction rather than the substance of the financial service provided to the consumer. While this ensures that the detail of the regulation is tailored to the product type (for example, the emphasis on security of tenure in the product regulation for SRB), it leaves gaps in the patchwork of consumer protection, particularly as any new product must be judged a proportionate risk to consumers—most likely because it has caused detriment to actual consumers—before the process of seeking to regulate is likely to be triggered; and a further delay while the regulatory regime comes online.[267] The issue of financial innovation and the regulatory perimeter has recently been challenged at the macro-prudential level,[268] with a shift towards focusing on the economic substance and the risks posed by systematically significant financial institutions, rather than on their legal form, when determining whether they fall within the regulatory perimeter.[269] The Government noted that

> it is vital that the authorities identify these [new] risks as they emerge and, if necessary, put in place an appropriate framework of oversight and regulation. To this end, the Treasury will ask the FSA to update it about relevant aspects of financial innovation, including areas where the FSA's scope of authority or existing powers are not sufficient for it to fulfil its statutory objectives. In response, the Government will give full consideration to any legislative changes that may be necessary.[270]

Yet even with a responsive regulator and a willing legislator, so long as the scope of the regulatory regime at the consumer protection level is determined by product definitions (rather than the economic substance of the transaction), there will inevitably be a time-lag between the emergence of new risks and the regulatory response.

[267] The issue of developing products was noted in FSA, *Regulation of Home Reversion and Home Purchase Plans—Feedback on CP06/8 and final rules, Volume 1, Policy Statement* (Policy Statement 06/12) (London, FSA, 2006) para 2.4; online at <http://www.fsa.gov.uk/pubs/policy/ps06_12.pdf>.

[268] HM Treasury, *Reforming Financial Markets* (Cm 7667) (London, TSO, 2009), paras 4.85, 5.25; online at <http://news.bbc.co.uk/1/shared/bsp/hi/pdfs/08_07_09_markets.pdf>.

[269] *Ibid*, para 6.28.

[270] *Ibid*, paras 6.33–6.34.

Once a regulatory regime is in place, the extent to which it provides effective protection depends on a range of factors, from the compliance of firms in the sector to the effect that the shape and size of the sector has on the administrative agency's ability to monitor compliance and promote good practice (contrast the relatively small number of lifetime mortgage and home reversion providers with the very fragmented market for SRB). The issue of time-lag is also extant in cases where the regulator investigates the misconduct of individual firms. Wadsley illustrated this problem with reference to the litigation in *Investors Compensation Scheme v West Bromwich Building Society*,[271] where the Building Societies Commission[272] investigated complaints that investors had been given negligent advice. The case resulted from a financial scandal in the early 1990s involving 'home income plans', an early equity release product targeted at retired people and in which the owner mortgaged his or her property to secure a loan of up to 50 per cent of its value, with interest on the loan rolled up and added to the debt. The pinch-point for the consumer was that when the debt reached two-thirds of the property's value, the building society could repossess the property, leading to considerable consumer detriment.[273] The product was regulated under the Building Societies Commission's jurisdiction, but the regulator's response demonstrated one of the weaknesses of the regulatory model in protecting consumers:

> Regulators approach the problem from the point of view of the stability of the organisation. Controls, if they are instituted, may incidentally prevent harm to individual customers, but that will not be the primary aim of the regulator. In fact, regulation is a clumsy tool for dealing with individuals. The regulator will need an opportunity to ascertain that there are failures in the procedures and that these are bad enough to threaten its stability; and, once it decides to act, there will be a time lag before controls can operate effectively ...[274]

In the *Investors Compensation* case, it was acknowledged that the regulator had been aware of the risks posed to consumers from an early stage, had frequently expressed concern and underwent extensive discussions with the lender over several months before determining to take action. Administrative enforcement agencies in the UK have typically focused on negotiation with firms, with court action seen as a last resort[275]; however, by the time the *Investors Compensation* case was litigated, many more consumers had suffered detriment as a result of negligent advice and the high-risk nature of the product.[276]

Even where providers are compliant, the nature of the protection which the regulator seeks to provide (for example, where this is primarily oriented around information and advice rather than suitability) may not be the most effective means of avoiding the harms which it seeks to prevent.[277] The emphasis on proportionate responses also underlines the

[271] [1999] Lloyd's Rep PN 496.

[272] The Building Societies Commission was one of the agencies whose functions were taken up by the new FSA after 2000.

[273] In the 1990s, a period of rising interest rates and falling house prices, this trigger-point was quickly reached.

[274] J Wadsley, 'Bank lending and the family home: prudence and protection' [2003] *Lloyd's Maritime and Commercial Law Quarterly* 341 at 357–58.

[275] P Rott, 'The Protection of Consumers' Interests After the Implementation of the EC Injunctions Directive into German and English Law' (2001) 24 *Journal of Consumer Policy* 401 at 421; see also C Scott and J Black, *Cranston's Consumer and the Law*, 3rd edn (London, Butterworths, 2000) 61.

[276] Wadsley, above n 274.

[277] See section (4)(a) for discussion of the effectiveness of the FSA's regulation of the UK lifetime mortgage market. For similar findings in other jurisdictions, see also P O'Shea, 'Consumer credit disclosure: does it work?'

fact that regulatory approaches do not seek to cover all risks, or to avoid all harms to consumers. Llewellyn has argued that

> [e]xpectations about what regulation, monitoring and supervision can achieve need to be managed to realistic levels. There needs to be a recognition (including by consumers) of the limitations of regulation; that it has a limited role; that even in this restricted dimension it can fail; and that not all risks are covered. Above all, the optimum level of regulation and supervision falls short of eliminating all possibility of consumers making wrong choices in financial contracts.[278]

The fact that regulation does not seek to prevent all harms is generally justified on the grounds that to do so would create a 'zero consequence' environment, where consumers do not need to evaluate the soundness of the firm or the reasonableness of the transaction. The FSA argued that 'Consumers would be free to buy ever more risky products knowing that if these failed, they would not lose money.'[279] The regulator must strike a balance between the need to protect vulnerable consumers, the level of protection that can be achieved within the available resources, the costs that may be passed on to the consumer and the desire to 'retain some incentive for consumers to exercise their responsibilities'.[280]

The FSA's approach to regulating housing equity transactions has shown, however, that when the consumer cohort for a particular product is likely to be especially vulnerable, where that vulnerability is directly associated with an increased risk that those consumers will make wrong choices, and where the detriment or impact of wrong choices is particularly severe, the idea of the consumer as a self-responsible financial and legal subject is undermined, and the responsibility for ensuring that the transaction is appropriate or 'suitable' for the needs, objectives and circumstances of the consumer can shift to the provider. This shift in perspective has been played out in recent years through the debates relating to responsible lending and responsible borrowing in the conventional mortgage market.

The image of 'owners' as self-responsible consumers[281] was consistent with a neoliberal, market-led ideology which opposed stronger government intervention in macro-financial markets, and which has been widely challenged following the global financial crisis.[282] Much of the debate that has followed the crisis in the UK has focused on macro-prudential strategies to restore and maintain confidence in the stability of financial

(2008) 16 *Journal of Banking and Finance Law and Practice* 5 (Australia); E Renuart and D Thompson, 'The truth, the whole truth and nothing but the truth' (2008) 25 *Yale Journal of Regulation* 181 (USA); S Block-Lieb *et al*, 'Disclosure as an imperfect means for addressing overindebtedness: an empirical assessment of comparative approaches' in J Niemi and W Whitford (eds), *Consumer Credit, Debt and Bankruptcy* (Oxford, Hart Publishing, 2009).

278 D Llewellyn, 'Principles of effective regulation and supervision of banks' (1998) 6 *Journal of Financial Regulation and Compliance* 312 at 314.

279 FSA, *Reasonable Expectations*, above n 258, para 4.27.

280 *Ibid*, para 4.30.

281 See S Nield, 'Responsible Lending and Borrowing: Whereto low-cost home ownership?' (2010) 30 *Legal Studies* 610, for analysis of the concepts of responsible lending and borrowing in home finance, and the impact of the *Turner Review* on the concept of lender responsibility; see further discussion of legal subjects as responsible risk-takers in ch 4.

282 See generally, Tomasic, above n 112; eg, his argument (*ibid*, at 106) that 'The notion that government should not intervene in markets has led to an almost blind-faith in the power of the "invisible hand" to ensure that markets are self-correcting. It also traumatised governments and regulatory agencies, and prevented them from assuming greater responsibilities in the face of excessive risk taking behaviour in the market.'

institutions,[283] although both the *Turner Review*[284] and the FSA's *Mortgage Market Review*[285] focused on irresponsible lending as a key factor giving rise to the crisis. This has resulted in a series of regulatory initiatives which suggest a stronger commitment towards lender responsibility in the conventional mortgage market, through affordability checks, better quality product information and arguments for minimum product standards.[286]

The responsible lending rule was part of the original FSA strategy for mortgage market regulation, both for conventional and lifetime mortgage sales.[287] The effectiveness of this strategy has been widely criticised: for example, an FSA survey in 2008 found that some lenders, especially those lending to consumers with impaired credit, were not making the necessary checks on income statements or self-certification; that some lenders' policies on responsible lending were vague as to how they determined a customer's ability to repay, and, significantly, that they did not assess ability to repay where the mortgage was scheduled to run past retirement.[288] Since housing equity products targeted at older consumers do not generally involve loans which are scheduled for repayment,[289] the idea of 'responsibility' in this context takes on a different form, although arguments for greater lender responsibility in the conventional mortgage market[290] also reflect changing perspectives on consumers as financial and legal subjects, which coincide with the shift towards greater lender responsibility in relation to the most marginal housing equity consumers (that is, those who enter SRB transactions).

In housing equity transactions, 'affordability' hinges not on the ability to repay but on a range of factors, including the future asset value of the property, interest rates and mortality rates.[291] Indeed, it is arguable that housing equity products should not even be regarded as a loans, particularly where (as in most cases) there is a 'no negative equity guarantee', meaning that the provider will have no recourse to the borrower's estate in the event of a shortfall. Nevertheless, affordability remains an important part of the suitability rules for housing equity products. For example, in advising a customer about a lifetime mortgage, a firm must explain that its assessment of the suitability of the product takes account of:

a) current interest rates, which might rise in the future; and
b) the customer's current circumstances, which might change in the future.[292]

Where a customer is consolidating debts, the firm is also required to take account of:

[283] The Government's 2009 White Paper, above n 268, focused on four key objectives: dealing with firms deemed 'too big to fail'; strengthening the UK's regulatory institutional framework; identifying and managing systemic risk at a macro-level; and learning and applying the lessons of the current financial crisis.

[284] Above n 255; the *Turner Review* was commissioned to look into the lessons from the financial crisis for the FSA.

[285] Above n 255.

[286] See Nield, above n 281.

[287] Consultation Paper 186, above n 61, para 5.11; this applied whether sales were advised or non-advised.

[288] FSA, 'FSA reiterates call for firms to treat customers fairly in current market conditions'; online at <http://www.fsa.gov.uk/pages/Library/Communication/PR/2008/087.shtml>.

[289] Lifetime mortgages are included under the responsible lending rules because they are classified as regulated mortgage contracts, although in most cases where interest is rolled up and no regular payments are made, the requirements do not apply; see FSA, *Mortgage Market Review: Responsible Lending* (London, FSA, 2010), para 2.80, online at <http://www.fsa.gov.uk/pubs/cp/cp10_16.pdf>.

[290] See generally, Nield, above n 281.

[291] The creditworthiness of the individual is not a factor for the lender, so there is typically no 'credit risk' attached to these products.

[292] MCOB 8.5.10; <http://fsahandbook.info/FSA/html/handbook/MCOB/8/5>.

a) the costs associated with increasing the period over which a debt is to be repaid;
b) whether it is appropriate for the customer to secure a previously unsecured loan; and
c) where the customer is known to have payment difficulties, whether it would be more appropriate for the customer to negotiate an arrangement with his or her creditors than to enter into an equity release transaction.[293]

The good practice guidance adds, however, that in assessing suitability for a lifetime mortgage, the firm is *not* required to consider whether it would be preferable for the customer to:

a) trade down rather than enter into an equity release transaction;
b) rent a property, rather than purchase one or enter into an equity release transaction on his or her existing property; or
c) delay entering into an equity release transaction until a later date on the grounds that property prices would have changed in the intervening period, or that the interest rate in relation to a lifetime mortgage would be lower, or both.[294]

As the discussions in sections (4)(b) and (c) have shown, with home reversions and SRB, providers have been required to go much further in assessing the needs, objectives and circumstances of the individual consumer, and in the case of SRB to take responsibility for the suitability of the transaction whether the sale is 'advised' or not.

Recent reviews of the regulatory approach to conventional mortgages have emphasised the need to articulate better what is required from lenders to ensure responsible lending and responsible borrowing. This has prompted a raft of discussion concerning the nature and extent of the provider's responsibility for the suitability of the transaction (both in terms of the product design and in terms of its suitability for the individual borrower's needs and circumstances) and for adverse outcomes that may result when borrowers make bad choices.[295] The importance of the individual consumer context was also underlined in the Treasury's White Paper *Reforming Financial Markets*, which stated that 'every effort must be made to help consumers get the products that are right for their needs and circumstances'.[296] In the cognate area of consumer credit,[297] the European Consumer Credit Directive[298] has given Member States 'a deliberately large margin to design a duty to assist consumers in order to decide which credit product is the most appropriate for his needs and financial situation',[299] and the White Paper *A Better Deal for Consumers* refers to

[293] MCOB 8.5.11; <http://fsahandbook.info/FSA/html/handbook/MCOB/8/5>.

[294] MCOB 8.5.15; <http://fsahandbook.info/FSA/html/handbook/MCOB/8/5>.

[295] See FSA, above n 289; OFT, *Irresponsible Lending—OFT Guidance for Creditors* (OFT 1107) (London, OFT, 2010), online at <http://www.oft.gov.uk/shared_oft/business_leaflets/general/oft1107.pdf>; and for details of the EU consultation on *Responsible Lending and Borrowing*, see <http://ec.europa.eu/internal_market/finservices-retail/credit/responsible_lending_en.htm>; Nield, above n 281.

[296] HM Treasury, above n 268, para 8.51.

[297] Although the Directive does not apply to FSA-regulated transactions; see Department for Business, Enterprise and Regulatory Reform ('BERR'), *Consultation on Proposals for Implementing the Consumer Credit Directive* (London, BERR, 2009) paras 1.7, 1.11, 5.12, online at <http://www.bis.gov.uk/files/file50962.pdf>.

[298] Directive 2008/48/EC, Art 5(6), Recital 27.

[299] European Commission, *Public Consultation on Responsible Lending and Borrowing in the EU* (Brussels, European Commission, 2009), para 13. Art 5.6 of the Directive is clear that it is the consumer's responsibility to determine whether or not a product is suitable for his or her needs and financial situation. The creditor is responsible only for providing such explanations as might be necessary in order to put the consumer in a position to make this decision. Nevertheless, the UK's BERR welcomed the opportunity that implementation of

'responsibility' only in the sense of 'consumers [being] enabled to exercise greater personal responsibility ... helped to do so through greater transparency and information provision'.[300] In its recent report on responsible lending and borrowing, the European Commission noted:

> The requirement to assess the suitability of mortgage products to the personal circumstances of the consumer is set out in the national law of Austria, Belgium, Hungary, Ireland, Malta and the Netherlands. In the UK the requirement to assess the suitability of the product for the borrower is only relevant where advice is given.[301]

Nevertheless, it was noted that 'The issue of suitability is ... one that may need to be addressed.'[302]

In the mortgage context, the validity of a strategy for responsible borrowing that rests on information disclosure to enable informed consumers to make rational choices has been thoroughly undermined,[303] signalling the emergence of a more paternalistic approach from the FSA 'to protect consumers from themselves'.[304] The value of disclosure regulation has long been criticised as based on an 'unrealistic, rational actor model of borrower behaviour',[305] described as a 'protection for the middle classes',[306] with Wilhelmsson describing 'measures based on the information paradigm [as liable to] reproduce and even strengthen existing social injustice'.[307] Protections based on information are unrealistic (inasmuch as they require consumers, armed with the information, to protect themselves[308]) and likely to be of least benefit to those who need them most, both because they are least well-placed to manage their own risks based on information, and because they are likely to have little choice due both to pressing financial pressure necessitating the transaction and the limited range of products available to them.[309]

There are several strands to the FSA's new approach, including a move from general standards of lender behaviour to prescriptive product regulation, increased lender responsibility for affordability and suitability, and a rebalancing of decision-making responsibilities between borrower and lender[310]; as well as continued efforts to improve the quality of rational decision-making through strategies for consumer education and financial capability. Nield has observed that in taking forward these issues, the FSA has preferred

the Directive offered for reviewing the concept of lender responsibility in consumer credit, since 'we have freedom to decide the lengths to which lenders should go to achieve the stated aim': BERR, above n 297, para 4.4.

300 HM Government, *A Better Deal for Consumers: Delivering Real Help Now and Change for the Future* (CM 7669) (London, TSO, 2009) 13.

301 European Commission, *Public Consultation on Responsible Lending and Borrowing in the EU* (Brussels, European Commission, 2009) para 3.1; online at <http://ec.europa.eu/internal_market/consultations/docs/2009/responsible_lending/consultation_en.pdf>.

302 *Ibid*, para 3.1.

303 See Nield, above n 281, at 616–17.

304 FSA, *Mortgage Market Review*, above n 255, para 6.12.

305 L Willis, 'Decision making and the limits of disclosure: The problem of predatory lending: Price' (2006) 65 *Maryland Law Review* 707, 741.

306 G Day, 'Assessing the effects of information disclosure requirements' (1976) 40 *Journal of Marketing* 42 at 49; G Howells, 'The potential and limits of consumer empowerment by information' (2005) 32 *Journal of Law and Society* 349, 357.

307 T Wilhelmsson, 'Consumer law and social justice' in I Ramsey (ed), *Consumer Law in the Global Economy* (Aldershot, Dartmouth, 1997) 224.

308 For discussion of varying abilities to manage risk, see ch 3.

309 'Information is only useful if it can be acted upon. The poor may rationally decide not to make use of information, if they feel no alternatives will be available to them.': Howells, above n 306, at 357.

310 See Nield, above n 281, at 622 *et seq*.

measures which focus on the suitability of particular products for particular individuals over 'product regulation *per se*',[311] thus appearing to respond to Gray's analysis of the failure of the UK's pre-crisis model of financial regulation, that 'in its design, techniques and consequences financial regulation has failed to acknowledge the essential humanity of its subject matter and its subjects'.[312] Nield argued that requirements that lenders in the conventional mortgage market take on more responsibility for the affordability of the transaction for the individual consumer reflect a shift in the balance of responsibilities, such that 'lenders would be required to look beyond their own interests and take the mortgagor's interests into account. No longer can lenders be self-interested players within the neo-liberal market model.'[313] At the same time, the content of these responsibilities remains focused on the objective question of whether the mortgagor is likely to default (that is, the borrower's 'creditworthiness') rather than on the broader issue of the consumer's financial well-being[314] (including whether the loan is affordable and sustainable into the future).

The distinctions between the meaning of lenders' responsibilities for 'affordability' in the context of acquisition mortgages and for 'suitability' in housing equity transactions, are also undergirded by an important difference in the qualities (as well as the extent) of the risks taken by the consumer. If leveraging future value through a conventional mortgage 'buys you a glimpse of a prosperity you haven't really earned',[315] the use of housing equity involves trading on the security and prosperity which the older owner has 'earned' through years of acquisition mortgage repayments, but which must now support his or her needs into an uncertain future. While the exposure to risk of vulnerable consumers has prompted greater sensitivity to contextual factors in the regulation of home reversions and SRB, the regulatory philosophy adopted in relation to the lifetime mortgage market has been closer to that applied to the conventional mortgage market (albeit that a considerably higher proportion of lifetime mortgages are advised sales). It is not yet clear whether the shift towards greater lender responsibility and emphasis on suitability for individual consumers in the conventional mortgage market will carry across to lifetime mortgages, in light of the differing meanings of 'affordability' in these contexts, and to the extent that the considerably greater impact of conventional mortgage defaults on the economy as a whole has justified raising the regulatory bar.

(6) Conclusions

In the wake of the global financial crisis, MacNeil and O'Brien argued that 'it has become essential that basic flaws in risk-based regulatory techniques be remedied and that the

311 *Ibid*, at 623.
312 Gray, above n 112, at 134.
313 Nield, above n 281, at 629.
314 *Ibid*, at 626.
315 M Lewis, 'Wall Street on the Tundra', *Vanity Fair*, 4 March 2009; quoted in J Gray, 'What Next for Risk-based Financial Regulation?' in I MacNeil and J O'Brien (eds), *The Future of Financial Regulation* (Oxford, Hart Publishing, 2010) 139.

integrity deficit in regulatory frameworks be addressed'.[316] While some of this work involves legal rules to ensure that the lender's role and responsibilities are articulated more clearly, as well as more rigorous supervision by the administrative agencies charged with responsibility for financial regulation to monitor and enforce these rules, it is also widely recognised that the 'inevitable gaps' in any regulatory framework must be addressed through additional (legal or non-legal) measures which reflect 'much clearer concepts of accountability and integrity applicable to individuals, entities and markets as a whole'.[317] Gray has argued that this must include rethinking the model of 'financial citizenship' which has developed in recent decades, taking account of how people view issues concerning 'money, wealth, status, entitlements and senses of security and fulfilment, for it is people, not institutions, processes, models and technical elites, that matter most as the ultimate stakeholders in financial regulation'.[318]

The shift to a stronger regulatory framework for equity release and SRB provides an important layer of consumer protection which adds substantially to the general legal framework to safeguard marginal older consumers in housing equity transactions. These protections are premised on three factors: the high-risk nature of the products themselves; the high vulnerability of the consumer base; and recognition of the detrimental impact of adverse transactions on the consumer. Each of these factors interacts with the idea of the older consumer as a legal and risk subject, although not always directly. The products themselves are viewed as inherently high-risk due to their complexity, although the fact that they are targeted at older consumers and the detrimental impact of financial losses (particularly linked to the owned home) late in life are also intrinsic to the decision to regulate. Most significant, perhaps, is the distinction between the approach to SRB—with its customer base of marginal, but not necessarily older consumers—and the regulated equity release products.

The idea that older consumers cannot be left to 'take the rough with the smooth' is evident in the more rigorous regulation of equity release products (evident in the weight attached to suitability, whether in the requirements of advised sales[319] or in the filtering questions for non-advised lifetime mortgages, which reflect the risks of 'mis-buying') compared to the more minimal regulation of conventional mortgages, which reflects the impact of losses on this consumer group and, by implication, the vulnerability of the consumer base in the decision-making process. Yet, as the effectiveness review has revealed, the mechanisms for advising consumers in lifetime mortgage transactions have no evident impact on the quality of decision-making, which is more likely to be determined by the existing social capital of consumers, ie their ability to research the products, to consult with others, and to make planned and informed decisions discrete from any input from the mortgage provider or adviser. The light-touch approach to high-pressure sales also appears to reflect an assumption that lifetime mortgage consumers are not predominately marginal, therefore not particularly vulnerable, so that no additional protections are needed. This is despite the evidence, discussed in chapter six, of older consumers' particular vulnerabilities, for example in relation to high-pressure sales.

[316] I MacNeil and J O'Brien, 'Introduction: The Future of Financial Regulation', in MacNeil and O'Brien (eds), above n 315, at 1.

[317] *Ibid*, at 2.

[318] Gray, above n 112, at 140.

[319] Combined with the heavy (and successful) steer towards advised sales for lifetime mortgages.

It also leaves those older owners who are vulnerable within this consumer base (those who lack the cultural capital to research and plan their own decisions) most exposed.

While the home reversion provisions refer to consumer vulnerability and risk in terms of both the decision-making process and the impact of adverse outcomes, they place particular emphasis on the high-risk nature of the product (that it involves a *sale* of the property rather than merely a mortgage). The regulation of home reversion plans was also influenced by attempts to shift towards high-level principles at the time the regime was developed, although that policy has now been somewhat overtaken by events. The crux of the 'suitability' requirements for home reversion was the requirement that providers ensure that the consumer has received independent legal advice (widely discredited as a panacea for vulnerability) before completing a sale. Of course, individualised advice as the mechanism for protecting consumers comes at a cost to the consumer. Terry and Gibson have estimated that the costs of advice for a consumer entering into an equity release transaction range from between £1,300 and £2,500 charged by the provider, and about £400 for customer's own legal expenses.[320] This financial cost underlines the practical implications of default legal rules concerning the allocation of responsibility for ensuring suitability/appropriateness, between the provider and the consumer.

The SRB provisions take a different approach in as much as they require the provider to bear responsibility for suitability rather than imposing the costs of advice directly on the consumer. While it was recognised that this creates additional costs for firms (and indirectly for consumers), the FSA reasoned that this was appropriate in light of the high-level of risk it attributed to SRB products.[321] Consumers in SRB transactions are strongly directed towards sources of free independent legal advice, for example from Citizens' Advice,[322] on the basis that it is not reasonable to expect the customer base for SRB to pay for advice[323]; providers are required to bear the costs of valuation despite the fact that this must be completed before the cooling-off period and that the consumer may opt out of the transaction leaving the provider out-of-pocket. The FSA was not swayed by industry feedback concerning the costs that this would impose on providers, reiterating that the valuation was a key element of the process for SRB consumers, and that since most SRB consumers could not afford to pay upfront (and incurring charges that would be repayable to the provider in the event they 'cooled off' could unduly influence their decision and result in an unsuitable transaction), it needed to form part of the information considered during the cooling-off period. It therefore concluded that 'firms will have to treat valuations as a cost of business, and model costs accordingly'.[324] The SRB

[320] R Terry and R Gibson, *Can Equity Release Help Older Home-Owners Improve Their Quality of Life?* (York, Joseph Rowntree Foundation, 2010) 16, fn 30.

[321] 'Rules on treating customers fairly and complying with guidance on excessive charges would have costs to firms, including a loss of sales and a reduction in income from excessive charges, but this would have associated benefits to consumers arising from not undertaking an unsuitable transaction.': FSA, *Regulating Sale and Rent Back: An Interim Regime*, CP 09/6 (London, FSA, 2009), Annexe 1, para 10, available online at < http://www.fsa.gov.uk/pages/Library/Policy/CP/2009/09_06.shtml>.

[322] See, eg, the Consumer Financial Education Body factsheet on SRB, available at <http://www.moneymadeclear.org.uk/pdfs/sale_and_rent_back.pdf>, which firms are required to provide to, and explain to, consumers: *FSA Handbook*, MCOB 4.11.2, online at <http://fsahandbook.info/FSA/html/handbook/MCOB/4/11>.

[323] FSA, *Sale and rent back (full regime), Feedback on CP09/22, made rules and consultation on reporting* (CP 10/04) (London, FSA, 2010), para 3.35, online at <http://www.fsa.gov.uk/pubs/cp/cp10_04.pdf>.

[324] *Ibid*, para 3.36.

transaction provides the strongest example to date of the extent to which the responsibility for ensuring that a transaction is 'suitable' can shift from consumer to the provider. This clearly responds to the emphasis not only on the product risks, but on the specific decision-making vulnerabilities of the marginal consumer base, including evidence about the effects of situational vulnerabilities on the capacity for SRB consumers to act as rational, self-responsible legal subjects.

With indications that the lifetime mortgage and home reversion markets generally work well for most consumers, the idea of taking a more rigorous approach to lender responsibility in the regulation of these products is likely to be viewed (within the regulatory cost–benefit analysis) as disproportionate. However, this perspective does not (neither does it seek to) address those older owners at the margins of the equity release market, who embark on equity release transactions in circumstances of financial pressure, or where the transaction does not form part of a rationally-planned strategy for financial well-being in retirement. The FSA has recognised that marginal older consumers are susceptible to the same types of consumer risk (situational vulnerability in the decision-making process and disproportionate impact of detriment) in equity release transactions as SRB consumers; the justification for a different approach between these products is primarily based on the proportion of the consumer base who may be regarded as vulnerable in the decision-making process.

This raises further issues in relation to the limits of the regulatory regime discussed in section (5) above, and, more specifically, the advantages and disadvantages of the regulatory approach for older consumers as a cohort. On the one hand, the regulatory approach is an attractive legal approach for the protection of older consumers inasmuch as it is oriented around prevention rather than cure: the framework created by the Financial Services and Markets Act 2000 is primarily focused on regulating providers' conduct rather than protecting consumers directly through the provision of remedies,[325] although it has been noted that in certain circumstances redress in the form of compensation may be available under the FSCS or from the FOS.[326]

The preventive approach is particularly suitable for older consumers in light of the detrimental impact of financial harms and the limited opportunities they are likely to have to recover,[327] as well as evidence to indicate that they are less likely than the general consumer population to bring actions for redress.[328] Qualitative research with older consumers has indicated that they 'felt they had few options for redress when faced by problems with services. The research suggests that older people lack the confidence, skills and stamina necessary to pursue complaints, so feel simply unable to effect change.'[329] The research found that older consumers were 'particularly averse' to using law to seek

[325] See s 151(2), which states that 'No … contravention [of the regulatory regime] makes any transaction void or unenforceable.'

[326] See section (4)(d) above.

[327] See, eg, G Crosby, A Clark, R Hayes, K Jones and N Lievesley, *Financial Abuse of Older People: A review of the literature carried out by the Centre for Policy on Aging on Behalf of Help the Aged* (London, Help the Aged, 2008) 23.

[328] While there are many cases on issues relevant to older consumers, there are relatively few reported cases on housing equity transactions brought by older people. Research has also shown that the practical barriers to accessing 'safety-net' protections may be much higher for low-income consumers; see T Wilson, N Howell and G Sheehan, 'Protecting the Most Vulnerable in Consumer Credit Transactions' (2009) 32 *Journal of Consumer Policy* 117, 126.

[329] F Butler, *Rights for Real: Older People, Human Rights and the CEHR* (London, Age Concern, 2006) 9.

solutions, as it resonated with a 'compensation culture'; they did not believe that it should be necessary to use courts to resolve problems; they lacked faith that the law would produce a positive outcome; and they lacked confidence that they had the knowledge or skills to negotiate the legal process to seek redress.[330]

Another advantage of the administrative model of regulation is that it is capable of achieving more widespread results than individual litigation. Willett has observed that where individual consumers act, 'these will be individual victories and will not serve to discipline what traders offer in general'.[331] Individual litigation carries financial and emotional costs, including shame and humiliation for the older person, who has to admit that he or she has made a bad decision or exercised poor judgement.[332] An environment of individual responsibility and control over one's own financial affairs can leave problems undetected if older people do not talk to others about what has happened.[333]

There are at least three possible avenues along which the legal regulation of housing equity transactions might progress. The first would be to do nothing: to accept that there are inevitably gaps in the reach of the regulatory approach and in the remedies it offers, and that harm to some individual consumers is a necessary *quid pro quo* for the opportunities that spending housing wealth offers older consumers to improve their quality of life in retirement. The acceptability of this approach depends on a number of factors, including the extent to which the vulnerabilities of older consumers are thought to justify additional legal protection, particularly in a public policy context which presses older owners to spend their housing equity. If it is accepted that there is a need to enhance the protection of older consumers in this context—whether as a fairness-based response to potential vulnerability; under the strategic goal of generating a 'safer' environment and so achieving the public policy objective of encouraging older owners to release equity to meet welfare and pension needs; or to address the risk of older consumers who enter into unsuitable transactions being thrown back on the State for support—this might be achieved by strengthening the regulatory framework and/or by considering alternative routes to protection in the general law.

The second approach is to look to alternative grounds of protection for older consumers in the general law. While it has been noted that the regulatory approach does not extend to invalidating the transaction and so restoring the 'housing as home' to the older consumer, these gaps might, to some extent, be patched by the equitable remedies and/or through a shift in judicial policy (from freedom/autonomy to vulnerability/responsibility-based approaches) in the application of provisions under the general law. The suitability of equitable relief for addressing the harms associated with housing equity transactions is discussed in chapter ten, although it is noted that as a general principle, the equitable

330 *Ibid.*

331 C Willett, *Fairness in Consumer Contracts: The Case of Unfair Terms* (Aldershot, Ashgate, 2007) 25.

332 Research into financial abuse of older people has reported that it can be difficult to detect because victims are reluctant to report; because they are embarrassed to admit that they have made a poor decision; because of stigma and loss of personal dignity; because they do not know where to turn for help or do not have the mobility to access help; because they consider the situation to be their own fault or part of the normal risk of transacting; or because they do not realise that an actionable wrong has taken place: see, eg, JI Kosberh and D Nahmiash, 'Characteristics of Victims and Perpetrators and Milieus of Abuse and Neglect' in LA Baumhover and SC Beal (eds), *Abuse, Neglect and Exploitation of Older Persons: Strategies for Assessment and Intervention* (London, Jessica Kingsley, 1996); CL Dessin, 'Financial Abuse of the Elderly' (1999) 36 *Idaho Law Review* 203, 211–13.

333 Dessin, above n 332, at 214.

remedies are typically regarded as available only in 'exceptional' cases,[334] and therefore may not provide a mainstream solution to generic problems.

Lastly, and alongside such debates, a third approach would be to enhance the appropriateness of the protections conferred on older owners through the regulation of housing equity transactions. There are a number of ways in which this might be achieved, in line with the current ideological shift towards greater lender responsibility and the re-casting of consumers as potentially vulnerable rather than as self-responsible legal subjects. In 2010, the Coalition Government announced plans to set up a new Consumer Protection and Markets Authority (CPMA), which will inherit the FSA's responsibilities in respect of the regulation of authorised financial firms providing services to consumers and ensuring good conduct of business in retail financial markets.[335] This move forms part of a strategy to separate the functions of macro-prudential regulation, prudential regulation of individual firms[336] and consumer issues[337] into a tripartite system. The Government's statement setting out these proposals claimed that 'The CPMA will regulate the conduct of all firms, both retail and wholesale—including those regulated prudentially by the PRA—and will take a proactive role as a strong consumer champion'[338]; while its Consultation Paper claimed that 'The creation of a regulator with specific responsibility for consumer protection will ensure that the interests of consumers are not forgotten about or subordinated.'[339] The statement also referred to transparency as a key objective, and revealed the Government's intention to 'ensure that this body has a tougher, more proactive approach to regulating conduct and its primary objective will be promoting confidence in financial services and markets'.[340] The Government's Consultation Paper on the new institutional approach was explicit in emphasising that under the proposed CPMA, consumer confidence would be the first-order objective, with factors such as the efficient and economic use of CPMA resources, the principle that the burden of regulation should be proportionate to the resulting benefits, and the potential impact of policies or regulatory decisions on consumer lending, all specified as second-order considerations.[341]

The Consultation Paper also outlined the Government's intention to build on recent FSA initiatives which are shifting the UK approach to consumer protection towards a

[334] See, eg, S Waddams, 'Protection of weaker parties in English law' in M Kenny, J Devenney and L Fox O'Mahony (eds), *Unconscionability in European Private Financial Transactions: Protecting the Vulnerable* (Cambridge, Cambridge University Press, 2010) 27: 'The categories of … "fraud and undue influence" suggest rare and closely defined instances, scarcely affecting the general principles of contract law … [There is also a tendency] to suggest that it is not directly relevant to the most basic principles of contract law, and that relief on the ground of unfairness is conceptually exceptional.'

[335] See 'Statement to the House of Commons by the Financial Secretary to the Treasury, Mark Hoban MP, on Reforming the Institutional Framework for Financial Regulation', 17 June 2010, online at <http://www.hm-treasury.gov.uk/statement_fst_170610.htm>; HM Treasury, *A new approach to financial regulation: judgment, focus and stability* (Cm 7874) (London, TSO, 2010), online at <http://www.hm-treasury.gov.uk/d/consult_financial_regulation_condoc.pdf>.

[336] Macro-prudential regulation will be taken over by the Bank of England Financial Policy Committee, with responsibility to look across the economy at the macroeconomic and financial issues that may threaten stability, while the Bank of England will also set up a new Prudential Regulation Authority (PRA) headed by the Deputy Governor to conduct prudential regulation of sectors such as deposit-takers, insurers and investment banks.

[337] The Consultation Paper also raised the question of transferring the OFT's consumer credit responsibilities to the CPMA to create a single regulatory regime for consumer credit and financial services: Cm 7874, above n 335, para 4.56.

[338] 'Statement to the House of Commons by the Financial Secretary to the Treasury', above n 335.

[339] Cm 7874, above n 335, para 1.22.

[340] 'Statement to the House of Commons by the Financial Secretary to the Treasury', above n 335.

[341] Cm 7874, above n 335, paras 4.6–4.12.

more interventionist and pre-emptive regulatory philosophy, including the work carried out under the *Mortgage Market Review* and in the area of responsible lending.[342] This philosophical recalibration is clearly based on rejection of the abstract concept of self-responsible, autonomous consumers in favour of a new model that recognises the reality of consumers as potentially vulnerable subjects, although the emphasis remains on product risk rather than consumer risk, as indicated by the explanation that

> [t]hese initiatives recognise and respond to some of the distinctive characteristics of retail financial services that call for a more intrusive approach, such as long-term product payoffs, product complexity and asymmetry of information between consumers and producers.[343]

While it is anticipated that the new institutional structure will be in place within two years, the Consultation Paper leaves scope for further debate into the question of responsibility, with the establishment of the CPMA described as 'present[ing] a key opportunity for a frank and open debate about achieving the appropriate balance between the regulation and supervision of firms, consumer responsibilities, consumer financial capability and the role of the state'.[344] It remains to be seen how effectively the CPMA applies the concept of 'responsible lending' in addressing the needs of vulnerable consumers, although the tone of the Government's Consultation Paper suggests that the post-crisis environment will provide an opportunity to re-think the philosophical assumptions underlying the regulatory regime, with potential implications for a regime based on a more responsive and realistic model of the consumer as legal subject.

The nature and quality of the advice offered to equity release customers continues to come under debate. In 2010, the Society of Equity Release Advisers (calling for a ban on telephone sales in response to the FSA's *Mortgage Market Review*) emphasised the importance of face-to-face advice to ensure that consumers are legally capable and that they understand the risks of the transaction.[345] The question of how consumers pay for this advice remains controversial: while the FSA has proposed a ban on providers rolling up fees and charges into the debt, which it identified as an unfair charging practice,[346] the Society of Equity Release Advisers (SERA) has argued that this would reduce the ability of many equity release consumers—who by definition tend to be cash-poor at the time of the transaction—to avail themselves of advice.

Meanwhile, there is also useful work to be done in honing the 'information and advice' to make it as effective as possible in serving the needs of older consumers. The FSA's current approach to lifetime mortgages, for example, places considerable emphasis on the training and competence of staff, who are required to take appropriate examinations administered by the Financial Services Skills Council (FSSC) to ensure that they have an adequate level of knowledge and understanding of both products and processes.[347] The examinations to qualify as an equity release adviser include the Chartered Insurance

[342] *Ibid*, para 4.24.

[343] *Ibid*, para 4.24.

[344] *Ibid*, para 4.25; see also paras 4.50–4.52.

[345] See D Singh, 'Sera wants equity release recognition', *Financial Times Adviser*, 4 February 2010; online at <http://www.ftadviser.com/financialadviser/regulation/regulators/fsa/news/article/20100204/2442ba1a-0f25-11df-ba8b-0015171400aa/sera-wants-equity-release-recognition.jsp>.

[346] See *Mortgage Market Review*, above n 255, ch 8, Table 3.

[347] See *FSA Handbook*, TC 2.1, online at <http://fsahandbook.info/FSA/html/handbook/TC/2/1>; see also FSSC website for details of the appropriate examinations at <http://www.fssc.org.uk/appropriate_exam_list.html>.

Institute's Certificate in Equity Release, the IFS School of Finance's Certificate in Regulated Equity Release, and the Chartered Institute of Bankers in Scotland's Equity Release Mortgage Advice and Practice Certificate. The FSSC also offers a Later Life Adviser Accreditation Scheme (LLAA), which is awarded to individual advisers in recognition of their demonstrating best practice, appropriate knowledge and older client-care procedures.[348] This is not a necessary qualification to give equity release advice, although its development does reflect the growing awareness of the need for bespoke services for older consumers. This approach remains at the self-regulation stage,[349] although the LLAA has set standards for the application of soft skills and knowledge (that the adviser has a good working knowledge and understanding of the needs, capacity and issues of dealing with older clients, with an emphasis on behaviours which must be demonstrated, such as understanding of the consumer); and the equity release section of the syllabus includes as learning objectives that the adviser understands the types of consumers at whom equity release is targeted and their personal requirements, understands the impact on consumers' future options, and can apply suitable equity release solutions according to the circumstances of different clients. The Society of Later Life Advisers, founded in 2008, seeks to promote good practice in later life advice, as well as promoting Later Life Accredited Advisers to consumers and their families.[350]

In 2009, the Financial Services Consumer Panel (FSCP) published a scoping paper on *Financial Services and Later Life*,[351] which reported that while significant progress is being made towards addressing consumer detriment in later life, there is still a need for a proactive approach to address current market failures; and that the landscape of financial decision-making for older consumers is likely to grow only more complex into the future. The report noted that the development of new and increasingly complex products designed for the 'decumulation' stage of financial life places older consumers at risk of making poor choices, and could lead to individual detriment as well as to increased costs for the taxpayer.[352] The FSCP's findings have strengthened its commitment to continue working with the FSA/CPMA and the Government to develop appropriate consumer protection for older consumers. Particular areas for attention include the need for a bespoke advice standard for later life advice, and achieving a better understanding of how 'mainstream' projects, such as the financial capability work, need to be adapted to address the specific needs of older consumers.[353] The project's work on decumulation products identified product types which are regarded as higher-risk than equity release,[354] although it was noted that while 'FSA sales regulations limit the volume of misselling … where it does occur the consequences for the consumer can be severe, extremely stressful and in

[348] See <http://www.fssc.org.uk/later_life_adviser_guide_web.pdf>.

[349] See <http://www.ship-ltd.org/uploads/qualificationtable.pdf>. Equity release intermediaries are also represented by a number of trade bodies, including Specialist Advisers for Equity Release (SAFER), online at <http://www.specialistequityrelease.org/>; Independent Equity Release Adviser Alliance (IERAA), online at <http://www.ieraa.co.uk/>; and SERA, launched in November 2009.

[350] See website at <http://www.societyoflaterlifeadvisers.co.uk/>.

[351] J Wells and M Gostelow, *Financial Services and Later Life: A Scoping Project for the Financial Services Consumer Panel*; available online at <http://www.fs-cp.org.uk/publications/pdf/fscp_laterlife0609.pdf>.

[352] *Ibid*, at 1.

[353] Eg, much of the financial capability agenda is delivered through new technologies, which is likely to reduce its reach amongst older consumers.

[354] Eg, annuities.

some cases difficult to remedy.'[355] Its research into information, guidance and advice found that older consumers are often excluded from the growth in consumer-oriented information due to their lack of access to new technology, lack of mobility or social isolation, lack of trust in financial institutions or preference not to ask for help.

While it is widely accepted that the extension of mandatory regulation of housing equity products through the FSA has significantly reduced the risks that such transactions pose to older consumers, there are gaps in the protection offered by the current regulatory regime.[356] In the recent FSCP report, which 'traffic lighted' both the materiality and the probability of detriment resulting from:

a) inappropriate equity release products;
b) high charges/costs; and
c) emotional/psychological harm resulting from equity release transactions;

the 'traffic lights' remained orange (moderate level of risk/medium probability) on five of the six variables, with only the probability of high costs/charges coded as green (level of risk insignificant).

The area of equity release has also come under consideration by the European Commission, which in 2009 published a study on the issues and laws governing equity release schemes across the EU with a view to considering whether EU action is justified in this area.[357] The report concluded that legal conditions for equity release in the Member States are 'generally favourable'. Although 'consumer protection law may require some adjustment since some information obligations are not entirely appropriate',[358] the UK is offered as an example of an 'advanced maturity' market.[359] Nevertheless, it was recognised that 'the vulnerability of the customer base will mean that this market will always be supervised as having a high risk of consumer detriment'.[360] A question which remains is the extent to which the remaining gaps in the protection of older consumers in housing equity transactions should be addressed solely through improvements to the regulatory supervision regime, or whether there is any scope for applying the 'general law' more proactively within the vulnerability/responsibility paradigm, to improve the redress available to vulnerable older consumers in this context.

[355] Wells and Gostelow, above n 351, para 1.4.

[356] The FSCP report also noted that 'the FSA continued to identify cases of mis-selling well beyond the introduction of sales regulation': *ibid*, para 5.1.5.

[357] U Reifner, S Clerc-Renaud, EF Pérez-Carrillo, A Tiffe and M Knobloch, *Study on Equity Release in the EU* (January 2009); available online at <http://ec.europa.eu/internal_market/finservices-retail/docs/credit/equity_release_part1_en.pdf>.

[358] *Ibid*, Executive Summary, V.

[359] *Ibid*, Part II, Country Reports, at 6; available online at <http://ec.europa.eu/internal_market/finservices-retail/docs/credit/equity_release_part2_en.pdf>.

[360] *Ibid*, at 36.

10

Equitable Remedies and Older Owners

(1) Introduction

To the extent that vulnerable older owners are recognised as being susceptible to harm in housing equity transactions, the primary vehicle of legal protection has been the development of the regulatory regimes linked to targeted housing equity products. The arguments in favour of targeted protections in housing equity transactions, as identified through the regulatory regime, are based on a combination of transaction risk (with emphases, for example, on the complexities of particular products) and consumer risk (which has been linked to a range of factors, including decision-making or procedural vulnerabilities of older consumers as a group, situational vulnerabilities where (marginal) older consumers enter into transactions under financial pressure, and the disproportionate impact of adverse financial transactions for older and/or marginal consumers). As the analysis of these protections in chapter nine has revealed, the regulatory approach, which is primarily focused on regulating providers' conduct rather than protecting consumers directly through the provision of remedies, is particularly appropriate when the potentially vulnerable party is an older owner, not least because with limited time and resilience to recover from harm, the prevention of bad outcomes is preferable to curing them through remedial action. Nevertheless, there are limits to the reach of the regulatory regime which circumscribe the range of products covered by the regulator: some transactions fall outside the scope of the regulatory regime. Regulatory approaches do not seek to respond to all risks, or to avoid harm to all consumers, and the administrative model of remedial enforcement is focused on achieving results for the market as a whole (or a proportionately critical section of the market to justify expending the administrative agencies' limited resources) rather than on the individual consumer.

An alternative way of looking at housing equity transactions is to focus on the nature of the relationships between the parties to the transaction, recognising that transactions between parties to certain types of relationship attract particular scrutiny from the courts. There are at least two distinct types of housing equity transaction in which the courts may be called upon to scrutinise the relationship between a creditor/equity provider and an older owner. The first is a 'three-party transaction': for example, where an older owner agrees to the use of the home as security for the debt of a younger relative, and where the relationship under scrutiny is that between the older and younger relatives, with the bank's potential liability based on failure to discharge the responsibilities that flow from being 'put on inquiry'. Since the regulatory framework extends only to those transactions in which the older owner purchases a specifically defined equity release product, and consumer credit protections are potentially relevant only when the older owner is acting as a consumer within a specified credit transaction, neither has any bearing on those *inter vivos* transactions (by contract or gift) into which an older owner may enter, often in favour of a family member or close friend. A second type of transaction considered in this chapter is the 'two-party transaction', in which the provider's potential liability is direct, based on its own relationship with the older owner, and where any equitable intervention may be (depending on the nature of the transaction) layered on top of the protections discussed in chapters seven, eight and nine. Both types of transaction are of interest for the analysis in this book, not only because they offer a potential avenue of practical relief to older owners who suffer losses resulting from adverse financial transactions, but because they reveal a set of norms with respect to the paradigm of the older owner as a legal subject, the meanings attributed to 'vulnerability' within the equitable domain, and the willingness of English courts to hold commercial (and social) parties responsible for their conduct when transacting with older owners.

In *Niersmans v Pesticcio*,[1] a deed of gift executed by an older owner was set aside for undue influence. Mummery LJ recognised that—following a flurry of attention focused on the 'surety wives' cases—the phenomenon of *inter vivos* transactions dealing with the housing equity of older owners presented a new set of issues for the courts in applying the undue influence principles:

> With the increase in home ownership and the rising value of residential property, more people have more property to dispose of in their lifetime and on death, and more people expect to benefit substantially from inheritance. As people live longer, the inheritors have to wait longer. There is, however, the unwelcome prospect that the longer the wait, the greater the risk that even a modest estate will be seriously diminished by the high cost of care in the old age or infirmity of the home-owner, and by the impact of inheritance tax on death. The elderly and infirm in need of full-time residential care are vulnerable to suggestions that they should dispose of the home to which they are unlikely to return. In my view, these social trends are already leading to a renewed interest in the law governing the validity of lifetime dispositions of houses, both in and outside the family circle, by the elderly and the infirm.[2]

While this book has focused primarily on transactions between older owners and credit providers, when seeking to evaluate law's responses to the older owners as legal subjects it is also instructive to consider claims of undue influence or unconscionability involving family or friends, as these transactions provide much of the fact base for the equitable jurisprudence concerning older owners. From a practical perspective, an equitable wrong between the parties to an *inter vivos* transaction (for example, a suretyship arrangement between an older owner and younger family member) may form the basis of a claim that a transaction is voidable against a third-party provider, so determining the scope of the provider's responsibility in the transaction. Further, the provider itself may be subject to direct liability for undue influence or unconscionability in 'two-party cases' where it is deemed to have 'crossed the line' in procuring the transaction, again with implications for the scope of the provider's responsibility towards potentially vulnerable customers.

This chapter examines the scope of the doctrines of undue influence and unconscionability as an additional 'safety-net' for older owners who suffer a loss as a result of a housing equity transaction. These doctrines were described by Capper as the most useful from the 'patchwork quilt of protection' that contract law's vitiating factors offer to vulnerable people who have entered into 'financial transactions they would do better to

[1] [2004] EWCA Civ 372.

[2] *Ibid*, at [4].

avoid'.[3] The aims of the equitable remedies echo the functions of regulatory redress in so far as they seek to protect vulnerable parties from being taken advantage of, and to deter such conduct.[4] However, the nature of the remedy offered by these vitiating factors is distinctive in that (when successfully pleaded) its enables the claimant to avoid the transaction. In the housing equity context, this means its offers the possibility of recovering the home itself, rather than compensation for financial loss. Undue influence—which Capper described as having 'done the bulk of the work in protecting the vulnerable, at least in England'[5]—will be the primary focus of this chapter,[6] although the prospects for developing arguments under the broader concept of unconscionable dealing are also considered in section (3).

While the prospect of avoiding the contract altogether represents a potentially significant outcome for older owners who have suffered harm as a result of adverse housing equity transactions, it is important to bear in mind that these remedies are typically viewed as 'marginal' in the sense that they are intended to remedy 'exceptional' or 'pathological'[7] cases where something goes badly wrong, not to function as a routine mechanism for ensuring the safety of transactions. Even those commentators who disagree on the jurisprudential basis of undue influence are agreed that it arises only in 'exceptional' circumstances. For example, Birks and Chin, describing the nature of undue influence, stated that 'The relationship must be such as to impair the autonomy of the weaker party to a serious and exceptional degree',[8] and later that

> the degree [of impairment] in question is exceptional. Although adults are in reality of widely differing intelligence and personality, by and large they must be presumed equally able to cope with their own affairs. Similarly, adults come under all sorts of different influences, and again they have to be assumed able to cope. The law relieves only an extreme loss of autonomy.[9]

This was echoed by Bigwood who, when describing his proposed reconceptualisation of the defendant's fault-base in undue influence as 'transactional neglect', claimed:

> Obviously, only 'serious' vulnerability or dependency can give rise to the possibility of exploitation, and this must especially obtain in this context where the very security of bargain transactions is at stake—hence the legal threshold tests of 'serious' mistake, 'excessive' trust, 'special' disadvantage and the like.[10]

[3] D Capper, 'Protection of the vulnerable in financial transactions—what the common law vitiating factors can do for you' in M Kenny, J Devenney and L Fox O'Mahony (eds), *Unconscionability in European Private Financial Transactions: Protecting the Vulnerable* (Cambridge, Cambridge University Press, 2010) 182.

[4] T Wilson, N Howell and G Sheehan, 'Protecting the Most Vulnerable in Consumer Transactions' (2009) 32 *Journal of Consumer Policy* 117, 126.

[5] Capper, above n 3, at 183.

[6] This focus on undue influence also provides an opportunity to consider the protection of vulnerable older owners in transactions which do not directly benefit the owner himself or herself, but where he or she acts as surety for a younger relative or caregiver.

[7] M Chen-Wishart, 'Undue Influence: Beyond Impaired Consent and Wrongdoing towards a Relational Analysis' in A Burrows and A Rodger, *Mapping the Law: Essays in Memory of Peter Birks* (Oxford, Oxford University Press, 2006) 201.

[8] P Birks and NY Chin, 'On the Nature of Undue Influence' in J Beatson and D Friedmann (eds), *Good Faith and Fault in Contract Law* (Oxford, Clarendon Press, 1995) 69.

[9] *Ibid*, at 87.

[10] R Bigwood, 'Contracts by Unfair Advantage: From Exploitation to Transactional Neglect' (2005) 25 *OJLS* 65, 86, fn 105.

Bigwood later added that his reconceptualisation of undue influence as breach of the dominant party's responsibilities in respect of an obligation of reasonable care 'would continue only exceptionally to apply … at the expense of security of contract'.[11]

The view that equitable remedies should apply only exceptionally at the expense of security of contract reflects, of course, a commitment to a particular model of contract law that is 'freedom-oriented', and that fits within a broader liberal ideology and conceptualisation of the legal subject which has itself been subject to some criticism.[12] The liberal model of contract is reinforced by reference to policy goals concerned with facilitating commercial transactions, with the possibility that a contract could be invalidated by any vitiating factor highlighting the tensions between competing goals of fairness towards vulnerable parties, on the one hand, and transactional certainty on the other. Limiting equitable relief to exceptional circumstances under doctrines which are demarcated by clear rules and requirements promotes the classical contractual values of stability, certainty and predictability,[13] while accepting that some deserving claimants may be excluded; in contrast, if the vitiating factors are conceived as more flexible, as offering broad general principles, it is more likely that relief will be available in all deserving cases, but at the expense of transactional certainty.[14]

In his seminal analysis of unconscionability, Waddams claimed that the goal of achieving substantive fairness in any given case is always manifest (even if not articulated) in the decisions of any 'civilised system of law',[15] but that courts have sometimes been 'reluctant to admit as a controlling factor any notion so vague as reasonableness or fairness [because] it was easier, intellectually, to accept a rigid rule without apparent rational basis, than a general power of control'.[16] Waddams argued that the effect of an explicit commitment to certainty over fairness is to create rigid rules that are at once both over- and under-inclusive, and lobbied for greater judicial clarity in the articulation of what he identified as an (implicit) general doctrine of unconscionability, to make explicit (and so more certain) the underlying policy considerations that influence the exercise of the court's general power. Capper has supported this argument for elucidation, on the basis that cases are better argued when litigants and advisers understand the issues around which to organise their evidence and arguments, and where stronger or better-resourced

[11] *Ibid*, at 89.

[12] See especially ch 4, ch 6 section (7), and ch 8, section (2). Critics of the liberal model of contract are less concerned than its proponents with the 'exceptional' nature of the equitable remedies; see, eg, D Kennedy, 'Distributive and Paternalist Moves in Contract and Tort Law, with Special Reference to Compulsory Terms and Unequal Bargaining Power' (1982) 41 *Maryland Law Review* 563, in which Kennedy justifies paternalist interventions to overrule the choice of another, based on the party's 'capacity to make this decision', so shifting the focus from the importance of respecting the individual's choice, however misjudged, to the consequences of the parties' particular choice. Kennedy argues, with particular resonance for older owners in housing equity transactions, that a salient consideration should be whether intervention will in fact make the person more dependent, or whether he or she will be able to learn and grow from non-intervention, or to live with his or her mistakes, and so on.

[13] See, eg, MJ Trebilcock, 'The Doctrine of Inequality of Bargaining Power: Post-Benthamite Economics in the House of Lords' (1976) 26 *University of Toronto Law Journal* 359; *(Alec) Lobb (Garages) Ltd v Total Oil GB Ltd* [1985] 1 WLR 173.

[14] See S Waddams, 'Unconscionability in Contracts' (1976) 39 *MLR* 369; D Capper, 'Undue influence and unconscionability: A Rationalisation' (1998) *LQR* 479, 501; and Lord Denning's proposal for a general doctrine of inequality of bargaining power in *Lloyd's Bank Ltd v Bundy* [1975] QB 326D; see below, section (3).

[15] Waddams, above n 14, at 370.

[16] *Ibid*, at 371.

parties are prevented from delaying litigation with obscure or unmeritorious points.[17] Against this view, Cretney expressed alarm at the proposition that transactions could be impugned on broad and general grounds such as 'fairness', arguing that 'soft' grounds of relief tempt the weak into litigation,[18] which while 'certainly preferable to personal violence as a means of dispute resolution … is not an intrinsically desirable activity'.[19]

Yet, notwithstanding Cretney's general caution that 'soft law' approaches encourage litigation, judicial action is unlikely to be an obvious, attractive or 'easy' option for vulnerable older owners. Equitable remedies, like regulatory redress, depend on the injured party initiating action to trigger the possibility of protection, which in turn depends on their being aware of the options and having the necessary resources (financial and personal) to instigate and pursue legal proceedings.[20] This has particular implications for vulnerable (for example low-income, older) consumers.[21] One of the vulnerabilities identified in the context of elder abuse is that older people are less likely than the general population to 'go to law' for solutions to their problems.[22] This was reflected in discussions of consumer credit remedies in chapter eight, and of the regulation of specific targeted products in chapter nine, both of which highlighted the relatively low volume of reported case law in which older consumers have utilised formal mechanisms for legal redress. While some might perceive lack of litigation as evidence of an absence of harm—that the system works well to protect its constituents—this explanation seems unlikely in light of the evidence concerning (marginal) older owners' vulnerability in financial transactions, and the higher proportion of cases brought by older consumers through non-judicial avenues, for example the Financial Ombudsman Service (FOS).[23] A more likely explanation is that reluctance to pursue formal legal remedies is a result of the high levels of stress and anxiety that vulnerable consumers experience in dealing with legal issues and processes, leaving them ill-equipped to embark on litigation.[24]

In order for older consumers to pursue a remedy they must be aware that they have rights, or at least that something is not fair; they must have access to advice or resources to help them assess whether any remedy is available; and they must have the capacity to pursue those rights.[25] It has been widely accepted that this is most difficult for low-income or vulnerable consumers.[26] The Office of Fair Trading (OFT) has suggested that, in reality, vulnerable debtors are rarely likely to seek relief from the courts, due to receiving no, or

[17] Capper, above n 14, at 503.

[18] SM Cretney, 'Mere Puppets, Folly and Imprudence: The Limits of Undue Influence' [1994] *Restitution Law Review* 3.

[19] *Ibid*, at 12.

[20] T Wilson, N Howell and G Sheehan, 'Protecting the Most Vulnerable in Consumer Transactions' (2009) 32 *Journal of Consumer Policy* 117, 129.

[21] *Ibid*, at 127; H Genn, *Paths to Justice: what people do and think about going to law* (Oxford, Hart Publishing, 1999) 101.

[22] See discussion in ch 6, section (4).

[23] See ch 8, section (7)(c).

[24] R Moorhead and M Robinson, *A trouble shared—legal problems clusters in solicitors' and advice agencies* (DCA Research Series 8/06, 2006).

[25] Wilson *et al*, above n 20, at 130.

[26] See, eg, DTI, *Extortionate Credit in the UK: A Report to the DTI*, by E Kempson and C Whyley (London, DTI, 1999), available online at <http://webarchive.nationalarchives.gov.uk/+/http://www.dti.gov.uk/ccp/topics1/extortionate.htm>.

inadequate, legal advice, or because they are unaware of their rights.[27] Vulnerable debtors may also lack the financial resources to bring a case to court, or experience practical, psychological or cultural barriers to litigation.[28] In the case of older people, barriers to litigation resulting from victimisation may include social isolation, deteriorating physical health, loss of independence, financial loss, adverse impacts on relationships with family and friends, emotional distress, humiliation, loss of self-confidence and depression.[29] This represents a major barrier to the effectiveness of remedial responses to older owners' vulnerability (which seek to provide a 'cure' rather than prevention, and which require the injured party to bring an action in his or her own right) when compared to the regulatory strategy of empowering institutional agencies to monitor, negotiate with and litigate against firms when standards are breached. Consequently, remedial strategies may have limited value for vulnerable older and marginal consumers, compared to the regulatory approach which emphasises the prevention of harm.

Nevertheless, the nature and extent of the safety-nets provided by the equitable remedies—and specifically the doctrines of undue influence and unconscionable bargains considered in this chapter—merit analysis for two core reasons. First, since the regulatory regime is targeted at particular types of transaction, and within that at particular product types, it inevitably leaves certain types of financial transaction involving the older owner's housing equity outside its reach. Across the patchwork quilt of legal responses to housing equity transactions, it is valuable to map the options that may be available to older owners in different circumstances, and to evaluate the effectiveness of differing approaches with respect to the specific issues raised when older owners transact on their housing wealth. Secondly, these doctrines, and the evolving jurisprudence that supports them, provide useful insights into the ways in which the ideas of vulnerability and responsibility—identified in this book as key referents for the conceptualisation of the older owner as a vulnerable legal subject—have been articulated and developed within the domain of equitable remedies.

(2) Undue Influence

The scenarios in which claims of undue influence have been raised following a property transaction by an older owner include cases in which the older owner has made a gift of money or property to a person on whom he or she is functionally dependent; where the older owner transfers property to a relative or friend to ensure accommodation and care in old age (and to avoid institutional care); where the older person forms a romantic

27 OFT, *Protecting Vulnerable Consumers—A note by the Office of Fair Trading in response to the DTI's consultation document on extortionate credit* (London, OFT, 2003), para 24, online at <http://www.oft.gov.uk/shared_oft/press_release_attachments/extcredit.pdf>.

28 DTI, above n 26, at 31–32.

29 A Mowlam, R Tennant, J Dixon and C McCreadie, *UK Study of Abuse and Neglect of Older People: Qualitative Findings* (2007), available online at <http://www.dh.gov.uk/en/Publicationsandstatistics/Publications/PublicationsPolicyAndGuidance/DH_078333>. In another study, 29% of those who had been financially abused reported 'wishing their life would end', compared with only 8% in the rest of the sample: E Podnieks, 'National survey on abuse of the elderly in Canada' (1992) 4 *Journal of Elder Abuse and Neglect* 5; cited in G Crosby, A Clark, R Hayes, K Jones and N Lievesley, *Financial Abuse of Older People: A review of the literature carried out by the Centre for Policy on Aging on Behalf of Help the Aged* (London, Help the Aged, 2008) 14.

liaison, leading him or her to make a gift of property; where the older owner transfers property to a relative working in the family business; or where the older owner transfers or mortgages property for the purpose of raising income or capital, which may then be gifted to another.[30] While the primary focus of the analysis in this chapter (and throughout the book) is whether, and to what extent, commercial creditors or housing equity providers are 'responsible' for the risks undertaken by vulnerable older owners in these transactions, in the realm of undue influence the idea of the older owner as a vulnerable subject, and the responsibilities that vulnerability engenders on those who contract with the older owner, have largely been developed in 'two-party' cases in which the defendant is either a 'friend' or a family member.

Commercial parties may be fixed with indirect liability for undue influence in 'three-party' cases, for example where an older owner acts as a 'non-commercial surety' by agreeing to the use of his or her owned home to secure the debts of another, often a younger relative or caregiver.[31] Within this category, there is evidence to indicate that transactions which enable young adults to leverage parental financial assistance to enter the homeownership sector[32] (with parental contributions viewed as 'an early inheritance or living bequest'[33]) are increasingly prevalent in the UK, although they do not always take the form of a traditional surety/guarantee arrangement. Innovative products such as the 'Lend a Hand' deal from Lloyds TSB, which allowed borrowers to take out a mortgage with only a 5 per cent deposit 'plus the backing of someone who wants to help you onto the property ladder by putting their savings up as additional security for the mortgage',[34] enable parents to leverage their own housing wealth to support adult offspring. Alternatively, older people may provide financial support by using their housing equity as security for a younger family member's business liabilities.[35] Depending on the circumstances, these transactions may potentially be avoided (and so rendered unenforceable against the commercial provider) if it can be established that the older owner acted under undue influence in entering into the transaction, and that the third party creditor/provider is tainted by the undue influence.

The role of older owners in supporting younger family members is, of course, additional to demands that may be placed on housing equity to meet an older owner's own needs. It might be thought that an older person who can afford to use his or her property to support others rather than meeting his or her own needs is not likely to be a 'marginal' owner, reinforcing the argument that 'the beneficiaries of the relief that contract law can give are rarely the very poor. They are people with something to lose, and

[30] The role and influence of adult offspring in the older owner's housing decisions was considered in ch 4, section (4), which noted that what tends to be 'inheritable' on the part of younger family members is the function of housing as an investment asset rather than housing as home.

[31] Fiona Burns has termed this practice 'intergenerationally transmitted debt'; see, eg, F Burns, 'Protecting Elders: Regulating intergenerationally transmitted debt in Australia' (2005) 28 *International Journal of Law and Psychiatry* 300; F Burns, 'Legally regulating intergenerationally transmitted debt' (2005) s24 *Australasian Journal on Ageing (Special Issue: Ageing and the Future of Elder Care)* 46.

[32] See M Andrew, 'The Changing Route to Owner Occupation: The Impact of Student Debt' (2010) 25 *Housing Studies* 39.

[33] G Chamberlin, 'Recent Developments in the UK housing market' (2009) 3(8) *Economic and Labour Market Review* 29, 34.

[34] See <http://www.lloydstsb.com/mortgages/lend_a_hand.asp>.

[35] These transactions are often voluntary on the part of the older owner, involving the gift of capital to a family member, or the voluntary assumption of liability for the borrower's debts.

with the means and energy to seek to regain it.'[36] Yet the growth in marginal homeownership in the latter part of the twentieth century[37] created a significant cohort of older owners who have something to lose but not necessarily the wherewithal to recover it, and the undue influence case law includes a raft of cases in which older owners have 'pauperised' themselves,[38] or been left with no resources to support themselves for the remainder of their lives.[39] Indeed, when marginal owners put their homes at risk by agreeing to act as surety for the debts of another they are not likely to expect that the outcome will be the loss of their homes, so that the conflict between the older owner's own future needs and the debtor's need for asset security may not be evident at the time of the transaction.

Whether the party against whom the claim of undue influence is brought is a friend or relative, a commercial creditor/provider which has itself overstepped the line in procuring the transaction, or a commercial party which has failed to discharge its responsibilities in relation to undue influence exerted by another, the first matter to be addressed is whether the transaction has been procured by undue influence. It is generally accepted that undue influence is 'normally applied to transactions within a relationship in which one person has come to trust the other. The essential element of the doctrine has been described as taking "unfair advantage" of the other or assuming "a role of dominating influence".'[40] While English courts have resisted the articulation of 'neat and tidy definitional rules',[41] the categories which have evolved through judicial application of the equitable doctrine include a distinction between actual and presumed undue influence.

Actual undue influence (Class 1) exists where it can be proven that undue influence or pressure was in fact exerted[42] to bring about the transaction. In the small number of reported cases where older claimants have successfully avoided transactions due to actual undue influence, both the vulnerability of the claimant and the fault of the defendant have been patent. For example, in *Clarke v Prus*,[43] old Mr Clarke gifted property worth £1.9 million to the younger Mrs Prus over a period of 20 years in which she became increasingly aggressive in her demands, waging an 'emotional war of attrition'[44] that led the court to find that 'what started out as Mr Clarke's folly ... finished up as Mrs Prus' victimisation at the end of his life'.[45] There was clear evidence both of Mr Clarke's

36 S Waddams, 'Protection of weaker parties in English law' in Kenny *et al* (eds), above n 3, at 41.

37 See ch 1.

38 See, eg, *Allcard v Skinner* (1887) 36 ChD 145.

39 *Langton v Langton* [1995] 2 FLR 890.

40 Law Commission, *A Private Right of Redress for Unfair Commercial Practices* (London, Law Commission, 2008), para 2.73, quoting *National Westminster Bank plc v Morgan* [1985] AC 686 at 707b, *per* Lord Scarman; see also *Royal Bank of Scotland v Etridge (No 2)* (hereafter '*Etridge (No 2)*') [2001] 4 All ER 449.

41 In *National Westminster Bank plc v Morgan*, above n 40, Lord Scarman claimed (at 709): 'There is no precisely defined law setting limits to the equitable jurisdiction of a court to relieve against undue influence. This is the world of doctrine, not of neat and tidy rules ... It is the unimpeachability at law of a disadvantageous transaction which is the starting point from which the court advances to consider whether the transaction is the product of one's own folly or of the undue influence exercised by another. A court in the exercise of this equitable jurisdiction is a court of conscience. Definition is a poor instrument when used to determine whether a transaction is or is not unconscionable: this is a question which depends upon the particular facts of the case.'

42 Actual undue influence typically involves improper pressure or coercion, eg deliberate concealment of material facts or threats to prosecute.

43 [1995] New Property Cases 41 (Ch).

44 F Burns, 'The elderly and undue influence *inter vivos*' (2003) 23 *Legal Studies* 251, 258.

45 *Clarke v Prus*, above n 43.

'vulnerability' (he suffered from dementia, a severely paranoid personality and a disordered irrational suspicion towards his children) and of 'fault' on the part of Mrs Prus, whom the court described as having 'a well developed capacity to persuade which she freely and successfully exercised'.[46] In *Langton v Langton*,[47] the plaintiff was recognised as vulnerable due to his dependence on the defendants to care for him in light of his poor health and mobility. Investigating a transaction in which he gifted his home to the defendants to ensure that they would continue to care for him within his home environment (so preserving his housing as home), the court held it to be voidable based on evidence that the defendants had exerted such pressure on the plaintiff that he felt he had no choice but to transfer the property to them in order for them to continue looking after him.

While actual undue influence tends to involve explicit pressure, presumed (or 'relational') undue influence cases are typically more subtle. Presumed undue influence arises when there is a relationship of 'trust and confidence' between the parties to the transaction, and a 'suspicion of abuse' of that relationship (evidenced by demonstrating that the transaction 'calls out for explanation').[48] In *Royal Bank of Scotland v Etridge (No 2)*, Lord Bingham described an inverse relationship between the presumption that flows from the relationship and the explicability of the transaction, so that 'the greater the disadvantage to the vulnerable person, the more cogent must be the explanation before the presumption will be regarded as rebutted'.[49] The category of presumed undue influence has generated a substantial body of case law in recent decades, including an increasing judicial recognition of the specific vulnerabilities of older people to relational undue influence,[50] which, in turn, has sustained an upsurge of scholarly interest in the jurisprudential nature of the doctrine. This section considers these analyses as they relate to the issues explored in this book. Specifically, it considers whether, and to what extent, the competing accounts provide a useful conceptual framework within which to develop the discursive tropes of vulnerability and responsibility, and so to shore up the value of undue influence as a potential safety-net for vulnerable older owners.

(a) Presumed undue influence and older owners

While analyses of actual undue influence[51] emphasise the exercise of coercion or application of pressure,[52] presumed or relational undue influence involves a 'relationship of influence' which is 'both the context and the cause of the alleged victim's vulnerability to the exploitation of which he or she subsequently complains'.[53] It is this emphasis on the *relationship* as the cause of the vulnerability that narrows the scope of the doctrine,

[46] *Ibid*, *per* Knox J.

[47] [1995] 2 FLR 890.

[48] *Etridge (No 2)*, above n 40, at [14].

[49] *Ibid*, at [24].

[50] See discussion of *Niersmans v Pesticcio*, above n 1, discussed at text to nn 1–2; Burns, above n 44.

[51] Birks and Chin argued that actual undue influence could be subsumed with duress: see Birks and Chin, above n 8; Devenney and Chandler proposed the doctrine of economic duress as a vehicle for the merger of the two categories: J Devenney and A Chandler, 'Unconscionability and the Taxonomy of Undue Influence' (2007) *Journal of Business Law* 541, 553; while Capper has suggested that it is duress which should be expunged from the common law vitiating factors: D Capper, above n 3, at 175.

[52] R Bigwood, 'Undue Influence in the House of Lords: Principles and Proof' (2002) 65 *MLR* 435, 440.

[53] *Ibid*, at 440.

appearing to exclude vulnerabilities which are extant and independent of the transactional relationship (for example, contextual or situational vulnerabilities). The relationship of trust and confidence is presumed in two types of cases (previously known as 'Class 2A' and 'Class 2B'): where the relationship between the parties is one of the 'well established categories of relationship' (examples typically given included the influence of a parent over a child, a doctor over a patient, solicitor over client, or religious leader over disciple)[54]; and where the relationship between the relevant individuals is, on the individual facts of the case, one of 'trust and confidence', so that a presumption of undue influence is raised.[55]

One of the common instances in which a gift or surety transaction is made by an older person in favour of a younger adult is where a parent uses housing equity to benefit his or her adult offspring. While the relationship between a parent and child gives rise to an irrebuttable presumption that the parent has influence over the child, even into the adulthood of the child,[56] the converse does not apply: if a parent (or other older relative) seeks to avoid a transaction in favour of an adult offspring (or another younger relative),[57] he or she must establish the relationship of trust and confidence as a matter of fact. In *Inche Noriah v Shaik Allie Bin Omar*,[58] where a nephew exerted undue influence over his elderly aunt, the court emphasised that such a claim

> depends upon the circumstances of each individual case and requires some evidential foundation. A relationship between a parent and a child varies over time. At an early stage it may be the child who is under the influence of the parent and it may be that, when the parents are elderly ... the parents come under the influence of one or more of their children.[59]

While the relationship is viewed as one that *may* involve 'trust and confidence', the law makes no presumption to this effect but requires that it be proven in the individual case.

If the presumption is raised, a claimant must also satisfy a second requirement: that the transaction 'calls for explanation'.[60] While the House of Lords previously suggested that 'disadvantage'—financial or any other form—should not be an essential ingredient for a finding of undue influence,[61] in *Etridge (No 2) Lord Nicholls* observed that

[54] The appropriateness of these 'typical' Class 2A categories was criticised in Devenney and Chandler, above n 51, which argued that the old 'Class 2A' presumption should be abandoned in favour of establishing a *de facto* relationship of trust and confidence.

[55] '[I]f the complainant proves the *de facto* existence of a relationship under which the complainant generally reposed trust and confidence in the wrongdoer, the existence of such a relationship raises the presumption of undue influence.': *Barclay's Bank plc v O'Brien* (hereafter, '*O'Brien* (HL)') [1994] 1 AC 180 at 189, *per* Lord Browne-Wilkinson.

[56] *Bainbrigge v Browne* (1881) 18 ChD 188, where an impoverished father prevailed upon his inexperienced children to charge their reversionary interests under their parents' marriage settlement with payment of his mortgage debts; *Powell v Powell* [1900] 1 Ch 243, where strong moral pressure was applied by a stepmother to a 21-year-old girl who was regarded as not capable of dealing irrevocably with her parent or guardian in the matter of a substantial settlement. See also *Etridge (No 2)*, above n 40, at [84]–[85], *per* Lord Nicholls.

[57] Presumed undue influence has been asserted in a wide range of familial relationships: *Vale v Armstrong and another* [2004] EWHC (Ch) 1160 (nephew over aunt); *Cheese v Thomas* [1994] 1 All ER 35 (great-nephew over great-uncle); *Williams v Williams* [2003] EWHC (Ch) 742 (brothers); *Watson v Huber* (unreported, Chancery Div, 9 March 2005) (half-sisters); *Pesticcio v Niersmans* [2003] 2 *Planning & Compensation Reports* D22 (sister over brother); *Randall v Randall* [2004] EWHC 2258 (nephew over aunt); *Jennings v Cairns* [2003] EWCA Civ 1935 (niece over aunt).

[58] [1929] AC 127.

[59] *State Bank of India v Soni* (CA, 17 February 1997), *per* Hobhouse LJ.

[60] *Etridge (No 2)*, above n 40, at [14] *per* Lord Nicholls.

[61] *CIBC Mortgages plc v Pitt* [1994] 1 AC 200.

> in the nature of things, questions of undue influence will not usually arise, and the exercise of undue influence is unlikely to occur, where the transaction is innocuous. The issue is likely to arise only when, in some respect, the transaction was disadvantageous either from the outset or as matters turned out.[62]

This formulation helpfully allows for the unanticipated risk that materialises after the transaction. In determining whether a transaction calls for explanation, the court may take account of a range of contextual factors, including

> the nature of the alleged undue influence, the personality of the parties, their relationship, the extent to which the transaction cannot readily be accounted for by the ordinary motives of ordinary persons in that relationship, and all the circumstances of the case.[63]

At the same time, as the discussion in section (2)(c) below will illustrate, the application of this part of the test is heavily dependent on the perceived norms attributed to the relationship between the claimant and the beneficiary of the transaction or—in cases where the claimant is the beneficiary as in a two-party housing equity transaction—the presumed normalcy (including likely motivations) of the transaction for such a claimant.

Although there is no 'special protection' for older owners (either generally or in their relationships with younger adult relatives),[64] there have been many cases in which older owners have successfully avoided disadvantageous contracts on the basis of undue influence,[65] and the age of the claimant (and other individual characteristics) has often been noted by the courts as part of the evidence base for considering whether the claimant was vulnerable (within a relationship of trust and confidence) on the facts.[66] While this fact-led approach recognises the heterogeneity of older owners, it has left to academic commentators the tasks of piecing together the bases on which vulnerabilities are recognised by the courts, and assessing whether age plays a significant role in this process.

(b) The relationship of trust and confidence

The age of the claimant has long been recognised as a relevant factor when a claim of presumed undue influence is made,[67] although both its weight and the direction in which

[62] *Etridge (No 2)*, above n 40, at [12].

[63] *Ibid*, at [13].

[64] Reflecting the legal principle that all adults are assumed to have contractual capacity unless their ability to make a valid transaction is impaired; see Burns, above n 44, at 264. Since this book is concerned with *inter vivos* housing equity transactions, this chapter excludes consideration of testamentary undue influence, although it is noted that there has been no specific protection afforded to older testators in this context either: see R Kerridge, 'Wills made in Suspicious Circumstances: The Problem of the "Vulnerable Testator"' (2000) 59 *Cambridge Law Journal* 310; P Ridge, 'Equitable Undue Influence and Wills' (2004) 120 *LQR* 617; F Burns, 'Elders and Testamentary Undue Influence in Australia' (2005) 28 *University of New South Wales Law Journal* 145.

[65] See, eg, *Cheese v Thomas* [1994] 1 All ER 35; *Hammond v Osborn* [2002] EWCA Civ 885; *Meredith v Lackschewitz-Martin* [2002] EWHC 1462 (Ch); *Mortgage Agency Services Number Two Ltd v Chater* [2003] EWCA Civ 490; *Williams v Williams* [2003] EWHC 742 (Ch); *Niersmans v Pesticcio* [2004] EWCA Civ 372; *Vale v Armstrong* [2004] EWHC 1160 (Ch); *Humphreys v Humphreys* [2004] EWHC 2201 (Ch); *Watson v Huber* [2005] All ER (D) 156 (Mar); and where an older adult has acted as surety for a younger adult: *Greene King Ltd v Stanley* [2001] EWCA Civ 1966; *Wright v Cherrytree Finance Ltd* [2001] 2 All ER (Comm) 877; *Portman Building Society v Dusangh* [1999] EWCA Civ 1331; discussed below.

[66] See discussions in Burns, above n 44; Burns, 'Protecting Elders: Regulating intergenerationally transmitted debt in Australia', above n 31; Burns, 'Legally regulating intergenerationally transmitted debt', above n 31.

[67] Age was considered as part of all the circumstances in the case in *Cooke v Lamotte* (1851) Beav 234; *Elgie v Campbell* (1865) 12 Gr 132; *Symons v Williams* [1875] VLR 199; see Burns, above n 44, at 265.

it weighs in the balance is heavily dependent on all the other circumstances of the case. For example, while in *Avon Finance v Bridger*, the court's assessment that the claimants were vulnerable was explained on the basis that they were 'old-age pensioners, much less well educated than [the defendant] was',[68] in *Portman Building Society v Dusangh*[69] the Court of Appeal held that while Mr Dusangh was elderly, illiterate and on a very low income, with a limited understanding of spoken English, he had failed to prove by affirmative evidence that he was accustomed to repose trust and confidence in his son. In some successful cases the older owner was highly dependent on the beneficiary, due to mental or physical frailty,[70] although it does not seem necessary to prove frailty, as the courts have recognised that 'a fit and mentally alert elder may be transactionally dependent on a person in some situations, but not in others'.[71] This idea of 'transactional dependency'—which may be specific to the particular transaction under scrutiny—also allows for the possibility that older owners may establish the necessary relationship of trust and confidence in a bilateral transaction with a credit provider where the older owners are the beneficiaries and where they did not have a relationship with the provider prior to the transaction, if the facts show that the claimants ('not financially sophisticated people and not in a position, without the advice of persons more expert than themselves, properly to judge the risks involved'[72]) relied completely on the provider's advice in the transaction.

This highly contextualised approach reflects the reality that while age may be a factor in rendering parties susceptible to undue influence, it is rarely age alone which makes people vulnerable but other factors which may be associated (but not exclusively) with advancing age. These may be internal to the individual (for example, failing health), external and situational (for example, living alone), or a combination of the two (dependency on a particular person for care and support). A 2005 survey examining the susceptibility of older people to 'undue influence' identified a wide range of factors which predispose a person to financial exploitation, including advanced age (75+), being female, being unmarried, organic brain damage, cognitive impairment, physical, mental or emotional dysfunction (especially depression), recent loss of spouse or divorce, living alone, social isolation, being estranged from children, being financially independent with no designated financial carers, being in the middle or upper income brackets, taking multiple medications, and frailty, fear of change of living situation (ie, transfer from home to institution), an implied promise by the perpetrator to care for the elderly person if funds or material goods are transferred, an elderly person who is subject to deception (misrepresentation/concealment of information for selfish gain), an elderly person who is subject to intimidation (perpetrator induces dependency with fear of rejection if demands are not met, or creates fear by threat of physical or emotional harm or abandonment).[73]

[68] [1985] 2 All ER 281 at 287, *per* Brandon LJ.

[69] Above n 65.

[70] *Meredith v Lackschewitz-Martin*, above n 65.

[71] Burns, above n 44, at 268; discussing *Goldsworthy v Brickell* [1987] 1 Ch 378.

[72] *Investors Compensation Scheme v West Bromwich Building Society* [1999] Lloyd's Rep Professional Negligence 496 at 513; for a more detailed discussion of this case see ch 9, section (5)(a).

[73] RCW Hall, RCW Hall and MJ Chapman, 'Exploitation of the elderly: undue influence as a form of elder abuse' (2005) 13 *Clinical Geriatrics* 28. These factors are drawn from several studies: CJ Heisler and JE Tewksbury, 'Fiduciary abuse of the elderly: A prosecutor's perspective' (1991) 3 *Journal of Elder Abuse and Neglect* 23; B Shiferaw, MB Mittelmark, JL Wofford *et al*, 'The investigation and outcome of reported cases of elder abuse: The Forsyth County Aging Study' (1994) 34 *Gerontologist* 123; Subcommittee on Health and Long-Term

While these factors might be viewed as rendering an older person vulnerable in *any* relationship, particular categories of close relationship between older people and younger family members have also been highlighted in studies of financial abuse. While undue influence is both wider (in that it does not necessarily involve exploitation in the sense of deliberate wrongdoing on the part of the defendant) and narrower (in that it is focused on the subtler sphere of influence rather than criminal abuse) than financial abuse, the field of potential defendants in both cases can include family, close friends, care workers, neighbours and acquaintances, as well as 'strangers' (for example, a financial services provider) whom the older person meets for the first time when the transaction takes place. Over 50 per cent of financial abuse is perpetrated by a son or daughter, and nearly 70 per cent by a family member,[74] and this is broadly reflected in the high volume of reported undue influence cases where the defendant is a family member.[75]

It is the very normalcy of both the relationship and the transaction, against a liberal backdrop in which undue influence is viewed as 'exceptional' or 'pathological', which raises the bar in judicial applications of the undue influence tests. For example, in identifying a 'relationship of trust and confidence' between parent and child, Burns argued that English courts are looking for something that is not 'normal' in the relationship,[76] so reflecting the view that the equitable doctrines are not intended as a routine mechanism to ensure the safety of transactions but as a safety-net for 'exceptional' or 'pathological' cases where something goes wrong. Yet Burns noted that a case in which the necessary relationship was identified based on the fact that 'the daughter had assumed responsibility for the mother and the mother lived in the daughter's home'[77] does not seem particularly unusual or 'abnormal', especially in light of changing family arrangements in response to increasing longevity.[78] In contrast, in *Portman Building Society v Dusangh*, the Court appeared to require much more affirmative evidence to establish a relationship of trust and confidence between the parties.[79] The building society had granted a 25-year repayment mortgage to the defendant, then aged 72 and retired, secured against the defendant's home, and to fund his son's business venture. Although there was evidence that the defendant was a vulnerable individual,[80] the claim of undue influence was rejected on the basis that the defendant had failed to provide affirmative evidence of trust and confidence in his relationship with his son.

The difficulties in drawing inferences in relation to a close relationship such as that between a parent and child are paralleled, to some extent, in the 'surety wives' cases. Brandon LJ highlighted the analogy in *Avon Finance v Bridger*[81]:

Care, Select Committee on Aging, US House of Representatives, *Elder Abuse: Questions and Answers* (Washington, DC, Subcommittee on Health and Long-Term Care, Select Committee on Aging, 1990); County Welfare Director's Association of California, *Protecting the Silent Population: Remedying Elderly and Dependent –Adult Abuse* (Sacramento, CA, CWDA, 1988); Podkieks, above n 29.

[74] Crosby *et al*, above n 29, at 9.

[75] These statistics do not necessarily suggest that family members are less trustworthy than non-family, since the volume of cases may be skewed by the increased likelihood that a relationship of trust and confidence will exist between an older person and a family member, and that a financial transaction will occur between the parties.

[76] Burns, above n 44, at 265.

[77] *Ibid*, referring to *Davies v Dobson* (ChD, 7 July 2000).

[78] See ch 4, section (4), for discussion of the role of adult offspring in providing care and support.

[79] *Portman Building Society v Dusangh*, above n 65.

[80] He had a poor understanding of spoken English and was illiterate.

[81] Above n 68.

> [W]hile the relationship between husband and wife may be one in which it is more obvious that the husband will have influence over the wife, the relationship between a son in the prime of life and parents in the evening of life is equally a relationship in which it should be appreciated that the possibility of influence exists.[82]

In *Avon Finance v Bridger*, the court held that the age of the claimant, combined with the close relationship of parent and child, 'heightened the possibility of undue influence'.[83] Yet while the courts have admitted a 'special tenderness' towards surety wives based on the close relationship with a partner,[84] advancing age and the parent/child relationship together provide only a 'preliminary basis' for the relationship of trust and confidence, so that 'additional evidence about the relationship will be required'.[85] In adducing that additional evidence, the courts may look to the older person's state of mental and/or physical health, his or her (lack of) business or commercial experience or expertise, and other sources of vulnerability and dependence, such as the desire to avoid institutionalised care.

Burns argued that, on the whole, the court's assessment of all the facts of the case has tended to focus on 'the extent of the independence of the elder rather than simply the age of the elder'.[86] This approach emphasises the personality of the older owner, for example, whether he or she was 'independent-minded',[87] rather than the context in which he or she entered into this particular transaction. Burns has cautioned that 'there is a danger that the elder's reputation for independence will mask either the true context in which the elder entered into the transaction or the elder's actual vulnerability'.[88] This approach also reveals an implicit normative suggestion that appears to equate dependency with vulnerability, defining these as the absence of autonomy and the inability to make decisions.[89] A requirement that older persons prove themselves to be dependent (or lacking autonomy) to qualify as 'vulnerable' colours the tenor of undue influence arguments, requiring older claimants to identify themselves within a model of vulnerability that emphasises their personal limitations and internal characteristics (specifically, their lack of autonomy in a context which views autonomy as a prerequisite for subjectivity). It also shapes how we understand the vulnerabilities of older people, both in this context and in legal contexts more broadly.

The emphasis on older persons' (lack of) independence within their relationships echoes the more heavily litigated and analysed area of 'surety wives'. The 'surety wives' cases have dominated the judicial development of the undue influence doctrine in the English courts in recent decades, certainly so far as 'three-party' cases involving commercial parties are concerned. Considerable scholarly attention has also been focused on the issues that arise in cases involving 'surety wives', which raise analogous issues in respect of many of the themes discussed in this chapter (although the specific nature of the

[82] *Ibid*, at 288.
[83] Burns, above n 44, at 266.
[84] See, eg, *Grigby v Cox* (1750) 1 Ves Sen 517, 27 ER 1178; *O'Brien* (HL), above n 55, at 190, *per* Lord Browne-Wilkinson.
[85] Burns, above n 44, at 267.
[86] *Ibid*.
[87] See *The Estate of Brocklehurst* [1978] 1 Ch 14; *Forsdike v Forsdike* (CA (Civ), 21 February 1997).
[88] Burns, above n 44, at 267.
[89] This 'legal' understanding of a spectrum of dependency/autonomy is inconsistent with psychological accounts, which also underpin relational feminist analyses of autonomy, and which distinguish between the distinct spectrums of dependency/independence, and autonomy/heretonomy: see ch 5, section (3).

relationship between the parties, and significantly, the bases for finding older owners to be vulnerable are distinct). Common questions across both types of case include the nature and source of any vulnerability attributed to the claimant, and the issues this raises for the characterisation of categories of claimant as dependent, lacking autonomy or even lacking capacity; the extent to which transactions for the benefit of partners or offspring are (always) explicable on grounds of natural love and affection; the responsibilities of third party creditors through their duty of inquiry; and the underlying policy questions concerning use of the occupied home as an investment asset (whether to secure the (business) liabilities of another, or to release equity for the owner's benefit).[90] The remainder of this section focuses on the value of analyses examining the purported 'vulnerability' of surety wives in informing the parallel inquiry for older owners.

While there is no 'Class 2A' presumption of trust and confidence in respect of 'surety wives',[91] the courts have been explicit in articulating a judicial policy which shows 'tenderness' towards wives in relation to undue influence,[92] suggesting that the relationship between spouses has 'never been divested completely of what may be called equitable presumptions of an invalidating tendency'.[93] The Court of Appeal in *Barclay's Bank plc v O'Brien* suggested that married women who acted as sureties for their husband's debts should be treated as a specially protected class,[94] although this approach was beset by difficulties and the argument that married women are an especially vulnerable category for the purposes of undue influence[95] was rejected on appeal to the House of Lords. The House of Lords held that the proposition that spouses could be treated as a special category of litigants, particularly vulnerable to undue influence exerted by their husbands, was not supportable,[96] and that individual sureties would have to establish the necessary

[90] Lord Browne-Wilkinson highlighted the 'important public interest' competing with the desire to protect vulnerable wives, 'viz, the need to ensure that the wealth currently tied up in the matrimonial home does not become economically sterile', since it was deemed 'essential that a law designed to protect the vulnerable does not render the matrimonial home unacceptable as security to financial institutions': *O'Brien* (HL), above n 55, at 188. Against this, commentators have questioned whether it is 'an essential aspect of freedom that persons should have unrestricted power to borrow money on the security of their assets, or are some restraints acceptable or desirable, and if so what restraints, and on whom, and in respect of what assets?': see Waddams (2010), above n 36, at 36. See also A Barlow, 'Rights in the Family Home—time for a conceptual revolution' in A Hudson (ed), *New Perspectives on Property Law, Human Rights and the Home* (London, Cavendish, 2004); R Auchmuty, 'Men Behaving Badly: An Analysis of English Undue Influence Cases' (2002) 11 *Social and Legal Studies* 257.

[91] See, eg, *Howes v Bishop* [1909] 2 KB 390 at 395, *per* Lord Alverstone CJ; *Kingsnorth Trust Ltd v Bell* [1986] 1 All ER 423 at 427, *per* Dillon LJ; *O'Brien* (HL), above n 55, at 190, *per* Lord Browne-Wilkinson.

[92] '[E]xamin[ing] every such transaction between husband and wife with an anxious watchfulness and caution, and dread of undue influence': *Story's Equity Jurisprudence* (1835) at 995, para 1395, referred to by Scott LJ in *Barclay's Bank plc v O'Brien* [1993] QB 109 (hereafter '*O'Brien* (CA)').

[93] *Yerkey v Jones* (1939) 63 CLR 649 at 675, *per* Dixon LJ. In *O'Brien*, Lord Browne-Wilkinson noted that 'In *Grigsby v Cox* Lord Hardwicke, whilst rejecting any presumption of undue influence, said that a court "will have more jealousy" over dispositions by a wife to a husband.' (*O'Brien* (HL), above n 55, at 190).

[94] *O'Brien* (CA), above n 92.

[95] *Ibid.* 'And, in the culturally and ethnically mixed community in which we live, the degree of emancipation of women is uneven. The likelihood of influence by a husband over his wife and of reliance by a wife on her husband to make the business decisions for the family was the justification in the first place for the tenderness of equity towards married women who gave their property as security for their husband's debts. In my opinion, that justification is still present' (*ibid*, at 139, *per* Scott LJ). This approach was criticised by one commentator on the grounds that 'the conferment of special protection on married women, differentiating them from all other sureties, is unacceptably patronising and wholly inconsistent with modern notions of the status of women.': G Battersby, 'Equitable fraud committed by third parties' (1995) 15 *Legal Studies* 35, 36.

[96] 'Should wives (and perhaps others) be accorded special rights in relation to surety transactions by the recognition of a special equity applicable only to such persons engaged in such transactions? Or should they enjoy only the same protection as they would in relation to their other dealings? In my judgment, the special

relationship of trust and confidence to raise a presumption of undue influence.[97] Yet, at the same time, their Lordships acknowledged 'the underlying risk of one cohabitee exploiting the emotional involvement and trust of the other',[98] suggesting that 'surety wives' cases *are* considered more likely to be tainted by undue influence than 'the ordinary run of cases where no sexual or emotional ties affect the free exercise of the individual's will'.[99]

There are two interlocking bases of vulnerability in these cases: one is the status of the individual (as an older person, or a (married) woman); the other is that person's relationship with the beneficiary. The surety wives cases tended, however, to conflate these two bases: while the courts were ostensibly concerned with the relationship between the parties, the idea of a special protection was criticised on the basis that it treated the individual, as a (married) woman, as vulnerable in the sense that she was 'weak', unable to consent or lacking in autonomy. The issues raised in cases involving older owners in housing equity transactions resonate with those which have emerged in the debates concerning appropriate protections for 'surety wives',[100] including the argument that it is inappropriate to base a judicial policy on the presumed 'weakness', or 'weak-mindedness', of women/older people.[101] The House of Lords in *O'Brien* recognised that the proposition that a surety wife be presumed to be vulnerable to pressure from her husband presented a 'Catch 22' between protection and paternalism: while the court was reluctant to adopt an overly paternalist approach towards wives, it was also concerned to ensure that those female spouses who did look to their husbands for guidance in business matters could 'reasonably look to the law for some protection when their husbands have abused trust and confidence reposed in them'.[102]

The challenges to applying a concept of vulnerability in this context include reconciling appropriate protection for vulnerable sureties with the undesirable consequences of

equity theory should be rejected. First, I can find no basis in principle for affording special protection to a limited class in relation to one type of transaction only. Second, to require the creditor to prove knowledge and understanding by the wife in all cases is to reintroduce by the back door either a presumption of undue influence of Class 2(A) (which has been decisively rejected) or the Romilly heresy (which has long been treated as bad law).': *O'Brien* (HL), above n 55, at 195, *per* Lord Browne-Wilkinson.

[97] 'Although there is no Class 2(A) presumption of undue influence as between husband and wife, it should be emphasised that in any particular case a wife may well be able to demonstrate that *de facto* she did leave decisions on financial affairs to her husband thereby bringing herself within Class 2(B), ie that the relationship between husband and wife in the particular case was such that the wife reposed confidence and trust in her husband in relation to their financial affairs and therefore undue influence is to be presumed. Thus, in those cases which still occur where the wife relies in all financial matters on her husband and simply does what he suggests, a presumption of undue influence within Class 2(B) can be established solely from the proof of such trust and confidence without proof of actual undue influence.': *ibid*, at 190, *per* Lord Browne-Wilkinson.

[98] *Ibid*, at 198, *per* Lord Browne-Wilkinson. His Lordship added that 'Now that unmarried cohabitation, whether heterosexual or homosexual, is widespread in our society, the law should recognise this' (*ibid*).

[99] *Ibid*, at 191.

[100] These were discussed in detail in the context of vulnerability and 'difference' in ch 6.

[101] 'In parallel with these financial developments, society's recognition of the equality of the sexes has led to a rejection of the concept that the wife is subservient to the husband on the management of the family's finances. A number of the authorities reflect an unwillingness in the court to perpetuate law based on this outmoded concept', *O'Brien* (HL), above n 55 at 191.

[102] *Ibid*, at 188, *per* Lord Browne-Wilkinson; '[A]lthough the concept of the ignorant wife leaving all financial decisions to the husband is outdated, the practice does not yet coincide with the ideal. In a substantial proportion of marriages it is still the husband who has the business experience and the wife is willing to follow his advice without bringing a truly independent mind and will to bear on financial decisions. The number of recent cases in this field shows that in practice many wives are still subjected to, and yield to, undue influence by their husbands.' (*ibid*).

treating women as lacking autonomy; although the root of the problem in fact lies with the conflation of 'autonomy' and 'independence', and with the assumption that autonomy is an inherent, internal condition rather than a contextual or situational factor.[103] Feminist critics of the 'special protection' have highlighted the need to define women as 'victims', as well as the danger that legal protections against undue influence could undermine the capacity of women to offer valid consent to surety transactions and so to participate fully in the 'public sphere' activity of exchange transactions.[104] On the one hand, the fact that women are often negatively affected by structural socio-cultural inequalities in relation to their rights in the home raises an argument for providing an additional, counterbalancing protection when they act as sureties for their partners[105]; yet at the same time, the suggestion that women should be treated with 'special tenderness' in law has undesirable connotations of female dependency, lack of capacity and lack of autonomy. In order to succeed in establishing that a transaction was procured by undue influence, Fehlburg suggested that a claimant was required to 'fit herself within a stereotype of the down-trodden and uninformed housewife'.[106]

This dilemma also echoes some of the issues that arise in relation to presumptions concerning the capacity to contract of other potentially vulnerable groups. In the context of surety wives, the stark choice between capacity/autonomy and incapacity/no autonomy prompted some feminist critics to argue that if the price of legal protection was to treat women as being less capable of giving a valid consent to contracts for credit then that price was too high[107]: 'In the end, we would rather be constructed as a person who can move in and out of private and public roles than as one who inevitably needs the particular tenderness of equity. We do not want always to be victims.'[108] The idea that it would always be 'manifestly disadvantageous' for a woman to put her home at risk in a surety transaction because of her particular role as homemaker was similarly problematic,[109] as it appeared to require that the female surety's only route to legal protection was to construct herself within a model of vulnerability which eroded her autonomy: since it is the surety's lack of independence that crystallises the claim, a successful claimant must not have brought an independent mind to bear on the transaction.

The discussion of lack of capacity and loss of autonomy for older owners in chapter six, while acknowledging that incapacity is an issue in a small proportion of cases, identified a range of vulnerabilities which may be extant in housing equity transactions but which do not rely on the claimant (or his or her representative) proving the older person to be 'weak-minded'. In the case of surety wives, this raises the question of whether once the status of the individual as a (married) woman is stripped away there are any remaining

[103] See discussion in ch 5, section (3).

[104] See, eg, R Auchmuty, 'Men Behaving Badly: An Analysis of English Undue Influence Cases' (2002) 11 *Social and Legal Studies* 257; B Fehlburg, 'The Husband, the Bank, the Wife and her Signature—the Sequel' (1996) 59 *MLR* 675; B Fehlburg, *Sexually Transmitted Debt* (Oxford, Clarendon Press, 1997); K Green and H Lim, 'Weaving Along the Borders: Public and Private, Women and Banks', in S Scott-Hunt and H Lim (eds), *Feminist Perspectives on Equity and Trusts* (London, Cavendish, 2001); D Morris, 'Don't Blame the Bank, Sue Your Solicitor' (1999) 7 *Feminist Legal Studies* 193.

[105] Fehlburg (1996), above n 104, at 694.

[106] *Ibid*, at 679.

[107] Green and Lim argued that 'if the only alternative is for all married women automatically to be "protected" by being treated as vulnerable to oppression—and safely confined to their silent towers—we might accept that the woman should not win against the bank': Green and Lim, above n 104, at 98.

[108] *Ibid.*

[109] Auchmuty, above n 104, at 267–68.

grounds to justify special protection based solely on the relationship. In the realm of presumed or 'relational' undue influence, courts and commentators have often underlined the need for any legal response to be rooted in the *relationship* between the parties to an alleged undue influence.[110] If this approach is adopted, the focus of scrutiny is not on the alleged weakness of the unduly influenced individual (whether because of age, or because she is a married woman) but on the characteristics of the relationship between the parties which, to attract the protection of the doctrine, must expose them to a sufficient degree of vulnerability to justify legal intervention.

Yet it is also questionable to what extent it may be considered advisable, or even possible, to disentangle the individual's transactional experience from the relationships that shape that experience. Indeed, as the discussion in section (2)(e) below will indicate, the courts have moved towards a more transactional approach to undue influence by fixing third parties with a duty of inquiry to discharge specific responsibilities in all cases of non-commercial sureties (albeit, in light of the nature of the responsibility, with limited impact for vulnerable parties).[111] This transactional approach, which treats all creditors as put on notice where the relationship between the surety and the debtor is 'non-commercial', emphasises the risks associated with the transaction rather than the inherent weakness or vulnerability of the influenced party, or the nature of the relationship between influencer and influenced. A transactional approach also potentially offers an opportunity to reflect the reality of vulnerabilities that are contextual or situational, rather than inherent or relational.[112]

The ways in which vulnerability is understood and articulated in the context of undue influence depend to a large extent on the jurisprudential basis of the doctrine, a question which has itself attracted much scholarly attention in recent decades, with competing schools of thought positioned on a spectrum that runs from a 'claimant-sided' emphasis on the 'impaired consent' of the unduly influenced party to a 'defendant-sided' focus on exploitation of the vulnerable claimant. This spectrum itself is also challenged by the emergence of relational analyses which advocate a more contextual approach to the transaction. These perspectives, and their implications for older owners in housing equity transactions, are considered in the next section.

(c) The jurisprudential basis of undue influence

The meaning of 'undue influence' is often described as 'elusive'.[113] While judgments from *Allcard v Skinner*[114] to *Royal Bank of Scotland v Etridge (No 2)*[115] have resisted or refused opportunities to define its meaning with precision,[116] Lindley LJ may have marked the outer limit of the doctrine with his famous observation that 'Courts of Equity have never

[110] See below, section (2)(c).

[111] *Etridge (No 2)*, above n 40.

[112] See ch 6 for analysis of these distinct types of vulnerability in the context of older owners' housing equity transactions.

[113] Birks and Chin, above n 8, at 57.

[114] (1887) 36 ChD 145 at 183, *per* Lindley LJ.

[115] [2001] 4 All ER 449.

[116] Birks and Chin noted that 'In the intervening century, the doctrine has enjoyed remarkable success in resisting attempts to pin it down': Birks and Chin, above n 8, at 57; and later that 'The ideas involved in this area of law are elusive. It is always difficult to find the right language, and always dangerous to make too much of any single word or phrase … Judges have fought shy of definition, even of exposition…': *ibid*, at 86.

set aside gifts on the ground of the folly, imprudence, or want of foresight on the part of donors.'[117] The absence of a clear judicial statement has provided fertile ground for doctrinal debate, notable contributions to which include Birks and Chin's claimant-sided, impaired consent theory,[118] Bigwood's defendant-sided, exploitation/transactional neglect theory[119] and Chen-Wishart's hybrid relational theory.[120] This section does not attempt to resolve the debate on doctrinal terms, but rather to consider the extent to which the competing perspectives offer opportunities to shape an appropriate safety-net for older owners who are vulnerable in housing equity transactions, around the discursive tropes of vulnerability and responsibility.

Central protagonists in this debate have variously suggested that the underlying conceptual justification for undue influence would not usually make a difference to the outcomes of cases in practice[121]; but it remains significant nonetheless to the extent that it influences how arguments are framed by litigants, and specifically the arguments that claimants presenting themselves as 'vulnerable' are willing to make about themselves. As such, the jurisprudential basis of the doctrine has a bearing on the instrumental value of discourses of undue influence to the problem of vulnerability in housing equity transactions. While alternative accounts of undue influence generally recognise that its purpose is to protect the vulnerable,[122] with emphases shifting across the presence (or not) of consent, capacity, exploitation, wrongdoing, fault and (latterly) responsibility, little explicit reference has been made to the source or nature of the claimant's vulnerability, or to how competing accounts of the doctrine can provide the most effective protection for vulnerable persons.[123] This discussion differs fundamentally from these analyses both in methodology and objective inasmuch as it starts not from the law as developed through the cases, but from the vulnerable person in need of legal protection. From this perspective, the value of the competing discourses lies in their pragmatic potential to shape a doctrine which appropriately reflects the underlying vulnerabilities of the people who seek to rely on it.[124] To do so, it adopts the conceptual lenses of vulnerability and responsibility

[117] *Allcard v Skinner*, above n 114, at 182–83.

[118] Birks and Chin, above n 8.

[119] R Bigwood, 'Undue Influence: "Impaired Consent" or "Wicked Exploitation"?' (1996) 16 *OJLS* 503; Bigwood, above n 10.

[120] Chen-Wishart, above n 7; M Chen-Wishart, 'Undue Influence: Vindicating Relationships of Influence' (2006) 59 *Current Legal Problems* 231.

[121] See, eg, Birks and Chin, above n 8, at 62–63. Bigwood argued that 'a paradigm shift from exploitation to legal neglect ought to make *no difference* to the way in which the doctrinal criteria are formulated, and the cases administered and decided, in this area of the law' (above n 10, at 68); 'Shifting to a negligence-based liability approach will only create a better fit between what the courts *say* they are doing in the decided cases—regulating against exploitation—and what they are *actually* doing in that name—regulating against transactional neglect.' (*ibid*, at 89–90).

[122] See, eg, Bigwood, who argued that 'the goal here is to protect the contracting "vulnerable" when their (serious) vulnerabilities are sufficiently known to their bargaining opponents': Bigwood, above n 10, at 94.

[123] Although Bigwood discussed the moral 'duty to protect the vulnerable' from harm to her welfare or autonomy interests, in the context of the liberal conception of contract and its scope for recognising 'agency-responsibility' on the part of the defendant: *ibid*, at 85–88. This theme is discussed further below.

[124] This not to propose bending the doctrine out of shape in the interests of one specific group (older owners) to the potential detriment of other potentially vulnerable claimants; however, since (as noted above) the undue influence scholarship has frequently emphasised the mutual compatibility of the 'competing' analyses, with differences being in emphasis only, this instrumental approach presents no more of a risk to the stability of the doctrine than the competing conceptual justifications.

to bring the doctrine, specifically as it avails potentially vulnerable older owners in housing equity transactions, into theoretical focus.[125]

(i) The 'claimant-sided' perspective

The distinction between 'claimant-sided' and 'defendant-sided' justifications for undue influence was marked out by Professors Birks and Chin in their seminal essay 'On the Nature of Undue Influence'.[126] In this paper, they described a doctrine as 'claimant-sided' if it focused on the quality of consent of the weaker party, for example by invalidating a transaction because the claimant was deemed to have 'impaired consent'. In contrast, a 'defendant-sided' perspective places the conceptual emphasis on the wrongful abuse or exploitation of the weaker party by the stronger party (caricatured by Birks and Chin as 'wicked exploitation' on the part of the defendant). Birks and Chin argued that the 'true' nature of undue influence is impaired consent (rather than fault on the part of the defendant[127] or a substantively unfair outcome),[128] with influence deemed to be 'undue' where it precludes the exercise of free and deliberate judgement.

While a 'claimant-sided' perspective focuses on the claimant's vulnerability, Birks and Chin's impaired consent theory does not readily map onto the vulnerabilities of older owners as they have been developed in this book. Rather, impaired consent was identified by Birks and Chin as a species of 'impaired autonomy', by direct comparison with other cases of 'substandard capacity' due to 'personal inequality' such as the impaired autonomy of children, 'persons of impaired intellect', the mentally ill, intoxicated persons and what Birks and Chin refer to as 'persons under socio-economic disadvantage' or 'socio-economic disability'.[129] The claimant is cast as lacking judgemental capacity,[130] an approach which (doctrinal issues aside) places the emphasis on the very feature of undue influence doctrine to which feminist scholars have been unable to subscribe in relation to 'surety wives'. While Birks and Chin recognised that, in practice, the undue influence cases tend to involve some unconscientious exploitation of this weakness, fault on the side of the defendant should not be regarded as a condition of relief; rather 'that relief is simply given on the ground of the impairment itself, not on the ground of its unconscientious exploitation'.[131]

The case law involving older people suggests that it has not always been necessary to plead 'impairment' in order to obtain relief for undue influence, although cases involving illegitimate pressure, such as *Williams v Bayley*[132] (in which a father yielded to pressure to give security over his colliery to repay losses incurred by his son through criminal acts,

[125] By starting from the person, not the law, the relevant points of comparison for this inquiry are those other legal contexts in which the older or otherwise potentially vulnerable party is protected against the risks inherent to housing equity transactions (rather than, as for contract and restitution scholars, other vitiating factors or the broader concept of unconscionability).

[126] Above n 8.

[127] Although they acknowledged that the case law, including seminal House of Lords opinions, has used the 'defendant-sided' language of abuse, fraud, wrongful, victimisation and exploitation.

[128] 'It is certainly impossible to draw a final inference of unconscionable conduct from the mere fact that a transfer has been obtained on terms which are highly favourable to one party and correspondingly disastrous to the other.': Birks and Chin, above n 8, at 61.

[129] *Ibid*, at 62–63; 89.

[130] *Ibid*, at 63.

[131] *Ibid.*

[132] (1866) LR 1 LH 200.

and, according to Birks and Chin's model, fear of the consequences for his son deprived the father of free agency) and *Re Craig*[133] (in which a bullying housekeeper extracted gifts from an old man), are classified by Birks and Chin as examples of actual rather than presumed undue influence. Birks and Chin argued that 'relational' or presumed undue influence rarely involves pressure, but that 'the relevant weakness of the plaintiff is that, within the relationship, by reason of excessive dependence on the other person, he or she lacks the capacity for self-management which the law attributes to the generality of adults'.[134]

Presumed undue influence, according to the claimant-sided perspective, must be based on impaired autonomy, sub-standard judgemental capacity and excessive dependence.[135] Indeed, many of the cases which Birks and Chin cited in support of this perspective involved older people whom they described as suffering a loss of autonomy, whether through diminished mental capacity combined with dependence on the defendant,[136] or simply as a result of advancing age and dependence.[137] By the same reasoning, the converse also applied: in *Re Brocklehurst*[138] the wealthy estate owner was held not to be under undue influence when he made a gift, because even in old age he was a strong-minded and independent person, and—by Birks and Chin's analysis –

> there was nothing to suggest a surrender or impairment of the donor's autonomy … Neither his age nor his relationship with the defendant impaired his capacity to make his own choices or to manage his own affairs … There was no cession of autonomy, no excessive dependence.[139]

Adopting the claimant-sided perspective locates the basis for presumed undue influence squarely within the claimant's inherent vulnerability. This focus on capacity/autonomy would naturally limit the scope of the doctrine to those cases involving that particular type of vulnerability; and exclude from its scope other forms of vulnerability (for example, situational vulnerability).

According to the claimant-sided perspective, while actual undue influence required the claimant to *prove* his or her lack of autonomy, relational undue influence was based on a *presumption* of lack of autonomy. This requires an emphasis on the claimant's 'dependence' on the defendant, as a result of the claimant's lack of autonomy within the relationship. Thus

> the reason for restitution in cases of relational inequality is that the morbidly dependent party is, or is presumed to be, unable to think freely for himself. His dependence on the judgment of the other means that he lacks the standard capacity for managing his own affairs and defending his own interests … [thus] impairing the integrity of the plaintiff's decision-making process.[140]

Birks and Chin do not claim that the 'impairment' is internal to the claimant, but they do require as a condition of relief that the claimant has 'to a sufficiently extreme degree, a

133 [1971] 1 Ch 95.

134 Birks and Chin, above n 8, at 67.

135 *Ibid*, at 67–69.

136 *Simpson v Simpson* [1992] 1 FLR 601.

137 Eg, *Goldsworthy v Brickell* [1987] 1 Ch 378, in which the elderly owner was in good health but dependent on the defendant, leaving him with an impaired ability to judge what was in his own best interests; for discussion, see Burns, above n 44, at 253.

138 [1978] 1 Ch 14.

139 Birks and Chin, above n 8, at 70–71.

140 *Ibid*, at 81.

sub-standard judgmental capacity, and the source of the impairment is the character of the relationship in which he finds himself'.[141] The emphasis remains on the relationship between the parties as it has affected the claimant's judgemental capacity to render him vulnerable to undue influence.

There are particular vulnerabilities associated with surety or guarantor transactions by older owners which leave even 'competent' or capable older people less able than the general population to protect their own legal and financial interests.[142] These include physical or mental decline falling short of incapacity, but which impairs the ability of the older person to protect his or her own interests, with examples drawn from the Australian case law including situations where the older person was suffering from depression,[143] mental illness[144] and physical conditions which cause poor concentration and memory loss.[145] Burns has argued that older people may also experience a particular form of situational vulnerability in surety transactions which, rather than being rooted in their own pressing financial needs, arises from feeling 'morally obliged to enter the guarantee or fear abandonment and alienation',[146] particularly where they are dependent on the caregiver or family member for care and support. In these cases, she argued that context (rather than *internal* factors) affects capacity, so that 'the social "context" giving rise to the elder entering into the guarantee may prevent a rational and clear evaluation of whether it is in the elder's best interests'.[147]

Burns claimed that, when dealing with older owners, a middle position has emerged between capacity/autonomy and incapacity/lack of autonomy, where older people are viewed as being particularly *susceptible* to undue influence due to an impaired ability to judge what is in their own best interests.[148] She argued that undue influence has developed from the nineteenth century, when the doctrine did not confer any 'special status' on the elderly, to increasingly recognise that the context in which older owners enter into transactions may require the grant of relief using the mechanism of undue influence.[149] Although Burns stopped short of claiming that there is yet a comprehensive or logically coherent approach to elders and undue influence, she argued that 'elders (or their representatives) have raised undue influence *inter vivos* in a wide variety of factual situations because in hindsight the transaction was not considered in the elders' best interests',[150] whether because of mental decline, impaired ability to judge their own best interests, or where even an apparently healthy and capable older person is subjected to the pressure of emotional manipulation (just as a younger person may be).[151]

[141] *Ibid*, at 89.

[142] Burns, 'Legally regulating intergenerationally transmitted debt', above n 31. This echoes the discussion of vulnerabilities in ch 6, particularly in relation to older people's susceptibility to financial abuse.

[143] *Mitchell v 700 Young Street Pty Ltd* [2001] VSC 116 (Cummins J, 23 April 2001).

[144] *Ashbourne v Melbourne Money Pty Ltd* [1992] ANZ ConvR 95.

[145] *Tessman v Costello* [1987] 1 Qd R 283.

[146] Burns, 'Legally regulating intergenerationally transmitted debt', above n 31.

[147] *Ibid*.

[148] Burns, above n 44, at 253–55.

[149] *Ibid*.

[150] *Ibid*, at 253.

[151] Eg, in *Goldsworthy v Brickell* [1987] 1 Ch 378, an 85-year-old man who was in good health (reported to be 'in full possession of his faculties') but who was functionally dependent on his farm manager for advice and help in running his farm, was able to avoid a disadvantageous tenancy by establishing a presumption of undue influence based on the confidential relationship between the two men. The Court of Appeal held that it was not necessary to prove dishonesty, conscious abuse of power or domination by the party exerting influence. It was

While Burns's model allows greater scope for older people to establish claimant-sided undue influence, the argument that older people have an impaired ability to judge what is in their own best interests differs only in degree from the claim that older people lack capacity/autonomy. The claimant-sided model relies on the proposition that undue influence is based on a relational inequality that leaves the vulnerable party 'morbidly dependent' on the defendant. The limitations of this model are underlined by the distinction drawn between 'dependent' subjects and 'vulnerable' subjects in chapter six. Dependent subjects are often portrayed in policy and legal discourses as failing to display the neoliberal virtues of commitment to work, family responsibility and competition, and so attracting social and moral opprobrium[152]; or, as discussed above, as inherently 'weak'. This characterisation of dependency is not only unattractive and demeaning, it is also in diametric opposition to the contemporary construction of older owners as active and responsible consumers; the claim that older owners have impaired ability to judge what is in their own self-interest is merely a gradation of dependency. This book has argued that a more appropriate perspective on housing equity transactions—both in theory and in practice—would focus on the vulnerability of older owners not because they lack capacity or autonomy, but in response to the contexts and situations in which older owners sometimes enter into housing equity transactions. On this ground, the vision of undue influence offered by the claimant-sided perspective is both unattractive and unhelpfully narrow in its response to the real transactional vulnerabilities of older owners.

(ii) The 'defendant-sided' perspective

Birks and Chin argued that while there may in fact be moral blame on the part of the defendant to a successful undue influence claim, the fault of the defendant is superfluous to a finding of undue influence[153]; while they acknowledged that the existence of the doctrine may act as a prophylactic against unconscionable conduct,[154] they argued that this was not a necessary condition of their 'claimant-sided' relief. At the same time, Birks and Chin acknowledged that their approach and the 'defendant-sided' view of undue influence differ primarily in emphasis and degree, since

> [d]ependence and influence are two sides of the same coin … a degree of reduced autonomy on the part of the one and a corresponding degree of control or ascendency on the other … Where there is too much influence on one side there is too little autonomy on the other, and it is that insufficient autonomy on which the relief is founded.[155]

Thus, while the outline sketch of the undue influence scenario remains the same, the defendant-sided perspective picture fills out in more detail the necessity of wrongdoing to

sufficient that the farm manager was 'in a position to influence' the older owner into entering into the transaction, and not necessary to show that a 'dominating influence' had been applied to secure the transaction. Once the presumption had been raised, the court held that a manifestly and unfairly disadvantageous transaction thence executed was voidable unless 'The party allegedly exerting influence had … proved that the tenancy had been granted after full, free and informed thought.'

[152] T Ross, 'The Rhetoric of Poverty: Their Immorality, Our Helplessness' (1991) 79 *Georgetown Law Review* 1499.

[153] Citing in support a range of cases in which the court found the transaction voidable for undue influence even though there was no suggestion of 'improper conduct' on the part of the defendant, including *Cheese v Thomas* [1994] 1 All ER 35; *Allcard v Skinner* (1887) 36 ChD 145.

[154] Birks and Chin, above n 8, at 80.

[155] *Ibid*, at 86–87.

establish undue influence, shaping the doctrine into a fault-based, or *responsibility*-based, model. Nevertheless, according to its principal proponents, this approach remains aligned with the classical model of contract, inasmuch as it maintains that the common law does not disappoint contractual expectations unless the party to be disappointed is guilty of some wrongdoing which makes its expectations less than fully legitimate.[156]

The 'defendant-sided' perspective acknowledges that any distinction that might be drawn with Birks and Chin's caricatures of 'impaired consent' and 'wicked exploitation' is 'superficial at best', as the concepts are inextricably linked.[157] The defendant-sided perspective has focused, however, on the degree of 'wrongdoing' required for undue influence. Some commentators have argued that active wrongdoing is not required but that 'passive acceptance of benefits when the claimant knows or should know that the other party is vulnerable' suffices.[158] Bigwood's early analyses identified the required element of 'fault' on the side of the defendant as objectionable advantage-taking or 'exploitation' of the claimant,[159] which went beyond the 'manipulative capacity' which is tolerated in contractual dealings. The objectionable aspect, he argued, resulted from the stronger party exploiting, actively or passively (by not correcting the power imbalance), its relative contracting power. This defendant-sided approach shifted the emphasis of the inquiry away from the claimant's capacity/autonomy/ability to give valid consent, to focus on the defendant's responsibility for the claimant's vulnerability. The justification for avoidance of the contract was based on the idea that, in light of the claimant's vulnerability, his or her individual responsibility or self-responsibility as a contracting party was shifted onto the defendant; and that the defendant who did not act to redress that imbalance failed to discharge his or her own responsibility towards the claimant as a contracting party.

For the defendant-sided model, the 'act' of exploitation begins with the claimant's vulnerability, but the 'exploitation' is crystallised by the defendant's failure to discharge the responsibility or 'duty to protect' that arises when transacting with a vulnerable party.[160] By emphasising the defendant's responsibility towards the claimant, the locus of liability was shifted from proof of the claimant's inherent weakness to the behaviour of the defendant, 'who wrongfully provides an ordinarily free and rational person with what appears to be reason for doing what the influencer desires'.[161] The defendant-sided analysis does not require that the claimant is proved or presumed to be incapable of consenting or lacking in autonomy. This is because, within this rationale,

[156] N Enonchong, *Duress, Undue Influence and Unconscionable Dealing* (London, Sweet & Maxwell, 2006); R Bigwood, 'Conscience and the Liberal Conception of Contract: Observing Basic Distinctions: Part 1' (2000) 16 *Journal of Contract Law* 1.

[157] Bigwood, above n 119, at 504.

[158] Capper, above n 3, at 167.

[159] Bigwood, above n 119, at 507.

[160] Bigwood argued that 'all acts of exploitation begin with a plaintiff's peculiar vulnerability. What is objectionable about exploitation is that a defendant chooses, freely and knowingly, to benefit from the relative position of power resulting from such vulnerability, and that the defendant's gain—in this context, the right to a contract—results from the exercise of that power. So, in the context of a law "designed to protect the vulnerable", the exploiter is guilty not merely of "neglecting" his or her protective responsibilities, but of *negating* them.' (*ibid*, at 509). The negation of the defendant's duty was underlined by the claim that 'Characteristically, an exploiter plays for advantage in the face of a strong moral-cum-legal duty actually to protect …' (*ibid*).

[161] *Ibid*, at 511.

> the will of the victim of undue influence is not 'overborne'. There may have been misplaced trust or reliance, but the victim still acts 'intentionally', perhaps even acceding to the transaction euphorically. Whether by threats, nondisclosure, argument, entreaty, intercession, importunity, or persuasion, what the ascendant party does in the undue influence context (*like* the coercer in the duress context) is wrongfully make the option put to the subservient party (ie, of entering into the transaction in question) appear to be a reasonable thing to do in the circumstances.[162]

Bigwood's model of undue influence did not require that the *claimant* should have weakness of mind but that the *defendant* has (actively or passively) used wrongful means to persuade, where otherwise the vulnerable party would not have entered into the transaction. The source of the claimant's 'weakness' was that he or she had 'let down their guard' to the stronger party, and it is on this basis that 'such vulnerable persons are excused from that level of "individual responsibility" ordinarily expected and required of the generality of contracting parties'.[163] Indeed, Bigwood's emphasis on the stronger party's 'special responsibility' to act in the interests of the vulnerable party led him to argue, in subsequent work, that the wrongdoing requirement can be met where the defendant is guilty of 'transactional neglect', ie where he failed to discharge his responsibility to protect the claimant, which responsibility flowed from the defendant's 'agency responsibility' towards potentially vulnerable parties.[164]

While Bigwood endorsed the liberal view that contracting parties are entitled to promote their own self-interests, and the only limitation on this is that they observe the rules of the bargaining process,[165] in the context of undue influence he suggested that

> the courts should err on the side of liberality when settling (and administering) the conditions preliminary to activation of a presumption of undue influence … [because] as an empirical fact, people tend not to complain about substantively fair transactions. This would indicate that a liberal presumption of undue influence is unlikely to be abused by those who simply regret fair bargains or moderate gifts.[166]

Using the idea of a relationship with fiduciary characteristics,[167] Bigwood argued that the dominant party is under a duty not to misuse his or her influence over the vulnerable party. The subtleties of persuasion were reflected in the characterisation of the 'influential fiduciary' as potentially 'a coercer, but typically … a wrongful *persuader* who works *with* his victim's will rather than against it'.[168]

In *Etridge (No 2)*, Lord Nicholls described the cases in which there is a 'classically fiduciary' relationship as

> when one person places trust in another to look after his affairs and interests, and the latter betrays this trust by preferring his own interests … it was the duty of one party to advise the other … or where one party owed the other an obligation of candour and protection.[169]

162 *Ibid.*
163 *Ibid*, at 510.
164 Bigwood, above.
165 See Bigwood, above n 156; and R Bigwood, 'Conscience and the Liberal Conception of Contract: Observing Basic Distinctions: Part 2' (2000) 16 *Journal of Contract Law* 191; discussed in detail in ch 4.
166 Bigwood, above n 52, at 449.
167 *Ibid*, at 437.
168 *Ibid*, at 440.
169 *Etridge (No 2)*, above n 40, at [9] *per* Lord Nicholls.

His Lordship went on, however, to state that the category of presumed undue influence 'is not confined to cases of abuse of trust and confidence. It also includes, for instance, cases where a vulnerable person has been exploited.'[170] This appeared to have potentially broadened the scope of presumed undue influence by allowing a more 'direct' route to protection based on the claimant's vulnerability, distinct from the relationship between the parties. Bigwood criticised the distinction between these routes, arguing that all cases of presumed undue influence are underpinned by the fiduciary principle, at least at the moment of the transaction; and that exploitation of vulnerable parties independent of a 'trusting and confidential relation' is more appropriately dealt with through other legal and equitable doctrines.[171] At the same time, Bigwood recognised that fiduciary responsibility is conceptually broad and is 'but one of a species of a more generalised duty by which the law seeks to protect vulnerable people in transactions with others'.[172] Indeed, while 'vulnerability' was referenced within the terminology which Lord Nicholls used to describe presumed undue influence,[173] it remains the case that transactions must be challenged by establishing the constituent elements of the doctrine. Once this is achieved, Bigwood argued, the ability of one party unduly to influence the other in itself constitutes the relationship as 'fiduciary',[174] such that the '"relationship of influence" … is both the context and the source of the alleged victim's vulnerability to the exploitation of which he or she subsequently complains'.[175]

The 'defendant-sided' nature of undue influence was endorsed by Lord Nicholls in *Etridge No 2*, when he stated that 'Undue influence has a connotation of impropriety. In the eye of the law, undue influence means that influence has been misused.'[176] However, and consistent with his view that undue influence should be liberally understood and applied, Bigwood has developed his theory of 'misuse' to include not only cases of 'pure advantage-taking', where the defendant took advantage of some 'ready-made' weakness in the claimant, but also cases of 'transactional neglect', where the nature of the defendant's 'fault' was failing to discharge a corrective liability to take reasonable precautions against the risk of foreseeable transactional harm to the claimant.[177] Bigwood argued that transactional neglect, rather than exploitation, provides the prevailing justification for interference with contracts in pure 'unfair advantage' cases,[178] and serves as a more appropriate paradigm in this context.[179]

The development of his transactional neglect theory moved Bigwood's defendant-sided approach further away from the claimant-sided concern with autonomy, and towards a doctrine based on transactional responsibility. Where 'exploitation' implied that the

[170] *Ibid*, at [11] *per* Lord Nicholls.

[171] Eg, coercion, actual undue influence, deceit, mistake and unconscionable dealing; Bigwood, above n 52, at 443.

[172] *Ibid.*

[173] Presumed undue influence was described as arising in relationships involving 'trust and confidence, reliance, dependence or vulnerability on the one hand and ascendancy, domination or control on the other': *Etridge (No 2)*, above n 40, at [11] *per* Lord Nicholls.

[174] Bigwood, above n 52, at 444.

[175] *Ibid*, at 440.

[176] *Etridge (No 2)*, above n 40, at [32] *per* Lord Nicholls.

[177] Bigwood, above n 10.

[178] *Ibid*, at 67.

[179] *Ibid*, at 68. The idea of a 'duty of transactional care', generated by relational circumstances that make exploitation a possibility, was described as having 'superior explanatory potential' compared to anti-exploitation theories.

defendant must have had knowledge of the claimant's vulnerability, with the object of the exploitation viewed in terms of the claimant's '*autonomy* interests—her capacity or opportunity to act as a free and rational self-directing agent—rather than in terms of her material welfare interests per se',[180] transactional neglect resonates more authentically with the empirical and theoretical analyses of older owners' vulnerabilities in chapter six, and with the proposition advanced in that discussion that the appropriate response to such vulnerabilities is framed in terms of responsibility—whether on the part of the State, on law as an institution of the State, or on the market through the standards of conduct that the State (though law) requires from market actors. The 'agency responsibility' which Bigwood attributes to transactional parties in respect of potentially vulnerable claimants is an obligation of 'reasonable transactional care'. While he takes care to indicate that this is not a 'full-blown legal duty' in the sense that it would generate a positive claim-right against the defendant, he argues that it would strike a better balance between the interests of the parties[181] by providing an 'immunity' against losing resources under the contract without fully responsible consent.[182]

Bigwood characterised the role and function of the equitable doctrine of undue influence as achieving a 'just' or 'fair' balance of responsibilities, between the parties' interests as free agents and as potential victims, and taking account of wider social interests in private contracting as a valued activity.[183] The transactional neglect theory remains fault-based (or defendant-sided), but 'fault' is identified where the defendant fails to meet the relevant standard of conduct. By moving away from the claimant-sided, autonomy-based model, Bigwood also adopts a broader understanding of 'harm' which encompasses the vulnerable person's 'welfare interests, autonomy interests, or both'.[184] This approach to undue influence sits more comfortably within the theoretical framework of vulnerability and responsibility developed in this book. The reconceptualisation of the underlying justification and rationale of undue influence around a 'duty' of precautionary care against transactional neglect also resonates with evolving ideas of market responsibility within the UK's regulatory approach to financial transactions. Lastly, while Bigwood is at pains to emphasise that his aim is positivist rather than normative—to improve the justification rather than to change the outcome to decisions—by re-framing the doctrine in this way he also liberates potential undue influence claimants from the objectionable requirement of demonstrating incapacity or lack of autonomy in order to avoid a transaction.

(iii) Transactional risk and relational norms

A third approach to presumed undue influence offers to shift the doctrine yet further towards the contextual or situational approach to vulnerability outlined in chapter six. This model, principally advocated in Chen-Wishart's analyses of the defendant's abuse of relational norms,[185] echoes to some extent Capper's argument that presumed undue

[180] *Ibid*, at 79.
[181] Where the bar is set for 'fault' in the defendant's conduct depends on 'the precise "game" that the parties are (or think they are) playing': *ibid*, at 76, 77.
[182] *Ibid*, at 86.
[183] *Ibid*, at 87–88.
[184] *Ibid*, at 86.
[185] Chen-Wishart, above n 7; Chen-Wishart, above n 120.

influence is neither claimant-sided nor entirely defendant-sided but requires both defective consent and unconscionable conduct.[186] Capper's analyses of the vitiating factors in contract advanced the view that conceptions of undue influence (and unconscionability) are dependent on context,[187] and this is also echoed in Wightman's relational analysis of unconscionability in terms of 'transactional risk'. Wightman argued that certain characteristics of particular kinds of transaction, in interaction with the conduct of the parties, create unusual risk for one party,[188] requiring a legal response that moves away from the individual conduct of either the claimant or the defendant, to focus on the nature of the transaction and the appropriate balance of responsibilities of contracting parties in transactions which generate specific and significant risk. Similarly, when Halfmeier and Rott argued that transactional risk is endemic in financial services contracts, they concluded that this requires a more substantive approach to fairness in determining the enforceability of such contracts.[189] Considerations of transactional risk are particularly cogent to older owners' housing equity transactions in light of the specific situational vulnerabilities and risks identified in this book, associated with transactions that draw upon the owned home as a financial asset to spend.

Wightman argued that the transactional risk approach has 'affinities with some regulatory techniques',[190] by imposing specific responsibilities on defendants based on the context of the transaction and without requiring proof of wrongdoing in any particular case. The scope of the commercial credit or equity provider's responsibility in both 'three-party cases' (where the alleged undue influence is between two non-commercial parties) and two-party cases (where the commercial party itself 'crosses the line') is discussed in section (e) below. The *Etridge (No 2)* approach—of requiring that the bank discharge a responsibility towards the surety in *all* cases where it is aware that the relationship between the surety and the borrower is non-commercial—demonstrates a transactional risk approach to undue influence which Capper has argued should displace the 'first stage' requirement of making out the elements of undue influence between the claimant and defendant.[191] This argument for bank responsibility, regardless of the conduct of the parties,[192] drew upon the Australian doctrine of unconscionability[193] which, while in this instance applied to surety wives, was described as 'potentially ripe for extension to other persons in emotionally vulnerable relationships'.[194]

[186] See D Capper, 'Undue Influence and Unconscionability: A Rationalisation' (1998) 114 *LQR* 479. Capper (above n 3, at 176) argued: 'What this means is that the defendant has obligations imposed upon him by the nature of the parties' relationship and also carries an evidential burden of proving that he was not in breach of those duties. If he is in breach he has not committed a wrongful act for which he may be sued but he is liable to suffer the loss of the transaction he cannot show to have been procured without undue influence.'

[187] *Ibid.*

[188] J Wightman, 'From individual conduct to transactional risk: some relational thoughts about unconscionability regulation' in Kenny *et al* (eds), above n 3.

[189] A Halfmeier and P Rott, 'Kickback payments under MiFiD: substantive or procedural standard of unconscionability' in Kenny *et al* (eds), above n 3.

[190] Wightman, above n 188, at 100.

[191] '[I]t would not expect too much of banks to make them accountable for what they do anyway and it would offer sureties some protection against the myriad of problems they face when asked to execute these guarantees': Capper, above n 3, at 180.

[192] See D Capper, 'Banks, Borrowers, Sureties and Undue Influence—A Half-baked Solution to a Thoroughly Cooked Problem' (2002) 10 *Restitution Law Review* 100.

[193] *Yerkey v Jones* (1939) 63 CLR 649; reaffirmed in *Garcia v National Australia Bank Ltd* (1998) 194 CLR 395.

[194] Capper, above n 3, at 180.

The argument for a relational approach to undue influence itself (as opposed to third-party liability) based on transactional risk was specifically developed by Chen-Wishart, who argued that 'the main source of confusion over the nature of undue influence is one of language: its key concepts do not mean what they appear to mean'.[195] While the requirements of undue influence variously purport to require transactions which are not explicable, in which claimants lack capacity/autonomy or in which defendants have behaved unconscientiously, Chen-Wishart argued that the underlying rationale for undue influence is that the transaction is regarded as objectively unacceptable because it breaches relational norms.[196] Chen Wishart rejected the 'either or' approach of claimant-sided versus defendant-sided rationales for undue influence on the basis that, despite 'the attraction of conceptual simplicity, clarity, and easy marketability ... it misses the target when simply superimposed on the subtle and complex dynamics of trusting relationships'.[197] Chen-Wishart sought to establish a theory of undue influence that steps outside the 'false dichotomy' of the dominant perspectives,[198] on the basis that 'any credible theory of undue influence must accommodate a multi-dimensional approach', in which the 'conduct and motivation of *both* participants *and* ... the outcome of the transaction, [are] all judged against the *norms* of the *relationship* between the parties'.[199]

In this way, Chen-Wishart located the 'pathology' of undue influence outside the specific faults or failings of either party but in the situational context of the transaction, judged by a set of normative standards which determine the parties' responsibilities towards one another. She argued that relationships of 'trust and confidence' are necessary to human flourishing and the pursuit of a 'good life': the existence of, and reliance on, such a relationship does not constitute a pathology on the part of the claimant or fault on the part of the defendant; but 'the law requires the defendant to have due regard for the *substantive and procedural norms implicit in the relationship of influence* he shares with the claimant when he transacts with her'.[200] When these norms are violated, a claimant may be relieved of responsibility for a transaction, notwithstanding his or her consent to it, due to the circumstances or context surrounding the consent[201]; and a defendant may be deemed responsible despite the absence of bad faith or 'wrongful' conduct,[202] on the basis that, objectively speaking, he or she has failed to meet the 'high standards of Equity' in acting to protect the claimant's interests.[203]

While Chen-Wishart framed her theory of undue influence according to relational norms, its reference to the balance of responsibilities between claimant and defendant is substantively similar to Bigwood's 'defendant-sided' theory based on 'transactional neglect'. The key difference is that Chen-Wishart was explicit in foregrounding the importance of the context of the parties' relationship in establishing implicit substantive and procedural norms, violation of which constitutes a failure to safeguard the claimant's

[195] Chen-Wishart, above n 7, at 202.

[196] 'In reality, the claimant's consent may not be defective, the transaction may be quite explicable and the defendant's fraud may be "constructive", his abuse "passive", and his liability to make restitution strict.' (*ibid*)

[197] *Ibid*, at 203.

[198] 'Since the defendant-sided version is concerned with the defendant's role in distorting the *claimant's consent*, it is reducible to the same rationale as the claimant-sided version.' (*ibid*).

[199] *Ibid.*

[200] *Ibid.*

[201] *Ibid*, at 206.

[202] *Ibid*, at 206–07.

[203] *Ibid*, at 216.

interests and so renders the contract voidable. Furthermore, while Bigwood's commitment to the liberal model of contractual relationships required him to reconcile the positive obligations of avoiding 'transactional neglect' and a 'liberalisation' of the doctrine of undue influence with his vision of the legal subject of contract as an autonomous, self-responsible individual,[204] Chen-Wishart's use of relational contract theory as an analytical framework provided a more convincing and consistent perspective on the 'normative expectations' that arise from certain contractual relationships.[205]

A key feature of Chen-Wishart's relational approach to undue influence is her rejection of the 'detached' model of autonomy represented by the 'stripped-down' liberal autonomous subject.[206] Rather, she adopted the relational meaning of autonomy as developed in psychology and feminist theory,[207] which recognises that to trust others in relationships 'is not pathological, it shows a healthy ability to connect with significant others'[208] and is necessary to lead a 'good life'. As such, the relational approach recognised that the claimant's welfare interest and his or her specific transactional autonomy interest are difficult to separate.[209] Where the claimant-sided approach to undue influence focused on consent (or, specifically, the claimant's inability to give a valid consent), Chen-Wishart argued that there are 'values at work' within the vitiating factors other than consent.[210] These values (or 'relational norms') may be invoked to justify relieving a claimant from responsibility for a transaction, despite the presence of consent, 'where the claimant engages with reason in consenting to the transaction, but should nevertheless be excused from responsibility in the circumstances'.[211] Chen-Wishart based her account of this shift from self-responsibility to legal intervention on Joseph Raz's version of 'positive autonomy', which (in contrast to 'negative autonomy' or 'non-interference') valued the freedom to make worthwhile choices, to enable people to live good, autonomous lives.[212] This perspective echoes the theories of progressive property and the freedom-promoting approach to property discussed in chapter four,[213] which in turn supported the argument that the legal regulation of older owners' housing equity transactions should be viewed through the lenses of vulnerability and positive responsibility rather than according to the liberal norms of (negative) autonomy and individualism.

Chen-Wishart's justification for law's interference in cases of undue influence was that it 'responds to harm to the autonomy-enhancing social form of relationships of influence'.[214] These trusting relationships, which are inherently valuable because they are necessary to the pursuit of a good life, trigger 'implicit relational norms about how people in such relationships treat each other',[215] and it is these norms which determine whether influence

[204] See discussion of Bigwood's liberal conception of contract in ch 4, section (3). Bigwood achieves this by adjusting the 'rules of the game' by which contracting parties must play if the contract is to be enforceable, to include a responsibility to avoid transactional neglect, rooted in the fiduciary characteristics of the relationship; see above, section (2)(c)(ii).

[205] Chen-Wishart, above n 7, at 220–21.

[206] See ch 4, sections (3), (4) and (5).

[207] See ch 5, section (3); and ch 6.

[208] Chen-Wishart, 'Vindicating Relationships of Influence', above n 120, at 244.

[209] *Ibid*, at 221.

[210] *Ibid*, at 246.

[211] *Ibid*.

[212] J Raz, *The Morality of Freedom* (Oxford, Oxford University Press, 1986).

[213] See ch 4, section (5).

[214] Chen-Wishart, 'Vindicating Relationships of Influence', above n 120, at 249.

[215] *Ibid*.

is 'undue'. The following section considers how the relational norms of undue influence have developed, specifically in relation to older people, for example in determining the circumstances in which a transaction will be viewed as 'calling for explanation', and the nature of the responsibility that shifts to the defendant/third party when undue influence is successfully established. To the extent that courts, when called upon to find undue influence, are willing to recognise the nature of the risks and harms 'at play' in housing equity transactions, it argues that the relational perspective offers the most theoretically satisfactory and pragmatically promising analysis of the role of equity in protecting potentially vulnerable older owners through the concept of responsibility.

(d) Does the transaction call for explanation?

The 'elements' of undue influence require that, having established the relationship of trust and confidence, the older owner must also show that the transaction 'calls for explanation' before it can be set aside for presumed undue influence. The explicability of the transaction depends on the circumstances, and will naturally vary according to the perceived norms of a spectrum of relationships, from older parents/adult offspring, to older owners' relationships with other younger relatives, friends and carers, and with creditors or housing equity product providers or advisers. While the forerunner to 'explicability'—the pre-*Etridge* 'manifest disadvantage' test[216]—raised some problematic questions, including whether a gift could ever be regarded as not manifestly disadvantageous,[217] the explicability test involves the more readily comprehensible inquiry of whether the transaction was normally to be expected within this type of relationship; 'not readily explicable by the relationship of the parties,'[218] or 'not to be reasonably accounted for on the ground of friendship, relationship, charity, or on the ordinary motives on which ordinary men act'.[219] So, for example, Lord Nicholls indicated that it would be 'absurd' for the law to presume that every gift from parent to child was procured by undue influence; if it did, 'The law would be rightly open to ridicule, for transactions such as these are unexceptionable.'[220]

The explicability test requires that the transaction have 'something amiss', 'something more', 'something which calls for an explanation'. Lord Nicholls reasoned that 'When that something more is present, the greater the disadvantage to the vulnerable person, the more cogent must be the explanation before the presumption will be regarded as rebutted.'[221] Yet by requiring that the transaction is explicable *only* by undue influence,[222] the second stage of the inquiry appears to shift the focus back to the relationship between the parties and the effect of that relationship, rather than other factors such as the broader contextual or situational vulnerabilities that might press the claimant towards the transaction. Burns argued that 'courts have not confused an elder's personal or subjective

[216] See, eg, *Bank for Credit and Commerce International v Aboody* [1990] 1 QB 923.

[217] Birks and Chin, above n 8, at 83.

[218] *Etridge (No 2)*, above n 40, at [21] *per* Lord Nicholls.

[219] *Ibid*, at [22], quoting Lindley LJ in *Allcard v Skinner* (1887) 36 Ch D 145 at 185. Bigwood suggested, however, that the question of whether a transaction calls for explanation is more difficult in respect of contracts, where commercial self-interest is assumed to motivate the parties: Bigwood, above n 52, at 447.

[220] *Etridge (No 2)*, above n 40, at [24] *per* Lord Nicholls.

[221] *Ibid*.

[222] *Ibid*, at [30] *per* Lord Nicholls.

motivation for entering into a transaction with the explicability test',[223] because the test is concerned with whether the transaction can reasonably be accounted for outwith the alleged relationship of influence. However, Chen-Wishart's 'relational norms' analysis posited that the application of the explicability test reveals some contextual sensitivity on the part of the courts. This may be viewed as less concerned with the subjective motivations of the owner, or with whether the transaction can be 'explained' as fitting within a spectrum of 'normal' transactions, as with an objective assessment of the effect (adverse impact) of the transaction on the particular individual. The relational norms applied to any given case vary according to the nature of the transaction, the context and the impact on the (vulnerable) older owner. For example, Chen-Wishart argued that 'Gifts which seriously jeopardise the claimant's future autonomy or are widely incompatible with the parties' relationship also "call for explanation"',[224] although the courts have been able to identify such explanations in certain circumstances.[225]

Chen-Wishart claimed that the most 'suspect' type of transaction is a substantial, outright gift where the owner obtains no countervailing benefit (a gift 'so improvident that it cannot be accounted for on grounds of love, friendship or gratitude'[226]). Yet the presumption of advancement in English law is based on the contrary idea, that when fathers (but not mothers) make gratuitous transfers to their adult children, such gifts can, by virtue of the relationship, be readily accounted for.[227] This may be contrasted with the Canadian approach, in which the presumption ceases to apply when a child reaches adulthood, so that gifts from parents to adult children are presumed to be held on a resulting trust in favour of the parent.[228] In *Pecore v Pecore*, the Supreme Court of Canada noted that

> it is common nowadays for ageing parents to transfer their assets into joint accounts with their adult children in order to have that child assist them in managing their financial affairs. There should therefore be a rebuttable presumption that the adult child is holding the property in trust for the ageing parent to facilitate the free and efficient management of that parent's affairs.[229]

Although both doctrines are rooted in intention, the court applied a pragmatic perspective –without falling back on the parent's capacity (or not) to formulate intention—perhaps because the starting point for advancement is the dependency of the *offspring* rather than the parent.[230] Indeed, the 'strong expectation' that parents will make gifts of their property to benefit offspring is also significant in respect of undue influence,

[223] Burns, above n 44, at 272.

[224] Chen-Wishart, 'Vindicating Relationships of Influence', above n 120, at 257.

[225] Eg, in *Re Brocklehurst's Estate* [1978] 1 Ch 14; *Campbell v Campbell* (Ch, 21 February 1996); *Glanville v Glanville* [2002] EWHC 1587 (Ch).

[226] *Langton v Langton* [1995] 2 FLR 890 at 905.

[227] In *Lavelle v Lavelle* [2004] EWCA Civ 223 at [48] it was assumed that a presumption of advancement would apply to gifts to an adult daughter; see J Glister, 'The presumption of advancement to adult children' [2007] *Conveyancer and Property Lawyer* 370.

[228] *Pecore v Pecore* [2007] SCC 17 (Sup Ct (Can)); *Madsen Estate v Saylor* [2007] SCC 18 (Sup Ct (Can)), discussed in Glister, above n 227.

[229] *Pecore v Pecore*, above n 228, at [37], *per* Rothstein J.

[230] There is, of course, also considerable scope to consider the broader context of the transaction when assessing whether the presumption has been rebutted.

inasmuch as it lends the appearance of 'normality' to such transactions.[231] As Chen-Wishart has observed, 'In truth, a legally relevant relationship of influence … is more *ordinary* than extraordinary.'[232] Nevertheless, Burns has argued that 'where elders have been concerned, courts have applied the former manifest disadvantage test and the explicability test rigorously',[233] by focusing on 'the necessity or practicality of the transaction from the elder's point of view'.[234] This resonates with Chen-Wishart's claim that undue influence cases reflect concerns with 'future autonomy',[235] and with Burns' claim that, 'Courts have not considered that it is in the best interests of elders in their twilight years to transfer significant assets to their children and relatives without some real and practical benefit to the elder which is legally protected.'[236]

In recent years, and particularly following the acknowledgement of transactional risk in all 'non-commercial' surety cases, placing one's home at risk in any transaction to benefit an adult child or relation should presumably be viewed as suspect.[237] Yet in close family relationships, the risks taken by the owner are often indistinguishable from reasons for entering into the transaction. As Lord Scott recognised in *Etridge (No 2)*, a wife's willingness to act as surety is

> a natural and admirable consequence of the relationship of a mutually loyal married couple … To regard the husband in such a case as a presumed 'wrongdoer' [is not] consistent with the relationship of trust and confidence that is a part of every healthy marriage.[238]

The 'normalcy' of the relationship of trust and confidence between the claimant and the defendant is therefore 'something of a two-edged sword. On one side, it helps to explain the gift. On the other, it provides the opportunity to take unfair advantage.'[239] A similar claim might be made of the ageing parent who is prepared to subjugate his or her own needs for those of a much-loved child. Chen-Wishart has argued that even under the new formulation, 'care must be taken lest the shorthand of "calls for an explanation" misleads the Court into denying relief simply because a gift appears to be perfectly explicable by the claimant's commitment or allegiance to the defendant.'[240]

From the perspective of relational norms, the explicability test may be understood as based not on the existence of a plausible subjective explanation or motivation for the transaction (which in cases of family relationships could almost always be found), but on 'an implicit judgement about the *objective acceptability* of the transaction in the context of the parties' relationship'.[241] According to this analysis, when applying the explicability test the court is in fact applying an objective standard against which 'abnormality' is judged.[242]

[231] See L Frolik, 'The strange interplay of testamentary capacity and the doctrine of undue influence: Are we protecting older testators or overriding individual preferences?' (2001) 24 *International Journal of Law and Psychiatry* 253, 261, discussing the US courts' 'unstated, but strongly felt, cultural norms about the "proper" distribution of an estate'.

[232] Chen-Wishart, above n 7, at 209.

[233] Burns, above n 44, at 273.

[234] *Ibid.*

[235] Chen-Wishart, 'Vindicating Relationships of Influence', above n 120, at 254.

[236] Burns, above n 44, at 273.

[237] *Ibid*, at 272.

[238] *Etridge (No 2)*, above n 40, at [159] *per* Lord Scott.

[239] *Randall v Randall* (Chancery Div 28 May 2004), [42].

[240] Chen-Wishart, above n 7, at 213.

[241] *Ibid*, at 213–14.

[242] *Ibid.*

Chen-Wishart identified a series of contextual[243] considerations which she claimed operate as norms in respect of the explicability test, and which include, for example, considerations of future autonomy or future freedom: where a transaction fails to provide for the contingency that different choices might later be made,[244] for example where a transaction 'would leave the claimant without adequate resources to meet the contingencies of old age'[245]; or the 'appropriateness' of the transaction in light of the specific nature of the parties' relationship.[246]

These norms are also shaped by the housing paradigms discussed in chapter five, which provide the frames within which older owners use and/or transact with their housing (as home, as inheritance and as an investment-asset-to-spend). For example, the 'normalcy' of the pressures that older owners may feel to act as surety for younger family members is shaped by the paradigm of owned housing as inheritance. Furthermore, this is a pressure that may not necessarily flow from the relationship: research in the UK has indicated that while many adult offspring have expectations of inheritance, they do not view it as an 'entitlement'; although some parents may feel a pressure—or at least a desire—to provide, many are pragmatic in relation to their own needs from their housing equity.[247] The traditional assumption that assets would flow down the generations has also been challenged by the dominance of the paradigm of housing as investment-asset-to-spend in political and policy agendas,[248] while the care needs of older people—as well as the limited capacities of their children to meet those needs—have altered relational norms between older people and their adult offspring.[249]

One (albeit high-risk) way of reconciling these competing demands on housing equity is through the use of the older owner's home as security or surety for the younger person's financial activities. This type of transaction—in contrast to an outright transfer—appears to allow older owners to satisfy a range of competing paradigms, retaining their own housing as home, and perhaps providing the possibility for spending equity to meet their own needs in the future, while offering the equity for use as leverage (perhaps in lieu of inheritance) in the short to medium term. In addition to the traditional suretyship, chapter five noted the ways in which the growing practice of parents leveraging their own housing wealth to help children on to the housing ladder has been enabled through a range of new mortgage products.[250] Burns described the practice of older people leveraging their assets for younger relatives' financial transactions as 'intergenerationally transmitted debt'.[251] She claimed:

> Longevity may result in the delayed inheritance of assets ... Elders may be perceived as burdens on both families and social resources. Therefore, intergenerationally transmitted debt may be a

[243] 'What qualifies as a transaction "calling for an explanation" is not a simple matter of disproportionate exchange measured against some objective market price.': Chen-Wishart, 'Vindicating Relationships of Influence', above n 120, at 253.
[244] Chen-Wishart, above n 7, at 214, citing as illustration *Allcard v Skinner*, above n 219.
[245] *Ibid.*
[246] Chen-Wishart, 'Vindicating Relationships of Influence', above n 120, at 254.
[247] See ch 5, section (4).
[248] See ch 2.
[249] See ch 5, section (4).
[250] See ch 5, section (4).
[251] Burns, 'Legally regulating intergenerationally transmitted debt', above n 31; adapting Fehlburg's famous description of transactions involving 'surety wives' as 'sexually transmitted debt'—see Fehlburg, above n 104.

> convenient way of resolving the financial problems of the younger generations—a premature unlocking of future economic potential in the form of a guarantee of their present liabilities.[252]

Of course, a major distinction between the use of housing as testamentary inheritance and 'housing as inheritance' *inter vivos* is that if the security of the older person's home is called in during that person's lifetime, the older owner risks losing both his or her home and his or her main financial asset, with potentially disastrous consequences for future financial well-being. The countervailing benefits of the transaction for the older person tend to be emotional rather than financial. The older owner may derive no (financial) benefit from the transaction, and is likely to have little control over whether the borrower defaults on the debt, leading the creditor to realise the security (that is, the older person's home).[253]

Nevertheless, and notwithstanding the high level of transactional risk associated with transactions in which older people agree to act as sureties or allow their owned homes to be used as security, it is difficult to cast these transactions as 'abnormal', or to determine when the 'normal' level of influence that children might be expected to have over their ageing parents' financial decision-making becomes 'undue'. Yet another remove is added when a third party is implicated in the offspring's undue influence. The evolution of the courts' approach to third-party responsibility for undue influence in cases involving older owners is examined in the next section.

(e) The nature and scope of the creditor's responsibilities

(i) Third-party liability

The nature and extent of a commercial third party's obligations towards a potentially vulnerable older owner depend on the type of transaction. In surety cases, the decision in *Etridge (No 2)* adopted the simple approach of putting all creditors on notice of undue influence where the relationship between the surety and the debtor is 'non-commercial', so requiring them to take appropriate steps to discharge the obligation.[254] These 'appropriate steps', set out in detail in Lord Nicholls's speech, are primarily oriented around ensuring that the surety has received adequate independent legal advice concerning the nature of the transaction and the risks taken by allowing the property to be used in this way. In these 'three-party cases', and following the decision in *Etridge (No 2)*, the function of independent advice in non-commercial surety cases is to shift the obligation to protect the claimant to a third party (the independent adviser),[255] whose responsibility, in turn, is to explain the nature of the transaction to the claimant, but 'not … to veto the transaction, even if it seems seriously unwise'.[256] This may be contrasted with 'two-party cases' (in which the commercial party is not merely 'put on inquiry' of undue influence exerted by another but

[252] Burns, *ibid.*

[253] *Ibid.*

[254] Lord Nicholls explained that 'if a bank is not to be required to evaluate the extent to which its customer has influence over a proposed guarantor, the only practical way forward is to regard banks as "put on inquiry" in every case where the relationship between the surety and the debtor is non-commercial': *Etridge (No 2)*, above n 40, at [87].

[255] See Chen-Wishart, 'Vindicating Relationships of Influence', above n 120, at 260.

[256] Capper explained that 'This goes beyond giving a formal explanation of the nature of the documents to be signed and requires advice as to the state of the borrower's account and the economic risks the surety is running': Capper, above n 3, at 179.

has itself 'crossed the line'), where the function of the independent advice is to 'emancipate the weaker party from the undue influence'.[257]

The circumstances in which commercial parties have been deemed 'responsible' for the undue influence of another have evolved considerably in recent years, with the *Etridge (No 2)* approach representing the latest in a line of judicial norms which appear to have progressively curtailed the substantive responsibilities attributed to commercial parties in respect of unduly influenced claimants. Prior to the decision in *Barclay's Bank v O'Brien*,[258] third-party liability for undue influence had been based on an implied agency relationship between the creditor and the principal debtor,[259] with the concept of the creditor 'using' the husband to exert pressure on the wife to sign placing an onus of responsibility on the creditor to 'abide [by] the consequences' where the wife's agreement was impugned.[260] For example, in *Avon Finance v Bridger*,[261] a son misled his elderly parents concerning the nature of the transaction, to procure their signatures as sureties for a loan from a finance company secured against the retirement home they were in the process of acquiring with the help of their son. When the son defaulted on the loan, the finance company sought to enforce the security and the parents attempted to avoid the transaction. A majority in the Court of Appeal[262] held that the charge was voidable in equity because the finance company was affected by the undue influence which the son enjoyed over his parents.[263] Applying the principle that third-party liability for undue influence was based on the agency principle,[264] the Court of Appeal held that the finance company should not be allowed to take advantage of its agent's (the son's) deceit. Brandon LJ was willing to deem the finance company responsible for the harm that resulted from the transaction, on the basis that it was the party that principally benefited from the suretyship.[265] The agency principle supported a construction of the transaction as one in which the son ('a young accountant in the prime of life') was appointed by the finance company to procure the surety from his parents. While the vulnerability of the parents was clearly noted,[266] and despite clear evidence of the son's wrongdoing,[267] fault was clearly

[257] *Ibid.*

[258] [1994] 1 AC 180.

[259] See *Turnbull & Co Ltd v Duval* [1902] AC 429 (PC); *Chaplin & Co Ltd v Brammall* [1908] 1 KB 233.

[260] *Turnbull & Co Ltd v Duvall*, above n 259 at 435, *per* Lindley LJ; see also *Chaplin & Co Ltd v Brammall*, above n 259, at 238, *per* Vaughan Williams LJ; *Kingsnorth Trust Ltd v Bell* [1986] 1 All ER 423 (CA); *Barclay's Bank plc v Kennedy* [1989] 1 FLR 356, and *Midland Bank plc v Shephard*, [1988] 3 All ER 17 at 22 (CA), where Neill LJ held that 'The court will not enforce a transaction at the suit of a creditor if it can be shown that the creditor entrusted the task of obtaining the alleged debtor's signature to the relevant document to someone who was, to the knowledge of the creditor, in a position to influence the debtor and who procured the signature of the debtor by means of undue influence or by means of fraudulent misrepresentation.'

[261] [1985] 2 All ER 281.

[262] After dismissing the defence of *non est factum*, on the basis that the parents had signed the charge without exercising reasonable care.

[263] Lord Denning MR agreed that the transaction was voidable, but by an extension to the principle of inequality of bargaining power, on the basis that the terms of the transaction were very unfair; the parents' bargaining power was impaired by their ignorance of the true situation; the son had brought undue pressure to bear by misleading his parents; and the parents had not received independent advice.

[264] *Turnbull & Co Ltd v Duval*, above n 259; *Chaplin & Co Ltd v Brammall*, above n 259.

[265] 'It was for the plaintiffs' benefit to have this security because they are in business for money lending, and they wanted a good secure money-lending contract.': *Avon Finance v Bridger*, above n 261 at 287.

[266] '... both of whom were old-age pensioners, much less well educated than he was': *ibid*, at 287, *per* Brandon LJ.

[267] Lord Denning claimed that 'It is plain that the son was a very bad lot. He went missing. He owed debts all round.': *ibid*, at 285.

attributed to the finance company for its use of the son, who—the Court held—should (normally) be expected to have some influence over his elderly parents.

The agency approach to third-party liability was rejected in *Barclay's Bank v O'Brien*, where the House of Lords described the doctrine as artificial and inappropriate, and held that, in the vast majority of cases,[268] the proper basis of third-party liability for undue influence was constructive notice.[269] In identifying the factors that would 'put a creditor on inquiry', the House of Lords focused (in light of the slew of 'surety wives' cases) on the nature and extent of the third party's responsibilities in surety transactions. The *O'Brien* judgments placed considerable emphasis on the particular susceptibility of wives (and other partners to a 'stable emotional and sexual relationship')[270] to be unduly influenced by their husbands (or partners), giving rise to a substantial risk that, in procuring the wife to act as surety, the husband has committed a legal or equitable wrong that entitles the wife to set aside the transaction.[271] This risk, combined with the transaction not being on its face to the financial advantage of the wife, was deemed sufficient to put the creditor on inquiry.[272] While this (contextualised) use of constructive notice appeared to shift responsibility for the probity of the transaction onto the creditor, the burden was relatively easily discharged by the creditor taking 'reasonable steps' to satisfy itself that the surety's consent had been properly obtained and by advising her to take independent advice.[273] Lord Browne-Wilkinson reasoned that this approach would 'hold the balance fairly' between 'wives' and creditors,[274] and would coincide with 'good banking practice'.[275]

The scope of the creditor's responsibility was revisited by the House of Lords in *CIBC Mortgages Ltd v Pitt*,[276] where the court held that the creditor did not have constructive notice of Mr Pitt's undue influence over his wife because the transaction (a joint loan rather than a surety) was not to her financial disadvantage.[277] The impact of a (broadly-drawn) special protection for surety wives on the 'usability' of the home as security was influential on the House of Lords' reasoning, with Lord Browne-Wilkinson concerned that

[268] Although the House of Lords accepted that there may be occasional cases in which the principal debtor acted as agent for the bank in procuring the surety's signature: 'Of course, if the wrongdoing husband is acting as agent for the creditor bank in obtaining the surety from the wife, the creditor will be fixed with constructive notice of its own agent and the surety contract can be set aside as against the creditor.'; *O'Brien* (HL), above n 55, at 191, *per* Lord Browne-Wilkinson.

[269] The House of Lords held that 'when a wife offered to stand surety for her husband's debt in a transaction which was not to her financial advantage and which carried a substantial risk of the husband committing a legal or equitable wrong entitling the wife to set aside the transaction, the creditor was put on inquiry and would have constructive notice of the wife's rights unless he took reasonable steps to ensure that her agreement to stand surety had been properly obtained': *ibid*, at 180–81.

[270] See, eg, *AIB plc v Byrne* [1995] 2 FLR 325 (ChD); *Midland Bank plc v Massey* [1994] 2 FLR 342 (CA).

[271] *O'Brien* (HL), above n 55, at 196, *per* Lord Browne-Wilkinson.

[272] Lord Browne-Wilkinson stated that 'if, but only if, the creditor is aware that the surety is cohabiting with the principal debtor, in my judgment the same principles should apply to them as apply to husband and wife': *ibid*, at 198.

[273] It was noted that the traditional means of satisfying the standard of inquiry would be inappropriate in this context: 'Normally the reasonable steps necessary to avoid being fixed with constructive notice consist of making inquiry of the person who may have the earlier right (ie the wife) to see whether such right is asserted. It is plainly impossible to require of banks and other financial institutions that they should inquire of one spouse whether he or she has been unduly influenced or misled by the other.': *ibid*, at 196, *per* Lord Browne-Wilkinson.

[274] *Ibid*, at 197, *per* Lord Browne-Wilkinson.

[275] *Ibid*, at 198.

[276] [1994] 1 AC 200.

[277] '[S]ince there was no indication that the transaction was anything other than a normal advance to husband and wife for their joint benefit, the plaintiff was not put on inquiry and could not be fixed with constructive notice.': *ibid* at 200.

if constructive notice of undue influence were to be imputed in every transaction between spouses, 'such transactions would become almost impossible'[278] because the burden of responsibility on the creditor (to advise the co-debtor to take independent legal advice) would discourage creditors from accepting matrimonial property as security.[279] The policy question concerning the extent to which creditors may be, or ought to be, required to take positive action to protect vulnerable sureties—and the implications for use of the home as an investment asset—resonates with the emergence of creditor responsibility for housing equity transactions in the regulatory context.[280] Yet, as the case law dealing specifically with older owners and the discussion in this chapter have demonstrated, the policy issues raised in their housing equity transactions—including, particularly, the impact of an adverse transaction on the older owner's future autonomy—are somewhat different from those which have influenced the 'surety wives' cases.

The application of the constructive notice principle in an older owner case came before the Court for consideration in *Portman Building Society v Dusangh*[281] where, perhaps in response to changing norms following the financial and equity upheavals of 1990s Britain, the Court showed no sympathy for the circumstances in which Mr Dusangh, an older parent, put his home at risk to provide security for the business debts of his child. The building society had granted a 25-year repayment mortgage to the defendant who was then aged 72 and retired. The purpose of the mortgage was to fund his son's business venture, and the mortgage was secured against the defendant's home. The Court noted that the (Indian) father's understanding of spoken English had remained poor, and that he was illiterate. However, the claim of undue influence was rejected at the first hurdle, on the basis that the defendant had failed to prove 'by affirmative evidence that [he] was accustomed to repose trust and confidence' in his son. In fact, the Court held that 'Such evidence as there is tends to suggest that Mr Dusangh Senior did not have trust and confidence in his son.' The Court focused wholly on the (limited evidence of the) relationship between the parties, and did not consider the context surrounding Mr Dusangh Senior's decision to enter into the transaction to be significant. This strict approach was also reflected in the Recorder's findings concerning the question of whether the building society had been put on notice of the alleged undue influence.

Applying the principle of constructive notice[282] which (similarly to the explicability test) drew on judgments concerning what is 'normal' or 'abnormal', the Court held as follows:

[278] *Ibid*, at 211, *per* Lord Browne-Wilkinson.

[279] 'On every purchase of a home in the joint names, the building society or bank financing the purchase would have to insist on meeting the wife separately from her husband, advise her as to the nature of the transaction and recommend her to take legal advice separate from that of her husband. If that were not done, the financial institution would have to run the risk of a subsequent attempt by the wife to avoid her liabilities under the mortgage on the ground of undue influence or misrepresentation. To establish the law in that sense would not benefit the average married couple and would discourage financial institutions from making the advance.': *ibid*, at 211, *per* Lord Browne-Wilkinson. See also *Midland Bank Ltd v Greene* (1993) 27 *Housing Law Reports* 350 (ChD); *AIB plc v Byrne* [1995] 2 FLR 325 (ChD).

[280] See ch 9.

[281] [1999] EWCA Civ 1331.

[282] Prior to *Etridge (No 2)*, it was necessary for the claimant seeking to establish third-party liability for undue influence to show that the bank had constructive notice of the undue influence between the principal debtor and the surety; *O'Brien* (HL), above n 55.

> It does not seem to me that an application for a re-mortgage by an elderly man of probable Asian origin, guaranteed by his son, was something which should have put Portman on notice of a possible equity the father might have against the son. Such things as an application containing different writing, a shaky signature, how access to the property is to be arranged seem to me of little significance. None of those things say anything about the relationship between Mr Dusangh Senior and Junior.[283]

The Court in *Dusangh* applied the tests set out by the Court of Appeal in *Etridge (No 2)*,[284] which pre-empted to some extent the emergence of the explicability test when that case was heard by the House of Lords. The Court's reasoning for enforcing the transaction included the rationale that it could not be said that the transaction was 'so extravagantly improvident that it was difficult to explain in the absence of impropriety'. Brown LJ described the transaction—despite the contextual vulnerabilities of Mr Dusangh—as

> reasonably … explained on the basis of a borrower/father's wish to help his son purchase and run a small business, that he was doing this out of natural love and affection. The notion that it is common for parents to make financial sacrifices for their children, whether or not within the Asian community, is commonplace. Indeed that is what I conclude happened here.[285]

In this sense, it is arguable that *any* transaction in which a parent releases equity to support the needs of offspring is 'reasonably explained', notwithstanding its potentially catastrophic effect on the older owner's capacity to meet his or her own needs into the future (with obvious consequences for his or her future autonomy in a neoliberal welfare context). According to the *Dusangh* view, it was 'not "manifestly disadvantageous" to this appellant that he should be able to raise money by way of re-mortgage so as to benefit his son'.[286] While the Court of Appeal acknowledged that Mr Dusangh Senior was elderly, illiterate and on a very low income, and that the transaction was an improvident one, the judge concluded that 'I simply cannot accept that building societies are required to police transactions of this nature to ensure that parents (even poor and ignorant ones) are wise in seeking to assist their children.'

The shifting terms of the elements of undue influence in the last three decades—particularly the evolution of the tests applied to determine whether a third party is affected by undue influence between an older owner and a younger relative—have, taken together, created an inconsistent and piecemeal approach to the broader question of responsibility for transactions procured by undue influence as applied to older owners. In *Dusangh*, the Court of Appeal was clear in spelling out that the building society did not bear a responsibility to protect Mr Dusangh Senior against this highly adverse transaction for the benefit of his son. The Court's unwillingness to hold the creditor responsible for the harm to Mr Dusangh was particularly stark in light of the fact that the creditor had failed to follow its own policies and procedures for responsible lending when it granted a 72-year-old man on a very low income a 25-year repayment mortgage with no evidence of how he would be able to service the debt. Brown LJ justified the Court's approach by

[283] *Dusangh*, above n 281, *per* Brown LJ. The Court therefore held that the Building Society was entitled to proceed against the property on the basis that the defendant had received legal advice, and it was entitled to assume that the advice was competent.

[284] [1998] 4 All ER 705 at 719.

[285] *Dusangh*, above n 281.

[286] *Ibid*.

claiming that the purpose of the bank's lending policies was not to define their responsibilities towards customers; they

> exist to protect the building society's interests, not their borrowers. That it was commercially unwise for the [building society] to put their trust in the appellant (and his son) is not to say that it was morally culpable for them to do so.[287]

This approach is indicative of the paradigmatic legal subject as a self-responsible consumer. It patently denies the contemporary belief—in the regulatory realm at least—that lenders bear at least some responsibility towards their customers for their lending decisions, which has been particularly evident in the emphasis on responsible lending in the wake of the recent financial crisis.[288] Neither did the Court acknowledge Mr Dusangh Senior's evident vulnerabilities, or the catastrophic impact that the transaction would have on his financial—and more general—well-being in retirement. *Dusangh* may, in this respect, be viewed as a high-watermark of non-intervention in cases of this type. Yet, as the discussion below will show, the formal acknowledgement that third parties bear *some* responsibility in undue influence cases, particularly towards 'non-commercial sureties', has not necessarily translated into substantive protections for vulnerable claimants.

A final pre-*Etridge* (HL) illustration of the norms of explicability as they have been applied to older owners may be found in *Wright v Cherrytree Finance Ltd*,[289] where the claimant's son-in-law procured her consent to use her home as security to enable him to buy shares in a company (of which he became director), although in fact he used the money to discharge existing liabilities and to make a loan to the company. The court held that her agreement to act as surety for his debts was procured by actual undue influence and misrepresentation; that this was a material factor in her decision to apply for a loan and execute the mortgage; that Cherrytree Finance Limited had constructive notice of the undue influence, although not of the misrepresentation; and that Cherrytree Finance did not take sufficient steps to dispel the effect of undue influence, of which it had constructive notice. The older owner's vulnerability in the sense of capability for financial decision-making was acknowledged when the judge noted that 'the claimant had recently lost her husband, with whom she had lived in matrimonial harmony for some thirty years or more, and on whom she had depended in all financial matters'.[290] The court also noted that 'She was unacquainted with commercial affairs'[291] and that her dependence on her husband had been transferred on to her daughter and son-in-law:

> [A]fter her husband's death the claimant had relied on Mr and Mrs Scott … both accepted that, particularly during the period following the death of her husband, the claimant had placed trust and confidence in them and that she was dependent on them in relation to financial affairs … [she] had no one else to turn to for advice.[292]

Although the court accepted that the degree of pressure placed on Mrs Wright was 'comparatively slight', it placed considerable emphasis on her pre-existing vulnerabilities. The court held that

[287] *Ibid.*
[288] See ch 9, section (5).
[289] [2001] 2 All ER (Comm) 877.
[290] *Ibid*, [16].
[291] *Ibid.*
[292] *Ibid*, [18].

> because of the relationship between the claimant and her daughter and son-in-law, because of her vulnerability immediately following her husband's death, because of her commercial ignorance and because of the misrepresentations made to her and because this arrangement was plainly to her manifest disadvantage in that she was putting up her house as security for money which was to be used and enjoyed by Mr Scott and, indirectly, to some extent at any rate, by Mrs Scott, alone, this was a transaction which was procured by undue influence.[293]

In addition to the 'inherent' vulnerabilities resulting from Mrs Wright's 'dependence' on the Scotts for guidance in financial matters, the court also viewed the nature of the transaction—and particularly its potentially adverse impact on her future autonomy—as determinative in finding that the finance company was affected by undue influence between an older mother-in-law and her son-in-law.

Applying the explicability test, the justification for non-enforcement was expressed in terms of the 'normalcy' of the transaction, although the potentially adverse outcome and its particular impact on this older owner were explicitly referenced by the court. Sir Christopher Staughton, giving the judgment of the Court of Appeal, stated that 'for a recently widowed lady to mortgage forthwith the house in which she lived, which, so far as we know, was her only asset, would seem to be a matter that would normally raise inquiry'.[294] The Court's concern with the high level of risk involved in this type of transaction (jeopardising one's home, the only major asset in retirement, to support the enterprises of an younger relative) for an older person underlined the implicit role of context and the guiding influence of relational norms relevant to the particular type of transaction in determining cases in which older people 'use' their housing wealth to support the activities of younger relatives.

Reorienting this analysis within a frame of vulnerability and responsibility, the relational norms approach to undue influence would present both stages of the test to establish presumed undue influence—that there is a relationship of trust and confidence, and that the transaction 'calls for explanation'—as not in fact concerned with the quality of the claimant's consent, or the defendant's 'wrongdoing', but with a contextual, relational analysis of the nature of the transaction, including an objective assessment of the responsibilities which the defendant must discharge, in light of his relationship with the claimant. These responsibilities are, in turn, shaped by a contextual assessment of the claimant's vulnerability in entering into the transaction, including the harms resulting from the transaction as they are likely to impact on the claimant's future autonomy. The final stage of the inquiry is then concerned with the steps that parties affected by undue influence must take to discharge the responsibility or obligation to protect the claimant, and so ensure the enforceability of the transaction.

It is with reference to the 'reasonable steps' that are necessary to discharge the third party's duty of inquiry once it has arisen that the decision in *Etridge (No 2)* has significantly curtailed the *substantive* responsibilities of commercial parties to transactions procured by undue influence. Critics of the *Etridge (No 2)* model of creditor responsibility have highlighted its emphasis on procedural steps without regard to the substantive effect of advice on the surety's free exercise of consent. The pre-*Etridge* authorities indicated that the bank could reasonably leave it to the surety's solicitor to perform its professional

293 *Ibid*, [25].

294 *Ibid*, [19]. See also *Watson v Huber* [2005] All ER (D) 156, in which the court held that the number and size of the gifts called for explanation.

duties properly,[295] and to provide any information and advice necessary to counteract the undue influence or misrepresentation,[296] even when the surety's solicitor also acted for the debtor[297] or for all three parties: surety, debtor and creditor.[298] The subject matter of the advice was left to the solicitor.[299] The 'reasonableness' of the steps taken was assessed from the creditor's perspective, with 'the true question … not how [the surety] regarded the transaction, but how it appeared to the bank and whether the bank should have taken further steps'.[300] While *Etridge (No 2)* set out in much more detail the steps to be taken to discharge third-party liability for undue influence, the courts' approach continues to 'focus on the issue of the victim's comprehension but completely ignore[s] the primary issue of influence'.[301] This factor has been judicially acknowledged on many occasions: for example, in *Banco Exterior Internacional v Mann*,[302] Hobhouse LJ focused on the surety's *response* to any advice given, noting that information and advice does not necessarily place the unduly influenced surety in a better position, since 'The problem is … not lack of intelligence or education, but lack of independence.'[303] His Lordship thus reasoned that 'The steps taken have to be directed to freeing her of that influence or, at the least, providing some counterbalance'.[304] Indeed, in *Credit Lyonnais Bank Nederland NV v Burch*,[305] the Court of Appeal recognised that independent advice may not be sufficient to displace the *effect* of the undue influence in 'exceptional cases',[306] since 'the same influence that produced her desire to enter into the transaction would cause her to disregard any

[295] *Bank of Baroda v Shah* [1988] 3 All ER 24; *Lloyd's Bank plc v Egremont* [1990] 2 FLR 351; *Midland Bank v Massey* [1994] 2 FLR 342; *Bank of Baroda v Rayarel* [1995] 2 FLR 376; *Midland Bank plc v Serter* (1994) *26 Housing Law Reports* 612.

[296] 'The bank was entitled to assume that [the] solicitors would act honestly and would give proper advice to the defendants if the solicitors were, as they represented, acting for the defendants': *Bank of Baroda v Shah*, above n 295, at 24.

[297] *Midland Bank v Massey*, above n 295. In *Wilis v Barron* [1900–03] All ER Rep 876 at 882, the House of Lords acknowledged that 'A wife usually has no solicitor of her own apart from her husband, and I think she is *prima facie* entitled to look to her husband's solicitors—the solicitor of her husband's family—for advice and assistance until that solicitor repudiates the obligation to give such advice, and requires her to consult another gentleman.'

[298] *Midland Bank plc v Serter*, above n 295. The Court of Appeal in *Royal Bank of Scotland v Etridge* [1998] 2 FLR 843 at 852, suggested that 'It is obviously unwise for the solicitor who is acting for the bank to advise the wife, unless the solicitor is instructed to act for the bank only in a ministerial capacity at completion; for the bank's interests are necessarily in conflict with those of both husband and wife.' Nevertheless, the bank is entitled to assume that, whomever else the solicitor is acting for, he will regard himself as owing a duty to the wife alone when giving her advice: *Barclays Bank plc v Thomson* [1997] 1 FLR 156.

[299] *Midland Bank plc v Massey*, above n 295, at 347, *per* Steyn LJ. See generally, B Fehlburg, 'The Husband, the Bank, the Wife and Her Signature—the Sequel' (1996) 59 *MLR* 675, 685 *et seq*; D Morris, 'Wives are Told: Don't Blame the Bank, Sue Your Solicitor' (1999) 7 *Feminist Legal Studies* 193.

[300] *Banco Exterior Internacional v Mann* [1995] 1 FLR 602 (CA) at 609, *per* Morritt LJ.

[301] M Oldham, '"Neither a borrower nor a lender be"—the life of *O'Brien*' (1995) 7 *Child and Family Law Quarterly* 104, 118.

[302] Above n 300.

[303] *Ibid*, at 611, *per* Hobhouse LJ. 'An understanding of the document may be the first step in the exercise of a free choice whether or not to sign it, but it is not the point at which the law of undue influence is directed. A person may be fully informed as to the content of the document and its legal effect and yet be acting under the undue influence of another when she signs it. The two considerations are distinct. As Lord Browne-Wilkinson points out, it is the undue influence not the lack of comprehension that gives the wife the defence.': *ibid* at 612–13, *per* Hobhouse LJ.

[304] *Ibid*, at 614, *per* Hobhouse LJ.

[305] [1997] 1 FLR 11.

[306] Millett LJ stated that taking independent legal advice is neither always necessary nor always sufficient to rebut the presumption of undue influence; *ibid*, at 22.

advice not to do so.'[307] Nevertheless, Millett LJ held that creditors seeking to avoid constructive notice of undue influence could do so by ensuring that the surety received 'competent and independent legal advice', reassuring creditors:

> If [the surety] does so, and enters into the transaction nonetheless, the third party will usually escape the consequences of notice ... because he is normally entitled to assume that the solicitor has discharged his duty and that the complainant has followed his advice.[308]

Similarly, in *Royal Bank of Scotland v Etridge*,[309] the Court of Appeal acknowledged that 'the protection which ought to be afforded to the wife by the provision of independent legal advice has in many cases proved illusory'.[310] The Court's emphasis was placed, however, on the quality of the advice, rather than on the ineffectiveness of advice *per se*.[311] Again, however, the risk of inadequate advice clearly rested on the vulnerable surety, with the bank held to have discharged its duty by telling the solicitor to give advice, 'notwithstanding that the advice was either inadequate or even not actually given'.[312] The Court was not prepared to place any *substantive* responsibility for the surety's vulnerability on the creditor. When *Etridge (No 2)* was heard in the House of Lords, Lord Nicholls stated that

> under the current practice the legal advice is often perfunctory in the extreme and ... everyone, including the banks, knows this. Independent legal advice is a fiction. The system is a charade. In practice it provides little or no protection for a wife who is under a misapprehension about the risks involved or who is being coerced into signing.[313]

Nevertheless, the House of Lords concluded that this 'fiction' and 'charade' of protection was, with a little additional unpacking as to the precise steps to be taken, sufficient to discharge the bank's responsibility towards the vulnerable claimant:

> The furthest a bank can be expected to go is to take reasonable steps to satisfy itself that the wife has had brought home to her, in a meaningful way, the practical implications of the proposed transaction. This does not wholly eliminate the risk of undue influence or misrepresentation. But it does mean that a wife enters into a transaction with her eyes open so far as the basic elements of the transaction are concerned.[314]

Although the Court of Appeal had envisaged the possibility of transactions in regard to which having ensured that legal advice was given would be insufficient to discharge the bank's responsibility, the House of Lords disagreed.[315] While this view might be defended,

307 *Ibid*, at 23, *per* Millett LJ.
308 *Ibid*.
309 [1998] 2 FLR 842.
310 *Ibid*, at 846.
311 'The advice which the wife has received has often been perfunctory, limited to an explanation of the documents and yet inadequate to dispel her misunderstanding of the real extent of the liability which she was undertaking, and not directed to ensure that she was entering into the transaction of her own free will rather than as the result of illegitimate pressure from her husband or blind trust in him.': *ibid*.
312 D Morris, 'Wives are told: don't blame the bank, sue your solicitor' (1999) 7 *Feminist Legal Studies* 193, 195. Morris concluded that 'the practical result of *Etridge* is that where a solicitor acts for a wife, no matter who instructs, pays or retains that solicitor, the bank is entitled to assume that the wife has been properly advised and that the charge is binding. By simply adopting the administrative procedure of asking the wife to obtain independent legal advice, the bank will usually find its back covered.': *ibid*, at 202.
313 *Etridge (No 2)*, above n 40, at [52] *per* Lord Nicholls.
314 *Ibid*, at [54] *per* Lord Nicholls.
315 *Ibid*, at [63].

from a regulatory perspective, as pursuing a proportionate risk-based approach, by setting out a simple method by which third parties can avoid liability it strikes the balance for proportionality on the side of a market-oriented preference for enforceability, and without adequate consideration for the real nature of the surety's vulnerabilities, or for whether the balance struck by the law ensures a fair outcome.

The House of Lords argued that its goal was to strike a balance between the interests of the vulnerable claimant and the interests of the lender,[316] with arguments on the side of the lender emphasising the importance of enabling and generating confidence in this type of securitisation.[317] The discussion in section (2)(b) above identified a range of cognate factors between 'surety wives' cases and older owners' housing equity transactions, which included the political and policy arguments that support facilitating the use of the owned home as an investment asset. While the main thrust of the policy agenda relating to older owners has been concerned with the release of equity for the owner's benefit rather than to secure the liabilities of another, there are clearly tensions between the older owner's own needs and the use of his or her housing equity as 'inheritance', or in some cases passing on the benefit of accumulated wealth during the older owner's lifetime rather than after death. The idea that older people's housing equity will operate as a source of capitalisation for small businesses has not emerged as a policy factor in the way that 'surety wives' transactions have typically been regarded; however, the growth in products to enable older owners to leverage their housing equity specifically to 'lend a hand' to younger relatives suggests that there is a market for this type of transaction. What is less clear is whether these transactions will necessarily fit the structural model of 'non-commercial sureties' so as to put the bank on inquiry that the transaction is not financially advantageous to the older owner. Yet while it remains necessary to establish, on the facts, that the duty of inquiry has arisen in 'non-surety' transactions (and this will continue to require a contextual assessment of the 'normalcy' of the transaction), it is questionable to what extent the procedural steps which are automatically triggered in surety cases provide real protections for vulnerable claimants.

Even if the bank is put on inquiry, the thrust of the *Etridge (No 2)* approach was to set out the rote-responsibilities that banks must follow to avoid liability, rather than to identify and provide an appropriate level of protection for vulnerable sureties.[318] Morris argued that the judgment 'pushes the scales most heavily in favour of [banks and solicitors]'.[319] While banks have 'positive duties', 'the judgment provides a practical framework which should not prove too onerous to implement … A formulaic approach should allow banks … to have a reasonable degree of assurance that the security will be enforceable.'[320] The bank is 'put on inquiry' when in any transaction a person in a non-commercial relationship with another offers to stand surety for the debts of that other. Once put on inquiry, that bank can discharge its responsibility by taking 'reasonable steps to satisfy itself that the [surety] has had brought home to her, in a meaningful way,

[316] M Oldham, 'If at first … Undue Influence and the House of Lords' (2002) 61 *MLR* 29.

[317] *Etridge (No 2)*, above n 40, at [34]–[35].

[318] See discussion of Australian position in CYC Chew, 'Another Look at the Giving of Independent Advice to Sureties: Some Uncertainties and Evolving Concerns' (2006) 18 *Bond Law Review* 45.

[319] D Morris, 'Surety Wives in the House of Lords: Time for Solicitors to "Get Real"' (2003) 11 *Feminist Legal Studies* 57, 64.

[320] *Ibid.*

the practical implications of the proposed transaction'.[321] This is achieved by the bank advising the surety that it will require, for its own protection, written confirmation from her solicitor that the solicitor has fully explained the transactions and its implications to her, and that the purpose of this measure is so that she cannot subsequently dispute the transaction. The bank must not proceed until it has received an 'appropriate response' from the surety.[322] Between the bank and the solicitor, the bank must disclose all relevant financial details relating to the debtor. Furthermore, if the bank suspects that the surety is actually being misled or is not entering the transaction freely, it should require that she receive separate advice.[323]

Similarly, the solicitor's duty is to advise on the transaction, not to ensure that the surety is acting freely or to 'veto' the transaction if it is not in the surety's best interests,[324] unless it is 'glaringly obvious' that the surety is being 'grievously wronged'.[325] The procedure for the meeting between the solicitor and the surety was set out in detail: it must be in person, and the explanations must be provided in non-technical language; the solicitor must explain that the purpose of the meeting is to ensure that the bank can rely on the surety, explain the nature of the documents and the consequences if the surety signs them, highlight the serious risks involved and the nature and extent of the surety's liability, advise the surety that she has a choice and that the choice is hers alone, and ask whether the surety is happy to proceed on the basis of the proposed terms, whether she wants the solicitor to negotiate terms or whether she wants to withdraw from the transaction.[326]

While the discussions above suggest that the courts have some sensitivity to the potential vulnerability of older owners in transactions involving their housing equity, and to the potentially catastrophic impact of losing assets after retirement,[327] the *Etridge (No 2)* approach to third-party 'responsibility' for such vulnerabilities in surety transactions sets a low standard, 'impos[ing] no more than a modest obligation on banks and other creditors'.[328] The House of Lords successfully presented its strategy as a 'workable compromise', with commentators accepting that 'even though the threshold is low, the steps required to avoid liability are clear, simple, and sufficiently formulaic to keep compliance costs within manageable bounds'.[329] The outcome in surety cases is that the protection of vulnerable sureties has been placed in the hands of solicitors,[330] although there are also clear limits on the extent to which they, in turn, are required to respond to the real source of the vulnerability. The outcome is that the balance has been decisively tipped in the banks' favour, so that 'Preservation of the market value of the matrimonial

321 *Etridge (No 2)*, above n 40, at [54] *per* Lord Nicholls.
322 Oldham, above n 316, at 30.
323 For details of the steps which the bank must take, see *Etridge (No 2)*, above n 40, at [50]–[57] *per* Lord Nicholls.
324 Morris, above n 319, at 65.
325 *Etridge (No 2)*, above n 40, [62].
326 *Ibid*, at [58]–[68] *per* Lord Nicholls.
327 See section (2)(d), above.
328 *Etridge (No 2)*, above n 40, at [89] *per* Lord Nicholls.
329 See, eg, Oldham, above n 316, at 32.
330 P Giliker, '*Barclay's Bank v O'Brien* revisited: What a Difference Five Years Makes' (1999) 62 *MLR* 609, 612.

home as security has been at the expense of protection of the surety and the imposition of a considerable burden on any legal adviser ...'.[331]

From a relational perspective, the question of third-party responsibility would be framed in terms of the relational norms between the third party and the unduly influenced claimant: that is, what is the nature and extent of the responsibility normatively owed by the creditor to the claimant in the particular context? The post-*Etridge (No 2)* position suggests that the prevailing norms for third-party responsibility in surety cases are limited to formulaic procedural protections. This is striking in light of what Wightman described as the shift from individual conduct to 'transactional risk' when *Etridge (No 2)* broadened the duty of inquiry to cover all cases of non-commercial suretyship.[332] While Wightman argued that the post-*Etridge* approach demonstrates greater cognisance of the unusually high risk that suretyships as a particular type of transaction create for one party (the surety),[333] the norms that surround the responsibilities corresponding to that risk are clearly procedural rather than substantive, justified with reference to the absence of 'wrongdoing' (in the traditional, rather than failure-to-meet-normative-standards sense) by the third party, and the policy desire to facilitate these transactions notwithstanding their high-risk nature and potentially disastrous consequences for vulnerable sureties. While it is no longer necessary to demonstrate 'wrongdoing' through constructive notice for the duty of inquiry to arise in these surety cases, the simple, formulaic guidance for avoiding third-party liability is clearly informed by the goal of enabling creditors, and solicitors, readily to get 'off the hook'. Thus, while the test is 'formally decoupled' from proof of wrongdoing,[334] in seeking to provide a safe and easy route through the process for creditors (rather than attempting to devise a form of protection which goes to the heart of the surety's transactional vulnerability) it implicitly reinforces the view that law's priority is to protect third parties against litigation.[335]

Wightman argued that the ease with which undue influence can be established is 'explicitly geared to the degree of apparent substantive unfairness'.[336] Yet when it comes to third-party liability, while the low threshold and clearly articulated responsibility respond to the idea of transactional risk, the content of that responsibility and the trade-off between *effective* norms of responsibility to address the specific vulnerability that has been recognised[337] and the desire to facilitate transactions, reveal a balance struck on the side of market freedom, through procedural safeguards rather than the substantive protection of the vulnerable party. Thus, while Chen-Wishart argued that the relational model 'shows why undue influence is and should be concerned with outcomes as much as processes',[338] this concern with outcomes slips out of view when the focus shifts from the doctrine itself to the question of third-party liability.

[331] Ibid, at 613.

[332] J Wightman, 'From individual conduct to transactional risk: some relational thoughts about unconscionability regulation' in Kenny *et al* (eds), above n 3.

[333] '[T]he nature of the transaction itself creates an increased risk that the claimant will suffer disadvantage ...': *ibid*, at 113.

[334] *Ibid*, at 115.

[335] And, by extension, to facilitate the use of the matrimonial home as an investment asset against which small businesses can seek capitalisation.

[336] Wightman, above n 332, at 121.

[337] '... because a guarantor who is truly under the influence of a stronger spouse will not be effectively protected by the measures proposed': Waddams, above n 36, at 35–36.

[338] Chen-Wishart, 'Vindicating Relationships of Influence', above n 120, at 266.

The features which Wightman identified as characteristic of contracts with transactional risk are clearly present in many of the housing equity transactions into which older owners enter, whether the transaction takes the form of a surety, a joint loan or bespoke joint mortgage product, or a tailored equity release product (which may release a lump sum that is then gifted to another, perhaps under undue influence). These are: first, that while the benefit to the claimant may be immediate, the claimant's own performance (that is, the possibility of losing his or her home) is postponed into the future; secondly, that the transaction bears

> a degree of transactional complexity which makes it more than usually difficult for the claimant to make an informed judgment about what is in their interests [and which] combined with the element of futurity … may mean, as in the non-commercial surety example, that the precise performance that will be required of the claimant may be contingent on uncertain events the occurrence of which is difficult to calculate at the time of entering the transaction;[339]

and, thirdly, that there is a 'clear disparity between the parties in terms of their experience of entering such transactions'.[340] These features are collectively identified as placing the claimant at a disadvantage in negotiating transactions,[341] and making it 'especially difficult' for 'one-shot players' to make good decisions in their best interests without advice.[342]

Wightman drew on behavioural economics to argue that law should respond to the difficulties individuals face in making (economically) 'rational' choices in circumstances of high transactional risk.[343] Wightman argued that relational theory offers the possibility of crafting a normative response to transactional risk which may be based on such an 'exchange morality'.[344] In applying this approach to housing equity transactions, it would be necessary to make judgements as to the appropriate balance between protecting potentially vulnerable parties and facilitating transactions, developed by reference to a contextualised 'big picture', including the policy arguments in favour of transactions as well as an understanding of the older owner as a legal subject and the (financial and non-financial) costs of adverse outcomes. By weighing the transaction in this way, it should be possible to reach a principled basis on which to balance the competing values at stake and to make appropriate judgements, for example as to whether the protection offered by the law should be procedural or substantive, and as to the nature of law's strategic policy position on the practice of older owners (as distinct from wives) using their housing equity to support others (usually younger family members), potentially in conflict with their own needs and in a policy context which emphasises financial self-reliance after retirement. Against this goal, the 'transactional risk' approach to surety

339 Wightman, above n 332, at 123.

340 *Ibid.*

341 '… because they are likely to be (at least initially) unaware of the existence or nature of pitfalls which are well understood by defendants': *ibid*, at 123.

342 *Ibid.*

343 Although he accepted that 'behavioural economics is not oriented to address the larger normative question of what obligations are owed when an organisation that is very familiar with the pitfalls (and opportunities for exploitation) of a particular transaction routinely deals with parties who are traversing those pitfalls for the first time; this is ultimately a question about the form of exchange morality which is to be expressed in the law': *ibid*, at 124.

344 *Ibid*, at 125–26; although this relational approach relies on an idea of 'acquired familiarity' amongst a contracting community which is not typical in older owners' housing equity transactions.

transactions in *Etridge (No 2)* remains underdeveloped so far as older owners (as opposed to surety wives) are concerned.

Meanwhile, the distinction between transactions (such as a suretyship) which are not on their face to the financial advantage of the claimant, and those (such as a joint loan, perhaps using a targeted product, such as the 'Lend a Hand' mortgage)[345] which may not take the form of a traditional surety/guarantee arrangement and where the balance of 'financial advantage' may not be obvious on the face of the transaction, may well be one of form rather than substance. However, to the extent that the *Etridge (No 2)* formulation is considered useful for the protection of sureties, this distinction is now significant. The proposition advanced in *CIBC Mortgages v Pitt*—that the bank is not put on inquiry when a loan appears on its face to be for joint purposes, and that the constructive notice principle does not require the bank to bear any substantive responsibility towards (potentially unduly influenced) claimants on the grounds that it would be inappropriate for the bank to pry into their personal affairs[346]—continues to govern all three-party transactions with the exception of non-commercial sureties.[347] It remains necessary for non-surety claimants to establish that the commercial party was 'put on inquiry' of undue influence. The application of the constructive notice test is, in turn, likely to be shaped by expectations of 'normalcy' regarding the transaction, and the case law concerning older owners indicates that the courts' attitude towards this question is built on shifting sands. Non-commercial sureties, in contrast, were identified as involving a particularly high level of risk for the surety (in light of the lack of financial advantage involved in putting one's home at risk for the debts of another), and so required the articulation of a set of 'core minimum requirements' which creditors and solicitors must satisfy for the avoidance of liability.[348] But while, on the one hand, *Etridge (No 2)* lowered the threshold at which creditors would be regarded as 'put on inquiry', it also diluted the responsibility this triggered for creditors from a potentially substantive obligation to discover for themselves whether there had been undue influence, or to require confirmation that the solicitor was satisfied that there had been no undue influence, to a formulaic, procedural approach of ensuring that independent advice is given to all sureties. For solicitors, the shift is from potentially being required to advise the surety about the wisdom of the transaction, to spelling out clearly the nature and effect of the transaction and the choice that the surety makes by agreeing to it.

There is limited evidence, post-*Etridge (No 2)*, to suggest that in cases involving older owners the courts are prepared to extend to third-party liability relational tests based on the explicability of the transaction and its adverse impact on the claimant, so requiring the third party to take substantive steps to discharge its responsibility towards the vulnerable claimant. In *Greene King plc v Stanley*,[349] the debtor's parents—at the time of the charge

345 See above, n 34 and associated text.

346 The suggestion that a creditor could be placed under a duty to make such inquiries was dismissed on the basis that it would amount to 'unwarrantable impertinence on the bank's part', and an undue burden on the bank, which 'is not to be treated as a branch of the social services agencies'; *Banco Exterior Internacional SA v Thomas* [1997] 1 WLR 221 at 230–31, *per* Scott VC.

347 'On the other side of the line is the case where money is being advanced, or has been advanced, to husband and wife jointly. In such a case the bank is not put on inquiry, unless the bank is aware the loan is being made for the husband's purposes, as distinct from their joint purposes. That was decided in *CIBC Mortgages Plc v Pitt* [1994] 1 AC 200': *Etridge (No 2)*, above n 40, at [48] *per* Lord Nicholls.

348 *Ibid*, at [87] *per* Lord Nicholls.

349 [2001] EWCA Civ 1966.

aged 68 and 70, and by the date of the court hearing aged 76 and 78—agreed to the use of their home as security for their son's business borrowings. Their son had misled them as to his own financial situation and the nature and extent of their liabilities (they believed that the debt would be discharged within two years, as they planned to release equity to supplement their pensions and so needed the property free from incumbrance when they were both 70). The county court found that there was a relationship of trust and confidence between the parents and their son, as a matter of fact, and that the relationship was 'of such a nature that it is fair to assume that the wrongdoer abused the relationship in procuring them to enter into the transaction'.[350] The county court also found that the parents were 'relatively naïve in financial matters', while their son 'showed rather greater financial acumen'.[351] While the parents had received independent legal advice, the solicitor advising them had not been fully informed of the nature of and reasons for the son's indebtedness, and had not given the parents a proper explanation of the document, leading the court to conclude that he had failed to live up to what was expected of adequate legal advice, and consequently that Greene King was tainted with constructive knowledge of the son's undue influence over his parents.

The adverse impact of the transaction on this older couple was clearly noted by the court, and was ultimately determinative in the decision to grant the appeal. One strand of the argument on appeal related to Greene King's decision to capitalise its security, notwithstanding the likely impact that losing their home would have on the Stanleys.[352] In the Court of Appeal, the appellants objected to a statement from the original judgment in which the judge noted that it was not clear why a large public company was seeking to make an couple in their seventies homeless, rather than 'simply sitting on their charge and waiting until such time as the Stanleys are no longer occupying the house, having either through death or through inability to cope in their own home vacated it'. The judge speculated that the creditor was perhaps seeking to make an example out of them, but concluded that regardless of the reason for seeking action, it was entitled to realise its security over the couple's home.[353] While the county court judge's comments were highlighted in the appeal to support the appellants' argument that the court should not in fact have allowed the creditor to force the sale of the property, the Court of Appeal dismissed this objection, emphasising that

> the judge was going out of his way to make clear that whatever sympathy he might feel for Mr and Mrs Stanley, whose home was at risk, and whatever doubts he might have as to the need for enforcement proceedings against them, he would not be deflected from the task of applying the law to the facts as he found them.[354]

In an interesting contrast, the impact of the adverse transaction *was* deemed relevant to the undue influence claim. The Court of Appeal held that the Stanleys had been subject to undue influence; that the transaction plainly called for an explanation; and that the charge was unenforceable against Greene King because it was affected by undue influence between the Stanleys and their son. Parker LJ held:

350 *Ibid*, at [48].
351 *Ibid*, at [49].
352 See ch 7 for discussion of the lack of weight conferred on the impact of repossession and forced sale in cases where older owners in default are threatened with enforcement actions against their homes.
353 *Greene King v Stanley*, above n 349, at [87].
354 *Ibid*, at [88].

> Quite apart from the fact that it was their home, the Property was Mr and Mrs Stanley's only significant asset. To put it up as security for a business venture by David Stanley was, it seems to me, to confer a gratuitous benefit on David Stanley far beyond that contemplated by Lindley LJ [in *Allcard v Skinner*].[355]

While it might be argued that, on a 'plain English' understanding of the word, the decision of parents to sacrifice their own well-being to benefit their son might be 'explicable', the Court was clearly concerned not only with the subjective motivations of the transaction but with its objective and contextual impacts on this financially vulnerable (having put their home at risk) older couple.

The Court of Appeal held that Greene King was automatically put on notice (according to the recently decided *Etridge (No 2)*), so that the decision turned on whether it had taken 'reasonable steps' to discharge its responsibility towards the Stanleys. Greene King did not arrange the advice, receive confirmation that advice had been given or inquire as to the result of any advice. Since, in fact, the advice received was not adequate, the Court held that Greene King remained fixed with constructive notice of the undue influence.[356] Although it was argued that Greene King had taken no steps to ensure that the risks of the charge were brought home to the Stanleys, Parker LJ concluded that the decision ultimately turned on the inadequacy of the advice, which was attributed back to Greene King, so that

> even assuming that GK is entitled to take advantage in this connection of the steps [taken by its agent], and of the advice given [by the solicitor] the manifest and serious deficiencies which the judge found to exist in the advice which Mr Townend in fact gave, and his own lack of information about the transaction, seem to me to put paid to the argument that the giving of that advice is an answer to the allegation of constructive knowledge.[357]

The proposition that, in a case involving an older owner, the perfunctory provision of independent advice might not be sufficient to let the creditor 'off the hook' was also recognised by Mr Justice Collins in *Radley v Bruno*,[358] in which the 95-year-old claimant sought to avoid a 99-year lease executed over her home at a peppercorn rent in favour of Mr Bruno, a former lodger who had moved into the claimant's home after her husband had died in order to look after her. The court recognised, following *Etridge (No 2)*:

> The most usual way to rebut the presumption of undue influence is to ensure that the complainant received independent legal advice, and it will generally be sufficient if the practical implications of the transaction have been brought home to the complainant in a meaningful way ... although it was there recognised ... that there might be exceptional circumstances in which it was glaringly obvious that the complainant was being seriously wronged, in which case the solicitor should cease to act.[359]

The argument that this was such a case—and the court's acceptance of this proposition a triable issue—suggests that (in cases where the facts are sufficiently strong) there may remain some avenues through which the relational norms of third-party responsibility applied to a specific case will be determined by contextual factors, including the age and

355 *Ibid*, at [106], *per* Parker LJ.
356 *Ibid*, at [54], quoting the county court judgment.
357 *Ibid*, at [116], *per* Parker LJ.
358 [2006] EWHC 2888 (Ch).
359 *Ibid*, at [29].

degree of vulnerability of the claimant. In the same case, it was also noted that in 'a number of cases independent advice has been given, but this has not been enough to rebut the presumption of undue influence',[360] suggesting, again, that in a case demonstrating a suitable factual matrix, there may still be scope—even after *Etridge (No 2)*—for a contextual assessment of vulnerability and responsibility to determine the issue of third-party liability for undue influence.

(ii) Two-party cases

As noted above, there may be cases in which the transaction (surety or non-surety) is not executed to benefit a relation or family member in a position to exercise undue influence, but where—although the transaction is ostensibly for the benefit of the older owner—the creditor/provider 'crosses the line' and is itself subject to a direct liability claim for undue influence. While the discussions in chapters eight and nine have analysed the consumer credit and FSA/OFT regulation of financial services contracts, it was noted that the courts have been sparing in their use of the consumer credit legislation to counter unfair terms, and there are significant gaps in the reach of the regulatory approach. This section briefly considers the extent to which the equitable doctrine of undue influence, particularly as it is understood within a relational framework, might serve to bolster the protection of vulnerable consumers, and to develop our understanding of the legal responsibilities imposed on commercial parties who contract with them.

There are relatively few examples of cases in which commercial parties have themselves been viewed as 'crossing the line',[361] although this remains a possible outcome where the facts are sufficiently strong to support such a claim. In *Tufton v Sperni*,[362] Lord Evershed MR held that there is no need for a prior relationship between the parties for the 'relationship of trust and confidence' to arise; it can emerge in the context of a one-off transaction. The circumstances in which this heightened duty may arise[363] are positioned at the 'fiduciary relationship' side of the undue influence doctrine: in *Etridge (No 2)*, Lord Hobhouse described undue influence as a wrong, which

> may be an overt wrong, such as oppression; or it may be the failure to perform an equitable duty, such as a failure by one in whom trust and confidence is reposed not to abuse that trust by failing to deal fairly with [the other party] and have proper regard to her interests..[364]

The content of the doctrine and the nature of the 'equitable duty' to which it gives rise were discussed above in section (2)(c)(ii), where Bigwood's characterisation of undue influence as responding to situations in which the defendant was deemed responsible for the claimant's vulnerability resonated with Lord Nicholls's description of cases involving a 'classically fiduciary relationship'.[365] Where the creditor/provider is directly implicated in such a relationship, it faces a heavier burden than that in three-party cases: rather than

[360] *Ibid*, at [30], *per* Collins J; citing *Pesticcio v Huet* [2004] EWCA Civ 372.

[361] Cases from other Commonwealth jurisdictions in which the bank was held to have 'crossed the line' include *Bank of Montreal v Hancock* (1982) 137 DLR (3d) 648 (Ontario High Court of Justice); and *National Australia Bank Ltd v Garcia* (1998) 194 CLR 395 (High Court of Australia).

[362] [1952] 2 *Times Law Reports* 516.

[363] 'in certain circumstances the parties will be taken to be in such a relationship that one will owe a duty of care and candour to the other', BAK Rider, 'A Special Relationship on the Special Facts' (1978) 41 *MLR* 585, 586.

[364] *Etridge (No 2)*, above n 40, at [107].

[365] *Ibid*, at [9], *per* Lord Nicholls.

simply providing advice that explains the nature of the transaction, the commercial party is itself required to emancipate the claimant from the undue influence. It is therefore unsurprising that the courts require very strong evidence that:

a) the claimant reposed trust and confidence in the commercial party; and
b) the commercial party abused that trust by failing to deal fairly with the claimant;

before they will be satisfied that a commercial party to a one-off transaction has crossed this line.

In *Lloyds' Bank Ltd v Bundy*,[366] sometimes cited as a case in which the direct relationship between the bank and the claimant (an older owner) was regarded as one of 'trust and confidence', where the bank incurred direct liability by 'crossing the line', it was the trust which Mr Bundy (the debtor's father) placed in the bank that formed the basis for the undue influence claim. In fact, *Lloyd's Bank v Bundy* is also well known as the decision in which Lord Denning propounded the (somewhat discredited) doctrine of 'inequality of bargaining power', in which he suggested that 'English law gives relief to one who, without independent advice, enters into a contract upon terms which are very unfair'.[367] The close relationship (and some have argued, overlap) between undue influence and unconscionable bargains has been much scrutinised by equity scholars[368]; and indeed in *Bundy*, Lord Denning attempted to link undue influence and unconscionability under the general thread of 'inequality of bargaining power'. This proposed category was considerably broader than the doctrine of undue influence as it has been delineated in this chapter, most particularly in its focus on the situational or contextual vulnerabilities of the claimant. Bigwood has argued that while undue influence is concerned with vulnerabilities brought about by a 'special relation' relative to the defendant—and so, in the case of direct liability of a commercial party, requires evidence that, through its actions in procuring the transaction, the commercial party 'crossed the line' to generate a fiduciary-type responsibility in its relationship with the claimant—unconscionable dealings are triggered by 'some social or transactional disabling condition unassociated (at least initially) with the defendant'.[369] The scope for protecting vulnerable older owners against 'unconscionable' housing equity transactions is considered in the next section of this chapter.

(3) Unconscionable Bargain Doctrine

The potential for employing the unconscionable bargain doctrine to respond to the contextual vulnerabilities of older owners in housing equity transactions was explored in Fox O'Mahony and Devenney's 'The Elderly, Their Homes and the Unconscionable

[366] [1974] 3 All ER 757.

[367] *Ibid*, at 765.

[368] See, eg, Birks and Chin, above n 8; D Capper, 'Undue influence and unconscionability: a rationalisation' (1998) 114 *LQR* 479; A Mason, 'The Place of Equity and Equitable Doctrines in the Contemporary Common Law World—an Australian Perspective' (1994) 110 *LQR* 238; A Phang, 'Undue Influence Methodology, Sources and Linkages' [1995] *Journal of Business Law* 552; A Phang, 'Economic Duress: Recent Difficulties and Possible Alternatives' (1997) 5 *Restitution Law Review* 53; L McMurtry, 'Unconscionability and Undue Influence: An Interaction' [2000] 64 *Conveyancer and Property Lawyer* 573; J Devenney and A Chandler, 'Unconscionability and the Taxonomy of Undue Influence' [2007] *Journal of Business Law* 541.

[369] Bigwood, above n 119, at 514.

Bargain Doctrine'.[370] This essay examined the relatively greater scope for the unconscionable bargain doctrine (compared to the doctrine of undue influence) to protect older owners, in light of its greater sensitivity to the contextual (as opposed to specifically 'relational') influences identified in chapter six of this book as a major source of vulnerability for older owners. The unconscionable bargain doctrine resonates, to some extent, with the 'defendant-sided' or 'unconscionability-based' approach to undue influence.[371] The scope for developing a protection based on the tropes of vulnerability and responsibility within a 'defendant-sided' approach to undue influence was demonstrated in section (2)(c)(ii) above. Yet the requirement of 'relational risk'[372] presents a significant limiting feature in the use of 'conventional' undue influence as a vehicle for protecting vulnerable older owners against adverse transactions resulting from situational (rather than inherent or relational) vulnerability. In contrast, the unconscionable bargain doctrine, with its concern for the objective (rather than relational) vulnerability of the claimant,[373] as well as its explicit emphases on context[374] and public policy considerations,[375] appears to provide a better doctrinal 'fit' for the development of an equitable framework within which to respond to substantively unfair housing equity transactions, by reflecting the reality of vulnerabilities rooted in the socio-economic and policy contexts of contemporary housing equity transactions.

While the unconscionable bargain doctrine—which, although described as a 'living fossil' in England and Wales,[376] remains extant[377]—is described by Capper as 'clearly capable of offering relief against unfair transactions',[378] it has rarely been employed in English courts since the nineteenth century.[379] The historical cases, which often involved

[370] L Fox O'Mahony and J Devenney, 'The Elderly, Their Homes and the Unconscionable Bargain Doctrine' in M Dixon (ed), *Modern Studies in Property Law*, vol 5 (Oxford, Hart Publishing, 2009).

[371] See Devenney and Chandler, above n 368.

[372] See Wightman, above n 332.

[373] See *Cresswell v Potter* [1978] 1 WLR 255.

[374] *Mrs U v Centre for Reproductive Medicine* [2002] EWCA Civ 565.

[375] *Mutual Finance v John Wetton & Sons Ltd* [1937] 2 KB 389.

[376] J Ross-Martyn, 'Unconscionable Bargains' (1971) 121 *New Law Journal* 1159; cf Australia and New Zealand, where the doctrine has undergone a 'renaissance', see Capper, above n 368, at 479. For an illustration of the Australian approach, see *Commercial Bank of Australia v Amadio* (1983) 151 CLR 447, in which an elderly couple with limited understanding of written English executed a mortgage securing the debts of their son's company, after their son has misled them as to the extent of their liability. The court applied the unconscionable dealing doctrine to find that if the couple could show that they were subject to a special disability which was evident to the bank, the burden was then on the bank to show why it was not unconscionable to enforce the charge. See also I Hardingham, 'The High Court of Australia and Unconscionable Dealing' (1984) 4 *OJLS* 275; A Finlay, 'Unconscionable Conduct and the Business Plaintiff: Has Australia Gone too Far?' [1999] *Anglo-American Law Review* 470; for a specific application of the Australian doctrine to older owners, see FR Burns, 'The Equitable Doctrine of Unconscionable Dealing and the Elderly in Australia' (2003) *29 Monash University Law Review* 336. Burns demonstrates that, even under a more developed and broadly-based independent doctrine of unconscionable dealing in Australia, it can be difficult for elders to prove 'special disadvantage' and 'knowing advantage-taking'.

[377] Capper, above n 368, at 479.

[378] *Ibid.*

[379] Some rare modern applications may be found in *Cresswell v Potter* [1978] 1 WLR 255, *Alec Lobb (Garages) Ltd v Total Oil (Great Britain) Ltd* [1983] 1 WLR 87, and *Multiservice Bookbinding v Marden* [1979] Ch 84. See also *Backhouse v Backhouse* [1978] 1 All ER 1158, where the doctrine was considered but not applied; and *Credit Lyonnais Bank Nederland NV v Burch* [1997] 1 All ER 144, where the possibility of a distinct doctrine invalidating unconscionable bargains was suggested (*obiter*). See also A Siopis, 'Unconscionable Bargains and General Principle' (1984) 100 *LQR* 523.

claimants who were viewed as acting under a 'disadvantage' due to poverty and ignorance,[380] old age and eccentricity,[381] mental weakness,[382] and recklessness and improvidence,[383] clearly emphasised the vulnerabilities of the claimant. The sources of vulnerability in these cases were both contextual (eg poverty) and internal to the vulnerable party; thus, in *Fry v Lane*, the effect of the doctrine was that 'where a purchase is made from a poor and ignorant man at a considerable undervalue, the vendor having no independent advice, a Court of Equity will set aside the transaction'.[384] The prejudicial impact of this historical terminology was addressed in *Cresswell v Potter*, where Megarry J indicated that 'the euphemisms of the 20th century may require the word "poor" to be replaced by "member of the lower income group" or the like, and the word "ignorant" by "less highly educated"'.[385] Furthermore, while the decisions in *Boustany v Piggott*[386] and *Portman Building Society v Dusangh*[387] indicated a need for misconduct on the part of the defendant,[388] it is not sufficient that the transaction is objectively harsh, unreasonable or foolish.[389] The transaction must also be 'oppressive', although the court has been prepared to infer this from the terms and context of the transaction where the facts are sufficiently extreme to support such an inference.[390]

While an overarching equitable concept of unconscionability has often been identified by the courts and discussed by commentators,[391] in *Lloyds' Bank v Bundy*, Lord Denning MR attempted to articulate an independent doctrine based on 'inequality of bargaining power'. Lord Denning claimed that

> English law gives relief to one who, without independent advice, enters into a contract upon terms which are very unfair or transfers property for a consideration which is grossly inadequate, when his bargaining power is grievously impaired by reason of his own needs or desires, or by his own ignorance or infirmity, coupled with undue influence or pressures brought to bear on him by or for the benefit of the other.[392]

[380] *Evans v Llewellin* (1787) 1 Cox 333; *Wood v Abrey* (1818) 3 Madd 417; *Garvey v McMinn* (1846) 9 Ir Eq Rep 526; *Clark v Malpas* (1862) 4 De GF & J 401; *Baker v Monk* (1864) 4 De GJ & S 386; *Fry v Lane* (1889) 40 Ch D 312; *Rae v Joyce* (1892) LR Ir 500; *Cresswell v Potter* [1978] 1 WLR 255; *Harry v Kreutziger* (1979) 95 DLR (3d) 231; *Commercial Bank of Australia Ltd v Amadio* (1983) 151 CLR 447; *Alec Lobb Garages Ltd v Total Oil (Great Britain) Ltd* [1985] 1 WLR 173; *Nichols v Jessup* [1986] 1 NZLR 226; *Woods v Hubley* (1995) 130 DLR (4d) 119); cited in Capper, above n 368.

[381] *Longmate v Ledger* (1860) 2 Giff 157; and in Ireland, *Lydon v Coyne* [1946] Irish Jurist Report 64; *Rooney v Conway* [1982] 5 Northern Ireland Judgements Bulletin; see Capper, above n 368.

[382] *Grealish v Murphy* [1946] *Irish Reports* 35; *Blomley v Ryan* (1956) 99 CLR 362; *Buckley v Irwin* [1960] *Northern Ireland Law Reports* 98; *Louth v Diprose* (1992) 175 CLR 621; *Boustany v Pigott* (1995) 69 P & CR 298; see Capper, above n 368.

[383] *Slator v Nolan* (1876) IR 11 Eq 367; *Howley v Cook* (1873) IR 8 Eq 570; *Butler v Miller* (1867) IR 1 Eq 195; although Capper argued that these Irish cases are 'remarkable' in light of the stated principle that the law does not protect people from their folly: Capper, above n 368.

[384] (1889) 40 Ch D 312 at 322.

[385] [1978] 1 WLR 255 at 257, *per* Megarry J; see Fox O'Mahony and Devenney, above n 370, at 281.

[386] (1995) 69 P & CR 298 at 303, *per* Lord Templeman.

[387] [2000] EWCA Civ 142.

[388] *Alec Lobb (Garages) Ltd v Total Oil (Great Britain) Ltd* [1983] 1 WLR 87 at 94, *per* Peter Millett, QC.

[389] See also *Multiservice Bookbinding v Marden* [1979] Ch 84 at 110, *per* Browne-Wilkinson J.

[390] See, eg, *Fry v Lane* (1889) 40 ChD 312; and more recently, *Credit Lyonnais Nederland NV v Burch* [1997] 1 All ER 144.

[391] Described by Delany and Ryan as a 'unifying thematic touchstone in equitable intervention', see H Delany and D Ryan, 'Unconscionability: a unifying theme in equity' [2008] *Conveyancer & Property Lawyer* 401; Waddams identified unconscionability as the general principle behind undue influence and duress, S Waddams, *The Law of Contracts*, 3rd edn (Toronto, Law Book Co, 1993) ch 14.

[392] [1975] QB 326 at 339.

While Lord Denning's doctrine of inequality of bargaining power has been discredited,[393] Capper has argued that its three core features—inequality in the bargaining positions of the parties, transactional imbalance, and unconscionable conduct by the defendant—are sufficiently shared by undue influence to justify merging the two doctrines. Bigwood has similarly argued that undue influence and unconscionable dealing share a conceptual identity,[394] so bolstering his 'defendant-sided' analysis of undue influence as oriented around unconscionable conduct on the part of the defendant, which need not be overt but may be framed as an obligation or responsibility that is 'almost like a duty to take reasonable care to ensure that the claimant fully understands the implications of the transactions and thus fully consents to it'.[395] Bigwood has also argued that the unconscionable bargain doctrine could be better referred to by the 'gentler badge' sometimes used of 'unconscientious dealing'; and that, consistent with his analysis of undue influence, it should be based on a concept of 'transactional neglect' rather than requiring deliberate exploitation on the part of the defendant.[396]

Yet, notwithstanding its potential value in targeting the particular issues identified in this book as likely to lead to substantive unfairness in older owners' transactions, unconscionable dealing remains a relatively unfamiliar ground of relief in English law. For example, in *Portman Building Society v Dusangh*,[397] the Court of Appeal held that there was nothing unconscionable in the grant of a 25-year repayment mortgage to a 72-year-old man to support a loan to his son to set up a supermarket business: 'I simply cannot accept that building societies are required to police transactions of this nature to ensure that parents (even poor and ignorant ones) are wise in seeking to assist their children.'[398] Similarly, in *Jones v Morgan*,[399] the court held that it was not unconscionable for a stockbroker to lend an unsophisticated farmer £105,000 in exchange for 15 per cent interest plus a 50 per cent share in his company. Contemporary English courts appear to depart from other jurisdictions, and from the historical line of cases, in the extent of the wrong-doing required on the part of the defendant: the modern cases suggest that the defendant must have effectively imposed the contract on the claimant if equitable relief under this head is to be made available. For example, the three elements of 'unconscionability' set out in *Alec Lobb (Garages) Ltd v Total Oil (Great Britain) Ltd*,[400] were that:

a) one party was at a serious disadvantage to the other, 'whether through poverty, or ignorance, or lack of advice, or otherwise, so that circumstances existed of which unfair advantage could be taken';
b) that this weakness was exploited in a morally culpable manner; and
c) that the resulting transaction was 'not merely hard or improvident, but overreaching and oppressive'[401];

[393] The attempt to establish a general principle of inequality of bargaining power was rejected by the House of Lords in *National Westminster Bank plc v Morgan* [1985] AC 686.

[394] Bigwood, above n 52, at 438; see also R Bigwood, 'Conscience and the Liberal Conception of Contract: Observing Basic Distinctions (Part II)' (2000) 16 *Journal of Contract Law* 191, 221.

[395] Capper, above n 3, at 181.

[396] Bigwood, above n 10, at 93.

[397] Above n 281, discussed in sections (2)(b) and (2)(d).

[398] [2000] 2 All ER (Comm) 221, [2000] EWCA Civ 142.

[399] [2001] EWCA Civ 995.

[400] [1983] 1 WLR 87.

[401] *Ibid*, at 94–95.

thus suggesting that the impropriety that 'shocks the conscience of the court' must exist not only in the conduct of the stronger party but also in the terms of the transaction.

Capper has argued that English courts appear reluctant to return to the 'true nature of unconscionable dealing',[402] a move which he views as 'probably explicable in terms ... [of] the fear of opening the floodgates of discretion'.[403] The high threshold for unconscionability reflects, once again, the pull of the liberal model of contract, with its emphasis on the choices 'freely' made by legal subjects whose (present) 'autonomy' must be respected by giving effect to their bargains, however ill-advised, and regardless of the realities of transactional constraints on both their choices and their autonomy to select from within available choices. The concept of constrained choice was recognised in the historical case law: in one eighteenth-century case, the court recognised that 'necessitous men are not, truly speaking, free men, but, to answer a present exigency, will submit to any terms that the crafty may impose on them'.[404] Waddams argued that while even the historical doctrine of unconscionable bargain responded only to exceptional cases, so that 'the mere fact of a bargain being *unreasonable* ... [was] not a ground to set it aside in equity',[405] the 'fraud' that was required on the part of the defendant included 'unconscientious use of the power arising out of these circumstances and conditions'.[406]

Waddams's analysis of the historical case law also highlighted the particular tendency for equity to intervene in contracts for loans where the need for money was immediate and pressing and the claimant's proprietary interest was transferred for an undervalue. Indeed, there are some parallels to be found between cases involving 'expectant heirs' who borrowed against a future interest, and the modern housing equity transaction which promises to release cash now in exchange for security over, or title to, the property, under an arrangement whereby the occupier continues to live in the property (for the time being at least). In the 'expectant heir' cases, the unconscionable bargain doctrine was invoked to

> set aside the transaction unless the purchaser proved that he had given full value [because] the situation is one in which experience shows that a person, pressed with the immediate need for money, is apt to sell a future interest at an undervalue—sometimes at a gross undervalue: again, the need for money is immediate, and the interest given up seems remote.[407]

These features appear to suggest that the doctrine might provide a useful vehicle through which to seek to develop a more responsive and responsible approach to the contextual vulnerabilities of marginal older owners, not least by recognising the 'normality' of behavioural decision-making that might be viewed as 'irrational' within the classical liberal model. Waddams argued that the inequality of an exchange could entitle the court to 'presume, without any separate proof, that the disadvantaged party must have been labouring under some sort of mistake or disability, or else must have been influenced by necessity, or by some sort of pressure, or by a relationship with the stronger party',[408]

[402] Capper, above n 3, at 182.

[403] *Ibid.*

[404] *Vernon v Bethell* (1762) 2 Eden 110, 113.

[405] S Waddams, 'Protection of weaker parties in English law' in Kenny *et al* (eds), above n 3, at 28.

[406] F Pollock, *Principles of Contract at Law and in Equity* (London, Stevens & Sons, 1876) 154, quoting Hobbes, *Leviathan* (1660) Part 1, ch 15; quoted in Waddams, above n 405, at 29.

[407] Waddams, above n 405, at 32.

[408] *Ibid*, at 34; referring to *Earl of Chesterfield v Janssen* (1751) 2 Ves Sen 125; *Heathcote v Paignon* (1787) 2 Bro CC 167.

suggesting that the substantive disadvantage experienced by a claimant could itself provide evidence of 'wrongdoing' on the part of the defendant.

Yet at the same time, the balance may be countered by the fact that the 'explanation' which is called for by the inequality of the bargain might be provided by the inherent risk of the transaction.[409] Indeed, as the case law applying the CCA 1974 (as amended by the CCA 2006) has demonstrated,[410] when modern legal frameworks allow scope for consideration of the circumstances and risks on the lender's side, this can readily outweigh considerations of the claimant's vulnerability, combined with the power of policy considerations in favour of facilitating commercial transactions. This has meant, when claimants have attempted to argue that 'surety wives' transactions are 'unconscionable bargains', that once the public policy issues are weighed in the balance they outweigh the vulnerabilities of the individual parties.[411] Applying this doctrine to housing equity transactions would, in turn, raise a distinct set of policy considerations, which are likely to be determined not least by the nature of the transaction under scrutiny—which may either be one which facilitates the Government's policy agenda concerning housing equity use after retirement, or one which operates against this agenda, by 'dissipating' housing equity so that it becomes unavailable for these policy-led uses. Lastly, contemporary analyses of the doctrine have also identified the risks of associating vulnerability with weakness or paternalism (for example, in relation to surety wives), although the discussion in chapter six has demonstrated how feminist legal theory can be applied to negotiate through these issues.

Arguments in support of a revived (and wider)[412] doctrine of unconscionability generally draw on the tropes identified in the undue influence and unconscionability case law (Capper identified three elements of unconscionability: relational inequality, transactional imbalance, and unconscionable conduct[413]; Waddams identified threads of inadequate consent, wrongdoing, unjust enrichment and policy influences),[414] although views differ as to whether the doctrine would be primarily procedural or substantive in its focus. Capper argued that the expanded doctrine of unconscionability would be 'more concerned with procedural than with substantive unfairness' on the basis that 'Substantive unfairness is not likely to become an independent ground of invalidity so long as courts maintain the approach that they cannot make or remake a contract for the parties.'[415] While this pragmatic perspective undoubtedly has the advantage of 'swimming with the tide', it remains questionable whether, in situations of contextual vulnerability and constrained choice, a procedural fairness strategy based on the information paradigm provides an adequate response to the risks faced by vulnerable consumers. For Waddams, on the other hand, the reasons for developing a general doctrine of unconscionability

[409] *Mortimer v Capper* (1782) 1 Bro CC 156.

[410] See ch 8, section (7).

[411] 'From the public policy point of view difficult questions arise: is it an essential aspect of freedom that persons should have unrestricted power to borrow money on the security of their assets, or are some restraints acceptable or desirable, and if so what restraints, and on whom, and in respect of what assets?': Waddams, above n 405, at 36.

[412] Capper, above n 368.

[413] *Ibid*, at 500.

[414] S Waddams, 'Unconscionable Contracts: Competing Perspectives' (1999) 62 *Saskatchewan Law Review* 1; see also Waddams, above n 405.

[415] Capper, above n 368, at 501. Capper added that 'If a contract is substantively unfair, the obvious solution would be to alter it to make it fair, but with some very limited exceptions English law does not do this.' (*ibid*).

included the scope for such a doctrine to shift the focus of contractual enforceability away from classical 'consent' models, and to introduce a substantive fairness element to enforceability tests, recognising, for example, the realities of constrained choice wherein even a 'valid consent' may not indicate 'true assent'.[416]

In this vein, it is interesting to recall that the historical unconscionable bargain doctrine cases allowed relief where an improvident bargain resulted from what might now be described as 'mis-buying' rather than 'mis-selling'.[417] Yet while Waddams argued that the extent to which a court is willing to set aside agreements for unconscionability reflects its commitment to the egalitarian values of the welfare State,[418] and its acceptance of a 'duty' to relieve the most vulnerable members of its society from very disadvantageous contracts,[419] he claimed that it is important to recognise the limitations of private law, and specifically contract law, in addressing inequalities.[420] The 'practical' benefits of private law strategies are, of course, limited by a range of factors, including the requirement that the injured party take formal action, barriers to which are higher for vulnerable (older, marginal) consumers. As the discussion in the introduction to this chapter noted, contract law or equitable relief is often viewed as operating in the margins, not least because a strategy which offers only the possibility of cure is not likely to be viewed as a 'mainstream' solution for older people at risk of losing substantial financial assets and the roof over their heads, and for whom prevention of harm presents a significantly preferable strategy.[421]

Nevertheless it remains arguable, particularly in light of the inevitable gaps in the regulatory protections discussed in chapter nine, that there is still some potential for equitable doctrines—if appropriately framed—to play a role in relieving vulnerable litigants. This relief is, in the immediate sense, limited to those individuals who litigate, although it is important not to underestimate the function of (even private) law in disciplining parties towards particular relational norms, as well as shaping social norms through its expressive function.[422] The 'benefits' of developing appropriate legal approaches to respond to vulnerability and hold those deemed 'responsible' to account are not, therefore, exclusive to successful litigants but are likely to ripple through our understandings of social issues and the normative frameworks within which we seek to resolve competing claims. For this reason, Waddams's argument that 'the beneficiaries of the relief that contract law can give are rarely the very poor. They are people with

[416] Waddams, above n 405, at 36. For a discussion of the arguments in support of a substantive fairness test to determine the enforceability of contracts, see ch 4, section (4)(a).

[417] In *Earl of Aylesford v Morris* (1873) LR 8 Ch App 484, relief was granted even though the plaintiff 'comes into court to be relieved from the consequences of a course of very wilful and culpable folly and extravagance' (at 499, *per* Lord Selbourne).

[418] R Brownsword, G Howells and T Wilhelmsson (eds), *Welfarism in Contract Law* (Aldershot, Dartmouth, 1994); E Posner, 'Contract Law in the Welfare State: A Defense of the Unconscionability Doctrine, Usury Laws, and Related Limitations on Freedom of Contract' (1994) 24 *Journal of Legal Studies* 283; Waddams (1999), above n 414.

[419] Waddams, above n 405, at 40.

[420] Waddams argued that contract law is not a satisfactory tool for redistribution of wealth because 'Its scope of operation is restricted, on the whole, to granting relief to those who happen to have entered into disadvantageous contracts …' (*ibid*, at 40) and at most the relief it offers is to restore the *status quo*.

[421] Waddams also pointed to contract law's focus on individual transactions rather than the parties' overall wealth—that it is not a mechanism for redistribution of wealth more generally—as a limitation of private law strategies to address social inequality.

[422] See, eg, CR Sunstein, 'On the Expressive Function of Law' (1995) 144 *University of Pennsylvania Law Review* 2021.

something to lose, and with the means and energy to seek to regain it …'[423] overlooks the broader significance of contract law's approaches to issues that potentially affect vulnerable parties.

Indeed, Waddams himself recognised this dimension when he traced the transplantation of a concept of 'unconscionability' from the equitable jurisdiction to broader protective regimes, including the EU Draft Common Frame of Reference, which seeks to lay the groundwork for what may become a common contract code incorporating common law and civil law approaches.[424] If it is true that European developments for harmonisation are reshaping the paradigm of the private law subject, as the presumptive priority often given to consent, autonomy, enforceability and commercial interests in English law is tempered by greater concern for social justice in some European jurisdictions, these initiatives may provide a bridge between the 'limited' reach of the traditional equitable doctrines for vitiating contracts in English law and a broader strategy to address substantive unfairness. To this end, analyses which identify the theoretical, doctrinal, policy and practical bases for protecting vulnerable parties are likely to play an important role in informing the accompanying normative debates.

(4) Conclusions

Older owners' housing equity transactions raise a range of legal issues, and these are addressed in different ways by property law, provisions that seek to regulate contractual terms, financial services regulation, and through the equitable doctrines of undue influence and (to a very limited extent) the unconscionable bargain. The equitable doctrines may, in principle at least, be instrumental in determining the validity of the transaction, but relief under these heads depends in large degree on the claimant's willingness and capacity to pursue litigation, and—significantly for older people—does not *prevent* harm from occurring, although the extent of the relief may be considerable where the transaction is avoided and the roof overhead recovered.[425] The equitable doctrines have an important role to play, both in the specific circumstances to which they apply and as part of a bigger picture in which older owners are implicitly characterised as legal subjects.

The specific value of undue influence as a safety-net for older owners depends on the court's response to the particular factual matrix in any given case, as it maps against the doctrinal frameworks developed by various scholars. While Birks and Chin's 'claimant-sided' analysis of undue influence provides an awkward fit for the understanding of vulnerability and responsibility developed in this book, Bigwood's theory of transactional neglect, and to a greater extent Chen-Wishart's hybrid relational theory approach to the doctrine, offer considerably greater scope for both the provision of specific relief, and the development of a concept of undue influence that reflects the meaning of contextual vulnerability for older owners and a theoretically underpinned approach to a corresponding responsibility on the part of market actors who transact with them. The impact of

[423] Waddams, above n 405, at 41.

[424] See A Somma (ed), *The Politics of the Draft Common Frame of Reference* (Leiden, The Netherlands, Kluwer Law International, 2009).

[425] In contrast to relief under the regulatory regime, equitable relief offers the possibility of avoiding the contract and so retaining housing as home, rather than merely providing compensation for loss of the home.

relational norms on the judicial development of undue influence is particularly evident in the 'explicability' test, especially as it has been applied to transactions involving older owners. The perceived 'normalcy' of the transaction was also a significant factor in the application of the constructive notice test for third-party liability, whereby the commercial party is 'put on inquiry', or not, depending on whether the transaction raises the suspicion of an equitable wrong.

While the constructive notice test continues to apply to non-surety transactions, following the decision in *Etridge (No 2)*, all non-commercial suretyships put the creditor 'on inquiry', in recognition of the high level of transactional risk associated with putting one's home at risk for the benefit of another. This formally recognises that the creditor bears a responsibility towards the potentially vulnerable surety in this type of transaction; yet, in what was clearly a policy-based strategy to facilitate the use of the home as security for business debts (in the context of 'surety wives' at least), the nature and extent of that responsibility is procedural, formulaic and designed to enable creditors easily to 'offload' responsibility onto solicitors—who in turn are instructed in the steps to take to discharge the transferred responsibility. Indeed, the House of Lords recognised that the approach set out in *Etridge (No 2)* may well be ineffective in countering the claimant's vulnerability. It is, however, worth bearing in mind that while the leading cases in this context have been concerned with (and shaped by the policy issues raised in) transactions involving 'surety wives', housing equity transactions raise a distinct set of policy considerations, including the impact of adverse transactions on both the individual claimant and the welfare State on which that individual is likely to fall back once his or her owned assets have been dissipated.

There are several avenues through which the current landscape of equitable remedies for older owners might develop, as the issues raised in the context of housing equity transactions are likely to garner increasing attention in the years to come. One possibility is that the court's application of undue influence doctrine—and particularly of the principles for determining third-party liability—in cases involving older owners' housing equity transactions will move away from the 'surety wives' approach, in recognition of the different order of risk and the distinctive policy issues surrounding the transaction. There are hints of this possibility in cases such as *Greene King v Stanley* and *Radley v Bruno*[426]; the development of this line of argument may depend, in part at least, on the effective articulation of the policy issues at stake in these transactions, the acceptance of older owners as a contextually vulnerable population, and the recognition of a corresponding responsibility on the part of those who seek to enter housing equity transactions with them. A second avenue might involve greater use of the unconscionable bargain doctrine, although, as noted above, and as in the case of undue influence, the effectiveness of this strategy is likely to depend on the willingness of the courts to recognise the distinctive issues raised by these transactions, and to develop a response which strikes a new balance between the commercial party and the potentially vulnerable claimant. Again, the development of a theoretical framework and evidence base against which older owners may be identified as potentially vulnerable subjects (as opposed to self-responsible neoliberal consumers), and which leverages an understanding of both the risk context and the harm that flows from adverse transactions effectively to challenge the 'freedom-oriented'

[426] See discussion in section (2)(e)(i).

contractual norms that prioritise commercial claims and enforceability, may have a role to play in the evolution of a new discourse around the use of equitable remedies in this context.

Other possibilities have been suggested by commentators, including, notably, Fiona Burns, who presented a range of options for the development of a comprehensive approach to older people's vulnerabilities to intergenerationally-transmitted debt. These included invoking the knock-on effects of adverse transactions on the policy of self-provision in retirement, to justify a ban on older owners (or at least the very old, aged 80–85 or older, who are most vulnerable) standing surety[427]; to limit the liability of an older owner under any suretyship or guarantee to a fixed amount or a fixed proportion of the older person's assets; and/or to prohibit the use of the occupied home as security for a relative or caregiver's liabilities.[428] This echoes the debate concerning use of the family home to secure business debts in the 'surety wives' context, although, as has been noted, the policy arguments surrounding use of the older owner's home—particularly in light of expectations concerning housing equity use for the older person's own needs,[429] and the lack of opportunity older owners have to recover from financial setbacks—seem likely to tilt more strongly in favour of preservation of the home in this context.

Alternative strategies proposed by Burns included the development of specific, 'before-the-fact' procedural protections (for example, full and frank disclosure of risk, including the borrower's ability to repay) for surety transactions. Furthermore, perhaps with a view to reducing the risk of 'equity lending' (where the bank is happy to rely on the security even though enforcement of that security could ruin the older person), Burns proposed a 'property' solution in the form of a ban on enforcement where the property is the older person's family home, until the older person no longer needs to live there (dies or moves into care, as in home reversions/lifetime mortgages); although she acknowledged that even the existence of a charge against the property could adversely affect the older owner's ability to make decisions in his or her own interest, for example to move house or to sell, because remaining equity after satisfying creditors will be insufficient to meet his or her needs.[430]

One fundamental issue to address if the equitable remedies are usefully to be developed as a 'safety-net' for older owners relates to the idea that adverse transactions which do not involve explicit 'wrongdoing' should be dismissed as 'folly' on the part of the claimant, against which English law does not protect. This well-worn proposition is challenged by a clearer understanding of the nature of older owners' vulnerabilities[431] and the development of a more realistic model of legal subjectivity[432] than that on which the liberal model of contract law has been based. If English courts are indeed shifting from an individual conduct model towards a transactional risk approach to undue influence in the wake of *Etridge (No 2)*, then a contextually informed analysis could usefully draw on the normative foundations articulated in this book.

[427] F Burns, 'Legally regulating intergenerationally transmitted debt', above n 31, at 48; Burns recognised that this strategy would potentially raise issues of age discrimination.

[428] *Ibid*, at 48–49.

[429] *Ibid*, at 49.

[430] *Ibid*.

[431] See ch 6.

[432] See chs 4 and 6.

Conclusion

The growing trend for the use of housing equity to support a range of activities and needs raises complex issues, particularly for older owners. In a policy context which pushes older owners towards housing equity transactions to meet income and welfare costs, the options and products now available offer a bewildering range of opportunities, which 'self-responsible' owners must negotiate through the choices they make. The idea of home equity as a resource to spend in later life raises important questions concerning the legal frameworks of regulation and remedies surrounding various types of housing equity transaction, from 'trading down' and 'ordinary' secured and unsecured debt to targeted products including reverse/lifetime mortgages, home reversion plans and SRB agreements. This book has attempted to address these questions using a problem-led approach, which has drawn upon a range of theoretical, doctrinal, empirical and policy perspectives to locate the issues raised by housing equity transactions within contemporary socio-legal and political contexts.

The tensions between neoliberal policy ideals that construct older owners (particularly marginal older owners living in lower-value properties) as autonomous, self-responsible legal subjects, and their experiences as vulnerable consumers, are only exacerbated by the complexities of the housing paradigms (housing as home, housing as inheritance, housing as investment-asset-to-spend) they must negotiate as a result of their status as 'owners', and as financial and risk subjects. In evaluating the relationships between the risks which older consumers must negotiate as 'self-responsible consumers' and the nature and extent of legal protections against adverse outcomes, the book has sought to evaluate the extent to which the landscape of legal protection maps appropriately onto a range of vulnerabilities in financial transactions associated with age, including capacity, financial capability, contextual or 'situational vulnerabilities', and the disproportionate impact of financial losses for older consumers. Against the backdrop of this vulnerability analysis, the book has attempted to analyse the nature and extent of legal protections for older consumers in the UK, as they have separately developed through fairness provisions in contract and consumer credit law (for example, the Unfair Terms in Consumer Contract Regulations), through the FSA's regulatory regime, through property law and through the equitable remedies of undue influence and the unconscionable bargain doctrine.

A core question considered throughout the book concerns the conceptualisation of the older owner as a legal subject. Fineman's theory of vulnerable legal subjects offers a useful framework through which to critique the incorporation (or not) of contextual factors into the legal frameworks through which these transactions are governed, as a measure of the 'appropriateness' of existing legal provision, and the arguments surrounding 'special protection', for example the development of the lender's/provider's duty of care towards (certain categories of) borrower/consumer, for older owners in housing equity transactions. By employing Fineman's approach, this book seeks to develop a theoretical framework for protecting vulnerable consumers in financial transactions which moves away from the autonomy/no autonomy debate, or models of 'skilled' or 'flawed' consumers. Rather, it focuses on the impact of external factors resulting from older owners' situations within broader socio-economic, political and market contexts on their legal subjectivity, including their capabilities and vulnerabilities in financial transactions. Recognising that these contexts are both indicative and determinative of vulnerability in financial transactions, the book seeks to examine the responsibilities of legal and financial institutions to address the harms that result from adverse transactions.

To do so, it has been helpful to map the range of legal responses against the discursive axes of vulnerability and responsibility. The prominence, presence or absence of norms that reflect the older owner's vulnerability, or which hold the commercial party responsible for the 'safety' of the transaction, varies according to the type of housing equity transaction (conventional mortgage, unsecured debt, equity release), as well as the circumstances in which the dispute arises (validity or enforcement) and the nature of the complaint (for example, procedural or substantive unfairness). While chapter seven has demonstrated the absence of these tropes from property law discourse concerning housing equity transactions, chapter nine has shown how they have come to the fore in the arena of financial regulation, particularly following the most recent financial crisis. These differences in perspective are significant, not least because the choice of financial product by which older owners use their housing equity determines the 'arena' in which the transaction will be regulated, and this in turn is likely to be constrained by the choices available to the individual consumer, based on credit history, assets held, state of indebtedness at the time of the transaction and so on, determining whether he or she is labelled a 'prime' or 'marginal' consumer.

It is not yet clear how changing patterns of mortgage equity withdrawal across the life-course will affect the housing equity transactions of older owners in the coming decades. As the practice of releasing equity—both during working lives and in retirement—is primed for growth, the norms and expectations underlying legal responses to these transactions will become increasingly central to the welfare and well-being of older people. With this in mind, the case for conceptualising these norms in coherent and considered channels seems clear. Recent discourse in the arena of financial services regulation provides an interesting insight into the evolution of normative perspectives on the vulnerability of consumers, and the extent to which credit providers and regulators are held to have corresponding responsibilities. Yet the regulatory response to older owners' housing equity transactions has addressed only a limited category of transactions; and even in those areas which have been regulated (lifetime mortgage and home reversion markets), the view that the markets now generally work well for most consumers does not (nor does it seek to) specifically consider the needs of older owners at the margins of these markets, who embark on equity release transactions in circumstances of financial pressure or where it does not form part of a rationally planned strategy for financial well-being in retirement.

The FSA has recognised that marginal older consumers are susceptible to the same types of consumer risk (situational vulnerability in the decision-making process and disproportionate impact of detriment) in equity release transactions as SRB consumers, yet the nature and extent of the protections attendant on the transaction are determined by the product risk. This means that when these marginal owners purchase equity release products (a significant proportion of whom do),[1] the transaction is regulated according to a perception of vulnerability based on a *proportion* of the consumer base, rather than the particular consumer. While FSA research into the lifetime mortgage market has found that while current regulatory protections have had little effect, the market 'works well for most customers most of the time';[2] this is attributed not to the legal framework surrounding these transactions, but to the belief that majority of lifetime consumers conduct extensive personal research, weigh up the benefits and disadvantages of products, and discuss the decision with family members. Yet this reliance on consumer self-protection raises questions concerning the adequacy of the protections for those lifetime mortgage consumers who do not fit the model of capable consumers making planned equity withdrawals.[3] For vulnerable consumers—who are also likely to have less financial cushioning to fall back on[4]—the measure of adverse impact could be significant. Furthermore, these impacts include both financial and non-financial costs for older owners themselves, and system costs: for the market when perceptions of equity release as 'high-risk' are reinforced, and for the State when older people 'lose' the assets through which they were expected to self-provide.

More rigorous regulation and other forms of legal protection inevitably raise the issue of costs on the provider side, although it has been accepted as a matter of principle within the regulatory sphere that these costs are justified in the interests of the market (including market confidence) where the transaction is sufficiently 'high risk' and/or the consumer can be identified as 'vulnerable', so that responsibility for the appropriateness of the transaction shifts from the 'self-responsible' consumer to the commercial party seeking to profit from participation in this market, through the intervention of the regulators charged with ensuring that the balance of risk between consumers and providers remains appropriate. With this principle in mind, it is important, when evaluating the appropriateness of various legal protections across housing equity transactions, to ensure that the spectre of market costs does not close off the debate so that the occurrence and impact of losses for vulnerable older owners are ignored or dismissed. Rather, the vulnerabilities and responsibilities of the parties should be properly balanced in a principled and—in light of the importance of these transactions and post-retirement assets more generally for current government policies—policy-sensitive way.

While the concept of responsibility is increasingly identified as a regulatory norm, a question remains as to how—if at all—it might be possible to embed the ideas of vulnerability and responsibility—in the specific context of housing equity transactions—in broader legal discourses. Where the transaction falls within the realm of contract law, strategies that might flow from the vulnerability/responsibility analysis include challenges to the liberal legal norms that have shaped the 'self-responsibility' norms in that context, including the paradigm of the liberal legal subject. As the discussion in chapter four has demonstrated, a significant body of scholarship has sought to reflect a more realistic model of legal subjectivity within contract law norms. The

[1] The consumer base for equity release in the UK is heterogeneous: the financial circumstances of owners range from those who are finding it difficult to get by to those who are living comfortably; see L Overton, *Housing and Finance in Later Life: A Study of UK equity release customers* (London, Age UK, 2010).

[2] FSA, *Mortgage Effectiveness Review, Stage 2 Report* (London, FSA, 2008); online at <http://www.fsa.gov.uk/pubs/other/MER2_report.pdf>.

[3] See discussion in ch 9.

[4] See ch 1.

arguments for such developments include—as in the regulatory context—not only the impact of the adverse outcome on the vulnerable party but the policy agenda that relies on older owners entering into (good value) housing equity transactions for particular purposes (arguably, for example, to meet their own welfare needs rather than to support younger relatives and friends). In contrast to the 'surety wives' cases, where the policy driver to facilitate transactions is concerned with encouraging creditors to lend on the security of the family home, in the case of housing equity transactions, the driver is to encourage older owners to release their equity and so to 'self-provide' for their welfare needs. This distinction also underlines the 'moral hazard' issues discussed in chapter three, relating to the actions of both the commercial party and the consumer: in a context where the dissipation of housing equity in adverse transactions is likely to lead directly to the consumer falling back on welfare provision (as opposed to participating in the labour market to generate further financial resource), an excessively 'free market' produces incentives for both parties to take unjustified risks; which in turn will create costs for the welfare system and so undermine broader policy goals.[5] Indeed, Posner has argued that 'restrictive contract doctrines are appropriate means for deterring this socially costly behaviour'.[6]

As well as presenting an alternative model of legal subjectivity for older owners (which has been carefully crafted to avoid ageist or paternalistic overtones), this book has explored various ways in which this model might be implemented within the relevant principles and provisions applicable to housing equity transactions. Overarching the arguments for (what broadly speaking represents the prevailing current approach of) non-intervention is the classical commitment to 'freedom of contract'. Yet the arguments advanced in this book resonate with a growing movement within ('Europeanised') contract law scholarship, which challenges the 'freedom' approach as it has conventionally been understood. For example, Colombi Ciacchi has argued that the principle of 'unconscionability' should be understood not as an 'exception' to the overarching pursuit of 'freedom of contract'. Rather, she posited, we must understand freedom *from* unconscionable contracts as a mainstream element of the goals of contract law.[7] Colombi Ciacchi argued that fairness, solidarity and social justice considerations do not conflict with freedom of contract but are part of a modern, substantive understanding of freedom of contract which challenges the old formal understanding, just as substantive models of equality have replaced the outdated concept of 'formal equality'.[8]

This model of contract law allows significantly greater scope for consideration of the risk involved in particular types of transaction, the contextual constraints under which

[5] See E Posner, 'Contract Law in the Welfare State: A Defense of the Unconscionability Doctrine, Usury Laws, and Related Limitations on the Freedom to Contract' (1995) 24 *Journal of Legal Studies* 283.

[6] *Ibid*, at 285. Posner added (*ibid*, at 293) that 'the appropriate responses to welfare opportunism and to welfare circumvention converge on the policy of deterring the extension of high-risk credit to the poor. One approach to this policy is simply the non-enforcement of contracts extending high-risk credit to the poor.'

[7] A Colombi Ciacchi, 'Freedom of contract as freedom from unconscionable contracts' in M Kenny, J Devenney and L Fox O'Mahony (eds), *Unconscionability in European Private Financial Transactions: Protecting the Vulnerable* (Cambridge, Cambridge University Press, 2010) 7.

[8] On the substantive approach to freedom of contract, see also A Halfmeier and P Rott, 'Kickback payments under MiFiD: substantive or procedural standard of unconscionability', in Kenny *et al* (eds), above n 7.

some parties 'choose' to enter into transactions,[9] and the specific vulnerabilities and responsibilities of contracting parties. Colombi Ciacchi's emphasis on the importance of substantive freedom of contract echoes the fuller understanding of 'autonomy' articulated in chapter five of this book. She argued that it is 'Precisely because self-determination is crucial to private law [that] private law has to provide remedies for contracts that are the product of a factual subjugation of the weaker party.'[10] 'Taking freedom of contract seriously' requires a proper engagement with the contextual or situational vulnerabilities of the parties, and positive interventions through private law (specifically contract law) to correct the balance between the contracting parties.

This perspective also resonates with Teubner's claim that 'freedom of contract' is undergoing a subtle transformation, as the legacy of the excessive freedom claimed by the market has triggered a more reflective strand in contract law discourse, concerned with the need to check the balance between (formal) 'autonomy' on the one hand, and the complex array of social expectations and third-party interests on the other.[11] The tensions between the classical private law understanding of 'autonomy' and a desire to achieve substantive fairness and social justice are at the heart of modern European contract law discourse.[12] Meanwhile—and recognising that the power of the non-interventionist arguments waxes and wanes with the market[13]—the latest housing market crash and resulting recession have prompted a fresh decline in influence for proponents of strictly market-led strategies. At the same time, developments in regulatory perspectives are opening up the possibility for rethinking the neoliberal paradigm of the self-responsible consumer, and the correlating model of legal subjectivity. In this crucible, specific issues facing older owners in a new, largely unchartered context for housing equity transactions[14] merge with a policy agenda for housing equity use after retirement which underlines the need for transactions that release this wealth to require no more than an acceptable level of risk taking. As the post-crisis environment provides an opportunity to rethink the philosophical assumptions underlying current legal approaches to vulnerability and responsibility in 'private law' transactions, the analysis set out in this book will, it is hoped, be instructive in extending that review to include the conceptualisation of older owners as legal subjects and the adequacy of the legal frameworks within which they participate in housing equity transactions, with potential implications for the development of a more responsive and realistic model of the (older) consumer as a vulnerable legal subject.

[9] Colombi Ciacchi argued that 'Achieving substantive freedom of contract involves preventing and eliminating the harm caused by an unconscionable contract to a party who was only formally, but not substantively, free to conclude it.': above n 7, at 8.

[10] *Ibid.*

[11] G Teubner, 'In the Blindspot: The Hybridisation of Contracting' (2007) 8(1) *Theoretical Inquiries in Law* Article 4; see also T Wilhelmsson and S Hurri (eds), *From Dissonance to Sense: Welfare State Expectations, Privatisation and Private Law* (Aldershot, Ashgate, 1999); HW Micklitz, 'Principles of Social Justice in European Private Law' (2000) 19 *European Yearbook of Private Law* 169.

[12] M Kenny, J Devenney and L Fox O'Mahony, 'Conceptualising unconscionability in Europe: in the kaleidoscope of private and public law', in Kenny *et al* (eds), above n 7, at 386.

[13] D Reiss, 'Regulation of Subprime and Predatory Lending' in SJ Smith, M Elsinga, L Fox O'Mahony, SE Ong and S Wachter (eds), *The International Encyclopaedia of Housing and Home* (Oxford, Elsevier, 2011).

[14] In light of the demographic, socio-economic, political and policy pressures considered in chs 1 and 2.

Index

ageing:
affective decision-making, 172–73
ageing identities, 27–28
ageing population, 2, 5–6
ageing society, 1–5
'Agequake', 2, 5–6
'baby-boomer generation', 2
cognitive processes, 172–73
demographic context, 5–11,
economic decision-making, 170–78
fiscal aspects, 7–8
gender, 7
political perspectives on, 25–30
socio-economic context of, 12–21
structured dependency of, 26, 28
subjectivity, 28
wealth and income differentiation, 11, 26–27
asset-based welfare, 15, 25–26
autonomy:
autonomous lives, 90, 136–37
balancing autonomy with vulnerability, 38, 72, 165–66, 184–88, 196
decisional, 133–34, 166
dependence, 134–35, 165, 338
feminist meanings of autonomy, 136
future autonomy, 196, 350–51
'genuine' autonomy, 136–37
heteronomy, 134
impaired consent theory, 336–40
in liberal individualism, 80, 82–83, 135
older owners as autonomous consumers, 28, 41, 148, 194
procedural and substantive autonomy, 136–37
progressive property theory, 109–110
psychological meanings of autonomy, 135
relational contract theory, 94–94
substantive fairness, 89–90

Bankruptcy, 212–218
frequency among older owners, 214
'fresh-start' philosophy, 214–16
impact on older people, 191–92
judicial policy concerning age, 213–24
relevance of context, 217–18
US approach to older bankrupts, 216–17
Behavioural economics, 41–42, 55, 103–4
challenges to efficiency models, 87
consumer learning, 199, 294
endowment effect, 103, 127, 171
framing effects, 103–104
heuristics, 55
hyperbolic discounting, 103, 283
information paradigm, 88–89
limits of cognition, 120
loss aversion, 103, 127, 171
over-optimism, 103
perception of risk, 55, 119–120, 127
prospect theory, 103–104
rational choice theory, 103
transactional risk, 98, 364–65
Bourdieu, Pierre, 19

Capacity, 157, 160–66, 186
medical model of disability, 164
Choice:
burden of choice, 48, 52
choice under uncertainty, 173
constraints on choice, 69, 81, 136, 173, 204–05, 249, 373–75
context, 186–87
differential distribution of, 51
ethos of choice in care provision, 29
expansion of choice, 45, 156
feminist critique of rational choice theory, 195–96
independence through active exercise of choice, 122–23
individualism, 41
marginal older owners, 81, 204–05
paradox of choice, 173
rational choice theory, 101, 103, 224
Scanlon, T, 69
voluntariness, 55
Context:
contextual or situational vulnerability, 41–42
economic decision-making, 41–42, 197–98
extortionate bargains, 247–48
relational contract theory, 95–96
unfair relationships, 255–56
unfair trading, 258–60
Conventional lending, 59, 207–212
ability to repay, 208
actions for possession and sale, 210–212
age discrimination, 209–10, 243
arrears, 208–09, 221–22
conventional mortgage transactions, 67
lender's responsibilities, 208, 307–09
risks for older owners, 207–208
risks to lenders, 209–10, 249, 262
Corrective justice, 73–78
de-personalised rationality, 74–75
hybrid legal reasoning, 83–85
liberal legal theory, 79–82

Dependency, 159–60
undue influence, 340

vulnerable legal subjectivity, 201
Difference:
'abnormal persons' approach, 175–76, 182–83
'dilemma of difference', 175, 189, 194–95
feminist scholarship, 174–78
gendered harms, 189–191
politics of differences, 177
'social relations' approach, 177–78
special protection, 174
traditional rights paradigm, 176–77
Distributive justice, 82
hybrid legal reasoning, 83–85
Downsizing, 17–18, 121–23, 154–55, 204–06
economic drivers, 121–22
generational attitudes, 148–49
legal transactions, 205–06
non-economic factors, 122–23

Economic efficiency, 86–87
Equality, 37–40
critical legal realism, 85–86
fairness across the life-course, 39
formal equality, 85
inequalities across the life-course, 39
non-discrimination, 39
rights-based approaches, 38–39
unequal later life outcomes, 39
United Nations Principles for Older People, 37–38
Equitable remedies, 318–78; *see also* undue influence, unconscionability
Equity release, 269–317
attitudes to, 148–50
complexity of, 57
consumer risk, 56
decision-making/procedural risk, 56–57
development of market, 150–51, 165, 269–71
development of products, 270
everyday needs, 23–24
FSA regulation, 149–51, 186
generational differences, 149
gifts, 23
healthcare and nursing care, 23–24, 32–37
home maintenance and improvements, 23–24, 30–32, 58
lifestyle expenditure, 23
marginal owners, 24
market intervention, 151–53
mis-selling, 55
perceptions of, 57, 104, 268
policies in support of, 30–37
pricing, 60
product risk, 56, 235–36
purposes of, 23–24, 153–54
risks for lenders, 59
risks of, 54–60
role of the State, 61
SHIP, 150, 271–72, 273
tax liabilities, 24–25
uncertainty, 67–68
welfare benefit entitlement, 24–25, 60–61
withdrawal of products, 272
Equity withdrawal:
across the life-cycle, 20, 58
attitudes to, 20, 144, 148–49, 220
generational differences, 149

Fairness, 223–63
contextual approach, 223, 229–30, 236–40
economic efficiency, 91–92
procedural fairness, 57, 88, 223
substantive fairness, 57, 87–94, 223
transactional risk, 96
Financial Abuse, 178–84
isolation, 179
risk factors, 181–83
targeting older people, 178–79
undue influence, 179–83
Financial capability, 40, 166–170
assuming inappropriate risks, 168
'capability gap', 178
choosing financial products, 167–69
financial citizenship, 169, 310
impact of life events, 168
information and education strategy, 169–70
planning for the future, 167
younger people, 169
Financial products:
flexible mortgages, 220
uneven access to, 19
FSA approach, 266–68, 314–15
appropriate level of consumer protection, 265–66, 302, 305–06
consumer confidence, 265, 314
cost-benefit analysis, 267, 279, 304–05
Financial Ombudsman Service, 298–99, 322
Financial Services Compensation Scheme, 300
'light-touch' approach, 301–02, 310
limits of regulation, 301–09, 313
mis-buying, 302
product risk, 303
redress and remedies, 298–301
risk-based approach, 268, 303–05

Habitus, 19
Harm:
ability to prevent harms, 92
differential impact and special protection, 97, 187
directly attributable, 69–70
duty to prevent harm, 92–93
gendered harms, 189–91
impact of bad financial outcomes, 57, 90, 96, 246, 312–13
unfair terms, 225, 246
victimisation, 197
Home as self-identity, 52–53
Home ownership, 10–11
affluent older owners, 10–11, 27
burden of ownership, 131, 133–34
government promotion of home ownership, 17, 138
hybrid of money, materials and meanings 118
marginal older owners, 2, 10–11, 27, 56
ontological security, 130–31
proportion of older owners, 10

responsible citizenship, 21–22, 138, 147–48
rhetoric of ownership society, 104
risk-taking model of home ownership, 104–105

Home reversion plans, 284–90, 311
definition of, 285
information and advice, 287
market share, 286
regulation of, 286–90
risks of, 285–86, 288–89
suitability, 289, 307
valuation, 289

Housing consumption, 120–25, 147

Housing as home, 118, 125–38
ageing in place, 125–38
attachment to place, 128–29
health, 126
identity and wellbeing, 128–32
practical issues, 127
symbolic meaning, 127–28
tenure identity, 129–31

Housing as inheritance, 118, 138–46
attitudes to inheritance, 143–44 , 351
decision-making, 141
inherited asset, 142–43
inherited homes, 142–43

Housing as investment asset, 52, 104, 118, 138–39, 146–154
development of financial products, 147, 155–56, 220
meanings of home, 141–42
normalisation, 139
political expectations, 146–47
rationality, 144–45

Housing paradigms, 118–120;
see also *Housing as home; Housing as inheritance; Housing as investment asset*

Housing options services for older people, 123

Housing wealth, 15–21
accumulation and decumulation, 62, 104–05
fungibility of, 20
gender gap, 19
government policies, 17
market performance, 18
over-investment in housing equity, 16–17, 20
positive risk, 62
source of income, 18

Information paradigm, 53, 68, 119, 194
critiques of, 88–89
financial abuse, 183–84
FSA approach, 264–65
lifetime mortgages, 276, 279–80
marginal owners, 68–69
older people, 172–74, 178
responsible borrowing, 308

Intergenerational justice, 6–8, 39
generational contract, 7, 13
intergenerational debt, 141, 324, 351
intergenerational financial support, 139–40
supporting adult offspring, 145–46, 154, 324, 327, 349–50

Legal subjectivity, 66, 72–117
contextual vulnerability, 177
critical legal realism, 86–87
dependency, 159–60, 340
difference, 177, 192
entrepreneurial individualism, 66–67
feminist scholarship, 86, 99
liberal legal subjects, 22, 42, 57, 78–83, 86, 87–88
non-instrumentalism, 73–78
'personality', 73–78
rationality, 67, 100–04
Rawlsian political subject, 75, 79
reasonable foresight, 68
reasonableness, 66–67
'reasonable person', 75
uncertainty, 67

Liberal individualism, 80, 83
Dworkin, R, 80–81
'freedom promoting' approach to property, 110–11
market individualism and community interests, 105–06
property law, 106–07

Lifetime mortgages, 273–84, 310–11
cooling-off period, 281
drawdown mortgages, 273
effectiveness of FSA regulation, 282–84, 312
high-pressure selling, 280–81
information and advice, 275–77, 279–80
'light-touch' approach, 281–82
marginal consumers, 283–84
non-advised sales, 278–79
regulation of, 274–84
risks, 274–76
roll-up mortgages, 273, 275
shared appreciation mortgages, 273–74
suitability, 277–78, 306–07

Moral hazard, 60–61
paying for care, 35

National Strategy for Housing in an Aging Society, 11, 120, 126, 156, 188

Neoliberalism, 21–22, 28, 41
'skilled consumers', 29
autonomous consumerism, 65
FSA approach, 264
liberal subjectivity, 79, 193
privatisation, 48
rationality, 41
responsible citizenship, 29
risk, 65
self-responsibility, 29, 305

'No negative equity' guarantee, 152

Non-status lending, 243–47
situational vulnerability, 244–47
unfair practices, 245

Normalcy of transactions, 119, 142–43
mortgage equity withdrawal, 220
perception of risk, 154
unconscionability, 373–74
undue influence, 349–52, 358, 365

Older owners, 1–22
  access to credit, 206
  advising older clients, 315–17
  as an identity group, 49
  as consumers of care, 34
  as consumers, 21–22, 148, 183, 267–68, 305, 310
  as vulnerable legal subjects, 49, 310
  asset-rich but cash-poor, 30
  attitudes to litigation, 190–91, 312–13, 317, 322–23, 336
  common characteristics, 12
  consumer debt, 21, 206–07
  living in poverty, 18
  polarisation of poverty and affluence, 18
  relative financial well-being, 12–21
  savings and housing wealth, 15–21
  socio-economic heterogeneity, 18–19, 156, 186, 188
Owned home:
  as a consumption good, 17
  future utility value, 128

Pensions, 8–10
  attitudes to saving for retirement, 16
  Booth, C, 12
  contributory pensions, 13
  generational contract, 13–14
  limitations of market approach, 14
  pension shortfall, 9–10
  poverty and pensions, 12–15
  privatisation and individual responsibility, 14
  risks and uncertainties, 14
  role of housing equity, 9–10
  savings and housing wealth, 15–21
  self-provision, 8–9
  universal state pension, 13
  'wealth-fare state', 9
Possession Actions, 218–19

Rationality:
  deep rationality, 100–02, 107–08
  economic rationality, 101–02, 107
  in property law, 100–04, 106
  rational choice theory, 103
  rational legal subjectivity, 67, 102
Reflexive planning, 18–19, 45, 47–48, 50
  individualisation, 66
  inequalities, 51
  place attachment, 129
Relational contract theory, 94–100
  feminist scholarship, 98–99
  personal characteristic risk, 95–97
  relational risk, 95–97
  transactional risk, 95–98
  undue influence, 335, 344–48
Responsibility, 193
  ethos of self-responsibility, 33–34, 70, 305, 357
  outcome responsibility, 69
  progressive property theory, 109–10
  property theory, 108–14
  provider responsibility, 264, 296–97, 307–09, 312, 314, 353–68
  responsible borrowing, 307–08
  responsible lending, 187, 306–08, 315, 356–57
  responsible risk-taking, 193
  transactional responsibility, 343–44
Retirement, 3
  normal retirement age, 3–4
Risk society, 44–49
  'at risk' groups, 49
  Beck, U, 47
  conceptual framework of, 46–49
  expansion of choice, 45, 156
  fault, 46
  Giddens, A, 47, 54
  global financial crisis, 185
  individualisation, 48, 66
  legal responses, 64
  liberal subjectivity, 79
  ontological security, 45, 52–54
  ontological status of older people, 65
  reflexivity, 45
  regulation, 64
  responsibility, 44, 47, 70
  responsible risk-taking, 64
  risk in financial markets, 70
  uncertainty, 52
  unequal distribution of risk, 50–51
  universal risk subject, 50
  winners and losers, 19, 48

Sale and rent back, 84, 311
  adverse impact, 296
  advertising, 295
  affordability, 296
  appropriateness, 296
  cooling-off period, 296
  definition, 290
  landlord default, 293
  legal advice, 297
  marginal consumers, 292, 296
  market for, 290, 292
  procedural safeguards, 296
  provider responsibility, 264, 296–97, 311–12
  regulation of, 294–95
  security of tenure, 291–92, 297
  situational vulnerability, 292–96
  suitability, 264, 307
  terms, 291
  valuation, 291
Social ownership, 132
Special protection, 39–40, 49, 90, 97
  access to credit, 164–65
  arguments against, 165
  difference, 174, 176
  financial abuse, 182
  vulnerable legal subjects, 160
Suitability of housing stock for older people, 126

Tax:
  inheritance tax, 140
  tax consequences of equity release, 140

Unconscionability, 345

inequality of bargaining power, 369–76
unconscionable bargain doctrine, 369–76
Under-occupation, 123–5
ageing in place, 124
low-value properties, 124
older people, 123
use of housing, 124
younger households, 123–4
Undue influence, 141, 318–369
actual undue influence, 325–26
age and susceptibility, 329–30
agency principle, 353–54
autonomy, 320
constructive notice, 354–56, 366–67
contextualised approach, 329, 345, 369–76
dependency, 340
direct liability, 319, 368–69
downsizing, 206
exploitation, 337, 340–43
feminist critique, 334, 347
fiduciary responsibility, 342–43, 368–69
financial abuse, 179–181
hybrid relational theory, 336,
impaired consent, 336–40
indirect liability, 324, 352–68
jurisprudential basis, 335–48
legal advice, 358–68
marginal nature of remedies, 320–21, 330
paternalism, 333–35
presumed undue influence, 326–28
provider's responsibilities, 319, 324, 358, 362–63, 365–67
relational contract theory, 335, 364–65
relational norms, 328, 330–31, 344–48, 350–51, 358, 367–68
surety wives, 319, 330–32, 361
suretyship, 324, 351
transaction calls for explanation, 327–28, 348–52, 356–58
transactional dependency, 329, 331–32
transactional neglect, 320, 342–44, 346–47, 372
transactional risk, 96–97, 335, 345, 352, 363–64
'trust and confidence', 328–35
unfair trading, 258
Unfair relationships, 250–52, 254–57
contextual approach, 255–56
Unfair Terms, 224–54
core terms, 228
fairness approach, 224–25
Financial Ombudsman Service, 231, 252–54
freedom approach, 224–25
FSA approach, 231–35
good faith requirement, 229
Law Commission approach, 241–43
marginal owners, 225–26
non-core terms, 228–29
situational vulnerability, 243
'Treating Customers Fairly', 232, 298
Unfair trading, 257–60
contextual approach, 258–59

Voluntariness:
corrective justice 76, 82
in housing equity transactions, 34–35, 119
Vulnerability, 157–203
capabilities, 111–12
decision-making, 157–9
dependency, 159–60, 340
economic decision-making, 157, 166–78
financial abuse, 158, 180
impact of financial victimisation, 189
impact of losses, 158–59, 187, 188–192, 246–47
impaired capacity, 157
older owners as consumers, 21–22
opportunity to recover, 188, 199
responses to vulnerability, 57
situational vulnerability, 57, 96, 158, 179, 182–88, 192, 194, 197–99, 223, 339, 373–74
universal nature of, 192, 194, 201
victimhood, 184
Vulnerable legal subjects, 49, 90, 99, 160, 192–202
critique of consent, 199–200
special protection, 160

Welfare:
asset-based welfare, 15, 25–29, 156
benefit entitlement, 60–61
feminist scholarship, 195–96
private law, 73–75, 77, 81–84, 87–88, 102, 104–05, 344, 347
public provision for older people, 140
self-provision, 2–3, 20, 24, 38, 41, 139–40, 147